Direct Marketing Management

SECOND EDITION

Direct Marketing Management

Mary Lou Roberts

University of Massachusetts, Boston

Paul D. Berger

Boston University

Prentice Hall
Upper Saddle River, New Jersey

Acquisitions Editor: Whitney Blake
Editorial Assistant: Michele Foresta
Editor-in-Chief: Jim Boyd
Marketing Manager: Shannon Moore
Production Editor: Aileen Mason
Permissions Coordinator: Professional Book Center
Associate Managing Editor: John Roberts
Manufacturing Buyer: Diane Peirano
Manufacturing Supervisor: Arnold Vila
Manufacturing Manager: Vincent Scelta
Design Manager: Pat Smythe
Cover Design: Bruce Kenselaar
Illustrator (Interior): Professional Book Center
Composition: Professional Book Center

Library of Congress Cataloging-in-Publication Data
Roberts, Mary Lou.
   Direct marketing management / Mary Lou Roberts, Paul D. Berger. —
2nd ed.
     p.   cm.
   Includes bibliographical references and index.
   ISBN 0-13-080434-7
   1. Direct marketing.   I. Berger, Paul D., 1943–   . II. Title.
HF5415.126.R62   1999
658.8'4—dc21   99-10509
                                                CIP

Prentice-Hall International (UK) Limited, London
Prentice-Hall of Australia Pty. Limited, Sydney
Prentice-Hall Canada, Inc., Toronto
Prentice-Hall Hispanoamericana, S.A., Mexico
Prentice-Hall of India Private Limited, New Delhi
Prentice-Hall of Japan, Inc., Tokyo
Pearson Education Asia Pte. Ltd., Singapore
Editora Prentice-Hall do Brasil, Ltda., Rio de Janeiro

Printed in the United States of America

10 9 8 7 6 5 4 3 2

To Our Families:
Greg, Lynn, Ernie, Sam, Nina, and Cara
Susan and Seth

Contents

Preface

In the years since the first edition of *Direct Marketing Management* was published, the discipline of direct marketing has attained maturity. No longer the sole province of speciality businesses, its methods now form an important part of almost every marketer's toolkit. It is used by marketing departments, both large and small, who serve both the consumer goods and services sectors. It constitutes a major part of the marketing efforts of most business-to-business firms and nonprofit organizations.

The clear reason for the increasing prominence of direct marketing methods is top management's requirement that marketing expenditures be accountable for success or failure on a profit-and-loss or even a return-on-investment basis. Traditional marketing methods have a difficult time meeting this requirement. The built-in evaluation mechanisms of direct-response marketing activities are ideally suited to this environment of accountability.

Evidence of the increased importance of direct marketing can be seen in changing media patterns. The specialized media of direct mail and telephone have been added to the media plans of traditional marketers. An increasing number of the promotions found in both print and broadcast media can be characterized as direct response.

Most important, however, is the recognition, by marketers of all kinds, that the real power of the discipline lies in the *development and strategic use of the marketing database,* not in the media per se. This recognition has both derived from, and led to, additional availability of mailing lists, as well as increased ability to develop, enhance, and analyze customer and prospect databases. The marketing database makes possible two other key developments:

- *Relationship marketing,* with its emphasis on customer service and retention, is recognized as the keystone of profitable marketing for the foreseeable future.

- *Computer-based electronic media,* best exemplified by the on-line services and the World Wide Web, have suddenly emerged as a major marketing vehicles. Because users of the various services can be identified and their activities tracked, the new eletronic media are, by definition, direct marketing media.

These two developments have already made changes in the way leading-edge marketers do business. They will result in far-reaching transformations in marketing practice over the next few years. All these changes are reflected throughout the new edition, not just in one or two specialized chapters. The same is true of the increasing globalization of businesses in the direct marketing industry and of the spread of direct marketing throughout the economically developed countries of the world.

Keeping up with change of this magnitude is no small task. Both authors owe a debt of gratitude to students in many courses throughout the years who have provided examples, information, and insights. We are also grateful to clients who have allowed us to participate in the inner workings of this fascinating industry.

Last, but not least, we are indebted to the Direct Marketing Association, particularly to the Direct Marketing Educational Foundation (DMEF). The foundation's support of direct marketing education in general, and its publications and conferences in particular, have provided a broad range of assistance to academics who teach direct marketing.

We look forward to introducing a new group of students to this dynamic facet of marketing and to our continued association with the academics and practitioners whose daily activities create exciting advances in both theory and applications.

We hope that students and practitioners alike find that the second edition of *Direct Marketing Management* does full justice to the richness and excitement of the discipline.

Mary Lou Roberts
Paul D. Berger

Direct Marketing Management

CHAPTER 1

Contemporary Direct Marketing

As recently as a decade ago direct marketing was generally regarded as a fringe element of the economy, although it was represented by successful specialty marketers ranging from the Burpee Seed Catalog to American Express. When the words *direct marketing* were spoken, most people heard "direct mail." Even worse, it was frequently referred to as the "junk mail" industry.

Sometime in the mid-1980s the picture began to change. The number of businesses that promoted their products and services primarily through direct-response media skyrocketed. Many consumer goods firms added direct marketing techniques to their marketing repertoire. Business marketers were virtually unanimous in their adoption of direct marketing. Small businesses and fund raisers of all kinds discovered that they could operate successfully without a huge investment in mass media advertising. These developments occurred more rapidly in the United States than in most other countries, but direct marketing rapidly became a global phenomenon.

There were many reasons for this dynamic growth. Some of the most important were

- the rise of single-person, single-parent, and two-income households, all of which crave convenience as a key element of the shopping experience
- the fragmentation of markets and of media, represented by many consumer segments and an ever-increasing number of media vehicles catering to their special interests and needs
- the rapidly escalating costs of reaching customers through traditional means such as mass media and field sales forces
- the increasing availability and decreasing cost of sophisticated information technology, which enabled a major shift in marketing approaches

One well-known catalog marketer has a history that in many ways parallels the growth of the industry. L.L. Bean, the world-class marketer of outdoor clothing and equipment, was founded in 1912 by Leon Leonwood Bean in the small town of Freeport, Maine. He began by selling his own invention, the Maine Guide boot, by direct mail. Unfortunately, the stitching that held the leather tops and the rubber bottoms together came loose, and 90 of the first 100 pairs he sold were returned. L.L., as he was affectionately known, refunded his customers' money and set about making a better quality boot. The second version of the boot was a success, and his business was established. In short order, he opened a retail store to serve outdoor enthusiasts. Many of the fishermen and hunters were friends of L.L. and did not hesitate to wake him in the middle of the night to buy a new pair of boots or just the right fishing lure. By 1951 the retail store was open seven days a week, 365 days a year.

The company grew in both sales and reputation until L.L.'s death at the age of 94 in 1967. Since then the company has grown at a rapid pace under the guidance of grandson Leon Gorman. More than 16,000 products are offered through as many as 23 different catalogs each year. Sales are in the neighborhood of $1 billion from catalog and retail, domestic and international sources. The company has four retail stores as well as a customer service center in Japan and customers in countries throughout the world.

L.L. Bean is famous for the quality of its products, for its 100 percent satisfaction guarantee and the customer service that backs it up, and for a warehousing and order fulfillment operation that is a "best practices" benchmarking site for companies in many different industries all over the world.[1]

You probably know the name of L.L. Bean. Perhaps you carry your books to class in a Bean backpack. Even though many students are familiar with a number of the well-known mail-order firms, they tend to be surprised at the size of the direct marketing industry. They also may not realize that direct marketing continues to grow as a component of the overall economy. Table 1.1 contains current statistics for the consumer and business-to-business sectors of the direct marketing industry and predicted growth through the year 2001.

A Definition of Direct Marketing

There are several published definitions of direct marketing.[2] None of the existing definitions, however, captures all the dimensions of contemporary direct marketing. Therefore, we use our own simple but powerful definition:

---

[1]www.llbean.com, 12 June 1997.

[2]See Connie Bauer and John Miglautsch, "A Conceptual Definition of Direct Marketing," *Journal of Direct Marketing* 6, no. 2 (1992): 7–17 for a good discussion.

TABLE 1.1 Value of U.S. Direct-Marketing-Driven Sales Compared to Total U.S. Sales*

Direct Marketing Method	1991	1995	1996	1997	2001	Compound Annual Growth	
						1991–1996	1996–2001
Consumer direct marketing sales	**458.3**	**595.2**	**634.6**	**677.1**	**906.1**	**6.7**	**7.4**
Direct Order	154.0	196.4	208.6	221.6	289.6	6.3	6.8
Lead Generation	215.8	286.5	306.6	329.1	457.4	7.3	8.3
Traffic Generation	89.3	112.5	119.4	126.1	158.5	6.0	5.8
Total U.S. consumer sales	**4,166.3**	**5,212.9**	**5,423.9**	**5,675.7**	**6,925.1**	**5.4**	**5.0**
Direct marketing sales percent of total sales	**11.0**	**11.4**	**11.7**	**11.9**	**13.1**		
Direct marketing business-to-business sales	**349.1**	**493.5**	**543.0**	**596.7**	**879.8**	**9.2**	**10.1**
Direct Order	102.4	142.1	155.5	170.0	242.6	8.7	9.3
Lead Generation	218.6	312.6	345.4	381.2	574.2	9.6	10.7
Traffic Generation	27.3	38.6	42.1	45.8	63.6	9.0	8.6
Total U.S. business-to-business sales	**8,246.0**	**10,154.6**	**10,704.2**	**11,355.1**	**14,977.5**	**5.4**	**6.9**
Direct marketing business-to-business sales	**4.2**	**4.9**	**5.1**	**5.3**	**5.9**		

Source: Data from DMA Report—*Economic Impact: U.S. Direct Marketing Today,* 1996. Table reprinted from *Direct Marketing Association's Statistical Fact Book, 1997* (New York: Direct Marketing Association, 1997), 336. Reprinted with permission of the Direct Marketing Association, 1998.

Note: Due to rounding, totals may not exactly equal the sum of each column.

*In billions of dollars. These numbers have not been inflation-adjusted—they represent current (nominal) dollars.

> Databased direct marketing is an information-driven, relational marketing process that takes place in a context of concern for the privacy of customer data.

This definition represents a whole new way of looking at marketing, one that many businesses have only recently discovered. It concentrates on developing customer relationships that result in repeat sales over time. It does so by collecting and using customer data to generate marketing strategies that are sharper, more focused, and more individualized than traditional marketing efforts. However, the same information that enables marketers to remove the "junk" (the unwanted communications) from the process is also an issue of concern to many consumers and public-interest groups. How well marketers use their powerful new information tools will determine both the continuing success of the industry and the extent to which it comes under stringent regulation throughout the world.

Table 1.2 (p. 4) presents an overview of the differences between traditional mass media (general) marketing and direct marketing. Let's concentrate on the marketing tasks that direct marketing performs especially well as compared to general marketing. Direct marketing

TABLE 1.2 Key Differences between Direct Marketing and General Marketing

General Marketing	*Direct Marketing*
Reaches a mass audience through mass media	Communicates directly with the customer or prospect
Communications are impersonal	Can personalize communication by name/title and/or with variable messages
Communication is one way—advertiser to prospect	Communications can be interactive
Promotional programs are highly visible	Promotional programs (especially tests) relatively "invisible"
Amount of promotion controlled by size of budget	Size of budget can be determined by success of test/promotion
Desired action is either delayed or unclear	Specific action always requested by inquiry or purchase
Incomplete/sample data for decision-making purposes are taken from marketing research and/or sales call reports	Comprehensive database drives marketing programs
Data must be collected separately from the sales process	Marketing data are produced as integral part of the sales process
Analysis conducted at segment level	Analysis conducted at individual/firm level
Uses surrogate variables such as advertising awareness or intention to buy to measure effectiveness	Measurable and therefore highly controllable

- facilitates focused, targeted customer communications
- allows those communications to be personalized
- encourages the prospective customer to take immediate, specific action
- can make marketing strategies less visible to competitors
- is measurable, providing a degree of accountability for marketing expenditures that is not present in traditional marketing

These special competencies are in large part responsible for the continuing growth of direct marketing. We now take a more detailed look at each.

The Special Competencies of Direct Marketing

If you think about the things that direct marketing does particularly well, you will recognize that virtually all of them stem from the fact that the communications of direct marketers are targeted to specific individuals, not to segmented mass markets by way of mass media.

PRECISION TARGETING

Through the use of carefully selected mailing lists and the information contained in customer databases, the direct marketer can direct communications to an individual consumer or a specific business customer who has been identified as a viable prospect. This reduces the waste inherent in many other types of communications that cannot be so precisely targeted. A person who purchased several fruitcakes as holiday gifts (which the direct marketer knows because they were mailed to different addresses) can and should be solicited to repeat the purchase the following year. It may be helpful to remind the customer what he sent and to whom he sent gifts the preceding year. The direct marketing database contains this information.

PERSONALIZATION

The individual consumer can and often should be addressed by name, and the business customer can be addressed by name and title. The ability to personalize extends beyond the mere use of names, however. Information from the database can be used to select an appropriate appeal (for example, "April is the month to plant lily bulbs in New England" for the Connecticut resident who has previously purchased bulbs and perennials from the nursery) or to encourage additional purchases from a customer who has purchased previously (for example, "As a thank you to our loyal customers, we are offering a preview sale day before we open the doors to the general public.").

CALL FOR IMMEDIATE ACTION

Direct marketing copy calls for specific and immediate action, typically the purchase of a product or a request for more information about it. This call for immediate action works against the prospect's normal tendency to defer action, often permanently. "Limited Time Offer," "Will Not Be Repeated," and "Your Prompt Reply Is Requested" are all frequently used exhortations.

"INVISIBLE" STRATEGIES

The strategies and tactics of the direct marketer are less visible to competitors than are strategies that must be implemented in the mass media. Competitors make a point of keeping abreast of one another's activities by, for example, making sure to be on their mailing lists. However, by the time the competitor receives the communication, so have customers, and it may be too late to retaliate effectively. Lack of visibility is especially important when testing direct marketing campaigns. A traditional test market invariably tips off the competition; the test of a direct marketing program may go unnoticed by competitors. To make it even more likely that a test will remain unseen, direct marketers can suppress test mailings to zip codes in the immediate vicinity of competitors' headquarters on the assumption that the households of executives are likely to be in these zip codes.

MEASURABILITY

The most important advantage that direct marketing has over other marketing techniques is arguably its ability to track, and therefore to measure the effectiveness of, specific marketing actions. By knowing precisely what worked and what did not, the marketer can allocate marketing dollars much more effectively. For example, a 1-800[3] number may be specific to an infomercial run on a specific cable channel. The response coupon in a business publication has a tracking code that identifies the vehicle and the insertion date. A catalog has a 6- to 10-

---

[3]Throughout this book, "1-800" is used generically to indicate any toll-free dialing prefix.

digit code above the mailing label that may have a variety of information embedded in it, including the mailing list from which the name came.

Taking these special competencies into account, the direct marketer next needs to consider the set of decision variables that will be combined into a sound and effective promotional program.

The Decision Variables of Direct Marketing

In general marketing we talk about the 4 Ps—product, price, promotion, and place. In direct marketing we can identify a set of decision variables that parallel, although they are not exactly the same as, the 4 Ps of general marketing. We add a fifth decision variable, customer service, which is an essential component of the relationship marketing process.

> Offer (which includes the product)
>
> Creative
>
> Media (which includes lists when applicable)
>
> Timing/sequencing
>
> Customer service

These decision variables form the basic framework around which direct marketing programs, and therefore the chapters of this book, are structured. Because they are discussed in detail later in the text, we only introduce them here.

OFFER

The offer is the complete proposition made by the marketer to a prospective customer. It includes the product or service itself, the price at which it is offered, any adjustments to the price, and other elements of the positioning strategy for the product.

CREATIVE

The creative component of the direct marketing program includes the copy platform, the graphic design elements, any involvement techniques, and production considerations such as personalization.

MEDIA

The media available to direct marketing include all those used by general marketing as well as direct mail, telephone, and the new electronic media, especially the World Wide Web.

TIMING/SEQUENCING

Concerns about the timing and sequencing of direct marketing communications are in many ways similar to those for general advertising. These concerns include one-shot messages versus campaigns, pulsing versus a steady flow of communications, seasonal effects, and questions of how much repetition is enough. Direct marketers often have more control over media than do general marketers. The direct mail marketer can decide when to mail, whereas the marketer who uses magazines must adjust to publication schedules and space availability.

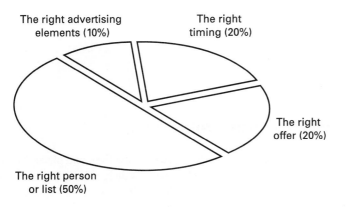

The right advertising elements (10%)

The right timing (20%)

The right offer (20%)

The right person or list (50%)

FIGURE 1.1 Importance of the List in Generating Response

How to take the greatest advantage of the timing variable is not well understood. One direct marketer suggests that there are four dimensions to consider.[4] The first is *recency.* Customers are most likely to buy again shortly after they have made a purchase. The second dimension is *frequency.* A customer who purchases multiple times (a multibuyer) is a better prospect than one who purchases infrequently. These two variables may sound counterintuitive, but their importance to direct marketing is well documented and is discussed in detail in chapter 4. *Seasonality* varies by the nature of the offer—for example, garden products in the late winter and Christmas gifts in the fall. Finally, *role transitions* such as the purchase of a home or the birth of a baby provide important indicators of a prospect's propensity to purchase.

Part of the conventional wisdom of the direct marketing industry is an estimate of the relative importance of these four decision variables in creating a response (see Figure 1.1). Reaching the right person accounts for 50 percent of a program's impact. The offer and the timing are next at 20 percent each. The creative elements account for only 10 percent. This estimate comes as a surprise to many people, especially those who are committed to the creative side of advertising communications.

Stop to think about it, though. If the message does not reach the proper target—the target for which it was designed—it has little chance of being effective. Likewise, if the product or the way it is valued is not right for the target customer, or if the message arrives at an inappropriate time, the probability of generating a response will be decreased. The creative elements, important though they are, cannot be effective unless the other variables are implemented correctly.

CUSTOMER SERVICE

The fifth major variable—customer service—has not been explicitly recognized in previous discussions of key direct marketing decision elements. This is true even though Lester Wunderman, one of the senior statesmen of direct marketing, is reputed to have observed long ago that "direct marketing turns a product into a service."

The importance of service cannot be overstated. The *types* of customer services offered—toll-free telephone numbers, free limited-time trial, acceptance of several credit cards, for example—are important techniques for overcoming customer resistance to buying

---

[4]Stephen Belth, "Timing: The Fourth Dimension of Direct Response," *DM News,* 15 May 1988, 38, 98.

Our founder, L.L. Bean, operated his business based on the following belief:

"Sell good merchandise at a reasonable profit, treat your customers like human beings, and they will always come back for more."

He personally tested his products in the field and backed them with a unique Guarantee of 100% Satisfaction.

Today, 86 years later, we still test our products in the field, still back them with the same Guarantee (which has become famous around the world), and still follow his Golden Rule.

FIGURE 1.2 L.L. Bean's Golden Rule

Source: Used with permission of L.L. Bean.

via direct-response media. Even more important is the *level* of customer service provided—the speed and accuracy of order fulfillment, handling of customer inquiries and complaints, and a guaranteed returns policy, for example. Next to the quality and performance of the product itself, the quality of the direct marketer's customer service is the prime determinant of customer satisfaction. The level of customer satisfaction is, in turn, a prime consideration in the decision whether to repurchase. L.L. Bean knew this from the very beginning, when he refunded the purchase price of those 90 pairs of Maine Guide boots that split open at the seams. The firm still abides by his "Golden Rule" of customer service. It is posted on their Web site, as shown in Figure 1.2.

Businesses that are notable for the excellence of their customer service are always looking for ways to further improve their services in ways that provide genuine value to customers. Federal Express now offers free software that allows its customers to schedule and track their own shipments via FedEx's Web site. Customers like this service because it saves time and gives them more control over their shipping operations. It saves customer service dollars for Federal Express, but even more important, it frees their well-trained customer service representatives to handle nonroutine customer issues.

Excellent customer service also includes problem prevention. Neiman-Marcus, the Dallas-based specialty retailer, goes to great lengths to try to prevent customer problems with merchandise ordered by mail or by phone:

Neiman-Marcus sends a first-class mailing to customers confirming the details of any complex order (e.g., engraved items). Customers are asked to immediately call the 800 number if any errors are found. This minimizes the shipment of incorrect orders (e.g., wrong message engraved) and thereby decreases the expense of responding to consumer complaints. During periods of peak telephone orders (e.g., Christmas), Neiman-Marcus sends a mailgram to ensure that customers are aware of their order's status.

Neiman-Marcus representatives who process telephone orders receive special briefings on product aspects which might lead to "unmet" customer expectations. For instance, if the actual color of a dress differs slightly from what is shown in the catalog, the telephone representative advises the customer of this difference. Also, representatives provide advice and help customers select clothes that will "go together." In this manner, product returns are reduced and consumer satisfaction is increased.[5]

As this example implies, and as many experts have found, expenditures on customer service may actually make operations more profitable instead of being a drain on profits. Certainly service that leads to satisfaction is an investment in relationships that lead to long-term customer loyalty.

Generic Objectives of Direct Marketing Programs

Each direct marketing program or campaign should, of course, have specific and measurable objectives. It is useful, however, to think about four broad types of objectives that direct marketing programs can achieve. These broad classes of objectives are

sale of a product or service

lead generation

lead qualification

establishment and maintenance of customer relationships

The nature of the specific objective or objectives of the program will be dependent on both the marketing and financial goals of the firm.

SELLING PRODUCTS OR SERVICES

Most of the direct marketing communications we are accustomed to receiving as consumers are designed to accomplish the sale of a product or service. The mail brings a solicitation for a preapproved credit card. The Sunday newspaper has an advertisement promising free compact disks if the consumer joins a club that offers recorded music. The television advertisement offers a tool that performs many difficult tasks with ease, provides a 1-800 number, and urges the viewer to order right away.

GENERATING AND QUALIFYING SALES LEADS

Business marketers, as well as consumer goods marketers, sell many products as a result of a single customer contact, but they are especially likely to be concerned with producing well-qualified leads (prospective customers) for their field salespeople. As we discuss in chapter 11, this has become increasingly important in recent years as the cost of a field sales call has

---

[5]*Consumer Complaint Handling in America: An Update Study, Part II* (Washington, D.C.: U.S. Office of Consumer Affairs, 1986), 14.

risen. It is also very important in the marketing of infrequently purchased consumer goods such as insurance, automobiles, and real estate.

Leads are generated when a prospect requests additional information as a result of a direct marketing communication. When prospects respond to a follow-up mailing, answer questions, or engage in any other behavior that indicates they have a genuine intention to buy, they become "qualified prospects."

A classic example of a multistep marketing program was carried out by Porsche Cars North America. The automobile marketer identified an initial 200,000 prospects who had the requisite income and other characteristics that identified them as potential buyers of the Porsche 944. Porsche mailed an invitation to each of these prospects to come in for a test drive. So far, not so unusual. What grabbed the attention of the prospects was the inclusion of a Porsche poster that had the individual prospect's name on the license plate of the car! Based on the success of the initial mailing, a total of 750,000 invitations were mailed over a 10-month period. The 6 percent response rate "exceeded our wildest expectations," according to a Porsche spokesman.[6] We would like to show you an example of this poster, but everyone we know who received one has kept it as a treasured conversation piece!

Porsche did not release the number of test drives that were converted into sales of the 944, but success can be inferred from the prominent role that direct marketing now plays in the marketing of many automotive brands. More generally, multistep, targeted, and customized programs are becoming increasingly important in both business and consumer markets and are discussed in more detail in chapters 3 and 11.

BUILDING AND MAINTAINING CUSTOMER RELATIONSHIPS

Direct marketing is uniquely able to engage in a continuing dialog with an identified customer in order to establish, grow, and maintain a customer relationship. Sometimes this type of effort is necessary to make a single sale, as in the Porsche example. More often, it is part of a program designed to promote repeat sales over a period of time. The process involved is often described as the *loyalty ladder.* As portrayed in Figure 1.3, the marketer's job is to move the customer through a series of steps that culminate in the customer being an advocate for the firm's product.

Suspects are prospective customers who fit the general profile of the purchaser of the product or service. They do not become *prospects* until they take some action that signifies interest, such as visiting a Web page or calling to request a catalog. *Customers* have purchased at least once over a specified period of time. *Clients* are customers with whom the direct marketer has opened a dialog; the client/customer provides information about wants and needs, and the marketer listens and responds. Finally, loyal customers become *advocates* and recommend the product to others.

To create long-term loyalty, the direct marketer needs to communicate with customers in ways that recognize their importance to the firm. To put it more bluntly, the marketer must communicate with the customer between attempts to sell something.

Fund-raisers have long known the necessity of telling their donors how their contributions are being used and how much good the money is doing for a cause about which the donor cares deeply. Television advertisements for various relief organizations have learned to link the donor/sponsor to a specific child and to provide the sponsor with periodic updates

---

[6]Janice Steinberg, "Direct Mail Becoming Hottest Incentive Conduit," *Advertising Age,* 24 July 1989, S-4, S-6.

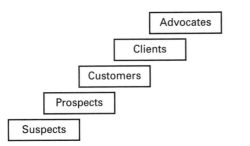

FIGURE 1.3 The Loyalty Ladder

on the child's progress. This is infinitely more effective than simply asking people to contribute to a rather faceless organization that assists unknown people in a faraway country. Similarly, you will find, when you graduate, that your school is eager to keep you informed about all the positive developments on the campus in the hope that you will become a donor sooner rather than later.

Businesses are also learning this lesson. However, with today's desktop publishing technology it is all too easy for companies to fill our mailboxes with newsletters and other communications of marginal value. A homeowner may open the mailbox to find a newsletter with helpful tips from the lawn-care concern and some checks making it easy to get a cash advance from the credit card company. The newsletter may be interesting and the checks may or may not be welcome, but they all fill up the mailbox and ask to be examined, if only briefly. The challenge is to engage the customer by providing information that is genuinely useful and to communicate it in a way that recognizes the customer as a unique individual.

The Media of Direct Marketing

The statistics in Table 1.3 (p. 12) describe the manner in which direct marketers divided their expenditures among the available media in 1996. Keep in mind that this media allocation varies greatly from country to country, depending on strategies used and the ability of available media to reach target groups. Although we cannot precisely separate expenditures for direct-response promotions from general media, these industry data help us understand the way direct marketers use the media.

Many people are surprised to learn that telephone is the largest advertising medium in the United States in terms of total expenditures. Telephone marketing experts estimate that approximately half of the almost $88 billion spent on this medium in 1996 was for outgoing calls, with the other half representing incoming calls for purchases and customer service. Television is next, followed closely by newspapers and then by direct mail. The miscellaneous category, which includes the Yellow Pages and outdoor media such as billboards, is also quite large. Radio and magazines are smaller in terms of total media expenditures.

Virtually all of the media shown in Table 1.3 can be used to transmit direct marketing offers. It is important to remember that, although many of the media are used by both general marketers and direct marketers, the direct marketer uses and evaluates the effectiveness of the media differently.

Let's take a brief look at each of the primary media and their roles in direct-response marketing. Developing and implementing direct marketing programs in each of these media are the subjects of several later chapters in the book.

TABLE 1.3 1996 Direct Marketing Media Expenditures Compared to Total U.S. Advertising Expenditures*

1996	Direct Mail Advertising Expenditures	Total Advertising Expenditures	Direct Marketing Percent of Total
Direct mail	34.6	34.6	100.0
Telephone marketing	57.8	87.9	65.7
Newspaper	13.9	38.3	36.3
Magazine	7.2	13.2	54.5
Television	15.5	39.1	39.6
Radio	4.7	12.0	39.5
Other	10.9	22.7	47.8
Total	144.5	247.8	58.3

Source: Data from DMA Report—*Economic Impact: U.S. Direct Marketing Today,* 1996. Table reprinted from *Direct Marketing Association's Statistical Fact Book,* 1997 (New York: Direct Marketing Association, 1997), 335. Reprinted with permission from Direct Marketing Association, 1998.

Note: Due to rounding, totals may not exactly equal the sum of each column.

*In billions of dollars, percent share. These numbers have not been inflation adjusted; they represent current (nominal) dollars.

TELEPHONE

The telephone is an indispensable medium for direct marketers of both consumer and business products. We are probably all familiar with many of the consumer applications of this medium. The consumer makes outgoing calls to obtain information, order merchandise, and request follow-up service. The consumer receives incoming sales and service calls, plus solicitations of many kinds from nonprofit organizations.

The telephone is especially critical to many business marketers today as they strive to make their sales effort cost effective. Telephone sales and service representatives are used in conjunction with a field sales force or, increasingly, they are taking over the entire responsibility for the sale of some business products. Telephone marketing is discussed in chapter 14.

DIRECT MAIL

Solo Mailings

A wide variety of marketing communications can be included under the heading of solo mailings. Solo mailings are generally understood to be any mailing piece that emphasizes a single product or service. The development of campaigns featuring one or more solo mailings is discussed in chapter 12.

Catalogs

Catalogs contain a line of merchandise—general or specialty, narrow or deep. Although we are all familiar with consumer catalogs, what many people do not realize is how extensively catalogs are being used as a sales tool in business-to-business marketing.

Business-to-business catalogs, both print and interactive, are covered in chapter 11, and the many issues involved in the development and management of consumer catalogs are discussed in chapter 13.

BROADCAST AND ELECTRONIC MEDIA

Direct-Response Television

Long the province of the late-night pitchman selling vegetable slicing machines, inexpensive sets of kitchen knives guaranteed to last a lifetime, and smokeless ash trays, direct-response television has gained respectability in recent years. It is now a vehicle for marketing a wide variety of goods and services. Large national advertisers from Time-Life in consumer markets to IBM in business markets have found prime-time direct-response television sufficiently effective to devote a portion of their promotional budget to it. Cable television has become an important medium for reaching targeted audiences of many kinds with direct-response offers.

In recent years there have been two important developments—television shopping programs and the infomercial—that have propelled the use of television for much more than traditional direct-response spot advertisements. Television shopping programs became popular in the mid-1980s and are now a staple feature of cable television services. As they have become established, the home shopping channels have broadened their merchandise offerings, provided more entertainment-oriented presentation of the products, and encouraged call-ins to give the programs human interest.

The infomercial is an even more recent development. The format is ordinarily 30 minutes, but it may be longer or shorter. From a few specialty advertisements shown to the insomniac market in the early morning hours, the infomercial has grown to encompass a wide variety of mainstream products and well-known marketers. Growth has been fueled by the expansion of specialized electronic media, especially cable television, which reaches many households, including upscale ones with a wide variety of interests. In 1996 the infomercial industry purchased $787 million of media time. Total sales of the electronic retailing industry, which includes radio and multimedia as well as television, were estimated to be $8 billion.[7]

Direct-Response Radio

Radio has not traditionally been considered a strong medium for direct-response marketing. The reasoning has gone something like this: "People usually listen to the radio while they are doing something else—working, driving, whatever. It is generally not convenient for them to stop what they are doing, find a pencil and paper, and write down an address or a telephone number. Besides, by the time they find the pencil and paper, the ad is over."

Radio has shown itself to be an effective direct-response medium from its early days, however, and even in the television era it has advantages to offer marketers. One attraction is its ability to reach highly segmented audiences. Furthermore, direct-response radio is cheaper than television.

Some products have an obvious affinity to radio, or more accurately, to the people on the move who are heavy radio listeners. Both paging systems and cellular telephones have been sold successfully by direct-response radio. Direct-response radio and television are discussed in chapter 16.

---

[7]www.nima.org, 10 June 1997.

Computers

The computer, specifically the Internet and the World Wide Web, are becoming major resources for customer information and service and, to a lesser extent, product and service sales. Less visible, but probably even more important, is the use of the Web by business marketers to interact with suppliers and vendors and to provide customer service. In the late 1990s the Web is still primarily an advertising (informative) medium. However, electronic commerce (translate that as "sales") is growing rapidly and may soon play an important role in the lives of many consumers. Business marketing on the Web is growing even faster, as we discuss in detail in chapter 11. We encourage you to use the Web to learn more about the activities and strategies of many of the companies mentioned in this book.

SPACE ADVERTISING IN PRINT MEDIA

Newspapers and Magazines

Display advertising in both newspapers and magazines is used by a wide variety of product and service marketers. You should examine your local newspaper as well as consumer and trade magazines to see the wide variety of companies using direct-response advertising for many different products. Notice which ones are attempting to sell products or services and which ones are encouraging readers to request additional information.

SPECIALTY ADVERTISEMENTS IN PRINT MEDIA

Newspaper Inserts

Daily and, especially, Sunday newspapers are vehicles for the dissemination of preprinted inserts, most often using four-color printing, often on glossy paper stock. These inserts are an important advertising vehicle for many branded products and mass merchandisers.

Bind-Ins and Blow-Ins

These advertisements, usually in the form of postal reply cards, are found in most magazines today (frequently hampering the reader's efforts to keep the magazine open to the desired page). These cards may support the adjacent advertisement; that is, the ad presents basic information about a sophisticated new printer, for instance, and the card invites the reader to send for additional information or to request a sales call. Frequently, though, the cards are stand-alone advertisements for a familiar product such as a subscription to a well-known magazine, perhaps the magazine in which the card is found. The cards can be stapled into the magazine (bind-ins)—a more expensive method, but the cards are less likely to be lost—or they can literally be blown in by specialized machinery—a cheaper method, but the cards are more easily misplaced.

Bingo Cards

Most trade journals and many general-interest magazines contain reader service cards, affectionately known in the trade as *bingo cards*. The reader can use these cards to send away for additional information from advertisers in that issue of the magazine. Bingo cards do provide a real service to readers and some advertisers, but they tend to attract many respondents who are merely information seekers, not potential purchasers. Advertisers often do not follow up these requests for information promptly and accurately, creating customer dissatisfaction.

SPECIALTY ADVERTISEMENTS IN VARIOUS MEDIA

A wide variety of miscellaneous direct-response devices exist. They are often used as inexpensive "ride-alongs" with products, bills, or other promotional materials. They may also be used to acquire new customers who are difficult to reach by more traditional media.

Bang-Tail Envelopes and Bill/Package Stuffers

Direct marketers are quick to take advantage of any opportunity to transmit a direct-response offer to a prospective customer without incurring postage cost. The package in which your last mail-order purchase arrived probably also contained a brochure, a mini catalog, or the current issue of the entire catalog. A bill from a retailer or a credit card company often contains a number of brochures and perhaps even a sample of perfume. In many instances, there is a noncompeting offer presented on the oversized (bang-tail) flap of the billing envelope.

Coupons and Samples

Both coupons and samples can be transmitted by a wide variety of media—newspapers, magazines, mail, and home delivery are frequently used options. Although coupons and samples seem not to qualify as direct marketing media, both are increasingly being used in ways that allow marketers to track them and to build and expand marketing databases with the information they provide.

The scanners used by supermarkets and mass merchandisers record coupon usage and, if the shopper is using a scanner card, information about the shopper and his or her purchases. Scanners also allow coupons to be printed out at the point of sale. This allows marketers to target purchasers of competing products without offering a price reduction to loyal customers who would purchase at full price.

This is only one of many ways in which direct marketers collect information about customer purchases and use it to develop more cost-effective direct marketing programs. Other aspects of database development and use are discussed throughout the book.

CONSUMER CONCERNS ABOUT PRIVACY

From the consumer's viewpoint, the good news about targeted, database-driven marketing is that it removes the "junk" from the communications stream, leaving offers and information that are uniquely relevant to the individual. The bad news, however, is that marketers must know a great deal about the behavior, characteristics, and even the financial affairs of the individual consumer to make individualized relationship marketing effective. Consumers are aware of the amount of information that business and government have about them, and they are concerned that it may be misused in a way that damages them. It is also important to note that this is primarily a concern of consumers, not business customers.

Since 1990, the credit-reporting firm Equifax and market-research firm Louis Harris have undertaken an annual study of consumer attitudes toward personal information. In 1996, 65 percent of respondents said that protecting the privacy of personal information is "very important." Forty-four percent expected privacy protection to worsen over the next three years, but 67 percent prefer the current situation of industry self-regulation over government intervention.[8]

---

[8]"Private Opinions," *Marketing Tools* (March 1997): 34–35.

To a greater or lesser extent, the issue of consumer data protection and privacy is of concern to consumers in advanced economies around the world. The exact nature and level of the concern varies from one country to another, often as a result of differing cultural values. The amount of current and potential government regulation also varies and can change rather dramatically over short periods of time as a result of the ebb and flow of political tides.

Over the past few years, direct marketers have become acutely aware that if the industry does not regulate itself in a way that satisfies consumers, the government is likely to do so. The Federal Trade Commission has been especially active in this area, holding hearings in July 1996 on issues of consumer data privacy and again in June 1997 on personal data collection on the World Wide Web (see www.ftc.gov for reports and useful references).

The Direct Marketing Association (DMA) is active in considering privacy issues in the context of governmental concerns and in recommending ways for its members to deal with consumer privacy concerns. Issues of data privacy are of special concern to many people who use the Internet, a subject that we examine in detail in chapter 17. In mid-1997 an industry group headed by Netscape proposed a standard for collection of information and consumer notification on the Web.[9] You may see other initiatives in the area of industry self-regulation as time goes on.

Consumer data privacy is also an important issue in the countries of the European Union (EU). The draft Data Protection directive, first proposed in 1990, would have required that consumers give permission before they could be contacted by direct marketers ("opt in") and would have prohibited most segmentation analysis and transfer of data outside the EU. Recent drafts of the directive have been less restrictive to the industry, but the status of personal data protection in the EU remains in question.[10]

Authors and consultants Don Peppers and Martha Rogers have a Web site called Marketplace 1 to 1 (www.1to1.com). They have a strong privacy statement (see Figure 1.4). As you visit Web sites, take time to see if the site has a statement of their privacy policy and examine the ones you find.

Direct Marketing as a Global Industry

The preceding discussion of privacy regulations points out one of the barriers to international direct marketing. Others include language, culture, customs, and business and communications infrastructure. However, the potential rewards are great, and direct marketers continue to venture outside the boundaries of their native countries.

As noted earlier, L.L. Bean has been successfully marketing its products in Japan for a number of years. The DMA estimates that Japan's catalog market was worth $21 billion in 1994 and that there are 500 catalog marketers competing for that market. A number of U.S. firms are among the successful competitors, driven by the Japanese desire for U.S. products and their need for convenience. However, firms who succeed often find that they must tailor their offer to special market needs. When Patagonia, an upscale marketer of outdoor clothing, entered the Japanese market, it found that the Japanese consumer prefers a brighter color

---

[9]"Netscape, Firefly and VeriSign Propose Open Profiling Standard (OPS) to Enable Broad Personalization of Internet Services," www.netscape.com, 27 May 1997.

[10]David Reed, "It's Still an Open Question in Europe: Will DMers Be Ruled by the Good Cops or the Bad Cops?" www.direct.com, 1 May 1997.

Our Privacy Pledge To You

Marketing1to1/Peppers and Rogers Group is a member of the TRUSTe program and is in compliance with TRUSTe privacy principles. This statement discloses the privacy practices for the entire Web site.

TRUSTe is an independent, non-profit initiative whose mission is to build users' trust and confidence in the Internet by promoting the principles of disclosure and informed consent. Because this site wants to demonstrate its commitment to your privacy, it has agreed to disclose its information practices and have its privacy practices reviewed and audited for compliance by TRUSTe.

When an individual visits a Web site displaying the TRUSTe mark, he or she can expect to be notified of:

1. What information this site gathers/tracks about him or her

2. What this site does with the information it gathers/tracks

3. With whom this site shares the information it gathers/tracks

4. This site's opt-out policy

5. This site's policy on correcting and updating personally identifiable information

6. This site's policy on deleting or deactivating your name from a site owner's database

Questions regarding this statement should be directed to Marketing1to1/Peppers and Rogers Group's webmaster, or TRUSTe for clarification.

Information this Site Gathers/Tracks

Our Site automatically captures IP addresses and Cookie ID's (which are set by this site). We keep a record on our server if a user knowingly provides the following information: first and last name, postal address, email address, daytime phone number, company name, gender, title.

Use of the Information this Site Gathers/Tracks

We use the information that we gather to register members so that they may enter our discussion forums. In addition, we use personal information to dynamically generate certain pages on our Web site and to send members our weekly e-mail newsletter if they so choose. We never sell or redistribute personal information.

Sharing of the Information this Site Gathers/Tracks

We do monitor sponsor click throughs, an activity which has received the approval of TRUSTe. If a user wishes to contact our site sponsors using our form-based feedback, an email gets sent to the sponsor, and a copy is kept on our server in its logs. We make personal information publicly available in only one context. If an individual posts to our discussion forums, it will show the individual's first and last name.

Opt-out Policy

If an individual posts to our discussion forums, it will show the individual's first and last name. If, however, the individual wishes to have their post removed, he or she can contact our webmaster and make that request.

Updating Profile

Once an individual signs into the site, there will be a link in our navigation bar to change his or her preferences. For example, if a member has chosen to receive our weekly newsletter, he or she may unsubscribe by changing that part of their preferences. If you have any questions, please contact our webmaster.

Deleting and Deactivation

If a member wishes to be removed from our site's database, he or she can contact our webmaster to remove them. Please note that some records may still exist in our logs. If a member has posted to our discussion forums, he or she must specifically request to have these removed.

Entire site copyright 1998 Marketing 1to1/Peppers and Rogers Group

FIGURE 1.4

Source: Marketing 1 to 1/Peppers and Rogers Group. Used with permission.

palette than does its U.S. counterpart. Patagonia also found that petite sizes and compact household items were important in meeting the needs of the Japanese consumer.[11]

Direct marketing is in the process of becoming a truly global industry. We discuss the activities of direct marketers based in Europe as well as the United States and Canada throughout the book. No statistics exist that accurately measure the total volume of cross-border direct marketing activities, but the spread of direct marketing around the world, in consumer and business markets alike, is unmistakable.

Summary

The direct marketing industry is made up of firms that rely exclusively on direct marketing and, to an increasing extent, firms that are engaged in both traditional and direct marketing activities. The growth of the industry has been stimulated by consumer needs for convenience and unique merchandise and by the demands of business management for greater accountability and effectiveness in its marketing efforts. The emerging electronic media, from cable television to the World Wide Web, have provided a fertile new global environment for direct marketing activities that encourages the prediction that the direct marketing industry will continue to grow for many years to come.

Discussion Questions and Exercises

1. In your own words, give a definition of direct marketing. How is direct marketing, as you have defined it, different from general marketing?
2. What is relationship marketing? How does it fit into the framework of direct marketing?
3. What does direct marketing do especially well compared to general marketing?
4. What are the decision variables of direct marketing?
5. Why is direct marketing growing so rapidly? Do you think this growth will continue? Why or why not?
6. Name some businesses that use aspects of direct marketing that are described in this chapter. Before reading the chapter, would you have thought of them as direct marketers?
7. The chapter discusses the privacy of customer data as a social and ethical issue with which the direct marketing industry must contend. Are you aware of any other ethical aspects of direct marketing?

Suggested Readings

Peppers, Don, and Martha Rogers. *The One to One Future.* New York: Doubleday, 1993.

Rapp, Stan, and Thomas L. Collins. *Beyond Maximarketing: The Power of Caring and Daring.* New York: McGraw-Hill, 1995.

Reitman, Jerry I., ed. *Beyond 2000: The Future of Direct Marketing.* Lincolnwood, IL: NTC Publishing Group, 1994.

Stone, Bob. *Successful Direct Marketing Methods,* 6th ed. Chicago: NTC Business Books, 1997.

Wunderman, Lester. *Being Direct: Making Advertising Pay.* New York: Random House, 1997.

---

[11]Rebecca Pinto Heath, "Think Globally," *Marketing Tools* (October 1996): 49–54.

Planning a Direct Marketing Program

C H A P T E R 2

Each direct marketing program (*campaign* is a synonymous term frequently used in the advertising industry) has an individual, detailed promotional plan. The plan is necessary to guide a complex activity that usually involves many people in various business functions, both inside and outside the firm. From a practical standpoint, a detailed promotional plan is generally part of the budget request that results in funding for a specific direct marketing program.

A direct marketing program plan is based on the business's marketing plan, which, in turn, is based on the corporate strategic plan. Figure 2.1 (p. 20) illustrates this relationship. The corporate strategic plan is a high-level plan that covers the entire organization and generally looks ahead a period of three to five years. The marketing plan is developed at the level of a business unit, such as a division of a large company, or a major product line. It is more specific in nature and usually covers a period of one to three years.

The direct marketing program plan deals with one specific promotional activity. This activity may last for just a few weeks or months or it might last for a year or more. A short program might be a one-time mailing to produce leads for an industrial equipment sales force. A longer program might be a multistep relationship marketing program, perhaps mak-

19

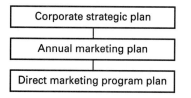

FIGURE 2.1 The Planning Hierarchy

ing use of multiple media, such as the Porsche program described in chapter 1. The length of time does not matter. What is crucial is that the program has a clear beginning and a definite point at which its success or failure will be assessed. We discuss program evaluation methods in several chapters, especially chapter 9. For the moment it is sufficient to remember that direct marketing is the only inherently measurable type of promotion and the measures to be used are an important part of initial program planning.

A Hypothetical, but Realistic, Example

Let's say that Sally and Martin, a young couple in their late twenties, have established a successful retail business in the downtown financial district of a midwestern city. With experience as a product manager and financial analyst, respectively, they succumbed to the lure of starting their own business. Called Fabulous Coffee, it began as a gourmet coffee shop and later realized an increased breakfast business when muffins, breads, and juices were added. When Sally and Martin decided to include gourmet salads and sandwiches, they also began to do a brisk lunch business. Almost all their business is take-out.

Sally and Martin realize that this business model has peaked in the current location. Extending their hours of operation is not feasible because this part of the city empties rapidly after 5 P.M. They have considered other retail locations. However, it is difficult to find good, affordable locations downtown, and there are few suburban locations that generate sufficient traffic made up of the office workers, executives, and professionals who are the majority of their customer base. Another issue is the presence of excess kitchen capacity at the existing location.

During the holiday season Sally and Martin solicited catering business, using some of their frequent customers as contacts. They were pleased with the results, in terms of their ability to service the events they booked as well as the profit margin they realized. They were confident that they could run a catering operation that provided high-quality beautifully presented food, and they exhibited the same kind of friendly professionalism that had made the retail operation successful. This holiday business had been generated by seasonal and corporate entertaining. They would have to broaden their target market for the catering business if they were to be successful on a year-round basis. The couple began to consider cost-effective options for reaching a different target market with a different product.

Stop and think for a moment about the informal type of planning that is implied by this example. Can you really tell what details are part of the corporate plan and what comes from the marketing plan? Not really. The good news is that Sally and Martin seem to be thinking carefully about the key issues that affect the growth of their business. The bad news is that too few small business owners write down explicit plans. Whatever their past practice, Sally and Martin decide that they need a detailed plan for this venture into uncharted territory.

The Elements of a Direct Marketing Program Plan

The process of planning a direct marketing program shown in Figure 2.2 probably looks familiar to you. What you are recognizing is that a direct marketing program plan has the same key elements as a corporate strategic plan or a marketing plan. At the program planning level, however, there is much more detail on communications strategy and program execution than you would find even in an annual marketing plan.

Ordinarily the program planning process will proceed on a step-by-step basis as outlined in Figure 2.2. Until the communications strategy is solidly in place, each step depends on decisions made in preceding steps. When the strategy has been agreed upon, budgeting, logistics, and creative development can proceed more or less simultaneously. In actual practice, they may be iterative, as when a creative execution is proposed that exceeds original budget estimates. In fact, the entire planning process should be thought of as iterative. A strategic insight at any stage of the process may cause the direct marketer to rethink earlier

FIGURE 2.2 The Direct Marketing Program Planning Process

- Establish communications objectives based on stated marketing objectives
- Evaluate the marketplace
  - Business environment
  - Competition
  - Customer market segments
  - Product and market fit
- Evaluate past experience and performance in similar programs
- Develop the communications strategy
  - Target market(s)
  - Positioning and desired brand personality
  - Key selling proposition(s)
  - Offer strategy
  - Media and list strategy
  - Message strategy
- Specify database development, use, and enhancement requirements
- Determine the program budget
- Establish the implementation timetable
- Develop creative prototypes
- Establish evaluation rules and methods

choices. The availability, or the lack of availability, of a particular mailing list or advertising medium may force the direct marketer to focus on a different market segment from the one originally targeted. Frequently, the approved program budget will cause the direct marketer to change the original scale or scope of the program. Insufficient budget may dictate targeting one segment rather than two or mailing less deeply into the chosen customer segment. We discuss the latter option in detail in chapter 5.

The first step is to establish the specific, measurable objectives that are the hallmark of direct marketing.

ESTABLISHING COMMUNICATIONS OBJECTIVES

Generic objectives for direct marketing programs are identified in chapter 1. The real challenge for the direct marketer is to develop measurable program objectives based on the marketing objectives of the firm or business unit. The marketing objectives, in turn, are dictated by the financial objectives of the organization as stated in the corporate strategic plan. There are many generic dimensions on which specific marketing objectives can be developed, as illustrated in Table 2.1. Marketing management translates these into precise objectives, as shown in the table.

Once the direct marketer understands which marketing objectives apply to the prospective program and the time frame within which they are to be achieved, planning the direct marketing program can begin. The choice between sales objectives, inquiry generation objectives, or relationship marketing objectives will be made in light of the marketing objectives. Share of market or revenue objectives will result in *sales* objectives. Increasing the number of dealers or retailers might suggest an *inquiry generation* program to provide qualified leads for a field sales force that calls on dealers or retailers. The sales objective would be stated in dollars or units of product or both. The objectives of the inquiry generation program would be stated as, first, inquiries and then, qualified leads. Inquiry generation program objectives should also include "conversions," the number of dealers or retailers (or "sales") that resulted from the program. Conversions are more difficult to measure than leads for two reasons. First, they take longer to achieve, and second, another group is involved, often the field sales force. Nevertheless, the direct marketer should seriously consider making the effort to track and measure the ultimate result of the program. We discuss this problem in more detail in chapter 11.

Less straightforward is the link between marketing objectives and *relationship marketing* objectives. In a generic sense, relationship marketing programs focus on acquiring new customers, retaining existing customers, or upgrading or cross-selling existing cus-

TABLE 2.1 Marketing Objectives

Generic Marketing Objectives	Examples of Specific Marketing Objectives
Share of market	Increase share of market from 12% to 15%
Sales revenue	Increase sales revenue by 10% to $110 million
Number of intermediaries	Increase number of retail outlets to 4,500
Price target	Maintain an average price of $72.50 per unit
Gross margin target	Achieve a gross margin of 40%
Profit target	Achieve a net profit of 28%

tomers. For example, a credit card company may try to upgrade an entry-level customer who has a satisfactory credit history by offering a higher-level product such as a gold card, or additional benefits such as a travel club membership. A bank engages in cross-selling when it offers mutual fund products to customers who have savings accounts. We discuss the profit impact of relationship strategies in detail in chapters 8 and 9.

The pricing, margin, and profitability objectives of the marketing function lend themselves well to secondary objectives for direct marketing programs, not to primary sales or inquiry generation objectives. The direct marketer needs to ensure that there are not so many different objectives that focus is lost, and that the objectives are complementary, not contradictory.

How do Sally and Martin go about setting objectives for a new business activity? They know that booking a catering account requires personal contact with the prospective customer. They also realize that their problem is to locate, out of the total population, the relatively small number of people who need catering services during a given period of time. This indicates an inquiry generation program of some type. Specific, measurable objectives will have to wait until they learn more about how to generate sales leads.

Once the direct marketer has established objectives, the next step is to study the market in which the program will be conducted. *Situation analysis* and *SWOT* (strengths, weaknesses, opportunities, and threats) *analysis* are terms often applied to the activity by which marketers evaluate both the external market and their own resources and abilities.

EVALUATING THE MARKETPLACE

As in all planning processes, it is necessary to have a thorough understanding of the market environment in which the direct marketing program will take place. The components of that environment, listed in Figure 2.2, are the business environment, the competition, customer market segments, and the product and market fit. The business environment and competition will be evaluated using secondary data obtained from either public or commercial sources. Customer market segments are best analyzed on the basis of internal data. The description of product and market fit will result from the direct marketer's own analysis. All of this must take place within the correct market framework—perhaps a regional area for a small or specialized marketer; nationally or even globally for well-established firms.

For a direct marketing program plan, the examination of the business environment should focus explicitly on factors that affect the market for the particular product or service, not on broader macroeconomic factors. The successful direct marketer has a clear understanding of the factors that drive his or her market. The catalog marketer who specializes in women's career clothing knows that fashion and price will be key short-term determinants of sales. The cataloger also knows that the level and type of women's participation in the workforce and longer-term style trends in the workplace (such as "dress-down Fridays") will affect the business over time. In recent years nonprofit fund-raisers have experienced difficulties resulting from donor concern over excessive operating costs attributed to some well-known nonprofits and overuse of fund-raising techniques including direct mail and telephone solicitations. The common thread is that these issues cannot be controlled by the direct marketer who must instead adjust programs to the realities of the surrounding environment.

In the same sense, competition is a factor the direct marketer cannot control but one that must be considered in program planning. Specific competitors must be identified, and their activities followed as closely as possible. The trade press is a key source of information about competitive activity as are commercial firms that specialize in this type of data. Direct marketers are careful to ensure that they are on the mailing lists of competitors—a key way to keep abreast of competitive activity.

Understanding the relevant customer segments is key to selection of the best target for the direct marketing program. Consumer segments are ordinarily described in terms of demographics, lifestyles, and product use behavior. Business segments can be described by industry characteristics, operating and decision-making styles, and product use behavior. The traditional marketing approach has been to conduct primary marketing research on an anonymous sample of actual or potential customers to understand segment characteristics and desirability. The direct marketer has a tremendous advantage in the database that has specific data on the product use behavior of identified individuals, households, or business firms. Segmenting these data is discussed in detail in chapter 5. Additional demographics can often be purchased from commercial suppliers of demographic data, either consumer or business. Customer surveys can be used to further enhance the database with attitudinal and lifestyle data.

Growth rate can be addressed at either the market or the segment level. However the direct marketer approaches the issue of growth, it is clearly more desirable to be in growing markets rather than stable or declining ones.

A final step should be to consider the degree to which the product or service fits the requirements of the market that has just been described. Does the product offer the features and services that the market wants? If not, can the product be modified? A clear and realistic view of the product being marketed is a necessary foundation for the development of a successful direct marketing program.

In a formal corporate plan the market evaluation or SWOT analysis may be lengthy, accompanied by numerous tables, charts, and graphs. Our entrepreneurs Sally and Martin may do it less formally, but they should do it no less carefully. They assessed the overall business environment in the metropolitan area as strong and growing based on information from library sources and from the economic research bureau at the local university. The listing of caterers in the local telephone directory was helpful, and they were able to obtain brochures, which helped them understand the services offered by many of their potential competitors and gave them some sense of price levels. They also talked to a number of meeting managers who frequently used caterers to find out more about their level of satisfaction with available suppliers. The most interesting thing they learned was that catering weddings was different from catering other events because clients often wanted a "package" of providers who were accustomed to working together and who could be overseen by a wedding consultant. The other segments they identified were individuals, meeting planners, and event sites that had no food service facilities.

Once the direct marketer has digested information about the marketplace, the next step is to study past experience with products and programs. This might be best described as the stage at which we do not reinvent the wheel!

EVALUATING PAST PERFORMANCE

The techniques used to evaluate program performance depend both on the objectives of the program and the past operating experience of the business. The evaluation modes must be a direct outgrowth of the objectives of the program. They also must be chosen to represent the overall outcome of the program, not partial results. This issue is discussed in detail in chapter 3.

TABLE 2.2 Some Measures Used to Evaluate the Performance of Direct Marketing Programs	
Measure	*Operationalization*
Response rate	Percentage of prospects contacted who replied
Number of inquiries	Number of requests for information
Number of qualified leads	Number of leads who expressed interest
New customers acquired	Number of purchasers who had not purchased before
Customer acquisition cost	Total marketing costs divided by number of new customers
Lapsed customers reactivated	Inactive customers who purchased
Average sale	Total sales divided by number of buyers
Product returns and adjustments	Dollar amount of returns and adjustments
Customer service requests	Number of post-sale service requests
Customer Lifetime Value	Net present value of a customer over a specified period of time

Some of the measures often used to evaluate performance are listed in Table 2.2. There are many other potential measures, some of them quite unique to the particular business. All valid measures have a potential place in the program plan. The final item on the list, Customer Lifetime Value, may not be familiar to you. *This is the single best measure of the success of any direct marketing program.* It is also a measure that is unique to databased direct marketing activities. Lifetime value is introduced and discussed in detail in chapter 9.

The direct marketer should look carefully at past programs for the product in question. This includes both the statistical program reports and the creative executions of each program. A careful examination will likely reveal both successes and failures and may suggest reasons that programs have worked or not. The direct marketer should select measures that have been used in previous programs in order to make results comparable. However, additional measures that reflect distinctive objectives of the new program should also be used. Again, the same caution applies as in the selection of objectives. There need to be a sufficient number of measures to adequately assess the success or shortcomings of the program but not so many that focus is lost.

Examining past programs will also reveal useful trends. Is response rate going down steadily over a period of time? Is it becoming more expensive to acquire a new customer? Trends such as this will send the direct marketer on a search for explanations that can improve the current program.

With a clear understanding of what has worked—and what has not worked—in the past, the direct marketer is much better equipped to establish strategy for the current program.

DEVELOPING THE COMMUNICATIONS STRATEGY

The communications strategy is the heart of the direct marketing program plan. It is made up of a number of elements, each of which must be presented in sufficient detail to provide a work plan for program execution.

Selecting the Target Market(s)

Target market selection requires an explicit statement of the market segment or segments that will be the focus of the program. This step may require considerable thought. Perhaps there are a number of attractive segments that the direct marketer has not yet penetrated but resources are insufficient to target all of them. Selecting the target market may be something of a foregone conclusion, as in the case where one of the principal objectives of the plan is to reactivate lapsed customers.

Sally and Martin can identify several potentially attractive segments, but they need to focus their limited time and resources on just one or two promising ones. Let's assume that they eliminate weddings and the meeting planner segment because they are convinced that without a successful track record in the catering business they will not be successful in those segments. They plan to make some personal contacts with event facilities but to concentrate most of their efforts on the segment of individuals who use catering services in their homes. This decision represents a good example of how a well-thought-out plan is often iterative. Sally and Martin now need to learn a great deal more about who these people are, what their needs are, and how to reach them.

Developing the Positioning Strategy and Brand Personality

The positioning of a product represents the manner in which target customers think about, or perceive, a specific product. Product positioning has two important components. One is the product features or benefits on which the customers make their judgments. The other is the set of competitive products to which customers make explicit comparisons.

Positioning a product in the most advantageous manner is an important activity. It is also one that is difficult to "fix" if it is done incorrectly or even when time passes it by. Several of the general merchandise catalogs that were very popular in the late 19th and early 20th centuries were unable to reposition themselves to serve a newly affluent suburban market after World War II. In the 1980s Spiegel did manage to successfully reposition itself to serve this more upscale market, but it took several years and presumably a large investment in marketing to do it. How to develop and execute a positioning strategy is discussed in chapter 3.

In recent years marketers have talked a great deal about a related concept—brand personality. Brand personality is a component of the broader construct of brand image. Brand image includes other elements in addition to brand personality, such as product features and benefits, corporate image, and images of other brands in the category.[1] Brand personality can be described as "those associations within the overall brand image that are typically called *brand personality,* which include (but are not limited to) associations with particular characters, symbols, endorsers, lifestyles, and types of users. . . . They make us think of a brand as if it were a person."[2]

Advertisers use a variety of techniques to create a personality for a given brand. A character that is closely associated with the brand—from the Pillsbury dough boy to Michael Jordan for Nike—conveys many things about the brand. Mass media advertisers also have a wide range of other techniques that range from the visual imagery of television advertising to the wonderful sensory stimuli of a cosmetics counter in an upscale department store.

---

[1]Rajeev Batra, John G. Myers, and David A. Aaker, *Advertising Management,* 5th ed. (Upper Saddle River, NJ: Prentice Hall, 1996), 320–321.

[2]Rajeev Batra et al., *Advertising Management,* 321.

Direct marketers have a wonderful opportunity to communicate directly with customers in a way that creates a unique and powerful personality. Patagonia, the catalog merchant and retailer of high-performance outdoor clothing, is a special case in point. The Ventura, California–based company was founded in 1973 by mountaineer Yvon Chouinard when he was unable to find the equipment he wanted. According to a company brochure, he chose a name for his company that "conjured romantic visions of glaciers tumbling into fjords, jagged windswept peaks, gauchos and condors." The catalog's positioning is derived from its obsession with quality, value, and lifestyles that feature adventure travel and extreme sports. It follows through on this positioning with an unusual focus on customers. The catalog's unique personality is embodied in long copy that features the performance of its products and photographs that show them being used by Patagonia customers. Most of the photos are taken by the customers themselves, who consider it a rare privilege to be included in the catalog.[3]

Sally and Martin know how they want customers to regard them. The first thing is that they have to become known as more than just a coffee shop. Because they want to benefit from the good reputation they have already developed, they decide to call the catering operation Fabulous Fare to link to the existing Fabulous Coffee name. They consider the key attributes of a successful catering service to be willingness to satisfy customer desires, products that are visually appealing as well as delicious, attention to detail, and friendly professional service in all aspects of the relationship. They realize that the professional competence and courtesy they want to be known for will have to be conveyed by their part-time service personnel as well as by themselves. Beyond these basic requirements for success, they want to develop a certain flair in both product and presentation that will distinguish them from other caterers.

Choosing the Key Selling Proposition

The key selling proposition is an integral part of the overall creative concept, which is discussed in detail in chapter 6. The key selling proposition states the overriding reason why customers should buy the product. Even though it is not a slogan or tag line, many advertisers believe that it should be brief and memorable. Yvon Chouinard, founder and CEO of Patagonia, wrote in a catalog introduction, "We think the future of clothing will be less is more, a few good clothes that will last a long time."[4] Key selling propositions like these form the basis for the entire creative effort.

Developing the Offer Strategy

The offer is a key direct marketing decision variable, as described in chapter 1 and discussed in detail in chapter 3. The offer includes the product (or service) itself, the price at which it is offered, any adjustments to the price, and other elements of the positioning strategy for the product.

The offer extended by Fabulous Fare, for example, will be tangibly conveyed by its menu, which will have three price ranges represented in each meal category. Low, medium, and premium price ranges will not be listed as such, but their presence will allow customers to tailor menus to their preferences as well as to their cost constraints. Their basic position-

---

[3]"The Anti-Marketers," *Inc.,* March 1988, 62; Robert Cross, "Wear on Earth: Patagonia Clothing Catalogues Capture the Spirit of Adventure in Style," *Chicago Tribune,* 7 September 1988, 29; "Patagonia: Where Less Is More," *Catalog Age* (September 1993): 94.

[4]"Patagonia: Where Less Is More," *Catalog Age* (September, 1993): 94.

ing strategy will be to deliver high-quality, beautifully presented food in a thoroughly professional manner that leaves no detail to chance. Sally and Martin are still wondering what they can do to differentiate their catering service from other reliable firms in the area.

The offer will be conveyed to the target market in the chosen medium or media by means of the message that is one product of the creative effort. Sally and Martin are aware that all promotions—in fact, all activities—of the new enterprise must convey the basic positioning of Fabulous Fare.

Formulating the Audience and Media Strategy

The media to be used in the program will be chosen based on the target market and the type of offer to be presented to them. If either direct mail or telephone is to be used, appropriate lists of prospects may be needed in addition to customer names from the company database. Locating, evaluating, and using mailing lists are addressed in chapter 4. Other direct response media are discussed in later chapters.

Even if only one medium, say magazines, is to be used, the media plan may become complex. There are thousands of magazines available, and there may be a substantial number that could reach a given market segment. In addition, the time frame of the program may be several months, permitting a number of insertions in the selected publications. To further complicate matters, the media planner may choose to place, say, three insertions in publications that are known to work for such offers and products and only one in a publication that is being tried for the first time during the specified period of time. A complicated schedule such as this requires careful planning and monitoring.

Even a simple media plan may require considerable effort. That effort should ordinarily begin with the customer database. People or companies who have bought before are usually the best targets for future marketing efforts. We discuss how we know this to be true in many contexts throughout the book. Sally and Martin provide one example.

In considering how to reach a target market of people who have a high likelihood of purchasing their catering services, they realize that people who know their existing business would be one set of good prospects for the catering operation. They did this informally with the Christmas party business by distributing flyers in the store. A logical extension is to produce an attractive brochure that can be placed in take-one holders in the store. Direct mail would be another way of distributing this brochure. Sally and Martin agree to think about how they might build a database of their retail customers at the same time they begin to look for one or more suitable local mailing lists. They recognize that proceeding slowly will, in fact, be in their best interest. They do not want to attract more business than they can handle effectively. This is a consideration in media planning and a particular advantage of some media. With a reasonable amount of historical data, the marketer can carefully regulate the flow of direct mail to generate just the right amount of business.

Crafting the Message Strategy

The message strategy is not synonymous with the completed advertising copy. The message strategy specifies what is to be said. It is meant to guide the writing of the copy as well as the other elements of the promotional execution such as the visual rendering.

As is discussed in detail in chapter 6, the message strategy is based on the desired positioning for the product and the key selling concept. The most important activity in this step is to identify the key benefit to be communicated to potential customers as the unique selling proposition. All aspects of the creative execution will work together to present this benefit—and perhaps one or two secondary benefits—to the prospect in a compelling manner.

The proprietors of Fabulous Fare know it is important to convey a single-minded message in all their communications with potential customers. After reexamining the promotional material of all the major caterers in their city, Sally and Martin come to the conclusion that none of them do a very good job of communicating a real customer benefit. They communicate features of the services offered—high-quality food, dependability, competent service personnel—but they do not really speak to how the customer benefits from these features. Each of them decides to talk to a few of their former college classmates and business colleagues whom they know have used caterers. The objective is to find out what using a caterer did for them that was deemed worth the money they spent. Sally and Martin talk individually to several of their friends. When they pool their information, they conclude that the key benefit their friends realized was a chance to relax and enjoy their social or business functions, knowing that the food and service was being handled in a way that reflected credit on them. The benefits Sally and Martin decide to emphasize are two-fold—relaxed, enjoyable entertaining and the esteem of friends and business colleagues. They translate this into a theme, "Carefree Entertaining with a Fabulous Flair."

When the message strategy has been established, the direct marketer has completed the communications strategy and is ready to plan the details of program execution, beginning with the manner in which the program will use the customer database and feed data back into it.

Specify Database Development, Use, and Enhancement Requirements

The database of customers and prospects is the cornerstone of direct marketing communications strategy. It provides information on which to base strategy. It allows the direct marketer to contact individual customers or prospects with offers and messages that are relevant to their needs, lifestyles, and business situations. Each contact with a customer or prospect provides useful information to be added to the database. How the direct marketer does these things is discussed in detail throughout the book, especially in chapter 8.

The established direct marketer should begin program development with an analysis of the database. For example, a catalog marketer may need to plan the regularly scheduled fourth-quarter mailing for a business supplies catalog. In this case the direct marketer will study the response to previous mailings from every possible perspective—by product, by industry type, by business size, by size and type of previous purchase, and by any other variable or combination of variables that explains differences in response rates.

On the other hand, a program may be motivated by a particular business problem. Routine management reporting may show a decrease in the rate at which cable television customers are signing up for profitable premium channels. The cable company thus may institute a program with the specific objectives of increasing the number of nonpremium subscribers who take at least one premium channel and increasing the number of premium channels to which current customers subscribe.

Both of these programs use information from the database to establish meaningful business and communications objectives. The business catalog marketer would use names and addresses from the database in executing the mailing and might also use rental lists, as described in chapter 4. The cable company marketer wants to present an offer to existing customers, for which one option is to communicate the offer by mail, again using customer information from the database. Both marketers must record all responses to their programs in the database. The catalog marketer will indicate exactly the products purchased by each customer who buys as a result of the mailing. The cable company will record new premium channel subscriptions for both billing and future marketing purposes. Both can analyze nonresponse data to see if they can determine patterns that suggest reasons for nonresponse. Alternatively, they can ask customers directly why the offer was not appealing and what customers want that is not being offered. All these opportunities for planning and executing programs and for communicating with customers exist because the database permits the marketer to know who customers are and how they react to specific offers.

This is a normal way of doing business for the relatively small number of businesses that have developed their customer database over several years. For new business, or for those that have just recognized the need for a database, the first task is to begin building a database. Sally and Martin vow to carefully record the names, addresses, telephone numbers, and preference information of all catering customers and contacts on their personal computer. They are also thinking about ways to build their base of potential customers more quickly. How can they collect names and addresses in the retail store without being too obviously mercenary? Could they offer a drawing for free office parties, perhaps for the first day of spring and later for Halloween? Would this give them the kind of prospect base they are looking for—busy, upscale individuals who have a reasonable probability of using catering services?

The database should also be used to provide as much information as possible for the personnel who will design the creative execution. This includes segment profiles as well as detailed information about the effectiveness of past programs.

DEVELOPING CREATIVE EXECUTION AND PROTOTYPES

With the communications strategy in place and the marketing database as an information resource, it is time to develop the creative execution. Specialized personnel, including artists, copywriters, and production experts, will become active at this stage.

It is useful to think of the creative process in two steps. First, the creative tactics must be specified. Are we designing a specialized catalog featuring one specific product line—children's apparel or home furnishings, for example? Or does the catalog feature several product lines such as outdoor equipment, casual wear, and home decorating items, for example? Does the catalog have a seasonal theme, is it targeted to a segment of the customer base, or is it a combination of both?

Having studied the creative strategy and all available information about the target segment, the creators of a direct-response print advertisement may translate the key selling proposition into a benefit-oriented headline. "Re-live a Magnificent Party of the Gilded Age" might be a headline for a collectible plate. "Manage Your Portfolio Like the Pros" could herald new software for personal investment management. Having established the central theme for the execution, the creative team goes on to the second step—generating the rough execution.

The creative team first makes its ideas tangible in prototype form. The prototypes are relatively inexpensive renderings that are sufficiently illustrative to be shared with program managers or clients for input and approval. For television spots the format is a storyboard consisting, in one column, of rough script that is paired, in the second column, with carefully selected frames from the proposed advertisement. The script is not complete, but it portrays the essential story line of the spot.

For a print advertisement or a direct mail package, the prototypes will consist of renderings that show headlines, perhaps line drawings of major visual elements, and blocks where the copy will appear. For a multiple-piece direct mail package, the creatives will produce a mock-up of each item so the functioning and appearance of each can be examined.

Sally and Martin decide that a brochure will be the most cost-effective marketing device for their catering services. They will place brochures in a take-one holder near the cash register in the store and will leave one, along with a menu, when they make personal sales calls. The brochure can also be the centerpiece of a direct mailing soon after Labor Day. They engage a local direct-response agency to design the menu and brochure, to advise them on rental lists to supplement their own database of prospects, and to plan and implement the mailing when the time comes.

When the creative tactics have been proposed, the major pieces are in place so that program planners can finalize the budget.

DETERMINING THE BUDGET

While evaluating past programs, the direct marketer should also uncover their budgets. Previous budgets are extremely useful in at least two ways. First, they show the manner in which budgets are typically presented in that firm. This can prevent a great deal of "rework" caused simply by not formatting the budget in the manner that company managers demand. Second, they can help avert mistakes arising from not including key cost components. This kind of error can make the difference between a successful direct marketing program and a disastrous failure.

Figure 2.3 (pp. 32–33) shows a sample budget for a hypothetical direct mailing. It is essential that the budget be broken down into individual elements, each of which can be costed separately. The mailing package in this hypothetical program, for example, requires a 4-page letter, a 16-page booklet, a reply card, a business response envelope (BRE), and an outer envelope. Each is treated separately because it involves different processes and perhaps even different suppliers. Note that each category includes a contingency amount. Also note the percentage of the total budget consumed by each element. These are general estimates; the past experience of the company itself will be an even better guide. For other general estimates of costs for a variety of direct-response media, you may wish to consult the *Direct Marketing Association's Statistical Fact Book.*

In planning an actual program, the guidance of suppliers is a critical element in good budget estimates. Whether you use an agency, as Sally and Martin decided to do, or you subcontract each element yourself, taking advice from experienced direct marketing professionals will prevent many missteps.

One thing you will quickly discover is that if your timing is off and everything becomes a "rush job," the costs will soar. Consequently, establishing a realistic timetable and sticking to it is essential.

ESTABLISHING THE PROGRAM IMPLEMENTATION TIMETABLE

Table 2.3 (p. 33) shows a time schedule for a relatively simple direct mail program using several different vendors. It lists each separate activity indicating the beginning and ending date for each one and its resulting duration. The date from which you plan is either the date you need to mail ("drop") the package or the date by which it needs to be delivered, whichever is most critical. Plan backward from the critical end date, indicating the time that will be required for each step. Do not forget to include weekends and holidays in your time allocation. Do consult with suppliers to get a realistic estimate of the time required and any special scheduling requirements.

Great North American Widget Corporation
Consumer Solo-Mailing Campaign
Two-for-One Widget Offer
(Approx. Net Quantity, 100,000 [100M]; Scheduled Drop Date, 7/28/95)
WORKING BUDGET*
Prepared by Frank N. Stine, Mar. 15, 1995

A. Creative
   1. Preliminary roughs and dummies $ 400
   2. Copy, including revises 3,570
   3. B&W computer mockup (headlines & text in place; illustrations 900
      and photos—position only)
   4. Contingency 500

   TOTAL $ 5,550   (6.71%)

B. Art & Preparation
   1. Photography $ 900
   2. Model fees 400
   3. Photo direction 500
   4. Line illustrations (7) 350
   5. Color computer mockup 600
      (final copy & art elements in position, incld. low res scans of
      photography)
   6. Color separations (2 randoms) 400
   7. Colorkeys 250
   8. Image assembly of film 600
   9. Contingency 1,000

   TOTAL $ 5,000   (6.05%)

C. Printing Production
   1. 4-pg. litho let., 8-1/2" × 11", 2 colors (105M @ $29.98/M) $ 3,150
   2. 16-pg. booklet, 5-1/2" × 8-1/2", 2 colors (105M @ $108.60/M) 11,400
   3. Reply card, 3-1/2" × 5-1/2", 2 colors (105M @ $14.46/M) 1,500
   4. BRE, #7-3/4, one color (105M @ $14.92/M) 1,550
   5. Outer env., 6" × 9", 2 color, cello window (105M @ $57.18/M) 6,000
   6. Contingency 2,400

   TOTAL $ 26,000   (31.44%)

D. Mailing Lists p
   1. Mail order respondents (tape) 70M @ $95/M $ 6,650
   2. Active magazine subs (tape) 45M @ $60/M 2,700
   3. Contingency 1,200

   TOTAL $ 10,550   (12.76%)

E. Computer Processing
   1. Reformatting, data conversion, etc. $ 450
   2. Merge/purge (115M @ $11.10/M) 1,300
   3. Code and run 4-up labels (100M @ $4.20/M) 400
   4. Reports & directory printout 200
   5. Contingency 450

   TOTAL $ 2,800   (3.39%)

(continued)

F. Lettershop Production
    1. Insert, label, sort, mail, etc. (100M @ $33.90) $ 3,400
    2. Affix bulk-rate stamps (100M @ $6/M)   600
    3. Audit & pull samples (100M @ $2.10/M)   200
    4. Contingency   300

               TOTAL $ 4,500   (5.44%)

G. Allocated Fees
    1. Ad agency $ 6,000
    2. Consultant   1,500
    3. Contingency   1,000

               TOTAL $ 8,500   (10.28%)

H. Postage
    1. 100M @ $198/M $ 19,800   (23.93%)

         BUDGETED GRAND TOTAL $ 82,700   (100%)

Source: Data from Shell Alpert, CMC, Alpert O'Neil Tigre & Co., 1995. Table reprinted from *Direct Marketing Association's Statistical Fact Book, 1996* (New York: Direct Marketing Association, 1996), 63. Reprinted with permission of the Direct Marketing Association, 1998.

*Rounded to the nearest $50
Budgeted Total without Cont. Reserves = $75,890

FIGURE 2.3 Sample Budget for a Direct Mail Program

TABLE 2.3 Reverse Calendar For Direct Mail Campaign Plan

	Event	Start Date	End Date	Working Days
11	Mail posted/delivered	10/5	10/14	7 days (3rd class)
10	Assemble, address, and imprint postage	9/29	10/2	3 days
9	All lists completed and delivered	9/25	9/28	1 day
8	All printing completed and delivered	9/15	9/28	10 days
7	Camera-ready art prepared and shipped to printer	9/3	9/14	7 days
6	Changes to text and design of mail piece final	8/31	9/2	3 days
5	Lettershop hired (if applicable)	8/31	—	—
4	Begin to write and design piece in-house or hire outside writer and designer	8/17	8/28	10 days
3	Start to compile in-house mailing lists and hire list broker to rent lists	8/13	8/31	13 days
2	Format and composition of mail piece determined	8/10	8/14	5 days
1	Set objectives, make plan, determine budget	8/3	8/7	5 days

Source: Pitney Bowes, *How to Grow Your Business Using the Mail,* 1992, p. 23. Reprinted with permission of Pitney Bowes, Stamford, Conn.

ESTABLISHING PROGRAM EVALUATION RULES AND METHODS

If the program has been well planned, some of the work of this stage has already been done. Program objectives were established with measurability in mind. Previous programs were examined, and the criteria used to evaluate them were noted. With these two considerations—program objectives and past experience—measures such as those described in Table 2.2 will be selected.

The plan must also specify the point at which the measures will be calculated. The responses to direct marketing programs may come in over weeks or even months. It is often impossible to wait until the last possible response has been received before conducting the initial program evaluation. Analysis of past programs should provide an estimate of the response curve. If 60 percent of the responses to a third-class mailing have historically been received within 6 weeks, 80 percent within 8 weeks, and virtually all responses within 12 weeks, the planner has several mileposts from which to choose. Response curves are highly dependent on the medium. A television infomercial is likely to have a response curve that stretches over only a few hours. A magazine may have one that lasts from a few weeks to a few months, depending on the life of the magazine and the pass-along readership. Whatever the appropriate time points, it is necessary to specify the measurement interval in advance and to stick to it.

In the same spirit, the manner in which the measures are calculated should be carefully specified in advance. Most of the measures in Table 2.2 seem pretty straightforward. However, issues such as returns and service expenses as well as definition of terms need to be clarified in the program plan. We discuss such calculations in chapters 3 and 9.

The Role of Service Agencies in Planning and Executing Direct Marketing Programs

Having now worked through the process of planning a direct marketing program, perhaps you can now see more clearly why several types of service agencies are commonly used by direct marketers of all kinds. In general, service agencies can be divided into two basic groups. The first comprises large agencies with multiple capabilities. Table 2.4 lists the 10 largest direct response agencies. Some of these names are familiar to you as traditional advertising agencies. To better serve their clients, traditional agencies have either acquired or built direct response units in recent years. Others retain the identification of the original direct response agencies. Notice that six of the top 10 agencies draw a substantial portion of their billings from outside the United States. Notice also that these billings include direct marketing services including database marketing, printing and lettershop functions, and telephone marketing.

The remaining four include the numerous specialty direct marketing service firms that offer these and other services. Some of the other services these providers include list brokers, creative specialists, fulfillment houses, and consultants. As specialists they perform critical services in the relevant portion of the direct marketing program.

TABLE 2.4 Direct Response Advertising Agency Ranking by Billings: 1994 vs. 1995

Agencies	Total Billings (in millions)		U.S. Billings (in millions)		International Billings (in millions)	
	1994	1995	1994	1995	1994	1995
Rapp Collins Worldwide[a]	934.4	1,183.8	461.0	552.5	473.4	631.3
Wunderman Cato Johnson	910.5	1,140.3	430.6	570.6	479.9	569.7
Ogilvy & Mather Direct	973.0	1,098.0	413.0	346.0	560.0	752.0
DraftDirect Worldwide, Inc.	493.7	655.6	259.8	413.5	233.9	242.1
Bronner Slosberg Humphrey, Inc./Strategic Interactive Group, Inc.[b]	333.5	450.2	333.5	450.2	NA	NA
FCB Direct	135.6	370.0	135.6	370.0	NA	NA
Barry Blau & Partners, Inc.[b]	261.6	332.6	261.6	332.6	NA	NA
Grey Direct International	312.3	331.1	184.3	186.1	128.0	145.0
DIMAC Marketing Corp.[a,c]	271.4	315.6	271.4	315.6	NA	NA
McCann Direct	215.0	275.0	50.0	90.0	165.0	185.0

Source: Data from DMA Research Department, September 1996. Table adapted from *Direct Marketing Association's Statistical Fact Book, 1997* (New York: Direct Marketing Association, 1997), 28–30. Used with permission of the Direct Marketing Association, 1998.

Note: These rankings were compiled from figures provided by 113 direct response advertising agencies. These agencies responded to requests made in 1996 for full year 1994 and 1995 U.S. and international direct response revenue and billings. This chart displays billings from standard direct response agency services (plus revenue from internal production capabilities).

[a]Billings include revenue from internal production capabilities such as printing, database operations, lettershop functions, and/or telephone marketing.

[b]Information was confirmed by an outside auditing firm.

[c]DIMAC Marketing Corporation's 1995 figure includes acquisitions of the McClure Group as of October 1, 1995; and Palm Coast Data, Inc. as of May 1, 1995.

Summary

Planning a successful direct marketing program is the heart of the direct marketing enterprise. It calls for knowledge of the marketplace, analytical skills, technical know-how, and good marketing judgment. Executing the program also requires substantial people management and a certain level of technical skills. The areas of knowledge about program planning and execution that are specific to direct marketing are the focus of the remainder of this book.

Discussion Questions and Exercises

1. What is the meaning of the term *direct marketing program*? How does it differ from an advertising campaign?
2. Discuss the steps a direct marketer should follow in planning a direct marketing program.
3. What are some of the objectives that might be established for a direct marketing program? Where do these objectives originate?
4. What are some of the variables a direct marketer can use to evaluate the effectiveness of a direct marketing program?
5. Name some of the types of service agencies or bureaus that might be hired to assist in a direct marketing program.

Suggested Readings

Goetsch, Hal. *Developing, Implementing, and Managing an Effective Marketing Plan.* Chicago: American Marketing Association, 1993.

Hiebing, Roman G., Jr., and Scott W. Cooper. *How to Write a Successful Marketing Plan,* 2nd ed. Lincolnwood, IL: NTC Business Books, 1997.

Luther, William M. *The Marketing Plan.* New York: amacom, 1992.

Roman, Ernan. *Integrated Direct Marketing,* 2nd ed. New York: McGraw-Hill, 1995.

3 CHAPTER Offer Planning and Positioning

At a Glance

In chapter 1 we briefly discussed the five decision elements of direct marketing—offer, creative, media, timing/sequencing, and customer service. Now we are ready to explore one of those elements—the offer—in depth. We defined the offer as the complete proposition made by the direct marketer to the prospect. The next step is to break down the offer into its component parts and examine each one.[1]

Elements of the Direct Marketing Offer

It is useful to classify the elements of the direct marketing offer into those that are *required* (must be present in all offers) and those that are *optional* (may be included or not, depending on strategy and costs). This classification assumes that the objective is order generation

---

[1]The authors wish to express their thanks to Connie Bauer of Marquette University for her helpful comments on an earlier version of this chapter.

TABLE 3.1 Elements of the Offer	
Required Elements	*Optional Elements*
Product/positioning	Incentives
Price	Multiple offers
Length of commitment	Customer's obligations
Terms of payment	
Risk-reduction mechanisms	

Source: Adapted from Herbert Katzenstein and William S. Sachs, *Direct Marketing* (Columbus, OH: Charles E. Merrill, 1986), 206; Caroline Zimmermann, "The Proposition," in Edward L. Nash, ed., *The Direct Marketing Handbook* (New York: McGraw-Hill, 1984), 81, 82.

on the basis of a stand-alone (often referred to as a "solo") offer. If the objective is, say, to have the prospect request information, all the elements listed as required in Table 3.1 may not be necessary. We return to that issue later in the chapter.

Figure 3.1 shows a customer acquisition offer made by America Online (AOL), the product being its on-line service. This particular version makes use of a cardboard mailing folder with a specially designed holder for the AOL disk. You may also have seen AOL offers shrink-wrapped with magazines, especially computer-related ones. The incentives are clearly "50 Hours Free" and a coupon book that helps new members find other offers on AOL. Terms of payment are described on the inside of the folder, although the amount of the monthly payment is not specified there. It also explains how to cancel without incurring the first month's fee—clearly an obligation of the customer—although there is no specific time commitment required. Inside the folder is the statement, "So easy to use, no wonder it's #1," which positions AOL as the industry leader. Notice also that AOL is attempting to get double mileage out of this promotion by including a pass-along coupon.

We can reasonably assume that this AOL mailing piece was not inexpensive because it was designed and produced to convey and protect a computer disk. By including all that a prospect needs to sign up for the on-line service, AOL is clearly attempting to acquire customers with this mailing alone—no additional steps required. Just sit down at your computer, insert the disk, and log on. However, they could have used a two-step program with a mailer promoting the service and a 1-800 number to call for a free disk. Ask yourself what you think the response might have been if the program had been designed in two steps: inquiry generation followed by a fulfillment mailing with the disk and additional information. Then ask yourself how that compares to the potential response when, as in this example, the prospect can immediately access the service.

THE REQUIRED ELEMENTS

Product/Positioning

Once the product for the direct marketing campaign has been chosen, the issue becomes how best to present the product to the target audience. How to create the desired perception of—how to position—a product is such an important topic that the last portion of this chapter is devoted to it. Suffice it to say at this point that the positioning chosen will define the product's image in the mind of the prospect.

FIGURE 3.1 AOL Customer Acquisition Mailer

Source: Used with permission of America Online.

There are times when the manager should consider changing the product itself to create a more effective offer. In the case of a tangible product, one or more of its attributes can be changed. For example, a catalog of art items may offer an expensively framed print that is not selling well, and management may decide to test an offer of the print alone without the frame. In the case of a service, changes are usually easy to make. A cable television franchise may find its customers resistant to the inclusion of a particular movie channel as part of the basic subscription package. If the franchise's agreement with the supplier does not prevent it, the cable company can offer the movie channel as an option. Both these actions will affect the price at which the product is offered.

Price

When establishing the base price for a product, direct marketers, like general marketers, follow one of three basic pricing policies:

1. A penetration price implies setting a low price to encourage a high volume of sales. In recent years, for example, direct marketers of discount office supplies have become an important element of that market.

2. A skimming price implies setting a high price in order to obtain a high margin on each unit sold. Prestige retailers can be just as successful in the direct marketing arena as in their stores. Neiman Marcus is an example of a retailer whose catalog not only generates substantial sales, but, through striking Christmas specials such as the "James Bond" BMW, actually adds lustre to its distinctive image.

3. A third policy, often referred to as sliding down the demand curve, implies establishing a high price for the initial offer and then making planned reductions in price for succeeding offers. Another important success story in direct marketing has been the sale of personal computers. This is a product category in which the initial version of a new model is usually given a premium price, which is reduced as the product ages and the appearance of a new model becomes imminent.

These policies obviously provide only general guidelines for actual price setting. A detailed discussion of the pricing process is beyond the scope of this book, but the topic is well covered in marketing principles and marketing management texts. Other pricing issues of importance to direct marketers are covered in retailing texts. Direct marketers, like general marketers, must remember that the perceived value of the good to the prospective customer and its costs to the marketer establish the upper and lower bounds within which the actual price must be set. They must also remember that price is one important determinant of the image of the product and the firm that offers it.

Length of Commitment

Offers can involve either a single transaction or a series of transactions over a period of time. Perfume purchased from a self-mailer sent by a local department store, a book bought through an ad in a trade magazine, or a piece of software purchased from a catalog are all examples of a one-time commitment. Offers that involve multiple transactions over a period of time are called continuity offers. There are a number of kinds of continuity offers:

Fixed-Term Offers   Newspaper and magazine subscription offers feature a fixed number of issues for a stated price, payable at the beginning of the service. For magazines, a year's subscription is fairly standard, with shorter terms used in introductory offers and discounts offered for longer-term subscriptions. Magazines are the classic example of a fixed-term offer; so much so, in fact, that other types of fixed-term offers are sometimes referred to as *subscription offers.*

Automatic Shipment Plans   In an automatic shipment plan, such as one that offers a shipment of different fruit each month for a year, purchase of the first item signals acceptance of the series and triggers automatic shipment of remaining items. Shipment of the series will continue until it is completed, as in the fruit-of-the-month example, or until the purchaser cancels. This type of offer is also referred to as a *till forbid* offer.

Club Plans   The true club plan, originated by the Book-of-the-Month Club, adds an element of choice to the automatic shipment plan. The advance bulletin allows the member to choose the recommended selection, an alternative, or no shipment at all for that time period. Most club plans use what is called the *negative option,* meaning the recommended selection will be shipped unless the customer *refuses* it within a stated period of time. It is also possible to structure a positive option, requiring the customer to reply affirmatively before any shipment is made, but experts agree that such a plan does not usually work because it makes it too easy for the customer to effectively say "no" by not replying. This is a violation of the basic direct marketing rule, "Make it easy to say yes!" Club plans may offer to ship more quickly if the customer does exercise the positive option, thus creating commitment to the purchase. Club plans have historically included a customer obligation to purchase a minimum amount of the product within a certain period of time. You may be familiar with clubs that offer compact disks (CDs) by mail order. Club plans in this highly competitive category may not have a minimum purchase requirement.

Terms of Payment   Most direct-response offers provide a variety of payment options, including cash, cash on delivery (COD), and credit cards. Direct marketers agree that the size of the average order is larger when customers use credit cards. Estimates of how much larger range from 15 to 30 percent. On the other hand, COD has become a less favored payment option because of its cost and inconvenience if the customer is not at home when delivery is attempted. Additionally, the rate of refusals of COD shipments is high.

Payment options have once again become an important issue with the advent of Internet commerce. The importance of credit cards to the direct-response marketer is in conflict with the concern felt by many consumers about providing credit card numbers over the Internet. Most experts expect this concern to abate with the advent of better encryption systems and, also perhaps, when consumers have more experience with Internet purchases. In the meantime, firms with their own proprietary credit plans may be the beneficiaries of this particular consumer concern because customers do not need to submit the charge account number with each order.

Risk-Reduction Mechanisms   There are many ways by which marketers can reduce the perceived risk of purchasing a particular product by direct response without first having had a chance to examine it. Guarantees, warranties, and free trial offers are among the most common. For example, Sears has operated from the very beginning with a "satisfaction guaranteed or your money back" policy. Free trial, ordinarily an opportunity to use the product in the purchaser's home or business for a specified period of time with the right to return it free of charge during that period, is also common.

For certain types of products, the seller may include some type of "value protection" in the offer. The concern that sells rare stamps may guarantee to repurchase them at the selling price for a stated time or even indefinitely. The "collectibles" firm may guarantee a stated value within a certain period of time or they will repurchase the item or series. Firms selling off-price or discount merchandise may offer to refund the difference if the purchaser can find the exact same merchandise at a lower price within a stated time period.

Perceived risk, which can be either economic or social in origin, can also be reduced by presentations that help overcome some of the disadvantages of not being able to see and touch the actual merchandise. In mailings or catalogs for furniture, fabric samples are sometimes included so that customers can evaluate both color and quality. Copy that describes the product in great detail helps lessen the sense of unfamiliarity. Perhaps most important of all, a well-known corporate or brand name lessens the perceived risk of purchasing without first examining the merchandise.

THE OPTIONAL ELEMENTS

The optional elements of the offer can best be described as ways of enhancing the value of the offer or reducing the perceived risk to the prospective customer. By providing a higher perceived value, these elements create a sense of urgency that helps to overcome the natural human tendency to defer a decision. Direct marketers long ago learned the lesson that a purchase postponed is most often a purchase not made.

Incentives

The variety of incentives that can be offered to make the proposition more attractive is limited only by the imagination and funds of the direct marketer. In a very general way, we might classify these incentives as free gifts, premiums, free information or samples, sales or discounts, and sweepstakes or contests.

Think carefully about what you intend to accomplish by including an incentive as part of the offer. Is it to reward the prospect for requesting information, for examining the product on a trial basis, or for actually purchasing the product? Do you want to use the incentive to increase the size of your average order—by offering merchandise at sale or discount prices, by offering an incentive for purchases above a certain amount, or by offering a series of gifts as the size of the purchase increases? Is it important to get a sample of the product itself into the hands of the prospect? Are you using the incentive to try to increase the response rate, or to build excitement and involvement, or both? Is the incentive a reward for continued purchases over a period of time?

With regard to free gifts, the generally accepted rule among direct marketers is that the gift should be related to the product being sold. Beyond that, creativity and cost take over. What will work best to achieve the stated objectives? Traditional marketing research—or even better, marketing research that takes advantage of the customer database and other strengths of direct marketing—can help refine the many possible options.[2] Then testing, as described in chapter 10, can answer that question with a specified level of statistical probability.

Some direct marketers recommend testing one gift; if that works, add a second, and keep adding them until you reach a point of diminishing returns. Fingerhut, a general-merchandise mail-order marketer, has long used multiple gifts successfully. They also use a great deal of personalization, even in acquisition mailings such as the one shown in Figure 3.2. This offer has incentives in addition to the six bonus gifts. The overwrap also offered, "Pay Nothing for 30 Days with a credit-approved order from this catalog!"

Sale or discount merchandise may be offered as a promotional activity, as part of normal merchandising practice, or for reasons related to other aspects of direct marketing strategy. Just as there are discount retailers, there are also discount direct merchants who make promotional prices a key part of their marketing strategy.

---

[2]Thomas M. Bodenberg and Mary Lou Roberts, "Integrating Marketing Research into the Direct Marketing Testing Process: The Market Research Test," *Journal of Advertising Research* (October–November 1990): 50–60.

FIGURE 3.2 Fingerhut Customer Acquisition Mailer

Source: Used with permission of Fingerhut Corporation.

Sales, especially discounts offered for promotional reasons, are quite frequent. A trade paper offers a limited-time subscription (two or three months, perhaps) at a steeply discounted price. A bank offers free checking accounts to new customers for the first two months. A coupon offers an especially attractive introductory price for a new consumer packaged good. A sports news service on the Web offers a month's free use before a subscription fee is charged.

Most direct marketers have overstocked, end-of-season, or just generally slow-moving merchandise that must be moved. This can be done by establishing outlet stores or selling the items in bulk to other firms. But frequently this merchandise is offered to the regular customer base as a sale or discounted item. You have probably noticed sale merchandise featured on special pages in the middle of many catalogs. Usually the cataloger compensates for the lower margin by putting more items on a single page, often in black and white instead of color. The length of the descriptive copy may also be shortened.

Occasionally, you will see merchandise offered at such a low price that your reaction is, "Either this is a really poor-quality product or there is another reason for the promotion." For many years cigarette marketers offered logo merchandise of significant value—T-shirts, caps, backpacks, and so forth—for minimal proof of purchase. Their objective was to capture the names and addresses of smokers. To smokers of their own brands they offered loyalty programs featuring attractive merchandise offers. To smokers of competing brands they offered tempting inducements to switch brands. This targeted direct-response promotional activity was useful during the years when no television advertising of cigarettes was allowed. When the final ban on media advertising went into effect—which is what many observers think that the industry had long been preparing for with its database-building efforts—the tobacco companies were left with much less room to maneuver in a promotional sense. However, they knew who their customers were because they had prepared well for the regulatory actions that had seemed inevitable for a number of years.

Multiple Offers

Often a mailing or a space advertisement will feature more than one product. Perhaps the most common type today, especially in business markets, is the card deck. Promotions for 20 to 30 different products, most printed on business reply postcards, are combined in a single mailing. These co-op mailings, which feature the products of many different manufacturers, offer a relatively low cost way to acquire new customers or to generate inquiries. Each offer stands on its own, but the set of offers is targeted to a particular market—business executives, doctors, computer professionals, and so on. For example, a card deck mailed to owners of small businesses might contain offers ranging from business cards to fax machines to office stationery to instructional videos for popular business software. Most of the offers are printed on postage-paid response postcards. Others might be more elaborate, such as a brochure, or on occasion the recipient will find samples of items such as a new brand of self-stick notes.

Another reason for developing multiple offers is product complementarity. A business marketer may offer computer software for medical billing purposes and include in the offer an initial supply of the preprinted business forms needed to produce the bills. The objective of this type of offer might be to increase the average order size or simply to enhance customer satisfaction by providing all the requirements for successful product use.

A financial services firm may include information about individual retirement accounts (designed for persons who wish to supplement their existing pension plans) or Keogh plans (designed for the self-employed) in a broadly targeted mailing. This type of offer should have "something for everyone" who is interested in retirement income planning, no matter what the person's employment status. The wise direct marketer then segments the respondents based on the nature of their response and the information they provide with it (people who are self-employed, employees of large corporations, people who are nearing retirement, and so forth). The direct marketer then has clear segments to which targeted offers can be directed.

Customer's Obligations

With some offers, the customer assumes an obligation by accepting the offer. A club mailing with a front-end offer of essentially free books or CDs obligates the customer to purchase a certain amount of product over a specified period of time. Other types of obligations are registration of warranties and a requirement to have periodic servicing performed. When the customer sends in the registration or warranty card, or when he or she registers electronically when installing a new piece of computer software, the direct marketer is building a database of customers. If you will stop and think about it, you will recognize that the marketer is usually collecting a small amount of additional data that will make future marketing programs more effective.

Clearly, the direct marker has a huge arsenal of techniques that can be used to develop any given offer. How is the marketer to know, out of all the possibilities, which ones are most likely to be effective? There are two types of guidance the marketer should follow. The first is the objectives of the offer. The second is the target market that has been selected for that particular direct marketing program.

Considerations in Designing the Offer

First we look at what kinds of objectives can be established for an offer and front- and back-end issues that arise from different kinds of objectives. Then we provide some guidelines on how many and what type of objectives to establish. Finally, we consider the effect of the target market on offer design.

OBJECTIVES AND THE OFFER

First the direct marketer must clearly establish the marketing objectives for the program. Some of the most common generic objectives include:

- to attract new customers, members, or donors
- to obtain repeat business from the existing customer base
- to reactivate lapsed customers
- to produce sales leads:
    for an established product
    for a new product
- to raise funds for a nonprofit organization

These are the general categories of direct-response objectives. However, stated in this manner, they are inadequate to guide a program. Specific objectives are needed, such as

- to obtain a sufficient number of new customers to achieve the target sales growth rate
- to get a specific percent of the one-year lapsed members to renew their membership
- to produce a specific number of sales leads for each sales representative or dealer/distributor

Numbers still need to be inserted into these more concrete objectives, which will then become measurable. Notice also that the second objective is very specific about the target market (members who have lapsed within the past year). Good objectives are developed with a specific target market in mind and may even specify the segment as part of the objective.

The marketer must also determine what financial objectives have been set, or what the customary objectives are for this type of offer in this industry or firm. Is the offer expected to product an immediate profit, or is profit dependent on repeat sales (e.g., continued purchase of tapes or records, heavy usage of a credit card)? Is the offer viewed as an investment in building the base of prospective customers? Is it part of a multistage sales process, such as sales-lead generation, that cannot be directly evaluated in terms of profitability? In other words, will the success of this specific offer be evaluated over a short or a long time horizon? We discuss the desirability of evaluating programs on the basis of long-term measures, especially Customer Lifetime Value, in chapter 9.

The direct marketer must clarify the marketing and financial objectives in order to make a decision that balances front-end (short-term) *responsiveness* against back-end (longer-term) *effectiveness*. An example shows why this is so.

Say that a magazine is deciding whether to offer a 3-month introductory subscription for $8 or a 12-month subscription for the regular price of $48. The 12-month offer would allow respondents to cancel at any time and receive a full refund for the unused portion of their subscription.

Assume that the magazine has a gross margin, before subscriber acquisition cost, of 10 percent, or $4.80, based on the regular price. The acquisition cost per subscriber for this magazine averages $6.

It is immediately clear that the magazine would not make money on 12-month subscriptions. It would lose even more money on the 3-month trial subscription:

Regular subscription revenue	$48.00
Less: gross margin	4.80
Product cost (12 months)	43.20
Plus: acquisition cost	6.00
Total direct costs (12 months)	49.20
Loss on 12-month subscription	(1.20)
Product cost (3 months; $43.20/4)	$10.80
Less: trial subscription revenue	8.00
	2.80
Plus: acquisition cost	6.00
Loss on 3-month trial subscription	(8.80)

This hypothetical example makes the economics of the 3-month trial subscription look very unfavorable. The example is oversimplified, however. For one thing, the response rate should be higher for the 3-month trial (less perceived risk!) than for the regular 12-month subscription, making the assumption of equal acquisition costs incorrect. The cost for a 3-month trial should actually be lower than $6, so the front end of the 3-month subscription would probably look acceptable. On the other hand, subscribers who accepted the 3-month offer would have to be contacted much sooner to renew their subscriptions, meaning increased renewal cost (which, by the way, should be considerably lower than the initial acquisition cost, assuming that the subscribers are satisfied and renew at a high rate). That is one of the back-end considerations.

Another back-end consideration is the number of cancellations on the 12-month offer. Cancellations can be quite high, making the loss greater than it appeared to be on the front end and, even worse, providing a smaller customer base for renewal efforts.

In this example no incentives were offered. Think about what might have happened if an attractive free gift had been included. The inclusion of a free gift with the 3-month offer would probably increase the response rate even further. That would be good—even though it makes the offer more expensive—if subscribers really like the magazine and renew over a period of several years. In other words, it could be a good investment in repeat business.

The inclusion of a free gift with the 12-month offer would probably increase the response rate to that offer also. That would also be good, wouldn't it? The 12-month offer brings in more revenue and doesn't incur renewal costs as soon, right? But remember, the 12-month offer has a cancellation privilege (and, of course, the customer gets to keep the free gift). What if a lot of people accept the offer just to get the gift, then cancel immediately? The answer is obvious—the magazine would lose a lot of money! This happens more often than you might expect, especially if the incentive is really attractive.

This illustrates the difference between a hard offer and a soft offer. A hard offer is one in which the product essentially stands on its own feet; there are no incentives, and perhaps even a small cost, such as furnishing the postage, attached to the reply. A soft offer is one that is as attractive as possible and that makes it as easy as possible for the prospect to take action. "Hard" and "soft" are not absolutes; they make up a continuum with many possible "hard_er_" or "soft_er_" offer configurations possible. Figure 3.3 (p. 48) contains suggestions for hardening or softening offers. The important point is that with a hard offer, the number of responses will be smaller but their quality will be higher; with a soft offer, there will be a large volume of initial responses but many of these responses will be unproductive.

There is one more way in which the marketing objectives can affect the choice between these two hypothetical offers. If one objective is to quickly ascertain the likelihood of success or failure of the product itself—say, the offer is for a new magazine—the 3-month trial offer will allow management to assess the renewal rate more quickly than will the 12-month offer.

It is clear that measurable objectives that take into account both front-end responsiveness and back-end profitability are critical to the success of direct marketing programs. Establishing a realistic number of objectives of the right kinds is necessary.

HOW MANY OBJECTIVES OF WHAT TYPES?

Before considering the question of how many objectives, it is useful to think about two different kinds of direct marketing objectives. A useful general guideline is that *primary* objectives should be measurable, direct-response objectives. *Secondary* objectives may be more communications-oriented, more long-term, and/or less easily measurable.

Primary Objectives

In chapter 2, we pointed out that marketing objectives are derived from the financial objectives of the business unit. Objectives for any specific direct marketing program are then derived from the overall marketing objectives. The direct marketing program objectives constitute the set of goals that guide offer strategy.

To Harden an Offer, You Can:

- Make it harder to order (telephone number not toll-free, business reply envelope not included, customer must ask for more information).
- Make payment terms more stringent.
- If price is not mentioned (e.g., a lead-generation offer), mention it. If price is mentioned, emphasize it.
- Tell more about the product, especially any negative features.
- Charge for something that could be offered free (charge for the first catalog, don't place postage on the business reply envelope).
- In a lead-generation program, tell them a salesperson will call.

To Soften an Offer, You Can:

- Make the payment terms less stringent.
- Offer advance credit approval.
- Offer an incentive. If you have been offering one incentive and find it is working, try offering two.
- Make it as easy as possible to respond (fill in the recipient's name and address on the postage-paid response card so all the person has to do is drop it in the mail; keep your toll-free number in operation 24 hours a day, 7 days a week).
- Add a game, contest, or involvement device—a rub-off spot, stamps that are to be stuck on the appropriate squares, a riddle or puzzle to be solved.
- Run a sweepstakes. Even direct marketers who personally dislike them admit they work.

FIGURE 3.3 Offer Hardeners and Softeners

Source: Adapted from Edward L. Nash, *Direct Marketing* (New York: McGraw-Hill, 1982) 74–75; Bob Stone, *Successful Direct Marketing Methods,* 3rd. ed. (Chicago: Crain Books, 1984) 58–60; Caroline Zimmermann, "The Proposition," in Edward L. Nash, ed., *The Direct Marketing Handbook* (New York: McGraw-Hill, 1984), 87–88.

As suggested at the beginning of this section, a specific program objective might be

- to add 5,000 new customers to the existing customer base during the third quarter of the current fiscal year.

There could be another primary objective that fits into this context, but the objective is so specific that there may not be. On the other hand, there may be secondary objectives that will advance the overall marketing objectives of the business.

Secondary Objectives

Not only do secondary objectives further the overall marketing goals, they should also help to integrate all marketing programs, whether direct-response or traditional. They might be brand-building objectives such as raising awareness or increasing the perceived value of the brand. They may be aimed at helping to decrease the perceived risk of purchasing through the mail or over the Internet. They may be associated with a corporate positioning or image-building strategy such as is described later in this chapter. Some examples of this type of objective might be

- to raise the level of unaided awareness of product X among members of the target market from y percent to z percent
- to make 20 percent of physicians in the appropriate medical specialty aware of the newly approved use for drug A
- to help position the Acme Corporation as the primary supplier for high-quality chemical reagent ZED

Secondary objectives that further overall marketing and communications objectives also help to guide the creative strategy for the direct-response program. In recent years marketers have placed great emphasis on having a consistent underlying theme and creative look in all facets of the marketing effort. This reduces customer confusion and provides more mileage for the marketing dollar.

The Question of "How Many Objectives?"

The question of "how many objectives?" is not an easy one to answer with any degree of certainty. Clearly there should be enough objectives to make the program robust, accomplishing as much as is feasible in a single undertaking. It is also important not to have so many objectives that the program loses focus and becomes confused (and is confusing to the prospective customer!). As a rule of thumb, consider the desirability of one or two primary objectives and two or three secondary objectives. Three to, at most, five objectives seems to be about all a single program can successfully achieve.

Objectives are critical in helping to guide offer construction. So is another key element of the direct marketing program plan—the target market.

DESIGNING OFFERS FOR DIFFERENT TARGET MARKETS

Ensuring that the product itself is appropriate for the target market or configuring a product or service to suit a particular target market are important marketing considerations. However, as you have just learned, the offer extends beyond just the product and its positioning.

Price, as you already know, affects the product and brand image. It also is a determinant of the amount of gross margin available to cover other elements of the offer, such as incentives. The length of commitment option may be used to make a product more attractive. If you are offering a relatively expensive product, such as a collectible plate, to a broad middle-class audience, you may want to offer terms of payment that commit the purchaser to, say, one-third with the order, one-third upon delivery, and one-third 30 days later. Committing the purchaser to three payments may make the product seem more affordable but it also gives the marketer the back-end problems of billing, collections, and perhaps a higher rate of cancellations and refunds. This type of strategy is clearly effective, however. Consider exercise equipment infomercials on television. The monthly payment amount is easy to discern, but the total cost may not be very evident. These two examples also suggest that offer elements are very interrelated; another way of saying they must all work together to appeal to the target audience.

The same goes for each of the other offer elements. The direct marketer must carefully consider the target market, for example, by offering a greater number of risk reduction factors such as incentives to prospective customers than to the existing customer base. This is good marketing strategy as long as you can keep the segments separate so your current customers will not know that you are giving a "sweetened" offer to attract new prospects. The careful direct marketer who is meticulous about the maintenance and use of lists can, in fact, accomplish this separation of segments much more effectively than the traditional marketer who must use mass media.

Designing an offer is not simple. There are a multitude of factors to consider and a multitude of techniques that can be used. Direct marketers will be much less likely to make major blunders in designing offers if they keep objectives and target markets, not the mechanics of the offer, paramount at all times. This is true of all offers, but it becomes especially important in a complex multistage offer.

Planning Offers for Multistep Programs

The classic multistep offer is a two-stage offer in which the prospective customer first requests more information and then is contacted by mail, telephone, or in person to close the sale. Actually, there can be more steps, perhaps several more: an inquiry, followed by a detailed mail package, followed by a qualifying telephone call, followed by a personal sales call. This is a common process in some high-ticket consumer markets such as automobiles and insurance. It is especially important in business-to-business marketing, and is discussed in greater detail in chapter 11.

Marketing and financial objectives play an equally crucial role in structuring multistage offers, just as they do in one-shot programs. Additionally, the direct marketer can plan a progression of incentives or can build up to a major incentive in a way that produces more qualified leads at each succeeding stage.

A few years ago, when the automobile industry was trying to ascertain how to advertise to the emerging women's market, Ford Motor Company turned to an approach called "Curriculum Theory." Based on theories of learning that you have probably studied in psychology or consumer behavior classes, Curriculum Theory argues that when the purchase is large or otherwise risky, direct marketers must move prospects through a carefully constructed series of steps that will culminate in a purchase.

> The [Ford Curriculum Marketing] program consisted of a series of three mailings, sent to 160,000 women car owners in San Diego and Dallas. A control group of 80,000 received no mail. The mailings and their follow-up were as follows:
>
> - A questionnaire and letter from the woman in charge of the program at Ford, personalized to acknowledge current car ownership, which discussed women's car-buying issues and Ford's intent to deal with these issues better.
>
> - Since an overwhelming number of women responded that they were not satisfied with their experience with dealership sales and service personnel, Ford established a training program. The second mailing, sent two months after the first to all questionnaire respondents, described the training program and invited the women to rate its success. It also offered a $25 incentive to visit a dealership and send in a rating form.
>
> - This "graduation" mailing, sent one month later to all rating form respondents, offered a dealer event for the respondent and a friend. It included a wine and cheese buffet, service seminars, help with financing, and a 14K gold bracelet for invitation holders who attend.

The results were exciting. After six months of tracking, 1,600 incremental car purchases could be attributed to the program. The sales rate for program recipients was almost three times that for nonrecipients.[3]

There are several things that are worth noticing about this program in addition to its success. One is that it obtained information from prospects at the very beginning. Ford learned that women were not satisfied with the way they were treated in the purchasing and servicing of automobiles. It seems reasonable to assume that the interest of the women prospects was piqued by this approach.

The information that Ford obtained forced them to take action—not just to develop a promotional program but to back up their claims with a program of dealer training. To be more precise, it was necessary to improve dealer responsiveness to women's concerns before making claims in a promotional program. Then Ford used another mailing to explain to prospects what they had done and to ask them to rate dealer effectiveness—additional involvement as well as additional information. The final mailing offered a substantial incentive, obtained additional names, and, most important of all, got the prospects to take action, to visit the dealership.

An approach such as the Ford Curriculum Marketing program pays attention to detail, dedicated follow-through, a commitment to obtain information from prospects and customers, and a requirement that the company act on the customer information. All of this takes place over a period of time ranging from several weeks to several months. These are demanding standards, even if they do carry with them a greater likelihood of success. Perhaps that is why we do not see more programs like it.

A Few More Words about Costs

In planning an offer, it is important to distinguish between its fixed and its variable costs. Whether we are discussing a mailing, a space ad, or a broadcast spot, fixed costs are those that do not change with the volume of responses, whereas variable costs do change with the volume of responses. In general, the same is true of telephone marketing costs, except that there we have the added factor of time expended per call.

Fixed costs generally include creative and production costs (copy writing, graphic design, printing, filming, recording, and so on) and some media costs (time in broadcast media, space in print media). Remember that these costs are defined as "fixed" for only one specific program. Once the direct marketer decides on a particular magazine in which to place the direct-response ad, the cost of the medium is fixed for that program. The direct marketer may, of course, choose a cheaper magazine (which may reach fewer prospects) or a more expensive one (which would be expected to reach more prospects or, at the very least, to provide a very desirable environment for the product being promoted). The direct marketer may also choose a simple presentation with a response coupon printed on the page, or the direct marketer may choose a more expensive presentation with a bound-in response card. Management should remember that

---

[3]Deborah Fain and Mary Lou Roberts, "Technology vs. Consumer Behavior: The Battle for the Financial Services Consumer," *Journal of Direct Marketing* 11, no. 1 (winter 1997): 44–54.

- once the production and media decisions have been made, the costs are essentially fixed for that program, whether it is successful or not

- high costs, or even high quality in a technical sense, do not necessarily make a direct-response program successful

Variable costs, as we have said, are those that vary according to the volume of either production or responses. Once an efficient production level has been reached, the cost of a direct mail package is usually directly variable on a unit basis. Postage is also a unit variable cost of *production*. Costs of merchandise and incentives will ordinarily vary directly with the number of *responses*.

Other costs will vary, but not necessarily directly. These are often the back-end costs of honoring guarantees, dealing with returns and/or cancellations, collection costs, and other aspects of customer service. Because these costs vary indirectly, they are difficult to predict. We cannot stress too strongly that these costs can escalate rapidly as a result of a poor-quality product or a poorly structured offer.

In the end, the degree to which prospects respond to an offer is affected by the offer itself, but it is more dependent on the degree to which the offer (and its presentation, which is discussed in succeeding chapters) answers the needs of the target market.

What Motivates Prospects to Respond?

There are many considerations in structuring an offer, and many individual elements that can be included. In the final analysis, the direct marketer can ascertain which of the available offers works best by testing alternative offers and going with the winner.

Testing, as we discuss in detail in chapter 10, is a critical aspect of the discipline of direct marketing. The ability to know which offer (or which list or mailing date or whatever) works best is the feature that most distinguishes direct marketing from general marketing.

Testing provides tremendous opportunities to improve the productivity of direct marketing programs. However, testing is not the entire answer. Direct marketers need to understand the attitudes, values, and motivations of customers and prospects just as general marketers do. Testing can only help select the best offer from the available set of offers. Understanding customer and prospect motivations and behavior will help the direct marketer structure better offers to test.

Marketing and consumer behavior texts frequently contain extensive discussions of motivation theory. Most students are familiar with Maslow's hierarchy of motivations, and many are also aware of other approaches to understanding human motivation. The problem for marketers is that these theories are borrowed directly from the behavioral sciences, and marketers often have difficulty in applying them to specific situations.

In 1978, Geraldine Fennell[4] set forth a marketing-specific typology of motivations that has been further developed by John Rossiter and Larry Percy.[5] Figure 3.4 shows the eight basic purchase motivations divided into three categories—negative, mildly negative, and positive.

---

[4]Geraldine Fennell, "Consumer's Perceptions of the Product-Use Situation," *Journal of Marketing*, 42 (1978): 38–47.

[5]John R. Rossiter and Larry Percy, *Advertising and Promotion Management* (New York: McGraw-Hill, 1987), 169–174.

Negative Origin

Problem removal	Prospect experiences problem; seeks product to remove it.
Problem avoidance	Prospect anticipates future problem; seeks product to prevent occurrence.
Incomplete satisfaction	Prospect not satisfied with current product; seeks a better one.
Mixed approach-avoidance	Prospect likes some things about product but not others; tries to find product to resolve this conflict.

Mildly Negative Origin

Normal depletion	Prospect is out of stock or low; seeks to maintain normal inventory.

Positive Origin

Sensory gratification	Prospect seeks physical gratification/enjoyment.
Intellectual stimulation	Prospect seeks psychological gratification; to explore or master situation.
Social approval	Prospect sees opportunity for social rewards/personal recognition through use of product.

FIGURE 3.4 Basic Purchase Motivations

Source: Adapted from John Rossiter and Larry Percy, *Advertising and Promotion Management* (New York: McGraw-Hill, 1987), 170.

For our purposes, it is sufficient to think of motives as forces that cause people to try to achieve a desired state of being. These forces, or drives, can cause a person to try to avoid a particular situation or outcome regarded as unpleasant or even dangerous (a negative motivation). If the situation or outcome is seen as pleasant or attractive, the person will be motivated to approach it. There are also times when the individual is motivated merely to maintain the status quo.

Home security systems are an example of a product category for which an avoidance motive—to prevent the negative outcomes resulting from fire or theft—is likely to be operative. Attractive travel opportunities suggest an approach motivation, whereas purchase of disability insurance may be motivated by a desire to maintain an established standard of living.

Thinking carefully about what would motivate the target prospect to respond to the offer will help the direct marketer develop more effective offers. There is one more thing to keep in mind when conducting this analysis. Motives affect both the decision to purchase a product category (disability insurance) and the decision to purchase a specific brand within that category (a specific firm's disability insurance policy). Sometimes the motivation will be the same at both category and brand levels; sometimes it will not be. Be sure to separate the two levels conceptually to be as clear as possible about motivations for purchase.

Marketing research is recommended to ensure that the hypothesized purchase motivations are the ones actually experienced by the prospect. This type of analysis will lead directly to a consideration of the appropriate positioning for the product.

The Importance of Positioning

The desired positioning for the product should be an important consideration throughout all stages of the development of an offer and its creative execution. According to Philip Kotler, "Positioning is the act of designing the company's offering and image so that they occupy a meaningful and distinct competitive position in the target customers' minds."[6] Positioning is relevant only to a clearly defined market—the target market and other stakeholders defined in the organization's planning process. The achieved position is relevant *only* to customers and other stakeholders; it does not matter whether persons outside the defined target market like the product's presentation or find it attractive. Only the stakeholders matter when evaluating the effectiveness of a positioning strategy.

There are two basic approaches to developing a positioning strategy. One is to rely on managerial judgment about what constitutes the most effective positioning. The other is to conduct marketing research at one or more points in the process of developing the strategy.

Unquestionably, marketing research is needed to develop the best positioning strategy. Experience suggests that managers often, perhaps even usually, would not select the positioning strategy that research finds to be best. One reason seems to be that managers find it difficult to view their own products objectively or in the same manner as prospective customers view them. The discussion of purchase motivations in the preceding section is based on consumer perceptions of the needs that products satisfy in actual use. However, the uses or needs of consumers may differ from management's expectations; hence managerial and customer perceptions of the product may differ.

A discussion of the techniques used to conduct positioning research is beyond the scope of this book. We will not complicate our discussion of positioning strategy by continually referring to the need for research and the types of research needed, but trust that you recognize that most of the issues we discuss in the remainder of this chapter can be more completely understood with the aid of good marketing research.

POSITIONING ALTERNATIVES

Conventional wisdom says that products can be positioned in terms of their benefits or attributes (a copying machine with automatic feed and collating), their particular uses or users (personal copiers for individuals or small businesses), or against a specific product category or competitor (the copier with the lowest repair frequency). However a study by C. Merle Crawford uncovered other types of positionings in widespread use among both consumer and business marketers.[7] Figure 3.5 contains a complete list of positioning alternatives that are available equally to general marketers and direct marketers.

Crawford called the new type of positioning he discovered surrogates or substitutes. The nature of this type of positioning is that "the marketer does not describe the features/benefits, but instead says something about the product that permits the reader/listener to reach individual conclusions."[8] Crawford reasons that this type of positioning is particularly effective because it lets the reader infer attributes or benefits of the product, presumably those the individual would most like the product to possess. Following Fennell's reasoning about

---

[6]Philip Kotler, *Marketing Management,* 9th ed. (Upper Saddle River, NJ: Prentice Hall, 1997), 295.

[7]C. Merle Crawford, "A New Positioning Typology," *Journal of Product Innovation Management* 4 (1985): 243–253.

[8]Ibid., p. 247.

Product Attributes/Benefits

Product Features: A characteristic, usually tangible, of the product itself.

Product Benefits: A satisfaction received from use of the product.

Direct—directly attributable to use of the product

Indirect—indirectly attributable to use of the product

Surrogates

Nonpareil: Without equal; top quality.

Parentage: Origin—maker, seller, performer, etc. A parentage positioning can be stated in terms of:

Brand—because it comes from that line of branded products

Company—because it comes from that particular company

Person—because it was created by a particular person

Manufacture: The manner in which the product is made. A manufacture positioning can be stated in terms of:

Process—how it is actually produced

Ingredients—the ingredients it contains

Design—superior functioning as a result of the way the product is designed

Target: Because the product was made specifically for people/firms like you. A target positioning can be stated in terms of:

End use—how or the situation in which it will be used

Demographic—created for a group of people who can be defined demographically

Psychographic—created for a group of people who can be defined in terms of lifestyle

Behavioral—created for a group of people who can be defined in terms of a specific behavior

Endorsement: Credible spokesperson(s) says it is good. Endorsement can be made by:

Expert—person with appropriate credentials/knowledge

Emulative/object of emulation—a role model or person the target would like to imitate

Rank: Market leader.

Experience: Long or frequent use gives credibility to its claims. The experience can be of several types:

Other market—in another market

Bandwagon—sheer numbers

Time—over an extended period of time

Competitor: Alike or similar to another successful product.

Predecessor: Similar to an earlier product that was popular.

FIGURE 3.5 Product-Positioning Alternatives

Source: Adapted from C. Merle Crawford, "A New Positioning Typology," *Journal of Product Innovation Management* 4 (1985): 243–253.

applying the purchase motivation categories to the development of positioning strategies, the surrogate positionings would allow for a broader positioning that does not rely on explicit claims about attributes or benefits. The result could be appeal to a broader target market. In Crawford's study, benefit positioning was used most frequently (32 percent) in the ads studied, followed by the general category of surrogates (23 percent), then attribute positioning (19 percent). Twenty-six percent of the ads had no identifiable positioning.

Crawford cites a number of strategic implications that emerged from the study:

- Surrogate positioning should be considered, especially for products with little or no physical differentiation.
- Positioning should be consistent over all elements of the marketing program.
- The positioning approach should be sustained over a considerable period of time.
- There will probably be more types of positioning developed as managers become more experienced with this powerful marketing tool.

THE PROCESS OF DEVELOPING A POSITIONING STRATEGY

The complex activity of developing an effective positioning strategy can best be handled by dividing it into distinct steps. Batra, Aaker, and Myers have provided a useful approach that can be modified slightly for the direct marketing environment.[9] It consists of six steps:

1. Identify the competitors.
2. Determine how the competitors are perceived and evaluated.
3. Determine the competitors' positions.
4. Analyze the customers.
5. Select the position.
6. Monitor the position.

Identify the Competitors

This step has already been accomplished as one element of the direct marketing program plan, which provides the basis for the more detailed analysis necessary to generate a positioning strategy.

Determine How the Competitors Are Perceived and Evaluated

Knowledge of how competitors are perceived and evaluated rests upon two pieces of information: (1) what attributes or benefits customers use to judge competitive products; and (2) how satisfactory customers perceive each product to be on each attribute or benefit. Because there are many attributes and benefits on which products can be judged, determining the few that are actually important to customers is not an easy task. This determination requires marketing research, and most research texts have detailed discussions on identifying and evaluating the attributes that customers perceive to be important.

---

[9]This section is based on Rajeev Batra, David A. Aaker, and John C. Myers, *Advertising Management,* 5th ed. (Upper Saddle River, NJ: Prentice Hall, 1996), 201–213.

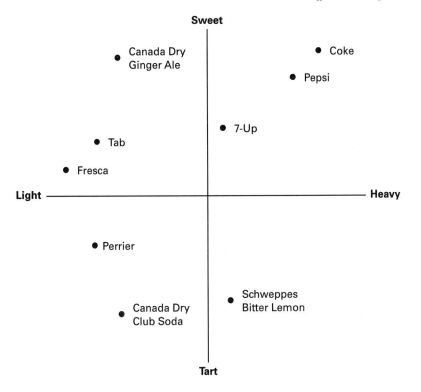

FIGURE 3.6 A Hypothetical MSD Map for Soft Drinks

Source: Glen L. Urban, John R. Hauser, and Nikhilesh Dholakia, *Essentials of New Product Management* (Upper Saddle River, NJ: Prentice Hall, 1987), 116. Reprinted by permission of Prentice Hall, Inc.

Determine the Competitors' Positions

Knowing how each of the competitive products is evaluated on each of the determinant (important) attributes or benefits effectively defines its positioning. This is often expressed as a mapping of products on dimensions that represent the important attributes or benefits. Figure 3.6 shows a hypothetical perceptual map for soft drinks in which taste (sweet or tart) and heaviness (light or heavy) are the dimensions (attributes) and a number of brands are arrayed on these two dimensions. Perceptual mapping is a technique commonly used by general marketers that is equally relevant to understanding competitive positions in a direct marketing environment.

Analyze the Customers

Customer analysis requires determining what segments exist in a particular market. The assumption, based on a great deal of research experience, is that customers tend to use the same set of attributes or benefits to evaluate all the products in a category, but that different segments of customers have distinctly different preferences for different sets of attributes and benefits. It is the difference in preferences that identifies market segments.

One way to approach the search for an unserved or underserved market segment is to look for a set of attributes or benefits that customers want, the firm can deliver, and its competitors cannot deliver. Once it is established that the firm's product can deliver those attributes or benefits, the question becomes: Will customers believe that it can deliver? If the attributes or benefits are not being successfully delivered by a competitive product, that is even better. Frequently a product will be able to establish a distinctive positioning simply by emphasizing desired attributes or benefits that no other product has seen fit to emphasize. Remember, this crucial step in developing a positioning strategy is based on understanding what customers want, not what management thinks they want!

Select the Position

Assuming that the product or service has some flexibility in its positioning approach, how does the marketer select the position?

The best way is to think in terms of a perceptual map such as the one in Figure 3.6, and look for "gaps" in product availability on one or more dimensions. Gaps indicate two possibilities. The first is that no product is serving that particular need or set of needs, which means an opportunity exists. The second is that no one (or at least not a sufficiently large group of customers) has that particular set of needs, which means there is no opportunity.

Even if an opportunity exists, questions remain. Management must ask: Are we capable of serving that particular segment of the market? Do we have the skills and resources? Is our image appropriate (or can we make it so)? Is the market segment attractive? Is it large enough to be profitable? Does it have a satisfactory rate of growth? Can we reach the purchase decision makers in a cost-effective fashion using lists or other direct-response techniques?

This discussion implies that the subject of positioning is always a product or a brand. However, it is also possible to reposition an entire company. In the fast-moving world of information and high technology, we may begin to see this happen frequently. An interesting example is provided by Guthy-Renker.

Guthy-Renker, the creation of Bill Guthy and Greg Renker, retains its headquarters in Palm Desert, California. The initial foray of these two individuals into the world of infomercials was largely accidental. Bill Guthy, who was running an audiocassette duplicating company in 1984, received a large order for tapes of a real estate investment course. When he learned that the customer was selling the tapes on television, his interest was piqued.

Guthy consulted with his friend, Greg Renker, who was working for his family's tennis resort business, and they considered what they might sell via infomercial. They were both fans of a self-help book published in 1937, Napoleon Hill's *Think and Grow Rich*. With capital of $100,000 they bought the rights to the book and audiotapes of Hill's lectures. They hired exquarterback Fran Tarkenton to promote the product and aired the infomercials on six small-market stations. Their first infomercial was an immediate success and grossed nearly $10 million by 1988.[10]

By 1996, the company was grossing $300 million a year with top-selling infomercials, including their PowerRider and Perfect Abs. They were also responsible for infomercials including Victoria Principal's line of skin-care products, Anthony Robbins's Personal Power instructional video, and Vanna White's Perfect Smile tooth-whitening product, and were aggressively expanding into the housewares market. They were more than a direct-response television producer; they designed and manufactured the skin care and personal improvement products sold via their infomercials. An increasing number of the products were sold at retail in the United States.

---

[10]Louis S. Richman, "Pioneers of a New Way to Sell," *Fortune,* 31 October 1994, 248.

Their business was also rapidly becoming a global one. They had businesses in New Zealand, Japan, and China, and used distributors to reach markets in other areas of the world. They entered the Japanese market in early 1996 with the Pressure Perfect cooking system; Pump-N-Seal, a hand-operated vacuum-creating device for preserving food; and the Perfect Abs device. The initial infomercials, produced in the United States with a Japanese voice-over, were deemed to be successful. The company planned to introduce more products and continued to add to its television reach, with a total of 23 million homes—about half the Japanese market—receiving its infomercials.[11, 12]

In China, the company began in late 1996 with the PowerRider, Perfect Abs, and Perfect Smile. According to press material quoted in a trade paper, Guthy-Renker rated the initial effort as extremely successful. They said that "within 20 minutes of its debut the inventory of PowerRiders was met with a buying frenzy, resulting in the depletion of its entire first month's supply."[13] They also noted that getting merchandise to customers still depends on primitive payment and delivery methods. Customers must pay either in cash or COD, and delivery is handled by privately commissioned taxi companies.

Guthy-Renker also was an early entrant onto the Internet. They founded America's Choice Mall on the Internet and were active in encouraging others to engage in business on the new medium, offering Internet seminars and opportunities to engage in product marketing in cooperation with Guthy-Renker. Their business also included catalog and direct mail marketing for a variety of products.

In short, the business was no longer a simple producer of television infomercials for exercise equipment. They felt they needed an image that accurately reflected the wide-ranging, global nature of their business. They discarded their original logo and replaced it with a stylized globe that can be put into motion on the television screen. According to the design firm, their challenge "was to create an identity that would symbolize television as the core of the business. It had to be 'ahead of the pack,' high tech and global in scope. Another design objective was that the symbol work independently from the name/logotype, allowing for a potential name change yet maintaining equity in the symbol."[14]

The logo change was an important symbolic move for a company that had come far from its original roots. Alone, however, it would not be sufficient to completely reposition the company within the global direct-response industry. Guthy-Renker has an active public relations operation and both of the original founders are active in industry activities, including taking a leading role in establishing the National Infomercial Marketing Association. As in all marketing activities, all these things work together to create the desired image and positioning for the firm.

Monitor the Position

Whether the task is to position a product, a service, or an organization, the positioning strategy needs to permeate all aspects of the marketing effort. The desired positioning will affect

- the manner in which the offer is structured and how the various elements of it are implemented
- the creative execution, which must portray in both words and visuals the desired image

---

[11]"Guthy-Renker Pushes Product on TV Tokyo," *DM News,* 15 July 1996, 18.

[12]"Guthy-Renker Expands Japanese Penetration," *Response TV*, Information Access Company, November 1996, 24.

[13]"Guthy-Renker Sells Infomercial Products on Shanghai TV," *DM News,* 23 December 1996, 3.

[14]www.Palmer-id.com, 1996.

- the choice of media vehicles, both to reach the chosen target market and to provide an appropriate context for the product as positioned
- the types of customer services offered

The degree to which the positioning of the product in the minds of the target market matches management's desired positioning should be evaluated at regular intervals to ensure that the positioning remains appropriate to the needs of the target market as it changes and evolves over time. Marketing research, both qualitative and quantitative, is needed on a planned basis to oversee the positioning that has been achieved and to recommend adjustments in strategy or execution as needed.

A FEW LAST THOUGHTS ON POSITIONING

If it is done well, positioning will create for a product or for an organization an image, perhaps even a "personality," as discussed in chapter 2. Positionings can be modified, but not easily, so much thought should be given to choosing an appropriate positioning strategy initially. When doing so, it will help to keep these points in mind:

- Don't try to be something you are not. Be realistic in assessing your firm's and your product's capabilities. You can be sure that your prospective customers will be!
- If the positioning is working, stick with it. Modified positionings—even worse, frequently modified positionings—cannot be as sharp and clear as a single positioning, maintained with absolute consistency. Because positions are expensive to achieve and difficult to change, the marketer should think as far ahead as possible when developing a strategy. The Guthy-Renker example is a good one, because they adopted a logo that would permit a name change at a later date if it is needed to further define their image.
- For maximum impact, see that the positioning permeates all your marketing communications.

Avoid these positioning traps:[15]

Trap 1: *Positioning head-on against the industry leader.* It is very difficult to compete with an established product on its own territory. Instead, establish your own territory.

Trap 2: *"Me too" positionings.* The positioning should not be a weak image of another product's position, offering some trivial differentiating feature or benefit. Again, carve out your own area of distinctiveness.

Trap 3: *Factory-driven positionings.* This trap arises when a firm produces a product to utilize manufacturing capacity or an available technology. It is difficult to position a product successfully if no one really wanted it in the first place.

Trap 4: *Being "something for everybody."* If you try to be something for everyone, you usually end up being nothing to anybody. An undifferentiated marketing strategy suggests an unsegmented market—a difficult thing to find today.

Trap 5: *Line-extension positionings.* A product that relies on a strong, preexisting product for much of its image in the customer's mind will obviously suffer if the original product declines in popularity.

Trap 6: *F.W.M.T.S.* This acronym stands for "forgot what made them successful." If it isn't broken, don't fix it!

---

[15]Al Ries and Jack Trout, *Positioning: The Battle for Your Mind* (New York: Warner Books, 1986), 34–114.

Summary

The offer and the product positioning it establishes are central to the execution of the direct marketing strategy. The direct marketer must choose carefully among the variety of offer options and positioning alternatives available. Both the marketing and the financial objectives of the program will affect the way in which the offer is structured. Marketing research can be used to refine offer options, and testing is often used to identify the offer that generates the greatest long-term profitability.

Discussion Questions and Exercises

1. What are the required offer elements? The optional elements? What role does each play in developing an offer?
2. What do the terms front end and back end mean? How are they relevant to offer planning?
3. Why would a direct marketer choose to use a hard offer instead of a soft offer?When might a soft offer be better? Would you describe the AOL offer at the beginning of the chapter as hard or soft?
4. Look at the motivations described in Figure 3.4. For each motive, can you think of a product that strongly appeals to that particular motive?
5. What is the meaning of positioning? How is it important in the process of offer development?

Suggested Reading

Brown, Herbert E., and Roger W. Bricker. "Just What Is a Direct Response Offer?" *Direct Marketing* (March 1988): 68–75.

CHAPTER 4

Mailing Lists: Processing and Selection

It has been said that you will lose money sending a terrific piece to a lousy list, but make lots of money sending a lousy piece to a terrific list. Perhaps this is a myth perpetuated by list managers, compilers, and brokers. Certainly product manufacturers would argue that the product is the key, and copy writers would probably insist that the copy is the important thing. Still, in the direct mail world, nobody denies that the list is a crucial (and most would say *the* crucial) ingredient in determining the profitability of the overall direct mail effort.

There are many definitions of a list, and quite a few of a mailing list. At this point, think of a mailing list as the names and addresses of prospects to whom your copy could feasibly be sent. Note the word feasibly as a qualifier.

Direct marketers should be aware of all feasible lists. However, it is even more important to select lists that are profitable, if not in terms of dollars, at least in terms of providing ample information that can be used to enhance future list selection decisions. But, even if we

limit the meaning of profitability to dollars, it is not always easy to specify the criterion function to be used in choosing among feasible lists. Should we use "response rate" as the guiding value? Or should we use "dollars of profit per name," or "dollars of profit per dollar
spent," or simply "total dollars"? The answer can be any of these, depending on just how we
formulate the choice. We have all heard the phrase from the Bill of Rights, "All men are created equal." However, all responses are *not* created equal. For example, responses from one
list may be more likely than from another to engender repeat business; if the "response" is a
request for more information, those from one list may result in a very different conversion
(to purchase) rate than those from another list. In chapter 9, we examine the criterion that is
considered the "ultimate" criterion in direct marketing profitability assessment, *Customer
Lifetime Value* (CLV), the net present value of all future revenues and costs associated with
an (acquired) customer. However, although the vast majority of direct marketers are in agreement about the merits of using CLV, at the moment the majority of direct marketing profitability assessments continue to be based on the *one-time* response rate or dollar profits of
the mailing or campaign.

   We begin this chapter by discussing the types of lists available and describing aspects
of each type. Then we walk down various paths through the list rental process. We next
expand upon a variety of list-related issues that are briefly mentioned in the discussion of
the list rental process. Finally, we consider the economics of mailing lists and the choice
among feasible lists. In chapter 5, we examine the key issue of list segmentation, which is
breaking out a list into subsets with different characteristics, notably, different profit, cost,
or response parameters. This allows different subsets to be treated differently in terms of
mailing decisions.

Types of Lists

There is no standard way to categorize the different types of lists. One way is to separate
them into consumer lists versus business lists. Within this classification, consumer lists are
most commonly broken down into response lists, compiled lists, and house lists. Business
lists can also be broken down into the same categories. Over the last decade, there has been
enormous growth in the number of lists available; on a percentage basis, the largest growth
has been in the area of business lists.

   Consumer *response lists* are lists of individuals who have some identifiable product
interest, such as martial arts equipment, investment advice, or X-rated videotapes, and have
a proven willingness (or at least not a total aversion) to buying by mail. The reason these lists
are called response lists is that the list members have indeed responded to a mailing. These
lists are, essentially, some other company's house list, or "subscriber" list. There are many
subcategories of consumer response lists, although the distinctions are not critical, and
indeed, not mutually exclusive: buyer lists—those who have bought a product or service;
subscription lists—those subscribing to a publication (who, therefore, have also bought a
product); donor lists—those who have made a contribution to a charity or other cause; and
others.

   There are many examples of consumer response lists. A recent examination of new lists
available notes the *Nordstrom Quality Women Apparel* list of about 500,000 purchasers of
apparel from Nordstrom during the past 12 months; the list is 87 percent female. Another new
list includes about 35,000 subscribers to *Sea Magazine*.

Consumer *compiled lists* are lists of individuals who we do not know are willing to buy by mail, but who have some identifiable characteristic or set of characteristics, such as being a lawyer, a male member of a bridge club, or a self-reported viewer of an UFO. The reason these lists are called compiled is that somebody (or a computer) has actually compiled them. That is, the names are generally not found in one place through any sort of "natural selection," as, say, a list of members of a gun club would be. The compiling usually is done from public records, often from phone books or other directories. Of course, the compiling may also be from private sources, such as hospitals or golf courses, but this occurs less frequently. After all, for example, it is not easy to contact every, or nearly every, hospital and acquire a list of all patients who, for example, had heart surgery; or to compile from golf courses a list of all Florida residents who have hired a golf teacher.

An enormous variety of compiled lists exist—indeed, some to an unexpected degree of "sub-sub-subcategorization" (i.e., specialization). Some are very large lists, and others are quite small. As we shall observe later in this and the next chapter, size plays a role in many types of list rental and segmentation decisions. For example, we could rent a list of college department chairmen (about 40,000); we can also rent a list of college department chairmen who are heads of language departments (about 3,000); we can also rent a list of college department chairmen of Spanish (language) departments! We can rent a list of women whose dress sizes are *petite* (about 2.4 million), of women who are wives of high-income male executives (about 66,000), and even of never-married women more than 21 years old who were born in Europe and eat kosher food (about 3,000)!

A *house list* is usually defined as a list of customers who have bought from the company. Actually a better way to express the notion of a house list is to say that it is a list derived from the company's own files. It may include, for example, the names of individuals who aren't really customers but who have once made an inquiry. Of all lists, house lists are probably the most important because, without doubt, they are the most profitable lists. This is not solely due to being the list engendering the highest response in aggregate (although this is almost always true), but also because it usually contains valuable information—that of previous purchase patterns—that other lists most often do not contain. This, in turn, allows increased ability to segment the list into subgroups, about which decisions are able to be more efficiently optimized. Actually, in addition, a house list is an asset—sometimes the most valuable asset the company owns! It can potentially bring in revenue by renting it to other parties. Naturally, many businesses, both big and small, have house lists; indeed, companies who had never kept a house list have finally seen the light and are now continually updating and maintaining a house list.

A *business list* is generally a list of individuals at companies, ideally including the individuals' titles. However, it can also be a list of businesses not including the name of individuals; in this latter case, the company is often called, and a request is made for the name of the relevant person to whom to send materials (or call). For example, a company selling janitorial services might call the company and ask for the name and title of the individual in charge of managing such services. A company selling business-to-business has, of course, its own house list. Unlike consumer lists, the majority of other business lists are not response lists, but compiled lists. They are usually compiled by SIC (Standard Industrial Classification) code, a classification that codes a company's type of business first into relatively large categories (e.g., mining, manufacturing, retailing), and then more detailed categories (e.g., the manufacturing [large] category corresponds to beginning numbers of 20 through 39; the manufacturing of computer-related devices corresponds to numbers beginning with 357; actually manufacturing computers corresponds to 3571, manufacturing computer storage devices corresponds to 3572, manufacturing computer terminals corresponds to 3577, and so on). Dun & Bradstreet is an example of a repository of many business lists.

Business lists also vary in their size and degree of specialization. An example of a compiled business list would be a list of public relations executives (about 45,000). One could perhaps debate whether this is a consumer list or a business list, but does it really matter what it is called? It probably should depend on the offer being sent. A compiled business list could also be a list of fabric shops (about 10,000), or a list of drive-in theaters (about 500). Examples of response business lists would include a list of home-based businesses that purchased Dillon Corporation's home employment software (about 9,000), or a list of businesses that purchased Internet products or services from Cyberbuilders (about 84,000).

Recently, new methods of list development have evolved that do not precisely fit any of the aforementioned definitions. These methods involve promotional activities that are planned and executed for the primary or near primary purpose of list development. This would include broadcast promotions; holding exhibits, seminars, and other events; or organizing Web sites that provide information and at the same time record the names registered at the Web site. It would also incorporate the use of coupons and other "gifts," sweepstakes opportunities, and special discounts—all done for the purpose of generating names, addresses, and other information that can be added to a profitable mailing (or telemarketing) list. Indeed, the ideal goal is to develop a highly qualified list that greatly supersedes routine compiled lists in profitability. Such a list cannot, strictly speaking, be called a house list (even though it has various similarities to a house list), and cannot, strictly speaking, be called a compiled list (even though it has various similarities to a compiled list). It is perhaps most similar to a response list, in that the commonality is a response, at least to the point of doing whatever has provided the name, address, and any other information. This list development process is very popular in Europe, where lists are nowhere near as plentiful as in the United States (primarily due to European governments' relatively high regard for what it sees as its citizens' privacy). In the recent past, these development methods have become increasing popular in the United States. These development efforts will be discussed in further detail in chapter 8, "Developing and Using Customer Databases."

The List Rental Process

More than 99 percent of all lists a company uses outside of its own house list are rented lists. Of course, some rental lists are house lists of other companies. On rare occasions, a list is bought rather than rented. Two companies might exchange house lists, or to maintain an equity of sorts, one company will exchange a number of names from its house list for a number of names from the other company's house list. The equity issue arises when, for example, one company's list is more up-to-date than that of the other company. For the most part, list exchanges can be lumped together with list rentals, in the sense that once the lists are exchanged, virtually all of the tenets and conditions involved are the same as for rented lists.

There are many steps involved in the list rental process, and as the number of lists proliferates (which seems to be happening at an ever-increasing rate), the process has become more complex and, in turn, has become more and more specialized. Depending on precisely how terms are defined, there can be as many as eight different "players" or parties involved in the list rental (and mailing) process. The first two are the two "end" parties; the others are, in some way, facilitators of the process between the two parties.

MAILER (LIST RENTER)

The mailer, or list renter, is, of course, the company or person who rents the list and uses it to solicit prospects (potential customers) by mail.

LIST OWNER

The list owner is the company or person who owns the list and receives the revenue, minus fees, for its rental.

LIST BROKER

The list rental process really begins with list brokers. These people provide a service analogous to that of a real estate broker. They work for both sides, the list renter and the list owner, and it is the latter who pays their fees, just as the seller of a home pays the real estate broker's commission. The list broker must be aware of most available lists; the general tendency is for list owners to make their lists available to any reputable broker who has a potential renter. This is similar to what is called "multiple listing" in real estate transactions. Some renters use one list broker; others use many list brokers. The list broker advises the renter which lists are good buys for the renter's needs and ideally provides some help in the entire direct marketing process. Brokers have a wealth of experience to offer the renter, partially based on their service to other clients, yet they are careful not to breach any confidence concerning the choices, results, and strategies of any other clients. Some brokers specialize in certain types of lists, such as business lists. Even when brokers don't *literally* specialize in certain types of lists, they may achieve a reputation for a particular type of list, such as political fund-raising lists, based on word-of-mouth after some particular success in helping a number of clients in one arena.

LIST COMPILER

Where do all these lists come from originally? Many are house lists of companies, but there are also many compiled lists. There are essentially two ways of creating a compiled list. Using telephone directories, government census data, and other sources of information, list compilers put together a list of people having some specific set of properties (e.g., female heads of households). Building up a list this way is the "older" method. Today many lists are compiled in a reverse approach. Instead of using many distinct sources to build up a list having special characteristics, large list compilers have an enormous master file of names, and by using computer technology they cull out a list with the desired special characteristics. The market for compiled lists now exceeds $1 billion annually. Donnelley Marketing, in 1990, had employees copy names from 4,700 white-pages phone books into a computer, from which it matched the names with other lists (driver's license data, birth records, and so forth) to create the product, DQI-2 Peoplebank. One can cull out relatively narrow subsets: for example, "'mail-responsive' 50-year-old women with a credit card who own a cat and a Porsche and like to travel."[1] This same article notes that American Business Information has every listing from every yellow pages in the United States, and "can list all the magicians in Miami and all the ravioli makers in New England."

---

[1]*The Wall Street Journal,* 19 November 1990, B1.

LIST MANAGER

A list owner may contact a list broker to convey that he has a list for sale. If the owner deals with several brokers, has several distinct lists available, or rents his lists somewhat frequently, he or she may prefer to hire a list manager who will interact with the list broker and keep track of all aspects of the process relevant to the owner. A list manager may be "in-house," that is, an employee of the firm whose house lists are being rented; this will often be the case when the firm's house lists are numerous, or quite large, and/or relatively frequently rented. About 20 percent of list managers are in-house. After all, for some firms renting its house lists is a substantial income generator. More often, the list manager is not an employee of the house list owner, but an outside person; on occasion, a list brokerage firm may have a "branch" or department that provides list management activities. A recent Direct Marketing Association survey indicates that about three-quarters of responding list owners utilized a list manager. Some people believe that it is not good practice to hire a list manager who is an arm of the list broker.[2] Bob Karl notes that being a good list brokerage firm does not at all guarantee that the company is a good list management firm.

Ideally, the list manager is not just an administrator but also an innovator who can suggest how the owner should market or segment the list. In theory, the list manager should evoke such trust that the owner is willing to delegate the approval of clients to whom the list is rented as well as other tasks (to be described later).

SERVICE BUREAU

A service bureau is a facility that performs data processing (for direct mailers and many other companies having nothing to do with mailing). With respect to direct mail activities, service bureaus have been in widespread use for about a quarter of a century. Indeed, the (mandatory) use of zip codes has forced direct mail firms to use the computer. Most of the direct mailers did not, 25 years ago, have the expertise to utilize the computer efficiently, and they therefore turned to service bureaus. Nowadays, some large direct mail firms find it sufficiently economic and have the expertise to perform the list processing in-house. Before the use of the computer, companies used devices such as stenciling to automate (to the degree possible) the process of addressing envelopes and other, at that time, laborious tasks.

The use of service bureaus has grown along with the entire direct mail/marketing field. Consequently, service bureaus have become more and more specialized. Some simply do list maintenance such as updating existing names with new data or adding names. (Of course, when we use the word *name,* we are referring to the entire "vector" of information being retained for that name, including, at a minimum, the address!) Some service bureaus simply do "merge/purge," a process that merges two or more lists but culls out (purges) any duplicates (merge/purge is discussed later in this chapter). Others actually send out the mail pieces (and do only that). Yet others are even more specialized; for example, doing one of the aforementioned tasks solely for college and university fund-raising.

Two parties perform tasks that may be done by a service bureau. One is an *inserter,* who performs the service of inserting (promotional) material into a company's invoices or actual products. (Have you ever received an American Express or other credit card invoice

---

[2]Bob Karl, "Finding the Right List Manager," *Direct Marketing,* March 1987.

without a spate of "bill-stuffer" offers for various products?) The other party is called a *lettershop,* which does specialized printing, inserting, packaging, and other tasks that get a piece "in the mail."

LIST RENTAL AGREEMENTS

Certain written and unwritten rules are typically part of the list rental process. Generally, lists are rented for one-time use. The renter may not retain any names for later use, except for the names of responders. The mailing piece generally must be agreed to by the list owner (or the owner's representative, perhaps a list manager) before it is mailed out; in a recent DMA survey, this was required by 87 percent of the list owners responding. Without this condition, an unscrupulous renter could offer a loss-leader deal just to get a large number of responders, and thereby get to keep a large number of names as his forever. (Actually, this could be a dubious economic decision for the renter, even if he could get away with it, because many people respond to loss leaders but do not "convert" when offered products on which the company would make a profit.) The list owner must also okay the date of the mailing. This condition allows the owner to make sure that sufficient time elapses between the renter's mailing and any mailing the owner may wish to conduct. It also protects the mailer; a not infrequently seen clause in rental agreements (about a third) provides that the list will not be mailed from one week before to one week after the current proposed mailing date.

How can a list owner or manager be sure that the renter will not defy the agreement and use the list more than once? The one-time use rule is so universally accepted that it would be rare for a renter to violate it; besides, the person or company that did breach the agreement would never again find a source from which to rent another list. Nevertheless, list owners and managers frequently seed lists, that is, insert a few dummy names, or names with an identifiable incorrect middle initial. Whenever these pieces are received, the owner is informed. The authors know one list manager whose dog gets a great deal of mail addressed to different variants of his name.

The price charged for a list rental depends on the list's quantity and quality. The quantity aspect is generally dealt with by pricing on a per-thousand basis. There are some exceptions to this rule for lists that are relatively small. Also, one must rent a minimum number of names so that fixed costs can be allocated over a sufficiently large base.

The quality aspect is more complex. It involves, among other factors, uniqueness (e.g., nobody else in the world has these names together on one list), specificity, and good old-fashioned supply and demand. What is the range of costs to rent a list? A look at a 1997 catalog of lists put out by Best Mailing Lists, Inc., showed a range of $50 per thousand names to $150 per thousand (actually, the $150 was for a total list of 1,133 religious libraries, for a cost, technically, of $132 per thousand). There are other small lists that are more expensive than that on a per name basis—for example, $85 for a list of 170 Army and Navy Post Exchanges (for a rate of $.50 per name or, if there were 1,000 names, a cost of $500). List rental prices per thousand names offered in the May 1996 issue of *Direct Marketing* included $50, $80, $90, $95, $110 (two), $119, $130, and $200. Interestingly, the lowest and highest were the two compiled business lists offered (about 64,000 sports executives at $50 per thousand, and about 210,000 names in the American Domain Name Registry [register of names for the Internet and World Wide Web] at $200 per thousand). That the more expensive list contains more names clearly indicates that rental price is not solely a function of scarcity (size of list).

Many lists, especially those available from large list compilers, offer a large number of "segmentation" options—for an additional price. A list renter often wants only certain zip codes, only women, only hotline names (people who made a purchase within the last 30 days or some other short-time period), or some combination of a large number of available segmentations.

Direct Mail List Rates and Data, a semiannual publication by Standard Rate and Data Service, Inc., located in Wilmette, Illinois, lists available lists and their rates. The lists are cataloged in a variety of ways (e.g., by market, by owner). There are other lists of lists. All contain data cards noting certain relevant facts about each list to be managed, rented, or brokered. The main elements of a data card are: (1) the number of names on the list; (2) the type of list; (3) the price of the list; (4) the source of the list; (5) the minimum number of names that must be rented; and (6) the segmentation options (the "selects" available). Data cards also contain some general facts about the list (e.g., percent women). For a sample data card, see Figure 4.1 (p. 70).

Typical selects are many. For example, the Best Mailing Lists, Inc., includes the following select options (all prices per thousand names):

*N*th name (for testing purposes)	no additional charge
Geographic select	$ 5.00
Title addressing	2.50
Key coding	1.00
Telephone numbers (when available)	10.00
Sales volume	10.00
Employee size	10.00
Carrier route presort	5.00
Specialty (e.g., attorneys, doctors)	5.00
Contact name (top executive)	25.00

In addition, there are minimum numbers of names that need be rented per order (often 5,000 names).

It is rare that a list owner insists that every name on a list provided be paid for. One exception has been the Metropolitan Opera House; at least as of 1995, it required a mailer to pay for all 100 percent of its subscriber list.[3] The usual rule *used to be* that a renter must agree to pay for a minimum of 85 percent of the names provided, even if only a smaller percentage is usable because of duplication or some other reason. A smaller percentage of usable names often occurs even after routine allocation of names to lists (e.g., if 10,000 [out of a larger number of] names are on the same two lists and no other list, then 5,000 names are allocated to each of the two lists). Nowadays, the more usual arrangement (about 60 percent in the DMA survey) provides that payment will be made only for names mailed; this method, however, still leaves the allocation issue to be determined in that a name not on the mailer's house list must be allocated to *some* rented list. It would be strange, indeed, if a name on two lists were deemed "free" to the mailer solely because the name is not unique to any one list; more about the allocation issue appears later in this chapter.

The "85 percent" arrangement or any other one in which there is a set minimum percent of names that must be paid for is called a *net agreement.* The newer type of arrangement,

---

[3]Edward L. Nash, *Direct Marketing,* 2nd ed. (New York: McGraw-Hill, 1995).

```
    36,813  LAST 3 MONTH BUYERS              95.00/M     NAMES THRU: 08/04/9
    72,646  LAST 6 MONTH BUYERS              95.00/M      POST DATE: 08/13/9
   233,699  LAST 12 MONTH BUYERS             95.00/M
   303,436  LAST 18 MONTH BUYERS             80.00/M    ——— UNIT OF SALE ———
   442,962  LAST 24 MONTH BUYERS             80.00/M    $70.00/AVERAGE
            PUBLISHER'S & FUNDRAISER'S BASE  65.00/M
            SPECIAL FOOD MAILER'S BASE RATE  75.00/M    ——————— SEX ———————
                                                        54% MEN/46% WOMEN
```

BROOKSTONE'S FAMOUS CATALOG OF HARD-TO-FIND TOOLS AND
OTHER FINE PRODUCTS FOR THE HOMEOWNER FEATURES PAGES   ——————— MATERIAL ———————
FILLED WITH UNUSUAL, HIGH QUALITY PRODUCTS FOR EVERY   4-UP CHESHIRE
IMAGINABLE USE. PRODUCTS ARE DESIGNED TO DO THE JOB   MAGNETIC TAPE*
FASTER, MORE EFFICIENTLY, OR SIMPLY TO BE THE BEST   9-TRACK 1600 BPI
AVAILABLE. THIS IS ONE OF THE BEST MEN'S MAIL ORDER   9-TRACK 6250 BPI
LISTS ON THE MARKET TODAY.   PRES. SENS. $7.00M

SELECTS: STATE, SCF, ZIP, SEX, CREDIT CARD $6.00M   ——— KEY CODING ———
         CANCEL FEE $50/L - DOLLAR SEE BELOW $3.00M
         $25+ $11.00M, $30+ $16.00M, $50+   UP TO 10 DIGITS
         $21.00M, $75+ $28.50M, $100+ $31.00M,
         PRODUCT, MULTIBUYERS $11/M, 30 DAY   — MINIMUM ORDER —
         RECENCY $22.00M; 60 DAY RECENCY   5,000
         $19.00/M-L 3 MO $16/M,L 6MO $11/M
                                                         — UPDATE SCHEDULE —
SOURCE: 100% DIRECT MAIL   LAST: 08/07/98
                                                         NEXT: 09/09/98
COMMISSION - 10% TO RECOGNIZED BROKERS.   UPDATES: MONTHLY
DOLLAR SELECT IS BASED ON CUMULATIVE PURCHASE.
NET NAME DEDUCTIONS ALLOWED:INTERNAL DUPES, BAD   — NET NAME POLICY —
ZIPS, PANDER DROPS, & MATCHES TO HOUSE FILE ONLY.   *50,000 MINIMUM
NCOA'D QUARTERLY. FILE IS 100% ZIP + 4 CODED.   85% + $6.00/M
    ** PRODUCT SELECTS **   (24 MONTH)   RUNNING CHARGE

```
AUTO ACCE (AUTO/GARAGE ACCESSORIES)     35% 153,182
BACKYARD LEISURE (LAWN FURN/HAMMOCKS)   13%  59,023      — MAG TAPE INSTR —
CHRISTMAS PRODUCT BUYERS                10%  42,911      *$20.00 NON-
GARDEN (GARDEN TOOLS/ACCESSORIES)       41% 179,968      REFUNDABLE CHARGE
HAND TOOLS/SHOP ACCESSORIES             23% 102,008      DO NOT RETURN TAPE
HOME COMFORT (HUMIDIFIERS/HEATERS)      45% 201,453
HOUSEHOLD (CLEANERS/DOORMATS/ETC)       23% 102,477      ——————— SUPPLIER ———————
KITCHEN (KITCHENWARE)                   14%  61,002      Millard Group, Inc.
LIGHTING (LAMPS/FLASHLIGHTS/BULBS)      14%  60,281
PERSONAL CARE/ACCE (GROOMING AIDS)      32% 140,212      ——— FULFILLMENT ———
SECURITY/SAFETY (HOUSEHOLD/AUTO/BOAT)    4%  19,083      DATAMANN
STATIONERY/DESKTOP (CLOCKS/DESK ACCE)   10%  43,545      LISA
TRAVEL (LUGGAGE/TRAVEL APPLIANCES)      13%  57,562      802-295-6600
                                                         802-296-3623
INTERNAL NOTES:
                                                         ——— PRINTED BY ———
20% COMMISSION - 10/10                                   JENNY ADAMS
AUT    CRE    DOM    GAR    TOO
```

FIGURE 4.1 List Card from the Brookstone Hard-to-Find Tools Catalog

Source: Brookstone Company, Petersborough, NH 03458. Reprinted with permission of Millard Group, Inc.

in which only names mailed are paid for, is called a *net net agreement*. This net net agreement allows the renter to do an independent analysis instead of relying on a priori selections. He can statistically or otherwise study the list, and then decide to whom to mail. It is not unusual today for renters to first rent a small portion of a list, mail it (after all merge/purge operations are completed), and determine whether the response rate warrants "rolling out" (renting more of or the rest of) the list.

Two other types of agreements should be mentioned here. The first has already been alluded to—exchanging lists. This can be viewed as similar to bartering, except that occasionally the issues of market share and competitive advantage become involved. Sometimes a company will exchange lists with another firm they would never allow to rent their list. In other words, reciprocity is a requirement. The second is cooperative mailings. In this case, a group of noncompeting companies each puts a piece in an envelope that is mailed out. A variation is a joint mailing, in which each company puts its own self-contained envelope into one larger envelope.

LIST PROCESSING

After a list (or a list segment) has been selected, arrangements must be made about the mechanics and format of the delivery (e.g., type of labels, location to which to deliver). Typical formats are cheshire labels (usually the default, no extra charge), pressure sensitive labels ($7 per thousand names additional in the Best Mailing List, Inc. catalog; all prices noted here refer to this catalog), magnetic tape ($25 per reel additional), 3" by 5" cards with name and address, and often telephone number and other information also available ($25 per thousand names additional), computer disks (inquire for pricing). The next step is often to call a service bureau or lettershop (or, perhaps, another party) to perform what we may call list processing. List processing comprises various tasks. One is to eliminate duplicates from a collection of more than one rented list, or between the rented list(s) and the mailer's house list.

There are other issues that need to be addressed in the processing of lists; one is list cleaning—getting rid of "nixies," or incorrectly addressed pieces that would be returned by the postal service. Actually, this is the job of the list owner or manager or broker; otherwise, the mailer is not receiving fair value. Indeed, often the list owner will provide a guarantee that at least 95 percent of the names will be deliverable; however, the guarantee may provide only a return of the expended postage for all mail pieces in excess of 5 percent that are returned by the post office. Usual agreements do not provide, and, indeed, may explicitly deny, providing any payment for "opportunity cost" (e.g., the number of nixies exceeds the guarantee, but the mailing is time sensitive and there is no time to remail to the correct address, if it can be determined, or to anybody else).

Another issue is that of list suppression—removing names with known undesirable characteristics. These include deadbeats, people who have requested that their names be removed from (all) mailing lists, and people who are willing to have certain companies mail them offers, but do not want their names to be rented to anybody else. In essence, list suppression is simply another case of performing merge/purge operations. One special list of names to be suppressed is that of the Direct Marketing Association "name removal list" (called a Mail Preference Service by the DMA). This list contains the names of people who have contacted this specially set up service, primarily to demonstrate to the government that there does not have to be government regulation, and the direct marketing industry can indeed police itself. It turns out, however, that the name removal process does not work as well as desired. This is because it is not mandatory that mailers pass their mail file through a merge/purge with the name removal list. Indeed, often it is only the very large mailers who make the effort to do so; actually, many more mailers indicate in surveys that they use the service than the data indicates actually do. As noted in February 1997 by Henry R. Hoke, Chairman of the Board of *Direct Marketing* magazine, "passing a thousand names through a 10,000,000 no-mail file didn't make economic sense." His comment was really in the context of a similar problem now arising in electronic mail, about which Steve Case, America Online's chairman and CEO, said that "junk e-mail" is the company's most serious problem. This, of course, is no surprise, as the "junk fax" problem cropped up long ago. Apparently, whenever there is new technology, direct "mailers" won't be far behind.

Data Overlay or Enhancement

The use of lists may also include data overlay or enhancement—matching names against certain response or demographic traits to increase the amount of information on each name available to be analyzed; this has become increasingly popular. What this involves, essentially, is "sending" your data disk or tape to a vendor (i.e., a list enhancer), who runs your list through his propriety database of (ideally) nearly all households and individuals in the United States. By matching his names and your names through a literal matching of names and addresses, or some other match code mechanism, the data he has on your names, or a subset of these data, get added to your names, and you receive back a data disk or tape that is much larger (it is "enhanced") than the one you sent to the enhancer in the first place.

Generally, between 80 and 90 percent of the names will be matched and enhanced by the large data enhancers. However, not every data element will be available for this, say 80 percent; thus, the percentage of names matched will be under the 80 percent for any individual variable. Naturally, the more data available on each name, the better one can segment the list (the subject of chapter 5) to more efficiently determine to whom it is economic to mail. The popular variables that direct marketers are more interested in having enhanced to their lists include telephone number; certain demographics, such as house value, income, age and education of head of household; lifestyle information, such as the frequency with which the household goes camping, or goes bowling, or drinks beer, or takes vacations; and psychographics, generally, attitudinal data, essentially a consideration of what is important to the consumer including the benefits a person wants from a product.

Data enhancement can be done at the individual level, or at the census tract or zip code +4 level. Naturally, at the individual level, the data are more "accurate" in that the value of the variable (e.g., number of children in household, income) attached to the name is directly associated with that name.

However, individual level data are more expensive, and some data are not always directly available on an individual basis. Hence, in some cases one uses, as a "surrogate," the aggregate value of the variable, usually with the least aggregation required. For example, if the income of an individual is not available, one would substitute the average income of the block group (on average about 300 homes) in which that individual resides; if, for some reason income is not available by block group, one might use the average for the census tract (on average about 1,300 homes), and so forth, "up the ladder" of aggregation.

The potential problem with aggregated enhanced data is that a particular household may not "mirror" the block group or census track in which it resides. Although nobody would deny a positive correlation between individual values and aggregated values (which, by the way, is the root of much of the enhancement that takes place—that "birds of a feather flock together"), the correlation is often nowhere near as strong as many assume. Indeed, a study by Marilyn Hill using individual level, block group level, and zip code level data from block groups and zip codes in the Chicago area, showed that the correlation coefficients between individual level data and both block group data and zip code data for a variable/attribute such as income did not exceed 0.3.[4] This indicated that the aggregated data (by either block group or zip code) explained only about 10 percent (i.e., the square of the correlation coefficient) of the variation in individual variable values.

REAL-WORLD EXAMPLE

The following discussion pertains to a real-world example of the list enhancement process, included as part of a list segmentation (again, the subject of chapter 5) consulting project undertaken by one of the authors. The company (Company X), involved in direct mail marketing, was a merchandiser of imported fine wines to individual consumers. It had a house list, with name, address, and very limited purchase data (e.g., recency of last purchase); the company had been somewhat lax in maintaining its customer database, except for name and address.

The list contained about 54,000 names (records), and tapes were sent to a well-established list enhancement bureau in Arkansas. About 42,500 of the names were enhanced (a match rate of about 79 percent). A total of about 4,000,000 elements were enhanced, or an average of about 94 data elements per record. However, the number of data elements actually added to *some* (i.e., at least one) records was much larger than this.

The reason was that the number of the 42,500 records that were enhanced by any one variable varied greatly: 90.1 percent of the 42,500 records were enhanced by the TRW gender of the head of household; but only about 15 percent of the records were enhanced by the actual NDL date of birth of head of household (DOBHH). (The "TRW" in front of the gender variable indicates that these data come from the company TRW; similarly for the NDL (National Demographics & Lifestyles) in front of the date of birth variable.) There were even smaller percentages than 15 percent; veteran status was about 3 percent.

The 15 percent for date of birth is itself misleading. This is because the list enhancement bureau has data from many different data collection, enhancement, or segmentation companies. What happens in practice is that many of the variables being enhanced are, in a sense, redundant. For example, Company X's records are enhanced by NDL DOBHH, TRW DOBHH, and TRM DOBHH, at 15, 26, and 30 percent, respectively. So, what percentage of the records are enhanced by at least one of the DOBHH variables? Actually, it is not clear because this piece of information was not readily available (although it was able to be determined if one wanted to take the time to specifically single it out). If we assume that the three databases were independent with respect to which records had the DOBHH and which did not, the answer is about 56 percent, based on working out the overlaps, using the formula $P(A$ or B or $C) = 1 - P(\text{not-}A$ and not-B and not-$C)$. However, the independence assumption is

---

[4]Marilyn Hill, "A Comparison of Zip Code and Block Group Demographics for Predicting Individual Characteristics," *Journal of Direct Marketing Research* 1, no. 1 (1986): 67–82.

probably not strictly valid (if a record has the information missing on TRW's database, it is probable that the same record is more difficult to find and that the information is more likely to be missing on the NDL database also). The right answer is likely in the 40 to 50 percent range. Incidentally, gender is usually represented on the databases by an M, an F, or a U for "unknown." DOBHH is generally represented by a six-element field: "YYMMDD," with six 0's for "unknown."

The list enhancement bureau, as is usual, provided various summary tables to Company X. For example, of the records enhanced, the table for the NDL (self-reported) home owner/renter was as follows:

Owner	85.2%
Renter	14.8%

and for dwelling unit size, the table was:

Single family dwelling	77.2%
Multi-family dwelling	22.8%

For a variable such as length of residence, the tables contain a much larger number of categories:

Less than one year	02.9%
One year	07.0%
Two years	06.4%
Three years	06.5%
Four years	05.7%
Five years	05.6%
Six years	04.7%
Seven years	04.6%
Eight years	03.2%
Nine years	02.7%
Ten years	02.1%
Eleven years or more	48.6%

Many of the variables added to the Company X house list records through the enhancement were valuable in deriving a statistical model that allowed more detailed segmentation concerning who would be more or less likely to purchase for a subsequent offer.

PREDETERMINED CLUSTERING ENHANCEMENT PROGRAMS

An alternative to enhancement of individual data elements (variables) is to contact a number of vendors who have proprietary clustering algorithms that divide the 37,000 or so zip codes or 275,000 block groups into a number of different segments or "clusters"; the goal of all of these clustering algorithms is to make the different clusters as similar as possible within each cluster, and as different as possible between clusters. In theory (and in practice), knowing the cluster membership of a household can help predict purchase behavior. In addition, these clustering techniques can sometimes link together with other useful databases.

One of the most well known of these clustering algorithms is PRIZM™ by Claritas, Inc. There are some different levels of clustering, but the standard system has 62 clusters, arranged at the macrolevel by socioeconomic status and neighborhood density, as well as by dominant characteristics of income, family type, age, education, occupation, housing type, and race or ethnicity. The clusters have catchy descriptive names, such as "Blue Blood Estates," "Urban Achievers," "Latino America," "Norma Rae-Ville," and so on. For each cluster, there is a comparison of the cluster with the United States overall. For example, for "Blue Blood Estates," there were (in 1994) 730,000 households, or about 0.8 percent of the U.S. population. Tables 4.1 and 4.2 show the education and race/ethnicity, respectively, for this cluster.

For each cluster, there is also a map of the United States indicating where the households of that cluster are located.

Another well-known clustering algorithm is ClusterPlus, originally developed by Donnelley Marketing, now named ClusterPLUS 2000 and owned by Claritas, Inc. From the description guide for this algorithm, ClusterPLUS 2000 classifies U.S. neighborhoods into

TABLE 4.1 The "Blue Blood Estates" Cluster—Education

Education	U.S. (%)	Blue Blood Estates (%)
4+ years college	20.6	61.0
1–3 years college	24.9	22.2
High school graduate	29.9	12.0
Less than high school graduate	24.6	04.8

Source: Adapted from a corresponding table in David Shepard Associates, *The New Direct Marketing,* 2nd ed. (New York: Richard D. Irwin, Inc., 1995), 342. Reprinted with permission.

TABLE 4.2 The "Blue Blood Estates" Cluster—Race/Ethnicity

Race/Ethnicity	U.S. (%)	Blue Blood Estates (%)
White American	80.1	92.0
Black American	10.6	01.1
Asian American	02.1	04.7
Hispanic American	06.5	02.0
Foreign born	07.7	12.2

Source: Adapted from a corresponding table in David Shepard Associates, *The New Direct Marketing,* 2nd ed. (New York: Richard D. Irwin, Inc., 1995), 343. Reprinted with permission.

TABLE 4.3 Cluster 1: Comparison for Educational Level Attained

Education	U.S. (%)	Established Wealthy, etc. (%)
No high school diploma	24.45	05.16
High school graduate	29.85	11.98
Some college education	25.09	23.64
Bachelors degree	13.32	31.39
Graduate degree	07.30	27.83

Source: Adapted from a corresponding table in David Shepard Associates, *The New Direct Marketing,* 2nd ed. (New York: Richard D. Irwin, Inc., 1995), 450. Reprinted with permission.

60 clusters, each with distinct product consumption, service usage patterns, and psychographic profiles. ClusterPLUS 2000 offers linkages to databases of other specialty research firms, such as Nielsen Marketing Research and Simmons Marketing Research Bureau. Simmons, for example, collects product and service usage information from about 20,000 households each year through a detailed questionnaire (paying them a nominal amount for their efforts). Thus, a ClusterPLUS 2000 user can choose those parts of a cluster that have a particular usage pattern (e.g., heavy users) for particular products or services. An example of the clusters of ClusterPLUS 2000 is cluster 55: younger, low income, mobile, Hispanic families. ClusterPLUS also provides comparisons between a cluster and the U.S overall. For example, for cluster 1 (established wealthy, highly educated, professionals, prestige homes), the comparison for educational level attained is shown in Table 4.3.

There are other clustering systems, and some companies that combine these clustering systems into their own "systems." The pricing structure may differ from one company to another. In some cases, a company will charge the same amount for enhancing any size customer file between 0 and 25,000, another amount for any size from 25,000 to 100,000, and so on; another company may charge, for example, one price per thousand for file sizes under 1,000, another (lower) price per thousand for file sizes between 1,000 and 1,999, another price per thousand for sizes 2,000 to 3,999, and yet another price per thousand for sizes of 4,000 or more. It should be noted that clustering systems are continually changing to reflect changes over time in the composition of zip codes and block groups. Correspondingly, the numbers in tables such as 4.1, 4.2, and 4.3 are also changing over time.

It must be remembered that the usefulness of any data enhancing is a function of the degree to which it leads to increased ability to predict who is more likely to respond (mail to this person!) and who is less likely to respond (do not mail to this person!). This will depend on what product is being marketed, what information is already available (in general, the more data available before the consideration of list enhancement, the less the marginal benefit of the enhancement, because more is "already known"), and the profit margin and cost of mailing trade-off.

A final note about list enhancement: we have been discussing list enhancement in the context of consumer lists. Enhancement of business lists is also possible, although it is not performed as frequently. Typical variables used in the enhancement of business lists include telephone number, number of employees, dollar sales volume, and SIC code.

Merge/Purge

We now discuss the concept of suppressing names from a list, and eliminating duplicate names when lists are combined. These activities are part of the general concept often referred to as *merge/purge.* There are many reasons for suppressing names; in addition, it is obvious that one would wish to eliminate duplicates. Thus, the concept of merge/purge and the different variables involved in making decisions concerning merge/purge alternatives have become central (or *should be* central—we discuss later some examples in which this is not happening to the degree it should) to the well-being of list management.

In essence, merge/purge is simply a matter of merging two (or more) lists, while detecting and eliminating duplicates. However, it is "easier said than done." In fact, a good merge/purge system will do some other desirable tasks, such as identify typographical errors with respect to zip codes (e.g., only four digits because one digit did not get typed, or five digit numbers that do not exist as zip codes), identify some names that are almost surely not correct (e.g., a name with six vowels in a row), or identify some addresses that are likely to be incorrect (e.g., mixed up or mistyped).

ASPECTS OF LIST SUPPRESSION

The most well-known task of a merge/purge system is to eliminate duplicates. Most decisions concerning the trade-offs among the attributes of different systems are based on the results of the elimination of duplicates. However, there are a number of other elements involved in the list suppression process. That is, there are a number of other sets of names that it is desirable to eliminate.

One set of names to eliminate is the Direct Marketing Association's do not mail list or name removal list. These are names of people who wish not to be mailed anything, and the names have been sent to the DMA and are provided to members and service bureaus. This process was set up by the DMA as a service to members. The stated purpose was to provide these names to DMA members, presuming (likely rightfully) that people who are so adamant against solicitation by mail as to send their names in will not become buyers, if they even open the envelope! However, this list, updated quarterly or so, has taken on a much larger role, and is part of the center of one of the biggest controversies in the United States, and to a degree worldwide, today—that of privacy. The DMA, representing many large member companies, wants, at all costs, to keep the government from passing specific laws about the privacy rights of consumers that would infringe upon the strategies of direct mailers. One argument that the DMA makes is that the existence of the name removal list enables anybody to keep from getting mailed (and, hence, no government regulation is necessary). There are two weaknesses with this argument. One is that most people do not know of the existence of this option, or if they do know of its existence, they do not know how to go about implementing it. This can be remedied through additional publicity. The other, perhaps more serious flaw is that only DMA members are likely to "see" the list, and even the members are under no legal obligation to suppress the names (although they would, if the cost is sufficiently low, because they know that it would be economic to do so).

Closely related to the name removal list is a list of people who are happy to receive mail from a company with whom they do business, but want to ensure that the company does not rent their name to any other company. In the past four or five years, there has been a clear indication that people are increasingly reluctant to give their names to any merchant (whether buying by mail or routine store location), because they know that most companies rent (or sell from the buyer's point of view) their names to other companies. These latter companies, in turn, send many solicitations by mail. Due to this reluctance on behalf of buyers, many companies are overtly offering to place the buyer's name on a list of names that will never be rented or exchanged with any other company.

Another set of names to eliminate or suppress from a rented list is that of your house list. Obviously, you do not want to send an offer to a rented list and include names from your house list. Why? Well, you may have sent them an offer a short time ago, or you may be using copy and an offer geared directly to (and only to) prospects who have never bought before. This phenomenon is, sadly, not so uncommon; and, it is often very irritating. At best, it makes a customer wonder about the "efficiency" of the company and whether the company is as "high tech" as it perhaps purports to be.

Other names to be eliminated or suppressed (i.e., purged) would include those who have not paid a previous bill. As stated earlier, another set of names to be eliminated are the nixies, those names that are undeliverable. These are usually names of people who no longer reside at the address on the envelope. There are lists of nixies that can be rented for the express purpose of purging them from your list. In some cases the new (i.e., correct) address can be determined and placed on the list; this is especially true when the name is included in the NCOA (national change of address) list organized by the U.S. Postal Service and rented to mailers. There are other special sets of names that specific companies might wish to purge. For some products, military addresses, prison addresses, or student addresses may be undesirable. Naturally, when making decisions concerning to whom to mail, other segments (e.g., those over a certain age) may be desirable to suppress. The elimination of names with specific demographics, previous purchase patterns, or other variables, is thought of as list segmentation (discussed in chapter 5), and generally not part of what is routinely thought of as merge/purge.

QUALITY OF MERGE/PURGE SYSTEMS

What distinguishes one merge/purge system from another (without reference to "platforms" and other factors on the technical side of computer science)? That is, what determines the quality of merge/purge systems? In essence, the attributes of quality are really the degree to which the system trades off the two kinds of "errors" that can be made in the detection and elimination of "duplicate names." Note the quotes around the words *duplicate names*. They are there because one type of error is to label (and eliminate) a name as a duplicate name when, in fact, it is *not* a duplicate name. The other type of error, of course, is to not label or identify a name as a duplicate, when, in fact, it *is* a duplicate name. The first type of error mentioned is like a "false positive"; the other type of error may be thought of as a "false negative."

In terms of the costs of these errors, it might be useful to consider three somewhat different cases:

1. Merging and purging two or more rented lists—a false positive is to not mail to a legitimate prospect; a false negative is to mail to the rented name twice (for the sake of brevity of discussion, we ignore, for now, the possibility of triplicates, and so forth).

2. Merging and purging a rented list with your house list—a false positive is again to not mail to a legitimate prospect; a false negative is perhaps more costly in that the person mailed twice is a current customer and, if alienated, represents, on average, a larger cost.

3. Purging the rented list of "undesirable names" to mail (i.e., comparing the names with another rented list of undesirables), such as the earlier noted DMA "do not mail names," nixies, or those

who have not paid their bills—a false positive is yet again to not mail to a legitimate prospect; a false negative is, on balance, more costly than case 1. Mailing to a nixie, a guaranteed nonresponder, or a DMA "do not mail," and generating potential major flack, or worse, mailing to someone who orders and doesn't pay the bill, is surely more costly than just nonmailing to a prospect.

It is not perfectly clear how to compare the cost of a false negative in case 3 with that of case 2; perhaps it depends on the loyalty of the customer and the frequency with which the error occurs.

What is the cost of not mailing to a legitimate prospect? In theory, if a direct mailer wishes to mail to a certain number of names, the false elimination of a name could result in the substitution by another, but less promising, name. (Remember, a direct mailer will first mail to those who are perceived as the best prospects, and each prospect eliminated would thus result in a substitution by the next name on the list, which is, by definition, a less promising name.) Another possible cost of a false positive—not mailing to a legitimate prospect—is that if the rental arrangement is on a net basis in which a minimum of 85 percent of the names must be paid for anyway, and you are under the 85 percent already, the false positive will have to be paid for as if mailed.

What is the cost of a false negative, the nondetection of an actual duplicate? For the merging of two rented lists, it is obviously the cost of mailing an "extra" package to the same person. Although the mailing of two packages may, in a particular case, *increase* the chance of a response, it is almost axiomatic that, in aggregate, doubling the mailing cost by mailing two of the same offer at the same time is not cost effective. In terms of merging a rented list with a house list, a false negative, in addition to the cost of sending two packages to the same name at the same time, may result in a current customer being upset that "their company" did not realize they were already a customer; if the company makes claim to being high quality in terms of customer service, the entire image may be destroyed. Also, current customers may take advantage of an offer meant only for new customers (e.g., a low introductory price), resulting in a loss to the company. In terms of purging a rented list of undesirable names, a false negative has the obvious potential consequence of mailing to those who will not pay their bill, or nixies, as alluded to before, or hurting the entire direct mail industry in terms of reneging on the promise not to mail to certain names.

The propensity of a merge/purge system to make the various types of errors can be determined by testing. Once the error rates are determined, a cost analysis can be performed to determine which merge/purge system minimizes the average cost of errors for a particular direct mailer.

Why are errors made by merge/purge systems? It is impossible for a system to be error free. Indeed, the two types of errors "trade off" with one another. If the system requires an exact match (of, say, each letter of a name, each letter of an address, and so forth) to label a name a duplicate, then it will be rare for the system to indicate a false positive; after all, if the name is not a duplicate, there is virtually no chance of an exact match in every way! However, the following examples, which are *almost certainly* duplicates, will be false negatives:

Maryann Jones   Maryanne Jones
112 Kenmore Avenue   112 Kenmore Avenue
Boston, MA 02215   Boston, MA 02215

Theodore S. Williams	Theodore S. Williams
10 Fenway Lane, #9	10 Fenway Lane, #99
Boston, MA 02215	Boston, MA 02215

In general, one would never devise a system that is so rigid in its definition of a match or duplicate.

Of course, there can be the opposite situation. Suppose that a system is very loose in its definition of a duplicate; that is, if there is any degree of similarity at all, label it a duplicate and purge the name. In this case, it would be rare to have a false negative; after all, if a name really is a duplicate, the system would virtually always label it as a duplicate. However, the following examples, which are very likely *not* duplicates, would be false positives:

Robert Clarke	Robert Clark
25 Oak St.	25 Oak St.
Plymouth, MA 02360	Plympton, MA 02367

Paul Jones	Paula Jones
69 Clintlock Way	69 Clinton Road
S. Wellfleet, MA 02663	S. Yarmouth, MA 02664

There are many decisions that can be implemented in designing a merge/purge system that result in the various stages of trading off the two types of errors. Yet, technologically, it is not a simple task to program the system to accomplish a particular degree of each type of error. One does not want false negatives, but how is a system to catch as duplicates the following names: James Cluff versus James Clough (or worse, Jim Clough)? It is likely that these are duplicates if the most of the rest of the address is the same; indeed, Cluff and Clough are likely homonyms (i.e., spelled differently but sound the same), and it is likely that some order-taker or clerk recording the name over the phone simply did not spell the name correctly. One of the authors remembers this exact name confusion for a high school classmate. If a system rightfully does catch Cluff versus Clough as duplicates, it is likely also to have many false positive results, unless the technology embedded is extremely sophisticated.

In business-to-business situations, the merge/purge process entails even more complex issues. A key issue is whether to call duplicates two names that are different, while the rest of the business address is identical. Clearly, the names are of separate individuals, but if the address is the same department, do we want to send both a catalog? Actually, the answer is not perfectly clear. It is an issue that generally doesn't arise in consumer mailing, where duplicates are most often considered at the household level. After all, do you really want to double mailing cost by mailing separate catalogs to a husband and wife? However, at the business level, the two names might be housed in different departments, or at different levels of the organization (especially if job titles aren't available), and it might be desirable to send to both.

Another issue in business-to-business mailing is exemplified by the fact that "AT&T" is clearly the same as "American Telephone and Telegraph." Yet, it is not simple for a merge/purge program to recognize this unless the two different ways of writing the company name are explicitly programmed into the software as duplicates. There are other complications in the business-to-business merge/purge process, which mostly revolve around the greatly varying ways an address can be configured in the world of business addresses. You can have a person's name or not; you can have the company name or not; you can have a suite or office number or not; and, these variations are on top of the more routine error-inducing aspects seen previously in the consumer mailing examples. Technology, especially pattern-recognition-linking technology, continues to be developed.

Many of these types of problems are exacerbated when considering lists in foreign countries. Some countries (Belgium, for example, as well as Canada to some degree) have two different "official" languages. Each country in Europe has a somewhat different postal format, although this may change over time as many aspects (e.g., currency) are moving toward standardization. The German postal format seems especially different from that of other Western European countries. It is likely that large parts of the structure and logic of merge/purge software would need to be very different for addresses in China or Japan. One of the main reasons for the continued technology development in merge/purge software is the growth in the use of direct mail in Europe and Asia (as well as in much of South America). The movement toward pattern recognition software is essential for merge/purge use in countries whose language is ideogram-based.

PAYMENT ALLOCATION TO THE MERGED (AND PURGED) LISTS

Suppose that two lists, A and B, of 1,000 names each are merged and purged, and the result is an ostensibly duplicate-free (the role of "errors" is irrelevant in this discussion) list of 1,600 names. Assuming that each list was duplicate-free to begin with (an assumption routinely made), there were clearly 400 duplicates. Do we give list A "credit" (and, thus, payment) for 1,000 names, and list B for 600 names? Or do we reverse the credit assignment for lists A and B? Or do we allocate 800 names to each list? Of course, the issue can be more complex when the lists are of different sizes, and even more so if there are three, four, or a higher number of lists.

One method of allocation is simply to split a name's credit equally among the lists on which a name appears. That is, if a name appears on two lists, each list gets credit for half of the name; thus, if there are 120 such names, each list receives credit for 60 of the 120 names. If 75 names appear on each of three lists, each of the three lists receives credit for 25 names.

Another way of allocating credit is with priority. For example, list A gets credit for any duplicates between itself and every other list. For duplicates involving list B (but excluding involvement with list A), credit goes to list B. The process can then continue through to the last list in the hierarchy. Of course, a method of allocation can combine the concepts of equal credit and priority; a not uncommon approach is to prioritize, but only between different groups, while granting credit equally among lists within a group. For example, with 10 lists, suppose that A, B, and C are "group 1"; D, E, F, and G are "group 2"; and H, I, and J are "group 3." A duplicate between A and C is allocated equally; a duplicate between B and E is allocated fully to B; a name shared by D, F, and J is allocated half to D and half to F. Remember that different lists rent for different prices. It is obviously economical for a mailer to negotiate an allocation priority that gives more priority to the less expensive lists. Often, however, the priority process is dictated (possibly, informally) by each list's success in the past for that mailer. A list that is a "proven winner" will often get priority over a list being tried for the first time; this makes some sense, if looked at from the perspective that the proven list would have been mailed whether the new list was rented or not, and hence, only names unique to the new list are credited to the new list. Another argument in favor of a priority system is that if a name's credit is evenly split among, say, two lists, and the lists rent for different prices, then *for the same name,* one list owner is receiving a different amount of money than another. This appears unfair to many.

It should be noted that the above discussion pertains to the issue of credit and payment to the "appropriate" list owner. In terms of information content, decisions about which names to currently mail, and future decisions concerning which lists to rent, the allocation situation is nearly irrelevant. Regardless of the allocation agreement, which, after all, is mechanical, once negotiated and decided upon, information concerning a name's "duplication status" should always be kept. How else could one discover, for example, that duplicates on three or more lists have a significantly higher response rate, or that duplicates on two specific lists are also high-level responders, or that duplicates on two specific other lists are poor responders. This type of information may have a major impact on decisions about to whom to mail, and which lists to rent in the future.

We end this section by noting that many companies do not do as good a job as they can in the elimination of duplicates. In one case, it is not clear that a company even attempts a merge/purge. One of the authors is a member of the GNC (General Nutrition Center) gold card program; if you join the program, paying a one-time $15 fee for a one-year membership, you receive 20 percent off on that day's purchase and 20 percent off on all purchases on the first Tuesday of each month. In addition, you receive the monthly magazine, *Let's Live.* The magazine has various health-related articles and promotes many GNC products, although not exclusively GNC products. On occasion, if a person makes a large purchase on a day other than the first Tuesday of the month, it may pay to "rejoin" the gold card membership and thus get 20 percent off that day's purchase and extend your membership to 12 months from that day. (Obviously, if one purchases more than $75 worth of product, the 20 percent discount more than offsets the $15 joining fee.) One of the authors has done this a number of times. This author now receives three copies of *Let's Live* each month! It is as if GNC never attempts purging (i.e., seeking duplicates) when it merges a new gold card membership with current members. The name and address on the three copies is identical in every way. Another example is more "forgivable." One of the authors has a "platinum plus" bank card from a very large, well-known bank. It is registered at his home address. However, he continually receives solicitations for this same card at his office address. Although this situation is perhaps understandable, the author recalls that the original application for the bank card did include (for credit-rating purposes) his office address. In an ideal merge/purge direct mail world, the databases could be linked in such a way as to catch this duplicate.

Economics and Selection of Mailing Lists

Before we take up the economics of mailing lists, we want to note that our discussion will be somewhat different for each of the following situations:

1. We are offered a list for rent. The list in question is not competing with any other choice, and the decision of whether to rent this list is independent of all other considerations.
2. We are choosing among many lists. We can choose, at most, only a subset of the available choices.

The first situation is cleaner, so we consider it first, and then extend the discussion to the second situation. We acknowledge that our description of situation 1 is a bit too idealized, in that it is unlikely that any significant decision is truly independent of other company decisions. However, our intent is to look at the economics of a mailing list in isolation.

Assume that we have an ongoing mail-order business and offer a specific product for which an order is virtually always for one and only one unit of the product and also that the lifetime value of a buyer is just the single sale. We have a good handle on our variable profit per order, which is revenue per order less variable costs per order (these costs include production costs and handling costs, both incoming and outgoing, and outgoing postage for orders). Further assume that we have never had a bad debt or a return. Given these conditions, should we rent the offered list? Let's detail the decision process:

Let $N =$ number of names on the list

$S =$ selling price of the one item making up an order (sum for all items if discussing multi-item order)

$H =$ handling cost per order

$M =$ variable profit per order (equals $S - H -$ manufacturing cost)

$R =$ rental cost per thousand names of the list

$C =$ in-the-mail cost per piece (name) mailed

$F =$ fixed cost associated with renting the list (can include any fixed costs involved in filling orders)

$p =$ estimated response rate (a value from 0 to 1)

Then, if we do rent the list, our overall gain, G, by having done so is:

$$G = p \bullet M \bullet N - N \bullet R/1000 - C \bullet N - F \qquad \textbf{(4.1)}$$
$$= [\, p \bullet M - R/1000 - C \,] \bullet N - F$$

If $G > 0$, rent the list.

Now consider what happens to G in equation (4.1) if we relax some of our earlier simplifications. If it is relevant to consider the lifetime value of a buyer, L, as opposed to just counting the profit of this one sale, M, simply replace M by L in equation (4.1). If it is thought that the list in question differs from the company's experience in terms of the value of M or L, the desired value will have to be estimated. If the M or L value is not the same for all customers, an expected value or average value is to be used.

If the customer is allowed to make returns, and $r =$ the proportion of purchases returned, by how much will profit be reduced? If we suppose that we return the customer's entire outlay, including the part due to handling, we reduce G by $N \bullet r \bullet p \bullet (S + H)$. We would then have

$$G = [\, p \bullet M - r \bullet p \bullet (S + H) - R/1000 - C \,] \bullet N - F$$

If a proportion, b, of the nonreturned orders will not be paid for (i.e., will be bad debts), the term $p \bullet M$ needs to be replaced with $p \bullet M \bullet (1 - r) \bullet (1 - b)$, and G would be

$$G = [\, p \bullet M \bullet (1 - r) \bullet (1 - b) - r \bullet p \bullet (S + H) - R/1000 - C \,] \bullet N - F$$

This expression may look complicated, but it really involves only plugging in values and performing arithmetic. The real problem is that we do not know the values of *p*, *r*, and *b*. These unknown values would have to be estimated by using the company's past experience to evaluate *G* and see if it is greater than zero.

If we do decide to rent the list, we would probably not mail to the entire list all at once. Instead, we would mail to an initial 5,000 or 10,000 (or more) names, note the values of *p*, *b*, and *r*, and then decide whether to mail to the rest of the list, to terminate mailing to the list, or to mail to another (larger) portion of the list. If we do mail to another portion of the list, we would then decide among the same three choices. This process is called *pyramiding* or *rolling out*. We shall discuss rollout decision making in more detail in chapter 10 on testing in direct marketing.

Because the list is to be tested, and not completely mailed if initial results are unsatisfactory, a simple decision based on whether *G* is greater than zero is not the mathematically optimal decision process if we include uncertainty and averages in our analysis. But for all practical purposes, *G* should be used for the decision. The *G* test is more conservative than the mathematically optimal decision process under uncertainty. Actually, the preceding analysis can be viewed in the context of the decision to rent the quantity that will be used in a test mailing. Certain terms of the equations would change to reflect the savings realized when test results are not as good as originally estimated, and the mailing is therefore terminated, as well as the gain in expected profit that would occur because only when initial results are encouraging enough do we go forward with a rollout. Nonetheless, the essence of the analysis would remain intact.

How would our analysis change if the issue is not the relatively simple one of deciding whether to rent a particular list, but rather one of choosing the optimal subset from a set of many eligible lists? First of all, why not just rent all lists with a *G* greater than zero? In considering this question, use the simplifying, although possibly unrealistic, assumption that each of the eligible lists contains no names that appear on any other list. Under this assumption, renting all lists with a *G* greater than zero (i.e., all profitable lists) seems to be the obvious answer. True, cash flow considerations might not permit us to rent all profitable lists, at least simultaneously, but this drawback could be overcome by setting a benchmark of *G* being greater than some modest positive value as a hedge against risk. Remember that we can envision the decision problem as one in which we must choose which lists to test, rather than which to completely mail.

In the real world, of course, our simplifying assumption that no list duplicates names on any other list would not hold. As more lists are rented for testing, the amount of duplication would increase. Duplication would be (in essence) eliminated by merge/purge techniques, but the merge/purge cost would have a negative effect on profitability. If we rented lists under an agreement to pay for a minimum of 85 percent of the names, regardless of the actual duplication rate, each additional list would likely yield a smaller and smaller rate of new names. Thus the rental cost per name would, in percentage terms, rise at a marginally increasing rate. If, on the other hand, we have to pay a rental fee for only those names to which we actually mail, this increased rental cost per name would not occur.

Summary

The list is an important element of the direct marketing mix. There are many types of lists; except for a house list, lists are usually rented on a one-time basis. There are professionals who specialize in facilitating the list rental process: list brokers, list compilers, list managers, and list processors or service bureau personnel. List rental agreements are generally pro-scribed in very specific detail.

The use of lists may include data or list enhancement; data on each name on the list (between 80 and 90 percent of names on most lists are able to be matched) are appended to the original data, adding a richness of information to the name; this aids decisions concerning whether it is economic for a name to be included in a mailing. There are many companies that specialize in list enhancement, both on an individual (name) level and on the basis of the name's zip code or block group of residence.

An important part of list usage activity is the merge/purge process. This is the process of merging two or more lists and purging the combined list of duplicates. The merge/purge process also usually involves purging some names without merging, often called name suppression. The goal here is to remove names that should not be mailed, either because they have requested not to be solicited or for a variety of other reasons (e.g., has not paid a bill that is way past due) are thought to be uneconomic to mail.

Discussion Questions and Exercises

1. Can you suggest some useful sources that can be used for compiling lists?
2. What are the key differences between consumer lists and business lists?
3. Why are some lists much more expensive (per name or per 1,000 names) than other lists?
4. Describe some key variables that the list enhancement process would frequently add to the information not usually available for names on a rented list. How does the list enhancement bureau get this information?
5. Describe in your own words why the merge/purge process is an integral part of the overall list processing procedure.
6. What do you believe is the most sensible way to allocate names to lists (for payment purposes) in the merge/purge process? Why?

Suggested Readings

Bailey, Marci. "Captivating Customers." *The Boston Globe,* 3 March 1997, B5–6.

Mammarella, Jim. "Psyching Out List Overlays." *Direct Marketing,* February 1986, 46–51.

New 1997 BEST Mailing Lists, Inc. (Catalog), 888 South Craycroft Road, Tucson, AZ 85711, Tel: (520) 745-0200.

Taybi, Paul, and Judy Frankel. "How You Can Make Compiled Lists Work." *Direct,* 20 June 1989, 19–24.

Wheaton, James, and Cynthia Baughan. "Evaluating Merge/Purge Systems." *Direct Marketing* (July–December 1987) (six part series).

Appendix

In this appendix we provide a list of the 62 PRIZM clusters, and some of their major attributes as of 1994, as adapted from a corresponding table in The New Direct Marketing.[5]

---

[5]David Shepard Associates, *The New Direct Marketing,* 2nd ed. (New York: Richard D. Irwin, Inc., 1995), 340–341.

PRIZM Clusters and Some of Their Major Attributes	
1. Blue Blood Estates	Wealthy, family, age 35–54, college educated
2. Cashmere and Country Clubs	Wealthy, family, age 35–54, college educated
3. Executive Suites	Affluent, couples, age 25–54, college educated
4. Pools & Patios	Affluent, couples, age 55–64, college educated
5. Kids & Cul-de-Sacs	Affluent, family, age 35–64, college educated
6. Urban Gold Coast	Affluent, singles, age 25–34, college educated
7. Money & Brains	Affluent, couples, age 55–64, college educated
8. Young Literati	Upper middle income, singles/couples, age 25–34, college educated
9. American Dreams	Upper middle income, family, age 35–54, college educated
10. Bohemian Mix	Middle income, singles, age <24, college educated
11. Second City Elite	Affluent, couples, age 35–64, college educated
12. Upward Bound	Upper middle income, family, age 25–54, college educated
13. Gray Power	Middle income, singles/couples, age >65, college educated
14. Country Squires	Wealthy, family/couples, age 35–64, college educated
15. Gods Country	Affuent, family, age 35–54, college educated
16. Big Fish Small Pond	Upper middle income, family, age 35–54, high school/college educated
17. Greenbelt Families	Upper middle income, family, age 25–54, high school/college educated
18. Young Influentials	Upper middle income, singles/couples, age <35, college educated
19. New Empty Nests	Upper middle income, couples, age 35–64, college educated
20. Boomers & Babies	Upper middle income, family, age 25–54, college educated
21. Suburban Sprawl	Middle income, family/couples, age <35, college educated
22. Blue Chip Blues	Middle income, family, age 35–54, high school/college educated
23. Upstarts & Seniors	Middle income, couples/singles, age: mix, college educated
24. New Beginnings	Middle income, singles/couples, age <35, college educated
25. Mobility Blues	Middle income, family/couples, age <35, high school/college educated
26. Gray Collars	Middle income, couples, age >35, high school educated
27. Urban Achievers	Middle income, couples/singles, age: mix, college educated
28. Big City Blend	Middle income, family, age 35–54, high school educated
29. Old Yankee Rows	Middle income, couples, age >55, high school educated
30. Middle Minorities	Middle income, family/couples, age 35–54, high school/college educated
31. Latino America	Middle income, family, age 25–34, <high school educated
32. Middleburg Managers	Middle income, couples, age >55, college educated
33. Boomtown Singles	Middle income, singles/couples, age <34, college educated
34. Starter Families	Middle income, families, age 25–34, high school educated
35. Sunset City Blues	Lower middle income, couples, age >55, high school educated
36. Towns & Gowns	Lower middle income, singles, age <35, college educated
37. New Homesteaders	Middle income, family, age 35–54, college educated
38. Middle America	Middle income, family, age 25–44, high school educated
39. Red, White & Blue	Middle income, family, age 35–64, high school educated
40. Military Quarters	Lower middle income, family, age 25–54, college educated

(continued)

PRIZM Clusters (continued)	
41. Big Sky Families	Upper middle income, family, age 35–44, high school/college educated
42. New Ecotopia	Middle income, families/couples, age 35–54, college educated
43. River City, USA	Middle income, family, age 35–64, high school educated
44. Shotguns & Pickups	Middle income, family, age 35–64, high school educated
45. Single City Blues	Lower middle income, singles, age: mix, mix educated
46. Hispanic Mix	Poor, family, age <35, <high school educated
47. Inner Cities	Poor, singles/family, age: mix, <high school educated
48. Smalltown Downtown	Lower middle income, singles/family, age <35, high school/college educated
49. Hometown Retired	Lower middle income, singles/couples, age >65, <high school educated
50. Family Scramble	Lower middle income, family, age <35, <high school educated
51. Southside City	Poor, singles/family, age: mix, <high school educated
52. Golden Ponds	Lower middle income, couples, age >65, high school educated
53. Rural Industria	Lower middle income, family, age <35, high school educated
54. Norma Rae-Ville	Poor, singles/family, age: mix, <high school educated
55. Mines & Mills	Poor, singles/couples, age >55, <high school educated
56. Agri-Business	Middle income, family, age >35, high school educated
57. Grain Belt	Lower middle income, family, age >55, high school educated
58. Blue Highways	Lower middle income, family, age 35–54, high school educated
59. Rustic Elders	Lower middle income, couples, age >55, high school educated
60. Back Country Folks	Lower middle income, couples, age >35, high school educated
61. Scrub Pine Flats	Poor, family, age >35, <high school educated
62. Hard Scrabble	Poor, family, age >35, <high school educated

Wealthy was defined as an average annual household income of at least $65,000; *affluent* as $50,000 to $65,000; *upper middle* as $37,000 to $50,000; *middle* as $28,000 to $37,000; *lower middle* as $20,000 to $28,000; and *poor* as under $20,000.

5 CHAPTER List Segmentation

Once you decide on a mailing list (whether your house list or a rented list), there is, of course, no rule that says that you must mail to every name on the list. You may choose a particular subset of your own house list for a specific mailing. Or you may have the option of renting only a specified portion of a broker's list—for example, just the males. Or you may rent an "entire" list, but choose afterward to mail to only a subset of the list (paying for whatever is called for in your list rental agreement). In any of these cases, the process of deciding the specifics of whom to mail is called *list segmentation.*

Market segmentation, in general, is a concept that has provoked a great deal of thought and attention in the literature. Its wide appeal derives, in part, from its power to aid in the design and implementation of marketing strategies that have higher efficiencies than less focused approaches. One might view a segment as a group of customers or prospects who have a similar probability of purchase when exposed to the same marketing mix.

Direct marketing offers a unique challenge and application of the segmentation concept because mailing lists are the "populations" from which the majority of direct marketers typically define their segments and select their target markets. To be formal, we propose the following definition of list segmentation:

> To break out a list into subsets with different characteristics; notably, different profit/cost/response rate parameters. Taken to the ultimate, each name becomes a "segment" with its own estimated response rate (probability of purchase), dollar purchase, or lifetime value.

Illustrating the Advantages of Segmentation

A SIMPLE EXAMPLE

What are the advantages of segmenting your list? If you mailed, say, to half the names on your house list, chosen randomly, you would generate about half the sales that would be produced by mailing to the entire list. Obviously, there is no advantage in this kind of segmentation. But suppose you could find a way to choose half the list so that the mailing generates 90 percent of the sales that would have been generated by mailing to the entire list. That would be an enormous advantage. In fact, depending on the economics of the situation, mailing to 50 percent of the list and generating 60 percent of the sales that would have come from mailing to the entire list could be quite an advantage.

Let's analyze how this could be done. Suppose you discover that when you break your list into five equally sized, mutually exclusive, and collectively exhaustive age groups, each promises to yield a different response rate for a particular offering. For simplicity, assume that profit per sale is the same for all responders and future considerations are negligible. Even though you cannot know the response rates prior to the mailing, by mailing a pilot sample of names and applying sophisticated statistical analysis, you can obtain a reasonably precise estimate of the five values; later, in chapter 10, "Testing Direct Marketing Programs," we discuss further the precision of sample estimates and related issues. Suppose the response rate values for the five age groups turn out to be as follows:

Group A	4 percent
Group B	3 percent
Group C	2 percent
Group D	1 percent
Group E	0.5 percent

Suppose further that the net profit per sale excluding mailing cost is $20, and the in-the-mail cost per piece is 28 cents. A little math will show why you would want to mail only to groups A, B, and C. For group A, expected profit per piece is .04 × $20 = 80 cents; for group B, .03 × $20 = 60 cents; for group C, .02 × $20 = 40 cents; for group D, .01 × $20 = 20 cents; and for group E, .005 × $20 = 10 cents. Clearly, you would not mail to groups D and E because the in-the-mail cost (28 cents) exceeds the expected profit for these groups. You might consider mailing to groups A, B, and half the names (randomly chosen) of group C, if you wanted to mail exactly half of the list (although A, B, and *all of C*—60 percent of the list— is your "optimal" choice). Thus, your mailing would be 50 percent of the total list—but this would be the *best* half of the list, not the random half discussed earlier. What percent of the sales that would be generated by mailing to the entire list will be generated by mailing to this best half of the list?

$$[4 + 3 + .5(2)] / (4 + 3 + 2 + 1 + .5) = 8/10.5$$

$$= .762$$

$$= 76.2 \text{ percent}$$

A MORE DETAILED EXAMPLE

In a typical situation, a test mailing would be executed using a relatively small sample from the total available, say, a house list. The response (purchase) or nonresponse of each individual in the test mailing is recorded and a list segmentation technique (of some kind—lots of discussion on this topic takes place later in this chapter) is then applied to "predict" a probability of response for the remaining names on the list. The simple preceding example can be cast into this mold by envisioning the response rates per age group to be indicated based on a small initial ("pilot") mailing and using the simple segmentation technique of predicting response solely based on age. Sometimes we segment by dollars of purchase, but the large majority of time segmentation in a direct mail campaign is based on probability of response; the logic is that virtually anybody who actually makes a purchase from our offer will result in a profit for the mailer—thus, identifying who will actually purchase is, in itself, a "win."

Once a probability of response is estimated, we rank order the probabilities, and the economics of the mailing (average profit per response, versus cost of mailing and the other parameters discussed in chapter 4—proportion who will return the purchase for refund, proportion who will not pay, and so forth) will determine how deeply we dip into the list. Table 5.1 is a hypothetical case to illustrate this point.

The first three columns of Table 5.1 (columns A, B, and C) show that the percentage of buyers that would be expected to occur in a given decile of a randomly ordered list con-

TABLE 5.1 Example Segmentation by Deciles

A	B	C	D
Decile	Percent of List's Buyers in Decile (random)	Cumulative Percent of Buyers (random)	Cumulative Percent of Buyers with Segmented Rank Order
1	10	10	20
2	10	20	35
3	10	30	47
4	10	40	59
5	10	50	69
6	10	60	77
7	10	70	85
8	10	80	92
9	10	90	97
10	10	100	100

Source: Adapted from T. L. Magliozzi and P. D. Berger, "List Segmentation Strategies in Direct Marketing," *OMEGA, The International Journal of Management Science* 21 (1993): 63.

forms to the cumulative percentage of the list; that is, 20 percent of the buyers are expected to occur in the top 20 percent of the list, 50 percent of the buyers in the top 50 percent of the list, and so on. Thus, no economic advantage derives from mailing to a portion of such a randomly ordered list. Mailing to 50 percent of the list, for example, will incur 50 percent of the expense of mailing to the entire list, and will capture 50 percent of the buyers on the entire list. Column D of Table 5.1 displays the results for an (assumed) successful list segmentation process. Here, a disproportionate percentage of buyers occurs for given deciles of the list. For example, 20 percent of the buyers in the entire list appear in the top 10 percent of the ranked-ordered list; 69 percent appear in the top 50 percent of the rank-ordered list, and so on. Thus, mailing to the rank-ordered list has advantages over mailing to a randomly ordered list, as illustrated in Table 5.2.

Assumptions regarding list size, response rate, and contribution per order are given at the top of Table 5.2. A standard strategy for a mailer who does not use list segmentation would be to mail to the entire list, the result of which is a net contribution of $50,000 (note that this result is better than the other choices—mailing to none of the list or a random portion of the list). The contributions associated with mailings to various depths of file are displayed in the lower portion of the table. These results have two important implications. First, they show that a mailing strategy using the list segmentation model yields a higher contribu-

TABLE 5.2 Results of Segmentation Analysis (in U.S. dollars)

Assumptions

List has 1 million names

Overall response rate: 1 percent = 10,000 buyers

Average contribution/order (before printing and mailing costs) = $50

In-the-mail cost = $.45/name

Mailing without List Segmentation

Total contribution (10,000 × 50)	$500,000
Printing & mailing cost	−450,000
Net contribution	50,000

Mailing with List Segmentation

Depth of file	Percentage of Buyers	Number of Buyers	Total Contribution	Cost	Net
.	.	.	.	.	.
30	47	4,700	$235,000	$135,000	$100,000
40	59	5,900	295,000	180,000	115,000
50*	69	6,900	345,000	225,000	120,000
60	77	7,700	385,000	270,000	115,000
70	85	8,500	425,000	315,000	110,000
.	.	.	.	.	.
100	100	10,000	500,000	450,000	50,000

Source: Adapted from T. L. Magliozzi and P. D. Berger, "List Segmentation Strategies in Direct Marketing," *OMEGA, The International Journal of Management Science* 21 (1993): 64.

*"Optimal" depth of file

tion (profit) than the strategy of mailing to the entire list; second, they show that an optimal strategy emerges—in this example, at the 50 percent depth of file—which yields a contribution that is more than double that of the nonranked mailing strategy ($120,000 to $50,000). Indeed, successful list segmentation offers opportunities for quite significant financial leverage.

Of course, the key questions that arise are, "What are the available segmentation techniques?" and "Which offer the best segmentation?" We soon address these questions.

Factors Affecting the Benefits of List Segmentation

Formerly, segmentation was done on the basis of "gut" feeling, without the aid of a computer. Even today, it is still done this way at some smaller companies. But high-speed computers that can deal with large lists in a relatively short time and relatively cheaply have revolutionized segmentation for large direct marketers.

Two whole new industries have developed, one to provide information for segmentation purposes (refer to the chapter 4 discussion of list enhancement/overlay), the other to perform the segmentation analyses. In the first, "simple" example, only one variable was considered in the segmentation process—age—and it had only five levels. In actual practice, segmentations may be based on hundreds of variables, each having many different possible values. We refer to a variable on which a segmentation is performed as a *major characteristic,* and to each of the levels of a major characteristic as a *category.* Typical major characteristics deal with previous purchase behavior (e.g., date of most recent purchase by mail of the company's products), demographics (e.g., age), geographical factors (e.g., zip code), and psychographics or lifestyle characteristics (e.g., degree of concern with nutritional eating habits).

Two major factors determine the benefit to be gained from performing a segmentation analysis. One factor is the amount of information available on each member of the list. The other is the sophistication (or ability to discriminate) of the statistical or other type of technique used to actually perform the analysis. Obviously, everything else being equal, the more information we have on list members, the greater is our ability to distinguish those who will respond from those who will not, or those who will provide large revenue from those who will provide small or no revenue.

Less obvious, perhaps, is the fact that some analytical techniques will yield better results than others, and that the computer hardware and software used might affect the analysis. There is, at present, no universal agreement about which techniques are better—in fact, not everybody will completely agree on what "better" means. By any definition of better, however, it is likely that no single technique or methodology is better in all instances.

Before discussing these two factors, we consider some basic facts about what segmentation will not do and the parameters that determine the amount of benefit one can expect from segmentation. First of all, segmentation will not make a buyer out of a nonbuyer. However, it should eliminate a number of nonbuyers from a mailing, and this is a clear advantage.

Second, segmentation will not change the underlying nature of the direct marketing economics of a company. If the mailing cost per piece is x percent of the revenue per purchase, this will not alter, unless the segmentation is geared toward identifying people who buy more when they do buy, instead of toward identifying people who are more likely to buy.

One parameter that is very important in determining the potential benefit of segmentation is the mailing cost. As we have seen, segmentation saves mailing costs by identifying and eliminating unlikely prospects from the mailing list. Where the mailing cost is very small per unit, of course, the savings will be less from segmentation. This does not mean that segmentation has no benefit, only that your cost-benefit analysis would probably show that it is not worthwhile to pay for extra-delicate discrimination.

Another important parameter is the extent to which a targeted customer exists. If the customer base is not very distinct, a segmentation analysis will result in a less focused profile. It will then be more difficult to break out the stronger names. For example, if males and females are just as likely to respond to an offering, then gender will not provide any discriminatory power. However, if males over 65 years of age are the most likely group to respond to an offer, then the major characteristics of age and gender will be good discriminators.

Segmentation Characteristics

Many major characteristics are routinely used for segmentation purposes. Others are used less often, mainly because of unavailability, and still others are specific to a particular company or list.

Within the group of major characteristics measuring previous purchase behavior (from the same company), the primary bases of segmentation are recency of last purchase, frequency of purchase (also known as multihistory), and monetary amount spent on the purchase(s). Most people consider these three variables—known as RFM—to be the most important in determining the likely profitability of mailing to an individual. In general, these variables are available only for names on a house list.

Recency of last purchase is represented by either the number of consecutive mailings without a response or the actual number of months since the most recent purchase. This variable addresses not only whether a customer is still in the market for the company's products, but also whether he is still at that address—or, indeed, whether he is still alive!

Frequency of purchase may be represented simply by the *number* of previous purchases made (by mail) from the company, or by the *proportion* of mailings to which the person responded. The former measure is used more often, but the latter may be more helpful, as it discriminates between the person who has responded three times out of six mailings received, and the person who responded four times, but out of ten mailings received. It is not clear which of the above buying histories suggests a larger chance of purchase this time: the former has a higher "response rate," 50 percent compared to 40 percent, but the latter has made 33 percent more purchases (4 to 3), which may speak to a higher brand loyalty.

Monetary amount may be represented by the total amount of dollars the person spent on all purchases or by an average dollar amount per purchase. Again, the former measure is used more often, but the latter may be more helpful because it discriminates between the person who has made ten purchases for a total of $100, and a person who has made four purchases for a total of $97.

Of the major characteristics in the demographic group, some of the most frequently used are sex, age, income, education, title code (e.g., Mr., Mrs., Ms., Dr., Rabbi), and family structure (e.g., number of people in household, number of children, number of wage earners). Of the major characteristics in the geographic group, some of the more frequently used are state of residence, zip code (more discriminating than state, but requiring a larger number of names on the list for statistical analysis to be of any value), sectional center, and overlay data pertaining to the neighborhood (or census tract or block group) of residence, (e.g., percentage Hispanic, percentage single-family households, educational level of the neighborhood).

The usefulness of major characteristics in the psychographic group depends on what information is available, and this varies considerably. Examples of psychographic and lifestyle characteristics pertaining to individuals are jogging, playing tennis, and degree of concern with nutritional eating. Examples pertaining to the neighborhood are mobility index (degree of stability of the residents of a neighborhood) and number of doctors per capita.

One other major characteristic that is often a good discriminator is the source code, that is, where the name came from (e.g., *TV Guide*'s subscription list, direct inquiry, house file of previous purchasers). This characteristic is especially useful when the list to be segmented is a combination of other lists, either rented, compiled, or in-house.

The decision concerning which major characteristics will be used in the segmentation process is based, first, on what information is available from the house list, and second, on whether it is considered desirable to purchase various overlay geographic and psychographic information. Once the major characteristics have been determined, the next step is to decide how to split them up into separate categories. This involves determining both the number of categories to be used and the class limits of those categories. A characteristic that is measured in "ratio scale" (in essence, for example, a value of 48 is double 24—a true statement for, say, age, but not true for, say, zip code, because a zip code, of 02050 is not "double" a zip code of 01025), such as frequency of purchases or recency of last purchase, can be treated either as a "continuous" (or ratio scale) variable, or split up into discrete categories. We discuss later why it is always superior to treat such a variable by splitting it up into discrete categories, sometimes called "binning." For example, it is superior to represent age not as a continuous single variable, say, X—the literal age in years—but as a series of variables, say, $X_1 = 1$ if the person is under 25, 0 otherwise; $X_2 = 1$ if the person is between 26 and 35, 0 otherwise; $X_3 = 1$ if the person is between 36 and 45, 0 otherwise; and so on, until $X_7 = 1$ if the person is over 75, 0 otherwise. Of course, this is simply an illustration. Perhaps there should be age categories by 5-year age groups, instead of 10-year age groups (excluding end categories); perhaps the age groups should be 21–30, 31–40, 41–50, and so forth, instead of 26–35, 36–45, 46–55, and so on; these are more detailed issues that are discussed later.

Segmentation Techniques

Once you know what major characteristics you will be using and how you will split them up, the next step in the segmentation analysis is to decide on a technique for actually performing the analysis. When you are using only one characteristic (variable), the decision is easy to make. Find the response behavior for different values (levels) of the variable, rank-order the values, and determine a cutoff point by considering expected profit, cost of mailing, and so on (as in the earlier discussion). However, when you have two or more major characteristics, you must choose among a variety of different statistical methods or techniques (or a combination of them). As noted earlier, there is no universal agreement about which method is the best in general, or even in any particular circumstance; in fact, there is no universal agreement about the definition of "best." In this section, we describe and discuss the most frequently used methods.

A SIMPLE TECHNIQUE

A simplistic method that has no formal name works as follows. (This is the method that was being used in 1981 by the first company with which one of the authors worked in the area of list segmentation.) You split each major characteristic into categories by gut feeling, scan your data set (names on the list to be analyzed), assign points to each category of each characteristic in accordance with its differential response behavior, and then add up the points for each name on the list.

For example, assume that the objective is to rank-order your list of names on the basis of available data so that you can decide who on the list should receive an expensive piece of mail. There are three major characteristics: time since last purchase (recency), number of purchases made in the last five years (frequency), and total amount of dollars spent in the last five years (monetary). You decide to consider the following categories of each characteristic:[1]

Recency	*Frequency*	*Monetary*
1. Within 6 months	1. 0	1. $0
2. 6–12 months	2. 1–3	2. 1–100
3. 12+ months or never	3. 4+	3. 101–500
		4. 500+

Assume that you are using data from last year's mailing at the same season as the mailing being considered, and response rate is the criterion of interest (i.e., you are looking at the category of a person immediately prior to last year's mailing and whether he or she responded to that mailing). Suppose that the overall response rate last year was 5 percent. Now look at each category of each characteristic to determine the category's response rate. Note that the response rates for the individual categories will likely not average exactly 5 percent because the categories are not generally of equal proportions in the list. Suppose that you obtain the following response rates by category:

	Response Rate	*Differential from 5%*
Recency		
1	7.3%	+2.3
2	5.2	+0.2
3	3.9	−1.1
Frequency		
1	2.1%	−2.9
2	6.3	+1.3
3	7.7	+2.7
Monetary		
1	2.1%	−2.9
2	5.1	+0.1
3	5.9	+0.9
4	8.1	+3.1

---

[1]For illustration purposes, we have used only a few categories. In the real world, each characteristic would often have more categories.

You are now able to classify each list member into one of the $3 \times 3 \times 4 = 36$ mutually exclusive, collectively exhaustive groups and add up the member's differential values. For example, John Smith with a recency of 8 months, a frequency of 2, and a monetary of $86, has a score of

$$S = +.2 + 1.3 + .1 = 1.6$$

Mary Jones, with a recency of 14 months, a frequency of 1, and a monetary of $531, is worse on the recency value, the same on the frequency value, and better on the monetary value. Her overall score would be

$$S = -1.1 + 1.3 + 3.1 = 3.3$$

Therefore Mary Jones is a better prospect than John Smith.

This method has one major advantage—simplicity. Its major disadvantage is that it does not account for *redundancy,* also called *overlap, double counting,* and, by statisticians, *multicolinearity.* For illustration purposes, a blatant exhibition of this notion was incorporated into the preceding example. The first category of frequency (0) and the first category of monetary (0) are complete synonyms: every person with a frequency of 0—and only those people—are in the monetary category of $0; and the only people with $0 monetary are those with 0 frequency. Note that each of the two categories has the same response rate of 2.1 percent. However, the $(2.1 - 5.0) = -2.9$ value is being counted *twice,* when it really should be counted only *once.* That is, if we consider all frequency and monetary combinations (ignoring recency for the moment), the 0/$0 combination would have a response rate of 2.1 percent and be 2.9 percent below the overall average of 5 percent, *not* $(2.9 + 2.9) = 5.8$ percent below this overall average.

Most double counting is not so complete as this one. This example contains partial overlap between the 0 frequency, $0 monetary, and 12+ or never recency categories. *All* of the 0 frequency $0 monetary people have 12+ or never recency; but only *some* of the 12+ or never recency people are the 0 frequency people. The only way there will be no double counting at all is when the major characteristics are all mutually independent. Characteristics are independent if the category a person is a member of in one characteristic gives no indication which category that person is a member of in the other characteristic. This is a condition one hardly ever encounters in practice in a direct marketing database, or any other, for that matter. To return to our example, if you know that someone's recency is 12+ or never, you surely also know that person is more likely to be a 0 frequency person than is a randomly selected person whose recency is not yet revealed to you.

All of the other segmentation techniques that we discuss have the ability to avoid this serious problem; in practice, however, the problem is usually tolerated to a minor degree, in return for other benefits.

MULTIPLE REGRESSION ANALYSIS

Over time, many forces came together to foster the use of sophisticated statistical techniques instead of simpler methods that were reasonably effective but left some room for improvement. (The method just described is one of these simpler methods, or simply using RFM, in categories, and noting the response rate for each category—in the previous example, for the 36 categories—and rank ordering them.)

Multiple regression analysis (MRA) is probably the most popular of the sophisticated statistical techniques. It is a technique that develops a scoring formula that predicts some aspect of purchase behavior. With our criterion of response rate, MRA would provide an estimated probability of response for each list member. For our example of three major characteristics, an equation in the following form would be found:

$$Y_p = a + b_1X_{12} + b_2X_{13} + b_3X_{22} + b_4X_{23} + b_5X_{32} + b_6X_{33} + b_7X_{34}$$

where a and the b's are constants mathematically derived (by the computer) to provide the best fit to the data, and X_{ij} is a 1 if the person is a member of category j of major characteristic i, and 0 otherwise. Note that one category of each major characteristic (category 1 of each) is not represented by an X variable; this is a purposeful omission and is part of the technique. For John Smith, who was in recency category 2, frequency category 2, and monetary category 2, we would assign for recency $X_{12} = 1$ and $X_{13} = 0$, for frequency $X_{22} = 1$ and $X_{23} = 0$, and for monetary $X_{32} = 1$, $X_{33} = 0$, and $X_{34} = 0$. For Mary Jones, who was in recency category 3, frequency category 2, and monetary category 4, we would assign $X_{12} = 0$, $X_{13} = 1$, $X_{22} = 1$, $X_{23} = 0$, $X_{32} = 0$, $X_{33} = 0$, and $X_{34} = 1$. The Y_p is the predicted probability that the person will make a purchase. A value of $Y = 1$ is used as input to the MRA if the person made a purchase from the (previous) mailing used as input data, and $Y = 0$ is used if the person did not make a purchase. MRA uses calculus to truly perform an optimization and determine the constants that best fit the data. It should be noted that having two categories that have 100 percent overlap is unwise; in fact, it adversely affects the performance of the regression analysis (overlap less than 100 percent, however, does not have the same adverse effect). If there were only one characteristic, the regression scoring equation would have coefficients for each category equal to the differential response rate of that category from the omitted category. The Y_p value for each category would equal its response rate. If frequency were the only characteristic in the earlier example, the resulting scoring equation would be

$$Y_p = .021 + .042X_{22} + .056X_{23}$$

Note the correspondence between the predicted probabilities of purchase and the actual response rates. A person with 0 frequency would have $X_{22} = 0$ and $X_{23} = 0$; Y_p is $.021 + 0 + 0 = .021$ (the response rate noted earlier is 2.1 percent). A person with frequency 1–3 has $X_{22} = 1$ and $X_{23} = 0$; Y_p is computed to be $.021 + .042 + 0 = .063$ (the response rate noted earlier is 6.3 percent). A person with frequency 4+ has $X_{22} = 0$ and $X_{23} = 1$; Y_p is $.021 + 0 + .056 = .077$ (again, same response rate as previously, 7.7 percent).

For all practical purposes, you cannot perform a multiple regression analysis without a computer and a software package that includes MRA. Once you have everyone's Y_p, the names can be rank-ordered and/or subjected to a variety of profitability analyses. Furthermore, the b coefficients provide information as to which categories auger better or worse for purchase likelihood (by their sign and magnitude).

Multiple regression analysis is considered by many to be the best and most versatile of all the statistical techniques available for direct marketing list segmentation.

An Important Digression

How can you evaluate the results or success of a segmentation analysis? In terms of response rate, you can construct a table that is similar, although not in identical form, to Table 5.2; in essence, for each decile (every 10 percent), or duodecile (every 5 percent), or percentile (every 1 percent), you can list the rank-ordered (say) decile, each decile's response rate, and each decile's cumulative response rate. Also, additional columns can denote cumulative actual number of responses (as a function of the number of names mailed, of course), and cumulative profit values. Actually, you can decide to list any column that you wish. An illustration of this is shown in Table 5.3.

Table 5.3 shows the results of an MRA-generated scoring model by decile being applied in validation mode; that is, the scoring equation is applied to a set of names that are not part of the set from which the scoring equation was generated. The results go well beyond response rate, and they consider sales and profits. The term "lift" refers to the ratio of decile cumulative result to the result if the total list is mailed (multiplied by 100). For example, the response lift of 304 (decile 1) is the ratio of 15.2 percent to 5.0 percent, multiplied by 100; the sales lift of 308 (decile 1) is the ratio of 6,252 to 2,031, again multiplied by 100. The sales lift values and response lift values are really the same, except for rounding. However, the profit lift values are not at all the same, again highlighting the leverage involved in direct mail campaigns.

Another way to get a quick look at the result of a segmentation is to derive a Pareto Curve, as illustrated in Figure 5.1. This is a curve on which the horizontal axis indicates the (top) percent of the rank-ordered list mailed (e.g., ".50" refers to mailing the top 50 percent by rank order). The vertical axis represents the number of responses realized as a fraction of the total number of responses that would be realized if the entire list were mailed (e.g., ".80" means 80 percent of the responses that would be realized from 100 percent of the list). The .50/.80 (or 50/80) point on the curve thus indicates that the top 50 percent of the rank-ordered list generated 80 percent of the responses of the entire list.

The Pareto Curve was named for the famous economist, Vilfredo Pareto, the originator of the famous "80/20 rule," which he introduced to illustrate that at that time 80 percent of the assets in Italy were controlled by the richest 20 percent of the people. This 80/20 rule has since been applied in many settings to express similar thoughts. For example, in total quality management (TQM), it is often noted that 80 percent of the defective items produced are caused by the top 20 percent of the causes. Even though the actual values in a setting often do

TABLE 5.3 Validation of MRA Segmentation/Scoring Model

	Response			*Sales*			*Profit*		
Decile	*Rate*	*Rate (Cum.)*	*Lift*	*Per 1,000*	*Per 1,000 (Cum.)*	*Lift*	*Per 1,000*	*Per 1,000 (Cum.)*	*Lift*
1	15.2	15.2	304	6,252	6,252	308	1,376	1,376	1,262
2	11.6	13.4	268	4,543	5,398	266	863	1,119	1,027
3	5.5	10.8	216	2,200	4,332	213	160	800	734
4	4.0	9.1	182	1,660	3,664	180	(2)	599	550
5	3.3	7.9	158	1,353	3,202	158	(94)	461	423
6	2.7	7.1	142	1,101	2,851	140	(170)	356	327
7	2.5	6.4	128	1,071	2,597	128	(179)	279	256
8	2.1	5.9	118	903	2,385	117	(229)	216	198
9	1.7	5.4	108	748	2,203	108	(276)	161	148
10	1.1	5.0	100	484	2,031	100	(355)	109	100

Source: Courtesy of Pamela Ames, Kestnbaum & Co., Chicago.

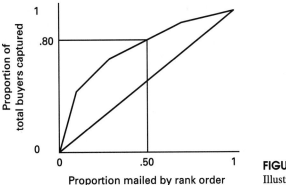

FIGURE 5.1
Illustrative Pareto Curve

not represent exactly 80/20, the results are usually still noted as examples of the Pareto principle. The label Pareto Curve in the direct mail–direct marketing setting was first used in an article by P. D. Berger and T. L. Magliozzi, which is discussed later in this chapter.[2]

MULTIPLE DISCRIMINANT ANALYSIS (MDA)

Another technique used for list segmentation is multiple discriminant analysis (MDA). MDA is useful only when the dependent variable is categorical—meaning, generally, when the dependent variable is response or no response—although it can also be used when the dependent variable is classified into more than two categories (e.g., no response, small monetary amount, large monetary amount), or into two categories that do not per se discriminate by response or no response (e.g., no response or response less than $10, response at least $10).

MDA, like MRA, yields a scoring equation (or more than one equation if there are more than two categories for the dependent variable) that relates to the probability of a person being in a particular category. The technique has many similarities to multiple regression analysis, especially when there are only two categories into which names are being classified.

LOG LINEAR MODELING/LOGISTIC REGRESSION

Another technique that results in a scoring equation is log linear modeling (LLM). LLM is a relatively new and complex technique. Like MDA, it is suitable for categorical data (as the variable to be predicted, called the dependent variable), but far less software has been developed for LLM than for MDA. The technique called logistic regression (LR), essentially the same thing as a logit model, is basically the same as log linear modeling. The key difference from these "log" models and traditional linear regression is that these techniques are using a nonlinear model. You can imagine the right-hand side of the equation as being the same as in the multiple linear regression section:

$$a + \Sigma\, b_i\, X_i$$

---

[2]P. D. Berger and T. L. Magliozzi, "The Effect of Sample Size and the Proportion of Buyers in the Sample on the Performance of List Segmentation Equations Generated by Regression Analysis," *Journal of Direct Marketing* (winter 1992).

However, the left-hand side is *not* simply the 0/1, or nonresponse/response, but instead the "log of the odds of a response." If the probability of a response is "*p*," then the odds of getting a response is defined as $p/(1-p)$ to 1; for example, if $p = .1$, the odds for a response is $.1/.9$, or $1/9$, or 9 to 1 *against* getting a response. If we set $\ln[p/(1-p)]$ ("ln" meaning natural logarithm) equal to the right-hand side, we get

$$\ln[p/(1-p)] = a + \Sigma\, b_i\, X_i$$

which leads to

$$p = \frac{e^{a + \Sigma b_i X_i}}{1 + e^{a + \Sigma b_i X_i}}$$

What is especially noteworthy about this equation is that p is always between 0 and 1, no matter what the value of $(a + \Sigma\, b_i X_i)$.

This nonlinearity (which, in a sense, is more general than an equation mandated to be linear, as used in MRA) leads to lots of discussion about which techniques are superior to others and the possible reasons for this. Many people argue that the nonlinear form is inherently superior for a variety of reasons. One reason is, indeed, the increased flexibility of being nonlinear; after all, one can say that a linear equation is simply a special case of the general case of an equation not restricted to be linear. Another reason often stated is that the "statistical assumptions" traditionally required to use a linear model are violated; to a degree this is true. For example, traditional linear regression assumes that the dependent variable (i.e., the variable we are trying to predict) follows a normal (bell-shaped) distribution. This is clearly not true for a variable such as response, which takes on only two values, 0 and 1. Another argument is that the predicted "probability of response" generated by MRA does not always come out between 0 and 1; they are correct, even though a probability is defined to be a value in this range.

Although these "criticisms" of MRA analysis sound serious, in the opinion of many (including the authors) they are not. Consider the issue of getting a predicted probability of purchase that is outside 0 to 1, nominally an impossible result. Think practically! If the indicated probability of purchase for a name is estimated to be (the impossible) 1.01, isn't it obvious we want to mail to that name? Of course! Likewise, suppose that a predicted probability of purchase is estimated to be –.01 (less than zero, and also impossible). Isn't it obvious not to mail to that name? Again, of course! The arguments about the statistical assumptions are also unimportant. It is generally agreed that many traditional measures of "goodness of fit" are simply spurious measures in the world of direct mail or direct marketing when it comes to evaluating the success of a segmentation analysis. Indeed, Berger[3] reports an example of a segmentation case in which the (multiple) coefficient of determination, the well-known R^2, came out .005 (quite low by most traditional benchmarks), and yet the segmentation power provided was excellent, yielding a dramatic "50/100" on the Pareto Curve (i.e., mailing to the top 50 percent of the rank-ordered list captured 100 percent of the buyers).

The relevant question when comparing different techniques is, "Which technique yields a superior Pareto Curve?" That is all that matters. If one method yields nearly all the

---

[3]P. D. Berger, "Some Issues in Direct Marketing List Segmentation," presented at the National ORSA/TIMS Conference, October 1988; repeated in P. D. Berger and T. L. Magliozzi, "List Segmentation Strategies in Direct Marketing," *OMEGA: The International Journal of Management Science* 21 (1993).

buyers when only the top 40 percent of the rank-ordered names are mailed, and another technique requires a larger portion of the names to be mailed to capture the same proportion of buyers, but the latter technique better satisfies the "statistical assumptions," which technique would you really prefer? A superior Pareto Curve puts money in your pocket. You can't put statistical assumptions into your bank account! A discussion of how LLM or logistic models and other techniques compare with respect to Pareto Curves takes place in the next section.

There are other techniques used for list segmentation that do not provide a scoring equation (which allows a complete rank ordering of an entire list of names). Rather, they attempt to cluster (bunch together) groups of names that will act similarly with respect to whatever dependent variable is used as the criterion, or, when no response-related data are available, to find groups with similar profiles. We discuss some of these other techniques next.

CLUSTER ANALYSIS

Cluster analysis considers the input data (generally geographic, demographic, or psychographic) and clusters names into like groups. Its main use in the area of segmentation is to identify groups with similar traits; cluster analysis might identify a certain neighborhood in Atlanta, another in Buffalo, and a third in Newark that should be clustered together for purposes of analyzing response behavior. As noted in chapter 4, cluster analysis is the general technique used by the list enhancement services that provide predetermined clusters, such as PRIZM by Claritas, Inc. and ClusterPlus, now also owned by Claritas, Inc., and others.

AUTOMATIC INTERACTION DETECTION

Another technique for list segmentation that belongs to the cluster family is automatic interaction detection (AID). AID is an exploratory data-analysis technique, developed at the University of Michigan's Survey Research Center, that considers the relationship between a dependent variable and a number of potential independent variables. It is very much like cross-tabulation analysis; it does not assume linearity (e.g., that the change in probability of purchase is a constant for each added year of age) or additivity (that the effects of different characteristics can be added, as opposed, for example, to requiring multiplication). Most other segmentation methods—MRA, MDA, and LLM—make at least some of these assumptions or make similar ones.

AID deals with categorical variables. Its main strength is its ability to discover interaction effects among the variables (i.e., the effect of one independent variable on the response variable not being the same for all levels of other independent variables). AID analysis is often referred to as a tree analysis because it subdivides the list of names into successive segments that are depicted as a pyramidal or tree-like structure. AID seems to require a relatively large database in order to provide useful results, but many lists and most databases in direct marketing applications are sufficiently large to use AID.

Indeed, current opinion is that AID or its extension, CHAID, which is discussed in the next section, is not the wisest choice of technique for the ultimate list segmentation, but is extremely useful to determine interaction effects that can then be input to the "main" segmentation technique of MRA, MDA, or LLM. One cannot model a segmentation to allow for the possibility of interaction between every pair of variables; the number of interactions involved would be prohibitively high. For example, if there were 20 major characteristics (even ignoring turning each into more than one variable by binning), the number of "two-at-a-time interactions" (called "two-way" interactions) is 190. For 40 characteristics, there would be 780! However, it is possible that certain interaction effects have the ability to provide significant additional segmentation. AID (nowadays, CHAID) is an excellent way to determine which few interaction effects should indeed be modeled. In this sense, it is an excellent intermediate step in the segmentation process.

CHI SQUARE AUTOMATIC INTERACTION DETECTION (CHAID)

An extension of AID is a technique called chi square automatic interaction detection (CHAID), developed by Gordon Kass. It overcomes one major limitation of AID in that it allows the finding of segments that are of three or more levels of a variable, whereas AID is limited at each stage to finding segments that respond either high or low. In fact, CHAID automatically determines just how many levels there ought to be and what those levels are. Statistical Innovations of Belmont, Massachusetts, has developed computer software for performing a CHAID analysis, called SI-CHAID, which, in 1998, was available as an addition to SPSS (Statistical Package for Social Sciences), one of the most popular statistical software packages.

Like AID, CHAID proceeds in steps to develop a "tree." First, the best partition for each X (predictor) variable is determined; if each variable is coded as a categorical variable (required in AID or CHAID), the program can determine just where, and into how many segments, to "split" the variable to maximize the differences (say, in response rate) among the segments. For example, if age is categorized into <21, 21–30, 31–40, 41–50, 51–60, 61–70, >70, the program might decide that the differences among the "segments" are maximized if there are three segments: AGE1, <31 (the first two categories); AGE2, 31–60 (the next three categories), and AGE3, >60 (the last two categories). Categories grouped together need not be contiguous categories. A chi-square statistic is used to determine maximum "statistical significance" and the decision where to do the splitting. The next step picks the best of these best splits to determine which X variable is the best single discriminator. If this were the age variable just described, this would be represented by the beginning of a tree, splitting the base into the three segments; see step 1 of Figure 5.2.

Subsequently, CHAID would consider each age segment as a starting point (i.e., would consider only the names in a given age segment), and find which other X variable is the best way to branch off from each age segment, and pick the best of the bests again. Suppose one of the other variables is gender, with two categories, GENDER1: male, and GENDER2: female (by the way, with only two categories, there was no need for CHAID to find the best split), and third (and last, in this small-scale example) is annual income, with best split INCOME 1: <$40,000, INCOME2: $40,000–$70,000, INCOME3: >$70,000. Suppose that for AGE1, the best segmentation available is by gender, whereas for AGE2 and AGE3, the best segmentation is income, and that the "best of the bests" is the gender segmentation of AGE1. This would lead to the tree in step 2 of Figure 5.2.

CHAID's next step would be to consider the four "end branches" at step 2 of Figure 5.2 and determine where the best further split now should take place. Note that at this point there are four segments: (AGE1, GENDER1), (AGE1, GENDER2), (AGE2), (AGE3). The algorithm continues to branch out and expand the tree until there are no further splits that pass a statistical test (i.e., no further splits that provide sufficient additional segmentation to

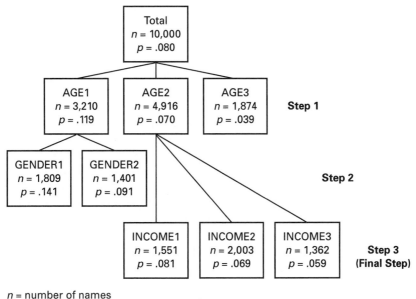

FIGURE 5.2 An Illustrative CHAID Analysis

warrant further steps). The final tree could, for example, look like the full Figure 5.2. In this case, the CHAID analysis has determined that there are six segments:

(AGE1, GENDER1—all incomes combined)

(AGE1, GENDER2—all incomes combined)

(AGE2, INCOME1—both genders)

(AGE2, INCOME2—both genders)

(AGE2, INCOME3—both genders)

(AGE3, all incomes and both genders)

Each segment has a somewhat different response rate, and can be differentially treated in terms of mailing strategy.

As input to a regression analysis or other analysis, the CHAID results also indicate that there are interaction effects between age and gender as well as between age and income; additionally, there is no indication of an interaction between gender and income. Thus, the two indicated interactions should probably be modeled in the regression (or discriminant, or log-linear, or whatever) analysis.

CLASSIFICATION AND REGRESSION TREES (CART)

Classification and regression trees (CART) involve a combination of elements of AID and CHAID and elements of multiple regression analysis. A treelike group of segments is formed, and MRA is used to split each division of the list of names into a further subdivision. CART has some advantages and disadvantages over CHAID. One advantage is that the

X variables do not need to be categorical, but can be metric. This is a minor advantage, because it is nearly always wise to represent variables as categorical, whether they are metric or not. The questions behind the reason for this advantage are conceptually simple: Why have to "guess" what functional form (linear, quadratic, logarithmic, and so on) of the variable best describes the relationship between the *X* variable (say, age) and response rate? Is it a straight line? Or is it concave (increasing at a decreasing rate, or decreasing at an increasing rate)? Or is it even "monotonic" (i.e., is response rate always going up or always going down as the age increases—or does response rate first go up with age, but then at some point decrease with age)?

The latter "nonmonotonic" relationship could easily be the case; for example, consider the response rate for a mail piece selling, say, lawn maintenance equipment. At younger ages, response may go up with age, because many people, as they grow older, are having children and moving into homes (with lawns!), and are physically capable of maintaining the lawn by themselves, and also perhaps are not able to afford to hire a lawn service anyway; eventually, an age may be reached where more and more people are less physically capable of maintaining a lawn by themselves, and at the same time can now afford to hire a lawn service. So, a graph of response rate against age would reveal a function that first rises, but then falls.

The key point is that coding an *X* variable, such as age, as a categorical variable, as earlier illustrated—even though it is, in its natural state, metric or continuous—removes the guess about the appropriate functional form; it allows the variable to seek its own functional form. After all, whatever the response rate of various categories, whether monotonic, curved, or whatever, it simply comes out the way it is. Just imagine a histogram representing the actual data—if you connect the tops of the histogram bars, you get what you get—there are no restrictions!

NEURAL NETWORK ANALYSIS

A method for performing segmentation analysis that is relatively new (at least compared to the other techniques mentioned earlier), and, to a degree, considered "chic," is a technique called neural network analysis, sometimes labeled "ANN [artificial neural network] analysis." A neural network analysis is an analysis that purports to simulate the way the human brain works. It does not involve statistical analysis, per se, but involves viewing the *X* variables as a series of inputs that are interconnected, weighted, and then pass through various nonlinear transformations, sometimes called "transfer functions" or "squashing functions." The network analysis then consists of "training," or the iterative adjusting and readjusting of the weights, until error (difference between, say, predicted and actual response pattern) is minimized. There are choices that can be made concerning how many "hidden layers" of "neurons" to use in the weighting, transformation, and training process. Indeed, this last sentence really highlights the major criticism of neural network analysis: it is, in the ultimate, simply a "black box," whose inner workings are nearly impossible to fathom in any meaningful way. Once the analysis has reached its "conclusions" about how to classify or segment names, it then applies this analysis to the "hold out" set of names, names that are not part of the set of data on which the network trains.

We discuss later in the chapter some comparisons and conclusions concerning the use of neural networks versus MRA and LLM or LR for list segmentation in direct mail.

Comparison of Segmentation Techniques

When we wrote the first edition of this text, there was not a great deal of literature comparing the various list segmentation techniques in a direct mail application. Since then substantially more has been written on the subject. In discussing these comparisons, we again maintain that what is important is how the techniques perform in (direct mail list segmentation) practice, not issues such as violation of assumptions, or other theoretical considerations. We use, whenever possible, the Pareto Curve results as the criterion for the model's effectiveness; of course, the Pareto Curve results have a "one-to-one" (i.e., unique and derivable) relationship to the individual response rates of, or cumulative response rates of, say, deciles.

Do not lose sight of the fact that for any segmentation to be possible using *any* technique, (independent) variables must be identified for which different values (levels) of these variables have differential "Y's" (response rates, dollars, repeat-response likelihoods, etc.).

TECHNIQUE COMPARISON STUDY
BY BLATTBERG AND DOLAN

A study by R. Blattberg and R. Dolan[4] compared (1) MLR with continuous independent variables; (2) MLR with dummy (categorical) independent variables; (3) first-order LLM (i.e., no interaction effects included); (4) saturated LLM (all interaction effects included); and (5) AID (indirectly). The primary criteria used in this study were the predictive abilities of the respective models. Secondary criteria were interpretability of results, simplicity of use, computer cost, and data-preparation cost.

The conclusions of the study were as follows:

1. The first-order LLM and the dummy variable MRA models dominated the other two models (continuous independent variable MRA and saturated LLM).

2. With respect to the two MRA models, the benefits of decreasing the number of parameters to be estimated are outweighed by the costs of misspecifying the model. (In particular, the assumption of a linear relationship between the independent variables, age and education, and the dependent variable, response rate, was clearly incorrect.)

3. With respect to the two LLM models, the introduction of the interaction terms (in going from the first-order model to the saturated model) reduced the performance of the model.

4. The first-order LLM model and the dummy variable MRA model performance about equally well.

When comparing LLM with AID, it must be noted that using LLM required a reduction in the number of independent variables, which using AID did not. However, even after this reduction, LLM generally outperformed AID by a sizable margin. For example, over a variety of examples in which the top-ranked 20 percent were mailed, LLM resulted in about 10 percent more respondents than AID. Both techniques, though, did far better than random selection.

---

[4]R. Blattberg and R. Dolan, "An Assessment of the Contribution of Log Linear Models to Marketing Research," *Journal of Marketing* (spring 1981): 89–97.

TABLE 5.4 Pareto Curve Results for Carter Study

Depth of File	Percent of Buyers Captured		
(Pareto Curve)	*AID*	*Geo-Demographic*	*MRA*
10%	17.7	19.1	23.1
25	38.7	40.9	47.6
50	71.6	65.3	74.8

Source: Adapted from J. F. Carter, "A Comparison of the Predictive Powers of AID, Regression, and Geo-Demographic Clustering," *Journal of Direct Marketing Research* 1, no. 2 (1987): 83–90.

Blattberg and Dolan reached three general conclusions: (1) LLM models do have a valuable application in marketing; (2) if the main concern is predictive ability with a dichotomous dependent variable, ordinary least squares regression with categorical X's may well be the most appropriate analytical tool; and (3) if the percentage of predicted probabilities falling outside the 0 to 1 range is small, regression with categorical independent variables is likely to be most effective. Conclusion (2) is based, in part, on those secondary criteria of interpretability, ease of use, and computer costs.

TECHNIQUE COMPARISON STUDY BY CARTER

A study by J. F. Carter[5] reports the results of two separate studies that compare AID, MRA, and geo-demography. In the first study, segmentations were conducted on a database with 21,036 names; half, or 10,518 names, made up the model sample (i.e., the names on which the techniques were applied), and the other half of the names were used as the validation sample (i.e., the names on which the results of the segmentation were evaluated). The variable to be predicted was the ownership of an IRA (individual retirement account), and the input (X variables) consisted of various purchase and demographic data from the Simmons Market Research Bureau, enhanced by additional household demographic data from the Donnelley Marketing residential database. The results of this study are shown in Table 5.4. As can be seen, MRA was superior at every level of the Pareto Curve.

Table 5.4 is also useful to point out an issue not yet mentioned: Sometimes it is not perfectly clear which Pareto Curve is superior. If one curve lies entirely above another, it is clearly superior; the MRA curve is an example. However, which of the other two curves is superior, the AID curve or the geo-demographic curve, is not clear from the table. At the 10 and 25 percent points (i.e., mailing to the top 10 or 25 percent of the names on the rank-ordered list), the geo-demographic segmentation is a bit better (ignoring, for now, the issue of statistical significance of the difference); at the 50 percent point, however, the AID segmentation has performed better. Which is truly the superior segmentation depends on the trade-off between the profit per response and the in-the-mail cost, as earlier illustrated in the analysis of Table 5.2.

---

[5] J. F. Carter, "A Comparison of the Predictive Powers of AID, Regression, and Geo-Demographic Clustering," *Journal of Direct Marketing Research* (spring/summer 1987): 83–90.

The second study performed by Carter involved response to a credit card mail promotion. The Pareto Curve details were not provided, although again MRA dominated the other two techniques.

SAMPLE SIZE AND "SALTING" STUDY
BY BERGER AND MAGLIOZZI

From 1992 to present, there have been a number of studies of different list segmentation issues and methods in direct marketing by Paul D. Berger of Boston University (one of the authors of this text) and some of his doctoral students. The first of these was a study of the impact of sample sizes and the number of buyers used in regression-based list segmentation models.[6] They considered the classic situation of having a house list to segment, and splitting the data into two parts (i.e., an "A/B split"), a model/regression sample (A), and a hold-out/validation sample (B). The data they used were from a U.S. catalog marketer of household tools, and consisted of 421,698 names from their house file. Data included purchase history, demographic information, and the (original) source of the name. There were 51 major characteristics, which turned into 220 categorical variables (0/1) when prepared for analysis. The variable to be predicted was response to a particular catalog mailing, and the model was based on the results of a previous mailing of a similar catalog.

First the researchers examined the impact of the n_A and n_B, holding them equal. They considered n's of 50,000, 100,000, and 200,000, and had many different runs on which to compute an average and to base their results; for example, when $n = 50,000$, there were 56 different runs, each of the 8 sets of 50,000 (there are 8 sets of 50,000 in 421,000 names) as the A sample, with each of the other 7 samples of 50,000 as the B samples. The Pareto Curve results are shown in Table 5.5 (p. 108).

Clearly, at both depths of the Pareto Curve, the segmentation was superior as the sample size increased; indeed, the differences for different n's were statistically different at $p < .01$. Perhaps it is not a surprise that increased sample size increases the goodness of the Pareto Curve; after all, more data often increase the reliability of results. What is especially interesting, however, is a comparison of this impact with the impact of "salting," or artificially inflating, for analysis purposes only, the response rate in the sample. *Salting* is the name Berger and Magliozzi gave to analyzing a portion of the database, but adding in extra buyers (similar to "salting" a gold mine with extra gold) to increase the information available on buyers in the previous mailing, which had a response rate of .75 percent (and, thus, only about 165 responders). The reason why the impact of salting could be important is that if salting the database can substitute for an increased sample size, a significant cost saving may be realized from having to maintain a smaller overall database and from having to mail to fewer lower purchase probability prospects.

They considered the impact of salting the A sample (which would perhaps allow the regression analysis to provide a superior model), and also of salting the B sample (which would perhaps allow more regularity or consistency in the results evaluated). The salting consisted of doubling the response rate from .75 to 1.5 percent by adding the names of buyers not part of the, say, 50,000 sample considered. The results were very definitive: salting the A sample (i.e., the set of names used to develop the scoring equation) significantly increased

---

[6]Paul D. Berger and Thomas J. Magliozzi, "The Effect of Sample Size and Proportion of Buyers in the Sample on the Performance of List Segmentation Equations Generated by Regression Analysis," *Journal of Direct Marketing* 6 (winter 1992): 13–22.

TABLE 5.5 Impact of Sample Size; Berger and Magliozzi Study		
Sample Size n	*25% Pareto Point*	*50% Pareto Point*
50,000	41.3	64.9
100,000	43.6	66.9
200,000	45.5	68.8

Source: Adapted from P. D. Berger and T. J. Magliozzi, "The Effect of Sample Size and Proportion of Buyers in the Sample on the Performance of List Segmentation Equations Generated by Regression Analysis," *Journal of Direct Marketing* 6 (1992): 13–22.

the Pareto Curve values; salting the B sample had no effect. Moreover, doubling the response rate by salting had just about the same positive impact on the Pareto Curve of doubling the overall sample size. It is not known whether this relationship would hold for other data sets, but the possibility is intriguing.

STEPWISE REGRESSION STUDY BY MAGLIOZZI AND BERGER

A second study by Magliozzi and Berger compared traditional MRA, where all of the *X* variables are used in the scoring equation (sometimes called "forced entry" regression because all of the *X*'s are mandated or forced to enter the equation), and stepwise regression, a form of MRA that results in a scoring equation that consists solely of *X* variables that are statistically significant.

In traditional MRA, by containing all of the *X* variables available, the scoring equation contains many variables that are not statistically significant; there is no argument that this obscures the importance and impact of individual variables because usually many of the variables are interrelated, or overlapping (i.e., correlated). When this "colinearity" occurs, the impact of a variable, as measured by its coefficient in the scoring equation, is not representative of its true effect on *Y*, the variable being predicted. We saw this illustrated early in this chapter in an extreme case of complete overlap, where there was an impact of –2.9 associated with having a frequency of 0 and also a –2.9 associated with a monetary of $0, yet the sum of the impacts was the same –2.9. Most examples are not as extreme as that, and indeed one cannot easily determine just how much overlap exists between variables, especially when there are a large number of variables and they might, and often do, overlap "every which way." For example, suppose that the impact of increasing age is positive on response probability for a given product. This positive impact may likely also reflect higher earnings (that positively correlates with age); indeed, age is positively correlated with many variables included in segmentation analyses: earnings, price of home, years at job, and others. Because each of these may be positively correlated with response probability, the regression equation will determine the impact of the "positively correlated package of variables" and split their impact among their respective coefficients, thus not yielding a scoring equation coefficient of age that truly reflects the increased response probability when one is older.

Stepwise regression is a technique that introduces variables into the scoring equation one by one, and prevents a variable from entering the equation if it has substantial overlap with variables already in the equation, thus not allowing strong overlap among the final set of variables. Also useful is that stepwise regression does not allow variables that have no relation at all with response probability to enter the scoring equation. It is well known statistically that if a scoring equation includes irrelevant variables, the equation's predictive power is weaker (its standard error of estimate is higher). It should be noted, however, that including variables that are good predictors of response probability, but do overlap, while obscuring the impact of individual variables, does not per se reduce the predictive power of the scoring equation. We have made the point that the only real way to tell if a technique is superior to another for direct marketing list segmentation is to study the Pareto Curves thus derived. Indeed, this is precisely what Magliozzi and Berger do in this study.

The study uses the same database as the previous sample size/salting study. Essentially various "*pins*" were tested. A variable's *pin* (really written as p_{in}, the *p*-value necessary to bring the variable *in* to the scoring equation) loosely represents a measure of how overwhelming the evidence is that the variable provides predictive value about response probability, above and beyond the variables already in the scoring equation. A variable that is, by itself, useful in the predictive process, but its usefulness is already captured by an overlapping variable already in the scoring equation, will not be permitted to enter the scoring equation—thus avoiding obscuring the impact of the variables already in the equation. A *pin* of 1 means to let in every variable; thus it is equivalent to traditional, forced entry MRA. The default *pin* on many stepwise regression software programs is .05 or .15.

Table 5.6 contains the Pareto Curve results found in the study for various *pins* at the 50 percent Pareto Curve depth. It is clear in Table 5.6 that the stricter criterion (i.e., the smaller the *pin*, and thus the more overwhelming the evidence would have to be that the variable provides predictive value before the variable is allowed to enter—hence, a "stricter" criterion) for entrance into the scoring equation, the better the results. Thus, a follow-up set of results were reported for even smaller *pins* (see Table 5.7).

TABLE 5.6 Pareto Curve Results for Magliozzi and Berger Stepwise Regression Study

	p_{in}				
Pareto Curve Depth	*.01*	*.05*	*.15*	*.40*	*1*
50%	75.9	67.6	65.3	64.9	64.3

Source: Adapted from T. L. Magliozzi and P. D. Berger, "List Segmentation Strategies in Direct Marketing," *OMEGA, The International Journal of Management Science* 21 (1993): 70.

TABLE 5.7 Extended Stepwise Regression Pareto Curve Results

	p_{in}		
Pareto Curve Depth	*.001*	*.005*	*.01*
20%	39.1	37.1	35.8
50	75.9	67.6	65.3
70	93.3	91.7	85.8

Source: Adapted from T. L. Magliozzi and P. D. Berger, "List Segmentation Strategies in Direct Marketing," *OMEGA, The International Journal of Management Science* 21 (1993): 71.

The same pattern emerged, that the more strict the criterion for entrance of a variable into the scoring equation, the more superior the Pareto Curve that results. This statement must, however, have its limitations ultimately, for a *pin* of (literally) zero would not let any variables into the scoring equation and the segmentation would then be no better than random choice (i.e., 20 percent depth captures 20 percent of the buyers, 50 percent depth captures 50 percent of the buyers, etc.). Of course, as in any similar study, it is not certain if these results would occur for other databases, with other sets of *X* variables, for example; yet, the results have added to the body of knowledge on which options a company should consider when deciding which technique to embrace.

NEURAL NETWORK ANALYSIS AND MRA COMPARISON STUDY BY LIX AND BERGER

As mentioned earlier, one of the relatively new techniques considered for use in direct marketing list segmentation is neural network analysis. T. J. Lix and P. D. Berger compared MRA (both forced entry and stepwise) with neural network analysis in the direct marketing list segmentation setting.[7]

Two neural network software packages ("NN1" and "NN2"; the specific names of the packages were not revealed) were tested, along with forced entry MRA and stepwise MRA at *pin* = .05. In all four "treatments," each of the independent variables was "binned" (i.e., each was coded into a set of categorical variables). NN1 was dedicated to direct marketing and was truly the proverbial "black box"; little detail was revealed about the neural network that performed the analysis. NN2 was not dedicated to any specific setting and allowed some meaningful choice in constructing the neural network to be used.

For all four treatments, the data set consisted of 5,000 physicians, and there were 44 categorical (0/1) variables in the analysis, including various demographic variables (e.g., home type, address, age), medical school history (e.g., year graduated, specialty), and current medical practice (e.g., years practicing, average number of hours worked per week, hospital affiliations). The data were split into set A (the "model" set) and set B (the validation set), by ordering the data by zip code and placing every other name in set A and the remaining names in set B. The dependent variable to be predicted was response to an offer for enrollment in new physician-oriented organization. As is always the case for any technique, but especially for neural network analysis, lots of data preparation (e.g., coding issues) and decisions concerning which variables on the database to include had to be made. In some sense one should include all variables that have the possibility of helping the prediction. However, some variables were clearly redundant (e.g., age and date of birth); others contained too many missing values to be of use; others had so little variation that they were useless (e.g., whether employed or not employed because virtually all of the 5,000 physicians were employed). Also, the neural network packages had limitations on how many variables could be included.

For each technique, there were two "A/B" runs; that is, first one half was used as the "A," and the other half as the "B," then the two halves reversed roles. Thus, there were two set of results to average (Table 5.8); naturally, the more results that are averaged, the more reliable the results. The key findings Lix and Berger reported from the results were that (1) neural network analysis can potentially outperform MRA (note results for NN1); and (2) not all neural network software packages perform the same (compare results for NN1 and NN2),

---

[7]T. J. Lix and P. D. Berger, "Analytic Methodologies for Database Marketing in the US," *Journal of Targeting, Measurement, and Analysis for Marketing* (February 1995).

TABLE 5.8 Pareto Curve Results for Lix and Berger NN/MRA Study

Pareto Curve Depth	NN1	NN2	MRA (forced)	MRA (step)
15%	41.7	27.6	36.1	26.5
30	74.1	55.9	72.3	54.8
50	94.2	77.9	87.9	78.1
70	100.0	91.9	93.5	85.6

Source: Adapted from T. J. Lix and P. D. Berger, "Analytic Methodologies for Database Marketing in the US," *Journal of Targeting, Measurement, and Analysis for Marketing* (February 1995): 237–247.

and one cannot simply "lump together" all neural network software packages. For contrast, if forced entry MRA is used, all software packages will yield the same exact results, except possibly, but rarely, for very minimal rounding errors. The same would be true for the use of stepwise regression.[8] Obviously, the same is not true for neural network software packages.

The other interesting finding from the above results is that stepwise regression performed a lot worse than forced entry regression. This contradicts the results found by Magliozzi and Berger in one of their earlier papers discussed previously. This mailing had a response rate of about 20 percent, much higher than what is usual in the industry. Perhaps this partially explains the difference in findings.

STUDY COMPARING LLM AND MRA FOR "PROSPECTING" BY LIX, BERGER, AND MAGLIOZZI

The latest of the series of papers by Berger and his doctoral students focused on the issue of list segmentation in direct marketing compared two variations of LLM and two variations of MRA (forced entry and stepwise).[9] However, there were some added elements of interest in this paper—they looked at list segmentation for the purposes of sending to noncustomers ("prospects") to acquire customers. All of the other studies were oriented around a house list, except the neural network study that used a compiled list.

Indeed, the comparison of the different techniques perhaps "takes a back seat" to the discussion involved in using commercially available external databases to identify superior prospects. The spirit of the process begins with taking a survey of, say, 5,000 people; the paper used survey results from two years of Monitor data, an annual survey of attitudes and behavior conducted by Yankelovich Partners, Inc., a well-known marketing research firm, of about 2,500 households annually. These survey results, in essence, provided the "*Y*," or

---

[8]There are a few different forms of stepwise regression, mainly (1) an algorithm as described in the earlier section in which variables enter the scoring equation one by one (with the possibility of deleting a variable that is entered, but then is rendered redundant by the entrance of subsequent variables); this is usually called "forward stepwise," or simply "stepwise"; (2) an algorithm called "reverse stepwise," or "backward stepwise," in which all variables are entered originally, and variables are deleted one by one, until no redundant variables remain. In direct marketing, the backward stepwise method is not practical, for there are usually too many *X* variables to use this form fruitfully. The statement about the consistency of results obviously assumes that each software package is performing the same form of stepwise regression.

[9]T. J. Lix, P. D. Berger, and T. L. Magliozzi, "New Customer Acquisition: Prospecting Models and the Use of Commercially Available External Data," *Journal of Direct Marketing* 9 (1995).

dependent, variable: various purchase behaviors and purchase attitudes (e.g., propensity to "buy green/environmentally"). The next step is to find these 5,000 people among the near 170 million individuals covered by the commercially available databases. The data on these databases provide, in essence, the "*X*" or independent variables. Then a scoring equation is found (the technique used to find the scoring equation is not central to this discussion) that uses only *X*'s available for most of the names on the commercial databases. This scoring equation can then be applied to the "millions" of names in the commercial databases to determine the prospects' predicted "*Y*" value (say, probability of response), and identify superior prospects to mail or market.

The paper considers four different dependent measures (whose results are averaged in the discussion of segmentation techniques that follows), and also considers two different ways of treating missing data (to be discussed subsequently). The different segmentation techniques tested were

1. MRA—stepwise with *pin* = .05
2. MRA—forced entry
3. LLM—first using CHAID to limit the number of variables in the analysis until the minimum cell size equals 1 percent of the sample being analyzed
4. LLM—first using CHAID to limit the number of variables in the analysis until the minimum cell size equals 5 percent of the sample being analyzed

The Pareto Curve results at the 20 percent depth point, averaged over the four dependent variables, and over the two different methods of treating missing data, are shown in Table 5.9. Note that the overall numbers are not "that high." This is because, of the four measures or dependent variables being predicted, three are attitudes (e.g., propensity to "buy green," as noted earlier, and propensity to "buy American") and not actual purchase behavior, whereas only one of them represents actual behavior (purchase or not during the past year of products by at least two direct marketing channels). It is well known that actual behavior is more directly able to be modeled compared to attitudes (i.e., behavioral *intentions*).

In terms of the efficacy of the different techniques, none of the results in Table 5.9 are statistically significantly different from any of the others. That the LLM results do not differ substantially from the MRA results is perhaps not a surprise, given that other studies (specifically the Blattberg and Dolan study) found that they performed similarly with respect to Pareto Curve results. That the forced entry MRA and the stepwise MRA performed about the same further confounds the issue of their comparison.

TABLE 5.9 20% Pareto Curve Results for Lix, Berger, and Magliozzi Study

Technique	20% Depth Pareto Curve Result
1	28.5%
2	28.1
3	27.2
4	26.9

Source: Adapted from T. J. Lix, P. D. Berger, and T. L. Magliozzi, "New Customer Acquisition: Prospecting Models and the Use of Commercially Available External Data," *Journal of Direct Marketing* 9 (1995): 16.

Commercially available external data typically have more missing data than a house list. There are two reasons for this. One is that you have control of your house list, and can exercise quality control (this is true even if you contract out the list maintenance task). The other, more compelling reason is that external data are made up of many different sources, and these different sources contain different data elements. People for whom credit card data are available would likely not have their annual incomes missing; however, certain purchase data may not be available. The source of data for other people may be their shopping behavior, from scanning methodology; extra purchase data might be available, but perhaps not their annual incomes. In most cases, but not all, both sets may be available. What should one do to deal with missing data? We cannot explore that question in this text; there are a number of 500-page books on this exact subject! The two missing-value strategies investigated in the Lix, Berger, and Magliozzi paper were

1. The construction of a separate category for "missing." For example, for the variable of gender, there would be three categories, not the "normal" two categories: M, F, X, where M = male, F = female, and X = missing data. The potential benefit of this coding is that it might be just as good as other possibilities (nobody has really explored this issue deeply, and not at all in a direct marketing context), and has the added potential advantage that if the data point is missing it may say something about the person (e.g., women of a certain attitude refusing to reveal their age), and the analysis can "capture" that.

2. The "substitution up the ladder" method. This method substitutes a missing value for an individual by the proxy value of the neighborhood; if the neighborhood value is missing, substitute the value of the carrier route; and so forth "up the ladder." If necessary use the zip code value, which is virtually always available. The logic here is that the method does the best that it can in terms of the variable's impact. Although the relationship between an individual's data and the data of his or her neighborhood, carrier route, and zip code is not as strong as some might believe (recall the discussion of this issue in chapter 4), there is still some positive correlation among these values at different points on the ladder. Why not capture it?

The study indicated that method 2, substitution up the ladder, outperformed method 1, using an extra category for "missing." At the 20 percent Pareto Curve depth, averaged over techniques and dependent measures, method 2 yielded a Pareto Curve value of 29.3, whereas method 1 yielded 26.1. More work is needed in this area of missing value strategy.

SHEPARD'S COMPARISON OF NEURAL NETWORK ANALYSIS AND LOGISTIC REGRESSION

David Shepard's excellent book on database marketing[10] contains an example comparing neural network analysis and logistic regression. The results do not appear to differ substantially. However, Shepard points out that each of the two models yields the "best" result when one particular variable is left out. Whereas there is no way to recognize the need to exclude the variable when performing the neural network analysis, the logistic regression analysis (as is the case for virtually all of the other techniques and analyses we have discussed) does give that indication and easily indicates that the variable should be dropped.

Shepard's book also includes a number of very specific modeling issues, such as the coding of zip code data and the incremental impact of adding overlay data (as discussed in chapter 4) to prospect models. It also mentions the modeling of dependent variables other than response probability, revenue or profit. For example, it reports on a Buchanan and

---

[10]David Shepard, *The New Direct Marketing: How to Implement a Profit-Driven Database Marketing Strategy,* 2nd ed. (New York: Richard D. Irwin, 1995).

Morrison study[11] on modeling falloff rates for third, fourth, and subsequent mailings based on the results of the first two mailings.

A recent article by J. Hess and G. Mayhew[12] considers the modeling of returns (i.e., sales cancellations) in direct marketing by methods similar to those discussed in this chapter in the more traditional setting of predicting response. However, Hess and Mayhew advocate using a "split adjusted hazard model" and suggest that it is superior to a regression model for their purposes, especially those involving the timing of returns (no concept of timing is part of traditional list segmentation models). Discussion of their hazard model is beyond the scope of this text; for details, see their article.

Other Considerations in Choice of Segmentation Technique

So which technique should one choose? The question is not easy to answer, in spite of the body of research that exists on the subject. The argument was made earlier in the chapter that the real determining factor in choice of a list segmentation technique is its performance in terms of Pareto Curve values. Nevertheless, the Pareto Curve evidence does not indicate that one technique dominates all of the others. Thus, we might turn to other considerations; here are some potential pros and cons for each technique that go beyond the strict issue of Pareto Curve values.

MULTIPLE REGRESSION ANALYSIS

pros:

widely understood

easy (easiest of all) to interpret

large amount of software available

no size limitations

cons:

violates many traditional statistical assumptions (viewed by this writer as a theoretical problem, not a practical one)

may yield predicted probability results outside the [0,1] range

traditional *t*-test and *F*-test not strictly appropriate due to violation of assumptions

MULTIPLE DISCRIMINANT ANALYSIS

pros:

none beyond multiple regression analysis

cons:

statistical assumptions violated by use of categorical X variables; impact on Pareto Curve not investigated

---

[11]R. Buchanan and D. Morrison, "A Stochastic Model of List Falloff with Implications for Repeat Mailings," *Journal of Direct Marketing* (summer 1988).

[12]J. Hess and G. Mayhew, "Modeling Merchandise Returns in Direct Marketing," *Journal of Direct Marketing* (spring 1997).

LOG LINEAR MODELING/ LOGISTIC REGRESSION

pros:

> superior "goodness" of fit when predicting very low response rates (but without hard evidence it translates to superior Pareto Curves)

cons:

> requires advanced statistical knowledge to run, by an order of magnitude above multiple regression analysis

> relatively difficult to interpret the coefficients

> relatively less software available

CLUSTER ANALYSIS/GEODEMOGRAPHY

pros:

> none, per se

cons:

> tends to use demographic and lifestyle variables and exclude previous purchase behavior (yet, the latter are usually the best predictors)

> demographic and lifestyle variables are less likely to be individually based

AUTOMATIC INTERACTION DETECTION, CHI-SQUARE AID, AND CLASSIFICATION AND REGRESSION TREES

pros:

> superior in detecting interaction effects

cons:

> contains relatively larger amounts of error

> generally requires larger amount of data relative to other techniques

NEURAL NETWORK ANALYSIS

pros:

> *potential* for breakthrough superiority

cons:

> more or less a "black box"—relatively little revealed

> relatively little software, although availability increasing rapidly

> high variability among software

To repeat the question, which technique should one choose? We repeat the answer: The question is not easy to answer. However, we do provide two qualified answers. (1) If forced to choose a technique in the abstract and having no opportunity to experiment, we would narrow our choice to first doing a CHAID analysis to identify interactions, and then doing either a stepwise MRA or a stepwise logistic regression. We would probably lean toward an MRA because of the "cleanliness" of the interpretations of the coefficients. (2) The other answer is that, if we had the opportunity—and there is no reason why we would not—we would test, test, and test some more. That is, we would recognize that there isn't only one answer as to which technique to use that works best in every situation. Due to the unique circumstances of a particular instance (with its concomitant set of available variables, products to be sold, and cost structure), the only way to determine which technique will work best is to test them.

In chapter 10, Testing Direct Marketing Programs, we discuss such issues as how to design an efficient experiment to perform testing of many types.

Summary

List segmentation, or mailing to a selected subset of a list, can improve the economics of mailing lists. A variety of variables in the areas of previous purchase behavior, demographics, psychographics, and lifestyles may be available as segmentation characteristics. Once these characteristics are chosen, there are many techniques that can be used to perform the segmentation analysis. These include some simple techniques, as well the more sophisticated techniques of multiple linear regression, multiple discriminant analysis, log linear modeling, cluster analysis, (chi-square) automatic interaction detection, classification and regression trees, and neural network analysis. Each may have certain advantages and disadvantages. There is statistical evidence that compares many of the techniques, although it does not appear to be definitive. All in all, this complex issue is, in the ultimate, best settled by testing the different techniques in the specific setting of interest.

Discussion Questions and Exercises

1. How important is it that a list segmentation technique provides a specific scoring equation?
2. After reading this chapter, what list segmentation research questions do you believe have not been addressed? Which do you believe have been addressed, but not sufficiently?
3. What does a Pareto Curve look like if the segmentation has provided no additional benefit? What does it look like if the segmentation has performed "perfectly"?
4. What is the relationship between the values on the vertical axis of the Pareto Curve and (a) the decile's response rate, (b) the decile's cumulative response rate?
5. What qualities would you look for in a list segmentation technique?

Suggested Readings

Bauer, C. "A Direct Mail Customer Purchase Model." *Journal of Direct Marketing* 2, no. 3 (summer 1983).

Hill, M. "A Comparison of the Zip Code and Block Group Demographics for Predicting Individual Characteristics." *Journal of Direct Marketing Research* 1, no. 1 (1986): 67–82.

Furness, P. "Applying Neural Networks in Database Marketing: An Overview." *Journal of Targeting, Measurement, and Analysis for Marketing* 1, no. 2 (1992): 152–169.

Shepard, D., and R. Ratner. "LRM and ANN: Can They Be Happy 'Together?'" *DM News,* 15 August 1994, 27.

Shepard, D., and R. Ratner. "Using Neural Nets with EDA and Regression Models." *DM News,* 23 May 1994, 27, 29.

6 CHAPTER Creative Strategy and Execution

As you read the title of this chapter, you may have said, "I can't draw and I don't want to be a writer, so why do I have to study the creative part of direct marketing?" That is a good question, and there are at least three good answers to it:

1. All direct marketing managers are involved in the creative process in some way. At the very least, they participate in the development of creative strategy and approve the final creative execution.

2. All direct marketing managers—all managers, for that matter—have opportunities to be creative, whatever their job titles. There can never be enough truly creative ideas for strategies, products, alternative offers, product positioning, customer services—in fact, for all aspects of direct marketing.

3. Most creative design work is now computerized. Preparation of layouts for print media is done on specialized CAD (computer-aided design) software. Video animation can be done using specialized software instead of the traditional hand-drawn frames. Software tools facilitate the

117

design and construction of Web sites. We even decorate our word-processed documents with computerized clip art.

There are two kinds of creativity that are important to successful direct marketing and to traditional marketing as well. The first is the kind businesspeople usually think of when they hear the word *creativity*. It involves a blend of layout, art, and copy that effectively communicates a message. The second has, in recent years, come to be known as *managerial creativity*. We might think of this kind of creativity as "finding new solutions to old problems."

Let's first look briefly at the subject of managerial creativity and then in more detail at the development and execution of creative strategy in various media.

What Is Creativity and Who Has It?

Many myths and false stereotypes interfere with the typical marketer's understanding of the subject of creativity. The purpose of this section is to help you break free from myths and stereotypes surrounding the subject and to understand that there is a simple process that all of us can use to enhance our creative problem-solving ability.

A DEFINITION OF CREATIVITY

There are many definitions of creativity, but the one set forth by Theresa Amabile gives considerable food for thought:

> A response will be judged as creative to the extent that (a) it is both a novel and appropriate, useful, correct, or valuable response to the task at hand and (b) the task is heuristic rather than algorithmic.[1]

The (a) part of the definition is pretty straightforward, but interesting for the emphasis it places on the applicability of the creative solution to the situation for which it is intended. Genuine creativity is not "creativity for creativity's sake," but a unique solution to a real problem. The (b) part contains two terms that sound like refugees from a statistics or a computer class: "heuristic" and "algorithmic." What do they mean in this context? Heuristics are rules of thumb, approximations that are used when precise solutions are either impossible for some reason or theoretically possible but prohibitively expensive to obtain. You might think of heuristics as commonsense rules or as decision rules developed on the basis of hard-to-quantify experience. Algorithms, on the other hand, are precise and mechanistic formulas or series of steps that will lead to the solution of a problem. Solve the formula correctly, follow the series of steps precisely, and you will have the answer to the problem. Because this is a mechanistic (though sometimes difficult) process, it does not qualify as creativity.

THE CREATIVE PROCESS

What, then, is the process an individual uses to come up with a unique and appropriate solution to a problem? Many processes have been suggested in the literature of the social sciences. These processes are based on various psychological theories or on observation and

---

[1] Theresa Amabile, *The Social Psychology of Creativity,* quoted in Michael Ray and Rochelle Myers, *Creativity in Business* (Garden City, NY: Doubleday, 1986), 4.

analysis of the way uniquely talented individuals (e.g., Charles Darwin, Marie Curie, Albert Einstein) approached major discoveries. Two marketers have synthesized a number of these theories and developed a five-step model of the creative process that is similar to a number of formulations you may have seen in other contexts:[2]

1. Sensing. The first activity is sensing a problem exists. This is the problem-recognition step. Assume that the product manager for a set of science reference works on CD-ROM, which is sold as a three-item continuity series targeted to families with secondary school students, recognizes a consistently decreasing response rate over several acquisition mailings. The response rate has declined steadily, and the most recent mailing barely broke even. Worse still, many of the initial purchasers are not completing the set, making the back end of the program unprofitable. Management has indicated that the series will be discontinued unless it can be returned to its former level of profitability within six months—a very clear problem definition.

2. Preparation. The second step in the process is preparation. In this state the manager or creative specialist gathers all information that is pertinent to the problem. Let's assume that our hypothetical product manager first analyzes the external factors, the market and the competition. The market is large and growing, based on the number of children in targeted age groups. There is only one direct competitor, who has an inferior product but a very attractive direct mail package.

The product manager then decides to commission focus groups with children and parents and a series of one-on-one interviews with secondary school teachers and professors of education who are known in the profession as experts in science curricula. The primary research uncovers no major flaws in the product; children and parents who are experienced users of the product report satisfaction and even enthusiasm. Children and parents who were not familiar with the product express a need for this type of reference and find the product attractive when it is demonstrated for them. The professional experts find it sound in both content and presentation.

3. Incubation. The product manager is ready for the third stage—incubation. In this stage the manager simply assimilates all the information, organizes it mentally, and attempts to understand its meaning and all its implications. The manager's conclusion at the end of this stage is quite clear: There is nothing wrong with the product; the marketing campaign has simply worn out. The product needs a new, attractive, hard-hitting mailing package.

4. Illumination. That was the easy part. Now comes the difficult question: What kind of mailing package will produce the results the manager needs? She is now seeking illumination—the "big idea" that will turn the situation around for this continuity program. She is convinced that incremental changes to the current package will not do the trick. A breakthrough idea is required.

At this stage experts recommend that if you are searching for a creative solution, you should get away from the problem for a while. The idea is not to keep struggling and trying to force a solution to emerge, but to simply turn the problem loose. Go on to another task; take a walk in the woods. Then, when you least expect it—while driving to work or while doing something else—inspiration will strike.

---

[2]Burton H. Marcus and Edward M. Tauber, *Marketing Analysis and Decision Making* (Boston: Little, Brown, 1979), 198–200.

There is much anecdotal support for this recommendation to get away from the problem for a while, but keep two things in mind:

1. None of the experts suggests that inspiration will strike unless intensive preparation has been done. The person seeking inspiration *must* become immersed in the facts in relation to the problem *before* sitting back and waiting for lightning to strike. This recommendation is in no way a prescription for laziness or for not doing one's homework!

2. There is a warning to managers inherent in this recommendation. It is counterproductive to force unrealistic deadlines on creative activities. Creative specialists must have time to absorb the available information, to let it gestate, and then to polish the creative concept that emerges.

This is not an argument for no deadlines, just for reasonable ones. Managers who consistently expect "instant creativity" will get just what they deserve—a poor creative product. At the same time, creative people who cannot meet deadlines will also achieve a rather predictable outcome—unemployment. The point is that good creative work demands cooperation and understanding between direct marketing managers and creative specialists. Figure 6.1 contains a set of guidelines to help managers encourage creativity within their own organizations. In general, they seem like good management practice. These guidelines are particularly interesting because they came from a monograph about creativity in the decision sciences—not an area in which most of us would expect to find discussion about creative issues.

After mulling over the situation with regard to the CD-ROM series, the product manager arrives at a solution. It centers around a new package format, a rewritten letter, the addition of a lift letter (discussed in chapter 12), and a totally new graphics approach. The "big idea" is to offer an incentive for *completing* the program, not as an *acquisition* device. The incentive is an attractive, well-designed holder for CDs given with completion of the set. This should encourage customers to take all three CDs, the key to profitability for the offering.

FIGURE 6.1 Fostering Creativity

Source: Adapted from James R. Evans, *Creative Thinking in the Decision and Management Sciences* (Cincinnati, OH: South-Western Publishing Co., 1991).

- Provide freedom to creative specialists
    - Allow things to be done differently
    - Take risks
    - Encourage individual initiative
- Create a supportive environment
    - Maintain only moderate work pressure
    - Loosen supervision
    - Set realistic work goals
- Include many persons in the decision-making process
    - Delegate
    - Give timely, constructive feedback
- Promote participation and interaction within and between work groups
- Encourage open expression of ideas

5. Verification. The final step is verification—evaluating the creative idea or concept that has emerged. By this we do not mean testing in the direct marketing sense (that will come later) but simply asking yourself whether the idea is novel, appropriate, useful, correct, and valuable in the current situation.

All the product manager's ideas for improving the CD-ROM offer seem reasonable. They will be tested in the direct marketing setting to see if they do indeed solve the problem. You may be saying to yourself that these ideas are not very original; they certainly do not seem earth-shaking. Yet in a real situation comparable to the hypothetical one we have just described, similar changes resulted in a campaign that exceeded its sales objectives by 10 times!

This hypothetical example illustrates an important point about creativity—a creative marketing *idea* can be the basis for the solution of a marketing problem. The idea can be an offer, a mailing package format, a product positioning or any of a number of other marketing variables. Whatever the idea is, it has to be carried out. The first step is to develop a creative strategy, and this will be followed by a creative execution.

Developing Creative Strategies

Every creative group, whether part of an agency, a service bureau, or a marketing client, has its own approach to developing a creative strategy. Figure 6.2 (p. 122) shows an overview of the creative process that takes into account the special capabilities of direct marketing, especially in the areas of databases and testing. As you examine the process, you will also recognize key elements that are part of any good planning processes.[3]

PROGRAM OBJECTIVES

A good planning process begins with the establishment of clear objectives. These objectives come from direct marketing managers and are based on overall marketing objectives. Whether they are stated in terms of customer acquisition, leads to be distributed to channel members, top-line sales, or any of many other possible objectives, there must be specific program objectives that contribute to the achievement of overall marketing and business objectives.

The direct mail promotion in Figure 6.3 (p. 123) promotes a newly expanded international shipping service offered by FedEx. The objective seems quite clear—to encourage businesspeople to try the new service. It seems equally clear that the target for this mailing was the established FedEx customer base because in the first paragraph it thanks recipients for their "understanding" and their "business" during a recent period of exceptionally high volume. FedEx might have sent this promotion to just a portion of its customer base— accounts that ship internationally. On the other hand, because the objective is trial, FedEx might have sent it to the entire base. This promotion is especially interesting because it uses a consumer promotional technique—a price-off coupon—in a business marketing situation.

---

[3]The material in this section is based on Don E. Schultz, Stanley I. Tannenbaum, and Robert F. Lauterborn, *Integrated Marketing Communications* (Lincolnwood, IL: NTC Business Books, 1992); William Wells, John Burnett, and Sandra Moriarty, *Advertising,* 3rd ed. (Upper Saddle River, NJ: Prentice Hall, 1995); Don E. Schultz, Dennis Martin, and William P. Brown, *Strategic Advertising Campaigns,* 2nd ed. (Chicago: Crain Books, 1984); and Michael L. Rothschild, *Marketing Communications* (Lexington, MA: D.C. Heath, 1987).

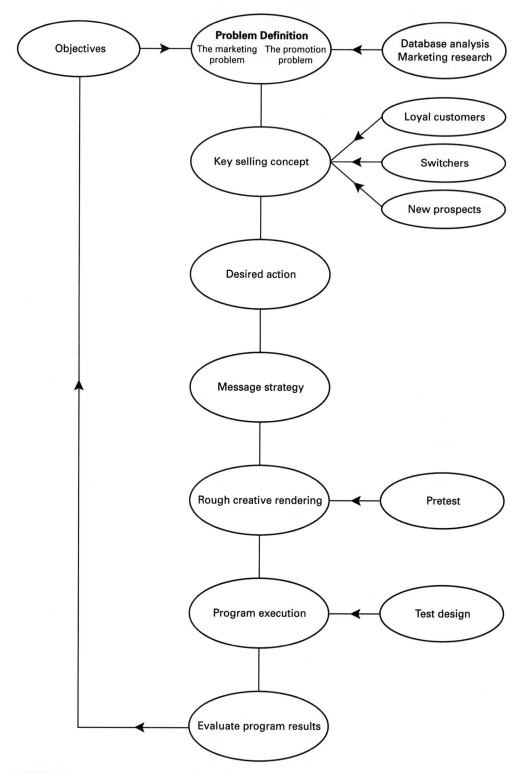

FIGURE 6.2 The Creative Strategy Process

FIGURE 6.3

Source: Used with permission of FedEx, Inc.

PROBLEM DEFINITION

Likewise, the marketing problem that is to be solved must be clarified first. The promotional problem will then flow from the statement of the marketing problem. Note that the marketing objective and the specific marketing problem come first, then the promotional problem definition and objective follow.

Direct marketers have a rich resource for all types of planning, including creative strategy, in the customer database that we discuss throughout this text. Assume for a moment that a catalog manager might have been growing its database for women's clothing until the segment of women who purchase career clothing is large enough to warrant the launch of a specialty catalog. The catalog merchant has analyzed the database and found the following profile of buyers of career merchandise:

Age	Over 60% between the ages of 24 and 34
	Most of the remainder under 50
Income	Primarily in the $25,000–40,000 range
Marital Status	Roughly 70% single
Geographic	Relatively evenly distributed throughout the U.S. with a skew toward urban zip codes and very little rural
Average Purchase	$87.22
Average Frequency	1.3 times per year

Further assume that, based on this and other corporate information, the catalog manager defines the marketing problem (or goal) as needing 50,000 purchasers to meet the breakeven target. The purchasers should be broken down into roughly one-half new buyers from rental lists, one-quarter one-time buyers from the existing customer base, and one-quarter repeat buyers from either source. These objectives also affect the list strategy, as discussed in chapter 4.

In defining the creative problem the management staff considers the profile of what will become their initial customer base, and carefully examines competitive catalogs and visits the retail stores of apparel chains that serve this target market. They describe the creative challenge as being:

> To design a catalog that appeals to the young or young-at-heart working woman. It must reflect the corporate policy of offering well-designed and constructed merchandise at a reasonable price. At the same time, it must reflect a profile that is younger, somewhat more upscale, and more fashion forward than the overall customer base of the firm. It must also differentiate itself from numerous other catalogs that target a similar market. The combined creative and offer strategies must be sufficiently aggressive to meet the total customer number specified by management.

A creative problem clearly specified provides initial guidance to the creative team. It also makes it obvious that various aspects of the overall catalog marketing program will have to intersect at and be implemented by the creative approach that is chosen.

KEY SELLING CONCEPT

The key selling concept is the "big idea" that will guide the creative execution. It is known by many names (each agency tends to have its own term), but you may know it as the "unique selling proposition." Whatever it is called, it is the key idea of the campaign.

Successful direct marketers have long known that an idea that emphasizes product *benefits* over product *features* has a much better chance of success. Figure 6.4 shows the front and back covers of a *Prevention* magazine mailing for one of its health-promotion books. With eight interior pages plus an insert containing the offer and response card, it is not clear whether this is a direct mail package without an envelope or a mini catalog. However, it is clear that the promotion features the benefit purchasers can expect to realize if they buy the book. The idea of "Switch Off Your Body's Fat-Makers" is then executed in a way that, in

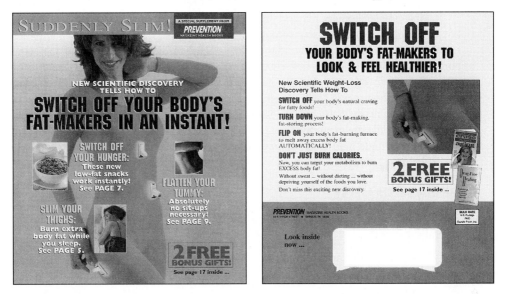

FIGURE 6.4

Source: Reproduced with permission of *Prevention Magazine.*

most people's minds, would qualify as creative. Why? For one thing, it is attention getting. More important, it dramatizes the benefit that is the core of the key selling concept.

Whether the "big idea" is centered around an offer as suggested in the section on managerial creativity, a creative execution as in the *Prevention* mailer, a new and innovative product or service, or any one of numerous other marketing variables, it needs to be based on information and solid marketing analysis, as portrayed in Figure 6.5.

DESIRED ACTION

The prospect behavior that the direct marketer wants to occur as a result of the promotional activity must be clearly stated. Often it is implicit in the objectives; it is clear that FedEx wants customers to try a new service, for example. To encourage this behavior, they are offering a coupon for the initial purchase. Because the targets are FedEx customers, they do not need to be told how to order a pick-up or use a drop box. They are, however, explicitly instructed to return the coupon with their payment invoice to receive the $20 discount.

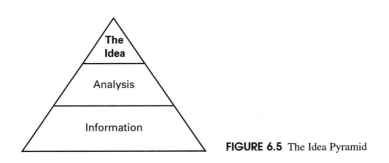

FIGURE 6.5 The Idea Pyramid

First-time customers may require more incentives, more instruction, or perhaps both. For a catalog that is being sent to both existing customers and new prospects, the creative solution may simply be a shiny gold sticker affixed to the catalog cover of the acquisition portion of the mailing. The sticker would make an offer for new prospects only ($5 off the first purchase, a year's free subscription to the catalog, and so forth). In that way the same creative execution works for both established customers and, with one simple addition, for new prospects. This is particularly desirable for the catalog because it represents a significant per piece cost and the marketer does not want to redesign it for different target segments. In the case of a simple mail piece, it may make sense to have substantially different executions for different segments.

MESSAGE STRATEGY

The next step in the creative process is to develop a detailed message strategy. This involves several substeps:

- Describe the target market
  - Demographics, geographics, and psychographics
  - Media use patterns
  - Purchase and use patterns for the product and/or brand
- Describe the selling task in relation to the competition
- Describe the selling task in terms of the product's benefits
- Give reasons why the product delivers the benefits
- Specify the desired tone or mood.

This information is based on the marketing plan or is a simple repetition of judgments made in earlier steps of developing the creative strategy. The exception is the specification of "reasons why" and tone or mood, which are both new. The significance to this step in the process is that it is the key point in the process at which the balance shifts from marketing managers to the creative team. The creative personnel need a thorough statement of the marketing and communications strategies that have been established. This statement will guide their execution of the creative approach.

We have already pointed out the importance of stressing product benefits over product features. The "reasons why" section of the message strategy elaborates on the key benefit by providing arguments that explain why the product delivers the benefit. Detailed supporting rationale for the key benefit is important to the writers as they develop the copy for the piece.

Reasons why may be linked to tangible features of the product: the materials from which it is made, its design, or the manufacturing process used. Credibility is often derived from the association with the company or brand name. Direct mail letters are usually signed by an actual officer of the firm, not by a hypothetical promotional character, for additional believability. Reasons why often come in the form of testimonials from satisfied customers. Creative personnel must be given access to this material, which may be drawn from research, customer letters, or other sources.

Finally, to complete the message strategy, the tone or mood of the program must be specified. The primary determinants of the desired tone or mood are the brand personality or image of the product and the key selling proposition. Legendary advertiser David Ogilvy says:

Products, like people, have personalities, and they can make or break them in the market place. The personality of a product is an amalgam of many things—its name, its packaging, its price, the style of its advertising, and above all, the nature of the product itself.

Every advertisement should be thought of as a contribution to the brand image. It follows that your advertising should consistently project the *same* image, year after year. This is difficult to achieve, because there are always forces at work to change the advertising—like a new agency, or a new Marketing Director who wants to make his mark.[4]

Direct marketing has historically been less concerned than general marketing and advertising with the issue of brand personality or image. However, as communications clutter has increased, these issues have become more important to direct marketers. They are especially important on the new frontiers of interactive marketing, as we see later in this book.

Think about the message strategy that underlies the ad in Figure 6.6. It is a tasteful execution of a message about a private subject, birth control. The ad comes from *Ebony,* a magazine targeted at African Americans. It gives a feeling of warmth and concern. The copy weaves in required information about possible side effects of the drug without making it seem threatening. Perhaps most interesting of all, it is a direct-response ad for a prescription drug that cannot be purchased over the counter. The marketer is clearly interested in providing more information than can be conveyed in a one-page ad and is probably building a database of interested consumers.

Advertisers have traditionally described the tone or mood of a promotion as either rational or emotional. There are a number of problems with these two terms: they are difficult to define and measure, no ad is entirely one or the other, and these two terms do not seem to correlate very well with purchase motivations, as discussed in chapter 3.

An improvement is the informational/transformational schema introduced by Christopher P. Puto and William D. Wells and subsequently expanded upon by Puto.[5] Consider the definitions of the two terms by Puto and Wells:

We define an informational advertisement . . . as one which provides consumers with factual (i.e., presumably verifiable), relevant brand data in a clear and logical manner such that they have greater confidence in their ability to assess the merits of buying the brand after having seen the advertisement. An important aspect of this definition is that an advertisement can be designed with the intention of providing information, but it does not become an informational ad unless it is perceived as such by consumers. . . .

For an advertisement to be judged informational . . . it must reflect the following characteristics:

1. Present factual, relevant information about the brand.

2. Present information which is immediately and obviously important to the potential consumer.

3. Present data which the consumer accepts as being verifiable.

A transformational advertisement is one which associates the experience of using (consuming) the advertised brand with a unique set of psychological characteristics which would not typically be associated with the brand experience to the same degree without exposure to the

[4]David Ogilvy, *Ogilvy on Advertising* (New York: Crown Publishers, 1983), 14.

[5]Christopher P. Puto and William D. Wells, "Informational and Transformational Advertising: The Differential Effects of Time," in Thomas Kinnear, ed., *Advances in Consumer Research, Vol. XI* (Provo, UT: Association for Consumer Research, 1984), 638–643; Christopher Puto, "Transformational Advertising: Just Another Name for Emotional Advertising or a New Approach?" in Wayne D. Hoyer, ed., *Proceedings of the Division of Consumer Psychology, 1985 Annual Conference* (Washington, DC: American Psychological Association, 1985), 4–6.

FIGURE 6.6

Source: Used with permission of Pharmacia & Upjohn Company.

advertisement. Thus, advertisements in this category "transform" the experience of using the brand by endowing this use with a particular experience that is different from that of using any similar brand. . . .

For an advertisement to be judged transformational, it must contain the following characteristics:

1. It must make the experience of using the product richer, warmer, more exciting, and/or more enjoyable, than that obtained solely from an objective description of the advertised brand.

2. It must connect the experience of the advertisement so tightly with the experience of using the brand that consumers cannot remember the brand without recalling the experience generated by the advertisement.

Puto and Wells present a 23-item scale that can be used to classify an ad as either high or low transformational at the same time it is either high or low informational. The scale has been tested and validated with television commercials. There seems to be no reason why it would not be just as effective when used in conjunction with print advertising or direct mail.

It is important to point out that the media most used by direct marketers are good at conveying information, but not particularly good at image building. This is especially true of both telephone and direct mail, perhaps because each appeals to only one sense (hearing and sight, respectively) at a time. Television is especially good at brand building, assuming a sufficiently large media budget and a consistent theme over time. However, as we discover in chapter 16, direct marketers ordinarily do not use television in an image-building mode. The conclusion that direct marketing is better at informational than transformational promotions seems inescapable. And this does seem to be true, except perhaps for the new interactive media, which may have substantial potential in the area of brand building.

ROUGH CREATIVE RENDERING

In earlier times—maybe 10 or 15 years ago—all of the rough creative was done by skilled artists. This usually took the form of one or more storyboards, sketches that showed major features of the ad including copy blocks and illustrated what the final layout would look like. Today, this is all done by computer. William Wells and his coauthors describe the situation as follows:

> The computer commonly is used for fast rough layouts, quick changes on storyboards, and even finished production for some black-and-white newspaper ads. . . . Assembling a mechanical, or a paste-up, of all the elements of an advertisement was once the work of the studio artists or an art director. . . . Enter the computer, with all the elements scanned into memory. The first mechanical might take 20 to 30 minutes. Each successive variation . . . might take only a few minutes.[6]

Individuals and small businesses can readily compete in producing this type of computerized artwork as a result of scanners and a plethora of software for creating page layouts and the individual components of the promotional piece.[7]

One important purpose of the rough creative is to gain initial approval of the creative concept from the client. The client may be internal direct marketing management, or at this stage the creative work may be in the hands of an external agency who will present the concept and rough execution to management. There are often pretests of the rough execution, especially if any aspect of the creative strategy has created controversy within the organization. Because time is of the essence and there is not usually a large budget for pretesting, focus groups often are used. Focus groups generally do a good job of exposing really bad concepts or confusing executions, but they should not be looked upon as an accurate barometer of the potential success of a promotional piece.

PROGRAM EXECUTION AND EVALUATION

Once the necessary approvals have been obtained, the promotion is executed. Most direct-response promotions have some sort of test associated with them. However, as we discuss in detail in chapter 10, the creative execution of the ad may or may not be the focus of the test. If it is, the results of the test will weigh heavily in the overall evaluation of the creative success of the program. Measures for evaluating program success, introduced in chapter 2, are discussed in detail in chapter 9 and the chapters dealing with individual direct-response media.

---

[6]William Wells, John Burnett, and Sandra Moriarty, *Advertising,* 3rd ed. (Upper Saddle River, NJ: Prentice Hall, 1995), 140–141.

[7]See Sunny Baker and Kim Baker, *Desktop Direct Marketing* (New York: McGraw-Hill, 1995), especially chapter 9, "Desktop Publishing—How to Produce Promotional Materials and Catalogs from the Desktop," pp. 203–230.

A FINAL WORD OF WARNING

This description of the creative strategy process does not explicitly take into account corporate requirements and restrictions, which can have an important impact, especially on execution. These requirements range from the extensive disclosure requirements that apply to many financial services and pharmaceutical products to internal corporate rules. These rules can govern everything from the required size of the corporate logo to printed information that must be included (the Internet address or 1-800 number are good examples). The creative team overlooks these requirements at its peril, because their omission will deny approval to the execution. The wise creative team learns what these requirements are early in the process so they will not cause difficult changes or unpleasant delays as the project nears its deadline.

Creative Execution

Once the creative strategy statement is in place, the translation of that strategy into the actual promotional piece can begin. Creative strategist Joan Throckmorton has a Basic Law of Creativity for direct marketers that we all would be well advised to heed. She states the premises that make up this law as follows:[8]

> *As direct marketers we're not here primarily to make a sale; we're here to get a customer . . .* our focus must be on the *lifetime value* of the customer—*repeat* sales rather than merely the value of a single sale. And to have that, you need a customer relationship. . . .

> *We set up a positive dialogue with our customers via direct response techniques. Through this dialogue we constantly test and measure to determine what "pleases" or appeals to the customer.* [The creative's] job is to discover the strongest appeals, the most compelling presentations, the most involving formats through testing, or by talking to the customers and prospects. . . .

> *Customer service is an important aspect of our business. Properly treated, the customer will continue to tell us reliably not only what to sell, when to sell, how much to sell, and the best offer to use.* Certainly all marketers should know this. But no one is equipped to demonstrate it better and more precisely than direct marketers, because direct marketers were the first to develop and utilize customer records [the database] to establish a productive customer dialogue or an ongoing, repeat purchase history. . . .

> *When we listen to the customer first, we can make money with considerable confidence. We can analyze customer information and learn not only where we are, but also where we can logically expect to be over the years ahead.* Marketers in every kind of direct marketing . . . have established formulas based on consistent behavior of specific customer groups. . . . [They] develop computer models based on these formulas and use them to draw up their long-range marketing plans.

> *Nothing must destroy our credibility with the customer. The customer takes us very seriously. The customer listens to us. The customer remembers. . . .* In direct marketing this premise is foundational. Every time we forget it or ignore it, we suffer.

---

[8]Joan Throckmorton, *Winning Direct Response Advertising,* 2nd ed. (Lincolnwood, IL: NTC Publishing Group, 1997), 30–34.

These all add up to Throckmorton's Basic Law of Creativity: *Whatever you say, however you say it, however you present it, first ask, "Does this make sense to the customer?"* Good advice, indeed. And note carefully that these rules for good creativity require that we consider the customer first, before we begin to craft the words, pictures, and layouts that will convey the sales message. These three elements—typically referred to as copy, graphics and layout—are the basic building blocks of the creative execution.

DIRECT-RESPONSE COPY

It is generally agreed that successful direct-response copy is different from general advertising copy. "It's long," is the difference most often mentioned. That is frequently true but very superficial.

John Caples, who spent more than 40 years in advertising and direct marketing at BBD&O, was regarded by many as the dean of direct-response copywriters. He had many strong opinions about what makes good copy in general and direct-response copy in particular:[9]

On length of copy: Ads with lots of facts are effective. And don't be afraid of long copy. If your ad is interesting, people will read all the copy you can give them. If the ad is dull, short copy won't save it. (p. 16)

On being straightforward: Direct writing outpulls cute writing. Don't save your best benefit until last. Start with it. You will have a better chance of keeping your reader with you. (p. 16)

On imagery: A skillful copywriter does not depend on the reader's imagination to visualize all the possible benefits of various product features. . . . He creates a word-picture that makes crystal-clear the specific advantages of every feature. (p. 84)

On product features and benefits: When you receive an assignment to write an ad for a product, your first step should be to study the product's features. . . . In writing your copy, your job is to translate these features into benefits. (p. 85)

On speaking directly to the prospect: Make believe you are writing a letter to your best friend. Put down the words "Dear Joe." Then tell Joe everything you want him to know about a wonderful new product you have just discovered. . . . Then turn your letter into an ad. (p. 180)

Caples was a student of all aspects of advertising—comparing ads that pulled well with those that did not, ads that were used over and over with those that wore out quickly, headlines that worked with those that did not, and words that improved ads with those that did not. After he learned what worked and what did not, he tried to find out why, and that is probably the secret of the success he enjoyed over his long career. Good direct-response creatives study the promotions of others as well as the results of their own work, learning from everything they observe. Joan Throckmorton's book has a chapter titled "A Gallery of the Good Stuff" that gives contemporary examples.[10]

---

[9]John Caples, *How to Make Your Advertising Make Money* (Upper Saddle River, NJ: Prentice Hall, 1983).

[10]Throckmorton, *Winning Direct Response Advertising,* pp. 251–316.

There are differences in writing copy for the various direct-response media, which we discuss in the chapters that deal with each medium. For now, remember that direct-response copy does not have as its primary objective to create awareness or to build an image. Rather, its primary objective is to incite the prospect to take the desired action. That is really what makes direct-response copy different.

GRAPHICS

The graphics of a direct-response promotion, whatever the medium being used (except, of course, radio) have a communications role to carry out, just as the copy does. There are several ways in which graphics can contribute to overall communications effectiveness:

- Communicating an important selling point quickly and effectively
- Attracting the attention of the target customer
- Directing attention to other elements of the promotion (e.g., the copy or a response device)
- Communicating an idea that is difficult to verbalize
- Showing the product in use
- Providing credibility for the selling points

There are two basic types of graphics: artwork and photography. Although artwork is used extensively in direct-response programs, photography is the norm in most applications because it offers greater detail and more credibility. This is especially critical when the objective is to close a sale on the basis of the direct-response promotion alone. Photography can be done either on location or in a studio.

To add excitement and to portray products in settings appropriate to their use, the trend in recent years has been toward on-location photography, especially for upscale catalogs. Shooting on location may well be cost effective, but remember it adds greatly to both the time and the absolute cost of developing the promotion.

Freeman Gosden suggests four myths about graphics that are well worth keeping in mind:[11]

Myth 1: Costly Graphics Produce Better Results   Whether we are talking about four-color, bleed pages, page after page of graphics, or any other expensive technique, the question is simply: Is it cost effective?

Before you spend a bundle testing a very expensive graphics approach, think about the nature of the costs being incurred. The photography, design, and production set-up costs are fixed, no matter what the size of your production run. Elaborate graphics will therefore add less per unit to a large mailing and might be more easily justified than they would for a smaller mailing.

Other types of graphics decisions may result in variable costs—manual insertion of an odd-sized piece into the envelope, for example, instead of machine insertion. This type of operation may be manageable and cost effective for a small program but not for a large one. The same is true for hand-addressing envelopes to create a perception of an upscale offer or

[11]Freeman F. Gosden, Jr., *Direct Marketing Success* (New York: John Wiley & Sons, 1985), 151–153.

of personal attention. It may not be possible to accomplish the hand addressing within the time line.

Myth 2: Graphics Always Improve Communications Effectiveness   A picture is not always worth a thousand words. Graphics are a wonderful communications device, but when they become overly elaborate, they can detract from the copy and harm overall effectiveness. Be especially careful of fancy type, particularly the kind with large serifs (the flourishes at the end of the main stroke on the characters of some fonts) and reverse type (light copy on a dark background).

Myth 3: A Picture Is Self-Explanatory   Not if people do not look carefully or if they misinterpret it! Picture captions help to ensure that the correct inference is made.

Myth 4: Color Is Always Desirable   Again, this is a matter of cost effectiveness. Let your decision on whether to develop an expensive program for testing be governed by common sense. Some products—food comes immediately to mind—need color for an effective (mouth-watering) presentation. Some objectives—lead generation for a business product, for example—may not require the impact of an expensive four-color presentation.

Gosden adds, "Year after year, the simpler packages seem to outpull the fancy, screaming, art-award generating, so called high-impact direct mail pieces."[12] It seems likely that, for many products, the prospect simply will not take the time or effort to unravel a complex or confusing piece. The consumer simply discards it, moving on to something else that communicates clearly and succinctly.

LAYOUT

Layout refers to the manner in which the various components of the promotional piece are arranged on the page. There are several generally accepted principles of layout design.

- *Balance* refers to a distribution of elements on the page that is visually pleasing. "Pleasing" does not necessarily mean symmetrical; in fact, total symmetry can be boring.
- *Clarity* suggests a design that is clean and straightforward, and conveys the message without confusion or misunderstanding.
- *Simplicity* implies that anything that does not contribute to the message should be eliminated. Prospects should be able to grasp the message of the visual elements just as readily as they read the copy.
- *Proportion* is the manner in which the various elements relate to one another and to the background on which they appear.
- *Eye flow or movement* describes the placement of the various elements so they lead logically from one to another.
- *Contrast* is obtained by using different shapes, sizes, densities, and colors or tints to provide appeal and interest.
- *Unity* means that the entire promotional piece works together as an integrated whole to convey the desired message.

---

[12]Gosden, *Direct Marketing Success,* 154.

A mechanistic approach will not produce an outstanding product. Batra et al. quote an art director who distinguishes between simply "arranging elements on a page" and "visualizing an idea." He states:

> The former is a designer's (or layout man's) feat; his innate sense of composition, balance, color is brought fully into play. On the other hand, presenting the clearest visual interpretation requires a strong desire to communicate with the audience, a flair for the dramatic, the ability to think in pictorial terms (usually referred to as "visual sense") and, probably most significant, a firm understanding of the advertiser's goal.[13]

Even in this era of pervasive computerization, a truly effective creative execution requires skill, taste, and good judgment. We have also tried to point out throughout the chapter that good execution also requires an understanding of the business objectives and those of the specific communications program. In the end, however, it is the direct marketing manager who must assess the creative execution, making judgments about the acceptability of the execution and its likely effectiveness in the marketplace.

Evaluating the Creative Product

Judging the creative execution is a difficult managerial task because there are no hard-and-fast rules, no "right" or "wrong." There are, however, executions that carry out the creative strategy and those that do not.

A good manager does not simply guide the development of the creative strategy, turn it over to the creative department, and wait for the final result. The good manager stays involved without interfering with the creative process.

One way to do this is to review the progress at several predetermined points. It makes sense to have a formal review of the creative concept, the rough execution, and the final execution. The checklist shown in Figure 6.7 suggests criteria that should be used at each stage in the review process. It is important to remember that primary research can be used at any stage in the evaluation process to supplement managerial judgment. Marketing research is especially useful at the rough execution stage. At this point the promotional piece is portrayed in sufficient detail to allow customers to appraise its likely attractiveness and effectiveness, but it is sufficiently incomplete to allow changes to be made without major time delays or added costs.

A Word about Business-to-Business Advertising

Business-to-business advertising has the dubious reputation of being the "creative wasteland" of the promotion industry. "Ninety-five percent of business print advertising is a bore,"[14] according to Rik Meyers, vice-president–creative director, Kerker Marketing Communications, Minneapolis. Ralph Rydholm, CEO of Euro RSCG-Tatham, Chicago, and chairman of the American Association of Advertising Agencies adds, "There are a lot of good

---

[13]Rajeev Batra, John G. Myers, and David A. Aaker, *Advertising Management,* 5th ed. (Upper Saddle River, NJ: Prentice Hall, 1996), 436.

[14]Adrienne W. Fawcett, "B-to-B Is Boring. On the Plus Side: It Can Only Get Better," *Business Marketing* (September 1977): 1.

Does the Execution Carry Out the Creative Strategy? The creative strategy establishes the overall direction which the creative execution should follow. Management should, however, be alert for the—very rare—"breakthrough" creative concept that suggests that the strategy itself should be revised.

Will the Execution Appeal to the Target Audience? It is not important that you personally or management in general "likes" the creative execution; it is vital that it strikes a responsive chord in the minds of the prospects.

Would You Say This to a Prospect in Person? If you wouldn't—either because it might be offensive or simply because you just wouldn't speak directly to the prospect this way—rethink the execution.

Is it Written from the Prospect's Point of View or from the Marketer's Point of View? Don't let ego get in the way!

Is the Execution Clear, Concise, Complete, and Convincing? These can be considered the "4 C's" of advertising and promotion.

Does the Execution Get and Hold the Prospect's Attention? Clutter exists in all media today—in the mailbox as well as on television. One important task of the creative execution is to break through that clutter.

If Time or Space Is Limited, Make the Message Single-Minded. It is better to present one compelling message than many weak ones which are not persuasive.

Make Sure Management Knows Exactly What the Creatives Have in Mind. Whether it is a complex mailing piece or a direct response television commercial, be sure that the exact nature of the finished product is clear.

If There Are Several Creative Pieces, Make Sure They All Work Together Effectively. This is not to say they should all be the same or similar, but that they should all contribute materially to conveying the desired image, the message, and/or to encouraging the prospect to take the desired action.

Does the Execution Overwhelm the Message? The substance of the message is more important than the manner in which it is conveyed. Great promotional pieces convey the substance in a way that strikingly draws attention to the message itself.

Is the Request for Action Clear and Specific? Don't leave the prospect guessing about the action requested . . .

If a Reply Device Is Used, Is it Simple and Easy to Use? . . . and make it easy for the prospect to take that action!

Do Let the Cost of the Proposed Execution Influence You. Don't accept an execution that has little chance of being worth its cost—and don't reject a great idea just because it will be expensive.

FIGURE 6.7 Checklist for Judging Creative Execution

Source: Adapted from Martin, Schultz, and Brown, pp. 283–287, and John M. Keil, *The Creative Mystique* (New York: John Wiley & Sons, 1985), 85–123.

print trade ads, but we shouldn't concentrate on the veneer of what's good. Take a look at what actually runs. It's awful."[15]

But the executive director of the Business Marketing Association points out that advertising in business markets is different. "Business-to-business and consumer ads serve differ-

---

[15]Fawcett, "B-to-B Is Boring," 1.

ent purposes. Business-to-business purchases are considered. They're usually made by more than one person, and usually for a lot more money. It's not something that appeals to the senses or emotions the way consumer advertising does, so consequently the ads look dull and boring. But if you're a widget buyer, it might be exactly the information you're looking for."[16]

Other business marketers and agency executives, however, disagree. They point out that there is no longer a sharp dividing line between business and consumer promotional techniques. That was shown earlier in this chapter with the FedEx letter and coupon. Marketers point out that businesspeople can be reached outside the office. They read consumer magazines, see billboards, and watch television. Industry statistics indicate that in 1996 more than 64 percent of the advertising dollars of business marketers went into non-business media, ranging from consumer magazines to national spot radio.[17] A natural result is an improvement in creativity in order to keep the business advertising from looking out of place in the consumer medium.

What about Creative Awards?

No chapter on creative strategy would be complete without mention of the continuing controversy surrounding awards for creative excellence. This controversy exists in direct marketing just as it does in general advertising. Are award-winning campaigns necessarily successful in meeting their objectives?

A highly regarded direct marketing copywriter, John Francis Tighe, comments:

> Don't try to equate winning a contest with sales results. A contest prize in a creative field means that a number of judges—your peers, usually—liked your work. It does not necessarily mean that more bakers will buy your shortening or more plumbers will buy your hardware. Your hard-nosed customers won't automatically be impressed with the things that impressed your judges. . . . With direct mail we don't really need a panel of judges. The marketplace is prosecutor, judge and jury, all in one.[18]

Perhaps the best description of creative excellence comes from a respected advertising executive, Malcolm McDougall. When asked what his expectations were of young people entering the creative end of the business, he replied that they should be fundamentally salespeople, not show-business people. They should love the business and use their talent, flair, and originality "to create a customer, not advertising."[19]

Summary

Creativity should be a vital part of all managerial activity. In direct marketing, high-impact creative work is increasingly important to break through media clutter. High-impact creative work does the selling job. It is the responsibility of managers, creative personnel, and other direct marketing specialists to work together to achieve this goal. Additionally, they must be

---

[16]Fawcett, "B-to-B Is Boring," 32.

[17]Adrienne W. Fawcett, "Creativity in Other Media Is Raising the Bar in Print," *Business Marketing* (September 1997): 32.

[18]John Francis Tighe, "Winning Ads Don't Always Sell," *Advertising Age,* 5 August 1987, 32.

[19]Interview with Malcolm McDougall, July 1987.

concerned about integrating creative strategy and execution into the overall creative approach of the firm. Managers have a special responsibility to understand, foster, and guide the creative process and to ensure that its final results are appropriate to the objectives of the direct-response program.

Discussion Questions and Exercises

1. What is the difference between "managerial creativity" and "creativity" in the everyday use of that term?
2. Explain the process of developing a creative strategy.
3. What are the three basic elements of a creative execution?
4. How should a direct marketing manager go about judging a creative execution?
5. Bring a direct-response promotion to class and be prepared to present your analysis of the creative strategy behind it and a critique of its creative execution.

Suggested Readings

Jones, Susan K. *Creative Strategy in Direct Marketing,* 2nd ed. Lincolnwood, IL: NTC Business Books, 1997.

Stein, Donna Baier, and Floyd Kemske. *Write on Target: The Direct Marketer's Copywriting Handbook.* Lincolnwood, IL: NTC Business Books, 1997.

CHAPTER 7 Fulfillment and Customer Service

"The best copy, the best graphics, and the wisest choice of lists are all sheer waste of money, time, and talent if it is not followed through with really outstanding fulfillment."[1] This quote by Robert Dorney expresses many people's views of the importance of the process of fulfillment. Fulfillment has been defined in a variety of ways by different people, but all definitions have at their core the activities involved in receiving a customer's order and fulfilling that customer's order after it has been received.

Fulfillment also includes *customer service,* a phrase that encompasses both servicing inquiries before an order is consummated and "physically distributed" (i.e., sent out), and

---

[1]Robert D. Downey, "Proper Fulfillment—Image with the Proper Stuff," *Direct Marketing* (July 1985): 28.

providing resolution to service issues that arise after the merchandise is distributed. Indeed, some definitions of fulfillment even imply an inclusion of the promotional and other activities that generate demand (for orders). These activities comprise the lead "subprocess" in the order management process, as described by D. Kamal and R. Agrawal.[2] In addition, fulfillment encompasses the following up of requests for information, and connected aspects of lead generation; discussion of this type of fulfillment is included under the banner of customer service (though, possibly, a more appropriate label for it might be "prospect service" or "Consummate the conversion! [from prospect to customer]").

Elements of Fulfillment

Some definitions of fulfillment encompass a larger circle of activities than others. The following list blends the most important elements contained in most of the various definitions:

1. order-form issues
2. receiving orders or requests for information
    a. mail orders
    b. telephone orders
3. processing of orders
4. inventory policy
    a. inventory costs
    b inventory management
5. warehousing issues
    a. site selection, sizing, configuration
    b. receiving
    c. storing, stock location
    d. picking
    e. packing
    f. shipping
6. customer service
7. planning and control
    a. data collection
    b. standards
    c. reports
    d. plans

Any system that is designed to deliver goods has aspects of communication, inventory, warehousing, and transportation. Order-form issues and, in part, receiving orders are in the communication category: they involve a direct connection of some sort with the customer. The processing of orders initiates what is sometimes called *physical distribution* or *physical*

---

[2]D. Kamal and R. Agrawal, "Re-engineering the Direct Marketing Organization Structure," *Journal of Direct Marketing* 11, no. 2 (spring 1997): 59–68.

fulfillment, and is a term that includes inventory, warehousing, and transportation issues. Customer service is another element of communication. Planning and control transcend this categorization and pertain to all aspects of fulfillment.

Some situations include a larger proportion of one aspect of fulfillment than of another. A magazine publishing operation may have no inventory or warehouse considerations (the magazines are sent from the printer directly to the customer), but may still have an extremely large concern with database management aspects of the order-processing element of fulfillment. To put fulfillment into perspective within the set of direct marketing activities, consider that what separates the "transactional" (selling) aspects of a direct marketing operation from most aspects of the fulfillment activities of a direct marketing operation is that the transactional aspects are essentially profit centers, whereas the fulfillment operations are primarily cost centers.

The fulfillment process aspects of order taking and physical distribution coordinate with other activities in the direct marketing process: They are preceded by the promotional aspects of the process, and followed by the customer service process (although technically we have included the latter under the wide umbrella of the fulfillment process). These days, all of the activities are tied together in terms of being recorded and processed on the computer.

As noted earlier, there is not universal agreement about what tasks in particular are part of the fulfillment process. Here we take the broader view and consider fulfillment to include many database operations and some activities that take place prior to receiving an order (e.g., ensuring that order forms are clear to the customer and that perforations tear neatly), as well as customer service, the handling of inquiries, and the planning and control function.

Order-Form Issues

For every offering, products for sale must be numbered, different variations (e.g., color, size) must be distinguished, and other facts (e.g., payment method, shipping method) often need to be indicated. Therefore, consideration must be given to the design of the order form, not only so that the customer will clearly perceive all aspects of placing an order, but also so that errors will be reduced in the processing of orders by the seller. When customers think of "quality," they mean not only traditional product quality, but also the quality of service. One important aspect of service is timely order processing, and this may not be possible unless the order form and all instructions that pertain to it are clear and simple.

Whether order-form issues are officially considered part of the fulfillment process is not really important. Certainly, nobody would argue that the people concerned with fulfillment operations should be involved in the designing and writing of the order form. No reference is intended here to the core of the creative process, nor to such decisions as pricing, payment options, and delivery options. These issues are covered elsewhere in this text. Our sole concerns here are clarity and simplicity.

Clarity ensures that customers will know precisely what it is they are purchasing. *Simplicity* involves devices such as separated check-off boxes (or their equivalent) for different sizes, colors, and other variations, and a specific place with sufficient space for a clear capturing of the buyer's name and address. A great many order-processing errors result from incorrect capturing of buyers' names and addresses. This fact seems to be fostering increased use of preaddressed labels. An alternative that seems to decrease errors in capturing correct names and addresses is to provide an individual box for each and every letter and number to be written (along with an instruction to please type or print).

What we have said so far pertains to mail orders. For telephone orders, the problems involve voice clarity and correct verbal transmission.

Receiving Orders

In the early days of direct marketing, nearly all orders were received by mail. Most current solicitations give customers a choice between mailing or phoning in an order. For many years, the percentage of orders that come in by telephone has been increasing, dramatically so for large mail-order firms. Virtually all direct marketers use toll-free numbers: nearly 60 percent as recently as 1992.[3] Many large direct marketers receive more than 90 percent of their orders by telephone. The majority of all catalog marketers receive more than half of their orders by telephone. The ease of obtaining low-cost 1-800 numbers is the key reason for this dominance of the order process by telephone.

MAIL ORDERS

Orders are not the only mail that a direct marketing firm receives. Hence, the first step in dealing with incoming mail is to sort it into categories. One possible set of categories is by function. For example

1. payments
2. orders
3. other correspondence

Another possible set of categories is by size. For example

1. postcard size
2. standard-size preaddressed material (usually for orders)
3. other sizes

Whichever category contains payments should be subdivided into different forms of payment. For cash payments, special logging-in procedures should be used to ensure adherence to laws pertaining to cash transactions (e.g., if product delivery will not take place within the allowable 30 days, the customer has to be informed and given the option to cancel the order) and to maintain supervision and security. For credit card payments, validation procedures must be undertaken for transactions exceeding a certain amount (this amount varies by firm). Once the transaction is validated, a set of procedures for logging the charge and transferring funds from the credit card agency to the firm is put into effect. Every firm has to have a policy concerning the clearing of personal checks. The time needed for check clearing adds a relatively large amount to the turnaround time of an order and needs careful monitoring.

---

[3]*Direct Marketing Association's Statistical Fact Book 1997* (New York: Direct Marketing Association, 1997), 296.

Machines can be bought or rented that slit envelopes; some even use suction to remove the contents from the envelope. Other machines can imprint checks and enhance quick check processing. One way or another, the mail orders need to be separated from the rest of the mail and be readied for order processing, and mail payments need to be separated by form of payment and sent on their respective paths of collection.

TELEPHONE ORDERS

The ideal is to have order-taking telephone lines answered 24 hours per day. If this is not economic, a decision has to be made whether to have a voice mail process in use during off-hours. Actually, in most people's opinions, whether to have voice mail is not the real decision (the decision should be to have it!); the real decision should be what type to have—one that takes the order (essentially an interactive voice process), or one that either offers to call back during business hours or, at least, apologizes for being closed and reinforces that the customer is important to them. Naturally, the 24-hour live order-taker decision as well as the voice-mail type decision have to be made in the context of the media used to communicate the offer and the complexity of the order taking process. For offers made through broadcast media, live ordering by phone must be immediately available; for direct mail offers, the timing is not so critical. For simple orders (e.g., there is only one product, with only one color, price, etc.), there is no reason the order cannot be taken in an automated way by requesting the name, address, and credit card type, number, and expiration, along with day and evening telephone numbers in case an ambiguity needs to be resolved. If more detailed ordering is required, an interactive system can be used; this system can prompt for responses, have them repeated by the computer (usually using a female voice), and even determine whether the items are in stock. In many ways, the process would not be unlike the use of an automatic teller machine (ATM).

If a live person takes a call, he or she should record all information directly onto a regular order form, or preferably, a mock order form on a computer terminal (the latter avoids handwriting errors). A frequent telephone-order-taking procedure has as the initial contact a recording that asks the caller to press a certain single digit if the purpose of the call is to place an order. This separates out the order-giving calls from the remaining calls (the latter follow different routes). Once this digit is dialed, a person comes on the line and solicits the information required on the order form. Each order taker has an on-site terminal in front of him or her into which the information is entered (typed). As each piece of information is given by the buyer, it is repeated by the order taker to ensure correct vocal transmission. When the product information is given by item number, the order taker states the item description (which appears on the terminal a moment after the item number is entered). At the end of the entire order, the order taker reiterates all the information entered into the computer and asks the caller to confirm that it is correct. Of course, if the call originates in the few minutes after a major broadcast offer, the first step of pressing a digit if the purpose is to place an order would be omitted.

Whether a firm uses this system of entering the order into a computer while the caller is still on the telephone, or a system whereby the information is recorded (e.g., by voice mail) for later entry into the computer, the situation at this point is the same as that reached when the order is received by mail and then entered into the computer. (If there is no computer involved in the order-taking process [there should be!], the order entry takes place in an analogous way.)

Processing Orders

The first step in order processing has in many ways merged with the order-receiving process. In processing a mail order, the initial step is to enter it onto the computer. The same is true for a telephone order, although, as we have seen, the trend is to log it on the computer while taking down the customer's information. After the order is entered into the computer, the remaining steps of order processing depend on what the computer is programmed to do with the order data.

Ideally, the computer now performs a variety of parallel tasks. Customer files are checked to see if the customer made previous purchases or was already in the database for some other reason (e.g., made an inquiry). During this task, the computer can also be performing a credit check (if past data are available) and updating the customer's record if his or her name is already in the database, or entering the name with accompanying purchase information in the database if the name is new. If the dollar size of the order is sufficiently large, the computer can conduct an outside credit check. If payment is via personal check, the order may be sent to a holding file, to be uploaded to the main order file when bank verification is received. (Note that customer file maintenance has a longer-range purpose than processing the immediate order. It can supply current records whenever management wants to analyze the house list, rent it out, or generate reports based on it.)

Either simultaneously with, or just after receiving the results of the credit check, inventory files record decrements for the items ordered and any stockouts noted (plus any action taken with respect to customer notification). In a more sophisticated system, not only the items ordered, but also the inventory of boxes and/or other required packaging will be decremented. Depending on the size of the item(s) and mode of transportation (delivery), even an allocated slot within the delivery system could be decremented.

Concurrently, the computer will generate for the warehouse hard copy of picking documents and shipping labels, as well as invoices to accompany the order. Notification of other offerings is usually included with the order. Many direct marketers believe that the accuracy and promptness of the hard-copy portion of order processing is the key to timely and proficient fulfillment.

Inventory Policy

Even if the number of orders equals or (even better) exceeds expectations, and even if each order has a delightfully high contribution, there will be no immediate benefit—in fact, there may ultimately be a loss—if the items ordered are not in stock. If the customer cancels the order because he or she thinks there has been an unreasonable delay in shipment, there is an actual loss attributable to administrative costs, plus an opportunity loss attributable to forgone profit. Even if the customer does not cancel the order and the item is ultimately shipped, costs may be increased because, for example, the stockout item had to be shipped in a separate package instead of as part of a multi-item order.

The general concepts of inventory policy are similar in all inventory environments. In some cases, the inventory to be managed relates mostly to raw materials; in other cases, to goods in process; in yet other cases, to finished goods. Our discussion envisions a finished-goods environment in which, in essence, items are being resold to mail- or phone-order customers. This situation is equivalent to a traditional retailing company selling by direct marketing: the company "buys" the finished goods from itself and "resells" them to the customer.

INVENTORY COSTS

As is true of many marketing decisions, the inventory decision primarily involves balancing different costs. These are (1) stockout costs, (2) order costs, and (3) carrying costs.

Stockout costs are the costs associated with not having an item in stock at the moment it is needed. This item may be on order, meaning there will be a "lead time" between the placement of the replenishment order and its actual delivery, or not yet ordered, meaning there will be an even longer wait for replenishment. Stockout costs were mentioned earlier in terms of increased shipping costs and lost sales (when a customer cancels an order). The opportunity loss of a stockout is a difficult value to determine. In fact, as Paul Teplitz argues, if direct marketing managers are asked what harm occurs if a stockout arises, 9 out of 10 of them cannot provide an answer![4]

There are three basic possibilities to the customer's decision; each raises additional questions:

1. Will a specific customer cancel the order? If the customer cancels the order, will that customer also refuse to place any more orders with the firm? What is the value of future orders lost this way?

2. Will the customer be willing to substitute another product? If so, will it have been a wise choice by the customer? If so, the customer will be pleased; if not, he or she may return the substitute, and whether returning it or not, will not be pleased.

3. Will the customer accept a backorder? If so, will it actually be delivered in a timely way? Will it ultimately be canceled? If the customer cancels, will he or she go elsewhere?

Because of all these uncertainties, the opportunity loss part of the stockout cost must be looked at in a probabilistic way and expressed as an "expected value" or average value. Even then, the value arrived at is not very robust. There has been some recent research on what people buy in a lifetime (we address this issue head on in chapter 9, "Profitability and Lifetime Value"); in this case, the issue is what would have been bought in a lifetime but wasn't. This is not quite the same issue, in part because customers are *not* all the same, and different choices among the three above options will often be made, depending on the degree to which (1) the customer pays attention to his or her own lead time in terms of need for items, (2) the customer is an impulse item buyer, (3) it is the first purchase by this customer, or first stockout he or she has encountered.

As Teplitz points out, the probability that a customer encounters a stockout situation is not simply a matter of the "initial fill rate"—the proportion of items in stock at any one time. Many orders are for more than one item. If an order is for three items, and 90 percent of the items are in stock, the probability that the *order* encounters a stockout is (assuming each item's availability is independent from each other's)

$$1 - (.90)^3 = 1 - .73 = .27$$

[4]Paul Teplitz, "'Only the Shadow Knows' Shines a Light on Shadow Demand," *Direct Marketing* (March 1997): 28–30.

That is, the probability of at least one item in the order being unavailable is about 27 percent, or more than a quarter of the time! Indeed, if the 90 percent changes only 5 points to 85 percent, the 27 percent increases to about 39 percent!

One of the real problems faced with regard to this issue is that very few order entry or order taking systems provide any information on what happens when requested items are not in stock. Customer surveys should be considered to investigate this issue.

Order costs refer to costs that are proportional to the number of orders, without regard to order size. These would be such costs as paperwork, the fixed-cost portion of telephone calls, materials handling, and certain transportation costs. It is not easy to arrive at the specific value of the order cost. What is the cost of somebody's time filling out paperwork if that person is on salary? Nobody would say that it is zero, even though it may result in no overt incremental cash outlay. Certainly, a significant portion of the order cost can be determined only by an allocation of fixed costs, and most allocations of fixed cost are somewhat arbitrary. Nevertheless, a ballpark figure can be determined.

Carrying costs involve costs such as warehouse rental, capital cost (i.e., forgone interest), insurance premiums, any taxes levied on inventory, and costs due to deterioration, pilferage, and obsolescence. In other words, a carrying cost is any cost that varies proportionally with the average or maximum level of inventory. All of the carrying costs mentioned above are at least approximately proportional to the average inventory level, except for the warehouse rental cost, which often is proportional to the maximum level of inventory.

INVENTORY MANAGEMENT

Inventory policy is primarily concerned with determining, for each item, the answers to two basic questions:

1. How often should we order the item to be replenished?
2. What quantity should we order?

There are two basic systems for managing inventory: the Q system and the P system. Under the Q system, the amount (of a certain product) to be ordered is fixed (i.e., the same for every order), but the time between orders varies. In other words, whenever the inventory level falls to a predetermined level, an order is placed. The amount that should be ordered each time so as to minimize total inventory-related costs is called the *economic order quantity* (EOQ). What level of inventory will trigger a reorder depends upon the lead time for the order to be delivered as well as on the expected demand pattern during the lead time.

Under the P system of managing inventory, the time between orders is fixed; the amount ordered each time varies. The inventory level at the trigger time is noted, and an order is placed for that quantity that will bring the level up to a predetermined amount. This predetermined amount depends on lead time and (anticipated) demand during lead time.

Each system has certain advantages and disadvantages. The Q system requires much closer monitoring of the inventory levels. Usually, high-priced items are good candidates for the Q system because they tend to be closely monitored anyway. Indeed, the advantage of the Q system is that it generally requires less safety stock, or "buffer inventory," the difference between what is on hand and what is expected to be demanded before replenishment. This safety stock is a positive value (as opposed to being zero) precisely because of the stockout cost discussed earlier in this section. The optimal level of safety stock is determined by the relative cost of a stockout. In general, with everything else equal, a lower level of safety stock will increase probability of stockout but result in a lower overall carrying cost.

Entire texts have been written on the subject of inventory policy. Precise treatment depends upon questions such as whether lead time for delivery of an order is variable or fixed, whether demand is reasonably constant over time, whether quantity discounts are available, and some other product-specific issues (e.g., perishability). Detailed treatment of this material is beyond the purpose of this text.

In an environment with a very large number of items, inventory policy will often lump together groups of items, so as not to have to actually monitor each and every item with respect to EOQ or reorder times. Sometimes it is useful to institute an A, B, C system in which there are different classes of items, and all that fall within a specific class are treated alike. The most popular classification is by the magnitude of an item's carrying cost. An item's carrying cost, in turn, is usually closely related to its wholesale or retail price—a fact that makes items easy to classify.

Ideally, a firm does ongoing demand forecasting so that inventory management can take place in a maximally informed environment. The issue of the accuracy of these forecasts has taken on more importance in recent times, as several U.S. companies have been adopting a fulfillment inventory policy that resembles the Japanese system of *kanban,* in which inventory is reduced to nearly zero by a combination of accurate forecasting of demand and careful planning of manufacturing and deliveries.

There are additional considerations that can be brought to bear on inventory decisions in a direct marketing environment. Actually, these additional considerations are not unique to direct marketing, but are especially well suited to a direct marketing operation. One set of considerations focuses around *redistributing* inventory among products, by (1) adding an amount to the nominal stockout cost to reflect the cost of lost customers, not solely the order in question; and (2) finding out (by survey, perhaps) which items are more time sensitive to customers, and adding additional "stockout cost" to them. Another set of considerations isn't directly connected to inventory decisions, but is related to them, and focuses on increasing the probability that a customer accepts a substitute, by (1) making certain that order takers are able to quickly make suggestions for substitutions and support them (by using software that makes the task user-friendly to the order taker), or (2) providing a gift of some kind, perhaps called a "bonus," to a customer who accepts a substitute. A third set of considerations involves inducing the customer to wait for the item to arrive in stock, by (1) building up a reputation of "telling it like it is" in terms of when the item is likely to be available, and (2) promising to send it by a faster delivery method (e.g., air mail or express mail) at no additional cost.

Warehousing Issues

The core of what is usually referred to as *physical fulfillment* involves all the activities connected to the warehouse operations. This set of activities begins with receiving incoming items at the warehouse.[5] After the received items are processed, their *storing* in the warehouse takes place and the location is noted for later reference. When an order comes in for

---

[5]The term *warehouse* is used here to denote any generic storage location.

one or more items, the next step is *picking* and gathering the items from their respective locations. The items then need *packing*. Finally, the package needs *shipping*. We discuss each of these activities in this section. Our level of discussion is that of describing the variables that need to be considered, their trade-offs, and, in a few cases where choices seem clear cut, some specific recommendations. Books with hundreds of pages each discuss these issues in great detail.

In a start-up situation, of course, all of these activities are preceded by consideration of where to locate the warehouse, its size (volume), and its dimensions. These start-up issues can be very complex. We discuss them only briefly, from the perspective of the different costs and other considerations that must be traded off. This perspective should provide some insight into the activities of physical fulfillment.

SITE SELECTION, SIZING, AND CONFIGURATION

When it comes to choosing a *site* for one or more warehouses, the main factors that need consideration are of two types. One type concerns the macro location of the facility (e.g., which quadrant of which state); the other type concerns the particular site within that location. In most cases, a warehousing operation will involve more than one location. Many times, the total area being served is broken down into separate territories, each to contain one warehouse. Thus, each warehouse is able to be independently located within a territory. There then are several so-called single-warehouse-location problems. The basic objective is to choose locations that minimize incoming and outgoing transportation costs. This, of course, requires knowing or forecasting points-of-origin of demand. The choice of the individual site involves a trade-off between the costs of land rental or purchase, real estate and other taxes, and such factors as adequacy of utilities, community attitude, and potential for expansion.

The *size* of the warehouse refers to its volume. Determining a minimum size is a complicated issue affected by many factors, such as the materials-handling system employed, the (anticipated) throughput of volume per time period, and the particular unit size of the items stored (beyond the total throughput volume). Certainly, the lower limit on minimum required size is the anticipated maximum volume of inventory.

The *configuration* of the warehouse first involves determining the ceiling height. Here there is a trade-off between construction and equipment costs and materials-handling costs. Once the height is determined, the next step is to decide on the best length and width, assuming the product of the two (the area) is fixed. That is, should the warehouse be a square, or if not, which particular rectangular shape should it be? This determination involves a trade-off between materials-handling costs and perimeter construction costs. It also involves consideration of dock requirements and design.

Now you can see why start-up issues are complex. We assume for the rest of this section that the warehouse already exists with a definite size and configuration.

RECEIVING

Items arrive at the warehouse from a variety of sources. They have to be logged in, they have to be inspected for quantity and possibly quality, and they have to be stored. The basic objectives are to record arrivals accurately, to be able to easily and quickly call up an item's location, and to minimize subsequent handling of items either for purposes of relocation or retrieval for shipment.

The issues involved in receiving items at a warehouse are really no different from those involved in receiving food deliveries at a restaurant or office supplies at a work station. In all these situations one must be concerned about the receiving workers' purposeful recording of incorrect amounts of goods received, as well as about security during the receiving process.

STORING AND STOCK LOCATION

Once goods are received at the warehouse, they must be stored. The particular choice among storing units (e.g., various types of shelving and racks) and the related lift equipment will depend on the size and configuration of the warehouse. A firm or division whose prime focus is on direct marketing should rely on the advice of a person with warehousing experience when making these choices because they are more qualitative than others considered in this section.

The issue of stock *location* is more amenable to analytical resolution. Indeed, this issue is so appropriate for quantitative analysis that for the past thirty years it has been the subject of a great deal of attention in the literature, including the *Harvard Business Review* and the very quantitative journal, *Management Science*.[6] There have been three approaches to determining stock location: intuitive, heuristic, and algorithmic.

The *intuitive* approach basically involves two criteria: (1) more popular items are located nearer the outbound point (i.e., the higher the item's turnover rate, the nearer the item's storage location is to the outbound point), (2) items are located according to size (i.e., the smaller the size, the nearer the item's storage location is to the outbound point, resulting in the largest number of items being near the outbound point). A third criterion, used on occasion, is a blend of the first two: the distance from the outbound point is rank-ordered by the ratio of volume to turnover. The larger the ratio, the nearer to the outbound point the item is stored. This criterion would rank two items equally if one item had half the turn-over of the other, but also half the volume of the other. None of these criteria guarantees an optimal solution in terms of cost and time minimization, but they are superior to having no system at all for choice of location.

The *heuristic* approach implicitly recognizes the difficulty of finding a truly optimal solution. A heuristic is a rule that has been shown empirically to often result in a solution not too far from the optimal solution, but with much less computational time (and therefore less expense) than needed to find the optimal solution.[7]

The third type of approach to this problem of warehouse or facility layout is the algorithmic approach. An algorithmic solution usually refers to a rule (most often mathematical) for solving a problem that results in an *optimal* solution in accordance with some predetermined criterion. For the problem at hand, the usual methodology proposed is in the linear programming or graph theory family. This approach almost always requires high-speed computer facilities and very accurate knowledge or forecast of demand.

In the direct marketing environment, where the products being sold or the demand patterns are often undergoing modest if not continual change, either an intuitive or a heuristic approach to warehouse layout is warranted.

---

[6]The first discussion of stock location in the marketing literature was by Ronald M. Ballou, "Improving the Physical Layout of Merchandise in Warehouses," *Journal of Marketing* 31 (1967): 67.

[7]An early heuristic model was CRAFT (computerized relative allocation of facilities technique), discussed, among other places, in E. Buffa, G. Armour, and T. Vollman, "Allocating Facilities with CRAFT," *Harvard Business Review* 42 (April 1964). Other heuristics are noted in D. Bowersox, *Logistical Management,* 2nd ed. (New York: Macmillan, 1978); and D. Lambert and J. Stock, *Strategic Physical Distribution Management* (Homewood, IL: Irwin, 1982).

PICKING

Picking the individual items and combining them to make up the full order is an operation second in labor intensity only to the packing operation. Some of the decisions to be made in the picking operation are similar to those required in other multi-item order environments. We are all familiar with the ordering process for a traditional fast-food operation. Imagine that there are four registers and four workers, each qualified to work the register, to actually "pick" the order (i.e., gather all ordered foods and drinks together), or both. Should management assign two workers to be register persons only and two to be pickers only, or should there be four registers operating, each worker being both a register person and a picker, in sequence? If there are two register persons and two pickers, should a specific picker work only with a specific register person? This set of issues is usually analyzed and decided on the criterion of minimization of "expected time to (customer's) receipt of order."

In the warehouse environment the choice set is analogous. Should one person pick an entire order (individual order pick)? Or should different people be assigned to pick different sets of products or in different areas of the warehouse, all meeting at some central point? The answers to these questions depend on a variety of considerations, many of which are dealt with in the queuing theory and simulation literature.

PACKING

Packing is the most labor intensive of the physical fulfillment activities. It includes the boxing and packaging of individual items, boxing the different items in an order together, wrapping the order, and addressing or labeling the order. Sometimes, orders that are received at the warehouse need to be individually packaged (often referred to as prepackaging.) This packing of individual items can be done at the time of the item's arrival at the warehouse, at the time of the item's inclusion in the order, or at slack times (whether planned or not). The decision will depend upon the predictability of the demand for other labor activities as well as on such issues as how fragile an item is and the degree to which it is susceptible to spoilage.

The packing of an order often involves an assembly line. The particular division of labor (i.e., separation into different stations along the assembly line) may vary from one warehouse to another, but the following sequence is typical:

1. Check individual items to see if the order is correctly constituted and that each item is properly packaged.
2. Stuff the items together into a premade carton or other type of container and seal the carton.
3. Wrap the carton.
4. Label or otherwise address the package, and dispatch it to the shipping area for stamping or metering and the beginning of the delivery process.

SHIPPING

The final element in the physical distribution part of fulfillment is getting the package delivered to the customer. Most packages sent to consumers (as opposed to business-to-business transactions) by direct marketers weigh less than 50 pounds, and are often called parcels. Delivery of these parcels is generally arranged through either United Parcel Service (UPS) or the United States Postal Service (USPS). A 1995 study indicated that about 38 percent of catalog orders, 39 percent of retail store orders, and 12 percent of other mail order shipments are delivered using UPS, whereas about 43 percent of catalog orders, 59 percent of orders from retail stores, and 85 percent of other mail order shipments are delivered using the USPS.[8] The remainder are delivered by Federal Express, and similar (private) services. Stanley Fenvessey reports that in the mid-1980s, UPS delivered about 94 percent of mail order shipments.[9]

Some firms truck their packages from their warehouse to various post offices to qualify for lower postal rates. Some warehouse operations are sufficiently large to warrant UPS or USPS trucks coming to their warehouse for pick up. In fact, some warehouses actually contain USPS facilities (i.e., they actually contain a post office!).

Customer Service

If all the fulfillment elements we have discussed thus far were always carried out perfectly, and if no customers ever misunderstood the conditions of an order and never changed their minds, and if all products were of top quality and were never damaged en route, shipping would be the end of the transaction. However, in the real world, there are returns, lost and damaged shipments, missing and incorrect items in a shipment, and various other complaints, whether justified or not. All of these occurrences result in additional contact with the customer after the order is sent out. Handling these issues is a major part of what is called *customer service*.

Nobody argues against the importance of customer service. Indeed, Murray Raphael reports that an Arthur Andersen Consulting document concludes that in general two aspects of marketing provide the largest potential for improving business; one of the two is customer service, and the other is the improving of store merchandising.[10] Another view of the role of customer service is provided by Bradley Gale.[11] Gale argues that customers buy based on "value," and value is composed of two items: quality and price; and, in turn, quality comprises two items: product and customer service. Thus, customer service is one of the cornerstones of value (shown schematically in Figure 7.1).

But just what is customer service? The exact definition of, and duties covered by, customer service varies, depending on the company and customer. However, there is general agreement that it covers three basic components (and handling the complaints based on them):

- timing of deliveries
- availability of the product
- quality of the delivery

The timing of deliveries has been alluded to previously. If deliveries are not timely, the customer may decide to cancel the order and the company will have to forfeit the corresponding profit. Of course, this depends also on the reason for the "nontimely delivery." If the reason is a UPS strike, as occurred in summer 1997, customers tend to be more forgiving. If

---

[8]USPS Household Diary Study, 1995, as reported in the *Direct Marketing Association's Statistical Fact Book 1997*, 325.

[9]Stanley Fenvessey, *Fenvessey on Fulfillment*, Catalog Age, Stamford, Conn., 1988.

[10]Murray Raphael, "How a San Francisco Movie Complex Breaks Attendance Records with Database Marketing," *Direct Marketing* (March 1997).

[11]Bradley Gale, *Managing Customer Value* (New York: Free Press, 1994).

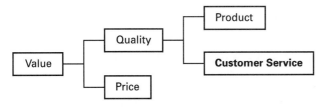

FIGURE 7.1 Customer Service: A Cornerstone of Value

Source: Adapted from Bradley Gale, *Managing Customer Value* (New York: Free Press, 1994), 29.

there does not appear to be a "justifiable reason," customers are less forgiving. Orders that were purchased on impulse are more likely to be canceled if delivery is not timely. Also, certain costs are incurred if, under the law, customers must be notified when delivery will be delayed by more than a given amount of time.

If a product is not available when ordered, the stockout will cause a delay in delivery. Also, extra costs are incurred here, due to the need for separate delivery of, and paperwork for, the items not in stock. There is often tension in the firm between people who want to realize cost reductions through reduced inventories and those who are responsible for traditional fulfillment.

The quality of delivery refers to many aspects of the transaction, especially the arrival of the correct items in the correct colors, size, and so on, as well as the condition of the merchandise upon arrival. The costs and benefits of this aspect of customer service involve not only the quantifiable costs of replacing the items, but also the qualitative costs of customer satisfaction. The real-world cost to ensure the maximum possible delivery quality is virtually always warranted.

L.L. Bean realized long ago that quality of delivery was a key to customer service and repeat sales. In 1983, H. Takeuchi and J. Quelch reported that L.L. Bean had a successful customer-driven quality program.[12] Their evidence came from the results of a survey of 3,000 L.L. Bean customers. When they were asked what they liked most about the company, 97 percent listed "quality." The following were noted as services L.L. Bean provided (and still does) to enhance customer satisfaction:

- They conduct(ed) regular customer satisfaction surveys.
- They track(ed) all customer complaints by computer.
- They guarantee(d) a full refund if the customer is not 100 percent satisfied.
- They ask(ed) customers to fill out a short form telling why they are returning goods.

An increasingly prevalent view of the role of customer service in mail-order operations is that excellent customer service will not compensate for an inferior product, but that inferior customer service can nullify a terrific product. This view certainly suggests having a proactive customer service program. L. Berry and J. Cooper listed four steps to follow when developing a customer service program:[13]

1. define the elements of customer service
2. perceive the customer viewpoint

---

[12]H. Takeuchi and J. Quelch, "Quality Is More Than Making a Good Product," *Harvard Business Review* (July 1983): 139–145.

[13]L. Berry and J. Cooper, "Improve Company Operations with Quality Control Programs," *Direct Marketing* 46 (1984): 50–60.

3. design a competitive package

4. establish performance controls

Step 1 involves determining what constitutes customer service: it includes, in one way or another, most of the fulfillment elements mentioned in this chapter. Step 2 calls for envisioning the benefits customers will realize from the elements of step 1. Step 3 involves doing a cost-benefit analysis of the different elements of step 1 and making the necessary trade-offs. In step 4 a specific activity is named (e.g., shipping); a measure of performance, or MOP, is specified (e.g., delivery time from the warehouse to any household in the continental United States); and a standard of performance, or SOP, is set up (e.g., 99 percent of orders will be delivered within five days, except during the Christmas season).

In 1990, Len Berry, this time with two other coauthors, developed "ServQual," a framework for examining a company's customer service performance, specifically, to inquire whether it is meeting customers' expectations.[14] The authors argue that there are five general dimensions to providing customer service (which cut across the aforementioned component areas of timing, availability, and quality):

- empathy
- assurance
- responsiveness
- reliability
- tangibles

The authors provide methods for conducting interviews to determine, for each of the above dimensions, the customers' expectations of service, and perceptions of service. Undesirable gaps can then be identified and, ideally, remedied.

Gale quotes an AT&T Universal Card Services' list of the elements of providing customer service (again, across the component areas of timing, availability, and quality) as[15]

- accessibility
- professionalism
- attitude
- efficiency

These elements are oriented toward the handling of customer inquiries and complaints. For example, "attitude" can be broken down into having customer representatives who

- are willing to help the customers
- treat the customers intelligently
- make customers feel comfortable
- are concerned about the customer

The prime functions of a firm's customer service operation are the handling of customer inquiries and complaints. Indeed, 54 percent of all (toll-free) calls received by a customer service department are inquiries, whereas 29 percent are complaints; most of the rest

---

[14]L. Berry, V. Zeithaml, and A. Parasuraman, *Delivering Service Quality: Balancing Customer Perception and Expectations* (New York: Free Press, 1990).

[15]Bradley Gale, *Managing Customer Value.*

of the calls concern new business.[16] Inquiries are made daily by potential customers who want information about products, warranties, costs, and other issues. Mail inquiries of this type must be separated from orders during the mail-sorting process. A similar sorting process is done for telephone inquiries. The importance of inquiry handling for the direct marketing firm is twofold. First, for some inquirers, the decision whether to become a customer ("convert") will depend not only on the substance of the information received but also on the quality of the service received in response to the inquiry. Second, an efficient inquiry-handling system both reduces the turnaround time for responding to an inquiry, which is especially important when sales are generated by leads that are followed up by sales telephone calls or visits, and improves the presorting of hot leads from dead ends.

Handling customer complaints has emerged as one of the areas of customer service receiving the most attention. The reason for this is exemplified by the results of a 1996 survey taken by Tibbett Spear of 1,179 randomly selected department store shoppers, which indicated that complainers have high loyalty and are very likely to stay loyal if the complaint is satisfactorily resolved.[17] Indeed, after a complaint is resolved satisfactorily, customers feel *more* loyalty toward the establishment. Most agree that the same principles apply directly, if not more so, to direct marketing transactions. The article went on to note that complainers are disproportionately over 45 years of age, and are evenly split, proportionally, among males and females.

The increased emphasis on customer service has apparently resulted in a decrease in complaints associated with direct marketing transactions. The number of direct marketing associated complaints reported to the Better Business Bureau in 1995 (the most recent year for which data are available) reflects a decrease of 28 percent from the 1994 number: 15,470 in 1995, down from 21,486. Incidentally, this 15,470 was less than two-tenths of one percent of all the complaints submitted to the Better Business Bureau in 1995.[18]

Nobody has claimed that establishing and maintaining a customer service program is easy. It is feasible, however, if management realizes that customer service is no longer the sole purview of the manufacturing or operations group and that "quality" is not limited in meaning to product quality. Only when quality is equated with customer service, and thus made a coresponsibility of the marketing function, will true success be achieved in the company's mission. The majority of firms have indeed (finally) realized this.

Kevin Clancy and Robert Shulman, in their widely quoted book, *The Marketing Revolution,* argue that in the 1990s and beyond, the companies that will thrive and grow are the companies that not only provide excellent customer service, but will continue to monitor that service (a topic addressed in the next section).[19] Clancy and Shulman also describe some of the issues and biases involve in performing this monitoring. For example, they note that mailed questionnaires are biased in that they are disproportionately responded to by "cheerleaders" and "gripers." They also point out that customer service (and satisfaction) should be measured relative to competitors and not be evaluated in absolute terms. Yet, Clancy and Shulman make a persuasive case that this does not mean that companies should "do anything" to retain a customer. They present a graphical depiction of profit as a function of the level of customer service (Figure 7.2, p. 154). Note in the figure that profit peaks at a value

---

[16]*Direct Marketing Association's Statistical Fact Book 1997,* 297.

[17]Tibbett Spear, "They Complain because They Care," *American Demographic* 18, no. 5 (1996): 13–14.

[18]*Direct Marketing Association's Statistical Fact Book 1997,* 293.

[19]Kevin Clancy and Robert Shulman, *The Marketing Revolution* (New York: HarperCollins, 1991).

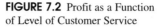

FIGURE 7.2 Profit as a Function of Level of Customer Service

Source: Adapted from K. Clancy and R. Shulman, *The Marketing Revolution* (New York: Harper Business, 1991), 240.

below 100 percent, perhaps between 90 percent and 95 percent, depending on the competition and cost structure of the industry, product, or company. Each company needs to make their determination of the right "percent satisfied" to choose. Figure 7.2 is based on the fact that customers often do not discriminate between "perfect" quality and "excellent" quality. Yet, the cost of moving from excellent to perfect can be high.

Planning and Control

It should be clear by now that a direct marketing operation involves many different functions and requires many different skills. Each of these functions has its own need for planning and control. Basically, *planning* is the activity of looking ahead to where you want to go and setting goals, and *control* is the activity of knowing where you are and measuring your growth toward these goals. There is usually one overall planning and control process for all the different elements of the fulfillment function, because of the need to treat this set of elements as a system to be globally optimized. For example, planning and controlling inventory management can be properly performed only in conjunction with planning for warehouse space, as well as with planning and control of stock location and virtually all the other physical fulfillment functions.

The planning and control process requires careful data collection and report generation. At a minimum, data are needed, by item, concerning sales, inventory, returns, customer service and satisfaction, credit, billing, and quality control. Data in these areas are broken down into operating statistics (e.g., daily number of orders received, weekly number of customer complaints, average number of days from order receipt to order shipping) and operating costs. Then the data are evaluated for degree of compliance with labor and other standards.

DATA COLLECTION

The operating statistics and operating costs should be collected by utilization of a software system, either one purchased off the shelf or one tailored to the particular fulfillment system (more about software a little later). General information such as the number of orders received should probably be collected on a daily basis. For some item-specific data, daily collection is called for; whereas for others, weekly or perhaps less frequent collection is sufficient, depending on the type of inventory policy employed and the turnover rate of individual items. Cost data should probably be tabulated over a somewhat longer time than sales-related data.

STANDARDS

Collecting and inspecting data would have little benefit unless there is a way of knowing what are "low numbers" and "high numbers," "good performances" and "bad performances." That is the reason for setting standards against which collected data can be sensibly compared.

Two types of standards are possible. One is a set of standards specific to the mail-order operation of a specific firm; the other is a set of standards conceived as necessary for the long-run success of any mail-order business. Initially (before any data are available) firm or product-specific standards must be estimated from knowledge of similar situations or firms. Soon, however, there are enough data to allow determination of reasonable standards for such things as time required to perform a task, proportion of items ordered that require backlogging, proportion of orders for which not every item is in stock, time from order processing to shipping, and time from shipping to receiving.

When the objective is to collect data on how long it takes workers to perform a given task, the process is called *work measurement.* Formulas exist that determine what sample size is required (i.e., how many times we need to time the duration of a task), and a vast literature addresses issues such as obtaining a random sample and margins of error. (Some of the formulas are discussed in chapter 10, "Testing Direct Marketing Programs," in a slightly different context.) A similar procedure is used for establishing standards for other metric quantities that do not, strictly speaking, come under "work measurement" (e.g., delivery time for an order once shipped, average number of items per order).

When the object is to collect data on the proportion of time a group of workers is engaged in a certain activity or set of activities, the process is called *work sampling.* A prominent example of work sampling is setting standards for the proportion of time workers engage in direct labor, indirect labor, and break times. This is a relevant notion for many aspects of a warehouse operation, and the literature abounds with formulas for required sample size and other useful considerations. (Again, chapter 10 contains some related discussion.) Steps involved in establishing standards for other categorical quantities, such as proportions, that are not, strictly speaking, labor-related (e.g., proportion of items ordered that are not in stock when the order is received) are quite similar to the procedures of formal work sampling.

Standards that pertain to the mail-order business or industry as a whole are of a different nature. These are basically a combination of the results of industry surveys and the opinions of experts. Typical standards are: "A customer should receive a response to written correspondence by the next calendar week," "No more than 4 percent of orders should be backordered," and "Customers should receive an order within 21 business days from phoning it in." These statements should be thought of as goals; if they are not considered achievable, there should be identifiable reasons why not. Some of these "standards" (really, "guidelines") may be identifiable from the yearly *Direct Marketing Association's Statistical Fact Book.* For example, the 1997 book reports that the average time on hold for phone calls in 1995 was 45 seconds, and the average length of the call was 3.8 minutes. These numbers were aggregated over many industries. The hold time averages varied from 18 seconds for health care establishments to 67 seconds for retail establishments. (Remember, these are averages, and self-reported at that! Selective memory probably yields the reader the memory of his or her 15-minute wait on hold!) The average call length varied from 3.3 minutes for financial services establishments to 6.6 minutes for retail establishments.

REPORTS

For purposes of control, we develop standards and collect data to compare with the standards (and possibly to use for continual revision of standards). The comparisons can take many forms. Control charts (*x*-bar charts, *R*-charts, *p*-charts, *pn*-charts, *c*-charts, and *u*-charts) are often used to study performances over time. They are especially geared for identification of trends. Many times, the objective is to monitor a process and to flag only when something is amiss or when an "outlier" or "unusual observation" occurs. This concept, usually referred to as *exception reporting,* saves much paperwork and yet keeps management informed whenever its attention is required.

PLANNING

The planning process must consider three notions: (1) a description of what has happened in the past (most of the preceding discussion focused on this); (2) a delineation of what is expected to happen in the future, assuming no action is taken to change anything; and (3) a determination of what the planners (management) want to happen. The first notion can be used to establish the relationship between input variables and output variables. The second notion concerns the extrapolation of this relationship for future values of input variables. The third notion involves a comparison of the projected values of the output variables with what management has concluded it would like the values to be, an examination of the cost required to bridge the gap, and a cost-benefit or risk-reward analysis to determine whether to continue toward the goal.

Using an Outside Contractor for Fulfillment Services

Most people would agree that business operations are becoming more and more specialized. This trend is apparent in direct marketing operations. A larger and larger number of direct marketing firms (or direct marketing divisions of firms) are hiring outside contractors to perform their fulfillment operations. Thomas Litle, president of Direct Order Sales Corporation of Nashua, New Hampshire, has listed the following significant advantages of hiring an outside contractor:[20]

1. It enables the hiring firm to concentrate on what it presumably does best—marketing and merchandising.
2. Fulfillment costs can be treated by the hiring firm as variable costs. These costs are then more predictable, and net profits will not vary so much with volume (and the firm will be exposed to less downside risk).
3. The hiring firm will have access to the best fulfillment software, which it otherwise might not be able to justify economically even if it has the personnel to take advantage of it.
4. The hiring firm will likely receive equivalent fulfillment services for a cost per order lower than the in-house cost per order.

Some of the advantages (especially number 3) have been reduced by the arrival of numerous fulfillment software packages at reduced cost. These packages can be purchased,

---

[20]Thomas Litle, "Integrating Product and Management Information Fulfillment Operations for Profit," *Direct Marketing Association Manual Release 1400.3* (1984).

or, if desirable, leased. Some examples of fulfillment software packages are *Order Power!* by Computer Solutions, Inc., of Miami, Florida; *PRO-MAIL*®*Fulfillment Processing Center* by Software Marketing Associates, Inc., of Rocky Hill, Connecticut; and *Take Control*™ *Customer Support/Help Desk,* by Brock International, Inc., of Atlanta, Georgia.[21]

The main disadvantage of hiring an outside contractor to perform the fulfillment function is loss of control and potential leaks of proprietary information.

As noted earlier, the proportion of direct marketing firms that have hired outside contractors for fulfillment services has been increasing. In fact, based on the 1995 DMA Consumer Magazine Customer Service Study, in 1995 a majority of firms exclusively used an outside source (service bureau) for customer service operations (57 percent), and another 19 percent used both an in-house and outside source. Selecting the right outside fulfillment contractor could have an impact on profits equal to that of other, more mainstream direct marketing activities.

Summary

Effective fulfillment involves many different skills and requires balancing many different considerations. Edward Nash lists the following four extreme "philosophies" of fulfillment and customer service:[22]

1. "Stop the deadbeat." (Giving highest priority to credit checking and the like, regardless of the resulting delays, cancellations, etc.)

2. "The customer is always right." (Giving highest priority to doing whatever the customer wishes, extending credit to everyone without a credit check, providing refunds without checking receipts, etc.)

3. "Cost efficiency *über alles.*" (Giving highest priority to cost minimization, regardless of customer service, delivery quality, etc.)

4. "A rolling stone gathers no moss." (Giving highest priority to maximizing turnover, regardless of costs, customer service, etc.)

A superior fulfillment operation is one that finds the right blend of these extreme philosophies, which correspond to the four key considerations of payment, customer service, cost, and sales volume.

An overview of the flow of the fulfillment process from the receipt of the order from the customer to the shipping of the order to the customer, along with the customer service and planning and control support activities, can be seen in Figure 7.3. Orders by mail and telephone are received and processed; payment issues are attended to and the central database is then notified about the particulars of the order. Warehouse documents are generated and the order is picked, packed, and shipped to the customer, and the inventory file in the central database is updated. Items are received from suppliers and stored in the warehouse; the inventory file is appropriately updated. Customer service activities are available to interact with the system; the planning and control functions are gathering data, generating reports, and monitoring the overall fulfillment process.

---

[21]Details of these packages can be found in the "1996 Software Guide for Direct Response Advertisers, Part 1," *Direct Marketing* (May 1996): 51–52.

[22]Edward Nash, *Direct Marketing,* 3rd ed. (New York: McGraw-Hill, 1995): 358–360.

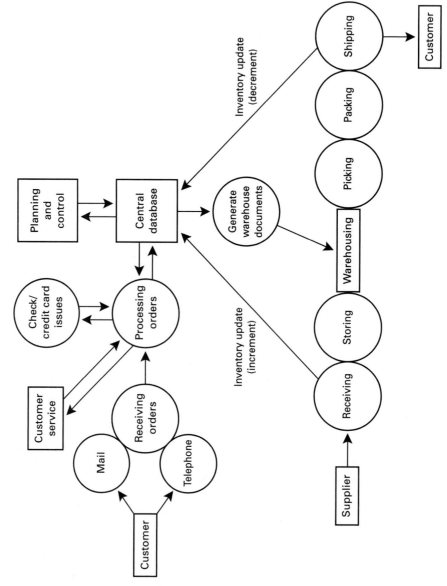

FIGURE 7.3 Flow of Fulfillment Process

Discussion Questions and Exercises

1. Describe situations in which fulfillment operations are (a) relatively more important and (b) relatively less important.
2. Why is there an increasing trend for the order taker, when taking orders on the telephone, to ask for the caller's telephone number?
3. Describe situations in direct marketing when demand patterns are (a) relatively more quick to change and (b) relatively more stable.
4. What are the merits of the different options for organizing the picking operation in a warehouse with regard to security?
5. Suppose that individual items making up an order are stored in different warehouses. What are the various costs that must be considered in deciding whether to send out the items in separate packages versus arranging for the items to be sent together in one package?
6. One reason for the increased emphasis on customer service is that it is generally agreed that a current customer is, on balance, worth much more than a new customer. In fact, Clancy and Shulman, as well as Philip Kotler (surely the most well-known author of textbooks in the field of marketing), say, specifically, five times more. What are some of the reasons for this?

Suggested Readings

Abramson, D. "What Retailers Must Learn about Fulfillment." *DM News,* 1 June 1984, 28.

Berry, L., V. Zeithaml, and A. Parasuraman. "Quality Counts in Service, Too." *Business Horizons* (May–June 1985): 44–52.

Churchill, G., and C. Suprenant. "An Investigation into the Determinants of Customer Satisfaction." *Journal of Marketing Research* 19 (November 1982): 491–504.

Dilworth, James. *Production and Operations Management,* 3rd ed. (New York: Random House, 1986).

Raphael, Murray. "Let's Examine Who You Are." *Direct Marketing* (July 1997): 54–55.

P A R T 3: SPECIAL TECHNIQUES OF DIRECT MARKETING

C H A P T E R 8

Developing and Using Customer Databases

In the late 1970s a small group of direct marketers at American Express was looking for a way to improve the response rate to direct mail credit card solicitations. At that time, American Express was the second largest mailer in the United States; only the Internal Revenue Service mailed a greater volume. The card division averaged a million pieces per day and used advanced demographic and geographic segmentation techniques to identify the top 5 percent of the population—the candidates for card membership. However, traditional segmentation was not adequate to identify, out of this demographic pool, prospects who had a sufficiently high probability of purchase to make the profitability of mailings satisfactory.

The direct marketers believed they could develop better segmentation models if they studied the purchase behavior of current card members. This information was available in the billing records of the company. They convinced management to assign statisticians and computer personnel to the project and were given a small budget to analyze this data.

They encountered numerous problems. There was a huge volume of data on the specific purchases of individual card members. The mainframe computers of the day were extremely slow by today's standards. The words "user-friendly" had not yet been applied to computer software. The data were formatted for billing purposes, not for marketing analysis. Worse, the database was essential for day-to-day operations; the marketers had to access it on nights and weekends.

The group persevered. They developed techniques, the predecessors of those described in chapter 5, that generated savings in mailing costs while maintaining or increasing the number of new customers acquired or lapsed customers reactivated. Management permitted them to reinvest cost savings in improved technology. Thus was born the discipline of database marketing.[1]

Today, an ever increasing number of companies are using database marketing techniques. Some of them are firms we would recognize as "traditional" direct marketers. Many are companies better known as mass media advertisers and members of conventional channels of distribution. Consider the following examples:

- Fingerhut markets household goods and apparel, primarily through catalogs and direct mail to a broad middle-class market; many of these people use Fingerhut's proprietary credit card. Fingerhut is well known for multiple offers and multiple purchase incentives as well as for personalized mailings that reflect the customer's purchase history and knowledge of personal events such as birthdays. According to their chairman, database marketing is Fingerhut's "core competency." They use the database to "test new product concepts, target offers, and build the customer relationship through every contact." In addition, the database permits Fingerhut to control credit risk, model a variety of marketing actions such as price changes, and target all marketing effort to those with the highest probability of response.[2]

- Religious publisher Guideposts noticed that it was selling an increasing number of books about angels. Marketing personnel conducted an analysis of their 19-million-person database and concluded that it held as many as 5 million prospects for a magazine about angels. The result is the publication *Angels on Earth*. It was expected to hit one million in circulation within two years of its launch. The publisher points out that careful database analysis helps prevent cannibalization of the flagship *Guideposts* magazine. Use of rental lists is expected to produce nine million more high-potential prospects.[3]

- Fielder's Choice sells seed corn direct to more than 7,500 farmers. It has a personal relationship, based on a sophisticated telephone marketing program, with each farmer. Fielder's Choice does not cold-call farmers. It uses a variety of media to generate sales leads, including direct mail, print advertisements, card decks, and package inserts. Response is by means of a postage-paid postcard. The farmer is called the day the card is received by Fielder's Choice. The telemarketer indicates that an informational package is being sent by priority mail. Two days after receipt of the mailing the farmer is called again to confirm receipt of the package and answer questions, or to explain the contents if the farmer has not yet reviewed the package. This level of attention signifies the concern paid to each farmer. All of the telephone reps either were farmers or were raised on a farm. They work on salary, not commission. Calls may last for as long as 30 minutes. Reps answer questions and ask for information that will allow them to recommend the correct

[1]John Stevenson, "The History and Family Tree of 'Databased' Direct Marketing," *Direct Marketing* (December 1987): 121, 150.

[2]Mollie Neal, "Fingerhut Movin' Ahead," *Direct Marketing* (September 1994): 30–32, 72.

[3]Doug Henschen, "Publishers Aggressively Plumb DBs for Brand Extensions, Yielding 3 Mags," *DM News*, 10 February 1997, 23.

product out of the 27varieties of hybrid seed corn offered by the firm. A sophisticated call-handling system linked to the customer database supports their efforts.[4]

- The Reel site on the World Wide Web (www.reel.com) is set up to help consumers identify movies they will enjoy. It intends to become an on-line video store. On a first visit to the site, the location called the Reel Genius asks the consumer to select a film genre (action, foreign, mystery, and so forth). It then gives a list of movies of that type and asks for a rating for all the ones the consumer has seen on a scale of 1 to 10. It combines all the ratings of people of similar tastes and comes up with a list of movies the consumer should like. Reel then asks for ratings of the movies it has suggested. Over time, it becomes better and better at picking movies that suit an individual's particular taste.[5]

- Joe Everybuyer has had a tough day at the office—the network was down, and the boss was grouchy. Late in the afternoon he realizes that it is his night to cook supper. The Jolly Green Giant has come to the rescue before; Joe hopes he can do so again. He surfs to the Green Giant Web site. The site recognizes Joe's address and queries its database. Joe has visited twice recently; both times he requested quick recipes from prepackaged products, and last time he chose the Garlic Pasta Chicken Salad. By the time Joe has finished clicking on the "What's New" section of the Web site a complete menu has been prepared—a recipe for Fiesta Chicken, suggested side dishes, and even a recommended wine. The site also identifies his geographic location and suggests nearby stores that have the supplies he needs for dinner.[6]

It is important to note two things about the final senario. Green Giant and its parent company Pillsbury do currently have substantial Web sites with recipes and nutritional information. However, the full range of capabilities described here are still a vision, not a reality. Would you like to wager that this type of capability will not be available within a few years? We do not think that would be a wise bet.

On the other hand, the first four illustrations are real examples of current database marketing activity. There is an important distinction between the first two vignettes—Fingerhut and Guideposts—and the next two—Fielder's Choice and Reel. Notice that the Fingerhut and Guideposts examples illustrate marketing programs based on traditional segmentation strategy. The difference is that the data for segmentation analysis were available in the customer database; they were not the product of marketing research, as has typically been the case. The traditional segmentation strategy can then be executed in a different manner. Because the database has the names and addresses of individual customers, and because it can assign each customer to a segment with a high degree of accuracy, these marketers can execute their segmentation strategy with personalized offers directed to individual customers who are members of the same segment. This, of course, contrasts with traditional execution in the mass media, which reaches both high potential targets and many others who have no interest whatsoever in the offer.

Both Fielder's Choice and Reel are using the customer database to develop programs for individual customers. The Fielder's Choice program uses conventional marketing media including print, mail, and telephone. Because it has a heavy telemarketing component, allowing reps to interact directly with individual customers and to tailor the communication to the customer's needs, Fielder's Choice is a good example of segment-of-one marketing. Reel, of

---

[4]"Fielder's Choice Plants the Seeds for Growth," *TeleProfessional,* June 1995, 40–42.

[5]Stephen H. Wildstrom, "Service with a Click," *Business Week,* 24 March 1997, 19.

[6]Michael Jay Tucker, "Poppin' Fresh Dough," *Datamation,* May 1997, 50–58.

course, takes place in cyberspace, where communication is inherently one-to-one. Notice the difference between interaction controlled by a knowledgeable human agent supported by a database and interaction entirely controlled by an electronic database. The human can readily and instantaneously adjust the dialog to meet the customer's needs. The electronic database must "learn" a great deal about an individual customer and the segment to which that individual belongs in order to make accurate recommendations. And it will be a long time before the database always gets it right!

There is another important lesson to be drawn from these examples of real-world database marketing. It is easy to talk as if database marketing supported only marketing communications activities. In fact, a robust customer database can affect all aspects of marketing effort. Table 8.1 presents a summary of ways in which the database can be used to develop or improve marketing programs of all kinds. The table points out strategic uses of customer data. These are generally types of analyses and activities that affect the long-run direction of

TABLE 8.1 Uses of the Customer or Prospect Database

Marketing Mix or Function Variable	Tactical	Strategic
Product	Analysis (sales, margins, by product line, region, etc.)	Trend analysis for forecasting and product development
Price	Price sensitivity by product, market segment Price incentive program planning	Pricing relationships across product lines
Promotion	Program evaluation by medium, vehicle Promotional program planning	Promotional effectiveness by medium
Channels	Targeted promotion to dealers Co-op manufacturer or dealer promotion to prospective customers or customer base	Channel or dealer effectiveness
Customer acquisition	Profile customer base or outside database overlay Qualification or sales programs from leads	Increase profitability of customer base
Customer service	On-line access to data by service reps Faster, more accurate order processing and fulfillment	Analysis of contracts, satisfaction levels
Sales force	Profitability analysis by territory or rep Lead generation and tracking programs Rep access for service and scheduling	Productivity programs
Customer relationship maintenance	Special promotions to customer base	Nonsales communications
Marketing research	Tightly controlled samples: higher response rates	Combine survey with internal and external databases for analysis and modeling

Source: Mary Lou Roberts, "Expanding the Role of the Direct Marketing Database," *Journal of Direct Marketing* 11, no. 4 (1997): 29. Copyright © 1997 by John Wiley & Sons. Reprinted by permission of John Wiley & Sons.

the business unit (opening up new market opportunities) or significantly change the way in which marketing activities are carried out (sales force productivity programs). It also lists tactical uses—analyses such as profiling customers and business accounts and developing marketing and promotional programs to meet their specific needs.

What Is a Database?

Chapter 4 discussed mailing lists and their role in direct marketing programs. A database is just another name for a mailing list, isn't it? No, it is not. Ownership of a mailing list may be the *first step* toward establishing a database, but it is *not* a database.

A database contains information about customers and prospects that has been collected over a considerable period of time. Consider for a moment just a few of the databases that contain information about you:

- *Student records.* Every school you have ever attended has records containing information on your background and academic performance. The Educational Testing Service has a more limited set of data that includes your college entrance test scores.
- *Employment records.* Every organization for which you have ever worked also has a record containing data on your background, salary, and the amount withheld from your wages for taxes.
- *Automobile registration records.* If you own a car, both the state in which the car is registered and your insurance company have records containing background information on you, descriptive information about your car, and a history of your traffic citations and accidents. Notice that the state and the insurance company are keeping essentially the same information related to your automobile, but they are keeping it for different purposes and probably in slightly different formats.

None of these examples mentions the word *computer.* Theoretically, the concept of a database does not require the use of a computer. Practically speaking, however, it is impossible to effectively maintain a database of useful size without a computer. It is safe to assume that all marketing applications involve computerized databases.

Also note that none of the examples we have cited is a database designed primarily for marketing purposes. But just consider the number of firms that would like to have the mailing list of students currently enrolled at or graduating from your school, or of persons who have just purchased new automobiles (which some states make commercially available).

An Example of a Marketing Database

Let's take the example of an airline that has designed a database to keep track of members of its frequent flier program, using the process displayed in Figure 8.1 (p. 166). This database has acquired a considerable amount of data on each member, including mileage accumulated under the plan, hotel and rental car usage, and mileage-based awards claimed.

Where and how does the airline obtain this information? The airline flight data originates from their own transactions (*customer contacts*). This is obviously rich data about how frequently members fly, destinations, length of stays, and number and types of tickets purchased. How do they obtain hotel and rental car data? They can ask; if members are given an incentive, such as additional miles, for answering questions about additional dimensions of their travel, a substantial percentage will respond to the marketing research effort. The same

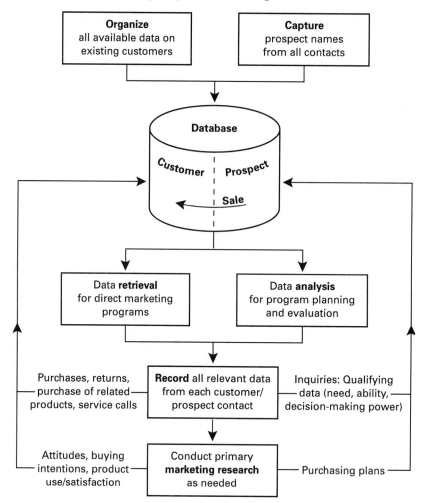

FIGURE 8.1 The Database Marketing Process

is true about asking members about travel on other airlines in order to obtain a more complete picture of members' travel activity.

The airline can manipulate (*analyze*) this data in a number of ways that will produce managerially useful information. It can analyze the travel patterns of individual members. By knowing that Mr. Smith travels frequently between Dallas and Chicago, for example, the airline can target him (*retrieval*) for information about special midweek fares between Dallas and Chicago or a tie-in promotion with a hotel in Chicago during the month of August. (The airline knows from the zip code of his home address that Mr. Smith lives in a suburb of Dallas, and therefore he may be interested in the Chicago hotel promotion but not in the corresponding one in Dallas.)

Because Mr. Smith is accessible, the airline may wish to collect data (*marketing research*) from him that goes beyond the behavioral data just described. They may also wish to ask for attitudinal data including his satisfaction with flight schedules and customer service, his level of satisfaction with other carriers, and his decision-making process for both business and pleasure travel. Because Mr. Smith can be addressed by name, because the airline can stress the value of his opinion as a member of the frequent flier plan, and because it can offer him meaningful incentives, the probability that he will reply to a request for information is far greater than if he were merely a randomly selected member of the general population. The information may also be used directly to develop products, services, and promotional offers that will be attractive to Mr. Smith and other customers like him.

The airline may segment its frequent fliers in a variety of ways to highlight especially pertinent information. If Mr. Smith has not flown on the airline for an unusually long period of time, the airline would be well advised to ask him why. If it is because of a change in his job requirements, there is nothing that can be done. If, however, he has changed his airline preference, knowing why he has done so may give the airline some insight into the success of competitive activities or the failure of their own.

In other words, the airline can manipulate the information it already has to help it better understand the behavioral patterns of its frequent customers. It can also collect and store additional information, which may be attitudinal as well as behavioral. This additional information can either be general (requested of all or most of the frequent fliers) or specific (requested of only those who have not flown on the airline for the past three months, for example). The airline can also overlay its database with information purchased from outside sources, as discussed in chapter 4. It can also add *prospects* to its database by running inquiry-generation programs or by using appropriate rental lists, such as a list of subscribers to travel magazines.

Using all the information, from whatever source, that is contained in the database, the airline can develop marketing programs that will appeal to precisely targeted segments of its frequent fliers. It can then promote these programs directly to the fliers who have a high probability of responding instead of wasting its promotional dollars on those who have a low probability of response.

By now you should have a feel for the wide variety of valuable marketing programs that can be carried out with great efficiency if a marketing database is available. You may have been wondering, though, if the cost and effort of establishing and maintaining a complex database are worth the benefits.

When Is a Database Cost Effective?

The cost of manipulating and storing computerized data is one of the few costs that have declined substantially in recent years. These cost decreases are quite significant, especially because computing power has been rising at the same time. Today, more firms have an opportunity to implement a wider variety of computer applications because processing time is shorter and costs are lower for any individual application.

Hardware, however, is not the only cost that management should recognize when considering whether to establish a marketing database (or any other computer application, for that matter). The software cost for the database management system (discussed in the next section) can also be substantial, particularly if the firm develops its own proprietary software or needs substantial customization of existing software packages. If the system is to be used in locations remote from the central processing facility, there will be additional costs for communications hardware and software and processing installations such as telemarketing stations.

There will also be human resources costs, both for additional training of existing personnel and for hiring new personnel, some of whom will be highly trained and experienced, and therefore command higher salaries.

Existing software and data files will probably have to be converted so they will work properly on the new database system. This can be expensive and time consuming, and can result in considerable inconvenience and delay to existing users.

Finally, there is an interesting phenomenon associated with successful system installations that is well recognized by information systems professionals but whose magnitude is difficult to assess. Successful applications breed ideas for additional applications, ones that were never envisioned until users began to use the system and to understand what it could do. As a consequence of this snowball effect, before long, a system that was more than adequate for the original applications is hopelessly overloaded. Management should consider buying either initial excess capacity or an easily expandable system (or both) to keep total long-run system costs in line.

Because total costs for a database system can be substantial, careful thought should be given to the types of situations in which a database will be especially valuable. Several such situations can be identified. For example, repeat-purchase situations have the following characteristics:[7]

- *Moderate to high dollar value.* The purchase must provide sufficient gross margin to cover all its promotion costs, including the database.

- *Purchase cycle of moderate length.* One-time or infrequent purchases do not present a need for databased marketing unless the infrequent purchase is so large and profitable that it is advisable to maintain the account history in depth. Also, very frequent purchases of convenience goods may offer little opportunity for specialized marketing promotions; neither have they proven to produce the margin needed to support those promotions. During the late 1980s, a number of consumer products companies tried to overcome this problem by accumulating data about household purchases of a wide array of branded data. However, in most cases the costs of collecting and maintaining data exceeded the benefits that could be derived from database marketing programs.

- *A segmented (or segmentable) market.* Few markets today are so small or so homogeneous that segmentation cannot improve marketing effectiveness. However, the stronger the segmentation in a particular market, the more valuable the database that allows the marketer to reach that segment directly with specialized offers and appeals.

- *Customers who cannot be reached cost effectively by mass media.* Despite the proliferation of specialized media, many valuable markets are identifiable only on the basis of behavioral variables for which there is no direct media counterpart (e.g., Rolls-Royce owners, ultra-prestige credit card holders, frequent business travelers).

- *Ability to obtain names and addresses of customers and prospects in machine-readable form.* Records in a database can, of course, be maintained by using only a unique identification number. Practically speaking, however, if the marketer wishes to collect information about the consumer or the business account over time, the name is needed. A unique identifying number will still be used because names are not unique. If the customer or prospect is to be reached by direct mail, a correct mailing address is obviously essential.

- *Opportunities to increase the volume of business from existing customers.* One such opportunity could be obtaining a greater share of these customers' purchases in product categories from which they are currently purchasing. Another could be cross-selling, that is, persuading customers to purchase additional products from the firm's product line.

---

[7]This list was adapted from promotional materials of Epsilon, a database consultancy.

Most organizations would find that at least some of these situations apply to their marketing experience, and many organizations would find that all or most of them apply. This suggests two things. First, most marketers will find a customer database valuable in making their programs more cost effective. Second, when an organization finds many opportunities for targeted marketing using databases, it should be possible to establish priorities on the basis of incremental profit (incremental revenues minus incremental costs).

Now that we have presented general ideas about the nature and usefulness of marketing databases, we look at both the marketing and technical requirements for the development, maintenance, and use of databases.

The Components of a Database System

A marketing manager does not have to be a technical expert to make effective use of database marketing. However, the manager must have a general comprehension of database technology and terminology to understand what it can do (and, at times, what it cannot readily do) and to be able to work effectively with information systems (IS) managers and technical personnel.

First, let's look at two definitions developed from an IS perspective:

A *database* is a collection of interrelated data items that can be processed by one or more application systems.

A *database system* is comprised of a database, general-purpose software—called the *database management system* (DBMS)—that manipulates the database, and appropriate hardware and personnel.[8]

These are straightforward and useful definitions, but we need to understand in some detail the context of today's database systems and their generic elements.

The operating environment for most database systems today is overwhelmingly based on a client-server platform. In its simplest terms, that means that a server computer stores the database and makes it available to client machines as requested. Client computers run their own application programs using data supplied by the server.

The clients, or users, often ask, "Why can't I have my own database? I only need a portion of the data, and it would be more convenient for me to store it on my own computer instead of having to access the server when I need a data set." Besides the technical issues, such as having enough storage space for both data and applications programs, there are a number of reasons why it is important to centralize the *maintenance* of the database even though its *use* may be widely distributed throughout the marketing organization.

Reasons why is it necessary to have a *centralized* customer database include[9]

- *Data independence.* The application program or user is protected from changes in the way the data are organized, stored, or accessed. The user should be able to continue to run the application program without even being aware that a change has been made in the physical or logical structure of the database.

---

[8]Gary W. Hansen and James V. Hansen, *Database Management and Design* (Upper Saddle River, NJ: Prentice Hall, 1996), 12.

[9]This discussion is based on Alfonso E. Cardenas, *Data Base Management Systems,* 2nd ed. (Newton, MA: Allyn & Bacon, 1985): 12–16, 83–93.

- *Shareability and nonredundancy.* All qualified users are assured access to required data via the database. This eliminates the need for the maintenance of similar data files in various parts of the organization (redundant data). It also means that users of the same data at the same moment in any part of the organization are provided current and valid data records. That is often referred to as *data integrity.*

- *Integrity.* The accuracy of the data must be ensured. This involves maintaining control over access to the data and over the editing of data. It also involves carrying out technical procedures that help to maintain the correctness and consistency of the data and maintaining back-up data and systems.

- *Relatability.* A record contains information about an individual (for example, your student record, as described earlier). Just as the data items on a single record are related to one another (in our example, they are related in the sense that they all pertain to you), so are records often related to one another. For instance, if either of your parents attended your school, there is a logical relationship ("child of alumnus") and the school should easily be able to represent this relationship in the database by linking the parent's and the child's records.

- *Access flexibility.* Access flexibility means being able to easily and efficiently access the data in a variety of ways suited to the needs of the user. It also implies the use of conventional software or English-like query languages to enhance the ability of the nontechnically trained user to retrieve data or to simply browse through the system. Access flexibility also makes the tasks of database administration easier because users can fulfill their own data needs without having to call on the services of a programmer.

- *Security.* The database must be protected against unauthorized or malicious access and actions. There are various types of access (read only, add/delete, and modify) that may be granted to an individual user. Users may also be allowed to access the entire database or only a portion of it. There must be procedures and personnel in place to assign, control, and remove permissions to access the database.

- *Performance and efficiency.* The system must function smoothly at a level of cost that is acceptable to users. The larger the database becomes and the more individual users are concerned only with small subsets of the data they can access frequently, the more strain is placed on performance and efficiency. High levels of technical skill are needed to maintain a large database at peak efficiency in the face of the often conflicting demands of different user groups. Also, the larger the database, the more difficult it is to make changes without disturbing the smooth functioning of the entire system.

- *Administration and control.* There must be centralized authority and responsibility for management of the system. Because of the large number of users, their different requirements, and their different levels of technical proficiency, it is imperative that responsibility for the system be vested in a highly skilled database administrator. This administrator must be a well-trained technical specialist who has the ability to work well with different user groups.

Figure 8.2 illustrates the various components of a database system that conforms to these requirements. The *database management system* is the heart of the system. The DBMS is software that handles requests for data and performs other functions for users and system administrators. As illustrated in the figure, the chief functions are the user query (request) and reporting subsystems, tools that assist the programmers in developing applications programs, a data definition and control subsystem (also called a dictionary/directory or a catalog), as well as subsystems for handling data security and integrity and for controlling simultaneous access by multiple users.

The *users* represent all individuals or groups who have access to data. Each user may have access to all or only a specific portion of the data. The section of the data that is rele-

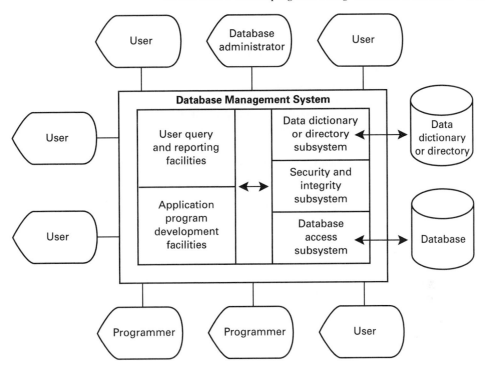

FIGURE 8.2 Components of a Database Management System

Source: Adapted from Gary W. Hansen and James V. Hansen, *Database Management and Design* (Upper Saddle River, NJ: Prentice Hall, 1996), 25. Reprinted with permission.

vant to each user or user group is often called a *view* or *user view*. Because each user has only the view that is relevant to his or her particular needs, each user is likely to be familiar with only a portion of the database and therefore to see (view) the database differently than other users. As suggested by Figure 8.2, user access to the system is controlled by the DBMS.

The *database administrator* is the highly trained technical specialist who acts as the main interface between the system and the users. The database administrator is responsible for the technical performance of the system. This individual is also responsible, in cooperation with the major user groups, for defining the data needs of the organization and specifying how the system is configured to meet those needs.

The *data dictionary/directory (DD/D)* catalogs all the data on the database. It stores the definition of each data entity in the database. It defines each item in terms of its name, its length, and the form in which it is stored. It also stores data about the relationships among data entities. (Data about data are called *metadata*.) The DD/D also keeps track of a great deal of other data that enables users to access data quickly and accurately.

Finally, the *database* is the software system where the data are stored. There are several types of true database systems. There are also systems that predate actual database systems. There are also applications programs, especially spreadsheets, that have some of the functionality of databases but that are not actually databases.

The precursor of contemporary database systems were file-based systems in which the records in a file had to be processed either *sequentially* (one after the other, in order) or *ran-*

domly (permits direct access to a specific record within a file). Whether sequential or random, these systems are frequently referred to as "flat file" systems. Processing of these systems is slow and cumbersome. It is very difficult for them to keep track of records that are related to one another—for example, two cars that are owned by the same household in the motor vehicle registration system. Flat file systems have been developed in conventional programming languages such as COBOL that require programmers who are skilled in that language to make any changes in the system. You will frequently hear of older systems, often written in COBOL and running on mainframe computers, referred to as *legacy* systems.

As database software has evolved there have been three primary types of database systems—hierarchical, network, and relational. To understand the essence of hierarchical and network models, think of a tree diagram such as a decision tree. In this case, however, the structure is made up of data items, and the tree specifies their relationship to one another. To locate a specific data item in a hierarchical system the software must start at the "base of the tree" and move through all the intervening branches to arrive at the desired data item. Network models have a more complex design that allows multiple data relationships and much better data access. However, when database systems become complex—say, 100 or more data items (customer purchase history) and many entries for each data item (the large green backpack, the bicycle shorts, and so forth)—even network systems become slow and cumbersome to manipulate. Consequently, the development of the relational model in the early 1970s was a boon to database processing in general and database marketing in particular.

The way the relational data model works is a little difficult for nonprogrammers to understand, but it is based on two reasonably simple ideas. The first basic concept is that the relationships between data items are represented in tables made up of rows and columns. For example, the bursar's view of the student database might use the data entity "student" as a column definition and have row entries such as "current semester tuition," "lab fees," and "dining hall meal ticket." So far, that is an easy concept. The second important principle is that tables can be linked together by specifying data relationships. Many tables can be linked together in this way. To continue with the student records example, the registrar has a different view of the student records database. For the same student data entity, the registrar needs rows that include data items such as "admissions test score," "current semester courses," and "current grade point average." At some point in the semester, data about courses for which the student is enrolled (from the registrar) need to be linked with tuition and fee data (someone has to be responsible for ensuring the accuracy of these data, perhaps the financial vice president) to produce the tuition bill for the bursar. This example offers some sense of how quickly data models can become complex in both design and use.

Think for a moment, though, about the three data items (out of many) listed as examples of the registrar's view of the student database. "Admissions test score" is a one-time entry that never changes but remains a permanent part of the student record. "Current semester courses," of course, does change each semester. However, the completed courses are not wiped off the record. They are moved to another section and the course grades added, all of which acts as an update to the student's official record. "Current grade point average" is a piece of data that also changes after the completion of each academic term.

It takes a lot of work on the part of both managers and IS technicians to set up a system such as this and to make it work properly. However, once that is done, the day-to-day operation of the system can be handled by clerical personnel who do not have extensive technical training.

This brief example is, on the one hand, an accurate depiction of what some parts of a student database might look like. On the other hand, it is a vastly simplified presentation. As we said at the beginning of this section, it is important for marketers to understand the basics of the technology if they are to work with it effectively. The good news is that the technical background is now available to marketing students in a way that it was not just a few years ago. Applications software has become so easy to use that most schools no longer have extensive technical prerequisites for the beginning database management course. Marketing students are frequently eligible to take the introductory database course when they have completed the required computer courses. We urge you to do so. You may never do hands-on database development or maintenance, but you will become a much more skilled database marketer if you take time to acquire some technical knowledge along with your marketing courses.

Having introduced you to the basics of the technical side of database marketing, we now look at database issues from the viewpoint of the marketing manager. We first suggest a marketing-oriented definition and then look at the processes involved in establishing, maintaining, and making profitable—and eventually optimal—use of a customer database.

A Definition of Database Marketing

There is no generally accepted definition of database marketing, so once again we use our own:

> *Database marketing* is a segmentation process carried out on a computerized database of customers and prospects using statistical analyses and models in order to target individuals instead of entire segments of customers or prospects.

We remind you that when we talk about "customers and prospects" we mean either consumers; business-to-business clientele; or the patrons, donors, and members of not-for-profit organizations. For brevity's sake we often use only the words "customer database," but the inclusion of prospective, as well as actual, customers is implied.

It is also important to remember that the database is dynamic, not static. Data are constantly being added to it, either as a result of interaction with the customer, by adding marketing research data collected from the customers, or by enhancing the database with outside, third-party data.

This all sounds deceptively simple. It is more difficult to implement database marketing in practice than it is to describe it on paper. Most of the reasons are organizational and have to do with the way the organization is accustomed to conducting its marketing activities.

Issues in Establishing a Customer Database

The process of establishing and using a customer database that was illustrated in Figure 8.1 describes a continuous process of data collection, refinement, and use. A well-designed system uses existing data to develop marketing programs, which in turn generate new data that, in time, lead to additional marketing programs.

One of the cardinal rules of database marketing is that *every contact with a customer or prospect should be captured and recorded in the database.* This is a deceptively simple idea that can be quite complicated in practice. The following situations are fairly typical:

- A firm that is organized around the concept of direct marketing (e.g., a catalog merchant) usually performs this function well. Each inquiry or order is recorded in the customer's file. Each contact also provides an opportunity to verify the accuracy of basic information such as mailing address.

- General marketers often do not perform this function well even though they may be in direct contact with some or all of their customers. This is frequently true of business marketers, for example. On the other hand, many traditional marketers are not in direct contact with their ultimate customers, and therefore constructing a database with information about them represents a formidable challenge.

- Retailers record every charge transaction in considerable detail. If they use scanners at the point of purchase they are recording all data, irrespective of manner of payment, in detail. This information is used for accounting and financial purposes, including customer billing, inventory control, and departmental profitability analysis. Retail scanner data are also a product themselves, sold to third-party specialists, who then sell it back to general marketers, as described in the preceding paragraph, who are not in direct contact with their final customers. Unfortunately, much retail data is relatively inaccessible to the marketing function, either because the financial functions have priority within the system or because the data are not organized appropriately for marketing's needs, or both.

- Financial services firms often provide another example of sequestered data. A single customer may have several kinds of accounts with a particular bank—a checking account, a money market fund, and a personal line of credit, for example. In most banks each of these financial products is the responsibility of a separate department, which has separate customer accounts systems. To further complicate matters, many households have a multiplicity of accounts set up in various names, as when parents set up a savings account or mutual fund to save for their children's college education. Consequently, it may be impossible to draw a complete profile of the business a customer does with the bank. This makes it more difficult to cross-sell other financial products—for example, to encourage the customer with a substantial money market fund balance to consider another type of investment vehicle such as a mutual fund. It also can make the organization look uninformed and uncaring when it contacts customers without knowledge of the full range of business the customer does with the institution. Some progress has been made on this front in recent years. We return to the subject briefly when we discuss the subject of data warehousing.

- Business marketers have similar problems. The order processing and accounts receivable functions often have a wealth of information about customer purchases that is not accessible to marketing management. Field salespeople also have a tremendous amount of information about current and prospective customers, but they often do not have a satisfactory way of providing that information to management, nor do they have sufficient incentives to do so.

Situations such as these make the processes of designing a database and creating an environment for its successful use challenging for many marketing organizations.

The contents of a database for a fund-raising application (presumably for a not-for-profit organization) are shown in Table 8.2. Examine it carefully, noting both the large number of individual data items and the fact that many of these items will have multiple occur-

TABLE 8.2 Fund-Raising Marketing Database Elements

Name Block	Address Block	General Donor Information	Donor Interactions	Market Research
Individual Name	Street Address	1. *Organizational*	1. *Gift History*	1. *Donor Profile*
Title and Suffix	(Name)	*Data*	Dates	*Survey*
Personal Salutation	City, State, Postal,	Approach Code	Amounts	Date of Response
Company or	and County Codes	Affiliations	Source Codes	Coded Answers to
Foundation Name	Date of Last Change	Chapter/Branch	Fund Allocation	Questions
	Business Address	Code	Use Code	
	City, State, Postal,	Donor/Member	Acknowledgment	2. *Secondary*
	and County Codes	Code	Code	*Database*
	Mail and Address	Origin Code, Date		*Classification(s)*
	Status Codes		2. *Pledge History*	PRIZM
		2. *Donor Profile Data*	Dates	
		Telephone Number	Amounts	3. *Demographic*
		(Home, Business)	Number of	*Profile*
		Special Interest	Payments	Occupation/Title
		Code	Interval between	Date of Birth
		Original Source	Payments	Sex
		and Date	Source Codes	Family Structure
			Fund Allocation	Education
			Use Code	
			Acknowledgment	4. *Psychographic*
			Code	*Profile*
				Program
			3. *Membership*	Preferences
			Date	Giving Motivation
			Amount	Interests and
			Begin Date	Lifestyles
			Expiration Date	
			Fund Allocation	
			4. *Tickets*	
			Date	
			Amount	
			Series	
			Section	
			Row	
			Seat Number(s)	
			Number of Seats	
			5. *Direct Mail*	
			Dates	
			Package Codes	
			Date Response	
			Received	
			6. *Memorial History*	
			Name and Date	
			7. *Volunteer History*	
			Name and Date	
			Assigned	
			8. *Activity History*	
			Fulfillment Action	
			Premiums Shipped	
			9. *Comment History*	
			English Comments	
			Date of Comment	
			Type of Comment	

Source: Copyright 9/1/84, Epsilon. Used with permission.

rences and therefore multiple entries. Once an organization begins to systematically collect data, it quickly finds itself confronted with huge amounts of data. Careful attention must be paid to collecting only data that will be useful in the decision-making process.

Making the Database Cost Effective

Database marketing has tremendous potential for making many aspects of the marketing process more cost effective, as can be seen in examples throughout this book. However, this does not happen by accident, nor is it a foregone conclusion. Database marketing requires a great deal of effort. Perhaps even more important, it requires a whole new way of thinking on the part of marketing personnel in most organizations. It is therefore imperative that, before database marketing is adopted, marketers ask themselves how the database will be useful. They can then measure prospective costs against potential benefits.

What follows is not an exhaustive list, but it does include many of the strategic questions to which a customer database can provide powerful answers. These questions include

- Who are our best customers?
- Where can we find other prospects like them?
- How can we convert these prospects to customers?
- What do our best customers buy from us?
- What else might they buy from us?
- What are they buying from our competitors that they might buy from us?
- Which ones were formerly good customers who have not bought recently?
- How can we reactivate them?
- Which medium- or low-value customers have potential for being upgraded to best customers?
- What is our investment in various customer segments?
- What is the return on that investment?
- How much is each customer worth in the long run?
- How are markets and customers changing?
- How can we identify price-sensitive customers or products?
- How effective is each channel of distribution and each channel member?

You may think of other questions to which the database will be able to provide answers, but these represent many of the most important ones. Some can be answered in other ways, such as through marketing research. Some cannot be answered without a database; a good example is "Who are our best customers?" Marketing research can develop a profile of best customers but, because of the anonymity associated with conventional marketing research, it cannot directly identify specific customers.

Another way of looking at the cost/benefit question is to ask whether it is becoming increasingly desirable to balance the costs involved in establishing a database and communicating directly with individual customers against the difficulty of reaching customers and prospects in a crowded and fragmented media environment.

It is difficult to argue that any marketing organization could not benefit from a database that meets its individual requirements. However, it is easy to argue that an organization must make a major commitment to database marketing over some period of time if the process is to be profitable.

A Word about the Future of Database Marketing

We have pointed out that database marketing has a rather brief history. From its inception in the late 1970s, both the technology and the uses have made spectacular advancements. Progress of this speed and magnitude makes it extremely dangerous to try to predict the future. However, there are three developments worth watching. Two are technical—the Internet and data warehousing. The other has social, political, and regulatory aspects—consumer privacy.

You are no doubt familiar with the Internet, especially the World Wide Web. In fact, you probably use it for purposes ranging from communicating with people via e-mail, to obtaining information for class projects and job interviews, to purchasing goods and services. Yet, as the Reel and Pillsbury examples at the beginning of this chapter illustrate, we have probably seen only the initial phases of what can be done on the Web and how it will affect our lives, both personally and professionally. You should keep a watchful eye on developments, especially those that affect products and industries that particularly interest you.

The other technical issue is data warehousing—another complex technology that we only touch on in this text. At several points in this chapter we have pointed out that organizations often have numerous databases, many of which are of interest to marketers and an equal number of which are relatively inaccessible. This is, in fact, true throughout the organization. Many units have information that could be useful to other groups that they cannot or do not share. Managers have referred, in considerable frustration, to "islands of information" throughout the organization.

Data warehousing is meant to deal with this problem. Building a data warehouse means taking existing data from many parts of the organization and combining it into one central data repository that can be accessed by anyone who has the proper clearance and can be used in a wide variety of data query or manipulation environments. It means other things, chief among them building an enterprise-wide data model out of the many disparate data views that exist within the organization. Technically, it means integrating the necessary data (not all existing data will fit into the enterprise model) into the data warehouse. Because these data exist on many different software and hardware platforms and have great diversity in their nature, detail, and integrity, this is a herculean task. However, it appears to be essential if organizations are to realize a satisfactory return on their investment in data and the required information technology.

Finally, we cannot end this database chapter without once again emphasizing the importance of the subject of consumer privacy. Databases contain a large amount of data about individuals. Some of these data have been collected with the individual's knowledge, as when a customer places an order or responds to a request for information. Even then, however, some customers do not realize that the information is being stored for future use. Other information is collected without the knowledge or permission of the user, as when software on Internet sites collect information about the user's location, computer system, and Internet activity.

Still other information is purchased or compiled by third-party data intermediaries. This kind of information transfer seems especially problematical to many consumers. Many consumers who do not object to typical list rental activities (and, we should note, a substantial number of consumers do object, at least mildly, to transfer of even name and address) do object to transfer of information. To be as precise as possible, one major issue occurs when companies use customer data for purposes other than those anticipated by the customer. An even more critical issue arises when companies provide information to other companies for purposes the customer never envisioned.

Database marketers are becoming more proactive in dealing with privacy issues. Most reputable companies have internal policies that control information use and sharing within and outside the company. Some companies have very specific policies that they share with their customers. This seems to be a very good approach, because unanticipated uses of data appear to be of the greatest concern to consumers.

Summary

Database marketing is the key to contemporary direct marketing. In recent years it has also become an important tool for many traditional marketers of both products and services. Successful database marketing requires technical prowess, focused marketing strategies, and a commitment to diffusing a new approach to marketing throughout the organization. Database marketing offers tremendous opportunity to sharpen both strategy and execution, but it is neither cheap nor quick. It is, however, both the present and the future for many successful marketers.

Discussion Questions and Exercises

1. Explain, in your own words, the meaning of the terms *database* and *database marketing*.
2. What are some of the ways a retail store can use its database for marketing purposes? a bank? a local historical museum?
3. Explain to the owner of a small business how to establish a database.
4. What does the statement, "Information is a strategic resource in today's world" mean? Do you agree or disagree with this statement?
5. For the next few days make a list of business activities you observe that could be providing information for marketing databases.

Suggested Readings

Blattberg, Robert C., and John Deighton. "Interactive Marketing: Exploiting the Age of Addressability." *Sloan Management Review* (fall 1991): 5–14.

Cespedes, Frank V., and H. Jeff Smith. "Database Marketing: New Rules for Policy and Practice." *Sloan Management Review* (summer 1993): 7–22.

Hughes, Arthur M. *The Complete Database Marketer.* Chicago, IL: Probus Publishing Company, 1991.

Jackson, Rob, and Paul Wang. *Strategic Database Marketing.* Lincolnwood, IL: NTC Business Books, 1994.

Nash, Edward L. *Database Marketing: The Ultimate Marketing Tool.* New York: McGraw-Hill, 1993.

Redstone, Ian. "Challenges in Strategic Database Marketing." *Journal of Financial Services Marketing* 1, no. 3 (1997): 249–259.

Roberts, Mary Lou. "The Disciplines of Database Marketing: How to Develop, Maintain and Use a Marketing Database Profitably." *The Journal of Database Marketing* 3, no. 2 (1995): 134–146.

Ventresca, Benjamin J., Jr. "Direct Marketing at Farm Journal, Inc." *Journal of Direct Marketing* (autumn 1991): 44–49.

CHAPTER 9

Profitability and Lifetime Value

In any business the bottom line objective is profit. This word, however, can have many different meanings and time horizons over which it is measured. Also, it is often a quantity that results from the optimization of other, intermediate criteria, these being quite different in various different activities. An example from general marketing is the choosing of advertising media to maximize *awareness,* then *recall,* and then the real bottom line: *response* (purchase), or *dollar profit from the purchase.*

Each area of direct marketing, from decisions to rent a list, to mail offerings, to qualify leads, to other areas, can be evaluated as if it were an auxiliary business of its own. An equivalent of a profit and loss statement can be generated to determine whether to expand or reduce an activity, or more generally, what the optimal (profit maximizing) choice of level or decision should be.

Some of the specific decision-making frameworks for profit maximization have been discussed in previous chapters. For example, the decision-making process with respect to whether to rent a given list of names, and that of how deep into a segmented list to mail (i.e., the "how deep to dip" decision), were addressed in chapter 5. In this chapter we consider some basic—and also some not so basic, but very important—issues in profitability analysis, both in general and in direct marketing in particular. We begin with a discussion of revenue, profit, and contribution considerations, including a very brief introduction to the concept of

Customer Lifetime Value (CLV) and its role in direct marketing decision making; indeed, its role is, or should be, considerable in *all* forms of marketing. Next we address some cost issues; then we put the two considerations together and discuss "profit and loss" statements for direct marketing offers or campaigns. Finally, we revisit the concept of Customer Lifetime Value, and provide an extensive examination of its determination and application.

Revenue, Profit, and Contribution

Robert Kestnbaum lists four basic growth strategies to generate higher revenue and profits in the long run:[1]

1. invest in new customer acquisition
2. invest in new media for presenting offers
3. add products or services to your line
4. expand the number of times customers and prospects are contacted

Each of these strategies can be utilized to achieve specific financial goals:

1. maximize sales
2. maximize profit
3. maximize profit as a percent of sales
4. maximize return on investment (ROI)

Kestnbaum goes on to say that the latter goal is the most meaningful in the long run. One key to achieving this goal is to make certain that no components of revenue, contribution, or profit are overlooked in the process of evaluating this return.

INTRODUCTION TO CUSTOMER LIFETIME VALUE

A core element in determining contribution and profit is to assess the lifetime value of a customer. Lifetime value (let's say for a new customer) is defined as the net present value of all future contributions to overhead and profit. It depends on a variety of considerations:

1. gross contribution (equal to revenue minus costs of sales)
2. relevant promotional costs
3. length of time over which values are projected
4. retention rate
5. discount rate appropriate for marketing investments

Each of these quantities (or at least 1, 2, and 4) is needed on a yearly or purchase cycle basis.

A major use of the calculation of customer lifetime value is for decision making in the areas of customer reactivation and customer acquisition. Julian Simon indicates how important this calculation is, by asking: "How much is it worth to you to get an additional customer? The calculation of the answer to this question is the most important calculation a mail-order merchant makes."[2] Indeed, according to Frederick Reichheld and W. Earl Sasser,

---

[1]Robert Kestnbaum, "Growth Strategies for Direct Marketers," Direct Marketing Association, Release 110.2, January 1984.

[2]Julian Simon, *How to Start a Mail-Order Business,* 4th ed. (New York: McGraw-Hill, 1987), 221.

in most cases companies do not know how much it really costs to lose a customer—primarily because today's accounting systems do not capture the value of a loyal customer.[3] Most companies focus on current period costs and revenues, and they ignore expected cash flows over a customer's lifetime with the company. Theoretically, CLV is the relevant amount to use to determine an upper limit for how much cost should be allocated to customer acquisition.

In the past, direct marketers would mistakenly consider only the initial profits from the current offering to represent the (potential) value of a customer. According to marketing theory, there are cases in which repeat business is not worth worrying about, and the current sale is the only real consideration. The usual example given is sales of encyclopedias. However, in direct marketing, repeat business is often one, if not *the,* major consideration. Most magazine publishers would never attempt to acquire any customers if they did not include repeat business in their calculations of "profit" or "contribution"—as part of the CLV. The profit made in the first year of virtually all magazine subscriptions is less than the one-time cost of setting up the account, plus the cost of the average number of "dry holes" per subscription achieved.

Looking at only the first sale is analogous to using the payback period as the criterion for investment decision making; it is a conservative criterion, one for which the risk is minimal but the opportunity loss is potentially very high. After all, if one decides to incur an acquisition cost only when it is less than the expected profit on the first sale, one will virtually never lose money in the acquisition process. Yet, quite often the decision would then be made not to attempt to acquire a customer when the latter's expected profit *over time* greatly exceeds the acquisition cost, but the *first-year profit* does not exceed the acquisition cost.

Note that we continue to talk about expected or average value of a customer. This is because usually we cannot be sure of the degree to which an individual new customer will be profitable (or, often, whether he or she will be profitable at all!). Statistical analysis can address the issue of predicting profitability, but it still will be a case of averaging, because two customers with exactly the same "profile" will not exhibit precisely the same purchase behavior. It is well known in the field of statistics that the larger the number of observations (e.g., people) comprising an average, the more reliable the average is.

Because of the need to go through an averaging process with respect to many of the parameters making up customer lifetime value, historical data are required for many previously acquired customers. Because we are usually desirous of projecting cash flows out a moderate or large number of years, we need the historical data that go back this same moderate or large number of years; for example, we cannot estimate what percent of our customers who have been with us for four years will remain with us for another year unless we have data on (or at least a list of) customers from four and five years ago.

Just how does one figure out the (expected) lifetime value of a new customer? We consider a simple example, and, at that, just sketch an outline of the process here. (In the appendix, we provide a detailed discussion of this topic.) Suppose that we assume that the margin is the same for all products we offer. This allows us to focus on total dollar sales, and multiply by a constant to determine contribution or profit. (Actually, we can arrive at the same point by taking a weighted average of the margins of the various products we offer, where the weights are sales dollars for each different margin. Let's ignore the difficulty of projecting margins into the future by assuming that these margins are constant over time.) Still, how

[3]Frederick Reichheld and W. Earl Sasser, "Zero Defections: Quality Comes to Services," *Harvard Business Review* (September–October 1990).

do we figure out the (lifetime) total dollars of a customer? Actually, we figure out an expected value of this quantity. We do this by using the average amount of total dollars per customer for each sale, multiplied by the number of repeats. We use our historical database to estimate the repeat rate. For example, in the case of a magazine subscription, we might simply assume that a constant percent of customers drop out each year. In a more general direct marketing situation, we may take a random sample of 200 customers and compute the average repeats per customer; for example:

(1) Number of Repeats	(2) Number of Customers	(1) × (2) Repeats • Customers
0	115	0
1	45	45
2	21	42
3	9	27
4	7	28
5	3	15
>5	0	0
	Total: 200	Total: 157

The average number of purchases per customer, *n,* then equals:

$$n = (200 + 157)/200 = 357/200 = 1.785$$

If it is possible that some of these customers will at some future time make another purchase, then this value could be a slight underestimate. By the way, we should take into consideration, and view as equivalent to repeats, any purchases that come from names of friends provided by the customer. Of course, we cannot always identify which purchases were based on the recommendations of other customers, or which purchases would not have occurred without the other customer; that is why some companies build in an added amount of sales accruing to them from an acquired customer, under the assumption that these "word of mouth" generated sales will occur. Ridgeway Fashions in Virginia assumes a referral rate of 5 percent in terms of assessing the value of a customer.[4]

To find the lifetime value of a customer one must project into the future. Courtheoux provides a methodology for projecting future customer performance, which involves seven steps:[5]

1. Segment customers into a manageable, but distinguishable number of cells, based on recency, frequency, or monetary considerations. Typically, there should be from 25 to 100 cells.

2. Choose a time period for tracking results. Six months is typical.

3. Estimate the contribution to overhead and profit by tracking all revenues and costs associated with all customers.

4. Describe movement of customers across cells.

---

[4] Arthur Hughes, "Evaluating Database Strategy by Lifetime Value," *Journal of Database Marketing* 1, no. 4 (1994).

[5] R. Courtheoux, "Estimating and Applying Customer Name Values," Direct Marketing Association, Release 620.2, January 1986.

5. Project the movement of 1,000 new customers over a number of periods into the future. Proceed enough into the future so that only a small amount of contribution is potentially remaining.

6. Use the number of customers projected for each cell (from step 5) and the financial performances for each cell (from step 3) to calculate the contribution for each period.

7. Apply the cost of capital and find the net present value of the contribution stream.

Courtheoux gives some examples of using this procedure and then goes on to incorporate the results into a variety of different decision-making situations.

PERFORMANCE MEASURES FOR PROFIT AND CONTRIBUTION

In addition to the concept of lifetime value, there are many traditional ratios and other performance measures used to evaluate a direct marketing campaign. Some of the more common performance measures are listed here:

$$\%R = \text{Percent response} = (\text{Numbers of orders/Total quantity mailed}) \times 100$$
$$OPM = \text{Orders per thousand} = \%R \times 10$$
$$CPM = \text{Cost per thousand} = \text{Total cost/(Quantity mailed/1,000)}$$
$$CPO = \text{Cost per order} = CPM/OPM$$
$$ROP(\%) = \text{Return on promotion} = [(\text{Contribution} - CPO)/CPO] \times 100$$
$$C\$R = \text{Cost per dollar raised (in a fund-raising campaign)}$$
$$DAP = \text{Total dollar amount purchased}$$

We note here that some contributions are qualitative (not able to be quantified). This appears to be especially true in the telemarketing arena. An example of this is reported by Stone and Wyman, who evaluate the economics of a GE Answer Center, a free telephone service provided by General Electric that allows customers to call with questions or comments about products, either before or after a purchase is made.[6] When Powell Taylor, then manager of the GE Center, was asked, "How do you know that the millions of dollars spent in building and maintaining the center have been worth it?" he answered, "Surveys have shown that 95 percent of surveyed dealers regard the GE Center to be a 'super idea.'" Obviously, there is no simple way either to quantify the value of the GE Center nor to have done a quantitative analysis prior to its being built. An a priori questionnaire about the center's impact on purchase behavior would have been speculative; likewise, an after-the-fact questionnaire to evaluate the incremental effect of having the center would also be of dubious value.

Costs

In the most general sense, contribution and profit are both defined as the difference between revenue and cost. Yet the terms are not interchangeable. Each is not defined consistently across disciplines, and often not even within the same discipline. The best and simplest working definition for us to use in the direct marketing environment is that *contribution is revenue less variable costs,* whereas *profit is contribution less fixed costs.* Fixed costs are those costs not affected by the amount of revenue (or number of orders or number of items); typical examples are rent and management salaries. Variable costs are costs that vary directly with items sold and are usually per order (e.g., paperwork), per item (e.g., wholesale cost of the item, postage), or per dollar of sale (e.g., taxes). Some fixed costs are called overhead.

---

[6]B. Stone and J. Wyman, "The Mathematics of Telemarketing," *Direct Marketing* (December 1986): 46–52.

One subtlety that needs mentioning is that some variable costs must be expressed as an expectation. For example, costs for bad debts (nonpayment) are incurred for some orders but not others. Yet, it is clear that if you had, for example, 20 weeks in which the number of orders were 200 per week, and another 20 weeks in which the number of orders were 400 per week, the average number of bad debts per week for the latter 20 would likely be about twice the average for the former 20. In other words, we cannot predict the cost for bad debt for a given order, but the total dollar cost surely varies, *on average,* with the number of orders. Bad debt cost, expressed as an expectation per order, is thus a variable cost. Costs for lost shipments, damaged items, and returned items are other variable costs that are expressed as expectations.

There are two key issues involved in correctly using costs in various decision-making situations. One is to make sure that all relevant costs of servicing the customer are included. The other is to include or exclude the fixed costs as relevant costs, as appropriate.

The list of all relevant costs for a direct marketing activity depends on the particular activity. In fact, there are different levels or hierarchies of costs. Consider, for example, a catalog operation. A higher level of costs might be the traditional costs, including the cost of the products sold, cost of shipping and handling, cost of bad debts, costs associated with returns, and so forth. One of the costs could be "cost of producing the catalog." At a level deeper in the hierarchy, we could list the detailed costs of producing the catalog: paper, printing, envelope, photography, consultants to produce copy, and others. At yet a deeper level in the hierarchy, we could detail the costs of the photography (say, into a time component, a black-and-white versus color component, or some other distinction) for purposes of making specific decisions about the catalog.

The most frequent error made in terms of wrong use of costs involves including the fixed cost in a decision situation in which it is unwarranted. (The converse—not including the fixed cost in a situation in which it is appropriate to include it—does not occur often.) This is a problem that pervades not only direct marketing decision making, but one that affects many areas of decision making. The entire notion of a "sunk cost" needs to be understood. Once a (nonrefundable) cost is incurred, it is no longer a consideration in deciding upon strategies for the future. Simon says this well by noting the adage, "Sunk costs are sunk."[7]

ILLUSTRATIVE EXAMPLE OF USE AND MISUSE OF FIXED COSTS

A typical example in which an inferior decision may be reached by misuse of the role of fixed costs is the decision regarding how deep into a segmented list to mail. Consider the following greatly simplified description of the parameters involved. Suppose we have rented a list to which we apply our proprietary segmentation algorithm. Anticipated response rates for the segmented list, rank-ordered by decile, are as follows:

Decile	Response Rate	Decile	Response Rate
0–10	.050	40–50	.027
10–20	.042	50–60	.024
20–30	.036	60–70	.021
30–40	.031	70+	.019

[7] Simon, *How to Start a Mail-Order Business,* 136.

Further, suppose that there is only one product offered for $50 per unit, there are no multiple orders, no returns, no "deadbeats," and no consideration of repeat business is relevant. The product cost is $22 per unit, and all other variable costs (front end and back end, including those that are expectations) total $10 per order. Thus, per order contribution to overhead is $50 – $22 – $10 = $18. Finally, suppose that the in-the-mail cost per thousand pieces mailed is $400.

The correct analysis to determine how deep into this list to mail is reasonably straightforward, given the simplified assumptions being made. In essence, we should mail any decile (we assume, without loss of generality for the point about to be made, that there is no way to segment more finely than by decile) for which the response rate, P, satisfies

$$18 \times (1,000 \times P) > 400$$

or

$$P > .022$$

This result corresponds to mailing the top 60 percent of the rank-ordered list; the 50–60 decile response rate is .024 (higher than .022), whereas the 60–70 decile response rate is .021 (lower than .022).

Now suppose that the decision how deeply into the list to mail is made by somebody who mistakenly includes some fixed (sunk) costs in the calculation. More specifically, suppose that the list rental cost is included, $63 per thousand names, with some selects. After all, one might reason, this is a cost that is associated "directly" with a name and is thus a variable cost. Of course, this reasoning is faulty, and does not reflect the realization that the (rental) cost is a sunk cost—it does not vary with the number of names we choose to mail from (i.e., how "deep we dip" into) the list. Suppose further that an additional $36 per thousand names is allocated to cost to cover such (other) traditional fixed costs as rent, management salaries, copy design expenses, and so forth. The cost figure that would now mistakenly replace the $400 value of the earlier analysis is

$$\$400 + \$63 + \$36 = \$499$$

With this value as input, we should mail any decile for which the response rate, P, satisfies

$$18 \times (1,000 \times P) > 499$$

or

$$P > .028$$

This result corresponds to mailing (only) the top 40 percent of the rank-ordered list. The 30–40 decile response rate is .031 (higher than .028), whereas the 40–50 decile response rate is .027 (lower than .028).

Note that the mistaken use of the fixed costs has resulted in mailing the top 40 percent of the rank-ordered list rather than the top 60 percent. Dollar contribution is reduced (i.e., money is lost!). Assume that the rented list consists of one million names. By not mailing the 40–50 decile, with response rate .027, and by not mailing the 50–60 decile with response rate .024, the number of orders forgone is

$$(100,000 \times .027) + (100,000 \times .024) = 2,700 + 2,400$$

$$= 5,100$$

This represents a lost contribution (excluding the in-the-mail cost) of

$$\$18 \times 5{,}100 = \$91{,}800$$

The in-the-mail cost is

$$200{,}000 \times (\$400/1{,}000) = \$80{,}000$$

and thus the resulting loss in *net contribution* is

$$\$91{,}800 - \$80{,}000 = \$11{,}800$$

In percentage terms, this $11,800 represents a decrease in net contribution of 8.6 percent, from $138,000 (if the top 60 percent of the rank-ordered list is mailed) down to $126,200 (mailing only the top 40 percent). In terms of the number of orders, the decrease is far more dramatic—28.3 percent, from 21,000 orders (if the top 60 percent of the rank-ordered list is mailed) down to 15,900 orders (mailing only the top 40 percent).

If there were a meaningful opportunity for repeat sales (which might suggest the use of customer lifetime value as a decision criterion, rather than the one-time contribution), the loss would be greater than $11,800.

Situations exist that illustrate when one would want to use the "fixed" list rental cost, and possibly other fixed costs (e.g., management salaries), in making a strategic decision. Suppose (somewhat hypothetically) that you have an opportunity to borrow the list at no cost, and note your segmentation results, before having to commit yourself to renting the entire list. The decision whether to rent the (entire) list would use the same optimal net contribution (excluding the rental cost) of $138,000 (by mailing the top 60 percent of the rank-ordered list), and subtract from it the total rental cost of $63,000 (a million names at $63 per thousand); this gives a value of $75,000. Because this amount (not the $138,000!) is greater than zero, the correct decision is to rent the list.

Now suppose (very hypothetically) that the entire business of this firm consists of the use of 10 lists, each identical to the one being discussed. At a $75,000 contribution per list, this results in a total contribution of $750,000. The decision whether this company should continue in business would be decided by taking the $750,000 and subtracting from it the total of all fixed costs (e.g., management salaries, utility bills); it should continue in business only if this difference (not the $750,000) is greater than zero.

If all relevant costs are included in a cost calculation, and fixed costs are not included when inappropriate, the analysis has an excellent chance of leading to the truly best decision. However, the actual implementation of decision analysis still requires adapting to the particulars of the decision situation. Decisions about how deeply into a list to mail involve very different costs and benefits than decisions about the number of products to include in a catalog, or decisions having to do with other areas of direct marketing.

Profit and Loss Statements

The most useful way to represent the results of many direct marketing activities is through a profit and loss worksheet or statement. This is a detailed table of sales (or revenue) and costs. It can also be used as the springboard for a spreadsheet analysis when different sets of assumptions are to be tested or explored. To construct a profit and loss statement one must be able to identify all relevant revenue sources and cost sources. (Note: the importance of the word *relevant* is the core of the previous cost section.) The statement is really just an organized format for assessing the prospects or results of an operation (e.g., promotion or offer, decision whether to rent a list, change of design for a warehouse). Indeed, producing a profit and loss statement is a general business tool that greatly transcends the field of direct marketing. In reality, it is a more narrowly focused version of what is called an *income statement,* a venerable part of any business's profitability summary for a period of time, usually a year.

There is no one design for a profit and loss statement; it depends on the operation being detailed. In fact, even for the same operation, two different people working independently would not arrive at the same exact design. Figure 9.1 lists the categories of a detailed profit and loss statement worksheet for a direct mail offer of one item, according to Pierre Passavant.[8] Passavant goes on to say that this list is too detailed and cumbersome if the objective is a quick review, so he proposes the categories of Figure 9.2 (p. 188) as a summarization.

---

1. Cash selling price
2. Deferred payment price
3. + Shipping and handling

---

4. Average gross order value
5. – Returns (10%)

---

6. Average net sale
7. Cost of goods per sale
8.   per unrefurbished return
9. Order receipt and processing
10.   Business reply postage
11.   Order process and customer setup
12.   Credit card fee (3.5%)
13.   Credit check
14.   Installment billing
15. Customer service
16. Shipping and handling
17. Returns postage
18. Returns handling
18A. Returns refurbishing
19. Bad debt (3%)
20.   Collection effort
21. Premium
22. Promotion (cost per order)
23. Overhead

---

24. Total expense
25. Profit before taxes
26. Profit % to net sales

FIGURE 9.1 Detailed Profit and Loss Statement

Source: Adapted from Pierre Passavant, "Direct Marketing Economics and Budgeting," Direct Marketing Association, Release 600.1, October 1979.

---

[8]Pierre Passavant, "Direct Marketing Economics and Budgeting," Direct Marketing Association, Release 600.1, October 1979.

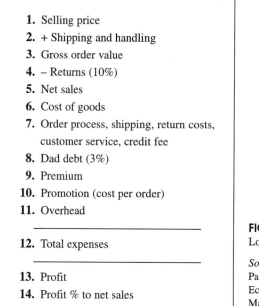

1. Selling price
2. + Shipping and handling
3. Gross order value
4. − Returns (10%)
5. Net sales
6. Cost of goods
7. Order process, shipping, return costs, customer service, credit fee
8. Dad debt (3%)
9. Premium
10. Promotion (cost per order)
11. Overhead
12. Total expenses
13. Profit
14. Profit % to net sales

FIGURE 9.2 Summary Profit and Loss Statement

Source: Adapted from Pierre Passavant, "Direct Marketing Economics and Budgeting," Direct Marketing Association, Release 600.1, October 1979.

Figure 9.3 presents the categories of a profit and loss statement put forth by David Shepard for a similar operation.[9]

Whereas the illustrations in Figures 9.1 and 9.2 are from about 19 years ago, the Figure 9.3 illustration is of more recent vintage (1995). Yet the two detailed profit and loss statements (Figures 9.1 and 9.3) are quite similar, although far from identical. It is natural that they are very much alike—after all, they are modeling the same operation. However, the fact that both statements include 26 entries is more a coincidence than something to be clearly anticipated; in fact, Figure 9.1 really has 27 entries, one being entry 18A. The two statements do differ in some ways. The precise names of the categories are not the same; for example, "Gross sales" on one statement has "Average gross order value" as its counterpart on the other statement. The order of the entries differ as well: "Gross sales" is the first entry on one statement, whereas its "Average gross order value" counterpart is the fourth entry on the other statement. The hierarchy of the categories is not identical on the two statements, either. Figure 9.3 lists all costs (e.g., product costs, order processing costs) as subsets of "Cost of sales," whereas Figure 9.1 has each major cost category in equal status to sales, with subset costs within each category on a lower level. Finally, each statement covers categories that the other does not; in Figure 9.3 there is no listing of profit as a percent of sales (category 26 in Figure 9.1); on the two statements the position of overhead differs, so that in Figure 9.1 the first profit or contribution measure (entry 25) has overhead already subtracted out, whereas in Figure 9.3, contribution (i.e., before overhead is subtracted out) is separately listed as entry 24, and profit is listed as entry 26.

The key point is that the profit and loss statement is for the user's benefit and should be designed to include not only all relevant revenues and costs but also any other costs or

---

[9]David Shepard, *The New Direct Marketing,* 2nd ed. (New York: Richard D. Irwin, 1995).

1. Gross sales

2. Shipping and handling

3. Total revenue

4. Returns

---

5. Net sales

---

6. Cost of sales

7. Product

8.   Net shipments

9.   Nonreusable units

10. Order processing

11.   Reply postage

12.   Setup costs

13.   Credit card costs

14.   Bad check expense

15. Shipping and handling

16. Return processing

17.   Postage

18.   Handling

19.   Refurbishing

---

20. Premium

21. Total cost of sales

---

22. Operating gross margin

23. Promotion expense

---

24. Contribution to overhead and profit

25. Overhead allocation

---

26. Profit

FIGURE 9.3 Profit and Loss Statement for a Single-Shot Promotion

Source: Adapted from David Shepard, *The New Direct Marketing,* 2nd ed. (New York: Richard D. Irwin, 1995).

combination of entries the user believes would be enlightening (e.g., "Profit % to net sales" in Figure 9.1, which is just the ratio of entry 25 to entry 6).

The important qualities for a profit and loss statement are (1) that it should correctly represent the relevant costs and revenues and (2) that the user understand precisely what assumptions correspond with the derivation of the "bottom line" profit measure, as yielded by the profit and loss statement. How costs are treated can totally turn around a go or no-go decision. Some of the potential confusion arises because of the different purposes for which (and different time frames over which) profit and loss statements are used. Assigning—and, thus allocating—overhead to operations is called *full costing.* For a wide variety of purposes, this is appropriate. Accountants argue that each operation must bear its "fair share" of costs, even if some of these costs are not *directly* connected to the operation. After all, if none of the operations were "charged" for items such as rent, salary of the company president, and so forth, every operation would be profitable, but the company would lose money! As noted earlier, however, there are many situations in which treating overhead as an expense against an operation can lead to a significantly reduced profit realization from what is optimal. At best, any allocation of fixed costs is arbitrary.

An alternative is to use what is called *direct costing,* which removes all indirect costs from an operation. This may often be more useful in the majority of decision-making situations. However, for routine reporting purposes, the Accounting Board of the American Institute of Certified Public Accountants has not sanctioned the use of direct costing.

What do and should companies do? They will often keep two sets of profit and loss statements; this may sound like the proverbial "keeping two sets of books," but it is exactly what they should do to capture all sides of the decision-making activity. In the long run, overhead expenses must be accounted for. In the short run, direct costing will more often lead to the correct decision.

As a final point, the reader should be reminded that the profit and loss statements presented were for situations in which no long-term profit considerations were present. For decision making in situations in which customers have lasting value (e.g., if you are examining the profitability of a particular rented list and you are permitted to enter on your house list all names who respond), the customer lifetime value, and not the net contribution or profit from sales on just this one promotion, could be the relevant consideration for the optimal decision to be reached. We treat CLV in detail in an appendix to this chapter.

Summary

Profitability analysis is a matter of considering the appropriate revenues and costs and determining the resulting contribution or profit. This analysis can be performed on a promotion-by-promotion (or list-by-list, item-by-item) basis or by grouping elements together. For example, we might evaluate three rented lists as a tandem. For catalogs, it is often considered more strategically useful to group items by merchandise category, and construct an aggregated profit and loss statement. Also, it may be beneficial in general to aggregate profit and loss statements by profit or cost center.

Profitability analysis potentially is both prospective and retrospective. As noted by John Groman more than a decade ago,[10] combined with the modern computer, profitability analysis can enable you to make outdated the famous quote attributed to Lord Leverhume: "I know I'm totally wasting half of my advertising expenditure but no one can tell me which half." Since then, there has been an increasingly strong movement toward the use of Customer Lifetime Value for the purpose of further refining the definition and delicacy of the concept of profitability.

The role of costs in affecting direct-marketing decision making is major, and is well illustrated by the common use of sending direct response ads through the fax machine. It is now routine for restaurants to fax menus to offices in the area and for florists to fax ads to various corporations. The key to this activity is cost. First of all, the cost of fax machines has

---

[10]John Groman, "Database Driven Marketing," *MDM Review* (April 1986).

been dropping dramatically. Second, "just about everyone" has a fax machine, far exceeding all predictions. Third, the customer pays a small portion of the transmission cost; the sender, of course, pays any expenses associated with the telephone call, but the receiver (customer or prospect) pays for the paper and cost of his fax. Compiled lists for fax machines are now routinely available. According to the *1997 DMA Statistical Fact Book,* fax marketing in 1995 accounted for 1 percent of all direct marketing budgets. Indeed, in 1996, the Operations Benchmark Report sponsored by *Catalog Age* reported that 85 percent of all catalogers who responded received 1 percent to 30 percent of their orders by fax, and 8.7 percent of the responding catalogers received 31 percent to 60 percent of their orders by fax. There already exists a spate of unlisted fax numbers!

As we revise this text, direct ("interactive") marketers are having spirited debate about how to assess the profitability and cost of Internet marketing; should Web sites and Web pages be paid for on the basis of "clicks" (i.e., essentially, inquiries) or on the basis of actual orders? What about folks who might inquire about products on the Web, but not order through the Web, perhaps using another vehicle? Do Web browsers and Web orderers have the same average profit margins as those who inquire or order through other channels? Are the back-end costs the same? We don't yet have a strong handle on these issues, but research is taking place to answer them. The ultimate marketing, ordering, and other uses of the Web, or any vehicle, depend on the profits and costs involved. How could it be otherwise?

Discussion Questions and Exercises

1. Give three examples in which it would clearly be incorrect to include fixed costs in a decision analysis. Give three in which it would clearly be correct to do so.
2. Explain the role of cost of capital in determining the lifetime value of a customer. If the cost of capital were larger, would the lifetime value of a customer rise or fall?
3. Give three examples of a business in which direct marketing customer acquisition decisions would dramatically change, depending on whether the company used Customer Lifetime Value or simply the one-time profitability of the initial purchase. Give three examples of a business in which there would be absolutely no change in direct marketing customer acquisition decisions.
4. Give three examples in which the contribution of a direct marketing activity is qualitative.
5. For the numerical example discussed in the Cost section of the chapter, why is it that mailing 33 percent fewer names than was optimal (mailing the top 40 percent rather than the top 60 percent) resulted not in a 33 percent drop in contribution but in only an 8.6 percent drop in contribution?
6. Discuss the similarities and differences between a profit and loss statement and the traditional income statement.

Suggested Readings

Blattberg, Robert C., and John Deighton. "Manage Marketing by the Customer Equity." *Harvard Business Review* (July–August 1996): 136–144.

Gale, Bradley T. *Managing Customer Value.* New York: The Free Press, 1994.

Geller, Lois. "Customer Retention Begins with the Basics." *Direct Marketing* (September 1997): 58–62.

Hughes, Arthur, and Paul Wang. "Media Selection for Database Marketing." *Journal of Direct Marketing* 9, no. 1 (winter 1995): 79–84.

Appendix: Customer Lifetime Value

Customer Lifetime Value (CLV) has been a mainstay concept in direct marketing for many years and has been increasingly considered in the field of general marketing. However, for the most part, what has been written about it has (1) extolled its use as a decision-making criterion, (2) put forth isolated numerical examples of its calculation and determination, and (3) discussed in general terms its proper role in customer acquisition decisions and customer acquisition or retention trade-offs. There has been little, if any, discussion of CLV from a systematic modeling perspective.

This appendix presents a series of models for determination of CLV and considers various insights about its use. The choice of which precise circumstances and models we describe is based on a systematic categorization and on assumptions grounded in customer marketing behavior. Specific selected managerial applications of CLV in the direct marketing arena are also offered.

Since the early 1980s, the field of marketing has undergone a major directional change in both its theory and practice, for the most part embracing many common direct marketing principles, especially that of relationship marketing.[11] At the core of relationship marketing is, of course, the development and maintenance of long-term relationships with customers rather than simply a series of discrete transactions. This is to be achieved by creating superior customer value and satisfaction; ideally, a "loyalty" that benefits both parties is fostered.

However, being overly enthusiastic about the concept of relationship marketing, many practitioners have become involved in losing relationships. Relationship marketing is costly. It might not pay to maintain long-term relationships, at least not all the time and not with all customers. Customers with low switching costs and short time horizons might not be financially attractive to the firm.[12]

Ultimately, marketing is the art of attracting and keeping profitable customers;[13] this is certainly true of direct marketing. A company should not try to pursue and satisfy every customer. What makes a customer profitable? Philip Kotler and Gary Armstrong define a profitable customer as "a person, household, or company whose revenues over time exceed, by an acceptable amount, the company costs of attracting, selling, and servicing that customer." This excess is exactly what Customer Lifetime Value is! Robert Blattberg and John Deighton acknowledge that *marketing talk is beginning to sound like direct-marketing talk.*[14] The *1997 Direct Marketing Statistical Fact Book* reported that, in 1996, 30 percent of the responders to the Annual List Usage Survey use CLV in their decision-making processes. Also, 50 percent of the responders to the *Catalog Age* Marketing Benchmark Report indicated that their CLV exceeded $200. In 1995, this had been indicated by only 42 percent of the responders.

DETERMINATION OF CLV

Determining the customer lifetime value, or economic worth of a customer, is, in principle, a straightforward exercise. To calculate customer lifetime value, you project the net cash flows that your firm expects to receive from the customer over time. Next, you calculate the

[11]R. Morgan and S. Hunt, "The Commitment—Trust Theory of Relationship Marketing," *Journal of Marketing* (July 1994): 20–38.

[12]B. Jackson, *Winning and Keeping Industrial Customers* (Lexington, MA: Lexington Books, 1985).

[13]P. Kotler and G. Armstrong, *Principles of Marketing,* 7th ed. (Upper Saddle River, NJ: Prentice Hall, 1996).

[14]Robert C. Blattberg and John Deighton, "Manage Marketing by the Customer Equity," *Harvard Business Review* (July–August 1996): 136–144.

present value of that stream of cash flows. In practice, however, estimating the net cash flows to be received from that customer can be a very challenging task. The questions to be answered before making the necessary computations are not always easy to handle: How many customers you can attract, given specific acquisition spending? How large will be the initial sale to a customer? What is the probability that a customer will buy additional products or services from your company over time? How does this probability change with the spending you make on promotion? When will a customer completely stop buying from your company? Some specific situations require yet additional sets of questions.

TYPES OF CUSTOMER BEHAVIOR

Jackson groups industrial buyers into two major categories: (1) "lost-for-good" and (2) "always-a-share."[15] Her lost-for-good model assumes that a customer is either totally committed to the vendor or totally lost and committed to some other vendor. In the second model, always-a-share, the customer can easily experiment with new vendors. The customer's cost to switch vendors (switching costs), which can be essentially zero, or can be very expensive (e.g., if you had previously bought large amounts of Macintosh equipment, consider the cost of switching to IBM), constitutes a major factor in implying one behavior or the other. R. Dwyer applied Jackson's ideas in direct marketing and showed its implications for CLV.[16] A customer retention model is used to model lost-for-good situations. In this model, a retention rate (or retention probability) is estimated, traditionally based on historical data. The retention rate is the probability that the account will remain with the vendor for the next purchase, provided that the customer has bought from that vendor on each previous purchase.

A customer migration model characterizes the always-a-share case. In it, the recency of last purchase is used to predict the possibility of repeat purchase in a period. The argument that one may use purchase history, including recency, to predict repeat purchase behavior is plausible. In the customer retention model, a customer who stops dealing with a company is considered as lost-for-good. Returning customers are therefore treated as new ones. Although this model might be more applicable in cases in which switching costs are higher and customer commitment is long term, other cases, in which customers may discontinue their purchase of a particular product or brand only temporarily, also exist. A migration model is likely more applicable in such cases.

CUSTOMER LIFETIME VALUE MODELS

The CLV models described in this appendix include typical cases of customer behavior. The two models offered by Dwyer are considered.[17] The first three discussed in this appendix address customer retention situations. Case 4 deals with a customer migration model. Case 1 is the simplest; it assumes yearly cycles of purchase (e.g., purchases every Christmas or yearly charitable solicitations). Of course, for many products, the relevant purchase cycle is not one year (e.g., automobile purchases or leases). The two parts of case 2 are direct extensions of case 1, for which the cycle is assumed to be shorter (case 2a) or longer (case 2b) than one year.

---

[15] Jackson, *Winning and Keeping Industrial Customers.*

[16] R. Dwyer, "Customer Lifetime Valuation to Support Marketing Decision Making," *Journal of Direct Marketing* 8, no. 2 (1989).

[17] Ibid.

Profits per customer are not necessarily constant per cycle. A major advantage in retaining customers is that the profits generated by them tend to accelerate over time. Reichheld and Sasser reported examples of accelerating profits in credit card use and other products and services.[18] They attributed the acceleration in customers' profits to four reasons. First, revenues from customers typically grow over time. For example, customers who newly acquire a credit card use it slowly at the beginning; in the second year and subsequently, if they stay with that company and card, they become more accustomed to using the credit card and balances grow. Second, existing customers are more efficient and this usually results in cost savings. Their familiarity with the company's products makes them less dependent on its employees for advice and help. Third, satisfied customers act as referrals who recommend the company to others (recommending, in addition, to *themselves* by cross-buying). Fourth, for some products, old (i.e., existing) customers pay effectively higher prices than new ones. This is sometimes due to the trial discounts available only to brand-new customers; this is extremely common in soliciting magazine subscriptions, for example. Case 3 specifically addresses situations in which profits per customer change over time.

Although acquisition costs, the costs incurred to attract (i.e., acquire) a customer, are obviously an important input value for a variety of direct marketing decision-making contexts, they are not specifically considered in our determination of CLV here. Direct marketing managers can, however, consider CLV as we compute it as the maximum value they are willing to incur as the acquisition cost per customer. Acquisition costs exceeding this value indicate the existence of unprofitable customers. We also do not consider fixed costs in determining CLV. To compute CLV, we discount the difference between the revenues and both "cost of sales" and promotion (e.g., direct mail) expenses incurred to retain customers. Cost of sales includes the cost of goods sold and the cost of order processing, handling, and shipping. Promotion costs incurred to retain existing customers, such as sending personalized greeting cards and gifts and general promotional expenditures, excluding those directly oriented toward acquisition, are referred to as retention costs.

Case 1

We start with a simple case to illustrate the concept. In this case we make three assumptions: (1) sales take place once a year, (2) yearly spending to retain customers and the customer retention rate both remain constant over time, (3) revenues achieved per customer per year remain the same. In subsequent cases, we relax assumptions 1 and 3, as well as the fixed retention rate in assumption 2.

In this case, as in the other cases with constant yearly net contribution margin per customer (cases 2a, 2b, and 4), we assume a specific timing of cash flows. Revenues from sales and the corresponding cost of sales both take place at the time of sale; the first sales transaction occurs at the time of the determination of CLV, which may be thought of as the "moment of customer acquisition." All promotional expenses (except for case 2b) are approximated relative to uniform dispersion to occur at the middle of the purchase cycle. This assumption results in slightly different discounting of these two sets of cash flows, as the models in the constant net contribution margin cases show.

---

[18]Reichheld and Sasser, "Zero Defections."

NOTATION

GC is the (expected) yearly gross contribution margin per customer. It therefore equals revenues minus cost of sales.

M is the (relevant) promotion costs per customer per year.

n is the length, in years, of the period over which you want to project the cash flows.

r is the yearly retention rate—the proportion of customers expected to continue buying the company's goods or services in the subsequent year.

d is the yearly discount rate (appropriate for direct marketing investments).

An illustration of cash flows in this case follows:

```
Now
I-----------*----------I-----------*----------I----------*----------I . . . . . . I----------*----------I
      Year 1                 Year 2                 Year 3                          Year n
```

where the **I**'s denote cash flows (both inflows and outflows) pertaining to sales transactions (i.e., *GC*). The asterisks indicate the approximate timing of promotional expenses. Therefore,

$$CLV = \left\{ GC \times \sum_{i=0}^{n} \left[\frac{r^i}{(1 + d)^i} \right] \right\} - \left\{ M \times \sum_{i=1}^{n} \left[\frac{r^{i-1}}{(1 + d)^{i-0.5}} \right] \right\} \tag{1}$$

The length of the projection period, *n*, highly depends on the industry or product. The *GC* and *M* cash flows are discounted differently because, as mentioned previously, they are assumed to take place at two different time instants. The exponent 0.5 in equation (1) reflects the approximation of the promotion expenses to all occur at the middle of each purchase cycle.

Numerical Example: A typical example of this case could be an insurance company trying to estimate its CLV. Suppose that the company pays, on average, $50 per year per customer on promotional expenses (e.g., mailing reminder cards and policy updates, retention-oriented commercials). The yearly retention rate is 75 percent. The period of cash flows projection is 10 years. The yearly gross contribution per customer is expected to amount to $260. An appropriate discount rate for marketing activities is 20 percent. Then, according to equation (1),

$$CLV = \left\{ 260 \times \sum_{i=0}^{10} \left[\frac{(.75)^i}{(1 + .2)^i} \right] \right\} - \left\{ 50 \times \sum_{i=1}^{10} \left[\frac{(.75)^{i-1}}{(1 + .2)^{i-0.5}} \right] \right\} = \$568.78$$

Case 2

Here we relax the assumption of case 1 that sales occur annually. The following cases are concerned with time periods that are shorter (case 2a) or longer (case 2b) than one year. The time periods are, however, still assumed to be equal in length.

Case 2.a We consider first the case in which sales occur more frequently than once a year. Let *p* be the number of cycles (i.e., "transactions" or sales) per year. For instance, *p* = 2 for semiannual sales, and $p = 4$ for quarterly sales; that is, p equals 12 divided by the cycle time in months. Then,

$$CLV = \left\{ GC' \times \sum_{i=0}^{pn} \left[\frac{(r')^i}{(1 + d)^{i/p}} \right] \right\} - \left\{ M' \times \sum_{i=1}^{pn} \left[\frac{(r')^{i-1}}{(1 + d)^{(i-0.5)/p}} \right] \right\} \qquad (2)$$

NOTATION

GC' is the (expected) gross contribution margin per customer per sales cycle.

M' is the promotion costs per customer per sales cycle.

r' is the retention rate per sales cycle.

As in case 1, d is the yearly discount rate (appropriate for marketing investments). The number of periods is pn; although it is not necessary that p be an integer (e.g., $p = 2.4$ for 5 purchase cycles per year), we assume that n has a value such that pn is an integer; this simply assures that the projection period does not conclude in the middle of a purchase cycle. The power of $(1 + d)$ is divided by the number of periods per year because d is indeed still the annual discount rate. The adoption of a nonannual discount rate would imply a change in the financial market; that is not the case here. The 0.5 is used in equation (2) because promotion expenditures in a cycle are assumed to occur in the middle of that cycle.

Numerical Example: A typical example of this case could be a health club trying to estimate its CLV. Suppose that customers subscribe for services on a semiannual basis. The company pays $25 per customer semiannually on promotion. The semiannual retention rate is 80 percent. The period of cash flows projection is $n = 4$ years. The gross contribution margin per semiannual subscription amounts to $125. An appropriate discount rate for marketing activities is 20 percent. Then, based on equation (2),

$$CLV = \left\{ 125 \times \sum_{i=0}^{8} \left[\frac{(.8)^i}{(1 + .2)^{i/2}} \right] \right\} - \left\{ 25 \times \sum_{i=1}^{8} \left[\frac{(.8)^{i-1}}{(1 + .2)^{(i-0.5)/2}} \right] \right\} = \$354.69$$

Case 2.b   In this case, sales transactions occur less frequently than once a year. In cases of durables, replacements often occur only every few years. Let q be the length of a cycle or the number of years between two consecutive sales. For example, if a car is leased every three years, then $q = 3$. Then,

$$CLV = \left\{ GC' \times \sum_{i=0}^{n/q} \left[\frac{(r')^i}{(1 + d)^{iq}} \right] \right\} - \left\{ M' \times \sum_{i=1}^{n} \left[\frac{(r')^{(i-1)/q}}{(1 + d)^{i-.5}} \right] \right\} \qquad (3)$$

We assume in this case that (1) promotion costs are approximated to occur at the middle of each year of the cycle, and (2) sales and the corresponding cost of sales occur once per purchase cycle, with the first transaction taking place at the time of the acquisition or determination of *CLV*. Cash flows are illustrated as follows (note that the number of purchase cycles, equals n/q):

Now

```
I---*---x---*---x . . . x---*---I---*---x---*---x . . . x---*---I . . . I---*---x---*---x . . . x---*---I
  Year 1  Year 2       Year q   Year q+1                                              Year n
```

where the **I**'s, the beginning of purchase cycles, denote cash flows (both inflows and out-flows) pertaining to sales transactions (i.e., *GC*). The asterisks show the approximate timing of promotional expenses (assumed to be the middle of each year). One may relax the assumptions concerning the timing of cash flows without major changes in the model. The value of r' pertains to a full cycle.

Numerical Example: Consider the case of a car dealership where customers lease cars for three years. The company pays $95 per year per customer on promotion. The cyclical retention rate is only 30 percent. The average gross contribution margin per car lease per cycle is $7,000. An appropriate discount rate is 20 percent. The company wants to project its CLV for the next 12 years (12/3 = 4 purchase cycles). In this case,

$$CLV = \left\{ 7,000 \times \sum_{i=0}^{4} \left[\frac{(.3)^i}{(1 + .2)^{3i}} \right] \right\} - \left\{ 95 \times \sum_{i=1}^{12} \left[\frac{(.3)^{(i-1)/3}}{(1 + .2)^{i-.5}} \right] \right\} = \$8,273.31$$

Note that the lessee likely pays the lease cost monthly. However, the lessor receives payment up front, irrespective of the lessee's financial choice.

To use equation (3), n/q, as noted in case 2a for *pn*, should be an integer. Again this corresponds with the projection period not concluding in the middle of a purchase cycle. The values of p and q are not chosen by the manager, but are based on the nature of the product and its related purchase cycle. However, the manager can always set n, the number of years over which he wants to project cash flows, in a manner that leads to the required integer value. Given that the manager is likely interested in estimating CLV for a certain number of complete purchase cycles, this "restriction" is generally a minimal one.

Case 3

In cases 1 and 2 (a and b) we assume that the gross contribution margin (*GC*) per purchase cycle and relevant promotion costs (*M*) per year per customer remain constant. In case 3, we address situations with *GC* and *M* per customer potentially nonconstant over time. For example, in the case of accelerating profits, one could have an S-shaped (increasing) customer life-cycle profit (*GC* – *M*) pattern—that is, one that first increases at an increasing rate (i.e., convex), and then, at some point, increases at a decreasing rate (i.e., concave).

Of course, to estimate customer lifetime value in this situation, one needs to estimate the specific customer profit function over time, $\pi(t)$. The example function for this case first grows at an increasing rate (up to point *g*), then at a decreasing rate, and has an upper asymptote. The upper asymptote reflects a ceiling that profits are not expected to exceed. (Note: $\pi(t)$ represents profit at time *t* and is not cumulative.)

$$\pi(t) = \pi_1(t) = ht^2 + v \qquad\qquad \text{for } t \leq g$$

$$\pi(t) = \pi_2(t) = \pi_1(g) + [N(1 - e^{-t+g})] \qquad\qquad \text{for } t > g$$

(4)

where h, g, v, and N are all positive constants. The rate at which profit grows over time affects the value of h. The value g is the time at which the inflection point in the profit curve occurs, and $[\pi_1(g) + N]$ is the expected ceiling for profits reached asymptotically. Companies typically use historical data to estimate those values. The intercept v is the company's gross contribution margin from the *first* sale. Sometimes, this value is not especially high; in some cases, it might even be near zero, and on rare occasion, negative. (Recall that we are not including acquisition costs; if we did include them, first year "profit" would often be negative.)

The *CLV* in this case is computed as follows:

$$CLV = \sum_{t=0}^{n} \left\{ \pi(t) \times \left[\frac{r^t}{(1 + d)^t} \right] \right\} \tag{5}$$

where $\pi(t)$ is the profit per customer in year t. In this case, as in case 1, we assume a yearly cycle. Applications to shorter or longer periods, as in cases 2a and 2b, are straightforward.

Based on equations (4) and (5), with g being an integer, we have

$$CLV = \sum_{t=0}^{g} \left\{ [ht^2 + v] \left[\frac{r^t}{(1 + d)^t} \right] \right\}$$

$$+ \sum_{t=g+1}^{n} \left\{ [(hg^2 + v) + N(1 - e^{-t+g})] \left[\frac{r^t}{(1 + d)^t} \right] \right\} \tag{6}$$

The case of accelerated profits was purposely chosen as the example of cases in which profits per customer change over time. This choice is based on the fact that increased profit over time was singled out by previous researchers as a frequently occurring case.[19] The same general approach of equation (5) can be applied to other cases for which change in profit over time exhibits other patterns, including decreasing ones.

As noted earlier, *profits* means *net contribution margin*. For simplicity, we did not separate gross contribution margin, *GC*, from promotional expenses, *M*. Given separate functions for *GC* and *M*, one can follow the same procedure applied in this case to discount *GC* and *M* separately, and then combine them, as in the previous cases.

Numerical Example: Consider the case of a credit card company that expects its profit per newly acquired customer to accelerate over time. Profit per customer starts at a low level of $20. This profit is, however, expected to grow at an increasing rate until year 5. Afterward, profit will continue to grow, but at a decreasing rate. Profit is not expected to exceed a ceiling of $200. The retention rate is 90 percent, and the discount rate is 20 percent. Profit per customer can be approximated as a function of time as follows:

$$\pi(t) = 4t^2 + 20 \qquad\qquad \text{for } t \leq 5$$

$$\pi(t) = 120 + [80(1 - e^{-t+5})] \qquad\qquad \text{for } t > 5$$

Note that $\pi(5) = \$120$. If this company is projecting its cash flows for the next eight years, then its *CLV* is computed as follows:

$$CLV = \sum_{t=0}^{5} \left\{ (4t^2 + 20) \left[\frac{(.9)^t}{(1 + .2)^t} \right] \right\}$$

$$+ \sum_{t=6}^{8} \left\{ [(4 \times 5^2 + 20) + 80(1 - e^{-t+5})] \left[\frac{(.9)^t}{(1 + .2)^t} \right] \right\} = \$212.163$$

---

[19]Frederick Reichheld, *The Loyalty Effect* (Boston: Harvard Business School Press, 1996).

TABLE A9.1 Purchase Probabilities—Customer Migration Model

Recency Cell	Probability of Purchase (P_{t-j}) (for the current year, t)
1 if last purchase was in year ($t-1$)	0.30
2 if last purchase was in year ($t-2$)	0.20
3 if last purchase was in year ($t-3$)	0.15
4 if last purchase was in year ($t-4$)	0.05
5 if last purchase was in year ($t-5$)	0.00

Source: Adapted from R. Dwyer, "Customer Lifetime Valuation to Support Marketing Decision Making," *Journal of Direct Marketing* 8, no. 2 (1989): 73–81.

Cases with accelerating customer profit show the importance of retaining customers. Any change in retention rate is expected to have a greater effect on CLV when profit per customer is accelerating than cases when profit per customer is constant over time. This is mainly due to the fact that the compounded retention rate is multiplied by a growing profit value in computing CLV. A. Hughes and P. Wang have shown the dramatic effect of a lower retention rate on CLV in the case of credit card customers.[20] In this example, dropping the yearly retention rate from 90 percent to 80 percent results in a drop of 37 percent in CLV (new *CLV* = $134.68).

Case 4

The previous cases assume a shrinking customer base over time, in which lost customers are treated as new ones if they return. In case 4, we use purchase history, particularly recency, to predict repeat purchase behavior. In his "Customer Migration Model," R. Dwyer uses the recency of last purchase to predict the probability of repeat purchase for the next period.[21] For ease of presentation, we first use Dwyer's example to present the case under discussion. We then provide the necessary equations to compute CLV. The sales cycle is assumed to be annual. The length of the cycle is not, however, a critical factor in constructing the model. We drop from Dwyer's model data on costs and earnings, and focus on the most critical factor in the model: the number of customers per year.

The model uses empirical evidence of purchase recency to predict repeat purchase behavior. From past data, the purchase propensities of each recency cell have been estimated. Table A9.1 summarizes the probability of purchase for members of each recency cell.

Figure A9.1 (p. 200) shows the number of customers over a four-year period after acquisition, starting with a base of 1,000 customers.

Equation (7) shows how to compute C_i, the number of customers in year *i*:

$$C_i = \sum_{j=1}^{i} \left[C_{i-j} \times P_{t-j} \times \prod_{k=1}^{j} (1 - P_{t-j+k}) \right] \text{ with } P_t = 0 \tag{7}$$

,

---

[20]A. Hughes and P. Wang, "Media Selection for Database Marketers," *Journal of Direct Marketing* 9, no. 1 (1995): 79–84.

[21]Dwyer, "Customer Lifetime Valuation," 73–81.

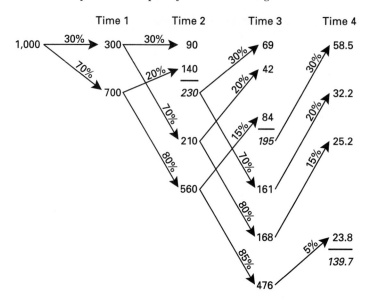

FIGURE A9.1 Number of Customers—Customer Migration Model

Source: Adapted from R. Dwyer, "Customer Lifetime Valuation to Support Marketing Decision Making," *Journal of Direct Marketing* 8, no. 2 (1989): 73–81.

For instance, the number of customers in year 4 in the example of Figure A9.1 is:

$$C_4 = [C_{4-1}P_{t-1}(1 - P_{t-1+1})] + [C_{4-2}P_{t-2}(1 - P_{t-2+1})(1 - P_{t-2+2})]$$

$$+ [C_{4-3}P_{t-3}(1 - P_{t-3+1})(1 - P_{t-3+2})(1 - P_{t-3+3})]$$

$$+ [C_{4-4}P_{t-4}(1 - P_{t-4+1})(1 - P_{t-4+2})(1 - P_{t-4+3})(1 - P_{t-4+4})]$$

$$= [C_3P_{t-1}(1 - P_t)] + [C_2P_{t-2}(1 - P_{t-1})(1 - P_t)]$$

$$+ [C_1P_{t-3}(1 - P_{t-2})(1 - P_{t-1})(1 - P_t)]$$

$$+ [C_0P_{t-4}(1 - P_{t-3})(1 - P_{t-2})(1 - P_{t-1})(1 - P_t)]$$

$$= [195(.3)(1 - 0)] + [230(.2)(1 - .3)(1 - 0)]$$

$$+ [300(.15)(1 - .2)(1 - .3)(1 - 0)]$$

$$+ [1,000(.05)(1 - .15)(1 - .2)(1 - .3)(1 - 0)]$$

$$= 58.5 + 32.2 + 25.2 + 23.8$$

$$= 139.7$$

Then, in general, in the always-a-sale case, applying the same assumptions of cash flow timing of case 1, company CLV is computed as follows:

$$CLV = \left\{ GC \left\{ C_0 + \left[\sum_{i=1}^{n} \sum_{j=1}^{i} C_{i-j} P_{t-j} \times \prod_{k=1}^{j} (1 - P_{t-j+k}) \right] / (1 + d)^i \right\} \right.$$

$$\left. - M \left\{ \frac{C_0}{(1 + d)^{.5}} + \left[\sum_{i=1}^{n} \sum_{j=1}^{i} C_{i-j} P_{t-j} \times \prod_{k=1}^{j} (1 - P_{t-j+k}) \right] / (1 + d)^{i+.5} \right\} \right\} / C_0,$$

with $P_t = 0$ $\qquad\qquad$ (8)

where C_0 is the initial customer base at the time of the determination of CLV (acquisition). Note that, in this case, we assume that sales, and the corresponding cost of sales, take place once a year; the first transaction is at acquisition. Promotion expenses occur at the middle of each year.

CONCLUSIONS

Companies are realizing that when operating in mature markets and facing stiffer competition, the development of a profitable relationship with customers is a critical success factor. To know whether a relationship is profitable, one needs to be able to quantify this relationship. CLV does this.

Determining CLV can help managers in making decisions through determining the impact of different courses of action on the value of CLV, including obtaining the difference in profitability among various market segments (e.g., different lists, different sources of customers, customers "reached" through different media—whatever the direct marketer wishes to consider a segment). The CLV determination can also help determine the effect of adopting a marketing strategy, with its resulting acquisition and retention rates, costs, and trade-offs. For example, the adoption of a price-skimming strategy typically results in a lower acquisition rate. Although fewer in number, however, these acquired customers might show a higher degree of persistence in their choice of a seller. The comparison of expected CLV in the case of price penetration to that of price skimming would enable a direct marketer, or any manager, to make a more informed pricing choice. CLV determination can also be used to decide how to allocate promotional budgets between acquisition and retention spending. Blattberg and Deighton have presented a procedure to determine the optimal acquisition and retention costs, based on the maximization of customer lifetime value.[22]

The basic insight that comes from looking at the economics of customer lifetime value is that one begins to view customers as ongoing relationships rather than transactions. Techniques that focus on a short-term impact of marketing strategies do not necessarily draw a correct picture for managerial use.

---

[22]Blattberg and Deighton, "Manage Marketing by the Customer Equity."

CHAPTER 10

Testing Direct Marketing Programs

Throughout this book you have read frequent references to the fact that direct marketing is the measurable element of the marketing discipline. This chapter covers another aspect of the measurability of direct marketing—the testing of many aspects of direct mail campaigns.

The basic philosophy of testing, as espoused by direct marketers, is a straightforward and very appealing one. Put simply, there is no reason to invest a large amount of resources in a direct mail program unless there is a high probability of success (or at least a high risk to reward trade-off). Because direct marketers have control over outbound communication to their customers and prospects (e.g., how many pieces are mailed and to whom) as well as inbound communication from customers and prospects (responses), they are able to estimate the probability of success with a high degree of accuracy. In addition, the expected (i.e., average) contribution per response can also be closely estimated. Marketing effort can then be allocated to programs with the highest expected value for those individual programs; or to programs with the highest (expected) lifetime value, as discussed in chapter 9; or to programs that optimize whatever criterion is chosen.

You may already realize that concepts from basic statistics courses are important in studying direct mail testing. Some of the concepts covered in this chapter are ones that you have already learned, but perhaps have not applied to marketing situations or to direct marketing situations in particular; other topics in this chapter are likely to be new to you. In addition, ideas about experimental design that are only briefly mentioned in most marketing research courses are introduced and applied to direct marketing testing situations.

What Should Be Tested?

There is universal agreement among direct marketers about the importance of testing. In fact, one can liken the adage in real estate about what is important in selling a piece of land or a house—"three things: location, location, location"—to what is of critical importance in direct marketing, and, especially in direct mail—"three things: testing, testing, testing." What should be tested? The conventional wisdom is to "test the big things." The list that follows comes from a compilation of suggestions in a variety of texts, augmented by the authors' experience:

> The product or service itself
>
> Positioning alternatives
>
> Media choices
>
> Selection of lists
>
> Whom on the list to mail
>
> Variations of the offer (e.g., price)
>
> Media options
>
> Format
>
> Copy
>
> Other creative alternatives
>
> Timing

Some of the listed items are more expensive than others to test. And, of course, the cost of testing must be considered in the decision of whether to test. It is rare that all of these items are relevant to any one direct response program. Ultimately, the decision of which items to test ends up being, to a degree, program specific. Yet, it is rare to encounter a program that would not be enhanced by testing *some* items (if not many of them). When more than one item is tested, the prospect of *interaction effects* (i.e., "synergy") among the items must be considered. Interaction effects may lead to a case in which individual testing of lists identifies list A as the best, and individual testing of positionings identifies positioning X as the best, but the (A, X) *combination* of list and positioning is not the best. This issue relates to what is called an "experimental design," discussed later in the chapter.

Sampling

The heart of any testing situation is *sampling*. We test by taking a sample; the whole point of sampling is that we want to get an idea of ("estimate," in more formal statistical parlance) what is likely to happen if we should "roll out" to the entire population of interest. Indeed, sampling is prevalent in our society. We take a small sample of blood to infer about the entire body's blood. We takes polls (basically another word for samples) on a myriad of things and see the results reported in the media. We get "marketing research" telephone calls soliciting our opinion on a variety of things; not *everybody* gets these calls about each particular item— at just one minute per call, it would take about 200 *years* to call 100 million people!

The fact is that we can usually get an estimate of what we want to know (e.g., the response rate if we choose this list or that list, or this positioning or that positioning) that is sufficiently close to the truth by sampling only a small subset of the entire group or population to which we wish to apply the results.

In general, when sampling, we want to take a *random sample*. This means, in essence, that the names mailed to, or the people broadcast to (in terms of, say, cities chosen) comprise a selection from the population to which an extrapolation is to be made, in which every subset of the population (of the selected sample size) has an equal chance of comprising the sample. After all, one is never sampling solely to find out who the buyers are *in the sample;* it is to be able to extrapolate, or generalize, to a larger (most often, very large) group, of which the sample is a subset. Random sampling guarantees an "unbiasedness" or "representativeness" of sorts, at least on average.

When direct marketers test, they often (or should) use a form of what is referred to as *systematic sampling*. In direct mail or telemarketing applications it is called N*th name sampling*. This technique involves having a complete list of names, picking a random starting point for a sample, and then selecting every 5th, or 10th, or, in general, N*th name, so that the desired number of names is obtained. If N is the number of names on the list, and n is the number of names to be sampled, we compute (N/n), round it off to the lowest whole number (integer), say R, and pick a random starting point between 1 and R (i.e., the equivalent of choosing a number out of a hat, from the integers 1, 2, 3, . . . R), and then sample each Rth name after that. For example, if we wanted to sample 5,000 names out of a list of 103,000 names, we would compute 103,000/5,000 = 20.6, and round it to 20. We would then pick a random name between the first and the 20th, and then each 20th name after that. This could result in taking, for example, names 13, 33, 53, . . . , 99,993 as the sample. This technique is actually *superior* to simply taking a random sample of 5,000 names from the 103,000. That is because lists are usually ordered in some specific way (the most common are by zip code; or by alphabet within zip code; or, for a list of purchasers, by time since first entering the list). The N*th name sampling method more or less guarantees a true cross section of names along the dimensions on which the list is ordered. Simple random sampling guarantees only that *on average* this representativeness is achieved. If the list is not ordered in any identifiable way, the N*th name method is, in essence, identical to simple random sampling.

Estimation and Sample Size

Before we explore the technical logic of formal statistical testing, it is useful to first consider the basics of sample size determination for the purpose of estimating a response rate, or the difference between two response rates. The subsequent section addresses the "economics" of whether we should sample and test. (Most often the answer will be "yes," but it is insightful to understand how that decision should be reached.)

The sample size needed to estimate an unknown quantity such as a response rate, p (or any quantity that is a proportion between 0 and 1), in a test situation depends on four basic quantities:

1. The accuracy desired, e; a typical value might be $e = .005$, meaning that we get an estimate $\pm.005$ from the true value of the unknown quantity, p. (Note: $e = 0$ means you must sample the entire list.)

2. The "confidence" you have of achieving this accuracy. The customary value for this confidence is .95 (95 percent), or possibly .90 (90 percent). (Note: a confidence of 1 [100 percent] means you must sample the entire list!).

3. The maximum value of p that is even remotely possible. Actually, it is the nearest possible value to .5, but in virtually all cases that means the maximum possible value. For example, if it is "incredibly unlikely that $p > .10$," use .10 as this maximum value. This value is called p_{max}.

4. The size of the population, N (i.e., the size of the entire list). If N is quite large, say, >100,000, we can ignore N.

Then, with a large N, and if the confidence value is chosen to be .95, it can be shown that

$$n = \frac{4 \times p_{max} \times (1 - p_{max})}{e^2} \qquad (1)$$

Then,

if $p_{max} = .03$, $e = .005$, then $n = 4,656$
if $p_{max} = .06$, $e = .005$, then $n = 9,024$
if $p_{max} = .06$, $e = .01$, then $n = 2,256$

If we change the confidence factor to .90, the 4 in equation (1) changes to 2.7, and the three sample sizes also change:

$n = 3,165$
$n = 6,136$
$n = 1,534$

With N not so large, or if $p < p_{max}$ is used, the required n is *smaller*. For a value of N that is "not so large," the value of n can be found by first finding the n in equation (1), calling it n^*, and then finding the actual n needed by

$$n = n^*\left(\frac{N}{N + n^*}\right) \qquad (2)$$

To see the impact on n of N, consider the following values, with $p_{max} = .03$ and $e = .005$:

N	n
large	4,656
20,000	3,777
10,000	3,177

To estimate the *difference between two response rates* (e.g., between two different positionings), equations (1) and (2) can be easily adapted. Basically, we simply double the values. However, we need to double the values for *each* "package"; thus, the total sample size, or number of names, is *quadrupled.*

Economics of Sampling

Why do we want to sample? We want to sample because possibly, after observing the sample results, our decision on how to continue (i.e., rollout the rest of the list, rollout a next portion of the list, or discontinue the list) may change from what we would have done had we been forced to decide at the beginning to send to the entire list or to send to none of the list. This is, essentially, *always* the reason for sampling—to obtain more information in advance before committing resources to an action whose results are uncertain, and therefore to make a more informed decision, with its concomitant higher "expected benefit." This logic is relevant whether it is a situation with monetary implications, or a situation of a candidate getting votes, or a situation of medical screening tests.

However, in general, there is a cost to sampling. That is, there is usually a fixed cost (i.e., setup cost) to properly make the arrangements to perform the sampling. Is this setup cost worth it? It depends. For example, if the anticipated response rate for a mailing based, say, on experience is way above the "break-even point," then it is virtually a guarantee that the decision will be to mail to the entire list; then it may not be economic to waste the extra cost of setting up a sampling process, when it is almost certain that the decision will be to mail anyway. Of course, if it is anticipated that the response rate for a list is too low, why waste the money to sample if there appears to be virtually no chance that the sample results will reveal that the decision will be to mail? However, there are many situations—likely the majority of cases—in which the decision to sample is economic. The following example illustrates the methodology to be used to make the proper determination.

Consider the following parameters in a sampling decision situation:

Average profit per order = $100
In-the-mail-cost per catalog = $5
Fixed cost to sample = $500
Size of the list (number of names) = 10,000

Originally, the response rate for a list being considered is not known with certainty; however, based on the best evidence and experience available, let's say that for this particular list, the probability distribution reflecting the belief about the response rate is

RESPONSE RATE (APPROXIMATE)	PROBABILITY
.06 (6%)	.60 (60%)
.05 (5%)	.20 (20%)
.04 (4%)	.10 (10%)
.03 (3%)	.05 (5%)
.02 (2%)	.05 (5%)

In other words, in the opinion of the "decision makers" (direct marketers), the response rate most likely will be about 6 percent, but there is a sizable chance in their view that it will be

TABLE 10.1 Profit If We Sample

Sample Result and Response Rate	Action	Expected Profit
.06	Rollout	$.06(10,000) \times 100 - 5(10,000) - 500 = 9,500$
.05	Either	$.05(10,000) \times 100 - 5(10,000) - 500 = -500$
		$.05(3,000) \times 100 - 5(3,000) - 500 = -500$
.04	Stop	$.04(3,000) \times 100 - 5(3,000) - 500 = -3,500$
.03	Stop	$.03(3,000) \times 100 - 5(3,000) - 500 = -6,500$
.02	Stop	$.02(3,000) \times 100 - 5(3,000) - 500 = -9,500$

only 5 percent, and about a 10 percent chance that it will be only 4 percent, and a one out of 20 chance (5 percent) that it will be only 3 percent, and even a one in 20 chance that it will be as low as 2 percent. Note that the probabilities add to 1 (or 100 percent), as they must—because at least *some* response rate will occur.

By solving the equation, $100b - 5 = 0$, we can solve for the break-even point, b, of .05.

Assume that if we sample, the appropriate sample size is computed to be $n = 3,000$. Based on the logic of the previous section, we can determine that this sample size has a 90 percent probability of yielding a result within .005 of the true response rate. Table 10.1 indicates, if a sample is taken, the possible sample results (rounded to the nearest .01), the decision or action to then be taken (by comparing to the break-even point of .05), and the expected profit on the entire venture when this optimal action is taken.

We can compute the average profit, or, as it is more formally known, expected profit, by weighting the profit values from Table 10.1 by the probabilities of their respective occurrence:

$$.6(9,500) + .2(-500) + .1(-3,500) + .05(-6,500) + .05(-9,500) = \$4,450$$

To determine whether the decision to sample is "optimal," we have to compare it with our expected profit if we do not sample. If we do not sample, the decision is either "send out the entire list" or "reject the entire list." We assume that rejecting the entire list is, essentially, a profit result of $0 (status quo). If we send out the entire list, Table 10.2 indicates the outcomes and corresponding profits.

TABLE 10.2 Profit If We Do Not Sample

Response Rate	Expected Profit
.06	$.06(10,000) \times 100 - 5(10,000) = 10,000$
.05	$.05(10,000) \times 100 - 5(10,000) = 0$
.04	$.04(10,000) \times 100 - 5(10,000) = -10,000$
.03	$.03(10,000) \times 100 - 5(10,000) = -20,000$
.02	$.02(10,000) \times 100 - 5(10,000) = -30,000$

We can, again, compute the expected profit by weighting the profit values from Table 10.2 by the probabilities of their respective occurrence:

$$.6(10,000) + .2(0) + .1(-10,000) + .05(-20,000) + .05(-30,000) = \$2,500$$

Clearly, this value of $2,500 is superior to (higher than) the $0 of rejecting the list.

Our last step is to compare the expected profit if we sample (which includes the fixed cost of sampling) with the expected profit if we do not sample. It can be seen that we are better off by sampling. In fact, even if the cost of sampling were, say, $2,000, we would choose to sample. (If the fixed cost of sampling were $2,000 instead of $500, the $4,450 expected profit if we sample would be $1,500 less, or $2,950—still higher than $2,500.) The expected value of sample information (EVSI), defined here as the maximum fixed cost we would be willing to incur for the sample, is $2,450, the difference between the expected profit had the sample no fixed additional cost ($4,450 + $500 = $4,950) and the expected profit if we do not sample, $2,500.

This example ignores certain "real-world" issues. For example, in some situations in which timing is critical, there may not be the option to sample. We have also ignored "back-end" costs (although we could argue that they are incorporated into the value used for "average profit per order"). In addition, we ignored somewhat the issue that the sample results may not exactly mirror the actual results experienced when the list is rolled out. This latter issue has generated a significant amount of discussion in the direct marketing (research) literature; there are some that believe that rollouts nearly always result in a lower than anticipated response rate, although the reasons for this are not well documented. One reason might be the concept of "regression to the mean," essentially that sample results that are higher than the list's actual rate are more likely to be rolled out than are sample results that are lower than the list's actual rate (because the former are more likely to exceed the break-even point). Even though this is clearly true, it is true in only a relatively small portion of the rollouts that occur, and it is an insufficient explanation to support widespread discrepancies between sample results and rollout results.

Nevertheless, in general, routine statistical variation does usually lead to some difference (positive or negative) between sample and actual list response rates. Thus, we often use a statistical analysis process called *hypothesis testing* to make rollout decisions, or any other decisions that are based on testing (i.e., when testing any facet of the offer, such as positioning or price, as discussed in the introduction to the chapter). To be conservative, it is usual to roll out or adopt a new strategy of any kind, only if we are highly confident that the rollout will yield a response rate that exceeds the break-even point, or highly confident that the response rate of the new strategy (e.g., new positioning) exceeds that of the old (or current) strategy.

The Testing Process: Hypothesis Testing

We set forth three simple rules for developing effective tests:

1. All tests should be measured against the criterion of expected profit. The measure of profit can be based on the one-time profit for this offer, or, as noted in chapter 9, preferably on a measure of lifetime value.

2. Decisions about the content of the test (e.g., which variables to test, when to conduct the test, for what period of time) should be based on sound marketing judgment.

3. Decisions about the design of the test (e.g., sampling method, sample size, experimental design, control of the probability of reaching incorrect conclusions) should be based on statistical theory.

Often, our testing involves the examination of whether a new strategy (or set of strategies) or a new package (e.g., a new positioning, a new price) is superior to the existing package. The existing choice, against which the new possibility is being tested, is often named the *control* in direct marketing tests. That is, the control is the package or strategy that thus far has performed best for the direct marketer. That package becomes the standard against which all other direct mail campaigns are measured. The package is generally used without change until it is clearly beaten by another package. In essence, direct marketers take the reasonable view of, popularly stated, "if it ain't broke, don't fix it." If a package "beats out" the control package, the former then becomes the control for future tests. This seems to be, and indeed is, a very simple concept. (The material at the end of the previous section has the same theme—in general, one does not change package or strategy, or adopt a new mailing list, or whatever, unless there is high confidence that the decision will be "a winner.") However, designing, conducting, and analyzing the results of tests to accurately determine if the new package is superior to the control package is a complex subject, and the focus of the following discussion. The subject is laid out in a series of steps, utilizing a real-world example as an illustration of the process. At the end of the discussion, we provide a list of the steps involved.

CHOOSE THE VARIABLES TO BE TESTED

The first step in any testing process is to decide which variables to test. We have already stated that nearly everything in a direct marketing campaign can be tested. However, one of the cardinal rules of direct marketing testing is to "test the big things." According to Stone, "Trivia testing, e.g., testing the tilt of a postage stamp or testing the effect of various colors of paper stock, are passé. Breakthroughs are possible only when you test the big things."[1] We earlier listed a number of areas in which testing can provide results that can materially improve the likelihood of the success of a direct mail program.

In testing the product or service itself, the direct marketer can test the appropriateness of a particular product for a given target market; for example, will this small portable kitchen appliance be a profitable addition to my catalog of housewares? Perhaps the major question might concern alternative product attributes, such as whether the product should be offered in avocado green as well as in off-white?

Product-positioning alternatives are derived from a study of the benefits and attributes of the product. For example, the marketer of the small portable kitchen appliance may have two major positioning alternatives: (1) focusing on a benefit of using the product, the marketer could choose a positioning statement centered around its ease of use; or, (2) taking a tangible attribute approach, the positioning statement chosen could stress its low price.

In most tests the direct marketer will mail to at least a portion of the house list. Beyond that, the possibilities seem endless. Ordinarily, the direct marketer will test several lists in a single mailing.

There are a huge number of possible offer variations. The direct marketer can test, among others, different price levels, different premium offers (or no premium at all), and different warranty options. Chapter 3 discussed the many alternatives that are available in constructing the offer.

As noted in chapter 1, all communications media are viable options for inclusion in a direct marketing program. Rarely, however, will all be used in a single campaign. Which,

---

[1]Bob Stone, *Successful Direct Marketing,* 4th ed. (Chicago: Crain Books, 1996).

then, will work best in a particular situation? In the context of testing, the important thing to remember is that the cost of testing varies from medium to medium. It is relatively cheap to test variations in telephone scripts or radio copy. Testing alternative lists is cost effective in both the direct mail and telephone environments. It is more expensive, but still usually quite feasible, to test variations in the direct mail package—whether to include a brochure or a lift device, or whether to use a plastic mailing sleeve or a printed, four-color mailing envelope. Testing different four-color magazine ads or different television ads can, however, become quite expensive. These costs go beyond the "setup cost" of sampling discussed in the earlier section on the economics of sampling, which referred to setting up a process for selecting a sample and did not include the cost of the alternatives, such as printing some brochures in a different size. Testing in print and broadcast media is discussed in chapters 14 and 15, because the techniques are quite different from direct mail testing.

There are two key issues for the direct marketer when testing media. The first is to consider not only the expense of testing but also the cost versus the benefit of continued promotion through a particular medium before deciding what to test. Second, the direct marketer should clearly distinguish between testing the medium itself (can this product be effectively sold by direct mail?) and testing a specific format in a specific medium (a mailing piece that executes a low-price positioning versus one that executes an upscale, ease-of-use positioning). The medium itself and the promotional formats that work in that medium are quite different questions, and the direct marketer should be clear about which is being tested. However, it is difficult to separate them even for purposes of discussion.

Nash suggests that while major creative alternatives such as a change in headline, illustration, or format are worth testing, "layout revisions or different copy treatments of the same theme usually show very little difference, presuming they were professionally executed in the first place."[2]

Timing can be a difficult issue when it comes to testing decisions. It is clear that timing can make a considerable difference in many direct-response situations. However, direct marketers must maintain a planned promotional schedule, which may not allow them to wait to run a test in a season that may be especially favorable. There is no simple solution to this problem. The element of timing should be built into the testing schedule in a manner that allows it to be studied, but does not seriously interfere with the promotional schedule.

Nash summarizes the difficulties of deciding what to test by pointing out that selecting variables to test must be done methodically on the basis of the expected value of the information. He states that "the big differences—200 and 300 percent lift factors—almost always come from product positioning, offer changes, or the selection of different lists or publications."[3]

SET UP THE HYPOTHESES

To make the concepts a bit more "concrete," let's choose as an example, the situation of testing a subscription acquisition mailing for a newsletter. A simplified statement of the revenues and costs of this newsletter, on a per subscriber basis, is shown in Table 10.3.

To keep our example as simple as possible, we use subscriber acquisition cost as the test criterion. We can justify using acquisition cost instead of profitability in this instance

---

[2]Edward L. Nash, *Direct Marketing,* 3rd ed. (New York: McGraw-Hill, 1995).
[3]Ibid.

TABLE 10.3 Single-Subscriber Revenue and Costs— Newsletter Example	
Subscription revenue (one-year subscription)	$10.00
Fulfillment cost (printing and mailing)	–$ 5.00
Gross margin	$ 5.00
Average subscriber acquisition cost	–$ 2.25
Operating costs	–$ 1.75
Net profit before taxes	$ 1.00

because it appears to be the only cost likely to vary across customers, and therefore to affect profitability.

Response rate can be justified as equivalent to profitability when both cost per person mailed and revenue per responder (customer) are the same for all. An example of this would be two mailings (with, say, different themes or graphic approaches) of equal cost to produce and mail, competing to be the winner, to then be applied to a large number of names from which the two test mailings were a random sample. Of course, whether the winner is, indeed, profitable enough to warrant mailing to this large number of names is a separate decision that will be based on various profit considerations.

Remember, though, that we are using average acquisition cost to keep the numbers as simple as possible. What we really should do is compute the lifetime value of a customer.

The testing situation is usually set within the framework of *hypotheses testing.* We specify two hypotheses about the "state of the world"; actually, most of the time, and certainly in our example, the hypotheses are more modest in scope, being about values of a "population parameter" (a specific value, albeit, unknown). Here the relevant population parameter is the expected subscriber acquisition cost of the new package. The null hypothesis is the statement that has to be disproved. In other words, unless the evidence is overwhelming—or, in statistical terms, "significant"—against the null hypothesis, we will continue to believe in the null hypothesis. A useful way to think about this idea is to view the null hypothesis as getting the benefit of the doubt. Indeed, this is the key way in which we insure not taking action unless we are highly confident of its success.

Assume that in this situation, the control package that has been delivering the best performance to date has an average acquisition cost of $2.25 (as seen in Table 10.3). Thus, when we hypothesize about the average of the *new* package's acquisition cost (that is the quantity we do not know), we should set up a null hypothesis that states that this average is no better (no lower—remember that lower is better for an acquisition cost) than for the control package. This will guarantee that unless the evidence is clearly in favor of the new package, we will stay with the tried-and-true control package.

In statistical terms, we state H_0, the null hypothesis, as

$$H_0: \text{new package mean} \geq \$2.25$$

Note again that this essentially says that the new package is not better (not lower) than the control. We do not want to reject this belief if the new is indeed no better than the control. However, there is always the chance that we could make this mistake. In statistical terms, this mistake is called a Type I error. How could this error occur? Well, what if the new package cost is higher than the control cost but by chance, this one experimental mailing gives us a result that shows a much smaller cost for the new package? Will we get misled? Sadly, the answer is yes, although we try to ensure that the chance of such a thing happening is very low. A corresponding example in the everyday world is that, although the average height of men is surely higher than the average height of women, in one particular sample the women could be taller just by the "luck of the draw."

The alternate hypothesis is essentially the complement of the null hypothesis; that is, the other possibility. Here the alternate hypothesis should have the meaning that the new package is indeed better than the control package by virtue of having a lower expected acquisition cost. In statistical terms, we state H_1, the alternate hypothesis, as

$$H_1: \text{new package mean} < \$2.25$$

We want to reject the null hypothesis, and thus accept the alternate hypothesis, when there is evidence that the average acquisition cost for the new package is less than that for the control package, which we know to be $2.25. Remember, our aim is to determine which package has the highest expected profit. We are using lowest acquisition cost as a stand-in for highest expected profit only because in the current situation they are equivalent.

CHOOSE A SIGNIFICANCE LEVEL

The significance level is the name we give to the probability that if the null hypothesis is true, we get test results that (sadly) mislead us into rejecting it in favor of the alternate hypothesis. In this example, the significance level refers to the probability of concluding that the new package has lower acquisition cost than the control, when, in fact, it does not. The person conducting the test gets to choose this value, which is usually denoted by the Greek letter, α. However, even though it would appear that the lower α is the better, there are some other subtleties that suggest otherwise. One of these is that all else being equal, the lower the α, the higher the sample size needed to achieve it. The other subtlety is that all else being equal, the lower the chance of a false rejection of H_0, the higher the chance of a false acceptance of H_0. After all, not only can we conclude that the new package is better when it really is not, but we might end up concluding that the new package is not better than the control package, when, indeed, the new package is better. Whereas, as noted earlier, concluding that the new package is better when it actually is not is called a Type I error, concluding that the new package is not better, when it really is better is called a Type II error; the probability of the latter is usually denoted by the Greek letter, β. The value of β cannot actually be determined because it depends on the unknown, the true acquisition cost. For example, intuitively, if the true acquisition cost for the new package were $1.00, it would be almost impossible that we would get sample results that tell us that the new package is inferior to (costs more than) the control; however, if the true acquisition cost for the new package were $2.21, it might be very possible that the results of our testing would mask the (slight) decrease from $2.25, leaving us to conclude that the new package is not better than the control.

The choice of a significance level, α, is often passed over quickly by using the traditional value of .05 (5 percent). However, the choice should be given more thought. If the cost of going with the new when, in fact, the new is not really better is unusually costly, then a wiser choice could be to go with a smaller value of α, say 2 percent or 1 percent. On the other hand, if the cost of staying with the control when, in fact, the new is substantially better has an unusually high opportunity loss, then a wiser choice could be to go with a larger value of

α, say 10 percent or even 20 percent. Sadly, there are also other considerations that are difficult to assess but bear on the best choice (for example, a priori beliefs about whether the new is indeed better). That is why people often simply go with the traditional value of 5 percent.

In our subscription acquisition example, let's assume that we are very risk averse and decide to choose a significance level of $\alpha = .01$. We know that the lower value for α will decrease our chance of selecting the new package if it is really no better than the control.

DESIGN THE TEST

Designing the test when there are a number of different variables to be tested can be a complex procedure. The latter portion of this chapter deals with test design and the corresponding analysis of the test results for these situations. We assume for the rest of the subscription acquisition example that there is only one variable, *package,* with two choices, *control* and *new,* being tested.

DETERMINE THE SAMPLE SIZE

We have already discussed the different factors involved in determining the appropriate sample size. Assume that in our case the standard deviation is known to be $1.00. With a choice of α of .01, we are stating that the desired confidence level is .99, or 99 percent. Suppose further that we decide that we wish our precision, e, to be .25; in other words, we are insisting on being 99 percent confident of being off by no more than $.25 (i.e., $\pm.25$) in our estimate of the true acquisition cost of the new package. (Remember from the earlier discussion, if you want incredibly tight precision, your sample size requirements will become impractically high.) The formula for determining our sample size here, even though relying on the same set of factors and inputs, is a little bit different than the one in the earlier section on sample size because we are using a criterion variable (acquisition cost) that is not a proportion, as was response rate in the earlier formula. The formula now is

$$ n = \frac{Z^2(sd)^2}{e^2} $$

The Z^2 value, which is 4 ($= 2^2$) for 95 percent confidence, as in equation (1), is $(2.6)^2 = 6.76$ for 99 percent confidence.[4] With $sd = 1$, and $e = .25$, we get a sample size requirement of

$$ n = 109 $$

With 109 responses needed, we must divide by the expected response rate to obtain the number to be mailed. We should choose the lowest response rate that seems realistic for this particular mailing to ensure an adequate number of responses. If a 2 percent response rate is the lowest reasonable expectation, we must mail

$$ \frac{109}{.02} = 5,450 \ \text{packages} $$

---

[4]When the standard deviation is assumed known, we use a standard normal distribution value. If the standard deviation is unknown, and estimated from a pilot sample, we should theoretically use a *t*-distribution value. However, when the pilot sample is at least 30 (and it always should be), the values from the two distributions are essentially equal. From here on in this chapter we use values from the standard normal distribution.

Actually, to be risk averse, we really should mail a few more than the 5,450, just in case the response rate is unusually low for this particular sample. So, as a practical matter, 10 percent should be added to this number, giving a total of about 6,000.

SPECIFY THE DECISION RULE

Next we must state the decision rule. A decision rule is simply a procedure that specifies the action to be taken for each possible sample outcome. That is, for which values of the sample mean acquisition cost should we accept the null hypothesis, H_0, and for which values should we reject H_0 and accept the alternate hypothesis, H_1? Clearly, sample means that lead us to reject H_0 should be ones that are lower than \$2.25—but not just any value under \$2.25, only ones that are enough below \$2.25 that it is likely they did not come out that way because of luck. After all, if the true mean of the new package is \$2.26 or \$2.27 (above \$2.25), we could still (easily) get a sample mean of, say, \$2.24. The decision rule requires finding a *critical value, C,* so that if \$2.25 is the true average acquisition cost for the new package, the chance is only 1 percent (the chosen value of the significance level, α) that we would get a sample mean below it. The formula for this critical value in this case is

$$C = 2.25 - \frac{2.33sd}{\sqrt{n}}$$

Assuming that we get 109 responses (the number needed), and recalling that $sd = 1.0$, we find

$$C = 2.25 - \frac{2.33}{\sqrt{109}} = \$2.03$$

or

$$C = \$2.03$$

We conclude that the new package has a lower acquisition cost than that of the control package (\$2.25) only if the sample mean acquisition cost is below \$2.03.

We note that the appropriate value from the Z table used in the preceding formula is 2.33, not the 2.6 we used earlier in determining our sample size. This is because we will reject H_0 only if the sample mean is *below* the critical value (which, in turn, is below 2.25); there is no corresponding rejection region above \$2.25. All of our 1 percent Type I error, α, is in the lower tail. Also, that is why we did not get a critical value of \$2.00 (.25 below \$2.25, in line with the ±\$.25 chosen as the precision). Our statistical analysis is portrayed graphically in Figure 10.1.

CONDUCT THE TEST

Once the parameters have been determined, the test must, of course, be carried out. This means, in effect, conducting the direct mail campaign to find the average acquisition cost for the new package. In fact, most testing generally is done as an additional activity in an ongoing direct mail campaign. Whether the test is full scale or smaller scale, all the planning, preparation, and execution that are necessary for a full-scale campaign are also necessary for a test. For even a small-scale test to be valid, it must be implemented just as if it were a full-scale campaign. That is, the conditions of the test must exactly replicate the campaign if the test is to be valid.

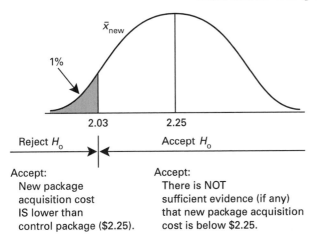

FIGURE 10.1 Statistical Analysis

RECORD THE TEST RESULTS

Of course, direct marketers always record the results of any contact with a customer in their database—correct? Yes, it is, but there is still a potentially fatal error lurking to catch the unwary direct marketer. The costs and revenues of the campaign itself (often referred to as the *front end*) are not the only issue. What goes on after the sale is made (the *back end*) can make a great deal of difference in the profit picture. An unusually high rate of returns or excessive service costs for products under warranty are two common examples of back-end costs that can quickly eat up profits. If the direct marketer fails to take these into account, the true results of the test can be grossly misstated.

For example, if we were testing two different pieces, for which one major difference is the prominent display of a toll-free number for no-hassle refunds, the mailing piece with the prominent display might induce a larger response rate (and thus a higher front-end profit), but also a larger number of returns for refund (and thus a far larger back-end cost). The mailing piece with the larger front-end profit could be the piece with the smaller overall profit if these back-end costs were (mistakenly) ignored.

MAKE THE DECISION

Returning to our subscription-acquisition example, let's assume that the results are that the average acquisition cost for the new (test) package is $2.10. The average acquisition cost for the test package is lower than the average acquisition cost of $2.25 for the control package. Is it significantly lower? Should we reject the null hypothesis that the acquisition cost of the new is (in reality) no lower than that of the control package, $2.25?

To answer these questions we must note whether the sample average acquisition cost falls into the acceptance region or the rejection (actually called "critical") region, these regions being established by our choice of significance level and sample size. Look at Figure 10.1—all we need to do now is to see whether our sample average acquisition cost, $2.10, is above or below the critical value of $2.03. Obviously, $2.10 is above $2.03, and falls into the acceptance region.

We therefore accept the null hypothesis. This means that the evidence that the long-run average acquisition cost of the test package is lower than that of the control package is not

TABLE 10.4 Steps for Carrying Out a Test
1. Choose the variables to be tested
2. Set up the hypotheses (for each variable)
3. Choose the significance level (for each variable)
4. Design the test
5. Determine the sample size
6. Specify the decision rule (for each variable)
7. Conduct the test
8. Make the decision (for each variable)

sufficiently strong. We will continue to use the control package for the bulk of our mailings. However, we may wish to continue to test other packages (or even this test package again if no other viable possibilities present themselves) in an attempt to find one with a lower average acquisition cost. The prevailing wisdom is to not adopt a new package (e.g., positioning, price), unless the evidence is *overwhelming*. We might, in the previous example, be tempted to bet that the new package is better; however, in traditional business, marketing, and direct marketing decision making, as stated, the evidence needs to be overwhelming, and the result of $2.10 is not—at least not by traditional standards.

Indeed, even if we had rejected the null hypothesis, and had concluded that the cost of the test package is lower than the cost of the control package, we might not choose to make a radical change without further testing. We might do another test mailing, perhaps with a larger sample, to see if the results were repeated. If we had been testing a list, further testing might take the form of rolling out to a larger number of names on the list. If a variation on some other promotional element had been tested, the variation might be tested on additional lists before we made a final decision to accept it as the control.

SET OF TESTING STEPS

The set of steps to be used in a testing procedure can be summarized by listing the steps just described in Table 10.4.

The Need for Efficient Test Designs

It should be clear from the preceding discussion of the testing process that the direct marketing manager welcomes information to support decisions on a wide variety of issues. The manager must identify the critical variables and test as many of them as possible. The limits of what can be tested are established by available funds and time.

The large number of variables that can be tested, coupled with the need to quickly develop and execute effective marketing programs in an increasingly competitive marketplace, puts a premium on efficiently designed tests. However, in the literature on the testing of direct-mail campaigns, two opposing arguments stand out: (1) you should test only one variable at a time; or (2) you should test a complete mail package all at once (e.g., different offers, premiums, lift devices). When you test just one variable, you can ascertain the effect of that variable with a known degree of certainty. When you test an entire mail package, you know which package works best even though you do not know the effect of individual variables.

The argument about "just one variable at a time" is clearly in conflict with generally accepted statistical and experimental design techniques. The second argument is somewhat more difficult to refute, at least on a practical basis. It is the second approach—testing an entire mail package—that we have taken in the previous section of this chapter. In describing a testing process focused on the average profitability of competing packages, we have been looking at the performance of entire packages, not of their component parts.

Without doubt, the overriding need of the direct mail marketer is to develop a package that works. There is simply not sufficient time to test even all of the variables that are likely to make a substantial difference in the profitability of the campaign. Creating a package that works is more important in the short run than finding out precisely what elements make it work (or, even better, *why* those elements make it work). Unfortunately, this approach—which might well be called "finding the whats, not the whys"—adds little to our store of knowledge about how direct marketing really works. Put in practical terms, it helps the direct marketer to *systematically* build a store of knowledge that will facilitate the rapid development of more effective direct mail campaigns.

Much of the remainder of this chapter is devoted to a discussion of ways in which we can make tests more efficient—that is, obtain more information in return for the resources of time and money devoted to the test—without sacrificing ability to make statistically sound judgments about test results. The application of statistical techniques with which you are probably already familiar, coupled with some simple principles of experimental design, enable us to develop a sense of what is possible. We still, however, will have only scratched the surface of the testing power that sophisticated multivariate analysis and complex experimental designs offer to the direct marketer.

One-at-a-Time Designs versus Factorial Designs

To better understand the issue of testing efficiency, we can look at an example that does not require numbers to make its point. Assume that our product is a small household appliance. We are faced with two issues: (1) the type of positioning to use (a convenience appeal versus a status appeal); and (2) whether to use an expensive or an inexpensive premium as part of our offer.

Let's assume that we take the "one variable at a time" approach. First we conduct a test, following all the steps described in Table 10.4, on the variable "appeal." To be consistent with experimental design terminology, from now on we refer to the variable as a *factor*. This factor has two levels, status and convenience. The term *levels* refers to the values that the factor may take. These levels may be quantitative (e.g., an offer price of $7.95 versus an offer price of $5.95), or they may be qualitative, as in this case: status versus convenience.

Because we are testing only one factor at a time, we hold the other factor constant. Assume that we decide to use the inexpensive premium and conduct the test on appeal by earmarking 20,000 pieces to receive the status appeal and 20,000 pieces to receive the convenience appeal, with all receiving the offer that includes the inexpensive premium. The particular profit values and response rates are not important to this example, so we simply note in Table 10.5 (p. 218) the number of mail pieces earmarked for the (so far) two cells.

TABLE 10.5 Number of Mail Pieces for Appeal Testing

Appeal	Premium	
	Inexpensive (I)	*Expensive (E)*
Status (S)	20,000	0
Convenience (C)	20,000	0

Now we consider testing the factor "premium," which has two levels, inexpensive and expensive. Again, we hold the other factor constant, and fix appeal at the level, status, when testing premium.

We conduct this test of the two premiums by earmarking an additional 20,000 mail pieces to receive the expensive premium–status appeal combination. We already have 20,000 pieces earmarked for the inexpensive premium–status appeal combination. Thus we have earmarked 60,000 mail pieces as shown in Table 10.6.

To test the two appeals, we can use the results from the (S,I) and (C,I) cells of Table 10.6; the (S,E) cell cannot be usefully included to compare appeals. We have the statistical strength of 40,000 mail pieces in terms of avoiding an erroneous conclusion about which level of appeal is superior.

To test the two premiums, we can use the results from the (S,I) and (S,E) cells of Table 10.6; the (C,I) cell cannot be usefully included to compare premiums. Again, we have the statistical strength of 40,000 pieces in terms of avoiding an erroneous conclusion about which level of premium is superior.

Now consider the earmarking of mail pieces shown in Table 10.7. With the same 60,000 mail pieces, in total, but allocated as in the Table 10.7, we can test appeal using all four cells, thus getting the statistical strength of 60,000 mail pieces in terms of avoiding an erroneous conclusion about which appeal is superior. Likewise, we can test premium using all four cells, here also getting the statistical strength of 60,000 mail pieces. Thus the experimental design depicted in Table 10.7 uses the same 60,000 mail pieces as depicted in Table 10.6, but results in a smaller probability of reaching an incorrect conclusion about which appeal level is superior and which premium level is superior, having the strength of 60,000 pieces, instead of only 40,000 pieces.

This reduced chance of erroneous conclusion is reason enough to prefer the experimental design in Table 10.7 to that of Table 10.6. Yet, there is another major advantage in the

TABLE 10.6 Number of Mail Pieces for Premium and Appeal Testing

Appeal	Premium	
	Inexpensive (I)	*Expensive (E)*
Status (S)	20,000	20,000
Convenience (C)	20,000	0

TABLE 10.7 Number of Mail Pieces for Premium and Appeal Testing—A Superior Alternative

	Premium	
Appeal	*Inexpensive (I)*	*Expensive (E)*
Status (S)	15,000	15,000
Convenience (C)	15,000	15,000

design of Table 10.7. What if, for example, the superior appeal for one premium is not the same as for the other premium? What if the superior premium is not the same for each appeal? It would then be possible to get an overall result that is suboptimal, in the sense of the best appeal, the best premium, but not the best appeal and premium combination. The one-factor-at-a-time design of Table 10.6 gives us no way to assess this possibility; but the design in Table 10.7 *does* allow us to examine that possibility. A situation in which the optimal level of a factor is not the same for all levels of another factor is called *interaction among factors*. As we illustrate later in this chapter, this interaction can be very important in determining the best overall combination of factors.

The design illustrated in Table 10.7 is called a *factorial design*. It permits the experimenter to evaluate not only the main effect of each factor, but the "synergistic" or combined effect of two or more factors. When all the combinations of all of the factors being tested are included, the design is called a *complete factorial design*. We use this design in the two examples of the next section. Later, we look briefly at *fractional factorial designs*—designs in which only a portion of all of the possible combinations are included. When there are many factors being tested, it is inevitable that the design will be fractional; otherwise, there are simply too many combinations of levels of factors to carry out the experiment in reasonable time and at reasonable expense.

The examples in the next section use the same two factors, appeal and premium. There will be the same two levels of appeal, status and convenience; however, for added richness of the example, premium will have three levels: no premium, an inexpensive premium, and an expensive premium. Thus, there are six experimental "treatments"—status–none, status–inexpensive, status–expensive, convenience–none, convenience–inexpensive, and convenience–expensive.

To avoid any timing bias, we must measure all experimental treatments simultaneously. Thus, the mailing is divided into six equal parts. One-sixth of the names will receive a package using each of the six treatments being tested. We can assume that Nth name sampling, as described in chapter 5 and earlier in this chapter, will be used to ensure that each treatment receives equivalent opportunities for response and profit (and the corresponding front-end and back-end costs).

Note that a control package is not required for this type of experiment. The dependent (response) variable is profitability of the mailing, although discussion of the precise meaning of this term will occasionally arise. If one can safely assume that order size and back-end costs are the same for each treatment, response rate can then be used as the appropriate measure to judge the different treatments.

By using this type of experimental design (in this case, a complete factorial design), we can measure the effect of the appeal factor as well as the effect of the premium factor. In addition, we can determine whether there is an interaction effect between the two factors. We will have done this with six experimental treatments, and we will have made all six experimental treatments from a single mailing, thus reducing the chance that unmeasured or uncontrolled variables will affect the results of the test. This could well result in a substantial saving of both time and money as well as in improved information for decision making.

The technique we use to analyze the effect of each factor and to determine whether interaction is present is called analysis of variance, often referred to as ANOVA.

Analysis of Variance

Analysis of variance, like regression analysis, is one of the statistical techniques that falls into the category of the *general linear model*. This model assumes an additive relation between the variable we wish to predict (the dependent or response variable) and the variables (factors) and interactions that may be its determinants (the independent or predictor variables).

Regression analysis, which was discussed in chapter 5, measures the impact of each independent variable upon the dependent variable (the regression coefficients) and the overall predictive success of the set of independent variables (the R^2). ANOVA asks a different question: What is the probability that a predictor variable could yield results different from simple random selection? It also allocates differences (i.e., variability) in dependent variable values for different experimental combinations to their sources (here: appeal, premium, their interaction, and other factors [i.e., noise or error]). Indirectly, ANOVA provides the same measures as a regression analysis, but generally not in the same form.

The logic behind ANOVA is precisely the same as that which underlies the concept of hypothesis testing, discussed earlier. We are, then, merely extending the concept of hypothesis testing in a way that can encompass more variables (additional factors).

We are preparing to analyze the results of a test with two factors, appeal and premium; hence we use a two-way analysis of variance. The three questions we intend to answer by performing this analysis of variance are

1. Are there systematic effects (i.e., differences in profitability) due to appeal alone (without any consideration of the possible effects of premium)?

2. Are there systematic effects due to premium alone (without any consideration of the possible effects of appeal)?

3. Are there systematic effects due neither to appeal alone nor to premium alone, but to specific combinations of a particular level of appeal with a particular level of premium?

Let's look at an example that illustrates the use of ANOVA and its interpretation. Assume that we have used Nth name sampling to assign each name to one of the six experimental treatments, conducted a test mailing, and achieved the results shown in Table 10.8.

Although the terms *profit per order* and *profit per piece mailed* both take account of production and mailing costs, the criterion we wish to use—the one that really corresponds to the profitability of the mailing—is profit per piece mailed. This criterion eliminates any problems that could arise if the number mailed in each experimental treatment is different (whether by plan or perhaps because some got destroyed accidentally), and accounts for any profit-per-order differences that may arise for whatever reason (perhaps because of back-end

TABLE 10.8 Results at Test Mailing

Experimental Treatment	*Number Mailed*	*Response Rate*	*Profit per Order*	*Profit per Piece Mailed*
Convenience–None	30,000	.009	$10.00	$0.09
Convenience–Inexpensive	30,000	.018	10.00	0.18
Convenience–Expensive	30,000	.020	9.00	0.18
Status–None	30,000	.013	10.00	0.13
Status–Inexpensive	30,000	.020	12.00	0.24
Status–Expensive	30,000	.016	12.50	0.20

costs). As we mentioned earlier, if production costs, mailing costs, and profit per order (including back-end costs) are all the same for each experimental treatment, then response rate is equivalent to profit per mail piece.

Table 10.9 presents the test results in terms of our criterion. To illustrate the ANOVA process, we next perform the detailed calculations by hand; most often the calculations are performed via one of many statistical software packages (they are also done routinely using Excel™ or Lotus™).

We can measure the total variation in our data (i.e., how different all the data values are from one another) by adding the squared differences between each data value and the overall, or grand, mean of all the data values. This sum of squared differences is called the *total sum of squares,* or *TSS*.

When performing ANOVA, one usually first states a statistical model, which simply sets up an equation stating how the total variation in our data (*TSS*) is to be partitioned into its various sources. As mentioned earlier, our sources in this analysis are appeal, represented by rows; premium, represented by columns; the interaction of these two factors; and error or noise, the impact of all other factors not controlled in this test (some of which we may not even know about). The model would be written as follows:

$$TSS = SSB_r + SSB_c + SSI_{rc} + SSE$$

TABLE 10.9 Test Results: Profit per Mail Piece (in dollars)

	Premium			
Appeal	*None*	*Inexpensive*	*Expensive*	*Row Means*
Convenience	.09	.18	.18	.15
Status	.13	.24	.20	.19
Column means	.11	.21	.19	
Grand mean				.17

That is, the total sum of squares (*TSS*) is equal to the sum of squares between rows (*SSB$_r$*), plus the sum of squares between columns (*SSB$_c$*), plus the interaction sum of squares (*SSI$_{rc}$*), plus the error sum of squares (*SSE*).

SUMS OF SQUARES

First we will compute *TSS*. Because the component parts of *TSS* are what we wish to find, we normally would not compute *TSS* except as an arithmetic check. Recall that we add together the squared differences between each data value and the grand mean:

$$TSS = (.09 - .17)^2 + (.18 - .17)^2 + (.18 - .17)^2$$

$$+ (.13 - .17)^2 + (.24 - .17)^2 + (.20 - .17)^2$$

$$= .0140$$

Do not think that there is not much total variability in the data just because *TSS* appears to be a "small" number. All numbers in ANOVA are relative. If the values in Table 10.9 were profit per 1,000 mail pieces instead of profit per mail piece, *TSS* would be 14,000.

Now we compute the *SSB$_r$*, the sum of squares between rows. We do this by subtracting the grand mean from each of the row means, squaring each difference, and summing; then we multiply this quantity by the number of data values in each row. There are three values per row in this case, the number of columns.

$$SSB_r = 3[(.15 - .17)^2 + (.19 - .17)^2]$$

$$= .0024$$

Next we compute *SSB$_c$*, the sum of squares between columns. The reasoning is the same as for *SSB$_r$*. We subtract the grand mean from each of the column means, square each difference, add them up, and multiply by the number of data values in each column. There are two values in each column, the number of rows.

$$SSB_c = 2[(.11 - .17)^2 + (.21 - .17)^2 + (.19 - .17)^2]$$

$$= .0112$$

We now calculate the interaction sum of squares, *SSI$_{rc}$*. This calculation is somewhat lengthy, but not difficult. For each cell value we subtract its corresponding row mean, also subtract its corresponding column mean, and add (back) the grand mean. We square the resulting value, and these squared values are then added up. You may not "see" how this is indeed measuring interaction, because the description

(cell value – row mean – column mean + grand mean)

is really a shortcut for

[(cell value – grand mean) – (row mean – grand mean) – (column mean – grand mean)].

In this latter expression, we take the amount by which the cell value differs from the grand mean (the first subtraction term), eliminate any of this difference due to the row in which the value is (i.e., adjusting for the row membership by the second subtraction term), and similarly eliminate any of the difference due to column membership. Putting aside the possibility of error for the moment, what could cause the value of this expression to be nonzero? The only answer can be that particular combinations of rows and columns have special incremental effects that are not captured solely by considering the row by itself and the column by itself. This is precisely what is called *interaction*. For our example, SSI_{rc} is computed as follows:

$$SSI_{rc} = (.09 - .15 - .11 + .17)^2 + (.18 - .15 - .21 + .17)^2$$

$$+ (.18 - .15 - .19 + .17)^2 + (.13 - .19 - .11 + .17)^2$$

$$+ (.24 - .19 - .21 + .17)^2 + (.20 - .19 - .19 + .17)^2$$

$$= .0004$$

Because there is no replication in this analysis (i.e., each cell has only one value), we are not able to compute a sum of squares due to error (*SSE*). Thus we must use the SSI_{rc}, which really reflects interaction *and* error here, as if it is entirely error. A later example in this chapter does include replication, and thus a separate SSI_{rc} and *SSE*.

Perhaps you have noticed that our three sums of squares add up to the *TSS* value: SSB_r = .0024, SSB_c = .0112, and SSI_{rc} = .0004, for a total of .0140. This fact leads us to the final concept that must be examined before we can perform ANOVA, that of degrees of freedom.

Each sum of squares must be normalized or averaged. Obviously, if there were 13 columns instead of the 3 columns we have in this example, we would have SSB_c be the sum of 13 terms instead of 3. To make SSB_c, or any other sum of squares term meaningful, we must take into account how many terms comprise the sum. After all, if we wanted to compare the incomes of a group of men and women, and the group consisted of 10 men but only 8 women, we would not compare *totals* of the incomes. We do this "normalization," more or less, by dividing by the number of terms in the sum. We say "more or less" because the proper number to divide by is not exactly the number of terms, but rather the number of "free terms" in the sum. It is this idea of free terms that requires us to explore the concept of degrees of freedom.

DEGREES OF FREEDOM

There is no straightforward verbal definition of the concept of *degrees of freedom* ("the total sample size minus the number of dependencies" doesn't seem that straightforward), but a simple example should provide sufficient understanding. In the computations we have just made, both the row and the column means were compared with the grand mean. According to Table 10.9, the grand mean is .17. The mean of the first row plus the mean of the second row, divided by 2, must equal the grand mean. If there are only two rows, and if we know the grand mean and the mean of row 1, the mean of row 2 has been uniquely determined; with the mean of the first row being .15, the mean of the second row can only be .19. No other value, added to .15 and divided by 2, could equal .17. In other words, when we know the grand mean and one row mean, the other row mean is not "free to vary." Consequently, we have one degree of freedom (*one* row free to vary, not *two rows* free to vary).

The same reasoning applies to degrees of freedom for the columns in our test results. If we know the grand mean, and two of the three column means, the third column mean is not free to vary; two of the column means can vary, but once they are determined, the third one cannot vary. For the columns, then, we have two degrees of freedom. In general, for n numbers squared around the mean of the n numbers, there are $(n - 1)$ degrees of freedom. Similar reasoning would indicate that the interaction term has a degrees of freedom number that equals the product of the degrees of freedom of the factors interacting. For error, the n numbers in a cell ($n = 1$ in our current example) provide us with $(n - 1)$ degrees of freedom per cell.

Returning to the basic model presented earlier in this section, we have

$$TSS = SSB_r + SSB_c + SSI_{rc} + SSE$$

The breakdown of degrees of freedom is equal to

$$(r - 1) + (c - 1) + (r - 1)(c - 1) + rc(n - 1)$$

where

r = number of rows

c = number of columns

n = number of replications (individual data values in a cell)

In this example, we have $r = 2$, $c = 3$, and $n = 1$. The degrees of freedom for error is thus 0, with $n = 1$. This corresponds with our earlier statement that with no replication (i.e., $n = 1$), we cannot compute a separate error term.

There is a helpful check for determining whether the degrees of freedom have been calculated correctly. The total number of degrees of freedom is always one fewer than the total number of data points used in ANOVA. There are six data points—the six cell values—in our example. The total number of degrees of freedom should therefore be five.

ANOVA SUMMARY TABLE

An analysis of variance is usually summarized in an ANOVA table. Let's construct an ANOVA table and continue the analysis of variance of the test results. Table 10.10 is an ANOVA table with the information we have already computed—all of the sums of squares (*SSQ*) and their respective degrees of freedom. We have three steps remaining:

1. Compute the mean squares (*MSQ*) for each source of variability by dividing each *SSQ* by its respective degrees of freedom. This is the normalizing or averaging step mentioned earlier. It can be likened to reducing all values to a per unit basis so they can be meaningfully compared to one another.

2. Calculate a value for F. The mean square for error reflects only error, assuming the most conservative situation—that the error plus interaction is all error. If we find significant differences under this assumption, then we know that they would also have been significant if we did not assume all the error plus interaction was error. The mean square for rows reflects error plus row differences. The F value is a ratio of the mean sum of squares for rows divided by the mean sum of squares for error. Hence, this ratio speaks to the issue of whether there

TABLE 10.10 ANOVA Table for Household Appliance Test

Source	Sum of Squares (SSQ)	Degrees of Freedom (df)	Mean Squares (MSQ)
Rows	.0024	1	.0024
Columns	.0112	2	.0056
Error	.0004	2	.0002
Total	.0140	5	

are row differences. It is similar for columns. The F value for rows is (.0024/.0002) and the F value for columns is (.0056/.0002).

If there are no differences in, for example, rows, the F value for rows should be near 1.0. However, the average weight of two different, randomly chosen, but ostensibly the same, sets of people would almost surely not be identical (and thus, analogously, the ratio will not equal exactly 1.0). We must decide how much above 1.0 is necessary before concluding that it is "beyond a reasonable doubt indicating real row differences." This is decided by a traditional hypothesis-testing procedure, and thus depends on various points on the theoretical F distribution. The shape of the F distribution depends somewhat on the degree of freedom values of the sums of squares involved, but for most degree of freedom values has the shape shown in Figure 10.2.

Most statistics texts have F table values for significance levels, α, of .05 and .01, and occasionally other significance levels. The value from the F table (a small portion of which is reproduced in Table 10.11, p. 226) is our critical value. Values of our calculated F ratio smaller than the critical value lead us to accept the null hypothesis, and to conclude that there are no differences between the levels of the factor under consideration. Values of the F ratio that are larger than our critical value lead to rejection of our null hypothesis, and to the conclusion that there are differences between levels of the factor under consideration.

3. Look up the F table value at the chosen level of significance and compare it to the calculated value of F. In Table 10.12 (p. 226), we carry out these three steps and complete the ANOVA table.

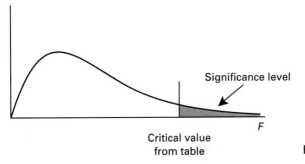

Significance level

Critical value
from table

FIGURE 10.2 The F Distribution

TABLE 10.11 Portion of *F* Table at α = .05

Denominator df	*Numerator* df									
	1	*2*	*3*	*4*	*5*	*6*	*7*	*8*	*9*	*10*
1	161.40	199.50	215.70	224.60	230.20	234.00	236.80	238.90	240.50	241.90
2	18.51	19.00	19.16	19.25	19.30	19.33	19.35	19.37	19.38	19.40
3	10.13	9.55	9.28	9.12	9.01	8.94	8.89	8.85	8.81	8.79
4	7.71	6.94	6.59	6.39	6.26	6.16	6.09	6.04	6.00	5.96
5	6.61	5.79	5.41	5.19	5.05	4.95	4.88	4.82	4.77	4.74
6	5.99	5.14	4.76	4.53	4.39	4.28	4.21	4.15	4.10	4.06
7	5.59	4.74	4.35	4.12	3.97	3.87	3.79	3.73	3.68	3.64
8	5.32	4.46	4.07	3.84	3.69	3.58	3.50	3.44	3.39	3.35
9	5.12	4.26	3.86	3.63	3.48	3.37	3.29	3.23	3.18	3.14
10	4.96	4.10	3.71	3.48	3.33	3.22	3.14	3.07	3.02	2.98
11	4.84	3.98	3.59	3.36	3.20	3.09	3.01	2.95	2.90	2.85
12	4.75	3.89	3.49	3.26	3.11	3.00	2.91	2.85	2.80	2.75
13	4.67	3.81	3.41	3.18	3.03	2.92	2.83	2.77	2.71	2.67

INTERPRETATION OF THE ANOVA TABLE

Now that we have completed the analysis of variance, what does it mean, statistically and managerially? First, we have already pointed out that the error term (as we have called it) contains both error and interaction. However, when we note how small the mean square is, .0002, relative to the other mean square terms, we can be assured that there is no practically meaningful interaction between the appeal and premium factors.

Second, it is clear that F_{calc} for rows is much smaller than the appropriate critical value of F, whereas F_{calc} for columns is much larger than its corresponding critical value. Consequently, we accept the null hypothesis for rows but reject the null hypothesis with regard to columns.

What does that imply? In ANOVA, the null hypothesis is always that "All _____ means are equal." For rows, then, it takes the form: "All row means are equal." Because we have accepted this hypothesis, we conclude that there are no differences between the various levels of the row factor. For columns, the null hypothesis is "All column means are equal," but we are rejecting it. We conclude that there is sufficient evidence in our results of differences among the column levels.

TABLE 10.12 ANOVA Table for Household Appliance Test

Source	Sum of Squares (SSQ)	Degree of Freedom (df)	Mean Squares (MSQ)	F_{calc}	F_{95}
Rows	.0024	1	.0024	12.00	18.51
Columns	.0112	2	.0056	28.00	19.00
Error	.0004	2	.0002		
Totals	.0140	5			

What are the managerial implications of the test results? Our conclusion that there is no meaningful interaction (if any at all) between the two factors, appeal and premium, in essence tells us that each factor's impact on profitability, if any, is independent of the other factor's level. Or, to state the conclusion in other terms, each factor's impact can be viewed as constant across all levels of the other factor.

We found no statistically significant difference in profitability between the two types of appeal. The reader must understand that although it is true that the resulting row means we observed are not equal, the difference between them (.15 versus .19) is not large enough to conclude that it happened for reasons other than the "luck of the draw." In other words, it is not beyond a reasonable doubt that the difference is "real." Therefore, the choice between the two types of appeal should probably be based on considerations not relating to dollar or profit issues. This does not mean that we should not test these two appeals ever again! Probably we should at some point.

We did find a statistically significant difference in profitability among the three levels of premium. We can have confidence that all three levels are not equally profitable. Yet, that does not totally solve our problem. Noting the three column means, our results are probably telling us: "Yes, the three are not equally profitable; no premium (column 1) is inferior to the two others, but most likely the difference in profitability between the inexpensive premium and expensive premium is too close to call."

To perform tests on subsets of levels of a factor requires other statistical concepts beyond the scope of this chapter. The interested reader can find other texts that cover this subject. The general topic is called multiple comparison testing.

An Example with Interaction Present

Let's assume that while the test mailing we have just described was being conducted and analyzed, the supplier of the appliance notified us that additional features had become available as a result of continued research and development. We can now have a timer added to the basic piece of equipment, and we can have the finish manufactured in either white enamel or stainless steel. There will be slight cost increases for both the stainless steel version and for the addition of a timer to either version. It is therefore important that the manager make a correct choice.

New features that force us to make additional decisions at this point are not particularly good news. We do not have time to do further test mailings to answer these product-design questions; the major selling season is near. Instead of testing, then, we make our decision on the basis of a small, laboratory-type experiment that can be carried out in the available time.

For this example, assume that an experiment was designed and that 16 consumers were recruited to participate in this research. That is much too small a sample on which to make a decision, but again, a large volume of data would have made our computations exceedingly tedious.

The consumers were shown product prototypes and asked numerous questions about their attitudes and actual and intended behaviors. We analyze only one question, however—the intention-to-buy question. This question was asked on a seven-point Likert-type scale, with 1 being "definitely would not buy" and 7 being "definitely would buy." The results are shown in Table 10.13 (p. 228). We randomly selected four consumers for each of the four cells.

Following the same computational procedure that we used in the preceding example, we find

$$SSQ_r = 30.250$$
$$SSQ_c = 12.250$$

TABLE 10.13 Results of Product-Feature Experiment

Finish	Timer		Row Means
	Without	*With*	
Enamel			
Individual responses	2,3,2,3	3,3,2,4	
Cell means	2.5	3.0	2.75
Stainless			
Individual responses	4,4,3,5	7,7,7,7	
Cell means	4.0	7.0	5.50
Column means	3.25	5.0	
Grand mean			4.125

Unlike the preceding example, however, we have replication in this experiment—four data points per cell. We can therefore compute both an interaction sum of squares and a separate error sum of squares.

As earlier, the SSI_{rc} is computed by subtracting from each cell mean its corresponding row mean and its corresponding column mean and adding back the grand mean. Each resulting quantity is then squared. These quantities (there will be as many quantities as there are cells, in this case, four) are added together and the result is multiplied the number of replications:

$$SSI_{rc} = 4[(2.5 - 2.75 - 3.25 + 4.125)^2 + (3.0 - 2.75 - 5.0 + 4.125)^2$$

$$+ (4.0 - 5.5 - 3.25 + 4.125)^2 + (7.0 - 5.5 - 5.0 + 4.125)^2]$$

$$= 4[(.625)^2 + (-.625)^2 + (-.625)^2 + (.625)^2]$$

$$= 4(.390625 + .390625 + .390625 + .390625)$$

$$= 4(1.5625) = .6250$$

The interaction sum of squares is 6.250. Now we compute the error sum of squares. Each individual data point is subtracted from its *cell mean*. The resulting quantity is squared. All these quantities (there will be as many quantities as there are individual data points, in this case, 16) are added together:

$$SSE = (2 - 2.5)^2 + (3 - 2.5)^2 + (2 - 2.5)^2 + (3 - 2.5)^2$$

$$+ (3 - 3)^2 + (3 - 3)^2 + (2 - 3)^2 + (4 - 3)^2$$

$$+ (4 - 4)^2 + (4 - 4)^2 + (3 - 4)^2 + (5 - 4)^2$$

$$+ (7 - 7)^2 + (7 - 7)^2 + (7 - 7)^2 + (7 - 7)^2$$

$$= 5$$

TABLE 10.14 ANOVA Table for Product-Feature Experiment

Source	SSQ	df	MSQ	F_{calc}	$F_{.95}$
Rows	30.250	1	30.250	72.54	4.75
Columns	12.250	1	12.250	29.38	4.75
Interaction	6.250	1	6.250	14.99	4.75
Error	5	12	.417		
Total	53.750	15			

The error sum of squares is 5. Now we are ready to construct the ANOVA table (Table 10.14). It is clear from Table 10.14 that there are significant differences between rows and between columns, and that there is interaction between the factors. Let's pay special attention to the interaction—to what it is and to how we should interpret it managerially.

We said earlier in the chapter that the third question we had to answer in an analysis of variance was whether there were systematic effects due to neither one factor alone nor the other factor alone, but only to the combination of a particular level of one factor with a particular level of the other factor. We are looking for a joint effect of two specific treatment levels that is different from the sum of the separate effects of each.

This is easier to understand if we portray it graphically, as in Figure 10.3. If there were no interaction, the lines in the figure would be parallel.

Looking back at the results of the product-features test, it is clear that the intention-to-buy score with the enamel finish increased only slightly when the timer was added (2.5 to 3, for an increase of .5). The intention-to-buy score with the stainless finish increased much more when the timer was added (3.25 to 5, for an increase of 1.75). This suggests the presence of interaction, and the analysis of variance indicates that it is significant.

In fact, ANOVA shows that the type of finish (without regard to timer) and the presence or absence of the timer (without regard to finish) are each also significant. Managerially, we can be confident that one particular level of each of these treatments creates a higher intention-to-buy score than the other, and the combination of the better levels of each factor creates yet a higher intention-to-buy score than the sum of the individual effects.

FIGURE 10.3 Graphic Representation of ANOVA Results for Product–Feature Experiment

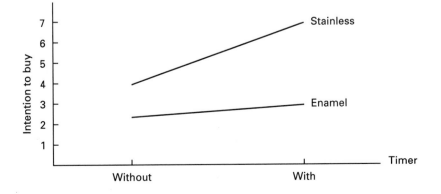

Consider the no timer–enamel cell in Table 10.13. As we add the timer, we gain .5; as we go from enamel to stainless steel, we gain 1.5; when we make both moves, we gain not just (.5 + 1.5) = 2, but 4.5 (i.e., 7 – 2.5). The manager would obviously want to select that combination of features—the stainless finish with the timer—for the appliance. This combination produces a significantly higher intention-to-buy score, so it would appear to be worth a slight cost increase to offer that version of the appliance. In this case, even without this positive interaction ("positive" because the gain is *more* than the sum of the two separate gains), the manager would still choose this combination.

A Word about Testing in the Real World

Except for the most statistically oriented among you, these examples of direct mail tests and experiments probably seemed complex. Actually, they were kept very simple and very "clean." Much of the reasoning behind certain steps in the ANOVA procedure was not discussed, the amount of data was very small, and the numbers tended to come out even or pretty close to it. Nothing happened to distort the results of our experiments. Apparently all of our mailings were delivered, product was available to fulfill them, and the research technicians followed instructions in the laboratory experiment.

Would that it were always so in the real world! Obviously it is not, and all sorts of problems can make the results of real tests difficult to interpret. For insight into some of these problems, and for a statistically more sophisticated approach to analysis of variance, you might wish to read Farley and Harvey's "Assessing a 'Real World' Mail Order Experiment."[5]

More Sophisticated Experimental Designs

This final section of the chapter provides a brief look at one advanced type of experimental design that holds great potential for the direct marketer.

Think for a moment about our last two examples. Instead of relying on a small laboratory test, it would have been nice if we could have tested the two new product features in the mailing in which we tested the appeal and the premium.

If we used a full factorial design and performed that test, what would it look like? We would have

3 levels of premium $\times$ 2 levels of appeal $\times$ 2 types of finish $\times$ 2 levels of timer
= 24 treatment combinations

It is not impossible to conduct a test that large, but it would be somewhat cumbersome and certainly expensive.

The alternative is simply not to take measures on every cell in the full factorial design. For example, we might construct a design that looked like Table 10.15 In the table the X's

---

[5]John U. Farley and Philip D. Harvey, "Assessing a 'Real World' Mail Order Experiment," in *Current Issues in Research in Advertising,* ed. James Leigh and Claude Martin (Ann Arbor: Division of Research, The University of Michigan, 1984), 123–139.

TABLE 10.15 Fractional Factorial

| | CONVENIENCE | | | | | | STATUS | | | | | |
| | Without Timer | | With Timer | | Without Timer | | With Timer | | | | | |
Premium	Enamel	Stainless Steel	Enamel	Stainless Steel	Enamel	Stainless Steel	Enamel	Stainless Steel
None	×	—	—	×	—	×	×	—
Inexpensive	—	×	×	—	×	—	—	×
Expensive	×	—	×	—	—	×	—	×

231

represent the cells for which measurements would be taken; the other cells (—) would not be measured. Reasonably enough, as noted earlier, we call this design a *fractional factorial.* Such a test would be less expensive, easier to manage, and probably completed more quickly than would the corresponding full factorial.

Would we lose anything by obtaining measurements for (in this case) only half the cells? Of course we would! The trick is not to lose anything important. What managers often consider unimportant is what statisticians call higher-level interactions. These are interactions resulting from combinations of three or more factors, above and beyond the effect of each factor itself, and each two-way combination.

For example, in the product-feature experiment we found a finish–timer interaction. If we combined the two experiments and did the full 24-cell factorial, we might find a three-way interaction—say, finish–timer–premium. Because we have four factors in the combined experiment, we might even find a four-way interaction: finish–timer–premium–appeal. Experience tells us, however, that in the real world the occurrence of higher-order interactions is infrequent. Also, would the direct marketer know what to do with that four-way interaction? Probably not; higher-level interactions are very difficult to interpret and for most people do not form a very comfortable basis for action.

If the higher-level interactions occur infrequently, and when they do they are not particularly useful, why spend time and money to measure them? Most managers would not want to do so. They do, however, want information about the main effects of the factors themselves—the effect of premium, the effect of timer, and so on—and, in many cases, of the two-way interactions (which occur reasonably frequently in the real world). The trick is to design fractional factorial experiments that unambiguously measure the main effects and as many of the interactions (nearly always two-way) as the manager wishes. In other words, the object is to measure all the potentially important effects and interactions, and accept as a penalty for not performing a full factorial the inability to measure the unnecessary ones.

The design in Table 10.15 is not necessarily efficient. That depends on which pairs of factors we can reasonably say do not interact. For example, there might well not be any interaction between the premium factor and the finish factor. To decide whether we could reasonably rule the interaction out, we would have to ask ourselves (or somebody else more expert, if appropriate) the following question: Do we believe that the *differences* in the response rates for the different premiums, whatever they are, will be about the same for each finish? Or equivalently, do we believe that the difference in response rate between the two finishes, whatever it is, will be about the same for each premium? The answer "yes" indicates that we can likely assume that finish and premium do not interact. The answer "no" suggests that we should not make that assumption.

This version of a fractional factorial is called a half replicate because it obtains measures for half the cells. It is also possible to do quarter replicates, one-eighth replicates, three-sixteenth replicates and, in fact, replicates of virtually any fraction that leaves us an integral number of cells. Done correctly, these designs could provide the direct marketer with a great deal of testing power relative to the resources required. However, it is beyond the scope of this text to go more deeply into these issues of experimental design. The suggested readings at the end of this chapter include some excellent texts on basic statistics and experimental design; however, none of them directly refer to direct mail or direct marketing. The article from the *Journal of Direct Marketing* examines, and goes beyond, many of the experimental design issues discussed in this chapter in a direct marketing context.

Summary

Testing is a powerful tool that allows the direct marketer to choose, with a known degree of statistical certainty, the most profitable mailing package or set of marketing variables. The testing process involves a number of steps: choosing the variables to be tested, setting up the hypotheses about these variables, choosing the significance levels for these variables, designing the test, determining the sample size, specifying the decision rule, conducting the test, and analyzing the results to make a decision about which package or which set of levels of variables to use. Good direct marketers test as many important program variables as possible, sometimes repeating tests on larger samples to ensure against statistical aberrations.

The principles of design of experiments can be fruitfully employed to increase the efficiency of tests. The application of these principles is relatively new to the field of direct marketing, but shows great potential for the future.

Discussion Questions and Exercises

1. Why do direct marketers test? What should they test?
2. Be able to define, in your own words, the following terms, and explain their relevance in the testing process: control, hypothesis test, significance level, full factorial design, fractional factorial design.
3. Do direct marketers accept the results of any given test as the final answer? Explain.
4. What does the use of experimental design principles add to the testing process?
5. Choose a direct marketing situation and outline an appropriate testing procedure.

Suggested Readings

Berenson, Mark L., and David M. Levine. *Basic Business Statistics: Concepts and Applications,* 6th ed. Upper Saddle River, NJ: Prentice Hall, 1996.

Berger, Paul D., and Thomas L. Magliozzi. "Experimental Design in Direct Mail and the Application of Taguchi Methods," *Journal of Direct Marketing* 7, no. 3 (summer 1993).

Brightman, H. *Statistics in Plain English.* Cincinnati: South-Western, 1984.

McLean, Robert A., and Virgil L. Anderson. *Applied Factorial and Fractional Designs.* New York: Marcel Dekker, 1984.

Rabb, David M. "List Tests: Less Reliable than You Think." *Direct Marketing* (March 1990).

11

Business-to-Business Direct Marketing

At a Glance

Business-to-business direct marketers use all the techniques described in the first three parts of this book and all the media we discuss in the final part. The chief differences are longer sales cycles for business products and the interaction between direct marketing and the field sales force, which has historically been the marketing mainstay of business marketers. With the cost of a personal sales call estimated to range from $300 to $800,[1] depending on the industry and source of data, the chief purpose of direct marketing in business markets traditionally has been to increase the productivity of the field sales force.

Consider the following examples from two very different companies:

> Dormont Manufacturing Co. is a small manufacturer of gas-appliance connections outside Pittsburgh, Pennsylvania. President Evan Segal wanted a way to showcase the diverse array of devices the company produced—everything from faucets to complex coupling devices. He wanted to produce a virtual factory tour so customers could experience their diverse product line but discovered that using virtual reality technology would cost at least $200,000. He settled for a multimedia tour of the Dormont factory, which includes animation, photographs,

---

[1] John M. Coe, "B-to-B Integrated Database Marketing," *The DMA Insider* (fall 1997): 29–32.

and video. Each of the firm's six salespersons carries the presentation on a laptop computer. Besides informative segments on various products in their line, it features Monty, a friendly gas-hose connector, who sings "Let's Get Flexible." Customers like the presentation because the segmented format allows them to choose the parts that feature relevant products.

At the same time the owners of Dormont wanted to make better use of their customer database. Instead of a standard contact manager program that keeps track of names, telephone numbers, meeting notes, and so forth, they chose newer opportunity management software. This type of system tracks sales at various levels ranging from an entire country to an individual customer.

Using the software, Segal realized that a few large customers in certain regions spent considerably less than their counterparts in the same industry in other regions. He ran a report and discovered that high-volume customers were buying a new safety valve in large numbers. The low-volume customers were buying none. Upon further inquiry, he discovered that some reps did not have a sufficient supply of sample valves to introduce it to all their customers. Dormont expects growth in sales of safety valves to exceed 50 percent during the current year, and attributes it to database information that helped identify a significant marketing omission.

With proper training and motivation, individual sales reps should be able to obtain this type of insight for themselves from the database and put it to work to improve their own individual results.[2]

A large and well-known corporation, Hewlett-Packard (HP), had a different type of problem.

"We want to build a relationship with customers to upsell and cross-sell, but it is so hard to determine the actual customer. Trying to identify the name of the user is the biggest problem," according to Judith Kincaid, worldwide customer information manager. The problem exists because job incumbents change rapidly in business markets and, in any event, the purchaser is often not the end user. Compounding the problem for HP is that many of its products are sold through channels, not directly through the field sales force.

Warranty cards or registration data filed electronically are two ways of getting data. Customers can be identified when they contact the call center or sales support personnel. HP also offers training programs and newsletters with information about product use. "A lot of b-to-b executives are very productivity-focused, so the best incentives are [tips about] how to do the job better, rather than giving away mouse pads," says Kincaid.

When a business becomes an HP customer, it receives an identification number, and every transaction and interaction is tracked. They calculate the support costs for a product, knowing that as a product becomes older, costs increase. That is communicated to the customer. Customers are likely to replace lower-end products such as printers and to upgrade higher-end products such as computers.

The Internet has been an important source for getting to know about customers and will be a source of sales in the future. "Privacy is a big deal on the Internet," says Kincaid. We manage customer information country-by-country. There are different privacy laws in different countries. The Web means customers surf from all over the world, and as our database becomes more global there are major implications for privacy."[3]

---

[2]Adapted from Sarah Schafer, "Supercharged Sell," *Inc. Tech 1997,* no. 2 (1997): 42–51.

[3]Adapted from Laura Loro, "HP Puts 'Data' in Database," *Business Marketing,* October 1997, 1, 24.

Whether the company is large or small, whether its products are sold through the sales force or through channels, the customer database is critical in driving the business-to-business direct marketing process.

Business-to-Business Direct Marketing Process

The basic activities—or as we called them in chapter 1, the generic objectives—of business-to-business direct marketers are

Sale of a product or service

Lead generation

Lead qualification

Establishment and maintenance of customer relationships

These generic objectives are precisely the same as those for direct marketing of consumer goods and services. However, the manner of implementation in business markets is often different. The primary reason for the difference is the nature of the decision-making process in business markets. In all decisions except for the very small or the completely routine, more than one person is involved in the process. People may act in many roles in the decision process—as initiators, influencers, gatekeepers (persons who exert control, especially over the flow of information), end users, or ultimate decision makers. This makes the marketing task more complex. At the same time, all businesspeople are human beings with individual outlooks and emotional reactions. The most successful direct marketing programs often operate at both levels, taking into account the complex group decision-making process and the equally complex individual objectives and reactions. This causes business-to-business direct-response activities to differ from similar efforts in consumer markets in a number of important ways:

1. *A single direct-response activity may require targeting several different people in the firm.* There are two primary reasons for this multiple targeting. The first is the multiple purchasing roles already mentioned. Each purchasing role may need different types and amounts of information. The design engineer wants to know, in considerable technical detail, how the product will make a particular job easier or more effective. The manager of manufacturing operations may be especially concerned about integrating innovations into operations without disrupting work flows; here again, much technical information will be required. The executive who will make the final decision whether to purchase may be more concerned about costs and about the impact of new technology or products on the organization as a whole. This executive may not have a technical background.

In some circumstances the direct marketer might be able to combine all this information into a single mailing or print advertisement, although a single message would probably be less effective than multiple, precisely targeted ones. A single message is impossible, however, when various participants have different backgrounds and training (engineering versus business management, for example); are differentially acquainted with precise technical terminology; and have preferences for lengthy, detailed information versus more concisely presented information that portrays the benefits and costs a decision maker must take into account. The presence of some or all of these three conditions creates a need for multiple versions of a program to target various participants in the decision-making process.

2. *Obtaining complete and up-to-date lists is often a problem.* There are more than 10,000 rental lists available to business marketers. However, in large firms personnel change their titles or physical locations so frequently that even the best maintained lists have a high proportion of incorrect addresses. One source estimates that "people change jobs in or outside a company at a rate of 62 percent a year."[4] Small firms come and go so quickly that they may not even engage in the kind of activities (such as undergoing credit checks) that would make them known to large business list sources such as Dun and Bradstreet. Moreover, the merge and purge operations are less effective for business lists than for consumer lists. Business lists contain four-line addresses—name and title; corporate name; corporate address; city, state, and zip code. However, there are many variations of this format as well as variations in spelling or abbreviating organizational titles and corporate names. Increasingly sophisticated computer software designed to deal with business addresses can catch some of the discrepancies—V-P and Vice President will be recognized as representing the same title, for example. Still, business address merge and purge are far from error-free.

2a. *Lists are often small.* Perhaps only a few thousand names are on a list in very specialized industries or occupations. In one sense, this is no problem if the direct marketer wants to reach the entire universe of interest. It may even make it possible to use more expensive promotions with greater impact. The small size of the total population presents one severe disadvantage to the direct marketer, however: The type of systematic testing and rollout, which is standard in consumer markets, is often impossible. This is why many business-to-business direct-response promotions go untested. It is also why more and more business marketers are turning to marketing research, especially to focus groups, even though their drawbacks are well known. Because they cannot test the programs with any degree of statistical rigor, they feel they must better inform the planning and development stages of their programs.

2b. *The business list situation is even more problematic in other countries.* Pan-European lists can give business marketers 5,000 to 30,000 addresses per country but are expensive at $200 to $500 per thousand. Business lists are also available for individual countries in Europe and may have from 15,000 to 100,000 addresses. They are even more expensive, ranging from $250 to $700 per thousand with additional charges for selects. There are multiple list compilers in every European country who make files available for either rental or purchase. According to a European direct marketer, "Specialized lists rarely contain more than a few dozen companies. . . .When searching for lists which include large companies prepare to adjust your definition of a large company. In the Benelux and many other countries in Europe, more than 50 percent of companies have nine or fewer employees."[5]

We must be careful not to exaggerate differences between business and consumer markets, however. The differences are mainly in degree, not kind. The wise marketer remembers that people do not cease being people the moment they enter their store, office, or plant in the morning. In fact, direct marketers of products that are not genuinely differentiated (such as office supplies) or of products in highly competitive markets (such as computer software) are increasingly turning to consumer marketing techniques, including colorful mailing packages and catalogs and price incentives of various types.

---

[4]Coe, "B-to-B Integrated Database Marketing," 31.

[5]Jim Foster, "Business-to-Business List Marketing in Benelux," *DM News International,* 11 November 1996, 16.

One of the differences of degree between business and consumer markets is the much greater use of multiple-step or lead-generation programs in business markets. Even though their frequency of use is considerably greater in business markets, remember that the same approaches are often used in consumer markets for expensive or infrequently purchased goods and services such as automobiles or financial planning services.

Lead Generation and Management Process

Although no statistics are available on this subject, it is commonly believed that lead generation is the single largest direct-response activity of business marketers. To be effective, these programs must be carefully planned and monitored. As we discuss each step in the process in detail here, keep in mind the primary purpose of a lead-generation program—to generate the highest volume of sales in the most cost-effective manner by focusing expensive field sales activity on the most qualified prospects.

Figure 11.1 presents a graphic portrayal of the process, showing that leads are generated, qualified, distributed to the field or to inside marketing programs, and followed up. At the same time, the effectiveness of each step in the process must be monitored and evaluated.

STEP 1: GENERATING SALES LEADS

Direct marketers often refer to sales leads according to the level of qualification they have achieved:

Suspects → Prospects → Leads → Qualified leads → Hot prospects → Customers

FIGURE 11.1 Lead Management Cycle

Source: Reprinted from *Marketing Tools* magazine with permission. © 1997, Cowles Business Media, Ithaca, New York.

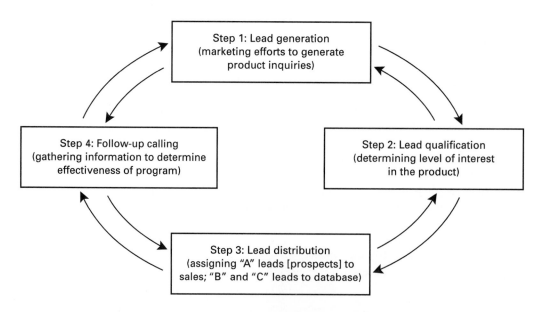

The first stage in the process is to locate a group of *suspects*. Suspects may be part of some broad business demographic group, such as Fortune 500 corporations, but nothing is actually known about their purchasing interest or likelihood to purchase. *Prospects* meet predetermined qualification criteria such as SIC code, which identifies them as a member of the industry group that is an appropriate target for the business's product or service. Many specialized prospect lists are available from list brokers; for example, there are lists of physicians (by medical specialty), real estate brokers (by residential or commercial), or owners of business aircraft (by type and size). The majority of these are compiled lists, although some response lists are available. The number of selects varies widely.

Leads are prospects who have indicated a minimum level of interest by some type of response, usually by requesting additional information. *Qualified leads* represent the next stage, leads who have been contacted and who have expressed interest in purchasing the product. *Hot prospects* add the intention to purchase in the near future. When a purchase is made, the prospect, of course, becomes a *customer.*

Suspects and prospects can be identified in a number of ways:

1. Traditionally, the most common way has been to *mail an inquiry-generation piece* to a rental list. Because this is unsolicited mail, it must get attention and compel the recipient to open and read it. One direct marketer advises:

> Phrases like "For more information . . ." and "To learn more . . ." should be banished from your marketing vocabulary. Instead, ask yourself: What specifically are we offering to send the reader? . . . Of the hundreds of direct mail campaigns to cross my desk in recent months, one of my favorites is a mailer from Pitney Bowes, the postage meter company, promoting their line of office copiers. In bold letters, the copy on the outer envelope reads: "Complete the enclosed Office Copier Downtime Survey and receive a FREE GIFT." What the folks at Pitney Bowes know . . . is that they're not going to sell copiers through the mail. They simply want to find people who are unhappy with their current machines. And what better way to identify those people than to present an attractive offer (in this case, a free coffee mug with their name on it) just for complaining?[6]

2. It is also possible to *use telephone cold calling* to identify prospects. Using the telephone as the first step has the advantage of being able to collect a small amount of data in the initial step. It has the usual disadvantage of cold calling—a high proportion of unproductive calls. In general, it is better to use mail first and let prospects self identify. Then a higher cost-per-contact medium, telephone, can be used to communicate in a more personal way with people who have expressed interest. On the other hand, if lists are unavailable or of poor quality, an initial telephone call to verify or create list data may be worth the effort to achieve a higher initial inquiry rate.

3. Another way of acquiring a large number of new names is through *advertising in trade publications*. The inquiry may come either as a direct response to an ad, by sending in a response device, by calling a 1-800 number, or through a reader service card, popularly known as a "bingo" card. The prospect sends the bingo card to an inquiry-handling service, which, in turn, passes it on to the advertiser. This can be quite slow, with the prospect losing interest in the interim. Direct response to the ad, either by mail or telephone, allows the marketer to respond to the inquiry more quickly. Business marketers often find that telephone response signifies a high degree of interest or urgency regarding the product.

[6]Howard J. Sewell, "Secrets of Successful Lead Generation," *DM News,* 17 February 1997.

4. Another common method of accumulating names is through *exhibits at trade shows*. When lead generation at trade shows is mentioned, many people immediately visualize the "throw a business card in the fishbowl" approach or the "sign up for a great prize" come-on. These broad-based techniques generally produce a large volume of highly *unqualified* leads. The poor quality of the leads is magnified by (or perhaps it is responsible for) the fact that relatively few leads are followed up—a true waste of time and effort.

Marketers have tried a number of ways to increase the quality of the names they collect at trade shows and to improve prospect follow-up. One is to use the exhibit booth as a screening device, qualifying prospects there and inviting them to another location for, say, a product demonstration. Another is to automate the process as much as possible. Many trade shows provide attendee badges with a magnetic strip that contains their mailing address and additional data from their registration form. The badge is swiped through a credit-card-like machine at the exhibitor's booth, producing an instant electronic database that leaves the show with the marketer and is available for immediate analysis and fulfillment.

5. Increasingly, marketers will *gather names over the Internet*. As in all lead-generation activities, the trick is not going to be to gather a large volume of names—that is easy, especially if a marketer disregards privacy issues and records electronic addresses without the visitor's knowledge or permission. It is always more difficult to collect names of high quality in terms of buying interest and intentions. Experience, however, reinforces the direct marketing maxim that, in generating leads, it is worthwhile to sacrifice quantity for quality. On the Internet that is being done by carefully targeting traffic-building advertising, including banner ads, and by requesting registration and some data—in effect, a slightly harder "offer" than simply entering the Web site without providing identification.

6. In the rush to acquire new leads, marketers often look for new names, disregarding the value of *looking in their own databases*. Pacific Bell, a unit of SBC Communications, has used sophisticated data mining techniques, including neural nets and statistical modeling, to identify business prospects for additional telephone lines.

> "We've maintained a marketing database for a few years and our customers' purchase history and usage history over a period of time is captured and saved. We found we could look at existing customers that have two lines today and travel back in time and see who started with one line, or even two or three lines, and group together customers who had demonstrated a certain behavior over time," says Bruce Pluchinsky, director of business marketing information support for SBC. . . . "We wanted to know, 'Can I predict which customers will buy two lines if they already have one line based on the behavior they are exhibiting today?' We could look at our database and find all one-line customers that exhibited all the characteristics of a business that would buy a second line," says Mr. Pluchinsky.
>
> More than 1 million businesses fell into that category last year. Knowing which ones, the telco approached them through a telemarketing campaign with the offer. . . . In a trial to test how predictive the model was, 30% of customers said they were aware they needed extra phone lines, and 10% actually purchased the service.[7]

This was by no means a no-cost approach to identifying prospects, but it had the advantage of speed over new-name acquisition methods and the even greater advantage of a predictive technique that provided prequalified leads.

---

[7]Laura Loro, "Pacific Bell Taps Database to Find Business Customers," *Business Marketing,* October 1997, 19.

STEP 2: QUALIFYING SALES LEADS

Whatever the technique used to acquire new names, if it is not accompanied by substantial data acquisition, a formal qualification step will need to be undertaken. Business-to-business direct marketers generally identify the basic lead qualification criteria as DNAM, an acronym for

Desire

Need

Authority

Money

Unlike models of the communications process, this emphasizes the importance of decision-making authority and ability to commit funds in the purchase decision process in business markets. Contact with the lead—either electronically or by telephone—is the best way to obtain qualifying information. It is important to use a low-cost-per-contact medium until the lead is identified as a hot prospect who has specific plans to purchase within an identified time period. If the size of that purchase is sufficiently large, this prospect should immediately be referred to the field sales force. Qualified prospects whose purchase is small or farther into the future should be handled by an inside marketing program, by either mail or telephone. Prospects should remain in a low-cost-per-contact marketing program until it becomes profitable to turn them over to the field sales force.

Questioning Prospects

The questioning needed to qualify a prospect need not be lengthy or complex. It should be a reasonably straightforward attempt to obtain the DNAM information. For example, substituting the specifics of the product or service in the brackets of the following basic questions yields a set of qualifying questions.

1. Does your firm [engage in a particular business activity]?
2. Do you intend to purchase [a specific product or service to carry out this activity]?
3. How much do you expect to spend for it?
4. When do you expect to buy [this product or service]?
5. Are you a decision maker in this selection process? If not, who is?
6. Has a budget been appropriated for this purchase?

The qualification may be done by telephone to gauge the quality of the lead and perhaps to get additional information that will help determine the exact contents of the fulfillment package. Alternatively, the same basic fulfillment package can be sent to all inquiries, and some or all of the qualifying questions can be asked as part of that step.

The Fulfillment Package

Whether used before or after the qualification contact, the fulfillment package plays a key role in the process of multistep direct marketing by answering the responder's request for information. There are several things to keep in mind when developing the package.

First and foremost, the package must be sent and received in a timely fashion, before the requester loses interest. Both the lead-processing system and the postage will affect the timeliness. The lead must be handled quickly, whether qualification is done before or after the package is sent, and transmitted to the fulfillment operation, which assembles the appropriate material and mails the package. The objective should be to mail the fulfillment package no later than 48 hours after receipt of the request for information. First-class postage will speed delivery, but is obviously expensive. The weight of the package, the value of the product being promoted, and the perceived quality of the lead are all factors to be taken into account when deciding between first- and third-class postage.

Electronic techniques are being used to meet the prospect's need for immediate information. Fax-back systems provide a special fax number that will automatically respond with the requested information. They are limited by the quality of the information that is returned, specifically its inability to use color and high-quality graphics. Fax-back systems, however, are ideal for some purposes, such as registration for conferences and trade shows. The Web can also be used to return information on demand. The marketer should keep in mind, however, that the quality of the material received by the prospect will be determined by the prospect's information system as well as by the quality of the material transmitted by the marketer. In both cases, the marketer may wish to provide basic material electronically and follow up with a complete mail package.

Second, the package should have a cover that clearly identifies it as information that has been requested. For a mail package, the envelope should contain a teaser indicating "Here is the information you requested." A fax cover sheet or e-mail message should also draw attention to the fact that it contains requested material. This is essential to separate the fulfillment package from all the unsolicited communications that cross the businessperson's desk each day. There is no need for elaborate identifying graphics because this is information sought by the recipient.

Third, a mail package should contain a bounce-back card. The card should ask whether the information is sufficient, and it often contains a toll-free customer service number. If the card is being used for even initial qualification purposes, the DNAM data should also be obtained. The electronic marketer may be able to obtain notification of successful delivery automatically. It may still be desirable to follow up by e-mail to ensure that the prospect's information needs have been satisfied.

STEP 3: DISTRIBUTING SALES LEADS

In this step an important distinction is made: Is the lead a hot prospect, which should be immediately referred to the sales force, or is it merely a qualified lead, which will be handled by direct marketing? Figure 11.2 shows the flow of leads as they are generated, qualified, and distributed.

As portrayed in Figure 11.2, the destination of the lead depends on analysis of the qualifying questions. If the prospect plans to purchase in the near future and plans to spend a sufficiently large sum of money, it will be awarded an "A" classification. If it plans to purchase at a more distant time, it will probably become a "B." Later requalification, triggered by an approaching purchase decision, may upgrade that prospect to an "A." "C" leads do not appear to have either a high likelihood of purchase or the ability to produce a sufficiently high gross margin to warrant further marketer-initiated contact. They will be sent a fulfillment package, and further contact will be left up to the prospect.

Clearly there is a great deal of work to be done to properly categorize each lead, assign it to the appropriate level of marketing effort, and follow up to be sure that the marketing program has been carried out. Leads "go stale" quickly; they need an initial response immediately and additional contacts as warranted until they either purchase or abandon the purchase

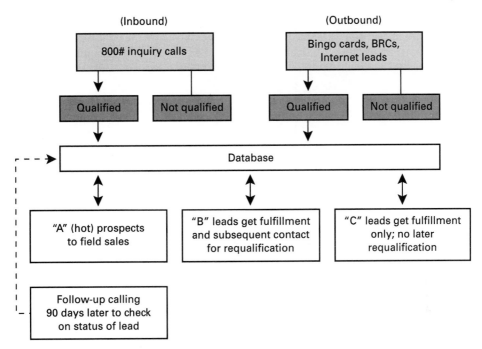

FIGURE 11.2 Lead Managment System

Source: Reprinted from *Marketing Tools* magazine with permission. © 1997, Cowles Business Media, Ithaca, New York.

process. Direct marketing and marketing communications managers also need timely reporting to assess the effectiveness of programs.

STEP 4: MONITORING AND TRACKING LEADS

Each lead should be tracked through each step as it moves from suspect to customer. Table 11.1 (p. 244) presents an example of tracking a relatively simple direct-response program that—according to column 4 in which only media costs are used in calculating the cost per sale—did not include referrals to the field sales force. In a more complex program, there might be additional columns, reflecting additional steps in the process. There might also be additional rows, reflecting additional sources of leads, which might be reflected in a higher cost per sale for sales closed by a salesperson, although if the size of the average sale were large enough that might not be true. You should also not be surprised if different media produced very different response rates and conversion rates, leading to great differences in the cost per sale for each medium. That is often the case.

This example is a good illustration of the simple financial ratios that form the basis of lead tracking and reporting. Data must be collected at each step and permit the comparison and analysis of data across and between steps if the measures are to be valid.

What the example of Table 11.1 does not consider is the issue of lead follow-up. Strange as it seems, one of the weakest links in the whole process in most programs is the contacting of qualified leads, either through direct marketing techniques or the field sales

TABLE 11.1 A Basic Lead Management Report

	Column 1	Column 2	Column 3	Column 4	Column 5
Media	Response Rate	Conversion to Prospect Ratio	Sales Ratio	Cost per Sale	Retention Rate (60 days after sale)
Formula	# Leads Generated	$\dfrac{\text{\# Prospects}}{\text{\# Leads}}$	$\dfrac{\text{\# Sales}}{\text{\# Prospects}}$	$\dfrac{\text{Costs of Media}}{\text{\# Sales}}$	$\dfrac{\text{\# Customers Still Active}}{\text{\# Original Sales}}$
Magazine Ad Publication 1	250	125/250	13/125 = 10.5%	$6,000/13 = $461	10/13 = 76.9%
Ratio Ad					
Direct Mail					

Source: Reprinted from *Marketing Tools* magazine, with permission. © 1997, Cowles Business Media, Ithaca, New York.

force. One source estimates that as many as 70 percent of all leads are not followed up.[8] The cost of generating those leads varies widely, but it is common for each one to cost more than $100, sometimes much more. That is a great waste. Even worse is the fact that many of those leads might have been converted into sales.

This seems counterintuitive; both field sales and direct marketing should be eager to follow up leads and increase their sales effectiveness. Yet, in many companies a new sales lead program produces only a cynical "been there, done that" kind of reaction, especially on the part of the sales force. Programs have come and gone, and they have not been productive. That becomes a self-fulfilling promise.

One group of experts has identified a number of common barriers to achieving successful sales lead programs:[9]

Barrier 1. Senior management does not care. Senior management is often unaware of the detailed follow-up and the cross-departmental cooperation that is required to make a lead program work.

Barrier 2. Salespeople remain unconvinced about the potential of successful lead programs. Salespeople may interpret the program as an implication that they are not doing their job, and sales managers may imply that leads are for slow days. Marketing may contribute to the problem by not thoroughly qualifying leads.

Barrier 3. Poor coordination hobbles marketing and sales. Direct marketing and marketing communications personnel are often unaware of issues crucial to the sales force, such as quota deadlines, sales contests, and balanced distribution of leads across sales territories. For its part, the sales force resents the additional paperwork generated by the reports necessary to monitor the success of the program.

Barrier 4. The company mismanages its prospect lists. "Inquiries become orphans in a netherworld between marketing and sales. As a result, the company sends the wrong information to inquirers, sends it late, and does not tailor it to inquirers' specific interests. Marketing collects limited and uninformative data and updates them infrequently. Marketing rarely compares separate databases—one for orders and one for inquiries, for example—much less merges them into a marketing information system."

Barrier 5. Management does not hold salespeople accountable. "Sales management does not insist on follow-up and new prospect status reporting, even though it fusses over detailed expense and call reporting."

Barrier 6. Management does not hold marketing people accountable. "Chief marketing officers do not . . . insist on program return-on-investment reports, . . . evidence that inquiry generation ties in with company sales goals, or analyses of inquiry source productivity."

A number of functional departments need to be fully engaged in each lead program. Direct marketing and sales management will always be involved. Direct marketing may include separate groups who are responsible for mail (lead generation, fulfillment, and follow-up), telephone (follow-up and inside sales), and direct response advertising (in trade

---

[8]Kate Bertrand, "High Tech Enhancements Fortify Trade Show Leads," *Business Marketing,* February 1996, 1, 4.

[9]Adapted with quotations from Bob Donath, James W. Obermayer, Carolyn K. Dixon, and Richard A. Crocker, "When Your Prospect Calls," *Marketing Management* (1994): 27–37.

journals and other media). All must be involved in the program, and the contribution of each must be measured if the program is to be a success.

The process just described can become a complex one for two reasons. First, there may be numerous steps in the process, which may occur over a considerable period of time, before a sale is actually closed. Second, various groups who are likely to be in the habit of working rather independently must be involved in a closely coordinated program. These two issues are exacerbated when a network of independent dealers or distributors is included in the program.

LEAD-GENERATION PROGRAMS FOR DEALER NETWORKS

The problems of motivation and control are magnified when a traditional lead generation program is executed on behalf of a dealer network instead of the firm's own field sales force. The dealers, as independent businesspeople, must be handled with special care. A carrot-and-stick approach usually works best. The carrot is genuinely qualified, fresh leads. The stick is some type of requirement of dealers that will give them a stake in the success of the program. This assumes that most lead-generation programs are initiated by the manufacturer; programs initiated and carried out by dealers themselves without some type of support from the manufacturer are comparatively rare. A number of issues must be resolved about the manner in which the traditional program will be implemented:

- *Who plans and coordinates the program?* Generally, programs are more effective if the manufacturer takes the lead in designing a program, receiving leads, and distributing them to the appropriate dealer.

- *Who bears the cost of the program?* If dealers bear at least some of the cost of the program, they are more likely to take an active role in it. This may involve a shared-cost program or it may be implemented by the manufacturer providing the promotional material customized with dealer information and the dealer taking the responsibility for generating prospect names and paying for the mailing.

- *Who processes and tracks the leads?* Although most dealers would like to see leads come directly to them, centralized control tends to be more effective. Just as is true with a field sales force, if leads are not tracked, they may not be followed up in a timely fashion or may not be followed up at all.

Technology, however, is rapidly changing the nature of the support that business marketers can provide to their dealers and distributors, taking it far beyond generic mail pieces and reply cards. At one level, custom printing techniques make it possible for the manufacturer to produce brochures or catalogs that feature the intermediary's logo, driving business directly to the dealer or distributor. At a slightly higher level of technology, it is possible to provide marketing material to business partners on a secure Web site.

IBM began its TeamPlayers program by offering its dealer-cooperative direct marketing campaigns. These mailing pieces, designed to build dealers' business for IBM products, were based on IBM's own successful direct-response programs. The lead-generation pieces, produced and mailed by IBM, featured the distributor's company logo, services, and a picture of the sales team. Prospects were asked to contact the distributor to place orders. Leads generated by this program produced more than $80 million in sales for distributors in 1997 and captured more than 80,000 new customer names. IBM maintains these names in a separate database and guarantees that it will not mail to them except on behalf of the distributors. Because some resellers are still concerned that IBM will solicit their customers, they may elect to maintain their databases through a third-party firm.

The program, although not directly profitable to IBM, was considered a success and expanded under the title Campaigns-on-Demand. This allows distributors, referred to by IBM as "business partners," to sign onto a special Web site (www.ibm-teamplayers.com). Here they can view predesigned direct mail pieces and customize them with dealer logos, maps to their location, and promotional offers. The pieces are laser printed and mailed by IBM. The partners receive lead tracking information for each program. They can also add prospect screening services or a dedicated toll-free number, which is handled by a call center. These programs are estimated to save distributors up to 90 percent of their direct mail costs.

According to IBM's director of brand direct marketing, "The typical business partner is really missioned to sell, and when it comes to marketing they don't have the time or the infrastructure. . . . Another corollary reason they like the program is that they are often too small to fund an aggressive marketing program. A third reason is that we can provide marketing programs at a lower price, because we are doing such volume. We are almost acting as an outsourced marketing department."[10]

Lead generation or business development programs that are jointly undertaken by manufacturers and dealers or distributors have many similarities to vertical cooperative advertising campaigns. These have long been a staple of consumer marketing and have more recently achieved prominence in business markets with campaigns such as "Intel Inside." In cooperative advertising there is potential for joint benefits to be realized that exceed the total of benefits accruing to the manufacturer and the dealer network acting separately and independently.[11] Although we know of no published studies that document the economics of shared lead-generation programs, direct marketers should be aware of the synergy possible as a result of these programs.

One of the issues in business-to-business marketing is who owns the end user database—the manufacturer, or the dealer or distributor who has direct contact with the user? Whether that database is the property of the manufacturer, through initiatives such as the Hewlett-Packard database-building program described at the beginning of this chapter, or whether it is the property of an intermediary, the database is crucial to the success of today's business marketer.

The Business-to-Business Database

Figure 11.3 (p. 248) represents the business-to-business database as a funnel. It is the direct marketer's job to capture the names, addresses, and data about a multitude of customers and prospects from many different sources. Even current customers should be considered as prospects for a forthcoming direct-response program. In fact, we know from our studies of Customer Lifetime Value that our current customers are our best prospects. Having identified prospects, the direct marketer's next job is to execute programs that will convert prospects into customers and customers into loyal repeat buyers.

We first look at a hypothetical but realistic performance of a business marketer's database in a test against rental lists. We then will look at a longer-term analysis of the revenue

---

[10]Denise Duclaux, "IBM Finds Success with TeamPlayers," *DM News,* 5 January 1998, 2; also based on "IBM Offers Its Partners Online Program to Simplify Direct Mail," *Business Marketing,* October 1997, 6.

[11]Paul D. Berger, "Vertical Cooperative Advertising Ventures," *Journal of Marketing Research* (August 1972): 309–312.

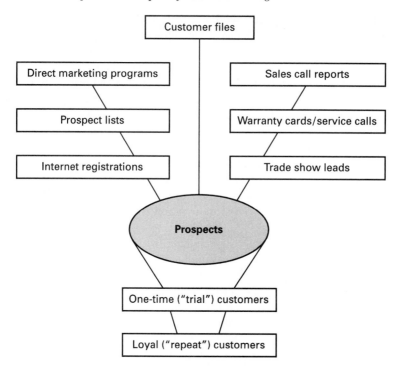

FIGURE 11.3 Business-to-Business Database

stream of an existing customer base. Both of these perspectives paint a compelling picture of the importance of the database to cost-effective business marketing.

Assume that a producer of external storage devices has typically achieved a response rate between 1 and 2 percent on its lead-generation direct-response programs, not an unusually low response for prospecting mailings. A radically new product, targeted primarily to the home office market, caused them to look for a more productive approach. They developed a mailing package that offered a paperback book on storage options. The book explained the concept of the new product, showed the benefits of its use in various applications, and told which options were important to which use. The mail package focused on the offer and encouraged recipients to return the reply card to receive a copy of the book. To test the offer, assume a mailing of slightly more than 20,000 pieces, approximately 5,000 each to rental lists from three relevant trade publications, and another 5,000 to prospects from the company's own database. The results that might be seen in such a test mailing are shown in Table 11.2.

We might attribute the overall lift in response rate to a relevant incentive that added value to a basic offer. As direct marketers, we can attribute the higher response rate from the firm's house list to the well-known phenomenon, "The direct marketer's best *prospects* are current *customers.*"

The same phenomenon is evident when the accounts in the database are analyzed in terms of their revenue stream over a given period of time, as shown in Table 11.3. Marketers who carefully analyze their sales patterns on an account-by-account basis are well aware of the 80/20 rule, which states that 20 percent of customers generate 80 percent of

TABLE 11.2 Hypothetical Test Results for Lead Generation Mailing for Storage Devices

List	Number Mailed	Number of Responses	Response Rate
Byte	4,995	431	8.6%
Entrepreneur	4,909	327	6.7
Inc	4,905	369	7.5
House prospect list	5,229	894	17.1
Total	20,038	2,021	10.1

sales (Pareto's law). These percentages, of course, are not absolute; a firm may be startled to find that 15 percent of its customers generate 95 percent of its business! However, the basic principle—that a small percentage of customers accounts for a large percentage of business—holds true across firms and industries, in consumer markets as well as in business markets. Thus the business marketer should carefully analyze its customer base, discover who its best customers are, and design programs based on this knowledge.

The analysis by revenue decile shown in Table 11.3 is based on 66,000 customers who generated $2 million in revenues. Only 3 percent (1,768) of the customers produce 20 percent of the revenues of this business. Whereas the average revenue per customer is just over $30.30 ($2,000,000/66,000), the average revenue per customer for the top 3 percent is $226.24 ($2,000,000 $\times$ .20 = 1,768). The company might ask itself whether the $11.41 in average revenue (not margin!) produced by the 17,535 customers in the lowest revenue percentile covers the cost of doing business with them. The answer is that it almost certainly does not. If that is true, the firm is losing money on a substantial proportion of its transactions!

TABLE 11.3 Revenue from Customer Base by Percentile

Number of Customers	Cumulative Number of Customers	Percent of Revenue	Average Revenue per Customer
650	650	10	$307.69
1,118	1,768	20	178.89
1,196	2,964	30	167.22
1,996	4,960	40	100.00
3,206	8,166	50	62.38
3,799	11,965	60	52.65
9,713	21,678	70	20.59
11,268	32,946	80	17.75
15,519	48,465	90	12.89
17,535	66,000	100	11.41

Source: Used with permission of Epsilon, Burlington, MA 01803.

Several marketing approaches are suggested by this simple analysis. The business marketer needs to go beyond this decile analysis and look at profitability by customer. Once unprofitable customers have been identified, there are at least two possibilities. The first is to attempt to make unprofitable customers profitable. A likely tactic is to switch them from a higher-cost-per-contact sales mode (probably field sales) to a lower-cost-per-contact mode (probably some form of direct marketing). Many businesses have done this in recent years, although these customers may not be very pleased. For that matter, the sales force may not be pleased initially, although it should be in their long-run best interest to serve more productive customers. The other option is to simply stop serving unprofitable customers who seem to have little likelihood of becoming profitable. That is painful for all concerned, especially if there have been personal relations between the sales force and customers or between the managements of the two firms. The impact can be lessened, however, if the marketer finds a new supplier for the former customer, one who can handle the business profitably.

Once unprofitable customers have been eliminated, the firm can begin to look at the remaining customers to see which ones are worthy of what kinds of marketing effort. The result is invariably a pyramid, such as the one shown with hypothetical data in Figure 11.4. Of the 250,000 customers in this hypothetical but realistic customer base, the account analysis shows that only a small proportion produce sufficient gross margin to justify being handled by the field sales force. A significant, but still relatively small, segment of the customer base generates margin that qualifies it for nonpersonal, marketer-initiated contact. A large proportion of the total customer base does not produce sales and margin that justify the cost of proactive marketing efforts.

Implementation of this type of approach is also difficult, both for the customers who are downgraded to non–face-to-face contact and for the sales force, which often faces a significant reduction in size. Yet, the cost of personal selling leaves little choice for the astute marketer. You should also note that this is the same type of reasoning that we applied to sales leads in the preceding section.

Figure 11.4 refers to the "potential" of accounts. This implies that all accounts have been analyzed, probably using a predictive model based on the characteristics of highest-performing accounts. Each account has been rated according to the level of sales it should produce with an appropriate marketing effort. Accounts that are not performing up to their potential are identified for upgrading. Upgrading can be accomplished either by selling the

FIGURE 11.4 Analysis of Hypothetical Customer Base

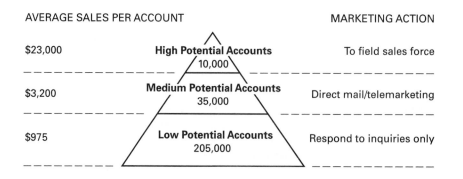

customers a greater volume of the products they are currently buying or by cross-selling, that is, selling them other products from the line.

The marketer should recognize that there is a strategic implication inherent in this type of analysis. It is certainly important to serve the existing customer base in the most efficient way possible. It is also true that acquiring new customers who have the same characteristics as the most productive existing customers is usually profitable. However, this type of reasoning does *not* lead the marketer to the consideration of new market segments that could be served profitably. Acquisition of new customer *segments* will require marketing programs over and above those that aim to achieve the greatest level of profitable sales from the existing customer base.

THE MEDIA OF BUSINESS-TO-BUSINESS DIRECT MARKETING

The dual needs of generating sales leads and serving the existing customer base in the most efficient fashion dictate that the direct marketer uses a variety of media. However, the media mix is quite different from that used by consumer marketers. As shown in Table 11.4 (p. 252), trade magazines account for the largest portion of business marketers' advertising budgets, with television not appearing as a separate category. Direct marketing—the combination of mail, telephone, and the Internet—accounts for a sizable proportion of expenditures, one that has been growing for a number of years.

Another way of looking at media costs is to consider the typical costs of reaching a customer in different media. According to Penton Research Services, as quoted in *Business Marketing* magazine,[12] cost per contact in various media might look like

Personal sales call	$277.00
Trade show	162.00
Telemarketing	31.16
Business letter	13.60
Direct mail	1.68
Internet	.98
Specialized business publication	.32

Bear in mind that these figures can vary substantially, depending on the purpose of the contact (e.g., customer acquisition, routine customer call) or the nature of the product, with high technology products and complex services often experiencing higher-than-average cost per contact.

Two aspects of business media are sufficiently different from consumer media to warrant special attention, trade magazines and business-to-business catalogs.

Trade Magazines

There are hundreds of specialized trade magazines published in countries around the world. Many are so focused on small industry segments that they have a circulation of only a few thousand. This makes them a very cost effective way of reaching business decision makers with brand advertising or sales lead generation campaigns. It also makes their subscriber lists valuable to business marketers.

---

[12]"Reaching Your Customers," *Business Marketing,* November 1997, 34.

TABLE 11.4 Media Breakdown of Business-to-Business Advertising Budgets		
	1996	*1993*
Trade magazine advertising	27%	22%
Trade shows	22	18
Direct mail	10	11
Promotion and market support	7	10
Dealer or distributor materials	6	13
General magazine advertising	6	2
Internet	6	—
Directories	5	6
Telemarketing or telecom	5	6
Publicity and public relations	5	5

Source: Adapted from "The Big Picture," *Business Marketing,* November 1997, 27.

Subscriber lists is not an entirely accurate term, however. Many trade publications are distributed by means of *controlled* circulation, not paid subscriptions. Controlled circulation requires potential recipients to *qualify* for the publication by supplying information such as industry, job title, lines of business, size of firm, and decision-making authority. This creates a pool of targeted recipients that is highly desirable to marketers who need to reach these specialized sectors. It enables the publications to be entirely supported by advertising, with subscriptions provided free of charge to qualified managers and technical personnel.

Business-to-Business Catalogs

Catalogs have been a staple of business marketing for a long time. Business catalogs have changed a great deal in recent years, however, from uninteresting printed pieces that were little more than price lists to attractive publications that use many of the techniques of the best consumer catalogs.

As catalogs have become more widely used in repeat-purchase, relatively low margin categories such as computer and office supplies, other changes have taken place. We discuss interactive catalogs in the next section. There also are also important innovations taking place in paper catalogs. Viking Office Products exemplifies these changes.

Viking was founded in 1960 in Los Angeles, where it retains its headquarters. The company has no retail outlets, and by 1995 mailed 140 million catalogs each year. The company is widely known as a leader in the use of database-driven one-to-one marketing in both the U.S. and international markets.

Viking president Irving Helford refers to their strategy as PRISM—personalized, regionalized and individual selection of merchandise. Viking personalizes its catalogs by inkjet messages on front and back covers and on selected interior pages. Even an inquirer who requests a catalog via the firm's Web site is greeted by name and welcomed as a prospective customer (see Figure 11.5). About half of all catalogs printed in the United States contain personalized content. Viking has also discovered that there are regional preferences in office products, and the catalogs cater to those preferences. Finally, Viking uses its database to create individual catalogs for customers based on their past buying behavior. A customer

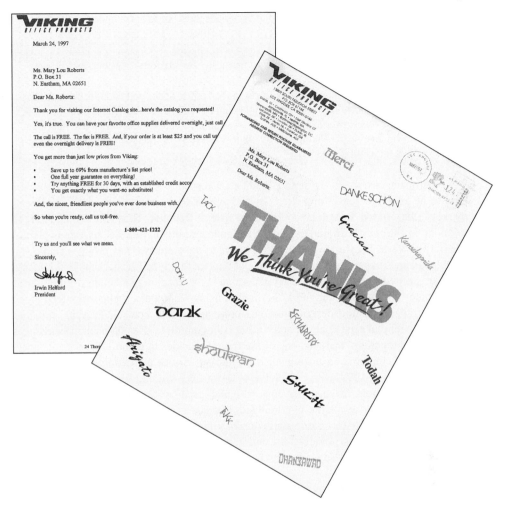

FIGURE 11.5 Viking Mailing Envelope with Personalized Greeting

Source: Used with permission of Viking Office Products.

who habitually buys one brand of ball-point pens gets only that brand in the personalized catalog; a lawyer gets advertisements only for legal software, not software for a CPA's office. The company saves money on paper and printing; more important, it makes clear that the customer's business is recognized and valued.

> As Helford puts it, Viking's goal is to service "customers beyond what they've ever seen or had before and earn their loyalty for future business."
>
> Servicing customers' needs has translated into what Helford calls "fanatical customer service." As he says, "People will forget what you say, they'll probably forget what you do, but they'll never forget the way you made them feel."[13]

---

[13]Patricia A. Scussel, "Catalog of the Year: Viking Office Products," *Catalog Age* (September 1996): 57.

He adds that, "Ninety-eight percent of our customers think we have the lowest prices, but we don't."[14]

A trade paper describes "the Viking formula" for customer service as follows:

in cities where they have warehouses (eight in the United States and eight in Europe), they deliver same-day if the order is received by 11 a.m. Not one of the superstores offers this type of service. And orders over $25 are free, whereas all their competitors have a $50 minimum. For those who live near a Viking facility, 98 to 99 percent of the orders are picked, packed and shipped for overnight delivery.[15]

European customers are generally not accustomed to this level of customer service and tend to be very favorably impressed. In addition, Viking caters to numerous international markets (the United Kingdom, Germany, Austria, Benelux, Scandinavia, and the Czech Republic in Europe; Australia; expansion to Japan and other countries in Asia is planned) in a variety of ways. They offer merchandise native to the country. They produce catalogs in the local languages, using their employees in Los Angles to do the translations. In Germany, catalogs are printed on the slightly larger paper that is the norm in that country. Viking produces visual material as well as copy in Los Angeles, using techniques such as digitized photography. Centralized catalog design promotes consistency and control. Printing and mailing, however, is done in each country, and Viking is beginning to use personalized messages and content in international markets, one of the first companies to do so.

Viking's emphasis on customer service and one-to-one marketing created sales of more than $1.3 billion in 1997, with 63 percent of those sales coming from international markets. Their average annual revenue per customer increased by almost 5 percent and customer retention, figures for which are not divulged, increased to the highest level ever.[16]

Is it also possible that companies such as Viking, who know how to create and use customer databases and to provide swift and accurate fulfillment, will be leaders as business moves onto the Internet? Some experts believe they will be.

DOING BUSINESS ON THE WEB

As we know by now, the origins of the Internet were in the defense and academic communities, and much of the explosive growth in the 1990s came from consumers and businesspeople searching for information. E-commerce has been slower to develop, but, by one estimate, business-to-business sales on the Internet will increase from $8 billion in 1997 to $327 billion in the year 2002.[17] Another source predicted that the figure would be more than $1 trillion.[18] Obviously, no one can give a precise figure, but most industry experts agree that Internet sales of goods and services to business markets will soon dwarf electronic sales to consumers. What are the reasons that businesses are moving so quickly to Web-based or Web-assisted transactions? In a single word, the answer is *productivity*.

---

[14]Barbara Drimmer, "Viking Chairman Attributes Winning Strategy to DB Marketing Techniques," *DM News*, 8 July 1996, 2.

[15]Bill Dean, "Viking Pillages Office Superstores," *Catalog Marketing,* 26 February 1996, 19.

[16]Dean, "Viking Pillages Office Superstores"; www.vikingop.com, 26 December 1997.

[17]"Forrester Research Finds Internet Business Trade to Jump to $327 Billion by the Year 2002," Press Release, www.forrester.com, 28 July 1997.

[18]John Borland, "E-Commerce Companies Struggle to Make Profit," www.cmp.net, 11 December 1997.

According to Blane Erwin of Forrester Research, "Businesses are aggressively adopting intercompany trade over the Internet because they want to cut costs, reduce order processing time, and improve information flow. For most firms, the rise in trade over the Internet also coincides with a marked decrease in phone and fax use, allowing salespeople to concentrate on proactively managing customer accounts rather than serving as information givers and order takers."[19]

Business marketers, large and small, have taken various approaches to Internet commerce. In *NetMarketing*'s first ranking of the 200 best business-to-business Web sites, a little-known distributor, Marshall Industries, achieved first place because, according to the publication, "This site has it all."[20]

Marshall Industries is a $1.3 billion distributor of electronic components. As early as 1994 the company recognized that information technology was revolutionizing business and began to design a enterprise-wide strategy that included the Internet. According to President Rob Rodin, "The Internet is not the end-all, but connectivity is."

Their definition of connectivity includes 24-hour call centers, 24-hour live help via interactive chat sessions on the Web site, and on-line services that are the equal of that found in any other distribution channel. Customers can search for a component by part number, manufacturer or product description. They can order the part, pay for it, and track the status of the order. Finally, they can expedite delivery by hot-linking to freight forwarders. If they wish, they can participate in live engineering seminars.

In making the commitment to this level of electronic commerce and customer service, Marshall made numerous organizational changes in an attempt to prevent friction between traditional channels and cyberspace. Chief among them, it eliminated all sales commissions and management incentives based on specific objectives and replaced them with a single reward criterion—corporate profit.

"Every marketing person has responsibility for the site and hundreds of people contribute," says Mr. Rodin. The site hosts about 33,000 visitors per month, each of whom clicks on 25 to 30 pages at each visit. Marshall spends about $2 million annually on Web development and maintenance costs. They do not, however, attempt to measure ROI on their Web site investment. "We don't see the Internet as a [profit and loss] center," he says. We don't have an ROI on every piece of literature, sales call or customer. We haven't been consumed by applying these issues to it."[21]

Small firms who are willing to start simply and do much of the work themselves can create an Internet presence cheaply by using off-the-shelf development tools. The two biggest cost factors then become how much of the content is already in digital format and the number of photographs to be included in the Internet catalog.[22]

At Boxer-Northwest Co., a supplier of food service equipment in Portland, Oregon, the firm's controller designed the Web site. "He simply downloaded a free piece of software from the Net; designing the site, he says, was no more difficult than using a word processor."

---

[19]"Forrester Research Finds Internet Business."

[20]"The NetMarketing 200," *NetMarketing,* November 1997, 18.

[21]Adapted from Russell Shaw, "The Best of the Best," *NetMarketing,* November 1997, 1, 22; Clinton Wilder, Bruce Caldwell, and Gregory Dalton, "More Than Electronic Commerce," *Information Week,* 18 December 1997.

[22]Joe Mullich, "Building a Net Catalog," www.netb2b.com, 28 December 1997.

Fortunately, Boxer's catalog data was already in electronic form. The biggest job was to add more copy for the 6,000 items included in the initial catalog. A local computer consultant converted the existing electronic data into the online format for a few thousand dollars.

Boxer says it costs them $25 per month to put the site on a local server and another $50 for a programmer to update data and add new items. Had they included digitized photos for all 6,000 products, initial costs would have increased by $20,000. They add that soon after establishing the Web site, they began receiving orders from the East Coast and other areas where they had not previously been able to market their products.[23]

Boxer's success in obtaining orders over the Web highlights some other important issues with respect to doing business there. Some items to which you should pay careful attention are[24]

- What are your objectives—providing customer service, giving additional technical information, conducting transactions?
- What is the offer that makes it worthwhile for customers to visit (and return to) your Web site—lower prices, more information, easier ways to locate products? "An online catalog has to be easier to wade through than a traditional catalog," advises Philip Pulver, president of Catalogs Online in Richland, Washington.

Focus groups can be helpful in understanding how customers search for information so you can categorize it in a way that facilitates their search.

- Are you able to fulfill immediately? "This is an ultra competitive environment and people have expectations that if they order something it will be there tomorrow," according to Alan Cohen, managing director for electronic commerce at IBM's Internet division.

Whereas some small firms are reveling in the "level playing field" furnished by the Internet, some large global firms are using their resources and technological expertise to explore new cyberfrontiers:

The Federal Express Corporation was founded in 1973 to provide overnight delivery of letters and small packages. Founder Fred Smith foresaw a business built, not just on airplanes and mainframe computers, but also on mobile computers, package tracking systems and sophisticated databases. From the beginning the company was predicated on information technology and made huge investments to keep a technological step ahead of its competitors.

The firm's COSMOS network provides real-time tracking of each item from the time it enters the FedEx system until it is safely delivered. In the early years it began to furnish free terminals to large-volume customers that allowed them to automate the entire shipping process. A few years later it started giving away dial-up software to customers so they could track their own packages on their desktop computers. By the mid 1990s its Web site (www.fedex.com) allowed customers to track packages and order shipments without calling a customer service representative. Far from being annoyed by having to perform this task themselves, customers were delighted with the control and instant gratification they received by being able to access the data themselves. FedEx saved $4 million a year ($2 to $5 per call) on customer service costs and built a transactional database of immense value.

By 1997 FedEx had 590 planes, 40,000 ground vehicles, over $11 billion in sales, and an annual expenditure of about $1 billion on information technology. And once again it was using that IT to change the way companies large and small conducted their business. The

[23] Adapted from Mullich, "Building a Net Catalog."

[24] Based on Mullich, "Building a Net Catalog."

concept is that of a fully integrated corporate partner that picks up, transports, warehouses, and delivers a company's entire finished goods inventory from its factory directly to its customers, with status data available at all times.

"We believe that information can replace inventory," says Laurie Tucker, senior VP of logistics, electronic commerce, and catalog, a $500 million FedEx unit. "We could just sit back and be the beneficiary of electronic commerce, but instead we want to be the catalyst for the customer to reduce costs." Two examples:

- Omaha Steaks chose FedEx for its exclusive delivery service before competitors offered two-day air service. It stayed when competitive services became available because of the IT links between Omaha Steaks and FedEx. Orders are sent to Omaha Steak warehouses and to FedEx at the same time. The orders are delivered to a FedEx hub and from that point on, the company has full access to delivery status data. It also lets customers track their orders on the Omaha Steaks Web site by means of a link to the FedEx Web-based tracking service.

- National Semiconductor Corp. outsourced its entire logistics system to FedEx in the early 1990s. Now virtually all of its products, which are manufactured in Asia in its own factories and those of subcontractors, are shipped directly to a FedEx distribution warehouse in Singapore.[25]

"They have the goods, they operate the warehouse, and they create everything necessary to process the order and then hand it off to the carrier—which of course is FedEx," says Larry Stroud, NatSemi's manager of logistics analysis. The result has been a significant improvement in customer service while lowering distribution costs. The average customer delivery cycle has decreased from four weeks to seven days, and distribution costs have declined from 2.9 percent of sales to 1.2 percent. They were also able to eliminate seven regional warehouses in the United States, Asia, and Europe.

By integrating its own IT with that of its customers, FedEx continues to create value-added services that promote a continuing relationship. For example, Cicso Systems, producer of networking equipment, lets its customers order FedEx services without ever leaving the Cisco Web site.[26]

Doing business on the Web is not just about creating your own Web site and devising ways to get customers to come to it. A number of companies are adding value for existing customers or creating whole new businesses by developing networks that allow customers to efficiently search for information about products and services and link to marketers who have them available for sale.

To easily understand the value of these megasites, think about the last time you looked for something using a Web search engine or did an automated search on one of the databases in the library. Chances are, one of two things happened. One possibility is that you came up with nothing or almost nothing. Perhaps your search criterion was too narrow or perhaps there just wasn't much there. The other common occurrence is to come up with hundreds, often thousands, of "hits"—far too many for you to examine. Either way, the search leaves you feeling frustrated.

Then suppose you are a professional purchasing agent or a businessperson who needs to acquire a specific item. If this is a nonroutine purchase, where do you start? The time-honored process is to consult industrial directories, purchasing files, or local Yellow Pages. Having accumulated a list of prospective suppliers, you contact each one of them, requesting

---

[25]Based on Monua Janah and Clinton Wilder, "Networking—Special Delivery—Think FedEx Is Only about Delivering Packages? Think Again." www.techweb.com, 28 December 1997.

[26]Todd Lappin, "The Airline of the Internet," *Wired,* December 1996, 234–240, 282–284; Janah and Wilder, "Networking—Special Delivery."

catalogs, brochures, or price lists. Then you must examine the sales material and try to determine which has the best value and can meet your delivery schedule. This is a time-consuming process, and one that leaves you with little assurance that the search produced the best possible purchase option. As the previous paragraph suggests, the Web has furnished another source of information, but it is not clear that it has improved either the quality or the timeliness of the purchasing process. Something beyond the commercial search engines is needed to provide the ability to filter information needed by the potential purchaser and to help marketers avail themselves of the huge potential market available on the Internet.

Manufacturing Marketplace

One such marketing site is Manufacturing Marketplace (www.manufacturing.net), established by Cahners Business Information, the U.S. subsidiary of British publisher Reed Elsevier. Cahners has long published numerous specialized trade magazines on narrow industrial segments with titles that range from *Auto Body Repair News* and *Cheese Market News* to *Biomedical Products* and *Broadband Systems & Design.* This gives them a base of both editorial content and advertisers who must target these narrow segments and provides a solid foundation for an electronic network.

According to Cahners's on-site promotional material, Manufacturing Marketplace is "the most comprehensive Web site for the manufacturing industry, integrating industry-specific information of interest to managers and other employees in the U.S. manufacturing sector."[27]

The scope of the site is shown in its home page, shown in Figure 11.6. Specific contents include

- A database of more than 30,000 manufacturers and service companies
- A directory of more than 6,000 new products, updated weekly
- On-line product information
- Links to the Web sites of some companies
- The ability to search based on product, company, or geographical region
- Editorial content from 12 Cahners publications that serve the relevant markets (these include *Metalworking Digest, Purchasing Magazine,* and *ScanTech News*)
- Content from the Lexis-Nexis database (also owned by Reed Elsevier) and additional content written solely for the site
- The ability to customize a personal page with relevant content identified by the user
- The option of receiving a weekly e-mail newsletter on user-specified topics
- Employment listings
- Discussion forums

The electronic product line also includes an international network called Kompass (www.kompass.com). In late 1997 that site indexed the products of 1.5 million companies in 61 countries, with material available in many languages.

Because Cahners's objective is to provide comprehensive listings in the relevant product categories, companies are not charged for the generic product listings. There are, however, a variety of advertising arrangements, some of which are bundled with the paper publications, that provide for a greater depth of information on the site itself and links to the advertiser's own Web site.

---

[27]www.manufacturing.net, 21 December 1997.

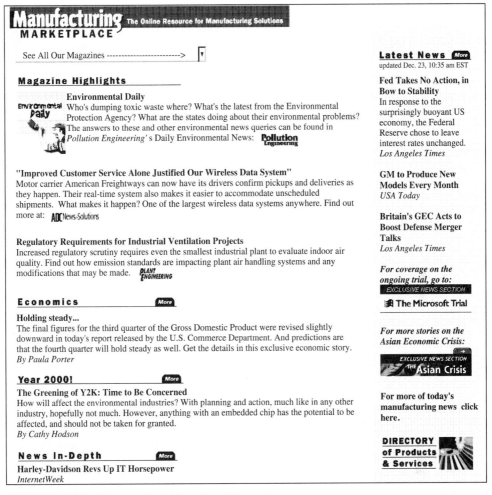

FIGURE 11.6 Manufacturing Marketplace Home Page

Source: Cahners Business Information, a division of Reed Elsevier, Inc. Used by permission.

At the time of this writing, Manufacturing Marketplace was a free service, requiring only registration to access all parts of the site. Having asked for these registration data, the company is explicit about its privacy policy. Item 5 in its terms and conditions statement says:

> Cahners provides advertisers whose Manufacturing Marketplace content areas are visited with demographic reports that include Members' names, registration profiles, and usage patterns. To opt out of this tracking mechanism, e-mail feedback@manufacturing.net, including the phrase "opt out" in the subject line. You must include your name, company, email address and username."[28]

Like most of Cahners' controlled circulation publications, the Web site it is supported by advertising. This allows them to provide a great deal of information free to all who wish to access it.

---

[28] www.manufacturing.net, 30 December 1997.

The Manufacturing Marketplace Web site sounds like a simple concept, and in some ways perhaps it is the electronic counterpart of the industrial directory. However, users of the Internet have developed high expectations concerning the level of assistance they will receive, and, according to one study, many business-to-business sites fail to live up to expectations.

IDG.net

International Data Group is a global publisher of computer-related periodicals including its flagship *Computerworld* and books including the highly regarded ". . . for Dummies" series. IDG and its market research subsidiary International Data Corporation, conducted in-depth interviews with more than 50 computer professionals who were familiar with technology sites. Their research yielded three basic conclusions:

- In general, people searching for information about computer hardware and software had a very hard time even getting close to articles about the products they cared about. They had a tough time even figuring out where to start.

- On the whole, the search engines were not designed in ways that helped actual human beings using the Internet. . . . Most large-content supersites, while they may contain much valuable information, give little thought to the actual experience of the visitor in navigating through their interface to the content they seek.

- The incidence of failure on the part of the computer system was high. More than half the time, the Web could not provide an answer that the human visitor found satisfactory. Visitors often gave up on a site before finding any content remotely helpful to them. . . . When they clicked on an ad, it tended to be because they were tired of trying to find the editorial content they had come to the site for in the first place.[29]

The IDG White Paper points out that most businesspeople search the Web for answers to specific questions such as the solution to a technical problem or the price of a product. Many Web sites, on the other hand, are better suited for casual browsing—for moving around from one page to another—than they are for quickly locating a specific piece of information. They suggest that this may have something to do with the way Web promotion is currently measured and compensated. One commonly used measure by which rates are set is the number of pages viewed on a visit to a site. Given the primitive state of promotional effectiveness measurement on the Web, the measure has some utility. However, it has little relation to the most valuable resource that businesspeople are using on the Net—their time.

Based on their research and numerous performance studies, the company created IDG.net (www.idg.net) to provide a user-friendly gateway to the content of their 140 separate sites, which contain content about computer-related issues all over the world. They also envision an on-line shopping environment that includes access to IDG product reviews and comparisons coupled with the ability to purchase the products electronically (www.web-shopper.com).

IDG.net also includes a specific statement under a "Personalization and Privacy" heading on their site:

> IDG.net's personalization system builds a profile of your interests, based on your evaluations of the relevance of stories you read. IDG.net will not release information about subscribers to any organization for marketing purposes, or use your profile to restrict your access to any stories.[30]

---

[29] White Paper, www.idg.com, 24 December 1997.

[30] www.idg.net, 30 December 1997.

TPN

Both Manufacturing Marketplace and IDG.net were established by publishers who serve well-defined markets and were in possession of a wealth of desirable content. Another site that is rapidly growing in popularity and prestige was initiated for a very different reason. General Electric Information Systems (GEIS) is the division of GE that specializes in Electronic Data Interchange (EDI). In 1996 the division initiated a project aimed at streamlining the parent corporation's procurement process. GE purchased some $30 billion in goods and services from about 25,000 suppliers in 1996, so making the system more efficient was an attractive prospective. The system they eventually devised was so successful that it was quickly commercialized and offered to external customers.

In 1994 GEIS began with an attempt to conduct an auction over the Internet for the Transportation Division. Not particularly satisfied with this approach, they looked for another way to harness the Net to generate purchasing efficiencies. In late 1995 they completed an Internet version of their EDI service and called it Trading Process Network (TPN) (www.tpn.geis.com).

Just a few months later,

> the new Internet-based bidding system paid off in dramatic fashion when some machinery broke down at a [GE] Lighting factory in Cleveland. . . .With no time to lose in getting repair parts, purchasing officials posted specifications and request for quotes on their Website [TPN]. Of the seven new suppliers that responded, Lighting chose one in Hungary, where GE now makes lamps. The Hungarian supplier charged $320,000, 20% less than the next-highest bid, and delivered promptly as well.
>
> The requisitioning process for machine parts, which formerly took more than seven days, has been reduced to two hours, reports Ronald J. Stettler, Lighting's manager of global sourcing. "Sourcing can now simply point and click and send out a bid package to suppliers around the world," he says. All the data are encrypted to keep them from competitors and hackers. After the bids are evaluated, orders can now go out in 24 hours instead of one or two months later, as in the past. Suppliers don't mind one bit.
>
> In the short time Lighting has used TPN, it has seen material costs decline as much as 20%. Paperwork has disappeared, and staffers have been freed for up to eight days a month to concentrate on strategic activities. Harvey F. Seegers, CEO of GE Information Services (GEIS), calls this latter accomplishment "freeing up the minds."[31]

After other divisions in the company achieved similar results, GEIS decided to offer the service to external customers. They quickly signed up more than 1,400 clients, most of them small to medium size manufacturers who presumably would have difficulty in creating this type of system for themselves. They also partnered with Thomas Register so users would have access to the publication's listing of more than 55,000 products.

Among the services offered by TPN are

- an electronic process for distribution of requests for quotes (RFQs) and bid awards
- a catalog-based purchasing service that can be used by both buyers and sellers
- a service that assists marketers in locating and bidding on marketing opportunities around the world

---

[31]"Sales Are Clicking on Manufacturing's Internet Mart" (excerpts from *Fortune,* 7 July 1997, by Gene Bylinsky); www.tpn.geis.com, 28 December 1997.

- help in establishing a Web presence
- miscellaneous services including discussion groups.

These services are very important to customers. Gloria D. Wandyez, a director of purchasing with Textron Automotive, a maker of automobile components, points out that "the costs of converting suppliers to TPN is borne by GEIS. GEIS takes our suppliers through an on-line and telephone training session. Then it takes maybe an hour to get comfortable with it. It's very user-friendly."[32]

Smaller companies who do not yet have a Web site can register for assistance in establishing one using on-line development tools. The customer fills out a few simple electronic forms, makes choices among colors and backgrounds, puts their products in the TPN electronic catalog, and they are ready to do business on the Net.[33]

This service emphasizes that, unlike Manufacturing Marketplace and IDG.net, TPN was established to facilitate electronic commerce, first between a company and its suppliers and then as a way to locate marketing opportunities on the network. These three electronic networks—each with a somewhat different perspective, but all with the objective of offering value-added services to a global marketplace—may well be an important harbinger of the future of the Internet for business marketers.

As we peer into the brave new world of electronically based direct marketing, there is one final aspect we need to consider. That is the new enterprise based solely on direct marketing using a variety of media.

"THE DIRECT MODEL"

In recent years a few notable businesses have been established using only direct-response promotion and the direct distribution channel. Companies such as amazon.com, E*Trade, Gateway 2000, and Dell differ from traditional direct marketers in important ways. Of these three, only Dell has primarily served business markets from its inception.

The story of Dell Computer, and its founder Michael Dell, is the stuff of business legend. The tale begins with a 14-year-old in a Houston, Texas, suburb who liked to take the top off his Apple II to check out its motherboard. The young Michael Dell entered the University of Texas, at his parents' insistence, as a pre-med major. During his first semester he began to buy obsolete computers from local retailers, upgrade them in his dorm room, and sell them door-to-door to local businesses. One day his roommate piled his large and growing inventory of computers and parts against the door. "He was kind of frustrated, I guess," remembers Michael Dell. "So I moved."[34]

Dell never returned for his sophomore year of college. Instead, he discovered that he did not need to upgrade old computers; he could buy parts and assemble machines himself. By marketing the computers directly to customers, he could sell them for a 15 percent price discount compared to established brands. The years since 1983 have seen Dell grow to the third largest manufacturer of computers in the world. About 90 percent of those are sold to businesses, from single units sold over the Internet to the reported 160 units per day purchased by Boeing.

---

[32] "GE's E-commerce Network Opens Up to Other Marketers," www.netb2b.com, 28 December 1997.

[33] Additional sources for this section are "PC Week's Top 10 E-commerce Sites," www.ZDNet.com, 28 December 1997; "GE to Move Purchasing to the Internet," www.techweb.com, 12 December 1997; www.tpn.geis.com, 28 December 1997.

[34] Andrew E. Serwer, "Michael Dell Turns the PC World Inside Out," *Fortune,* 8 September 1997, 80.

From the beginning, Dell Computer used traditional direct marketing media—mail and catalogs. Direct mail was used primarily for customer acquisition. "We have a large database, and we know which types of lists perform the best," says Anita Howard, manager of marketing communications.[35] Orders were taken over the telephone, by an inside sales and service force estimated to number about 700 people. Dell also has a sales force that calls on major accounts (Boeing has a dedicated sales representative on its own premises).

Because Michael Dell was an early proponent of using the Internet for transactions, the company's sales from its Web site had reached more than $1 million a day by mid-1997. These sales were mostly from two segments Dell had not penetrated deeply—individual consumers and small businesses. At this point relatively few of Dell's large customers had shifted their purchasing to the Internet, but the company was making a major effort to change that.

For major accounts it deployed individual Intranets that contain all the elements of Dell's relationship with the customer—from negotiated computer configurations and price points to technical support. For international customers, sites are built in native languages. "We're just scratching the surface," according to Scott Eckert, director of Dell Online. "We need to offer Premier Pages to thousands of accounts, not hundreds. We need to do this EDI stuff, and do asset management for customers, helping them maintain databases of systems."[36]

Dell hopes to migrate 20 percent of the firm's business to on-line by 2000. That could equal $2 to $3 billion in Internet sales. Dell does not discuss the cost savings that are realized by sales made and service provided over the Net, but they are believed to be substantial.

Observers also expect the Web to be an important part of Dell's global business strategy, providing both customer convenience and even greater cost savings than in domestic markets. Dell began its first international operation in the United Kingdom in 1987, and in 1997 had offices in 28 countries with products available in more than 140 countries. The aggressiveness of its direct marketing effort is evidenced by the introduction of a Japanese-language Web site in Japan in 1997, an effort to grow its small market share in the face of strong competition from Japanese computer firms.

Dell's build-to-order concept is an equally important aspect of what has come to be called "The Direct Model." Dell does not build a computer until the order is received, allowing it to produce the exact configuration requested by the customer—true one-to-one marketing! What is more, it does this quickly; it now ships in 24 hours from receipt of order. It achieves this by maintaining virtually no work-in-process inventories and by holding parts inventories on trucks at loading docks just a few feet from the start of the assembly line. Parts suppliers are required to maintain their inventory no more than 15 minutes from the factory for just-in-time delivery. As a result, Dell has an inventory turn that far exceeds others in the industry, no obsolete products in warehouses, and rock-bottom operating costs. Combine that with the absence of dealer margins, and you have a truly low-cost producer.

The important point is that the two functions are absolutely interdependent. Build-to-order production is feasible only if a firm is in direct contact with the customer, although that contact can be handled by a salesperson or a distributor. Speed in receiving and fulfilling orders is made possible by telecommunications or electronics and by production efficiencies.

---

[35]Denise Duclaux, "Dell Blazes New Trails in Selling on the Internet," *DM News,* 17 March 1997, 29.

[36]Dana Blankenhorn, "Dell's New Deal," www.netb2b.com, 28 December 1997.

Short channels reduce margins to a minimum. Dell's success can be attributed to the ability to put all the pieces together and, generally, to execute extremely well.[37]

Summary

Are Internet networks and the direct business model the future of business-to-business marketing? It is too early to say for sure. However, remember that we began this chapter by emphasizing the importance of traditional business-to-business direct marketing techniques in improving the productivity of the field sales force. We ended the chapter by looking at electronic commerce as another way of improving productivity in business markets. What we can say with confidence is that productivity is the key. Competition in global markets makes it difficult for manufacturers to raise prices. The only way profitability can be improved is to lower costs. Marketing must bear its share of cost reduction, and, for almost two decades now, direct marketing has played an important role. Business marketers will continue to explore new marketing approaches and to utilize new marketing media in the continuing quest for more effective marketing programs.

Discussion Questions and Exercises

1. What is the major role of direct marketing in business markets?
2. Lead generation programs are important in consumer markets as well as in business markets. Look for an example of a consumer lead program and be prepared to discuss it. Bring the ad or mailing package to class if possible.
3. How does the marketer qualify a customer? What does the marketer do as a result of the qualification process?
4. Discuss some of the differences in the way business marketers and consumer goods marketers use direct-response media.
5. What roles does the Internet play in business marketing today? Can you think of ways that may change over the next few years?
6. Visit one of the large network sites, either consumer or business (and you might stop and think about how you are defining a network on the Web), and be prepared to discuss your experience in class.

Suggested Readings

Morris-Lee, James. "Integrated Business Marketing in the US: A Case Study." *The Journal of Database Marketing* 2, no. 3 (1995): 205–217.

Peppers, Don, and Martha Rogers. *Enterprise One to One: Tools for Competing in the Interactive Age.* New York: Currency/Doubleday, 1997.

"The Web Changes Everything," www.idg.com/whitepaper/, no date.

Zeller, Loren, Richard Goldberg, and Bill Heenehan. "IBM Moves Towards Global Database Marketing." *The Journal of Database Marketing* 4, no. 4 (1997): 371–381.

---

[37]Additional sources for this section are "Dell Computer Bombards Japan," www.mediacentral.com, 15 October 1997; "Whirlwind on the Web," *Business Week,* 7 April 1997, 132–136; Eryn Brown, "Could the Very Best PC Maker Be Dell Computer?" *Fortune,* 14 April 1997, 26; www.dell.com, 10 April 1997.

CHAPTER

Developing Direct Mail Campaigns

When most people hear the term *direct marketing,* they are thinking "direct mail"—mailing pieces that vary from a postcard announcing a sale to glossy packages using four-color printing and a variety of physical and message components. The preceding chapters have emphasized that direct-response marketing is much more than direct mail, but direct mail is a key component of the industry—in some ways the standard to which all other types of direct-response efforts are compared.

In this chapter we discuss many types of mailing pieces, but catalogs—a type that could reasonably be included under the heading of "direct mail"—have become such an important aspect of direct marketing that we treat them separately in the next chapter.

Direct mail is a venerable part of the marketing efforts of major companies throughout the world. In the United States and Canada mail has been an established marketing channel since the early 19th century. Mail marketing also has a long history of successful use in Western Europe. In more recent years there has been an explosion of direct mail marketing in the rapidly growing markets of Asia and Central and South America. Today direct mail is a recognized part of the effort of marketers of all kinds—consumer, business, service, not-for-profit—throughout the world.

In the United States direct mail advertising expenditures were estimated to be $34.6 billion in 1996, which represented almost 24 percent of direct marketing promotional expenditures. Direct marketing promotion, in turn, represented more than 58 percent of all U.S. advertising expenditures.[1]

Special Characteristics of Direct Mail

Direct mail possesses all of the special competencies discussed in chapter 1. In addition, it has some unique advantages compared to the other media of direct marketing. According to Bob Stone, these *advantages* are[2]

- *Selectivity.* Because of the ability to rent mailing lists and to select especially desirable names from within those lists, as discussed in chapters 4 and 5, direct mail can engage in precise targeting of identified target markets.

- *Virtually Unlimited Choice of Formats.* Direct mail is extremely flexible, allowing for a wider range of choices of format than any other direct marketing medium. However, there are potential constraints resulting from the inability of production equipment to handle some formats or excessive costs resulting from unusual formats. (These are primarily constraints on creative execution, not strategy development.

- *Personal Character.* Direct mail communicates one-on-one with the recipient. It offers the marketer the opportunity to personalize the message or its delivery as desired.

- *No Direct Competition.* In other media, readers, listeners, and viewers are ordinarily perusing the medium for reasons besides consumption of the advertising. Once recipients open and read a piece of direct mail, there is no competition for their attention for the limited period of time they are focusing on the mail.

- *Most Controllable.* The direct mail manager is not dependent on the scheduling of other media for dissemination of promotional material. Barring error of some kind, the manager can control mail dates, the exact content of material sent, to whom it is sent, and so on. This also means that the direct mail medium lends itself to rigorous, statistically valid testing.

- *Unique Capacity to Involve the Recipient.* A wide variety of involvement devices can be used to stimulate and retain the interest of the recipient while a decision to respond is being made.

The direct mail medium also has some potential *disadvantages* that should be taken into account when considering it as a channel or as an addition to the overall marketing program:[3]

- *High Cost Per Contact.* Reaching a potential customer by direct mail is generally more expensive on a per prospect basis than is mass media. Keep in mind, however, that the selectivity of direct mail can help to make up for its high unit cost.

---

[1]*Economic Impact: U.S. Direct Marketing Today, Executive Summary,* 2nd ed. (New York: Direct Marketing Association, 1996), 5.

[2]Bob Stone, *Successful Direct Marketing Methods,* 6th ed. (Lincolnwood, IL: NTC Business Books, 1996), 315–316.

[3]Based on Iain Maitland, *How to Plan Direct Mail* (London: Cassell, 1996), 4–5.

- *Time Required.* The example in chapter 2 showed that even a rather small campaign involving only a few managers and suppliers takes time. Some of the activities can be compressed or carried out concurrently, but quality should not be sacrificed for speed. Because most mailers use one or many suppliers, as discussed later in this chapter, some timing issues are not entirely within the control of the marketer.

- *Variety of Knowledge and Skills Demanded.* Successful mail marketers must be familiar with details ranging from print production techniques to postal regulations in each of the countries in which they do business.[4] Good suppliers can be of great assistance in the myriad technical activities involved in planning and executing successful direct mail, but the marketer must know enough to select competent suppliers, to manage their contributions, and to make final decisions on the most technical of details. Technological developments that fall under the general heading of "desktop publishing," are enabling direct marketers to perform some of these activities in house, saving time, and in some instances, costs.

In spite of potential disadvantages, direct mail can be successfully used for a great variety of objectives and many target markets. It can be used to increase the value of present customers (e.g., cross-selling or upgrading), to acquire new customers (e.g., making initial sales or generating inquiries for additional information), with other relevant publics such as the stockholders of a corporation (e.g., informative enclosures with dividend checks), and with members of the channel of distribution (e.g., product and service updates).

When the medium is used to make a sale on the basis of the mailing alone, it is correctly termed mail order. (Actually, direct-response advertising in any medium that closes the sale on the basis of that ad alone is also referred to as *mail order.*) When direct mail is used for any purpose other than to close a sale, it is correctly termed *direct mail advertising* or *direct mail promotion.* In most instances in this chapter we use the more generic term *direct mail.* Keep in mind that when one of the other terms is used, it has a more precise meaning.

"Junk" Mail?

Despite the positive benefits direct mail offers to the marketer, it has a poor image in the minds of many people. It is frequently pointed out that "junk" mail is any mail that does not interest the recipient. Presumably, then, one person's junk is another person's treasure! The task of the marketer, using the list segmentation techniques discussed in chapter 5, is to send mail to the right people and not send it to the wrong people. This will not only raise response rates and lower costs, it will help to improve the image of the industry in the mind of the public.

DMA data show that in 1995, 68.7 percent of all adults in the United States ordered something by mail or phone from offers in magazines, newspapers, on television or radio, in catalogs, or from direct mail.

Table 12.1 (pp. 268–271) indicates that overall, these respondents are more likely to be female, married, between the ages of 35 and 54, college graduates, and to have a household income of $30,000 or more. Respondents in the Northeast and those in professional and managerial jobs were also more likely to buy by telephone or mail. Clothing and magazines are by far the most frequently purchased product categories, at 22.9 percent and 23.4 percent,

---

[4]See Pierre Desmet and Dominique Xardel, "Challenges and Pitfalls for Direct Mail across Borders: The European Example," *Journal of Direct Marketing* (summer 1996): 48–60 for a discussion of issues facing direct mailers within the European Union and between it and other countries.

TABLE 12.1 Percent of Total Population Ordering Products by Phone or Mail

	Total U.S. (000)	Total U.S. Product %	Cook-books	Children's Books	Other Books	Cosmetics	Magazines	Costume Jewelry	Clothing	Sporting Goods
Total adults	191,504	68.7	6.2	7.8	8.5	3.8	23.4	2.8	22.9	3.7
Males	91,938	64.0	3.0	5.2	7.1	1.2	20.3	1.1	15.1	5.5
Females	99,566	73.1	9.2	10.3	9.7	6.2	26.3	4.4	30.1	2.0
18–24	25,739	58.9	3.2	6.3	5.0	3.3	18.5	1.8	14.3	1.6
25–34	42,251	70.7	6.5	12.3	8.2	3.6	25.9	1.4	22.1	4.2
35–44	41,811	72.6	7.0	10.2	10.0	4.3	26.8	2.8	26.1	4.8
45–54	29,766	72.6	7.7	6.4	10.5	4.5	22.4	3.5	27.3	5.2
55–64	20,884	69.9	7.6	4.7	9.8	3.9	24.2	3.6	22.6	3.5
65 or older	31,054	64.4	5.1	3.5	6.8	3.2	19.8	4.5	23.0	2.1
Graduated college	38,819	80.6	6.3	10.3	11.5	4.4	29.9	3.0	33.7	6.0
Attended college	40,166	72.6	7.5	8.7	9.0	4.4	26.1	2.6	24.2	4.4
Graduated high school	75,202	66.8	6.3	7.4	7.7	3.6	22.1	3.0	20.4	3.1
Did not graduate high school	37,318	56.1	4.8	5.4	6.3	2.9	16.1	2.4	15.5	1.9
Professional	17,411	80.5	6.9	11.1	13.2	4.9	29.3	3.7	34.5	5.6
Manager/administrative	15,762	79.9	7.8	9.5	11.4	3.9	31.6	2.9	33.7	5.8
Technical/clerical/sales	36,449	72.1	6.8	9.2	8.7	4.5	25.9	2.2	25.9	3.5
Precision/craft	12,883	62.8	2.1	5.0	7.6	0.8	19.6	1.3	15.7	4.4
Other employed	36,482	65.7	5.4	7.4	7.2	3.5	21.5	1.4	18.0	3.9
Single (never married)	44,547	60.1	3.5	3.8	6.7	2.6	20.3	1.8	16.8	2.5
Married	111,238	73.2	7.1	10.2	9.4	4.1	25.5	2.8	25.9	4.5
Divorced/separated/widowed	35,719	65.5	7.2	5.4	7.9	4.4	20.6	4.2	21.3	2.7

Northeast	39,281	72.0	6.3	9.0	8.9	4.2	24.0	3.6	28.0	3.4
Midwest	45,111	69.3	5.9	7.2	8.7	3.7	22.6	2.7	23.4	4.3
South	67,006	66.7	6.3	7.2	8.3	3.5	23.6	2.4	20.9	3.6
West	40,107	68.2	6.4	8.4	8.0	4.1	23.3	2.9	20.8	3.5
Household income										
$100,000 or more	13,959	77.8	7.4	7.9	9.9	4.1	26.2	3.1	35.5	6.4
$75,000 or more	30,409	77.6	7.7	8.3	9.6	4.6	27.4	2.8	33.4	5.7
$60,000 or more	48,742	77.3	7.1	8.3	9.6	4.6	26.6	3.0	31.7	5.5
$50,000 or more	66,596	76.5	7.3	8.3	9.9	4.6	26.5	2.8	30.3	5.7
$40,000 or more	88,183	75.1	6.8	8.4	10.0	4.2	26.2	2.6	29.0	5.0
$30,000 or more	114,324	73.6	6.5	8.4	9.6	4.1	26.0	2.7	27.5	4.8
$30,000 to $39,999	26,141	68.6	5.7	8.4	8.4	3.7	25.6	2.9	22.4	4.1
$20,000 to $29,999	29,328	67.8	6.4	7.4	7.4	3.4	24.1	3.4	18.1	3.1
$10,000 to $19,999	28,929	58.8	5.6	6.6	6.4	3.2	18.2	2.5	16.1	1.7
Under $10,000	18,923	55.6	5.3	7.0	6.0	3.6	14.2	3.3	13.4	1.0
Household size										
1 person	23,976	66.5	5.3	3.1	8.9	3.3	22.9	4.6	21.9	2.8
2 people	61,622	70.9	7.9	4.5	9.7	4.3	25.0	2.7	25.7	3.7
3 or 4 people	76,480	69.1	5.4	10.9	7.4	3.5	23.3	2.3	22.1	4.3
5 or more people	29,426	65.0	5.7	10.8	8.3	4.0	20.4	2.9	20.2	2.9
Children										
No child in household	112,144	68.4	6.7	3.4	9.1	3.8	23.5	3.1	23.4	3.6
Children under 2 years	13,163	71.3	5.4	22.9	6.3	5.9	24.2	2.7	25.2	4.3
2–5 years	31,349	69.8	5.7	19.1	7.1	4.1	23.8	2.2	21.5	2.9
6–11 years	35,591	69.9	5.5	15.1	8.2	3.8	24.0	2.6	22.6	3.6
12–17 years	36,396	67.1	5.7	6.7	7.8	3.6	21.5	2.8	22.1	3.9
Residence owned	131,137	71.2	6.6	7.7	8.8	4.0	24.2	3.2	25.6	4.3
Residence rented	48,729	64.3	5.9	9.3	8.0	3.3	22.2	2.1	16.8	2.4

(continued)

TABLE 12.1 (continued)

	Toys	Cookware, Kitchen Accessories	Trees, Plants, Seeds	Curtains, Bedspreads, Linen	Compact Discs	Auto Accessories	Shoes or Boots	Audio Cassette Tapes	Travel/ Tour Information	Credit Cards	Videotapes
Total adults	4.5	6.0	6.6	7.2	13.4	4.4	6.5	8.1	10.9	9.8	8.0
Males	2.9	4.0	4.9	2.8	14.3	6.6	4.8	6.9	9.5	9.5	7.4
Females	5.9	7.9	8.1	11.2	12.5	2.4	8.1	9.2	12.3	10.0	8.6
18–24	2.6	3.8	1.5	3.2	19.5	3.5	5.2	7.8	5.5	9.2	6.8
25–34	6.4	6.4	4.9	7.1	18.6	5.0	4.9	8.3	10.1	11.5	8.9
35–44	6.5	5.6	8.5	9.0	15.5	4.9	6.2	8.0	13.2	11.7	8.4
45–54	4.1	7.6	8.5	10.6	11.0	4.8	7.5	8.8	13.8	11.2	8.2
55–64	2.8	7.5	8.2	6.3	7.8	5.1	7.4	8.6	13.4	9.6	8.1
65 or older	2.4	5.4	7.6	5.6	4.3	2.9	8.6	7.1	9.3	4.1	7.1
Graduated college	6.0	6.6	8.8	7.9	18.7	4.1	9.0	7.4	18.5	14.3	8.8
Attended college	5.0	6.7	7.4	8.5	17.6	5.3	6.7	8.6	13.3	12.4	8.8
Graduated high school	4.2	5.4	5.6	7.5	11.5	4.5	5.9	8.2	9.4	8.0	8.4
Did not graduate high school	3.0	5.9	5.4	4.3	7.1	3.7	4.9	8.1	3.8	5.7	5.7
Professional	6.5	6.3	8.8	8.5	20.5	5.6	7.7	8.4	17.3	13.6	10.0
Manager/administrative	5.7	5.7	8.3	9.0	18.8	4.7	8.3	6.6	18.0	16.8	8.9
Technical/clerical/sales	4.8	6.5	7.0	9.5	15.9	3.9	7.4	7.4	12.1	12.5	8.0
Precision/craft	3.5	5.0	4.0	4.3	17.0	7.8	3.8	7.6	9.1	7.1	7.6
Other employed	4.7	4.7	5.7	5.8	14.5	5.2	4.6	8.2	8.2	9.8	7.0
Single (never married)	2.6	4.5	2.9	3.8	18.0	4.5	5.3	7.8	7.4	10.4	8.2
Married	5.4	6.2	8.3	8.7	12.7	4.7	6.7	8.0	13.2	10.4	7.6
Divorced/separated/widowed	3.9	7.4	5.7	6.7	9.6	3.4	7.6	8.9	8.2	7.3	9.3

Northeast	5.9	6.5	8.4	9.3	14.3	5.0	7.9	9.3	13.1	9.8	7.8
Midwest	4.3	5.8	7.5	7.6	12.4	3.5	6.3	6.8	11.5	9.8	7.3
South	4.1	6.1	5.4	7.0	12.2	4.4	6.3	8.1	9.2	9.4	8.4
West	4.0	5.8	5.7	4.9	15.5	4.9	5.7	8.4	11.1	10.3	8.6
Household income											
$100,000 or more	5.3	6.4	7.6	10.9	17.9	6.8	8.8	7.1	21.1	11.9	6.7
$75,000 or more	6.1	6.6	8.5	9.6	18.1	5.9	8.0	6.4	18.6	12.5	6.5
$60,000 or more	5.4	6.3	8.1	9.2	17.4	6.1	7.2	6.7	18.2	12.7	6.9
$50,000 or more	5.5	6.0	8.2	9.0	17.7	5.8	7.0	7.2	17.3	12.6	7.6
$40,000 or more	5.3	5.7	8.0	8.6	17.3	5.5	7.0	7.7	15.8	12.2	8.0
$30,000 or more	5.0	5.8	7.6	8.0	16.6	5.4	6.8	7.6	14.6	11.9	7.9
$30,000 to $39,999	4.0	6.0	6.0	5.7	14.4	5.0	6.4	7.2	10.3	11.0	7.5
$20,000 to $29,999	4.1	6.2	6.4	6.7	11.1	4.2	6.2	9.7	8.2	8.8	9.3
$10,000 to $19,999	3.1	6.3	5.3	5.8	7.4	2.9	5.4	8.4	4.1	5.3	8.0
Under $10,000	4.3	6.9	2.8	5.2	6.3	1.4	6.7	8.1	4.0	5.3	7.0
Household size											
1 person	3.3	7.0	5.6	6.3	8.9	2.7	7.7	7.8	8.5	7.2	9.2
2 people	3.0	6.1	8.1	7.3	12.5	4.6	7.2	8.1	13.6	10.4	7.7
3 or 4 people	5.3	5.6	6.3	7.2	15.2	4.9	6.0	7.9	10.9	9.9	7.8
5 or more people	6.7	6.1	5.0	7.5	14.1	4.0	5.4	8.8	7.6	10.4	8.3
Children											
No child in household	2.6	6.2	6.9	6.4	12.0	4.6	7.1	7.8	12.1	9.5	8.1
Children under 2 years	9.1	6.6	5.2	9.5	17.4	2.3	6.6	9.0	9.7	12.1	11.0
2–5 years	9.4	−6.1	6.0	8.8	14.2	2.4	5.7	9.4	8.9	9.7	8.9
6–11 years	8.2	6.2	6.1	8.8	15.1	4.1	5.2	9.6	8.3	9.9	8.8
12–17 years	4.5	5.0	6.2	7.9	14.7	5.4	5.5	8.1	9.1	10.5	6.8
Residence owned	4.9	6.2	8.4	8.3	12.3	4.8	7.2	7.8	12.6	9.7	7.8
Residence rented	3.7	6.3	2.4	5.3	15.3	3.3	5.1	9.3	7.4	10.3	9.0

Source: Data from Simmons Market Research Bureau: 1995 Study of Media and Markets. Reprinted from the *Direct Marketing Association's Statistical Fact Book, 1997* (New York: Direct Marketing Association, 1997), 44–45. Reprinted with permission of the Direct Marketing Association, 1998.

respectively, of all adults purchasing in that year. The frequency drops off rapidly, with other books at 8.5 percent and children's books at 7.8 percent being the third and fourth most commonly purchased product categories. The selected product categories in Table 12.1 clearly indicate that the demographic profile of mail order purchasers differs from one product category to another.

An interesting study of consumer attitudes toward direct mail attempted to segment consumers on the basis of attitudes, including how they regarded issues of consumer privacy. Scenarios about the ongoing development of direct mail were presented to consumers. Two issues had to do with correct targeting and volume of mail received and two had to do with privacy—possible compensation for use of a consumer's name and requiring permission for its use. The three segments that emerged differed on both demographics and attitudes toward direct mail. One group, which was given the name "Potential Lobbyists," was primarily concerned about the volume of mail being sent and wanted compensation for the use of names. A second segment, characterized as the "Demanding Middle," was not concerned about the volume of mail but wanted it to be carefully targeted and also wanted compensation for the use of names. The final segment, called the "New Right"—a politically conservative, younger, and less well educated group—was concerned about all issues except granting permission for the use of one's name. The findings are in line with studies that emphasize the growing consumer concern about name use and exchange without the consumer's knowledge or control and suggest that direct marketers might find attitudinal data related to privacy concerns useful in further refining their targeting efforts.[5]

A similar study of attitudes toward direct mail in the United Kingdom shows that consumers there are also concerned about the potential invasion of the privacy of their personal data. This research found that the factors that contributed toward the perception of potential privacy problems were

- perception of excessive mailings
- concern over how they (direct mailers) know about me
- lack of informative value (of mailings received)
- the "age" dimension (concern increased progressively from younger to older consumers)
- ethics of direct mail
- amount of direct mail[6]

In both the United States and the United Kingdom the research indicates that the sheer amount of mail received is viewed as a problem by at least a segment of consumers. The negative perception seems to be even stronger when much of the mail is perceived to be improperly targeted and therefore of no interest to the consumer.

Data from the United States Postal Service (USPS) supports the perception that the overall volume of mail is increasing. Table 12.2 shows both total and per capita mail volume for 1994 through 1996. Although total volume is increasing steadily, per capita volume for this period grew, but erratically.

---

[5]George R. Milne and Mary Ellen Gordon, "A Segmentation Study of Consumers' Attitudes toward Direct Mail," *Journal of Direct Marketing* (spring 1994): 45–52.

[6]Martin Evans, Lisa O'Malley, and Maurice Patterson, "Direct Mail and Consumer Response: An Empirical Study of Consumer Experiences of Direct Mail," *Journal of Database Marketing* 2, no. 3 (1996): 250–262.

TABLE 12.2 Total and Per Capita Mail Volume in the United States, 1994–1996

	1996	*1995*	*1994*
Total mail volume (in billions)	182.66	180.73	178.04
First-class mail	97.28	96.30	95.33
Standard mail (A)	71.88	71.11	69.42
Standard mail (B)	0.96	0.94	0.87
Priority mail	0.96	0.87	0.77
International mail	1.00	0.80	0.86
Other	10.60	10.71	10.79
Per capita mail volume (in units)			
Pieces of mail	687.0	686.0	683.0
Percent change	0.1	0.5	2.9

Source: Adapted from *1996 United States Postal Service Annual Report,* pp. 39–40.

It is worth noting that, although the USPS reports on 11 different categories of mail, first-class, priority, and bulk business mail provided over 90 percent of mail volume in 1996. Standard mail (A), formerly called third-class mail, is part of the bulk business mail, as is standard mail (B) which is primarily parcels and bound printed matter.[7] First-class mail represents a great deal of personal mail as well as general business communications, and priority mail serves urgent communications of various types. These categories seem less susceptible to competition from electronic media, although e-mail may make inroads in years to come. On the other hand, bulk business mail may be liable to competition from a variety of electronic media, which may, in time prove to be more cost effective.

Clearly though, what matters most to consumers at present is the number of pieces of mail their household receives and how creative and relevant they consider them to be. Interestingly, however, one study found that, when questioned directly, consumers did not indicate that a high volume resulted in less chance of mail being opened.[8]

Households in Europe receive a much smaller volume of direct mail promotion compared to those in the United States. Notice that the figures in Table 12.3 (p. 274) reflect items per *year*. That would make the comparable figure for the United States approximately 1,092!

Let's now look at the type of promotional pieces that are most commonly sent through the mail.

COMMON DIRECT MAIL FORMATS

Earlier in the chapter we pointed out that the choice of formats available to direct mail marketers is virtually unlimited. Unfortunately, there is no generally accepted classification of formats to help us make sense of this boundless set of opportunities. However, industry usage and common sense suggest that we can meaningfully discuss the following:

- *Classic Consumer Format.* The classic consumer format comprises multiple pieces, usually including a sales letter, enclosed in an envelope.

---

[7] *1996 United States Postal Service Annual Report,* pp. 39–41, 70.

[8] E. Lincoln James and Hairong Li, "Why Do Consumers Open Direct Mail?" *Journal of Direct Marketing* (spring 1993): 34–40.

TABLE 12.3 Pieces of Mail Received by European Households	
Country	*Items per Year*
Switzerland	107
Belgium	85
West Germany	64
France	63
Netherlands	62
Norway	50
Denmark	50
Sweden	48
Finland	46
United Kingdom	39
Spain	24
Ireland	16
Portugal	9
European average	52

Source: Adapted from Diane Summers, "Personal Message," *Financial Times,* 18 May 1995, 19.

- *Business Mail.* The classic business mailing is often perceived to be a sales letter in a no. 10 envelope; in other words, something that looks like a business letter. This format can be varied with the addition of collateral material such as a brochure. As we discuss in chapter 11, business mail is also more frequently taking on the more overtly promotional characteristics of the classic consumer format.

- *Self-Mailer.* The traditional self-mailer is one or more 8-1/2 × 11 inch sheets, folded in half, with copy on all except one surface. That surface is reserved for mailing data, although it may also include a "banner" of promotional material.

- *Postcard.* Another relatively inexpensive format, the postcard is useful for simple announcements or reminders.

- *Invitation.* The invitation format appears to have grown in popularity over the past few years, especially for fund-raising applications and for lead generation in upscale markets.

- *Newsletter.* In an era of relationship marketing, the newsletter has taken on prominence because of its usefulness in keeping in touch with customers between transactions and in delivering a soft sales message.

- *Catalog.* Catalog-like formats are sometimes substituted for the classic format when there is a complex offer with a substantial amount of information to convey.

The selection of format should be guided by the objectives of the direct mail campaign. Table 12.4 presents an overview of which formats are useful for what types of objectives (X) and which are especially appropriate (XX).

Some direct marketers would argue with the inclusion of "general awareness" as an appropriate programmatic objective in Table 12.4. One reason for its inclusion is that there are many small businesses and nonprofit organizations that have limited access to mass

	General Awareness	Lead Generation	Immediate Sale	Retail Traffic	Relationship Building
Classic consumer format	X	X	XX		
Business mail	X	XX	X		X
Self-mailer	XX	XX		XX	XX
Post card	X	XX		XX	
Invitation	XX	XX		XX	XX
Newsletter	X	X		X	XX
Catalog	X	X	XX	XX	X

TABLE 12.4 Matching Direct Mail Format to Campaign Objectives

media for budgetary or geographical market reasons. They turn to direct mail, as did our young entrepreneurs in chapter 2. The second reason for including awareness as an objective is the role of primary and secondary direct marketing objectives as discussed in chapter 3.

The two main criteria that help the direct marketer match the format to objectives are the amount of information that can be conveyed and the cost of that type of format. For example, the classic consumer format is often required when the objective is to make the sale of a single item or a continuity offer. Both information and persuasion are required, and success will justify the higher relative cost. On the other hand, a complex, consumer-like format might be used to generate sales leads in business markets, but is the cost worth it? Might a sales letter accompanied by a brochure be more cost effective? Another situation that suits a format with lower information content is an invitation to attend a special sale or a promotional event in a retail store. Nonprofit organizations use newsletters (or more elaborate publications, such as the alumni magazines of universities and colleges) to strengthen relationships with members, donors, alumni, and so forth.

Because the classic consumer format is a useful standard against which we can compare other formats, it will be helpful to look at a typical execution in some detail.

The Classic Direct Mail Package

The basic contents of a direct mail package can be described as

- outer envelope
- letter
- brochure
- other inserts
- reply device

Each of these components can be executed in a wide variety of ways, and some, especially the insert category, can have multiple representation in a single package.

Figures 12.1 through 12.5 show elements of a complex package, some of which are quite straightforward and some of which are carried out in ways that emphasize the sales message and positioning of the product and the specific offer. *Highlights*® *for Children* is a well-known children's magazine whose basic sales proposition is that it is an educational product that children genuinely enjoy. This particular mailing contains a Christmas gift offer. Let's look at each component in turn.

THE OUTER ENVELOPE

Obviously, the outer envelope is the first part of the direct-mail package seen by the recipient. That makes clear the importance of getting the recipient to open the envelope. Otherwise, nothing else will happen except a quick trip to the trash can for the expensive direct mail package. Consequently, the envelope is an important creative issue that must set the tone for the sales message if the mailing is to be successful.

You have probably seen some envelopes that fit the following categories in your own mail:[9]

The Envelope with a Promise

Direct mail envelopes often carry a promise: "4 Books. 4 Bucks. No Commitment. No Kidding," from the book club; "Welcome Back with 12 FREE CDs!" on the renewal solicitation from the music club; "Your Personalized Return Address Labels Are Enclosed," from the nonprofit organization soliciting a donation; or the "No Annual Fee. 5.9% APR for the first twelve months," on the credit card offer. It is undoubtedly not accidental that these envelope teasers all contain a value proposition, either explicit or implied. The music club offers free CDs. The nonprofit sends free labels as an upfront incentive to encourage prospects to make a gift. Getting something for nothing is a basic human motive to which direct marketers often appeal with success.

The *Highlights for Children* envelope shown in Figure 12.1 is not actually an envelope, it is a plastic mailing sleeve. It was likely a cheaper alternative than a paper envelope. Perhaps more important, it allowed for good color reproduction in cheerful shades of yellow and red with an almost completely transparent back that allows the smile stickers to show through. The front of the envelope promises an immediate free gift, another incentive of a calendar, and introduces the Christmas gift offer. The back of the envelope allows the recipient to view the enclosed incentive before even opening the envelope. That is getting a great deal of creative mileage out of a single envelope.

The Important Envelope

As the name suggests, this type of envelope may cloak the sales message in an aura of great significance. The invitation format often makes use of a heavy envelope made of high-quality paper that mimics a personal communication, say a wedding invitation, to good effect. The dark side of this type of envelope is one that imitates an official communication—from the Internal Revenue Service, the U.S. Postal Service, and FedEx envelopes are often suggested—in an effort to make the recipient think this is a "must open" communication. Some direct marketers argue that if the envelope is opened it has accomplished its mission. We counterargue that if the recipient feels tricked when the envelope reveals its contents, the sales message is going to have a hard time being heard. It is also possible that the image of direct mail is devalued in the mind of the recipient, who feels misled by the appearance of the mailing piece.

---

[9]This section is based on Joan Throckmorton, *Winning Direct Response Advertising* (Lincolnwood, IL: NTC Business Books, 1997), 90–93.

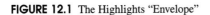

(front)

FIGURE 12.1 The Highlights "Envelope"

Source: Used with permission of Highlights for Children.

The Questioning or Challenging Envelope

Arousing the recipient's curiosity may increase the likelihood of the envelope being opened—"How you can make the new tax law work for you!" on a newsletter solicitation, for example. A challenging approach may have the same effect, such as "What If You Could Reduce Your Calorie Intake And Still Eat All You Like" on an invitation to subscribe to a magazine. Notice that teasers like this do not attempt to hide the sales purpose of the mailing, but instead give the recipient a preview of the full offer.

The Tell-It-All Envelope

This is an envelope that gives a strong summary of what is inside. A mailing package for a vacuum cleaner announces, "So Light, So Powerful, So Versatile. So Free!" and pictures one model of the product on the mailing surface. On the back surface it pictures another model of the product, stresses product benefits, and offers a free trial. You have no doubt that you are getting a vacuum cleaner offer when you open this envelope. A business mailing offers "Yours FREE! 'Tips & Techniques For Exhibiting Success,'" and pictures the incentive booklet on the front of the envelope. This approach qualifies the interested recipient as a marketer who is involved in planning exhibits at trade shows and conferences.

The Mysterious Envelope

This approach, often used when the company is not well known, provides a teaser to encourage opening the envelope. We often see "The Favor Of Your Reply Is Requested" or "Time-Sensitive Information Enclosed. Open Immediately," on such envelopes. You may also see a single word or phrase, such as "Sale," that gets attention or arouses curiosity.

The Blind Envelope

An even more extreme tactic, again often used when the mailer is not well known or when the recipient is not a current customer, is an envelope with no identification at all. Another variant is a simple, but impressive, two-line return address—no company name, just an address that sounds as if it might be prestigious.

THE LETTER

Inside the envelope are multiple pieces. The most vital of those is the sales letter. Direct mail experts agree that the letter is the most important part of the direct-mail package. It presents the offer and communicates the sales message. It urges the reader to take action immediately.

A four-page letter, such as the one in Figure 12.2, is common in direct mail, although there is no rule about letter length. There is, in fact, continuing dispute over whether "short" letters or "long" letters pull better. One study of letter length compared a one-page letter with a two-page letter in a mailing for a service contract on a consumer durable. There was not a significant difference in response rate between the two letters, but on a cost-effectiveness basis the one-page letter was slightly better.[10] The best advice seems to be to present your offer in a clear and compelling way, giving as much information as necessary to be convincing. At the same time, be respectful of the time of the busy reader; in other words, as long as it needs to be—no longer.

The *Highlights for Children* letter has many characteristics of a good direct mail letter, as set forth by copywriter Paul Bringe:[11]

- It uses *short words*—almost all the words in the letter are of one to three syllables. There is no jargon; no complicated technical terms; just simple, straightforward English.

- It uses *short sentences*. Bringe says that good sentences average about 12 words. Some will be shorter, some will be longer, but the average will be 12.

- It uses *short paragraphs*. The paragraphs in this letter are no more than one or two sentences long.

- It *looks easy to read*. That is partly the result of using short words, short sentences, and short paragraphs. It also uses a number of indented blocks of text. These break up the flow visually, creating more interest, and serve to highlight important parts of the sales message. Key selling points are underlined for emphasis.

If you are interested in ensuring that the readability level of your letter matches your target market in a more precise manner, there are many established metrics. One study of direct mail letters used the Flesch Reading Grade Level Score and the Dale-Chall to illustrate these techniques.[12] A later experiment varied the readability scores of letters sent to three target segments using these same two scales. This study did not find that the readability scores were related to levels of response.[13]

---

[10]John D. Beard, David L. Williams, and J. Patrick Kelly, "The Long versus the Short Letter: A Large Sample Study of a Direct-Mail Campaign," *Journal of Direct Marketing* (winter 1990): 13–20.

[11]Quoted in Julian L. Simon, *How to Start and Operate a Mail-Order Business* 4th ed. (New York: McGraw-Hill, 1987).

[12]John D. Beard and David L. Williams, "Increasing the Effectiveness of Direct Mail Copy through the Use of Readability Measures," *Journal of Direct Marketing* (spring 1988): 6–15.

[13]David L. Williams, John D. Beard, and J. Patrick Kelly, "The Readability of Direct-Mail Copy," *Journal of Direct Marketing* (winter 1991): 27–34.

FIGURE 12.2 Four-Page *Highlights* Letter

Source: Used with permission of *Highlights for Children.*

Notice some other things about this letter that are characteristic of a good direct mail letter:

- It uses a "headline" that represents an important benefit, perhaps even the positioning, of the product. It also uses a swath of smiley faces that are reminiscent of the smile stickers used as an incentive. Direct mail letters often use a boxed message (called a *Johnson Box* after pioneer direct mail copywriter Frank Johnson) summarizing the offer and main benefits as the beginning of the message. This might be considered another version of a headline.

- Its tone is personal. The letter is not "folksy or "cutesy," but is written as if one individual were speaking directly to another (just as a good salesperson would). This is not mass-media advertising; it is a letter to be read by one person at a time.

- It does not look typeset. Typewriter type in a common font is used—large, easy-to-read type at that.

- It has two postscripts. The first reminds the reader that she has already received a free gift of smile stickers. The second reminds the reader of the incentive gift the child will receive. Direct mail marketers know that even if most of the rest of the letter is not read, the postscript usually is. Use it for a final key message, which is often to restate the offer or for a call to action.

- It is signed by an individual in regular business-letter style.

- It displays awards and seals of approval that attest to the excellence of the magazine. Other direct mail letters include written testimonials from satisfied customers.

- It is slightly larger than the envelope, requiring that it be folded once through the center.

This letter is not personalized even though the envelope is personally addressed. Personalization is expensive and might add little to the offer. Another thing it does not have is "handwritten" notes in the margin. Handwritten notes are sometimes used to emphasize key points, but they should be used with care because they tend to give a downscale tone to the letter.

This letter is cheerful and upbeat, in keeping with the user of the product—children—but it manages to present a serious offer to adults concerned about the intellectual and social development of children in their lives.

So far, we have talked about the physical structure of a letter, aspects we can easily see and evaluate. These physical aspects merely implement the message the letter is designed to communicate. Now we consider the communications approach taken in a direct mail letter.

Many direct mail copywriters recommend following the AIDA model. AIDA stands for

Attention

Interest

Desire

Action

First you must get the prospect's *attention*. You do that by presenting the key selling point or offering the key benefit. In general advertising, this is often referred to as the unique selling proposition. "The gift that lasts all year long!" is a powerful selling message.

When you have the prospect's attention, you must then whet his or her *interest*. Do not just tell what the benefits of the product are, tell why—make the benefits credible. *Highlights for Children* has a registered mark, "Fun with a Purpose,"® which encapsulates the appeal to both the child and the adult giver. The letter presents that appeal in detail.

Next, instill in the reader a strong *desire* for the product. Show why the prospect, the prospect's family, or the prospect's business will be better off with this product, why they absolutely must have it. The *Highlights* letter repeatedly points out that children really want to learn and that this magazine promotes both intellectual development and social skills. The multiple support pieces in the package further develop this message. The letter also points out how easy it is to solve the Christmas gift-giving problem by ordering a magazine subscription.

The call to *action* is the key distinguishing feature of the direct mail letter. Do not forget it or let it be weak. Do not just imply that the reader should do something—tell the individual exactly what you want him or her to do and encourage immediate action. Do not leave anything to the reader's imagination; be very specific about what action and how to take it. The *Highlights* letter leads with the call to action. It emphasizes the involvement device—a YES sticker—and the gift order form. It repeats the YES theme at the end of the letter, "Just think about your favorite youngsters, then say YES to *Highlights*." It does not, however, promote a 1-800 number, nor is one mentioned in any other part of the package. Direct marketers make the choice about including a 1-800 number on the basis of cost (it adds to the overall cost of the program), availability of their own in-house call center or service bureaus, and the response behavior of their target customers. Use of a 1-800 number as an alternative reply method in a mail package should be tested to determine if the lift in response is worth the additional cost.

Stone suggests a seven-step approach to guiding a prospect through a series of stages that culminate in the desired action. His formula is not meant to stifle creativity, but merely to guide it. Like any rule, it can sometimes be broken by an experienced copywriter who thoroughly understands the product and the audience and who comes up with a creative substitute. Like other good rules of thumb, however, it provides a useful guide for the less experienced copywriter or for the manager who must judge direct mail copy. Stone's seven steps are[14]

1. *Promise a benefit in your headline or first paragraph*—your most important benefit. You are not writing an essay or a short story that builds to a climax. Unless you gain the reader's attention and develop interest at the very beginning, the reader probably won't be around for your ending!

2. *Immediately enlarge on your most important benefit.* A good salesperson drives home the most important points in an enthusiastic and believable manner. Your direct mail letter must do the same thing.

3. *Tell readers specifically what they are going to get.* Be specific about product attributes so the customer develops a correct set of expectations about the product. Emphasize the benefits that are delivered by these attributes. Do not assume, and do not leave it to the reader's imagination. Be specific.

4. *Back up your statements with proof and endorsements.* After all, the reader knows this is advertising and is likely to view it with some cynicism. If you can provide testimonials from satisfied users, objective test results, or expert endorsements, the credibility of your message will be increased.

5. *Tell readers what they might lose if they do not act.* Give powerful and compelling reasons that will help to overcome the normal human tendency to defer action.

6. *Rephrase your prominent benefits in your closing offer.* A good sales presentation has a strong closing in which the salesperson summarizes the main selling points. A good direct mail letter does the same thing.

7. *Incite action. Now!* Make the call to action strong and believable. If the reader puts the letter aside without acting, the battle is usually lost. Give good reasons why action should be taken, and make it easy to follow your instructions.

Even though a direct mail letter can be lengthy and can contain great detail about the product and the offer, there are things it should not be expected to do. Chief among these is to contain photographs or illustrations that can be persuasive and can be extremely helpful to the reader's understanding of the product and how it works. The brochure is the most common device for delivering this part of the message.

THE BROCHURE

According to Throckmorton, "A brochure's mission is to dramatize the benefits and illustrate the features of a product or service."[15] It is an essential part of a direct mail package with only a few exceptions:

---

[14]Stone, *Successful Direct Marketing Methods*, 333–334.

[15]Throckmorton, *Winning Direct Response Advertising,* 122.

- when you have a product or service with features that do not require illustration, such as a newsletter or newspaper.

- when you have a product so well known that it does not need visual description for most prospects—such as *Time* or *Newsweek* magazines, or the customer's expiring membership or expiring subscription to whatever.

- when you have a business-to-business promotion geared to qualify prospects by creating inquiries for "more information," which includes expensive brochures, charts, and diagrams.

- when you have the ability to write so well that your description does a *better* job than phrases and pictures because you can create a mental "framework" that lets your prospect move into a picture in his or her mind, and draw upon his or her own imagination! This works for entertainment, or self-improvement books and programs that help individuals achieve goals and aspirations; it doesn't work if you are selling widgets.[16]

There is no standard format for a brochure; in fact the "virtually unlimited choice of formats" phrase is nowhere more true than in brochure design. It is helpful to think of three key components:

- *copy*, which includes a headline, short copy blocks often arranged in columns, lists of key benefits, testimonials, and the guarantee or other risk reduction mechanism.

- *photographs, illustrations, or graphics*, which demonstrate product uses, benefits, and attributes.

- *folds*, which logically assist the flow of the message and permit the final product to fit comfortably into the chosen envelope.

The *Highlights* brochure shown in Figure 12.3 is the same size as the envelope, causing it to stand out in the package (along with the order form and the smile stickers, which are the same size). The cover of the brochure has a large headline that reinforces the benefits stated in the letter and illustrates children engaged in Christmas activities. When the reader opens the brochure, another headline, a large illustration of a magazine cover, and several smaller ones of magazine covers and stories to illustrate the variety of its contents is revealed. By opening the final fold, the reader sees copy that further reinforces the benefits of the product. The back cover reiterates the basic selling message, restates the offer, and presents testimonials from satisfied purchasers. All of this is done with liberal use of color and graphics. It presents the same cheerful, busy tone as does the rest of the package, but it is clear, well organized, and "tracks" the reader through the sales messages to the call for action.

Notice that this, as all good brochures, can stand alone if necessary. This might allow the marketer to use one brochure for a number of purposes. More important, if it is separated from the rest of the package (to show to a coworker or friend, for instance), it can function alone. For this reason, some brochures contain a reply coupon in addition to the larger, easier-to-use response coupon that is an important part of every package.

THE REPLY DEVICE

There are two important components of the reply device in a mail package. It must be made up of an order form and a mailing instrument of some sort. The marketer can execute these necessary elements in many ways. Some of the most common are

- *simple order form or reply card* with a return envelope. Whether the envelope is postage-paid depends on the hardness of the offer.

---

[16]Ibid.

(back)   (front)

(interior)

FIGURE 12.3 *Highlights* Brochure

Source: Used with permission of *Highlights for Children.*

- *self-mailer,* which is a mailing piece that does not have a separate envelope. It can be a reply card that has to be cut or torn out of the printed piece or a separate reply postcard. These are usually postage-paid, probably because most respondents do not have the correct postage for a postcard.
- *reply-o-letter,* which is a response card, often already filled out, inside a sleeve. All the recipient has to do is pull it out and drop it in the mail.
- *sticker or actual Rolodex card* to encourage telephone response.

Somewhat different in purpose but worth mentioning is

- *bang-tail envelope,* which is an envelope with a second flap—actually, a perforated elongation of the envelope flap. The tail is a response device for an offer ancillary to the main purpose of the mailing (a utility or credit card bill, for example).

The response device is so important that some direct-response copywriters design it before they write the main pieces of copy. Why? Once they have the response device in front of them, they know exactly what information the recipient must have and therefore are not likely to forget to include any important piece of information in the letter or brochure.

The reply device in the *Highlights* package comes in two pieces (Figure 12.4). It is a full-sized sheet because the respondent is being encouraged to give subscriptions to several children. It has a headline that echoes the ones on the letter and brochure. It contains the YES involvement device. It restates the offer, a critical element of a good response form. The graphic shows a year's worth of magazine covers, reinforcing the offer. And, instead of an "order form," the respondent is presented with a holiday gift list. The paper stock is lightweight because the entire order form is meant to be included in the standard, preaddressed, postage-paid envelope included in the package. The promotional copy is red and green—a not-too-subtle reminder of the Christmas theme of the mailing!

FIGURE 12.4 *Highlights* Reply Card

Source: Used with permission of *Highlights for Children.*

To make the reply device both attractive and functional be sure to

- design it so the eye moves easily through the form
- make sure it includes all the information the respondent needs to fill out the order or inquiry form accurately and promptly
- give the respondent plenty of room to write in the necessary information
- state the terms of payment clearly
- do not let the envelope flaps cover important parts of the form such as the instructions
- do not use strange shapes that are difficult to mail or colors or surfaces that are difficult to write on
- call the response device something other than an order form—such as a free trial certificate, an acceptance slip, a membership card
- make it look important—for example, like a bond certificate or a reply card in a wedding invitation.
- restate the offer, terms, and guarantee
- offer an opportunity to "trade up" (e.g., a two-year instead of a one-year subscription) or to order a "special"
- use an involvement device
- display your toll-free number prominently for people who are in a hurry or do not like to fill out order forms

In summary, the direct marketer needs a response device that is appropriate to the target market, the image and positioning of the offer, and the creative approach taken in the mailing package. It must also follow the direct marketing cardinal rule of making it easy for the customer to respond. Within these constraints, the direct mail manager can test different approaches to determine which specific reply device works best.

OTHER INSERTS

A wide variety of inserts can be added to the classic direct mail package to increase the response rate. (These add-ons are sometimes referred to as *peripherals*.) Brian Turley describes the following types of inserts:[17]

Circulars, Folders, and Product Sheets

Three terms—*circulars, folders,* and *product sheets*—are used interchangeably by many professionals to designate a type of insert that is factual, perhaps even technical in nature. This insert has no predefined format. It may be a single flat sheet; if folded, it usually unfolds to be no larger than the letter. It is designed to describe and give details about the product in a way that is more straightforward than the sales-oriented presentation of the letter or brochure. Consequently, it is less likely to be printed in four colors; ordinarily, two-color printing (or even black and white for product sheets) is used. Because this type of insert is supportive of a sales objective, it contains more detail than is usually considered desirable in an inquiry-generation mailing, so its use is most often confined to a sales-oriented package.

---

[17]Brian Turley, "Direct Mail Inserts," in Edward L. Nash, *The Direct Marketing Handbook* (New York: McGraw-Hill, 1984), 507–516.

Broadsides

A broadside, also found in a variety of formats, unfolds into a single large sheet, 17 by 22 inches or larger. Often it is inserted into a much smaller mailing package for impact. Its size provides a large surface on which to display product features, illustrations of the product in use, and numerous supporting blocks of copy. Sometimes it takes the form of a poster. Broadsides may contain an order form, but this order form should not take the place of a separate reply device.

The insert that promotes the additional incentive in the *Highlights* mailing is probably a broadside although it is a single unfolded sheet. It is, however, different in size from anything else in the package and the dominant color is dark blue, a color not used in the red and green Christmas scheme of the other major pieces. This is the only place in the package where the inclusion of "over 40 colorful stickers—a $6.95 value—FREE!" is described in addition to the Hidden Pictures Calendar, which is mentioned in the letter and on the order form. There is not enough room in other pieces or it breaks the flow of the sales message to describe the second incentive in this much detail—the reason for the inclusion of a separate piece to emphasize the incentive that will go to the child along with the magazine subscription.

Lift Letters

Often called publishers' letters because they were first used in that industry, lift letters are undersized inserts that frequently begin, "Don't open this unless you have decided not to accept this offer." Of course, the idea is that the reader will open and read it, providing one more opportunity to convince him or her of the value of the offer. The lift letter restates the offer, but from a different perspective. It should be signed by a different person from the individual who signed the main letter. Lift letters are reputed to sometimes generate substantial increases in response rate, perhaps as much as 25 percent.

The lift letter in the *Highlights* package (Figure 12.5) is typical. On an overflap (not shown), it asks, "Not sure?" and then advises, "Read this." A tiny back flap (also not shown) has the name and address of the chairman of the firm, the signer of the lift letter. When you open it, you find a short letter, which restates the offer and adds another benefit or two. For instance, the lift letter states that the giver never has to worry about violent or other questionable content in this magazine. It is a different size from anything else in the package and the paper color is a light green—a color used nowhere else in the package.

Gift or Discount Slips

Also called buck slips, gift or discount slips offer free gifts or price breaks or perhaps some last-minute information. Why make this a separate piece in the mailing? One reason is to test variations in the gift or discount without having to reprint expensive four-color components of the package. Another is that the slips can be implemented or discontinued quickly and cheaply, without changing the rest of the mailing package. Gift slips are usually smaller than other items in the package, and should be designed to stand out. The addition of a gift or discount will change the cost structure of the offer.

Miscellaneous Inserts

The marketer may also include a special purpose insert such as the smile stickers sheet in the *Highlights* mailing. This incentive also adds to the creative appeal of the plastic sleeve that is used as the envelope.

Remember that each insert—each piece in the total mailing package, for that matter—should serve a clear purpose. That purpose should be somewhat different from every other

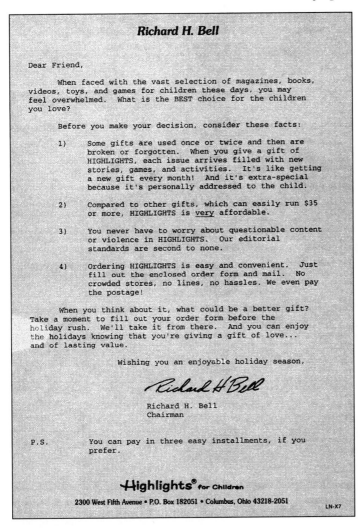

FIGURE 12.5

Source: Used with permission of *Highlights for Children.*

component of the mailing, but in terms of both offer and message strategy and of creative execution, each should be clearly related to the total. Note that each of the inserts in the *Highlights* mailing fulfills a separate function with respect to conveying the offer and the persuasive message.

If you decide to use one or more additional inserts, be sure they meet the following criteria:

- It is distinctive and stands out from the rest of the mailing. You may not even want to use the same type and grade of paper.
- It provides a different perspective on, not just a reiteration of, the selling points used in other pieces of the mailing.

- It can have a built-in response device in case it gets separated from the rest of the mailing. If that does not seem appropriate, include the mailing address or the 1-800 number.

- Its copy and visuals are supportive of the main message, sharp, and easy to follow.

- It can be inserted into the package mechanically. That is, it is not a strange size, shape, thickness, or weight that cannot be handled by the inserting machinery.

- It does not push the weight of the package over the limit for the amount of postage planned.

Other Aspects of Direct Mail Marketing

A number of other issues require decisions during the planning of the direct mail program or when the package is being designed. Some of these issues will be affected by the format chosen, whereas others will not.

PERSONALIZATION

Remember that one of the things direct mail does especially well is deliver a personalized message. Let's consider two different types of personalization: the use of the recipient's name and individualized content in letters or packages.

If you possibly can, address the package to a person (not "occupant" or "patron") and use the recipient's name in the salutation of the letter. For a business-to-business mail package, also use the title of the intended recipient in the address if it is available.

On the other hand, do not misuse the person's name! Do not use it (or the address) just to show you know it, rather than to enhance the sales message. If it looks forced or silly, it is not going to improve response to your package. The best rule of thumb may be to ask yourself if you would use the person's name this way in conversation. The second rule is to ask yourself whether you are using any information that will make the reader uncomfortable ("I didn't know this company knew that fact about me").

Lucille Guardala gives some do's and don'ts for name use:[18]

Don't	Mr. Matthew Smith will find 30 recipes each month in *Gourmet.*
Do	Mr. Smith, the next four-star dining experience people will talk about in Boston could very well be at 42 Southlake Dr. The talk might well center around your truffled chicken, one of the 60-minute recipes you'll find in our free bonus issue of *Gourmet.*
Don't	I'd like to send these slacks to 121 South River Dr. for a 15-day free trial, Mrs. Smith.
Do	What's the advantage of our 15-day free trial offer, Mrs. Smith? Something no store in Dallas will let you do. When the slacks arrive at 121 South River Dr., wash them, wear them. If you think there's a better value in Dallas . . .

---

[18]Lucille M. Guardala, "Direct Mail Personalization," in Nash, *The Direct Marketing Handbook,* 502.

Look carefully at the "don'ts." Would you talk to a person, face to face, this way? If you would not, why would you write this way in a direct mail solicitation?

Bear in mind that it requires a considerable amount of data gathering and list editing to make sure the personalization is accurate. Without accuracy, it loses all impact, becomes silly, or can be downright insulting. It is better not to personalize at all than to do it badly.

The direct marketer should certainly evaluate the cost effectiveness of personalization as well as taking into account the additional time required. However, experience suggests that in most instances personalized messages will out-pull nonpersonalized ones.

TIMING AND SEQUENCING OF MAILINGS

A truism of direct marketing is that you cannot mail too frequently to your own customer base. Although it is probably unwise to take that statement literally, many experts agree that most direct marketers could mail more frequently to their own customers and to their best rental lists. Precisely how frequently, though, is a question that has to be answered by each direct marketer through analysis of results of previous mailings. The first thing to understand is the response curve for orders (or inquiries) from mailings for a particular product or product line. In other words, how quickly do the responses come in? When can you expect to have received them all? Julian Simon quotes seven different studies of response timing.[19] Unfortunately, they differ widely. By taking three of the consumer mailings that seem to have some surface similarity and doing some interpolating, we get the following results:

end of first week	30–40 percent of responses received
end of second week	58–73 percent of responses received
end of third week	75–81 percent of responses received
end of fourth week	84–90 percent of responses received
end of twenty-sixth week	100 percent of responses received

Obviously, these ranges are far too broad to be of any real use, but they do give an idea of how quickly the curve tails off. Each direct mail manager must track his or her own response curve. By the way, direct marketers measure from the date the first response is received (to compensate for postal irregularities), not from the date the mailing is dropped. The information on response timing is important also for operating decisions such as managing inventory.

It is critical to understand the nature of the curve for your product if you need to estimate total response rate before all responses have been received. In fact, you will probably have to make a decision on remailing long before all responses have been received. Just how soon can you actually remail? Here again, unfortunately, the experts disagree. Simon quotes one as saying that if the response rate is twice break-even, mail again (the same offer to the same list) after 45 days. Another says after 70 days! Ed Burnett tells of "a well-known list buyer at a renowned membership fund-raising organisation who would not mail any list more than once a year. Yet, second mailings to his best lists, which were twice as good as average, would have provided him with more members at lower cost than using additional lists."[20]

[19]Julian Simon, *How to Start and Operate a Mail-Order Business* (New York: McGraw-Hill, 1987), 258–259.

[20]Ed Burnett, "How Not to Succeed in Direct Mail," *Journal of Database Marketing* 4, no. 3 (1997): 278.

Two facts seem clear: you can mail again more quickly than most people would expect; and the more successful the mailing, the more quickly you can remail the same offer to the same list. Again, the only way to know how frequently you can remail—and this question is most critical for your house list—is to test. Carefully matched sample groups and a considerable period of time will be necessary to arrive at a satisfactory answer. You are unlikely to ever have a "final" answer. The nature of the market may change. A different type of product may have a somewhat different response curve. Technology from time to time changes the nature of responses, and that may affect the speed of response.

The direct mail manager must also be aware of seasonal effects on response rates. The product itself may be seasonal—a gift item or cold-weather clothing, for example. Moreover, just as retail sales vary by month, so do mail-order sales. Table 12.5 presents a study of seasonality that has been conducted annually for the past 19 years. You may be surprised to note that for a majority of the product categories listed the best month for mail-order sales is December. "The Christmas season," you are thinking. For some categories, such as entertainment, that is a reasonable hypothesis. What about the business and finance category? And why is December the best month for cultural reading whereas June is the best month for general reading? Also notice that changes occur from year to year, especially in the second best month to mail for a particular category.

This category-based information is useful to the direct mail manager as a starting point, but it does not substitute for developing data that are specific to the firm and its products. You should also bear in mind two other issues. First, other considerations such as promotion

TABLE 12.5 Seasonality Study

SUMMARY OF TOP TWO MAILING MONTHS FOR THE YEARS

	1994–1995		*through*	1995–1996	
	Top Month	*#2 Month*		*Top Month*	*#2 Month*
Business & finance	December	June		December	June
Cultural reading	December	October		December	May
General reading	June	December		December	May
Self-improvement	September	April/May		September	December
Home interest	December	September		May	December
Parents & children	August	March		August	April
Hobbies/related subjects	December	June		December	June
Entertainment	December	January		December	June
Education	August	March		January	November
Fund raising	November	August		November	October
Health	December	June		June	December

Source: Data from The Kleid Company, Inc., 1996. Reproduced from the *Direct Marketing Association's Statistical Fact Book, 1997* (New York: Direct Marketing Association, 1997), 70. Reproduced with permission of the Direct Marketing Association, 1998.

schedules, frequency of mailings, and list availability can cause the marketer to schedule mail drops for times that are not optimal in terms of seasonality. Second, when evaluating results of mailings, seasonality effects should be taken into account.

SCHEDULING EXECUTION OF A MAIL-ORDER PACKAGE

The novice tends to seriously underestimate the time it takes to prepare a direct mail package. The result is that either the planned mail date is missed (which may well lower the response rate) or the package is more expensive or is shoddily put together because everything has been done on a rush basis. Plan ahead, and allow a little more time than you actually expect to take to prepare the package. The best advice for developing a schedule for the execution of a mail-order package is to start by estimating how long the most time consuming element will require. After you estimate the time each element will take, plan backward from the most time consuming element.

Chapter 2 presented a schedule for a simple mailing package. Figure 12.6 (p. 292) presents a detailed checklist that will be helpful in planning and scheduling a direct mail program. It also gives an indication of the number of suppliers that are ordinarily involved in preparing direct mail.

WORKING WITH SUPPLIERS

The DMA has developed codes that group its members into three categories—consumer products and service marketers, business product and service marketers, and direct marketing service firms. There are 32 codes in the service category. Many of them fall under the general headings of promotional agencies, media, and consultants. You have already become acquainted with list brokers and managers in chapter 4. In chapter 8 we pointed out that there were service bureaus that specialize in database services. Similarly, there are several important kinds of suppliers that specialize in functions that are necessary to direct mail. Here, we discuss each briefly.

Paper and Envelope Suppliers

The selection of paper and, to a lesser extent, envelopes is a complex and very technical subject that is beyond the scope of this book. DMA and specialized trade associations and publications are sources of useful information. For the novice, there are two important pieces of advice. One is to select a supplier who will take time to explain the relevant technical issues. The other is to check tentative decisions with your printer and lettershop to ensure that the paper and envelope chosen will not create problems in downstream processes. At the same time, you should recognize that no one of the specialized suppliers will be equally expert in all parts of the process.

Printers

Printing a direct mail piece involves several highly technical issues including choosing the right process and approving color separations. It is important to choose a printer who has the technical capability to produce the type and quality of work that you need. It is also equally important not to make a choice just because a particular printer does smashing four-color catalogs when your format calls for a two-color postcard.

All aspects of your print job should be checked and double-checked before the job goes to press. It is highly recommended that a representative of the client or client's agency also be present (no matter what the time of day or night) when a job goes to press. At the begin-

Lists

- Source
  - Manager
  - Broker
  - House
- Type
  - House lists
  - Compiled lists
  - Responder lists
- Review data cards
- Additional select costs
- Data appends
- Magnetic tape, PS label costs
- Key codes

Format

- Self mailers
- Double postcards
- Number of components and type
  - Outgoing envelope (OE)
  - Cover letter
  - Brochure(s)
  - Business reply envelope (BRE)
  - Business reply card (BRC), printed on mailable stock
  - Involvement devices
    - Pressure sensitive (PS) labels
    - Stamps
    - Coupons
    - Buck slip (a single slip of paper, the size of the envelope or smaller, with additional information about the product or offer)
- Number of colors per side of each piece
  - Process colors
- PMS colors
- Size of each piece
  - Postage
  - Press layout
  - Insertability
- Paper stock
  - Weight
  - Postage of total packages as a function of stock choice
  - Printing: web or sheet-fed
  - Folding/perfing strength
- Personalization method/location on each piece/how much
  - Laser
  - Ink jet (coated stock)
  - Pressure sensitive label (PS)
  - Cheshire label

Print Production

- Size of each piece
- Press sheet layout
- Paper stock availability/alternate stock options
- Paper stock and color usage
- Paper stock's durability for finishing
  - Grain direction for folding
  - Coated stock for four-color
  - Absorbability
  - Strength for perforating (make sure if you're perforating into a roll for personalization that the perforations will withstand the tension during the personalization process.)
- Press checks
  - Stock
  - Press layout
- Does each side "back-up" correctly?
- Color and register
- Last chance to check for typos!
- Cut and fold a sample
- Check for paper cracking
- Perforation and scoring positions
- Provisions for additional paper
- Have you confirmed delivery dates?
- Sign and date two samples

Computer Processing

- Data processing
  - Conversion (reformatting)
  - Hygiene
  - NCOA
  - DSF
  - Data appending
  - Merge/purge
  - Postal qualification presorts
- Key codes

Lettershop

- Folding
- Cutting
- Bursting
- Collating
- Addressing
- Inserting
- Labeling
- Sorting
- Affixing postage
- Postal costs
- Business return mail permits
- USPS 3602 form

FIGURE 12.6 A Direct Mail Project Checklist

Source: Reprinted from *Marketing Tools* magazine with permission. © 1997 Cowles Business Media, Ithaca, New York.

ning of the run, there is still time to correct problems. When the press run has been completed, it is too late. The elements to check are[21]

- Is the paper stock correct? Several of your pieces may use the same stock, or you may be using different types of paper for different pieces, as was described in the *Highlights* mailings.
- Is the press layout correct so that when multiple-surface pieces are folded, each surface will be in the correct place? Unfold a brochure or broadside and you will quickly see that the piece does not lie flat on press in the same order that the reader will examine it.
- Do two-sided pieces "back up" correctly? Pages should be aligned so that margins are the same, headlines are situated correctly, and all the copy reads in the same direction.
- Are the colors true to specifications?
- Are perforations and scoring (for folds) in the correct places? When a piece is folded, does the ink crack along the fold?

Sign and date two copies of the entire sample package. Leave one with the printer and take one with you. You should also be aware that all the materials used in the printing process are traditionally the property of the printer. If you think you might use any part of the job again, you should include in the original order a stipulation that all press materials become the property of the marketer.

Lettershops

Lettershops perform a variety of functions that result in the printed matter being prepared for and deposited into the mail stream. What you need from the lettershop depends on the format of the mailing. The functions performed include affixing mailing labels, cutting, folding, inserting the various pieces into the envelope, and applying postage if it is not preprinted. Contemporary lettershops are highly automated, and all of these activities are intended to be performed by specialized machinery. If your mailing is not planned properly, or if you consciously choose a format that requires handwork, the cost will soar.

The lettershop must also be extremely knowledgeable about postal regulations because another important function is to sort (i.e., by zip code and carrier route) the mailing so it will qualify for the largest possible discount from the post office or other carrier. You may also choose to ask the lettershop to obtain the necessary permits from the postal system.

There are two final recommendations: First, the set of suppliers you choose must work together to achieve a high-quality job on time and on budget. It is helpful to have an initial meeting of the creative and management personnel from the marketer with a representative of each of the suppliers to ensure a common understanding of the requirements of the job. Second, bear in mind that the types of suppliers we have just described might more appropriately be regarded as functions, rather than as discrete businesses. There is sometimes more specialization, and therefore more separate firms, than we have described. On the other hand, large suppliers may incorporate several of these functions into a single business. There is no substitute for knowing your suppliers well and working closely with them.

In chapter 2 we provided a detailed budget for a direct mail program. It specifies the roles of numerous suppliers, including an advertising or direct mail agency and suppliers of creative services.

---

[21]Based on Meg Goodman, "Getting a Direct-Mail Campaign from the Planning Stages to the Post Office," *Marketing Tools* (May 1997): 43–48.

Having done everything that is necessary to plan and execute a successful direct mail program does not complete the process. Results must be tracked and analyzed. The astute marketer learns as much as possible from past programs so that future programs can be improved.

After the Successful Direct Mail Package—What Then?

Because direct-response marketing allows the manager to know exactly what works and what does not, what is profitable and what is not, the search for something even better is unending. We close this chapter with two points of view, both very useful, on how to conduct that search.

In discussing testing (chapter 10) we stated a number of times that certain elements of a direct-response program can greatly affect response rate, whereas others will have little or no effect. For a direct mail package, the powerful elements are usually the product itself, the structure of the offer, product positioning, and list selection. How can you change any of these elements to make it more effective?

Stone suggests you ask yourself three types of questions as you try to develop possible improvements in your direct-mail package for testing:[22]

1. Can I *add* anything that will lift the response rate? An insert, a free gift, a contest, sweepstakes? Just be sure you do not lift the response rate at the expense of depressing the profit!

2. Can I *extract* anything from previous executions—some appeal, perhaps, that got buried in the earlier versions of the package, but which, if highlighted, might prove very effective?

3. Can I *innovate* with a new and different approach to marketing this product? A blockbuster idea may be needed when a mail package has become old and tired.

One or more of these approaches should be employed with every mailing in a continuing effort to develop a new package that will beat the control. John Stevenson takes a different perspective on developing a new winning package. Whereas Stone, correctly, encourages direct marketers to improve upon what they are already doing, Stevenson challenges them to look beyond their current approaches in an attempt to uncover new, untapped market segments. His reasoning is that if the "typical" (and, remember, there is really no such thing) response rate is 2 percent, what about the other 98 percent?[23]

You will recall from our discussion of mailing lists in chapter 4 that direct marketers improve productivity by selecting only the best names and mailing to them. Whether we have 98 percent nonresponse from a mailing or whether we do not mail to the lowest 50 percent of a list, we have many names that represent an essentially untapped market. Consider just two possibilities:

1. Perhaps the nonresponders are potential customers, but for some reason are not yet ready to become actual customers. In terms of a frequently used advertising model, they have not moved far enough up the "hierarchy of effects" (awareness, knowledge, liking, conviction, and purchase) to buy. If we approached them with a different mailing, one designed to coincide with their "readiness state" and move them along to the next stage in the hierarchy, could we gradually get them to the point of making a purchase? Experience suggests that we could,

---

[22]Stone, *Successful Direct Marketing Methods,* 350.

[23]John Stevenson, "98% Negative Database Holds Power of Expansion Benefits," *Direct Marketing* (March 1985): 38–47.

but success would require considerable knowledge about the individual prospect and a carefully designed campaign—not just a single mailing.

2. What if we decided to tap the 50 percent of our list of names who did not qualify for our initial mailing? Perhaps they have characteristics that would make them excellent prospects for another product in our line. Or maybe they would respond to another appeal or positioning. Our database contains a great deal of information about these people. Instead of just discarding them, we might conduct additional analyses to see if we could target them differently.

The point is to use everything you know and all the technology at your disposal to make your direct mail programs more productive. A good direct marketing manager is never satisfied, even with success!

Summary

Direct mail is the standard by which the entire direct-response industry is often measured, for better or for worse. Direct mail pieces can range from a simple postcard to a complex personalized mail package. Each part of the mailing must be appropriate for the target market and the direct marketer's objectives, and must be integrated with all other parts to deliver a cohesive message to the recipient. Continued testing and improved analytical methods hold the promise of increasing the productivity of the direct mail effort.

Discussion Questions and Exercises

1. What is the difference between direct mail, mail order, and direct marketing?
2. Why do you think the volume of direct mail received by households in various countries differs so greatly? Do you think some of the reason may have to do with privacy issues? Why or why not?
3. What do we mean by the "classic direct mail package"? What does it contain?
4. What are the most important characteristics of a good direct mail letter?
5. What are some of the additional inserts that may be included in a direct mail package? Why would a direct mail marketer use one of them?
6. What are some of the ways a direct marketer increases the pulling power of a direct mail package?
7. Bring one or two pieces of direct mail to class. Be prepared to discuss their format and contents in the light of the target market and the objectives for which they appear to have been designed.

Suggested Readings

See the *Journal of Direct Marketing* (winter 1994 and winter 1996) for articles on several aspects of international direct marketing.

Baker, Sunny, and Kim Baker. *Desktop Direct Marketing*. New York: McGraw-Hill, 1995.

Cohen, William A. *Building a Mail Order Business: A Complete Manual for Success*. New York: John Wiley & Sons, 1996.

Voekel, Jon. "Land Rover's Direct Marketing Programme: A Case Study." *Journal of Database Marketing* (summer 1993): 54–61.

CHAPTER 13 — Catalog Marketing

The Development of Catalog Marketing

In 1869, E. C. Allen of Augusta, Maine, had an idea. Americans had been buying products by mail from the time when Benjamin Franklin had offered his inventions by mail, but no company was wholly dedicated to sales by mail, and most of those that dabbled in mail orders usually carried only a single line of products. So Allen hit on a plan to sell nationally a selection of specialty items ranging from recipes for washing powder to engravings and to do it only by mail. He founded the *People's Literary Companion,* whose object, despite its title, was commercial, not educational.

In its second year, Allen's paper, priced at 50 cents a year, sold 500,000 copies. There was big money in the mails! The history of direct marketing does not record the fate of the *People's Literary Companion* beyond its successful second year of operations, but we know that some of its early competitors became mainstays of the American household.

The first of those U.S. institutions began when Aaron Montgomery Ward established a general-merchandise catalog in 1872. A single sheet of paper with a headline reading "The

Original Wholesale Grange Supply House," it was targeted at farmers in the Midwest who were upset by the high prices of goods they purchased compared to the low prices they received for their farm products.

The second came into being in 1886 when a Minnesota railroad agent named Richard Sears purchased an unclaimed shipment of $25 watches for $13 each and resold them to other agents along the line for $14 each. Encouraged by this success, he began a catalog of watches and jewelry in 1888. By 1896, Sears had formed a partnership with Alvah C. Roebuck, and they issued a 140-page general-merchandise catalog.[1]

The success of the Sears and the Ward catalogs can be attributed to the American farmer who found high prices and limited selections at the local general store, often after traveling several hours for the dubious privilege of buying there. The early catalog businesses were also bolstered by the development of the railroad network and the U.S. postal system.

Although no figures exist, it seems there was a steady growth in the catalog field during the first half of the 20th century. Several successful catalogs were established during this period, including those of Spiegel (1901), L.L. Bean (1913), and Eddie Bauer (1920).

The next major growth era in catalog marketing occurred after World War II with the establishment of successful specialty catalogers including Spencer Gifts, Sunset House, Foster and Gallagher, Hanover House, and many food and garden books. Most of these catalogs supplied household items, clothing, and gifts to the middle-class mass market.

The increasing affluence and sophistication of the middle-class market led to the explosive growth of catalog marketing in the 1970s and 1980s. The initiator of this movement was probably Roger Horchow, who established The Horchow Collection in 1974. This was the first in a wave of upscale catalogs that took the middle-class market by storm.

As the number of catalog firms has grown in recent years and competition has intensified, many catalog firms have come and gone—some so quickly that they left virtually no trace. However, some well-known catalogs failed, such as Alden's (1889–1983) and Sunset House (1949–1984). Montgomery Ward ended its catalog operation in 1985 and Sears ceased to mail its "big book" in 1993 after many years of trying to return it to profitability.

The typical reasons for failure include undercapitalization, lack of knowledge of the marketplace, insufficient customer base, and poor order fulfillment. Above all, it appears that the failure of catalog giants such as Alden's and Montgomery Ward can be attributed to their lack of recognition of the changing nature of the U.S. consumer marketplace, which had become too competitive for huge general-merchandise catalogs to remain profitable. Also, Alden's, with a downscale customer base, found it difficult either to remain profitable serving that set of customers base or to alter its merchandise and marketing efforts to serve a more upscale market. Image upgrading is not impossible, however, as witnessed by Speigel's successful turnaround during this same time period. The stars of the 1980s, however, were specialty catalogs targeted to niche markets, such as those of the Sharper Image (consumer electronics), Williams-Sonoma (kitchen equipment), Brookstone (hard-to-find tools), and Calyx and Corolla (fresh-cut flowers).[2]

In the 1990s the catalog landscape has changed once again, as can be seen by the 1995 listing of the 25 largest catalog merchants shown in Table 13.1 (p. 298). Dell Computer,

---

[1]Gordon L. Weil, *Sears, Roebuck, USA* (Chicago: Stein and Day, 1977), 61.

[2]This description of the history of catalogs is based on C. E. Bjorncrantz, "Sears' Big Book: Dinosaur or Phoenix?" *Direct Marketing* (July 1986): 71–75; "Ward Closes the Book," *Fortune,* 2 September 1985, 10; Stephen J. Sansweet, "Management Mistakes Plus Old Problems Led to Collapse of Alden's," *The Wall Street Journal,* 6 January 1983, 1, 13; Gregory A. Patterson and Christina Duff, "Sears Trims Operations, Ending an Era," *The Wall Street Journal,* 26 January 1993, B1, B8.

which was founded to sell microcomputers by mail order, leads the list. In fact, 5 of the top 10 catalogers are computer firms! Gateway 2000 and MicroWarehouse were also established as direct marketers. Digital Equipment and IBM have turned to catalog sales out of necessity; more about that appears in chapter 11.

The merchandise categories most represented by the top 100 catalog merchants are as follows:

CATEGORY	NUMBER OF COMPANIES
General merchandise	19
Apparel	17
Business, office, and industrial supplies	15
Computer supplies	9
Computer hardware	8

TABLE 13.1 Twenty-Five Largest Catalog Merchants

	Company Name	1995 Sales (in millions)	1994 Sales (in millions)	Category
1	Dell Computer	5,296	3,420	Computer hardware
2	JCPenney	3,738	3,817	General merchandise
3	Gateway 2000	3,676	2,600	Computer hardware
4	Digital	3,000[a]	2,550	Computer hardware
5	Fingerhut	1,826	1,719	General merchandise
6	Spiegel	1,751	1,742	General merchandise
7	MicroWarehouse	1,308	776.4	Computer supplies
8	IBM Direct	1,070	950	Computer hardware
9	Lands' End	1,030	990	Apparel
10	L.L. Bean	945	848	Apparel
11	Viking	920.7	673.6	Office supplies
12	Hanover	749.8	768.9	General merchandise
13	Deluxe Direct	678.5	665.3	Business supplies
14	Victoria's Secret	661	569	Apparel
15	J. Crew Group	640[a]	575[a]	Apparel
16	Global DirectMail	634.6	484.2	Computer, office, and industrial supplies
17	Computer Discount Warehouse	634.5	629	Computer supplies
18	Henry Schein	616.2	486.6	Dental, medical supplies
19	Brylane	601.1	578.5	Apparel
20	Newark Electronics	600	495	Industrial electronics
21	Blair Corp.	560.9	535.8	General merchandise
22	Damark International	500	477	General merchandise
23	Quill	500	416.5	Office supplies
24	Chadwick's of Boston	472.4	433.6	Women's apparel
25	Darby Group Cos.	430[a]	392[a]	Dental, medical supplies

Source: Adapted from www.mediacentral.com.

[a]Estimate

TABLE 13.2 U.S. Catalog Sales in $ Billions				
	Actual 1992	*Actual 1996*	*Estimate 1997*	*Forecast 2002*	*Compound Growth by Year: 1997–2002*
Consumer	33.6	45.5	48.3	64.6	6%
Business-to-business	19.8	28.2	30.3	42.2	6.8
Total	53.4	73.7	78.6	106.8	6.3

Source: Data from WEFA Group. Reproduced from the *Direct Marketing Association's Statistical Fact Book, 1997* (New York: Direct Marketing Association, 1997), 342. Reproduced with the permission of the Direct Marketing Association, 1998.

Business marketers, including those who supply the rapidly growing small business and home-based business segment, now have a large and growing presence in the catalog marketplace (see Table 13.2 for a catalog sales forecast). Quite a change from the early days of catalog marketing—or even from the go-go days of specialty consumer catalogs!

This chapter deals primarily with consumer catalogs; a specialized discussion of business-to-business catalogs is found in chapter 17. Bear in mind that the best business-to-business catalogs are far from the boring industrial price lists of years past. One of the reasons they have been so successful in recent years is that business catalog marketers have adopted many of the techniques of the most successful consumer catalog marketers.

Let's consider who is shopping from consumer catalogs and why customers find them so captivating.

The Appeal of Catalogs

From a survey with a nationally projectible sample, the Direct Marketing Association estimated that almost 59 percent of the U.S. population purchased from a catalog during the 12 months immediately preceding the study in 1995, buying in almost equal numbers by mail and by telephone (Table 13.3, p. 300). The demographics of catalog shoppers show a predominance of female buyers and an upscale profile in terms of education, occupation, household income, and home ownership. With an abundance of retail shopping opportunities, what accounts for the popularity of catalog shopping?

One study takes a generic look at the issue by examining consumer shopping orientations in terms of both retail store and nonstore shopping. They identified five different types of shoppers. *Catalog convenience* shoppers are concerned with saving time. *Catalog recreational* shoppers like to receive catalogs and to peruse them. *Store recreational* shoppers like to visit stores and malls even if they do not buy anything. *Merchandise intensive* shoppers indicate they are looking for a wide assortment of high-quality brand-name merchandise. *Impulse* shoppers buy without preplanning, whether they are shopping in stores or from cat-

TABLE 13.3 Catalogs: Purchases by Mail, Phone, or at Catalog Store in Last 12 Months

	Total	Bought from Catalogs in Last 12 Months		By Mail		By Phone		At Catalog Store	
	U.S. (000)	(000)	%	(000)	%	(000)	%	(000)	%
Total adults	191,504	112,904	59.0	70,735	36.9	74,355	38.8	10,191	5.3
Males	91,938	49,698	54.1	30,884	33.6	31,680	34.5	3,866	4.2
Females	99,566	63,207	63.5	39,851	40.0	42,675	42.9	6,325	6.4
18–24	25,739	12,308	47.8	7,955	30.9	7,441	28.9	1,046	4.1
25–34	42,251	25,693	60.8	15,965	37.8	17,922	42.4	1,914	4.5
35–44	41,811	27,360	65.4	16,822	40.2	19,718	47.2	2,773	6.6
45–54	29,766	18,806	63.2	11,530	38.7	13,393	45.0	1,637	5.5
55–64	20,884	12,441	59.6	7,724	37.0	7,719	37.0	1,231	5.9
65 or older	31,054	16,297	52.5	10,739	34.6	8,163	26.3	1,589	5.1
Graduated college	38,819	29,016	74.7	17,840	46.0	22,589	58.2	2,163	5.6
Attended college	40,166	25,357	63.1	16,249	40.5	17,598	43.8	2,221	5.5
Graduated high school	75,202	41,936	55.8	25,953	34.5	25,963	34.5	3,925	5.2
Did not graduate high school	37,318	16,595	44.5	10,693	28.7	8,205	22.0	1,881	5.0
Professional	17,411	13,037	74.9	8,221	47.2	10,369	59.6	1,100	6.3
Manager/administrative	15,762	11,630		7,208		9,174		606	
Technical/clerical sales	36,449	22,971	63.0	14,602	40.1	15,729	43.2	1,880	5.2
Precision/craft	12,883	6,935	53.8	3,882	30.1	5,079	39.4	587	4.6
Other employed	36,482	20,084	55.1	12,735	34.9	12,015	32.9	2,282	6.3
Single	44,547	22,597	50.7	14,990	33.6	14,280	32.1	1,632	3.7
Married	111,238	71,021	63.8	42,967	38.6	49,072	44.1	6,916	6.2
Divorced/separated/widowed	35,719	19,286	54.0	12,779	35.8	11,003	30.8	1,643	4.6
Northeast	39,281	25,193	64.1	15,804	40.2	17,168	43.7	2,148	5.5
Midwest	45,111	26,597	59.0	16,131	35.8	17,357	38.5	3,001	6.7

South	67,006	37,975	56.7	23,779	35.5	25,116	37.5	3,455	5.2
West	40,107	23,139	57.7	15,022	37.5	14,715	36.7	1,587	4.0
Household income									
$75,000 or more	30,409	21,724	71.4	12,411	40.8	17,661	58.1	1,426	4.7
$60,000 or more	48,742	34,610	71.0	20,211	41.5	27,032	55.5	2,323	4.8
$50,000 or more	66,596	46,581	69.9	27,488	41.3	35,381	53.1	3,289	4.9
$40,000 or more	88,183	59,803	67.8	35,515	40.3	44,956	51.0	4,617	5.2
$30,000 or more	114,324	75,190	65.8	45,589	39.9	54,614	47.8	6,377	5.6
$30,000 to $39,999	26,141	15,388	58.9	10,075	38.5	9,658	36.9	1,760	6.7
$20,000 to $29,999	29,328	16,150	55.1	10,648	36.3	9,003	30.7	1,590	5.4
$10,000 to $19,999	28,929	13,621	47.1	8,821	30.5	7,098	24.5	1,378	4.8
Under $10,000	18,923	7,943	42.0	5,676	30.0	3,641	19.2	846	4.5
Household size									
1 person	23,976	13,034	54.4	8,934	37.3	7,742	32.3	922	3.8
2 person	61,622	37,626	61.1	23,876	38.7	24,281	39.4	2,940	4.8
3 or 4 people	76,480	45,928	60.1	28,024	36.6	31,701	41.5	4,321	5.6
5 or more people	29,426	16,317	55.5	9,902	33.7	10,631	36.1	2,008	6.8
Children									
No child in household	112,144	65,251	58.2	41,713	37.2	41,641	37.1	5,204	4.6
Children under 2 years	13,163	8,400	63.8	4,878	37.1	6,074	46.1	882	6.7
2–5 years	31,349	19,036	60.7	11,492	36.7	12,938	41.3	1,924	6.1
6–11 years	35,591	21,621	60.7	13,261	37.3	14,829	41.7	2,392	6.7
12–17 years	36,396	20,900	57.4	12,695	34.9	13,884	38.1	2,527	6.9
Residence owned	131,137	81,302	62.0	50,111	38.2	55,616	42.4	7,557	5.8
Residence rented	48,729	25,812	53.0	17,034	35.0	15,045	30.9	1,903	3.9

Source: Data from Simmons Market Research Bureau: Study of Media and Markets, 1995. *Direct Marketing Association's Statistical Fact Book, 1997* (New York: Direct Marketing Association, 1997), 83. Reproduced with permission of the Direct Marketing Association, 1998.

Note: Most catalog purchases were made by phone, while the smallest proportion of catalog sales were made at catalog stores. Overall demographics show that buyers tend to be married, female, between the ages of 35 and 54, in the northeast region.

TABLE 13.4 Size of Shopping Orientation Segments	
Catalog convenience	25
Store recreational	118
Catalog recreational	86
Merchandise intensive	135
Impulse	18

Source: Reprinted from K. C. Gehrt and K. Carter, "An Exploratory Assessment of Catalog Shopping Orientations," *Journal of Direct Marketing* (winter 1992): 29–39. Copyright © 1992 by John Wiley & Sons. Reprinted by permission of John Wiley & Sons.

Note: Number of respondents; $n = 298$.

alogs. Table 13.4 estimates the relative size of these segments, based on the sample for this particular study.[3]

Another survey asked a national sample of catalog shoppers to rate the importance of 50 catalog attributes and how likely catalogs were to provide satisfaction on them. Both male and female respondents ranked guarantees as most important. This was true for both clothing purchases and sporting goods purchases. They ranked quality merchandise third in order of importance. Several convenience-related attributes made up the rest of the top six—accessibility, time savings, returns, and effort savings.[4]

When the question becomes loyalty, or why consumers engage in repeat purchasing from the same catalog, the results are similar. A study of repeat purchasers of photographic and video equipment found that three factors—price attributes, service attributes, and attributes related to the catalog shopping experience—discriminated between repeat and nonrepeat buyers.[5] A similar study of repeat purchasers from women's apparel catalogs found eight factors that describe shopper decision-making styles: quality, image, loyalty (to a set of apparel catalogs), value, fashion, recreation, emotion (impulse), and confusion (with the variety of catalogs available). Fashion and value-oriented shoppers switched between various catalogs for a majority of their purchases, whereas loyal shoppers bought more than half of their purchases from a single catalog. The loyalists were more likely to be married, to be older, and to buy less frequently.[6]

Taken together, these studies suggest a number of important issues relative to the catalog customer. The importance that customers attach to attributes that reduce perceived risk, through guarantees and positive corporate and brand image, is reinforced. Attributes that relate to shopping convenience are also highly prized by customers. It is also clear that these customers are looking for a positive price-value relationship, not just the lowest prices. What emerges is a picture of a relatively upscale customer who enjoys the activity of catalog shop-

[3] Kenneth C. Gehrt and Kent Carter, "An Exploratory Assessment of Catalog Shopping Orientations," *Journal of Direct Marketing* (winter 1992): 29–39.

[4] Mary Ann Eastlick and Richard A. Feinberg, "Gender Differences in Mail-Catalog Patronage Motives," *Journal of Direct Marketing* (spring 1994): 37–44.

[5] Michael J. Klassen and Karen A. Glynn, "Catalog Loyalty," *Journal of Direct Marketing* (summer 1992): 60–67.

[6] William J. McDonald, "The Roles of Demographics, Purchase Histories, and Shopper Decision-Making Styles in Predicting Consumer Catalog Loyalty," *Journal of Direct Marketing* (summer 1993): 55–65.

ping and values the convenience it offers but who is unwilling to sacrifice quality and who expects the highest level of service from catalog merchants.

This suggests a demanding environment in which to seek catalog marketing success. In considering the entire process, we can divide the marketer's concerns into three main areas:

1. The front end, which includes all marketing decisions—targeting and positioning, merchandise selection and presentation, pricing, and so on.
2. The back end, which involves order processing, fulfillment, and customer service.
3. The business environment, which includes postal, production, and regulatory issues.

Back-end operations, which are essentially the same for all types of direct marketing, are discussed in chapter 7. This chapter concentrates on the front end, or marketing, of a catalog. We also discusss important environmental issues currently facing catalog marketers.

The Crowded Catalog Marketplace

The day when a poorly targeted, poorly focused catalog could have even a minimal level of success is past. The consumer's mailbox is crowded by many marketers eager to sell their wares. To stand out in this mailbox clutter, a catalog must have a distinctive point of view and presentation.

But novel merchandise and creativity of presentation alone are not sufficient. The required investment in back-end operations, which include fulfillment, customer service, and database processing, is significant. The day of the kitchen table start-up is, to all intents and purposes, gone. Estimates of the amount of capital needed to start a catalog business typically begin at $1 million, but may be higher, depending on the planned scope of the business. One consultant has a list of success factors for catalog marketing that emphasizes this point. The items listed in Figure 13.1 are not necessarily in order of priority; however, they are all essential to catalog success.

FIGURE 13.1 Key Success Factors for Catalogs

Source: Adapted from Katie Muldoon, *How to Profit through Catalog Marketing,* 3rd ed. (Lincolnwood, IL: NTC Business Books, 1996), 63–64.

Enough **Money,** based on a solid business plan, to cover expenses and fund growth

Time to do the job right

Distinctive **Positioning** that cannot be copied easily

Total dedication to **Customer Service**

Complete understanding of all parts of the business based on thorough **Analysis**

Flexibility that permits adaptation to changing conditions

Timeliness in the product offering and presentation

Controlling Growth to sustain customer service and financial stability

Products with a reasonably **Short Repurchase Cycle** so that customers will need to return often

Database Construction and Manipulation because customer information is the lifeblood of the business

---

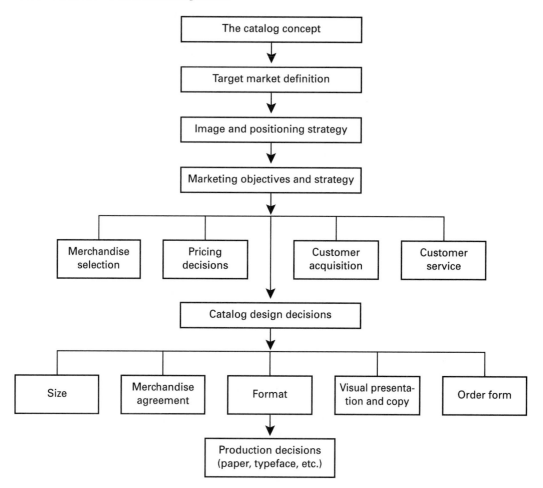

FIGURE 13.2 Catalog Development and Marketing Process

Catalog marketing has evolved from a romantic enterprise with low barriers to entry to a complex undertaking, requiring a wide variety of marketing, merchandising, and catalog production skills. Figure 13.2 presents the series of decisions that must be made by the catalog marketer.

Developing and Marketing Catalogs

DEVELOPING THE CATALOG CONCEPT

The distinctive point of view and presentation that are a major factor in the success of a catalog stem from the basic catalog concept. The catalog concept is a concise statement of the catalog's reason for existence. Many catalogers have presented to the public an explicit statement of their business philosophy that provides a description of the core concept of their business.

Brookstone describes itself very clearly on the inside front cover of its catalog:

Since 1965 . . . we have provided hard-to-find tools and other home solutions to our customers across the country. We search out the time-tested, the unique, the exceptional in quality, and even, when appropriate, the newest products and problem solvers. Our goal is to help
make your life at home, in the yard, in your workshop, in your car easier and more enjoyable.
We hope we can satisfy your needs in the years to come.[7]

The Brookstone catalog pictures a pair of lightweight overshoes on the front cover and
a magnetic ski carrier on the back cover. The laser-printed message on the address surface
exhorts the recipient to "Avoid costly snow & ice damage to your roof this winter. Order our
snow roof rake on page 3 and be prepared for winter's worst." Seasonal merchandise such as
snow removal tools, space heaters, and humidifiers are featured on the first few pages. Much
of the rest of the 64-page catalog comprises products for the car, the home, and the traveler
that have little or no seasonality.

A catalog's concept defines the limits of the business and identifies the area in which
the business intends to excel. Some, such as Brookstone, share their concept very explicitly with the prospective customer. Others, as shown in a subsequent section, present the catalog mission in a more image-oriented manner. Apparel catalogs are less likely to state the
concept in the catalog itself. Presumably the merchandise and its presentation make the
statement.

Developing a concept that is neither too narrow (limiting the catalog's appeal) nor too
broad (introducing irrelevant merchandise and confusing the catalog's image) is critical for
long-term success. The concept may be translated into a catalog theme—Norm Thompson's
"ESCAPE from the ordinary" is a good example.

The prospective customer knows what to expect from a catalog that states its purpose
clearly. An explicit statement of purpose also serves to focus the efforts of all personnel
involved in the production of the catalog.

DEFINING THE TARGET MARKET

As in all marketing endeavors, a clear profile and an in-depth understanding of the target customer are essential. The existing catalog operation should continually add to and refine its
knowledge, much of which resides in its database, about its customers, as discussed in chapters 5 and 8. The beginning catalog operation must define its target market on the basis of the
concept statement. This requires sound judgment supported by marketing research that helps
management better understand the needs and motives of the catalog shopper.

The need to understand the specific target market for any catalog is no different from
any marketer's requirement to fully comprehend all relevant dimensions of its market.
However, the catalog marketer, like all direct marketers, has a powerful advantage in the customer database.

IMAGE AND POSITIONING STRATEGY

Bob Stone has insightfully referred to the catalog as a "paper store."[8] This is a useful comparison because there has been a great deal of research identifying the major dimensions of
the retail store image.

---

[7]Brookstone Company, Inc., 1996 catalog.

[8]Bob Stone, *Successful Direct Marketing Methods,* 3rd ed. (Chicago: Crain Books, 1984), 305.

TABLE 13.5 Characteristics of Retail Store and Catalog Image	
Retail Store	*Catalog*
Merchandise assortment ————————————→	
Customer service ————————————→	
Pricing policies ————————————→	
Customer communications ————————————→	
Institutional reputation ————————————→	
Store clientele	Perception of catalog clientele
Store personnel	Customer service personnel
Physical attributes (atmosphere)	Appearance of catalog
Store location	

Source: Adapted from Barry Berman and Joel R. Evans, *Retail Management,* 3rd ed. (New York: Macmillan, 1986), 358–360; Jay D. Lindquest, "Meaning of Image," *Journal of Retailing* (winter, 1974–1975): 29–37.

What we mean by store image is "the way in which the store is defined in the shopper's mind, partly by its functional qualities and partly by an aura of psychological attributes."[9] Catalog image, then, would simply be the physical and psychological attributes of a catalog as perceived by its target customers.

Table 13.5 shows how the dimensions of a retail store image are duplicated in a catalog. Except for the fact that a catalog does not have a physical store location (even though many catalog companies do have retail outlets), catalog image can be evaluated on dimensions similar to those used for evaluating retail store image. What this tells the catalog marketer is that decisions concerning each of these dimensions will affect the image portrayed by the catalog.

For example, in establishing pricing policies, the marketer will have to decide such issues as the overall level of prices, the number of price points, whether to engage in comparison pricing, and whether to feature price reductions. Decisions to engage in premium pricing without explicit reference to competitive prices and not to offer merchandise in the catalog at sale prices will contribute to an upscale image. Be careful about implying too much from a single image dimension, however. Comparison pricing of moderately priced merchandise that is presented in a very attractive manner could be successful in creating a "value" image as opposed to a "downscale" one.

Many catalog marketers go further, attempting to create strong brand personalities for their catalogs. The Pyramid Collection, which calls itself "A Catalog of Personal Growth & Exploration" introduces a recent catalog with a quote from *The Celestine Prophecy* by James Redfield:

"THE MORE BEAUTY WE CAN SEE, THE MORE WE EVOLVE."

The message on the inside front cover goes on to say:

And when it comes to humankind's journey toward empathy and spiritual awareness, there's so very much beauty to appreciate and see.

---

[9] Pierre Martineau, "The Personality of the Retail Store," *Harvard Business Review* 36 (January–February 1958): 47.

In fact, we believe you'll find this issue of *The Pyramid Collection* contains some of the most beautifully conceived books, CDs, videos, tapes, and skillfully crafted jewelry, gifts, and accessories ever collected between the covers of a single catalog:

Prophetic narratives and calm-promoting gemstones and crystals. . . . Soothing sounds and stimulating scents to energize the spirit. . . . Page after page of ideas and objects that honor the world's great cultures and religions. . . .

Beauty to give and beauty to receive on your personal journey to inner peace and understanding![10]

Some catalogs use a personal approach to establish an image and a personality for their catalogs. Country Curtains, located in a picturesque small town in the Berkshire Mountains of Massachusetts, features a letter from cofounder Jane Fitzpatrick:

Dear Friend,

It's hard to believe Jack and I started Country Curtains in 1956 in Whitman, Massachusetts with only one style of curtain.

All of our curtains fit in the back of our station wagon when we moved to Stockbridge two years later. We soon outgrew the dining room of our new home, so in 1968 we purchased the famous old Red Lion Inn here in town, and moved our blossoming company there. When we needed still more space, we settled into our present building a few miles down the road.

Although we've grown by leaps and bounds, and now offer a huge selection, we still pay attention to the many details. Daughters Nancy and Ann, grandsons Casey and Alexander, and a marvelous staff, help us keep pace. Best wishes with your window decorating projects. I'll look forward to hearing from you soon!

Most Sincerely,
[signed Jane Fitzpatrick]

P.S. If you live in the Northeast or Mid-Atlantic areas, you would enjoy visiting a Country Curtains Retail Shop. Please see page 52 for the locations![11]

Also on the inside front cover of the catalog are two family pictures, "The Fitzpatrick family listening to grandson Casey, reading one of your letters," and "Daughter, Ann, and grandson, Alexander, missed the family photo; but Alexander sent a favorite photo of them taken while on a ski vacation." The overall impression is one of a family-run business that cares about knowing its customers personally.

A final example is a letter from the owner that helps to establish the image and personality of a catalog, but in a very different tone. J. Peterman calls his catalog of upscale apparel an *Owner's Manual*®. On the inside front cover of a recent edition, the following letter appears:

PHILOSOPHY

People want things that are hard to find. Things that have romance, but a factual romance, about them.

I had this proven to me all over again when people actually stopped me in the street (in New York, in Tokyo, in London) to ask me where I got the coat I was wearing.

So many people tried to buy my coat off my back that I've started a small company to make them available. It seems like everybody (well, not everybody) has always wanted a clas-

---

[10]Catalog Ventures, Inc., 1997 catalog.

[11]Country Curtains Mail Order, Inc., 1996 catalog.

sic horseman's duster but never knew exactly where to get one.

I ran a little ad in the New Yorker and the Wall Street Journal and in a few months sold this wonderful coat in cities all over the country and to celebrities and to a mysterious gentleman in Japan who ordered <u>two thousand</u> of them.

Well, the coat <u>is</u> something. Simple, functional, handsome, extremely well made, affordable and, yes, romantic.

I think that giant American corporations should start asking themselves if the things they make are really, I mean really, better than the ordinary.

Clearly, people want things that make their lives the way they wish they were.

J. Peterman[12]

As an aside, we will say more about this unique catalog later in the chapter. However, any business that has become a topic of conversation on Seinfeld, with the owner appearing in one segment, and has been satirized in a popular comic strip (*Doonsbury* featured a character called "J. Pretentious") has clearly established a compelling personality for the organization.

THE MARKETING STRATEGY

A strong image, portrayed clearly throughout the catalog, should be useful in helping to set direction for the marketing strategy. In developing a marketing strategy for a catalog, a basic set of marketing mix variables—merchandise selection, pricing, customer acquisition, and customer service policies—applies.

The objectives of a specific catalog stem from the catalog's place in the overall marketing program of the firm. This is true because it is unusual today for a single catalog to make up a business organization. More often, the catalog is part of a multiple-catalog firm, or has a retail counterpart, or is a supporting part of the marketing effort.

A catalog will usually have as its primary objective the sale of merchandise. Because many catalogers also have retail outlets, an equally important objective for these marketers may be to promote the retail stores, as you saw in the Country Curtains example. Some retailers use their catalogs primarily as vehicles to attract customers to their retail outlets. Sales made directly from the catalog are viewed as incremental and are not strongly pushed. Others, such as *Bloomingdale's By Mail* and *Neiman-Marcus Direct* are operationally separate and have their own separate sales objectives.

Large marketers of brand-name products and services often use sales incentive catalogs. General Mills has for many years used its Betty Crocker catalog to encourage repeat purchases. More recently, Pepsi has enjoyed great success with its "Drink Pepsi. Get Stuff" promotion. Our focus, however, is on catalogs that have objectives of either selling merchandise or driving traffic into retail stores.

Business marketers also use catalogs in a variety of ways: to make direct sales of lower-ticket merchandise, supplies, and accessories; to support the field sales force; and to support the dealer network.

Some aspects of the catalog will change—for instance, focus on image versus a stronger sales message, and more or less detailed and descriptive copy—according to the marketer's objectives, but the same general aspects of catalog marketing apply regardless of the specific objectives of the catalog.

---

[12]*Owner's Manual,* no. 47, The J. Peterman Company, 1997.

MERCHANDISE SELECTION

The importance of unique and appealing merchandise to the success of a catalog has already been stressed. How does the catalog marketer locate and evaluate merchandise to include in the catalog?

This question is more easily answered by the established than by the new cataloger for at least two reasons:

1. The profitability of each item from previous catalogs is known; profitable items will ordinarily be retained for the next edition.

2. The demographic and purchase profile of the catalog's customers is well known from analysis of the customer database.

The new cataloger must rely on judgment in selecting merchandise for the catalog, making it a much more risky venture.

Like retailers, catalog marketers can visit merchandise marts and shows in major cities including New York, Chicago, Dallas, Atlanta, and Los Angeles. Cities tend to specialize; for example, New York is well known for apparel and Los Angeles for gifts and home furnishings. Most of the exhibits, permanent or seasonal, are open to buyers only; consumers are not allowed. The new cataloger will have to seek out merchandise resources; the successful one will be besieged with manufacturers and inventors who wish to sell through a well-known catalog. Once attractive merchandise is located, however, both will face the same problem—choosing the correct assortment to appear in the next edition of the catalog.

The first step is to look at the profitability of each item in the preceding catalog. The basic process is to divide the total cost of the catalog, before any overhead allocation, by the number of pages. This gives a per-page cost. Then, assuming that the space allocation is roughly the same for each product, divide by the number of products on the page to determine the volume of sales each product must generate. Consider the following example:[13]

The catalog is 32 pages long and cost $160,000 for creative, production, lists, and postage.

$160,000 / 32 = $5,000 per page

The product appeared on a page that contained five items.

$5,000 / 5 = $1,000 required sales per item

The product cost $37.50 per item and sold for $75.00 (the keystone retail mark-up of 50 percent on selling price).

To find break-even on the catalog cost for this product: $1,000 (cost) / $37.50 (margin) = 26.66 = 27 units.

If a product did not break even in the previous edition, or if a new product cannot reasonably be expected to do so, including it in the catalog is a questionable decision. Other considerations for repeating a financially successful product include the ability of the vendor to maintain quality, meet delivery dates, and maintain a stable price. It is also important to consider the nature of the catalog's target audience. Is it trendy and upscale, always on the lookout for new merchandise? Or is it more conservative, perhaps feeling more comfortable with an item that has appeared in the catalog several times?[14]

---

[13] Adapted from Katie Muldoon, *How to Profit through Catalog Marketing,* 3rd ed. (Lincolnwood, IL: NTC Business Books, 1996), 107.

[14] Ibid., 107–108.

Will the **Quality** of the merchandise maintain the catalog image and delight the customer?

Is the **Price** within an acceptable range for your target customer?

Can the supplier guarantee product **Availability** at the time and in the quantities needed, and do you have a back-up source of supply?

Can you negotiate product **Exclusivity**?

Is the product **Unique** to the mail-order market?

Can you expect **Vendor Cooperation** on issues from helping to forecast sales to keeping sufficient back-up inventory?

Does the product have good **Photographic Potential**?

Will the item encourage **Cross-Sales** of other merchandise in the catalog?

Does the product fit well into your overall **Merchandise Mix and Assortment**?

Is the **Profit Potential** satisfactory?

FIGURE 13.3 Product Selection Criteria

Source: Adapted from Katie Muldoon, *How to Profit through Catalog Marketing* (Lincolnwood, IL: NTC Business Books, 1996), 107.

Stanley Marcus of Neiman-Marcus has been quoted as saying that "mail order works because it is a preedited selection of merchandise." By this he means that the skilled marketer makes the initial selection of an appropriate set of merchandise, thereby making the customer's final choice easier. The author goes on to say that "in a typical high-ticket catalog of thirty-two pages plus cover, an ideal maximum number of products would be 130 to 140."[15] Catalogers tend to err on the side of including too many items rather than too few. Crowding in too many items makes it difficult to display each to its best advantage. Figure 13.3 lists suggested criteria for choosing products to display in a catalog.

In choosing merchandise, select items for the most important pages first. The front cover is the most powerful location, followed by the back cover, the inside front cover, the inside back cover, the center spread, and the pages around the order form.

If merchandise is to be used on the cover, it should be selected with great care to excite interest and convey the overall image. Additionally, the inside front cover—the inside of the cover and the page facing it—helps set the tone for the rest of the catalog, as in the customer letters presented earlier in this chapter, and should display merchandise carefully chosen to be representative of the catalog theme, seasonality, merchandise categories, and price points.

The back cover has special importance because it may provide the customer's first view of the catalog. The center pages may get additional attention because the catalog easily falls open there. Similarly, the pages near the order form may receive closer scrutiny; these pages are an especially good location for impulse or sale merchandise.

---

[15]Jo-Von Tucker, "Catalog Sales," in Edward L. Nash, ed., *The Direct Marketing Handbook* (New York: McGraw-Hill, 1984), 667–668.

PRICING DECISIONS

Pricing often represents a difficult set of decisions for the catalog marketer because these decisions not only determine the financial viability of the catalog but are an important component of the image the catalog conveys. In making pricing decisions, the cataloger must consider the objectives of the catalog, select an overall pricing policy, and determine by what process actual prices will be set.

Catalog Objectives and Pricing Strategies

Pricing decisions are actually out of the hands of the catalog manager for two types of catalogs. Consumer catalogs whose main objective is to attract customers to retail stores will ordinarily use the prices set by the store and add shipping and handling charges for merchandise purchased through the catalog. Likewise, business product catalogs whose main purpose is to support the field sales force or the dealer network will use already established prices.

Like pricing decisions in any marketing environment, the catalog marketer has three major considerations when determining the overall pricing strategy:

- target market
- chosen image
- merchandise mix

For catalogs whose primary objective is to sell merchandise, the catalog manager will ordinarily be responsible for setting a broad approach to prices. The manager will have to consider financial objectives and constraints, such as return-on-investment targets, profit expectations, and investment pay-back commitments. Prices must also support the overall image strategy. A catalog that has to generate substantial cash flow to meet financial objectives and wishes to present a value orientation to a mass market should engage in penetration pricing. This approach to pricing involves using low prices to achieve a high volume of sales. Catalogs such as MacWarehouse and PCWarehouse follow a penetration pricing strategy for products that generally have established brand names and whose characteristics are known to knowledgeable buyers.

If there is no overwhelming pressure for immediate financial achievement and if the intent is to portray an upscale image for the non–price-sensitive customer, the catalog may practice price skimming. In this case, the catalog will set relatively high prices, relying on strong gross margins instead of high volume for its profitability. There are numerous home furnishings and apparel catalogs that fit into this category, including the well-known Williams-Sonoma (kitchen equipment, food, and housewares) and Garnet Hill ("The Original Natural Fibers Catalog").

There are, of course, many catalogs, just as there are many retail outlets, that follow a policy that might best be called value pricing. Their prices are neither noticeably high or noticeably low compared to similar merchandise offerings. They provide good value for the price. Some examples with which you may be familiar include J. Crew and Lands' End in the apparel field.

Approaches to Pricing

Once the broad price strategy has been established, there are several ways in which the catalog manager can approach the actual setting of prices. Although one orientation may take precedence, demand, costs, and competition must all be considered.

In a *demand-oriented pricing* strategy, prices are based on the quantity demanded at a specific price, almost irrespective of costs. Products may be given relatively high prices to appeal to a quality-conscious or prestige-conscious customer. On the other hand, if the customer is price-sensitive, products may have to be priced at a relatively low level, even at the sacrifice of higher margins.

Catalog marketers are often tempted to base their pricing decisions entirely on cost. It is easy to take merchandise cost, add catalog operating expenses and a reasonable level of profit, and produce a formula for computing prices. *Cost-oriented* pricing does have the virtue of being easy to implement, but this strategy fails to take into account either customer demand or the activities of competitors Consequently, even if it results in prices that enable the catalog to stay in business, it may not result in prices that produce an optimum level of profits. Still, it is obvious that costs provide a floor beneath which prices cannot drop over a period of time if the catalog is to remain viable.

The third strategy is to use *competitive pricing.* This will require comparison shopping to stay fully informed about competitors' prices for similar merchandise. Because catalog marketers cannot just walk into a rival's store and examine merchandise the way retailers do, wise catalog managers will make sure they are on the mailing list of all major competitors so they can monitor prices and other elements of strategy on a continuing basis. In fact, whatever the pricing strategy, the savy catalog marketer continuously monitors the product of all competitors. In addition, the marketer follows the catalogs of leaders in other merchandise categories, observing trends and getting ideas that might be applied in a different setting.

By this time, you have probably recognized that each of these pricing strategies has merit, but that practicing any one to the exclusion of the other two may result in ignoring factors that are important to marketplace success. Successful pricing policies consider all three strategies—demand, competition, and costs—and make the appropriate trade-offs among them in arriving at a final price for merchandise in the catalog.

CUSTOMER ACQUISITION

Attracting new customers and retaining customers are among the most important catalog marketing management activities. Catalog marketers may spend as much as 25 percent of net sales on customer acquisition. They obtain the names and addresses of prospective customers from many sources.

The House List

The house list is one of the chief assets of a catalog business. The catalog marketer must be concerned with three major issues in making decisions about uses of the house list.

1. *The house list should be complete and meticulously maintained.* This can be done either internally or by an external service firm. In either case, the catalog marketer should make sure that qualified technical personnel are responsible for database development and maintenance and that there is complete backup, stored off-site, in the event of a computer system crash or other disaster such as fire.

2. *The house list must be protected from misuse and overuse.* List rental, including ways of protecting the list from unauthorized use, is discussed in chapter 4. Catalogers have two specific concerns with regard to renting out the house list. The first is whether to rent to direct competitors. The dangers of renting the house list to direct competitors are obvious. The second concern is how frequently to rent the list. At some point the list's productivity will begin to suffer from too-frequent mailings.

3. *The house list should be subjected to ongoing analysis to ensure its most profitable use.* Employing list segmentation analysis, as discussed in chapter 5, enables the cataloger to mail more frequently to the most profitable customers or to mail specialty catalogs or other pieces to customers with the highest purchase probability for a particular set of merchandise.

The house list is an important profit center for many successful catalog marketers. It cannot remain so, however, if short-term list revenues are maximized at the expense of long-term merchandising profitability.

In addition to optimizing mailings, segmentation of the house file can benefit catalog marketers in another way. Catalogers watch the size of various segments on their house file. When a segment becomes large enough to support a separate specialty catalog, a new venture can be launched.

Foster & Gallagher (F&G) is a $450 million marketer of horticultural products with a catalog line that includes Spring Hill and Michigan Bulb. "We have a very strong core position in horticulture, but we're looking at our customer database to find what other products and services would complement our core businesses," according to the firm's president. The company purchased Walter Drake, which offers a wide assortment of personalized merchandise including pencils, mugs, and sweatshirts as well as health and personal care products. They went on to establish a new catalog, *Home Marketplace,* which features kitchen items and housewares and has "a strong appeal to many of F&G's customer profiles." The first mailing contained 70 percent names from the F&G house list and 30 percent from rental lists. The initial mailing was so successful that they doubled the planned size of the second mailing. They have also added two other specialty catalogs, the Popcorn Factory and Mauna Loa Macadamia Nuts.[16]

The better the match between the characteristics of the catalog and the rental list, the better the results are likely to be. Most catalogers constantly test new lists, but the most sophisticated list tests cannot overcome poor choice of lists to be tested. The Foster & Gallagher strategy is a good example of a firm that is offering a broader assortment of merchandise to its existing customer base instead of merely trying to increase the size of its house list.

Use of Space Advertising

An alternative method of acquiring new customers is to advertise in magazines. Actual or prospective customers acquired in this manner have already expressed their interest in the line of merchandise offered by the catalog. There are two basic approachs taken by catalogers to space advertising in magazines:

1. They use an "image" advertisement whose objective is to encourage the reader to request a catalog.
2. They use a product advertisement whose objective is to get the reader to purchase a specific piece of merchandise.

It is generally accepted that if a customer requests a catalog it is important to get the catalog to the customer while his or her interest is still aroused. Consequently, first-class postage is worth the extra cost because it usually arrives within three to four days instead of the two to four weeks it can take for a third-class mailing. Near a major selling season— Christmas, for example—it is especially critical that catalog requests be fulfilled immediately and mailed first class. To differentiate them from the rest of the mail, requested catalogs

---

[16]Doug Henschen, "Foster & Gallagher Forms Gift Group," *DM News,* 23 June 1997, 4.

are sometimes mailed in an envelope with a "This Is the Catalog You Requested" type of teaser to alert the customer to its arrival.

In addition, catalogs can be advertised in so-called catalog collections in major magazines. Each page of what is usually a two- or four-page spread includes up to 12 catalog promotions. This gives each catalog space for only a logo or picture of a cover page and a paragraph of copy. Insertions in a catalog collection are relatively inexpensive and have the advantage of being grouped with other catalogs targeted at similar audiences. If it is a particularly prestigious magazine, there may even be a "halo" effect. The reader returns the "bingo" card to the magazine, which in turn passes on the name and address to each of the catalogs requested. The result is that it can take several weeks for the consumer to receive requested catalogs.

Catalogers have instituted a number of mechanisms to make it easy for customers to request a catalog and to fulfill the request quickly. Many have installed special 1-800 numbers with automated voice-response systems and can also receive requests by fax and e-mail. Fulfilling these requests is outside the flow of the basic catalog process, and some catalogers have turned to outside service agencies to handle this task. A few agencies specialize in catalog request fulfillment, and their expertise and attention provide much quicker action. One client estimates that responses from people who requested catalogs has increased from about 2 percent to 6 or 7 percent as a result of faster fulfillment.[17]

Electronic Media

For a number of years a few of the larger and more broadly based catalog marketers have been doing a limited amount of television advertising. L.L. Bean has been a leader in using television spots at key times of the year, primarily back-to-school and Christmas, to encourage viewers to request a catalog. However, television is an expensive medium and is not sufficiently targeted to be a viable medium for specialty catalog marketers.

The World Wide Web is another matter, however. The Web provides a new medium for marketing products; we discuss that application in chapter 17. As marketers have been learning to use this new medium, encouraging visits to the Web page and then encouraging visitors to request a catalog has become important. Fulfillment of these requests then takes on the same characteristics as space advertising requests. Speed and identification as requested mail are important. In addition, the electronic request may give the marketer a better chance to personalize the fulfillment mailing. We discuss this opportunity in more detail in chapter 17. It is not yet clear what the quality, in terms of lifetime value, of names acquired electronically is going to be, but this is clearly a subject of great interest to catalog marketers.

Miscellaneous Customer-Acquisition Methods

There are a number of miscellaneous methods of customer acquisition that share the advantage of low cost. Used appropriately, they can be effective in adding to the house list. However, the volume of new names is not great, and they should not be depended on as the major way to build a list. However, the quality of the new names is often quite high, so these methods should not be ignored either.

Get-A-Friend offers are commonly used by catalogers. They range from a low-key item on the order form that provides space for several names and addresses to more visible promotions that may offer an incentive for providing names. The names obtained in this way are likely to have profiles similar to current customers, so they are typically high-quality additions to the house list.

---

[17]Renee Wijnen, "Quick Catalog Delivery Drives Profits at Fulfillment Firms," *DM News,* 4 August 1997, 1.

Package inserts are invariably included in a merchandise shipment to encourage repeat orders. They range from flyers through abbreviated catalogs to the complete current catalog edition. Inserts can be included in the outgoing orders of other firms for a promotional fee. This is relatively inexpensive, but the timing and even the demographics of the recipients are not controllable because no selects are available. Firms with a number of catalogs often cross-sell in this way with considerable success because customer profiles are similar from one catalog to another.

Catalog marketers frequently participate in *cooperative mailings.* Because these mailings, usually sent to "occupant" with only geographical selectivity, are primarily composed of cents-off coupons, catalog offers may not receive a great deal of attention.

Billings of bank charge cards and department stores offer the opportunity to present catalog offers by using *statement stuffers.* Costs are low because there is little incremental cost to the mailer. Selects may be available that will enable the catalog marketer to reach a specified target market with statement stuffers.

Free standing inserts (FSIs), discussed in chapter 15, also offer the catalog marketer access to large potential markets at minimal cost. The flexible nature of FSIs permits inclusion of promotional devices ranging from flyers to samples to minicatalogs.

Home delivery, usually consisting of multiple promotions enclosed in a plastic bag, is available but often relatively expensive. The cost depends on the weight of the insertion and also on whether particular addresses are specified or complete coverage of a geographical area is requested.

Finally, *publicity* can be a valuable source of new customers for the catalog marketer. It requires a great deal of effort, and both the timing and the actual content are outside the control of the cataloger, but publicity is received more credibly by consumers because it is editorial in nature, not paid advertising. Publicity gains in prestige and effectiveness when it appears in a popular or especially credible medium. This can range from feature articles in magazines, the trade press, or newspapers all the way to an executive interview on a highly rated television or radio talk show.

Whatever the source of the new name, it is important to record it for analytic purposes.

Tracking Customer Acquisition Cost

Customer acquisition costs should be evaluated separately for each medium. Both the cost of acquiring the name and the cost of converting the name to a sale should be calculated. When the effectiveness of each acquisition medium is evaluated individually, the catalog marketer can decide which media warrant the greatest expenditures. The faster catalog requests are fulfilled, and the more concerned and personal the follow-up appears to be, the higher the conversion rate should be. This will keep costs of acquiring names to a minimum.

RETAINING CATALOG CUSTOMERS

In recent years marketers of all kinds have become keenly aware of the high cost of obtaining new customers and the consequent desirability of spending the smaller amounts of money necessary to retain existing customers. Catalog marketers focus on customer service as their primary customer retention mechanism.

Customer Service Policies

The competitiveness of the catalog marketplace and the high expectations of sophisticated customers have increased the importance of excellent customer service in developing and maintaining customer loyalty. Earlier in this chapter we pointed out that the fulfillment of orders and the delivery of customer service are part of the so-called back end of direct mar-

FIGURE 13.4 Coldwater Creek Customer Service Commitment

Source: Used with permission of Coldwater Creek.

keting (discussed in chapter 7). Chapter 3 emphasized that excessive back-end costs could destroy the profitability of a direct-response offer. Savvy marketers recognize that well-designed and well-managed back-end operations can actually become a profit center instead of a cost center.

Coldwater Creek, headquartered in Sandpoint, Idaho, markets upscale women's apparel, gifts, and accessories. Dennis Pence, the company's president, attributes recent increases in sales and profitability to a commitment to customer service, described for customers on the catalog's order form (Figure 13.4). During a single year, Coldwater Creek saw the number of active customers increase from 801,000 to 1.2 million, sales almost double, and profitability more than double. "If you work very hard for seven years, these are the kind of numbers you can end up with," according to Pence. Some of that hard work has included

- installing bells that ring in the telephone call centers when more than two calls are on hold for more than 25 seconds
- cross-training returns personnel to handle overflow calls (returns personnel routinely staff the call center immediately after a catalog drop when call volume is high and returns are low)
- empowering customer service representatives to make many decisions without consulting supervisors
- refunding even small amounts of money when customers have overpaid
- sending flowers when a mistake has been made on an order[18]

---

[18]Renee Wijnen, "Back End Takes Credit as Profits Soar for Cataloger," *DM News*, 7 July 1997, 1, 58.

Perhaps this suggests that dollars wisely spent to achieve superb customer service should be regarded as an *investment* not a *cost!* You should also recognize that outstanding customer service is not attained quickly or easily—witness the seven years referred to in the preceding example. *This makes customer service a genuinely sustainable competitive advantage.*

Establishing policies to guide back-end operations that will achieve the desired level of customer service is an integral part of the development of marketing strategies for catalogers. Standards need to be set in the following operational areas:

- time to ship orders
- acceptable number of back orders
- time on back order
- fulfillment accuracy
- product quality
- telephone service level
- accuracy of customer service responses

Some companies combine these, and perhaps other, measures (weighting them if necessary) into a customer service index that they use to monitor service levels. This can be not only a useful measure but also a powerful way to communicate with employees about the success of customer service initiatives.[19]

The importance of customer service to the success of a catalog cannot be overstated, but a mistake need not be fatal to the customer relationship if it is corrected promptly and courteously. A survey conducted for the U.S. Office of Consumers Affairs found that, even in the case of consumers who had service problems valued at more than $100, 54 percent would remain loyal if their problems were satisfactorily resolved, whereas only 19 percent would repeat their purchase if the resolution was not satisfactory. With problems of lesser value, 70 percent would remain loyal if satisfied, whereas only 46 percent of the unsatisfied customers would repurchase.[20]

Catalogs lack the store ambiance and social aspects that make retail store shopping an enjoyable experience, at least for people who like to shop. As a result, catalog marketers recognize that exceptional customer service is necessary to build and maintain customer loyalty.

The catalog itself, however, conveys the initial impression to the potential customer. The catalog is "the store" and its design and production are important parts of the process.

Catalog Design

Decisions about the design of the catalog should be guided by its basic concept. A catalog's overall look and the way it presents merchandise are powerful contributors to the firm's image in the eyes of the consumer. Earlier in this chapter the catalog was referred to as a "paper store." Think of catalog design as akin to designing a retail store and arranging merchandise inside it to achieve the highest possible level of sales.

The basic design decisions are the size of the catalog, the layout format to be used, merchandise arrangement, visual presentation, and copy. In addition, an easy-to-use order form must be developed.

---

[19] "An Effective Way to Measure Customer Service," *DM News,* 4 November 1996, 13.

[20] Quoted in Christopher W. L. Hart, James L. Heskett, and W. Earl Sasser Jr., "Soothing the Savage Customer," *Harvard Business Review* (winter 1990–91): 17.

SIZE OF THE CATALOG

There are two commonly used catalog sizes—standard, 8-1/2 by 11 inches, and digest, 5-1/2 by 8-1/2 inches. There are other types of catalogs as well: the square, the oblong, and the slim jim are the most common variants. According to DMA statistics, well over half of all catalogs are standard size, and as many as 15 percent are digest size.[21] This is because these sizes are an exact fit on printing presses (you probably noticed that the digest size is half the standard size). Not having to trim odd-sized pages reduces paper waste and results in lower catalog costs.

The most common lengths of catalogs are less than 24 pages, 32 to 40 pages, and more than 64 pages.[22] The reason again has to do with the presses on which catalogs are printed, which do not print single pages but instead print a grid of eight pages at a time. Consequently, a number of pages that is evenly divisible by eight is the most cost efficient.

The primary consideration in deciding which size to choose is the number of items and the space each will require for effective display. Houseware catalogs often are digest size because each item does not need a great deal of space. This is especially true if items are not shown in a use setting or are shown without a background setting. Fashion apparel catalogs are more likely to be 8-1/2 by 11 inches to show the clothing to best advantage. Home furnishing catalogs have to be at least standard size to effectively depict their merchandise.

Catalogs may, of course, be larger than 8-1/2 by 11 or longer than 64 pages. Upscale apparel catalogers frequently make use of larger sizes, partly to permit stunning layouts and partly to provide greater impact in the mailbox. There are still a few companies, of which Spiegel is the best-known example, that produce a lengthy catalog for each selling season. Customers that score high on a RFA (recency-frequency-monetary amount) measure are the primary targets for a comprehensive catalog. Other customers, based on value of purchases or concentration by merchandise type, receive specialty catalogs.

CATALOG FORMAT

When you look at a catalog, you see two facing pages, called a spread. The pages that make up each spread are laid out as a unit because that is the way the customer views them.

There are two basic styles of format, a grid format or a less patterned arrangement that is referred to as either free-flowing or asymmetrical. Figures 13.5 and 13.6 illustrate each style.

The Williams-Sonoma spread (Figure 13.5) shows that "grid" does not necessarily equate to "boring." The layout is based on two equal-sized columns separated by a half-size column. The small center column provides a space for small-size merchandise, for copy, or—scattered throughout the catalog—tempting recipes or useful cooking tips. Illustrations may take up two columns or even stretch across the entire page without violating the underlying grid. The two pages in this spread are not mirror images of one another, but they are carefully balanced. Some catalogs use several complementary grid designs. This catalog used only the one basic grid design, but execution that varies from spread to spread and appealing photographs with a variety of backgrounds and presentations keep the catalog fresh and live-

---

[21]Direct Marketing Association, *1996 Statistical Fact Book* (New York: Direct Marketing Association, 1996), 98.
[22]Ibid.

FIGURE 13.5 Grid Format

Source: Used with permission of Williams-Sonoma.

FIGURE 13.6 Free-Flowing Format

Source: Used with permission of The Smithsonian Catalog.

ly. Whatever the format, it should be used consistently throughout the catalog to provide the recognizable look that becomes an integral part of the catalog image.

Figure 13.6 is a spread from the Smithsonian catalog, which is a unit of the Smithsonian Institution in Washington, DC. This catalog, one of a growing number of successful catalog ventures by not-for-profit organizations, uses an asymmetrical format. The nonstandard format and the fact that most of the merchandise is displayed without a photographic backdrop allows the inclusion of more merchandise, especially items of varying shapes and sizes, on each page. It requires a bit more design expertise to configure this type of page, but the efficiency of the presentation can make increased design costs worthwhile.

Notice two other good catalog practices that are illustrated on these spreads. The Smithsonian catalog has developed a special symbol that it uses to indicate exclusive merchandise. Both spreads include the catalog's 1-800 number, and the Williams-Sonoma catalog adds that its number is in operation 24 hours a day.

A special design, consistent with the overall catalog format, should be developed for the front and back covers. The cover format should be as distinctive and recognizable as creative design can make it. Within the basic cover format of prominently featuring the catalog name, logo, and slogan (Williams-Sonoma calls itself "A Catalog for Cooks," for example), the catalog designer can use colors, textures, and seasonal merchandise to provide freshness and excitement.

The number of possible spread designs is immense. Common sense, especially the recognition that too many items squeezed onto a page cannot possibly be effective, will eliminate the worst ones. Beyond that, testing is necessary to determine what works best. In this case, in-mail testing may not be the most effective method. Instead, eye-movement cameras are often used to analyze the movement of customers' eyes over the page. Designs that do not allow for smooth eye movement are unlikely to be effective.

MERCHANDISE ARRANGEMENT

The placement of merchandise within the catalog can be approached in a number of ways. One way is to arrange the merchandise by category—all shoes together, for example. This type of arrangement emphasizes the broad assortment of a product category the catalog has to offer. It also allows the customer who is looking for merchandise in that category to easily make comparisons among the items offered.

Another approach is to group items of merchandise according to typical customer use. For example, a spread might feature a man's business suit along with a matching shirt, tie, tie tack, and pair of shoes. This type of arrangement encourages multiple-item purchases.

Yet another way of looking at merchandise arrangement classifies merchandise as commodity items (items regularly used and therefore repurchased on a predictable cycle), shopping items (items for which both a need and an intent to buy exist), and impulse items (items for which customers do not engage in advance planning). Retailers place the planned purchase items (e.g., bread and milk in a supermarket) along the back or side of the store so that customers have to walk past many other items of merchandise to reach them. The same principle can be applied to merchandise arrangement in a catalog.[23]

---

[23]Brent John Bissel, "Catalog Merchandise Floor Planning," *Direct Marketing* (March 1987): 78–82.

Shopping items should be granted sufficient space for detailed graphics and persuasive copy. Because customers already have recognized a need for these products, they will be attentive to them. Consequently, the products can occupy space in some of the "lower-traffic" pages of the catalog.

Commodity products, such as business shirts for men and blouses for women, often complement a number of other products—both a suit and a pair of slacks, for example. They may be displayed several times in a single catalog, appearing each time with another item with which they are frequently used.

Impulse items should be displayed in "high-traffic" areas—the front and back covers, the inside covers, the center spread, and the pages surrounding the order form. For interest and variety, these pages can contain an equal mixture of impulse and commodity items.

All of these approaches to placement of merchandise emphasize the importance of understanding customer shopping and product-use behavior. Customer buying needs and behavior should be the key determinants of merchandise arrangement within the catalog.

VISUAL PRESENTATION

Most catalogs use photographs for visual presentation of their merchandise. A skilled professional photographer, preferably one experienced in catalog photography, is an absolute necessity if the cataloger wants photographs that do the best possible selling job.

Photographs can be divided into three basic categories:

- studio shots
- location shots
- stock photographs

If you are using original photography for the catalog—because you are presenting merchandise, most of it will be original—the choice is between photographing in a studio or on location. The studio has the advantage of a completely controllable environment. It is also cheaper than location shooting. However, location shots can provide atmosphere and context to your visual presentation that cannot be obtained in any other way. The problems, as well as the costs, of location shooting can be monumental, however. Ask a cataloger about shooting the bathing suit layouts for the summer catalog on a windswept beach in January!

Good photographs have the following characteristics:

- They show the details of the merchandise. The scenery or the pose of the model, no matter how attractive, should not obscure the details of the merchandise, however.
- They use props to enhance the presentation and establish the size of the merchandise when necessary. Many items need something to provide a sense of scale. Fill the vase with flowers, for example.
- The models are representative of the target market—or at least the way the target market would like to look. Some catalogs use their employees as models to provide a sense of reality, but most use professional models.
- The backgrounds and backdrops are attractive without overwhelming the merchandise, and are appropriate to both the items being portrayed and the catalog image.
- The colors are right.

The last point—color—involves two issues:

1. The colors should represent the merchandise accurately. If the actual color is different from the color shown in the catalog, many items will be returned. Getting the colors right requires an understanding of color separations.

2. The pages should be laid out in a way that allows the printer to control the ink flow so that color from one page does not bleed onto another. This requires working closely with the printer to understand which pages will be next to one another on the press (a relationship quite different from the order of pages in the catalog).[24]

Stock photographs come from a supplier who specializes in huge archives of shots of all types. Stock photographs might be used for cover pages or to lend interest to spreads inside the catalog.

There is one other way to present merchandise in a catalog. That is to use illustrations. Most catalogers choose to use photographs because they show the details of the merchandise very clearly and seem to lend credibility to the merchandise presentation. Simply because most catalogs use photographs, however, the use of illustrations differentiates the catalog from its competitors. The J. Peterman catalog is one of the handful that does this very effectively. Use of illustrations not only creates catalog imagery that is different from most of the competition, it also allows the artist to emphasize product features that are especially interesting or appealing.

CATALOG COPY

Because catalog copy must fit the space provided by the layout, it is the most disciplined form of direct-response copywriting. It must do the selling job and do it with no excess words.

Catalog copy begins with a caption or headline that focuses the reader's attention. This can be merely "Power Lawn Mowers" or "Our Best Power Lawn Mowers," for example. A label headline does little to advance the sales message.

A strong headline stresses the *benefits* to be obtained from using the product. The copywriter for the lawnmower could say, "Cut Grass-Cutting Time in Half," or even better, "New Contoured Blade Trims up to One Inch Away from Fences, Buildings." The second headline stresses a benefit and adds a reason (new contoured blade) that makes the benefit plausible. It also emphasizes a problem solution (getting close to structures without having to make a second pass with a trimmer). However, it may also take up more space than is available.

A sale headline stressing price and value is sometimes used. The headline for the lawnmower could also read "Compare at \$XXX.xx." Catalog copy that emphasizes price, or that uses comparative pricing, is subject to all the existing laws that regulate pricing to ensure that it is accurate and not misleading. In addition, many companies have strict internal policies that guide the establishment and verification of comparative prices.

Writing catalog copy that is complete, yet concise, and that sells but is interesting and fun to read is a large order. Like any good copy, it should emphasize the primary benefit, identify secondary benefits, and follow with selling points that support the benefit. The copy must end with all necessary ordering information; SKU (stock-keeping unit), size, weight, color, price, and so on.

[24]William A. Dean, "Catalog Imagery," Manual Release No. 1400.5 (New York: Direct Marketing Association, October 1986).

THE ORDER FORM

In catalog marketing, as in all direct-response marketing, one of the cardinal rules is: Make it easy for the customer to order. We could well expand this to: Make it easy for the customer to order correctly and completely. All the order form issues discussed in chapter 7 apply to catalog order forms.

The current preference is for order forms bound into the catalog. The order panel itself is on one side; when folded, it becomes a self-mailer with the firm's address printed on the envelope portion. Many variations on this basic form are possible. Just be careful that all aspects, including folding and mailing, follow the easy-to-use rule.

The information required on an order form is rather extensive, especially if credit card orders are accepted. Several of the suggested readings at the end of this chapter, as well as the references in the notes, provide extensive checklists to ensure the completeness of the order form.

Depending on space and design, the order form may also be used for marketing or customer service purposes. Apparel catalogs may provide size information to make ordering easier and less risky. Merchandise, probably impulse items, often are featured on one surface of the order form.

Producing the Catalog

The catalog marketer must deal with many technical issues as the catalog moves from design into production. These include deciding which type of printing process to use, obtaining camera-ready art, putting all material in the preferred form for the printer, and complying with postal regulations.

Other decisions are technical in nature but also affect the image of the catalog. The type of paper and ink used and the choice of typeface fall into this category.

Many of these activities are carried out by technical experts, such as printers and graphic artists, but the catalog marketer must have sufficient technical knowledge to deal with these experts in a professional manner. Entry-level catalog marketers often find themselves working on the technical aspects of the catalog, which is excellent experience. References cited in this chapter provide a wealth of information on technical aspects of catalog production. Seminars and professional meetings, as well as careful reading of trade periodicals, can also help the direct marketer become well versed in the technical processes and developments of catalog production.

We also repeat the advice given in chapter 6. Select suppliers well in advance and work closely with them, listening to the advice of experienced technical experts. Beginning this process long before material is actually delivered for production also increases the probability that issues that need to be dealt with in the design process will be handled correctly.

Catalogs and Retail Stores

Throughout this chapter we have used retailing concepts to help explain the catalog marketing process. As you are no doubt aware, many retail stores also make extensive use of catalogs; one source estimates that 36 percent of catalog firms now have a retail operation of some kind.[25] The blurring of the line between catalogs and retail stores in recent years may foster the mistaken impression that running a catalog business and running a retail store or chain of stores are very much alike, and therefore a firm that is successful at one should be equally successful at the other. Recent examples suggest that this is not so. Several well-known specialty firms, including Esprit and Eastern Mountain Sports, have shut down their catalog operations in the last few years to concentrate on their retail stores. Other catalog firms have deliberately not developed or expanded retail outlets so they can concentrate their resources on the business they know best. Chief among these is L.L. Bean, which chose not to expand its retailing operation beyond the phenomenally successful location in Freeport, Maine, in order to focus on its core catalog business.

There are, however, more instances of successful blending of these two different types of retailing than there are of failures. The successful blendings seem to fall into two categories: retail stores using catalogs to achieve retail objectives, and firms running both catalog and retail store operations simultaneously. In this section we focus on the simultaneous operation of a full-fledged catalog and a network of retail stores.

This is not a "chicken or egg" question. It does not matter which came first—the catalog or the retail stores. What is important is the realization that the two operations must be managed separately. Careful examination shows that many of the success factors for a retail store differ from those for a catalog operation. The proportion of operating expenses accounted for by various elements of cost also differs. There are differences in the timing of various activities between catalogers and retailers. Perhaps most important of all is the difference in the very nature of the two types of business.

SUCCESS FACTORS

Many of the factors that make a catalog successful are the same as those that account for the success of a retail store—carefully selected merchandise and concerned customer service, for example. Others are different, however:

- Because customers must come to retail stores, the location of a retail store is vitally important because most customers will come from the surrounding trading territory. Catalogs, on the other hand, take their "paper store" to the customer wherever he or she may be located.

- The catalog must accomplish all the tasks necessary to make the sale. Catalog marketers cannot offer customers fringe benefits such as the sheer pleasure of shopping in an attractive retail environment.

- A retail store relies to a great extent on media advertising to attract customers. A catalog relies on mailing lists.

- Retail stores provide their customers with instant gratification because purchases are available immediately. Because catalog customers must wait for their purchases, some type of added value such as convenience or unique merchandise is required.

COST FACTORS

Although retail stores and catalogs have essentially the same cost elements, the balance of these elements is not the same for the two types of merchandisers. The retail store will spend proportionately more on all costs associated with physical location because of the requirement for a desirable (high-traffic) location and an appropriate building with attractive interi-

---

[25]Paul Imbeirowicz, "Using MO Transactional Data to Drive Retail Sales," *DM News,* 16 June 1997, 23.

or furnishings and equipment. This means that the proportional investment in physical facilities will be higher for the retail store than for the catalog. The nature of the retail location, and perhaps also the required opening hours, will cause labor costs to be higher. A catalog will make relatively greater expenditures for customer acquisition, data processing, order fulfillment, and customer service.

OPERATING PHILOSOPHY

The retail store operation has traditionally been a blend of showmanship and marketing, with heavy emphasis on the showmanship. In recent years, rapidly changing consumer markets and intensifying competition have changed this balance to a certain extent. However, the ability to provide a pleasant experience—even a glamorous and exciting one in upscale retail stores—still plays a key role in the success of a retail store. This type of marketing activity is inherently unmeasurable. The location of many stores in retail malls also places noticeable constraints on operations and affects their level of expenses. For example, there are ordinarily mall-wide policies, including required hours of operations. Regular marketing expenses and the costs of special events are also shared by retail tenants in malls.

Catalog merchants, on the other hand, can choose locations based on costs and labor force availability. Catalogers require measurability in their marketing efforts. These efforts are based on analysis and projection, not on flair and showmanship.

This fundamental difference in approach between retail store and catalog management means that, at the operating level, it is very difficult to combine the two. Senior management must establish a coherent strategy for the dual businesses, but day-to-day operations must be managed separately.

SYNERGY

There are benefits to be gained from combining catalog and retail store operations under a single corporate umbrella that may indeed make the whole greater than the sum of its parts. They include heightened awareness levels created by the promotion of both catalog and store; easier retail expansion as a result of an established customer base; the ability of potential customers who are reluctant to shop by mail to visit the retail store; the opportunity to capture the names of retail store customers for the catalog mailing list; the ability of retail stores to facilitate mail-order returns and exchanges; and the ease with which a mobile customer can switch from store to catalog as location dictates.

The most important synergies arise from the customer database. Customers exhibit the same buying patterns whether they are shopping from a catalog or in a store. The existence of proprietary charge cards and scanner data enables the marketer to analyze the buying patterns of retail customers in detail. Customers or tightly defined market segments can be targeted for catalog promotions.

The catalog database is a rich source of data for improving retail operations. Analysis of the database can drive the location of new retail outlets, dictate the types of merchandising of retail outlets in various locations, and help to make retail promotion more cost effective.[26]

You may be wondering if retail stores do not cannibalize catalog business within their own trading territory. The long-term answer to that is "no." Firms such as Talbot's and Williams-Sonoma, who have substantial experience in running dual operations, agree that the

---

[26]Imbeirowicz, "Using MO Transactional Data," 23.

long-term effects are beneficial to both catalog and store. Catalog sales may drop for a time in a geographical area where a retail store has just been established, but the effect is neither great nor long lasting. Overall, sales increase, often substantially, when customers have the option of shopping either at retail or by mail. Customers, even those who are primarily retail shoppers, like to receive catalogs to help them plan their shopping expeditions. Mail-order buyers seem to continue in that mode and to make incremental purchases at retail.

Above all, however, it is the database that creates the basis for synergy. Dual operations give the ability to build a more comprehensive database, which is then used to offer purchasing options to the customer, to offer different lines of catalog merchandise that fit the customer's profile, and to make overall marketing efforts more cost effective.

THE GLOBALIZATION OF CATALOG MARKETING

It is difficult—in fact, it is dangerous—to make generalizations about global direct marketing. As we have pointed out in other chapters, each country offers its own specific challenges, as well as its opportunities, to direct marketers from other nations. However, the catalog as a mode of shopping is making great strides in many parts of the globe. A few examples give at least a flavor of the growth of this medium throughout the world:

- Eddie Bauer, the West-Coast marketer of outdoor equipment and casual clothing, has opened stores and initiated catalog operations in Japan, Germany, and the United Kingdom during the 1990s. In each country it has partnered with local firms that can support either fulfillment or marketing operations or both. From Germany it reaches markets in Switzerland and Austria, and the company is considering entering both the Korean and French markets.[27]

- Computer marketers Dell, Compaq, and Gateway are increasing their levels of activity in Australia. Dell has been successful selling into the commercial market for a number of years, but has found considerable initial reluctance on the part of Austrilian consumers to buy computers through direct channels. Gateway tried to overcome that reluctance by establishing a catalog showroom in Sydney. Australia is important as an opening to the entire Pacific Rim as well as for its own market.[28]

- The world's largest mail order firm, Otto Versand, is headquartered in Germany and is a major player in many world markets including the United Kingdom, France, and Japan (where it partners with Eddie Bauer). It has established an operation in Shanghai and planned to mail Korean and Chinese-language catalogs beginning in the fall of 1997.[29] It is also partnering with a division of the U.S. forest products manufacturer, Boise Cascade, in a venture into the German office products market. This is seen as a direct result of the success of Los Angeles–based cataloger Viking Office Products in Germany.[30]

- French apparel cataloger LaRedoute is actively challenging U.S. catalogers throughout Europe and in Japan. This firm, which is France's largest mail-order marketer, is also considering expansion into the U.S. market.[31]

- The Lands' End experience in Europe suggests some of the pitfalls of international expansion. This firm mailed catalogs in Germany, France, and The Netherlands in 1994, but did not contin-

[27]Thomas Weyr, "Eddie Bauer to Drop 500,000 UK Catalogs, Open Three Stores, This Fall," *DM News International,* 17 February 1997, 1, 4.

[28]"Dell and Compaq Expand Aussie Sales," *DM News International,* 13 May 1997, 3.

[29]"Otto Versand and LaRedoute Post Gains," *DM News International,* 13 May 1997, 3.

[30]"Otto/Boise Cascade to Challenge Viking in Germany," *DM News International,* 17 February 1997, 4.

[31]"French Catalogers Push Fashions in Europe, US," *DM News International,* 14 April 1997, 6.

ue unsuccessful first efforts there. Looking back, the firm indicates that it had neither the inventory nor the quality of operations to successfully service customers. After almost two years of preparation, it reentered the German market. The excellence of Lands' End telephone customer service and the fact that it is available 24 hours a day, 365 days a year created attention among the press and the public. Germany's stores usually close early, and customers voice concern over the level of service. Lands' End sees this as a competitive opportunity.[32]

These are just a few snapshots of the growing catalog market around the world. Experts point out that there are major untapped markets in Asia and Eastern Europe. Prospects for continued growth appear very bright.

It is important to keep in mind, however, that each country is unique. The typical marketing issues of language and culture are complicated for the direct marketer by additional issues of postal and telecommunications infrastructure. Planned expansion and controlled growth will be essential for success as companies from all over the world move into international markets.

REASONS FOR CATALOG FAILURE

Both domestic and international catalog marketers are well advised to consider one consultant's assessment of why catalogs fail. According to Maxwell Sroge, the top 10 reasons for failure are

- lack of a business plan
- difficulty in obtaining adequate financing
- no clear identity or market niche
- insufficient customer knowledge
- failure to understand catalog creative subtleties
- haphazard acquisition of new names
- underestimating the time it takes to build a profitable list
- lack of skilled financial management
- inadequate fulfillment and customer service
- lack of sound inventory control.[33]

Summary

The catalog segment of the direct-response industry contains some of the best known and most successful firms in the industry. Their success makes it clear that catalog shopping is a favored strategy for many customers throughout the world. Developing and marketing a catalog requires a well thought out concept, a clear definition of the target market and the desired positioning of the catalog, a sound marketing strategy, good catalog design, and careful attention to production issues. Once again we see that a sound customer database forms the core of the operations of catalog marketers and allied retailing units. Understanding the ways in which a database can enhance growth and profitability, coupled with specialized knowledge of the catalog field, are the essence of the successful catalog marketer.

---

[32]"Service Key to Lands' End German Success," *DM News International,* 21 October 1996, 15.

[33]Maxwell Sroge, *How to Create Successful Catalogs,* 2nd ed. (Lincolnwood, IL: NTC Business Books, 1995), 7.

Discussion Questions and Exercises

1. In your opinion, what is the nature of the appeal that catalogs have for consumers? What drawbacks do catalogs have in consumers' eyes?
2. What seem to be the reasons why some of the largest catalog marketers, listed in Table 13.1, have developed such large businesses?
3. What warnings or advice would you give to a friend who is considering starting a catalog?
4. Explain the steps necessary to develop and market a catalog.
5. What are the main similarities and differences between retailing and catalog marketing?
6. If you have not ordered something recently using a catalog's toll-free number, conduct a brief interview with someone who has. Exactly what went on during the call? Did it leave the customer with a good feeling toward the catalog company? Why or why not? Did the customer's later experiences verify the initial impression?

Suggested Readings

Desmet, Pierre, and Dominique Xardel. "Strategies for a European Catalog." *Journal of Direct Marketing* 8, no. 3 (summer 1994): 62–73.

Robles, Fernando. "International Market Entry Strategies and Performance of United States Catalog Firms." *Journal of Direct Marketing* 8, no. 1 (winter 1994): 59–70.

CHAPTER 14

Telephone Marketing

In chapter 1 we learned that the telephone is the largest of the direct marketing media, expected to account for more than $62 billion in promotional expenditures in the United States in 1997 and an anticipated growth rate of almost 8 percent per year into the next century. A total of $20.6 billion was spent in business-to-consumer promotion in 1997, and $41.5 billion was spent in business-to-business promotion.[1] Traditionally, inbound and outbound telemarketing have each accounted for about half the total telemarketing expenditures.

In this chapter we discuss the multiple roles telemarketing plays in direct response programs. You may be surprised to discover how deeply embedded telephone marketing is in the marketing programs of many successful firms.

---

[1] *Economic Impact: U.S. Direct Marketing Today, Executive Summary* (New York: Direct Marketing Association, 1996), 20.

The Example of Grolier, Inc.

Even if you are not familiar with the corporate name of Grolier, Inc., you probably know some of their products, which include the *Encyclopedia Americana,* the *Beginning Reader's Program with Dr. Seuss,* and the *New Book of Popular Science.* The company was established in 1895 as the Grolier Society in Boston. During its early years it focused on expensive leather-bound sets of books, which were sold by subscription to wealthy collectors. By the turn of the century it had moved to New York City and was marketing an encyclopedia in Britain and throughout North America. The purchase of the *Book of Knowledge* in 1910 and the growth of its direct-sales force formed the basis of the contemporary organization.

The company entered a new era when it moved to Danbury, Connecticut, in 1976 and began to concentrate on the direct marketing aspect of its business. The telephone marketing program was begun in 1978 as part of the Direct Marketing Division. A trade journal describes Grolier's award-winning program as follows:

> Grolier Telemarketing is a mass-volume outbound, business-to-consumer company. Its strategy features a soft-sell approach from a trained sales force to offer a variety of products to meet the customer's needs. Calls are restricted mainly to previous customers or names on specially targeted lists of consumers who have a need for educational products.
>
> To expand its services and meet objectives, Grolier has become an expert in testing sales concepts, in identifying and obtaining qualified prospects, and in training and coaching reliable people for its telephone sales force.
>
> In order to meet its objectives and remain competitive, Grolier sought to implement the following: 1) create a team-based organization, 2) provide ethical guidelines for employees, and 3) acquire new tools to support telemarketing efforts.[2]

Grolier was aware that other experiments with team-based approaches, such as quality circles, had frequently been unsuccessful. It believed that the reason was that these were considered adjuncts to a traditional organizational structure. Grolier management decided to establish the team as the basic work unit in the telemarketing center and to entrust the teams with important decisions about their work and its management. The result was greater efficiency and improved productivity.

A team of managers and sales representatives developed a set of ethical guidelines to ensure that all employees were treated fairly, honestly, and with respect in matters including timely disclosure, monitoring, work environment, career development, and team development.

Employees were provided with sales tools that included a customized computer system, a database for improved list selection, and automated tools to aid scripting and other aspects of the telemarketing program. Automation has freed representatives to concentrate on the needs of customers. The sales representatives are extensively cross-trained, and that, along with the team environment, has enabled the elimination of an entire layer of management in the center.

By 1995 the Telemarketing Division had become the most profitable division of Grolier Direct Marketing, with more than $40 million in annual sales. Call volume has increased 250 percent since the beginning of the program. Grolier believes that it benefits most from the flexibility telemarketing gives to assess the needs of prospects and to meet

---

[2]Angela Karr, "Grolier Telemarketing: Pursuing Success with the Aid of its Representatives," *TeleProfessional* (July/August 1995): 31.

them from its wide array of publications. Sales representatives provide additional data for the database as a result of their conversations with customers. They are able to provide better customer service and support and to deal with customer problems before they become serious.

Grolier attributes its success to the high quality of its products as well as its sales representatives. Training and empowerment have resulted in a high level of job satisfaction among its representatives, which stimulates them to present products in a positive light.[3]

This example suggests that a well-designed and managed telephone program can be an important and positive addition to programs that are composed of a variety of marketing approaches.

What Does Telemarketing Do Especially Well?

Telephone marketing possesses all the special competencies of direct marketing discussed in chapter 1. However, as the second most intensely personal promotional medium (personal selling, of course, is the most personal), telephone marketing does some things especially well:

- It provides *immediate feedback* in two ways:
  - The two-way dialogue of telephone communications allows a rapid assessment of which aspects of the marketing program are working and which are not.
  - Sophisticated monitoring equipment gives management an up-to-the-minute accounting of the effectiveness of telephone representatives.
- It provides *flexibility.* Aspects of the program that are not working can be changed overnight; program variations can be tested. Fixed programmatic costs are low (as distinguished from capital equipment costs, which can be substantial), so adjustments can be made immediately.
- It provides *incremental effectiveness* when used in conjunction with other media. The effectiveness may be more than just the sum of two contacts; often the combined result is greater than the sum of the two parts.
- It provides a method of *building and maintaining customer relationships* between sales. The telephone is especially effective to check on customer needs and satisfaction, especially for recently purchased products and services.
- It provides opportunities for *greatly increased levels of customer service.* Order verification, tracking, and complaint handling can all be done more quickly by telephone, increasing the level of customer satisfaction. It is important that customer and order databases be instantly available to telephone representatives to permit smooth and effective customer service. Later in this chapter we discuss automation techniques that integrate the database into an effective program of telephone customer contact.
- It provides an opportunity for *increased productivity and cost effectiveness.* Just how much the increases are depends on the medium to which telephone is compared. The usual comparison is to field selling, in which the number of calls per day and the cost per call are much higher, as we discuss in chapter 11. On the other hand, if you compare the cost per contact of direct mail to that for telephone, the cost per contact of mail is usually lower. Table 14.1 (p. 332) gives a range of cost per completed call (usually defined as reaching a decision maker in the household or the office).

---

[3]Karr, "Grolier Telemarketing," 31–32; "The Story of Grolier," www.grolier.com, 10 October 1997.

TABLE 14.1 Average Cost per Call	

Approximate Inbound Cost per Call

Category	Range of Cost
Business	$2.50 to $7.00
Consumer	$1.50 to $3.00

Approximate Outbound Cost per Decision-Maker Contact

Category	Range of Cost
Business	$6.00 to $16.00
Consumer	$1.15 to $4.00

Source: Bob Stone and John Wyman, *Successful Telemarketing,* 2nd ed. (Lincolnwood, IL: NTC Business Books, 1992), 152.

There is also a considerable difference in the number of calls per hour that a telephone rep can handle in an inbound versus an outbound environment. According to DMA estimates:[4]

Inbound calls	12 to 15 calls per rep per hour
Outbound calls	5 to 6 calls per rep per hour

There are many things that the telephone medium does well. However, there are a number of areas that are less positive.

What Are the Potential Downsides of Telephone Marketing?

The potential disadvantages of telephone marketing are

- *Telemarketing lacks prestige.* Many members of both the public and management have a poor image of telemarketing.

- *The number of prospects that can be reached in a given period of time is limited.* Productivity depends on the ability of the caller to reach qualified prospects, the complexity of the product, the nature of the offer, and the skills of the telephone communicator.

- *There may not be enough lists or enough good lists.* We pointed out in chapter 4 that there are never enough good lists. This is especially true for telemarketing because some mail lists are not available, either because they do not have telephone numbers or because their owners will not release them for telemarketing use.

---

[4]Direct Marketing Association, *1996 Statistical Fact Book* (New York: Direct Marketing Association, 1996), 140–141.

- *It may be difficult to hire and retain good telephone representatives.* Telemarketers must be able to tolerate both intense personal interaction and frequent rejection. Finding people with all the positive characteristics described later in this chapter and making it possible for them to feel rewarded and fulfilled in this kind of atmosphere is difficult. Turnover in telephone call centers is often quite high.[5]

A Definition of Telephone Marketing

Bob Stone and John Wyman say that

> [telephone marketing] utilizes sophisticated telecommunications and information systems combined with personal selling and servicing skills to help companies keep in close contact with present and potential customers, increase sales, and enhance business productivity.[6]

This definition suggests several aspects of a professional telephone marketing program:

1. Telephone marketing makes use of the latest technologies, including communications hardware and software and database technology.
2. Telephone marketing is well planned. It does not consist of making a series of hit-or-miss telephone calls. Rather, it is a carefully thought out and controlled marketing activity in which the persons or companies called have been identified as actual or potential members of the target market.
3. Telephone marketing is most often used as part of an integrated marketing communications program. It is not successfully used as a stand-alone medium.
4. One of the key advantages of telemarketing is that it allows a business to build and maintain satisfactory customer relationships. One-shot programs with only short-term objectives are not really telephone marketing.
5. Interaction with the customer or prospect is personal, even though not face-to-face. This interaction is most effective, as in the Grolier example, when it is carried out by well-trained and motivated personnel.
6. Judicious use of the telephone can often make marketing programs more effective at a lower total cost, but this is not to say it will make these programs inexpensive on a per customer contact basis.

True telephone marketing is not a boiler-room operation in which untrained or ill-trained personnel canvass a broad population to generate an immediate result. Even get-out-the-vote operations on election day are more sophisticated than that today. Political operations work from carefully honed databases of citizens who are known or likely voters for the party or the issue.

There are, however, real abuses that are perpetrated through the telephone medium. Its ease of entry and mobility makes it a prime candidate for unethical solicitors who prey on vulnerable populations. Telephone fraud has received a great deal of attention in the media in recent years. Hopefully this has provided a warning to consumers who are tempted to

---

[5]Based on Robert W. Bly, *Secrets of Successful Telephone Selling* (New York: Henry Holt and Company, 1997), 14–18.

[6]Bob Stone and John Wyman, *Successful Telemarketing,* 2nd ed. (Lincolnwood, IL: NTC Business Books, 1992), 3.

TABLE 14.2 Importance Rating of Telephone Sales Call Attributes (Mean Scores on a Scale of 1 to 6)

Attribute	Importance Rating
The salesperson is professional and courteous	5.254
A person, rather than a computer, calls	5.143
The company calling has a good reputation	5.011
The person calls at a convenient time	4.892
You have an interest in the product	4.679
You have had a good previous experience with the company	4.537

Source: Adapted from John Wyman, "A Survey of Consumers' Acceptance of Proactive Telemarketing," *Journal of Direct Marketing* (spring 1990): 38.

accept an offer that is clearly "too good to be true." There is little doubt that it has also lowered the reputation of the medium in the minds of members of the public.

It is important to note that telemarketing does not have an unfavorable image in business markets, where it is seen as an efficient way of doing business. It is the consumer market where an image problem exists. The magnitude of the problem is not a subject on which there is agreement within the industry.

ACCEPTANCE OF TELEMARKETING BY CONSUMERS

Much of the evidence about consumer perception of telemarketing is anecdotal. Many of us have personal experience with calling marketers and being called by them. Our friends, families, and acquaintances recount telephone experiences.

If you examine this anecdotal evidence carefully, you will probably find that the complaints center around being called, not around calling. DMA data and the results of research conducted by a telephone service bureau in 1990 and 1991 indicate that consumers are generally pleased with the results when they initiate the call. The most common reasons for consumer-initiated calls are to purchase something and to request information. Calling for repair service and to lodge a complaint are also mentioned. The majority of consumers report satisfaction with calls they initiate.[7]

There is little research on attitudes toward marketer-initiated calls, which is the apparent source of the image problem. One study found that, indeed, only 14 percent of the consumers questioned were receptive to proactive telemarketing. However, when they were asked to assume the existence of six calling attributes that had been identified as being important, the acceptance rate went up to 47 percent. The six attributes that appear to make marketer-initiated calls more acceptable to consumers are listed in Table 14.2.

It seems, then, that marketers have the ability to affect the image of telephone marketing by the manner in which they conduct outbound sales calls.

---

[7]Direct Marketing Association, *1996 Statistical Fact Book,* 145–146; Kathy Sisk, *Successful Telemarketing* (New York: McGraw-Hill, 1995), 14–16.

The Basic Types of Telephone Marketing

There seem to be as many ways of describing basic telephone marketing approaches as there are professionals who write and talk about the subject. We describe them as scripted, guided, and professional.

SCRIPTED TELEPHONE MARKETING

Scripted telephone marketing is just what its name implies. The caller works from a script that is complete from "Hello, my name is . . ." to "Thank you for your time." This type of telephone marketing is much more commonly used in consumer markets than in business markets. The major advantage of using completely scripted calls is that personnel require little training and become virtually interchangeable. Supervisory managers need not be highly skilled either.

This approach can work only for relatively inexpensive, routinely purchased products and for very simple offers, including straightforward fund-raising solicitations. Often it does not work very well even for these. One of our colleagues reports an experience he had with scripted telephone marketing. He had been buying *The New York Times* on his way to work every day for many years when he received a telephone call announcing that *The New York Times* was now available for home delivery in his neighborhood and asking if he would like to subscribe. He broke into the scripted call immediately and said that he would indeed like to subscribe. The caller replied a little huffily that she had to complete the sales pitch and went right on with the script. As he tells the story, he tried to break into the script two more times, saying that he was convinced and ready to subscribe, but finally just gave up and let the caller complete the pitch before taking his order!

Actually, it is possible to do rather complex calling using a script. Computer software, initially developed for marketing research applications, allows the construction of complex scripts that "branch" to different responses depending on the prospect's answer to each query. Script content can also be determined by information in the customer database. For example, when a college or university calls alumni to ask for donations, the amount given the previous year or the average gift over several years can automatically be made available to the caller and inserted in the script if appropriate. The caller will ask for a gift at a predetermined higher level and, if necessary, move down in established steps, trying to obtain a contribution that is no lower than last year's, and hopefully one that is higher. You may have participated in such a calling program at your school, either as a volunteer or as a paid caller. Higher-education fund-raisers recognize that the enthusiasm of students about their institution makes up for some rough edges in presentation.

GUIDED TELEPHONE MARKETING

Guided telephone marketing programs might be compared to depth interviewing in marketing research, in which the questioner or caller works from a topical guide instead of a script. The guide specifies the subjects to be covered but does not provide the actual words for the caller. Guided telephone marketing has a wide range of uses: from situations appropriate for scripted approaches all the way to those that require a professional selling approach. It is safe to say that the more knowledgeable and upscale your target market, the more important it is to move from a scripted to a more natural and spontaneous approach.

PROFESSIONAL TELEPHONE MARKETING

Professional telephone selling is essentially a personal sales call that takes place via the telephone. It requires a high level of skill and training for both telephone representatives and managers, and it should be carried out in an environment in which each representative has access to the marketing database. The professional telephone marketing approach is sometimes used in consumer markets and is fast becoming the norm in business markets. Figure 14.1 presents a summary of a hypothetical call to a professional customer that follows a seven-step process used in training telemarketers at AT&T.

Used well, telemarketing can be effective in a broader range of situations than many marketers realize. Not too many years ago, the belief among telephone marketers was that supplies, reorders, and sales of products under $5,000 could effectively be handled by telephone, but sales of higher-ticket (business) products could be closed only by a field sales representative. Now, there is virtually no limit to what can be sold using a properly structured telephone marketing program, especially when the focus is additional sales to the existing customer base.

FIGURE 14.1 An Example of the Seven-Step Selling Process: Call to Introduce a New Veterinary Drug to a Customer

Source: Bob Stone and John Wyman, *Successful Telemarketing,* 2nd ed. (Lincolnwood, IL: NTC Business Books, 1992), 168–169. Used with permission by NTC Contemporary Publishing Group.

---

1. Precall planning The telemarketer reviews the account file of the Whiteside Veterinary Clinic. He notes that Dr. Sargent ordered her usual order of drug supplies last month, but that she has not tried a new drug that L.L.M. Pharmaceutical has recently introduced via direct mail.

The telemarketer reviews his introduction briefly, takes a deep breath, and says "Smile!"

2. Approach/positioning "Hello. This is Mark Wiley with L.L.M. Pharmaceutical. Dr. Sargent is usually available about this time. May I speak with her?"

"Good morning, Dr. Sargent. This is Mark Wiley with L.L.M. How have things been going at your clinic since I last talked to you? (Pause) I'm certainly glad to hear that! Dr. Sargent, as a buyer of many of our quality products, I knew you'd be interested in hearing about one of our innovative new drugs. If you have a minute, I'd like to ask you a couple of questions . . ."

3. Data gathering "Doctor, your practice pretty much covers a suburban area, doesn't it?"

"Right now when a dog is suffering from hookworm, what drug are you prescribing?"

4. Solution generation "Many vets also used to prescribe that particular drug. Have you had many dogs suffering from various side effects from that drug?"

"Would you be interested in prescribing a new drug that has few, if any, side effects?"

5. Solution presentation "L.L.M. has introduced Formula XYZ that not only has fewer side effects, but extensive laboratory tests have shown that the medicine takes effect 24 hours more quickly than similar drugs."

6. Close "I'm sure that your customers would appreciate faster relief for their pets. Can I add a case of Formula XYZ to your regular order?"

7. Wrap-up "I'm sure that you will be pleased with the results, Dr. Sargent. We've gotten excellent comments back from many vets around the country. I'll get that shipment to you by early next week. Thank you for your business. I'll be calling you again the first of next month. Have a good day!"

This type of telephone selling works so well because of the increased professionalism of telephone reps and the growing understanding by managers of the requirements for managing an inside sales force (which we discuss in the next section). Telephone reps are being trained just as extensively and rewarded just as well as field sales reps. Some firms, in fact, are rotating personnel between the two types of selling. Others first place trainees in the telephone sales force, where they can receive more supervision and support, and later move them to the field sales force. It can work either way, if management handles it correctly. We discuss in some detail the problems that can arise between inside and outside sales forces in chapter 11.

Developing Telephone Marketing Programs

The basic decision variables for telephone marketing are the same as those for any other direct marketing program: the offer, creative, timing and sequencing, customer service, and implementation. There are, however, two special considerations in this medium: preparing the script or guide (which is essentially the copy aspect of the creative execution) and integrating the use of telephone with other media.

PREPARING THE TELEPHONE SCRIPT

Essentially, each telemarketing call is either a sales presentation or a search for information. Sales calls should follow the basic steps of introduction, qualification of the prospect, presentation of the sales message, meeting objectives, and closing. Some of the considerations to keep in mind when developing a telephone script include[8]

- *Anticipate encountering a gatekeeper and be ready to get through to the decision maker.* In a business setting, the gatekeeper is usually a secretary or receptionist whose job is to screen callers to prevent "nuisance" calls from going through to an executive. The caller must convince the gatekeeper that the decision maker will benefit from taking this call. Households do not usually have a gatekeeper, although more and more people are using answering machines for that purpose and the caller must be prepared to deal with that.

- *Establish credibility at once by introducing the caller and the company.*

- *If the prospect has (or should have) received promotional material, or if the prospect has been referred by a third party, mention it.* This should build credibility as well as jog the prospect's memory about your product.

- *Capture the attention and interest of the prospect by summarizing the major benefits up front.*

- *Qualify the prospect.* If the rep has not reached the right person, the time of both parties is being wasted. The dimensions on which a prospect (either business or consumer) is qualified are
  - Is the prospect's household or company a user of your product or brand?
  - Are further purchases planned? Within what period of time?
  - Is the person contacted the decision maker for the purchase? If not, who is? When and how can the decision maker be reached?

- *Make the offer and gain the prospect's acceptance of the concept, or better, of the offer itself.* Get the prospect to commit at least to the desirability of the offer. If the prospect is prepared to accept the offer, that is great. But more often the prospect will have questions or will raise objections.

---

[8]Adapted from Richard L. Bencin, "What's My Line?" *Direct Marketing* (June 1987): 94–101.

- *Answer the questions and respond to the objections.* Both questions and objections are pretty standard across prospects. The majority of these should have been anticipated and answers and responses prepared in advance and be readily available to the rep on the computer system. Some of the major objections—with the proper responses—are often included in a segment of the presentation that offers supporting evidence, which provides additional credibility for the offer. Remember, the answers and responses should be positive, never apologetic.

- *Repeat the order and all other relevant information* such as the customer's mailing address. Stress that this is being done to enable you to provide first- class service.

- *For incoming calls, try to get an add-on sale.* Many firms have one or more daily specials that all telephone reps offer to each customer. At the very least, the rep should suggest a complementary product; if the customer has ordered copier paper, for instance, the rep might ask if a toner cartridge for the copier is also needed. The customer who has ordered computer software is likely to be offered an impulse item such as a screen saver or a game at a promotional price.

- *Close on a positive note, paving the way for future calls.* Remember that important uses of the telephone include building customer relationships and enhancing the customer database. Not all contacts will produce a sale, but all contacts are an important part of the relationship-management process.

Figure 14.2 (pp. 340 and 341) presents a detailed example of a telephone script. Notice that although this could be described as a fully scripted presentation, there are many choices that have to be made by the representative. These choices are made on the basis of the responses of the prospect. The complexity of this script illustrates the necessity for thorough training of telephone communicators, even if their presentations are to be relatively structured.

If the call is not for the purpose of making a sale but for another objective, such as scheduling an appointment for field sales personnel or locating the decision maker in order to correctly address product information, some of the steps shown in Figure 14.2 will not be necessary. However, they form a sound foundation for building a customer contact program, whether it is scripted completely, partially, or not at all.

SCRIPTS VERSUS SURVEYS

Having looked at two types of telesales calls, you can recognize that telephone scripts do not closely resemble survey research questionnaires for marketing research designed to be administered over the telephone. Pure information gathering does have a role in a well-managed telephone marketing program but it is *never* appropriate to attempt to disguise a sales appeal as marketing research. The person called will not be fooled for long, and the reaction to the call will immediately become negative.

Firms that practice this type of deception—and it is deception—do themselves a disservice and do substantial long-term damage to both the telephone marketing and the marketing research industries. Misrepresenting the purpose of the call is just one of the unethical practices that the Direct Marketing Association has long tried to discourage. The DMA's guidelines for acceptable telephone practices are available on its Web site (www.the-dma.org). They are worthy of careful study.

ENABLING CONDITIONS FOR TELEPHONE MARKETING

It is also important to recognize two other developments that made this change possible: 1-800 numbers and credit cards.

The 1-800 number (WATS, or wide area telephone service) was originally viewed by businesses with a large volume of incoming (and outgoing) telephone calls as primarily a cost-saving device. The travel industry was the first to use it on a large scale as a marketing device, and many other industries soon followed. The first direct marketer to use a 1-800 number to facilitate ordering was JS&A in 1973. That is not very long ago when you consider how ubiquitous these numbers now are in direct-response space advertising and catalogs as well as on television.

Part of what makes the 1-800 number work so well is the ease of buying on credit cards. More than half of all U.S. households now use credit cards, and the buying power of those households is much greater than those that do not use credit cards. Put this together with the fact that calling a 1-800 number costs the customer nothing, and you have a recipe for explosive growth.

INTEGRATING THE TELEPHONE WITH OTHER MEDIA

We have already pointed out that the telephone is rarely used as a standalone medium. It is most effective if it is integrated into a planned program of customer contact that uses other direct-response media.

Television Advertising

Some of the early direct-response television ads were hucksterism at its very worst. However, as we discuss in detail in chapter 16, direct-response television (DRTV) advertising is now dominated by well-known firms marketing credible products and services. To a certain extent, this change happened because respectable firms discovered the power of direct-response advertising. It also happened because the telephone was available as a response mechanism. Without the ease and low cost of telephone response, DRTV would not have become a viable advertising medium.

Space Advertising

The 1-800 number and credit card have also.been partially responsible for the growth of direct-response space advertising. There is another important factor at work here, however. The print media offer marketers an opportunity to target selectively—for example, newspapers by geographic area, and magazines by demographics and, even more, by lifestyles and special interests.

Space advertising offers other ways besides the telephone to respond. The prospect can cut out the coupon, fill it out, find an envelope and a stamp, address the envelope, and mail it in. Or they can go to the Web address now listed in most space advertising to look for detailed information on the product or service. Mailing in a response device has the dual disadvantages of being complicated and slow. Information on the Web is, for the most part, not yet well integrated with other promotional media, perhaps leaving the inquirer frustrated because he or she cannot find specific information. When the prospect wants precise information and wants it quickly, telephone response it often the appropriate action.

Catalogs

Telephone ordering—especially the 24-hour-a-day, 7-day-a-week variety—has also been a boon to the catalog business. According to Stone and Wyman, catalogers report that the average telephone order is 20 percent greater than the average mail order. The primary reason is that the telephone rep can engage in consultative or promotional selling. Consider two examples:

Cross-Selling Existing Clients

STEP 1 Introduction

Good _____, I need . . . > to speak with Mr. (**last name**) please? (*Use first name cue if rapport has been previously established.*) Hello (**first or last name**), this is (**your full name**) with (**your company name**) and we're *located* . . . > (**territory, landmark, or location**).

STEP 2 Reference

My company requested . . . > I contact you personally. (Or) I'm contacting our distributor's customers to help keep their inventory up to date. (Or) I'm updating our distributor's accounts.

STEP 3 Request for Time

I hope . . . > I haven't caught you at a bad time ***have*** I? (*Assumptive*) Why don't I call you back in about an hour, would that be all right ***with*** you? (*Assumptive*)

STEP 4 Purpose of Call

We are reviewing our distributor's customer base and in order for us to ***continue*** offering the best products on the market, I need . . . > to ask you ***just*** a couple of ***quick*** questions, if you don't mind. (*Assumptive*) (Or) As I mentioned earlier, I'm updating our distributor's customer inventory (**or**) accounts and, in order to ***ensure*** you are getting the best service you're entitled to, I need . . . > to ask you ***just*** a couple of ***quick*** questions, if you don't mind. (*Assumptive*)

STEP 5 Probing

Q: How familiar are you with the variety of (*describe*) products we manufacture?
Q: Other than (*describe*), what other products do you offer your customers?
Q: What is your most popular product line?
Q: What is your least favored product line?
Q: Who do you order your (*describe*) from?
Q: Since you serve (*describe*), who do you order your (*describe*) from?
Q: What motivated you to choose XYZ competitor?
C: When was the last time you evaluated and cost compared ***ensuring*** you offer the best products while maximizing your profits?
C: Regarding (*describe*), what have you compared recently to determine . . . > the best (*describe*) available for your customers?

Easy Close

I respect that. (Or) Thank you for sharing the information with me. If I could ***send*** you information about (*describe*) you would have an interest in, what would that be? (*Assumptive*) Once you have had the ***opportunity*** to review the information, I would like to gain your feedback. Does that sound fair enough? (*Assumptive*)

FIGURE 14.2 Example of a Telemarketing Script (continued next page)

Source: Kathy Sisk, *Successful Telemarketing* (New York: McGraw-Hill, 1995), 349–351. Reproduced with permission of the McGraw-Hill Companies.

Talbots' . . . has developed an innovative way to make all their telephone communicators familiar with the apparel they sell. They have installed a moving dress rack adjacent to their telephone center. So when a customer calls and asks a question, the telephone communicator needs only to press a button. Presto—the apparel in question is in the communicator's hands and he or she can answer questions in an authoritative and meaningful way.

STEP 6 Restate

I want to be sure I have the information correct (*restate their answers*). Is that correct?

STEP 7 Features and Benefits

Based on the information I have on your account, I recommend you try using (*describe the feature you are selling*). Our (*describe the functions of the product*). How this benefits your customers (*describe the implied benefits*). More important, . . . > This offers continuity to customers ordering and increases your sales.

STEP 8 Get Reaction

How important would that increase be to your bottom line? (Or) How valuable would that be to your customers?

STEP 9 Trial Close

Great! I recommend that you try (*describe*). Start out with a test order, and see what kind of response you receive. Your distributors will check back within a couple of weeks to see how you are doing to ensure . . . > you don't run out of stock.

Does that sound fair enough? (*Assumptive*) (Or) Based on your current orders, I recommend (*describe*) to start out with, and if your distributor doesn't hear from you by (*offer time frame*), I will check back with you to see if we need to make any adjustments to your order. What else do we need to consider before I process your order?

STEP 10 Objections

See chapter 15.

STEP 11 Close

I will expedite your order today, and your distributor will be able to get that out to you by (*offer time frame*). Does that meet within your time frame?

STEP 12 Postclose

To process your order more efficiently, I need to go over the information to be sure I have everything correct. (*Go over your order form.*) Thank you for your order. We will be looking forward to gaining your feedback!

FIGURE 14.2 (continued)

> Hallmark . . . printed the following legend in its [Halls] catalog, "When you place your order by phone, ask our telephone communicator for the special of the week." . . . Depending upon the special of the week, up to 29 percent of those who placed phone orders added the special to their orders.[9]

The same authors point out the importance of presenting the 1-800 number properly, whether in a catalog, throughout which the number should be repeated at intervals, or in other direct-response media. Their rules are as follows:

> Always show 800 as an integral, inseparable part of your 800 service number. Use bold print for all 800 numbers and always include "1" before 800.

---

[9]Stone and Wyman, *Successful Telemarketing*, 70–73.

Hours available: Specify the hours during which operators are on duty to answer calls at your 800 number. Include the time zone. If the number is answered twenty-four hours a day, there is an advantage to stating this.[10]

Direct Mail

Telephone marketing is also a powerful force when combined with mail order. Joseph Fisher presents the results of a consumer market study that illustrates its value. The objective of the program was to sell preferred credit cards. The program tested preapproved credit versus a short application (not surprisingly, preapproved credit won), first-class versus third-class mail for packages that were otherwise identical, and telephone follow-up versus no follow-up, for a total of eight test cells.

Prospects who received the first-class packages were more likely to accept the offer than those who received the third-class packages (20.6 percent versus 17.8 percent, which was significant at the .07 level in a chi-square test). Overall, telephone follow-up raised response by 35.6 percent. Even more interesting, there was an interaction effect between telephone follow-up and first-class mail—an incremental effect of 5.1 percent over the effects of telephone alone plus first-class mail alone. This was reflected in the cost per order, which was 27 percent less than the overall average in the first-class and telephone follow-up condition.[11]

Results of a similar magnitude can be found in business marketing programs. A marketer of consumable supplies used an expensive four-color mailing package, which experienced unsatisfactory results (2.5 orders per thousand mailings) even though the free trial and money-back guarantee offer was sent to a targeted list from a trade publication. The marketer decided to add telephone to the mix and to look at two ways of using it.

- The first step was to use the telephone to qualify recipients. Callers identified the decision makers, qualified them as users of the product, and informed them that information was being sent. This strategy resulted in fewer but better qualified mailings and a substantial increase in the percentage of orders.

- The second step was a call-back to decision makers who had received the mailing but had not placed an order. This call was placed about three weeks after the mail had been dropped. The rep confirmed that the mailing had been received, provided a brief explanation of the money-back guarantee, and asked for the order.

Together, the two-step integration of telephone into the direct mail program resulted in 34 orders per thousand—a 14-fold increase over mail alone![12]

Internet

The Internet offers the possibility for a dialog between marketer and prospective customer that may take the place of some telephone interaction. This is especially true at the moment when the prospect is searching for information. In this early stage of Internet commerce, telephone contact seems to be playing two roles. One is to substitute for electronic transactions, either because customers are reluctant to submit credit card numbers over the Internet or because the site is not yet configured to handle transactions. The second role is to allow the customer to call for information that is not available on the Web site itself. In both

---

[10]Ibid.

[11]Joseph C. Fisher, "Getting the Most Out of Telemarketing," *Direct Marketing* (June 1987): 34–37.

[12]Bill Gessert, "Putting the Marketing Back into TeleMarketing," Teleprofessional (July/August 1995): 28–30.

cases telephone is merely being used as an alternative to activities that could, in theory, be conducted over the Internet. The long-term role for the telephone in conjunction with the Internet is not clear.

INTEGRATING THE TELEPHONE WITH A DATABASE-BUILDING PROGRAM

When you look at the media discussed in the preceding section, you realize that the only medium besides telephone that offers the possibility of a real dialog with the customer is the Internet. The other media offer only limited opportunities for enhancing the database. When customers call to inquire or to place an offer, there is a limited but significant opportunity to acquire useful information. According to one British telemarketer:

> The rule is that most consumers will answer a few questions, if those questions are relevant to their particular transaction. No company will be successful if the questions are not relevant to their own transaction with the consumer. Air New Zealand can ask if a consumer has a valid passport (to qualify consumers for last-minute travel promotions) and receive an unhesitating "yes" or "no." Princess Cruises can ask consumers if they have ever taken a cruise. Isuzu can ask when a consumer intends to purchase a new vehicle.

The telemarketer then goes on to suggest some steps that can maximize the ability of telemarketing programs to add valuable information to the database:

- Assure that telemarketing and database marketing work together to identify the most useful data.
- Design questions carefully so you will not overburden the call but will obtain the data most relevant to each customer segment.
- Train the telemarketers well and consider ways in which they can add value to the process.
- Test the questions and measure reactions to the process.
- Work with database marketing to identify the best prospects for follow-up programs.
- Watch for product or marketplace changes that should cause modification of the questions.
- Stay ahead of the competition.[13]

Telephone marketing can not only benefit from database information, it can add data that will be useful to future programs.

Establishing an Outbound Telemarketing Program

There are a number of factors that are key to the success of a telemarketing program and others that indicate a likelihood of failure. Table 14.3 (p. 344) summarizes these factors.

Even if the success factors are in place, establishing an in-house call center is a complex activity requiring both managerial and technical skills and a substantial upfront investment. Consequently, many firms test the viability of telemarketing by engaging a service bureau to conduct trial programs. The competence of the service bureau will affect the program's likelihood of success, and the manner in which it interacts with customers and

---

[13]Evelyn Schlaphoff, "Turning a Telemarketing Programme into a Competitive Database Marketing Weapon," *The Journal of Database Marketing* 4, no. 2 (1996): 187–191.

TABLE 14.3 Success Factors for a Telemarketing Program	
Positive Factors	*Negative Factors*
A well-targeted list Rental lists must be approved for outbound telemarketing	Lack of a clear plan with measurable objectives
A compelling offer that is easily communicated over the telephone	Lack of monitoring and evaluation of telephone representatives
Integrity of the product and the company offering it	Failure to track program productivity
	Unreasonable expectations by upper management

Source: Adapted from Laura Hansen, "Dialing for Dollars," *Marketing Tools* (January/February 1997): 47–53.

prospects will have an impact on the company's image. Selection of a service bureau is an important activity that should not be undertaken in haste.

Modern telephone technology makes it possible to locate large call centers in low-cost geographical areas where there is an abundant labor supply, irrespective of where clients are located. There are also service bureaus in most major cities. The major issue in choosing a distant call center over a local one is how important it is to have frequent face-to-face or on-site interaction with the services supplier.

Screen a number of potential suppliers before investigating two or three in greater detail. Your assessment should include one or more site visits. However, it would be foolish to choose a telephone service bureau without also conducting extensive interviewing over the telephone! Criteria for choosing a service bureau include[14]

- *The knowledge and professionalism of management.* Consider how you were treated the first time you called, the ease with which you reached a senior sales or account person, the depth of their inquiry into your business needs, and their ability to respond with sales support literature and a specific proposal.

- *The experience of the firm and its senior personnel.* Not only ask how long they have been in business but also request a list of repeat clients.

- *Areas of specialization.* Some service bureaus specialize in business markets, whereas others may concentrate on not-for-profit clients. A specialized market focus adds to the expertise the firm can bring to your telemarketing program.

- *Check references.* If possible, also locate clients who were not on the list the agency supplied to you and contact them.

- *The account managers who will be assigned to your account.* Do not judge the bureau on the basis of senior personnel alone. It is important to meet the account manager and lead reps who will be working on your account.

- *How the agency monitors its reps.* Find out if you can participate in training and monitoring off site. Ask about hiring, training, and evaluation policies. Inquire about the turnover rate.

---

[14]Adapted from Laura Hansen, "Dialing for Dollars," *Marketing Tools* (January/February 1997): 47–53.

- *Technology used by the agency.* Conduct a thorough evaluation of their technology. Predictive dialing and interactive voice technology (to be discussed in a later section) are both important in keeping productivity up and costs down. Find out if their computer system is compatible with yours and if you can transfer data electronically.

- *Membership in professional organizations.* Does the agency subscribe to the Codes of Ethics of the Direct Marketing Association and the American Telemarketing Association?

Once an outside service bureau has been selected to carry out your telephone marketing program, you must develop a plan for monitoring and exercising control over its activities. This plan will have many of the same characteristics as an in-house operation.

Establishing an In-House Telephone Marketing Center

Establishing an in-house telephone center is not a minor undertaking, even if the firm has substantial experience working with outside suppliers. Substantial investment in facilities and equipment is required. Personnel with the required level of skills may not be available in sufficient numbers, requiring significant retraining of existing staff or hiring additional people. The organization should also be sure that it has a sufficient volume of work to justify the high fixed cost of an in-house center.

Advances in telephone and computer systems make it possible to carry on outbound and inbound programs from the same call center. This increases the complexity of the management task, although it can reduce overall costs. Finally, most companies will need to make arrangements to handle peak volumes that cannot be accommodated by the in-house center at a reasonable level of investment. Telecommunications technology makes distance and national boundaries irrelevant in dealing with this type of issue.

For example, direct-response television is growing so rapidly in the United Kingdom that even rapid expansion of call centers has resulted in only 67 percent of calls being answered. Matrix Marketing, headquartered in Newcastle, U.K., is planning to route overflow calls to the United States—first to its center in Pueblo, Colorado, and then to other centers in Salt Lake City, Utah, and Omaha, Nebraska. Peak response times in the United Kingdom are during prime-time television viewing, which corresponds to midday in the central United States, a quiet time. Consequently, centers in the United States with slack capacity can handle overflow calls from U.K. consumers.[15]

Setting up a call center and managing an ongoing program involve

- obtaining the support of top management
- setting goals and objectives
- integrating telephone marketing with other promotional activities, including the field sales force
- developing scripts and guides
- recruiting and training telephone personnel
- supervising and motivating reps
- integrating telephone and computer systems
- designing a productive work environment

---

[15]"Matrix to Flip Calls from UK to Colorado," *DM News International,* 21 October 1996, 10.

- developing measurement systems
- testing systems and procedures
- reporting and controlling the operation

OBTAINING THE SUPPORT OF TOP MANAGEMENT

Whenever a new telephone marketing operation is established, there is a learning curve as personnel are trained, bugs are worked out of the equipment, lists are refined, and so forth. If top management expects a smoothly functioning and highly profitable operation overnight, it might lose patience and decide that telephone marketing does not work. It is the responsibility of direct marketing management to help top management establish a reasonable set of expectations.

One of these expectations has to do with the level of professionalism, and therefore the level of compensation, of telephone representatives. Top management may not equate the requirements for good inside salespeople with those of field sales personnel. It may view telephone marketing solely as support for the field sales force as opposed to a major element of the marketing operation with its own goals and objectives. It may also be justifiably concerned about the damage a poorly designed and managed program could do to the image of the firm and relationships with its customers.

Unless top managers are aware of the multiplicity of roles that professional telephone marketing can successfully play, they are likely to relegate it to second-class status. If they do this, it is unlikely that the telephone marketing program will obtain either the amount or the quality of resources necessary for success.

SETTING GOALS AND OBJECTIVES

Each telephone marketing program must have its own precise and measurable goals. However, there are a number of generic goals that telemarketing can achieve:[16]

- Sell products and services
  - Practice proactive outbound selling
  - Take orders from incoming calls
  - Upgrade or cross-sell
  - Reactivate lapsed customers
- Handle sales leads
  - Generate sales leads by outbound calling
  - Screen and qualify leads generated by other media
- Gather information by surveying customers and prospects
- Add information to the database from all customer and prospect contacts
- Improve cash flow
  - Perform credit checks
  - Collect accounts
- Perform a variety of customer service activities

---

[16]Based on Stone and Wyman, *Successful Telemarketing,* 187.

Well-trained telephone representatives can be involved in a lead qualification program for a period of time, then move on to a lapsed account reactivation program, followed by a survey of product use and purchasing activites by targeted prospective customers. Representatives who are handling inbound calls can, with proper technology, deal with calls stemming from a number of simultaneous promotional activities or product lines. However, it is difficult for an individual rep to mix being available to provide customer service with being responsible for a program of proactive outbound calling. Hence, the complexity of the management problem, requiring that call center managers understand not only the priority of the various marketing programs but the ability of the staff to deal with various demands on their time and skills.

INTEGRATING TELEPHONE MARKETING WITH OTHER PROMOTIONAL ACTIVITIES, INCLUDING THE FIELD SALES FORCE

We have already discussed the synergy that comes from combining telephone marketing with other direct-response media. This cannot happen without careful coordination to ensure that appropriate levels of training and staffing will be available from the telephone center when needed.

When a firm has both inside and outside sales forces, and especially when both are compensated wholly or partially by commissions, great care must be taken to see that the two forces work together cooperatively. Because this is most often a problem for business marketers, we discuss it at some length in chapter 11.

DEVELOPING SCRIPTS AND GUIDES

This activity was discussed earlier in this chapter. The process is the same for an in-house call center as when working with outside suppliers.

RECRUITING AND TRAINING TELEPHONE PERSONNEL

There are three basic personnel levels in a call center—representatives, supervisors, and managers. Representatives are the persons who will represent the company to its prospects and customers; they should be recruited, trained, and compensated accordingly. The telemarketing industry has grown rapidly in recent years; consequently, there is a persistent shortage of experienced supervisors and call center managers.

According to Sisk, there are three basic kinds of qualifications for reps:[17]

1. formal education and training coupled with relevant work experience
2. natural communication skills
3. self-motivated, self-starter

It is possible to provide product knowledge and other relevant information to reps who have the right characteristics. It is possible to sharpen the skills of people who have natural communications abilities. It is, however, rarely possible to train people to be effective communicators who have no innate ability. It is also unlikely that a negative personality with little drive to succeed can be turned into a model of positive, achievement-oriented behavior.

[17]Sisk, *Successful Telemarketing,* 176.

Look for the right basic characteristics and then provide all the necessary training, motivation, and support.

The initial training of telephone communicators will vary in length and intensity according to the objectives of the program. Some of the areas covered in most training programs are

- orientation to the company
- basic telephone selling skills
- product knowledge
- effective listening skills
- call center procedures, including call reporting

A good training program contains a great deal of role playing or sales simulations designed to let trainees practice their selling skills, reinforce their product knowledge, and become totally comfortable with the center's systems, call guides, and report formats. Such a program can take from a few hours for a completely scripted calling operation to several weeks for professional selling. Whatever the length, the trainee groups should be small enough to allow for adequate individual attention and practice.

Training does not stop with the initial program. In a well-managed center, training is ongoing. Training programs for existing personnel can perform a number of functions, including

- upgrading skills and preparing employees for promotions
- preventing formation of bad habits
- introducing new products and marketing programs

All good training sessions send employees back to their daily routine feeling stimulated and highly motivated to improve their performance.

SUPERVISING AND MOTIVATING REPS

The supervisor's basic job is to maintain quality, productivity, and work force morale. Good supervisors are actively involved with reps without creating a feeling of "breathing down their necks." They monitor calls from their stations and are a visible and positive force on the floor, demonstrating techniques and acting as role models for the reps. In addition, there is a heavy burden of reporting to evaluate and control the effectiveness of individual communicators, specific marketing programs, and the center itself.

This paperwork load can easily detract from activities designed to motivate reps and keep morale high (and, not incidentally, to control turnover, which can become a serious problem). Books on sales force management discuss many ways to motivate sales reps, including compensation, quotas, recognition, and incentives. A study of supervisory behavior and communicator job satisfaction provides evidence that the same principles hold true for a force of telephone reps.[18] The differences occur because everyone is "under the same roof," and information, including productivity comparisons, is transmitted quickly. Good

---

[18]Herbert E. Brown and Paula M. Saunders, "Predictors of Job Satisfaction among Telemarketing Sales Employees," *Journal of Direct Marketing* (spring 1990): 49–57.

supervisors are also aware that the intensity of inside selling greatly exceeds that of outside selling because inside salespersons are in almost continuous contact with customers and prospects. They plan work processes and environments so reps have regular breaks and an opportunity to "take a breather" after a particularly intense interaction.

INTEGRATING TELEPHONE AND COMPUTER SYSTEMS

The capital expenditures for an in-house telephone marketing center can be substantial. This initial expense is justified by greatly increased productivity if it results in effective linking of telecommunications, computer systems, and the marketing database. The industry calls this "computer telephony integration" (CTI).

The equipment available—including telecommunications devices, computer hardware, and many kinds of specialized software—is complex and seems virtually limitless. We can, however, gain an understanding of the basic elements of an integrated system and the acronyms for basic components that will prove useful in grasping the importance of the topic.

High levels of integration are especially important to timely and effective servicing of inbound calls, although database availability is also important to outbound callers. However, with inbound calls there is little time to prepare for a call. The caller is "there" and the call needs to be handled immediately and accurately.

As an example, assume an incoming call, originating in either a business or a household location, travels over the public telephone network to the marketer's premises. There it travels through an internal switch, often referred to as a PBX (private branch exchange), which routes the call to its proper destination within the firm. By connecting a number of PBXs in various locations, calls can be routed to available agents in any location without the customer being aware that the call has been switched to another location. (In fact, with the prevalence of 1-800 numbers for both ordering and customer service applications, the customer often has no idea of where the center being called is located or if there are several centers linked together to improve service and reduce the total number of reps required.) This type of switch does not offer much flexibility. It can transfer a call to an identified telephone number or to an available number within an identified set, and provide standard services such as call forwarding, but it cannot provide the degree of flexibility needed by a professional call center.

The next level of flexibility is the addition of an ACD (automatic call distributor). The ACD is a programmable server that can direct a call based on a variety of criteria or user-defined rules. These can include:[19]

- number dialed (customer service versus technical service)
- origin of calls (inside sales forces may be organized along geographical lines so inside and outside sales reps work as teams)
- caller-entered or spoken digits (more about interactive voice response in a moment)
- customer profile database look-up by
  - customer account number (used in business marketing applications)
  - social security number (used in financial services applications)
  - trouble ticket number (used in customer service applications)
  - ANI (automatic number identification; discussed later in this section)

---

[19]Based on Louis Volpe, "Taking Control of the Network," *Teleprofessional* (April 1996): 40–46.

- business rules (such things as different lines of businesses; mortgages versus consumer loans versus auto loans, and so forth)
- agent availability
- time of day (the center in one time zone may be closed when one in a distant zone is in full operation; this logic can be extended to move calls completely around the globe over a 24-hour time period)
- day of week
- cost of the call (a free 1-800-number call for basic levels of service versus a paid 900-type number call for customers who have subscribed to a service contract)

The presence of an ACD in the system is the beginning of sophisticated call center routing. It does not end there, however. Placing an IVR (interactive voice response) system between the incoming call and the ACD provides another level of efficiency.

You probably deal with IVR systems when you call your bank to check your balance, call the airline to see if a flight is on time, or even call your school to register for next semester or check your grades from the last one. These transactions have two things in common. They require access to a database of some sort, and when this access is provided, routine calls can be handled by an automated system without intervention by a human operator. This obviously is both fast and relatively inexpensive, and it has the potential to be less error prone than systems that require a human operator to access a database. You are also aware that if your needs exceed the limits of the automated system, the call is automatically transferred to a human operator.

The other major type of interface between the incoming call and the rep is an automatic number identification system. An ANI system takes identifying call information from the network and sends it to the database server, which uses it to access information that is keyed to the calling number. The call arrives at the rep's station at the same time as a "screen pop," a automated screen containing data that is relevant to the call—name, address, and previous ordering data, for example. This also improves the speed and accuracy of the order or service call. However, reps must be trained to use this information with courtesy: "Am I speaking to . . . ?" and never, "Hello, Mary!"

Outbound calling presents a different type of problem—how to maximize the number of completed calls per communicator per hour. Predictive dialing systems provide assistance with this aspect of improving productivity. According to Sisk,

> a predictive dialer is a computer system that dials a list of phone numbers and presents a steady flow of successful "connects" to available TSRs [telephone service representatives]. . . . The system configuration consists of a telephone line to TSR ratio of 3:2 or greater. For example, 16 TSRs could use a system with 24 phone lines dialing. The calls are dialed in anticipation of a TSR being available. Through a formula preprogrammed into the system, the dialer predicts the number of lines to dial at any point in time. It is an intelligent, self-adjusting system.[20]

Predictive dialing systems monitor the progress of the call through the telephone network. They can recognize rings, busy signals, voice answers, answering machines, business salutations, and various telephone company (telco) signals. If all reps are occupied, the system can terminate a call before it is connected at the customer's end, reducing nuisance calls.

---

[20]Sisk, *Successful Telemarketing*, 38.

Working with the PBX and ACD predictive dialers can even balance incoming and outbound calls direct to a common set of telephone reps.

Predictive dialers are complex systems that must be chosen to provide the functionality and the flexibility the center requires and that can be effectively integrated with the rest of the telecommunications and computer systems.[21]

A wide variety of software can be made available at the rep's work station to make a system more efficient and transparent to the caller. This includes query software that provides information from various operating databases (order status when an order number is entered, for example), branching software that provides responses based on data provided by the caller, and reporting software that reduces the time the rep spends filling out forms when the call ends.

This overview gives you some idea of the flexibility and functionality that can be built into the operating systems of a call center. It may also suggest to you how many technical systems have to work together to form a state-of-the art call center. You have also recognized that the objective of much of this technology is to get information from the database to the rep in an accurate and timely fashion, and to return data to the database as a result of each customer contact.

Arthur Hughes provides a vision of what call centers should look like in the era of database marketing:[22]

- On-line screens will be linked to a comprehensive relational database on a mainframe that contains the complete customer record from all sources.

- The customer record will be called up by ANI or by customer name and address whenever the customer is on the telephone.

- Telephone reps will be entering and retrieving a vast amount of relevant data about each customer. Much more than most can do now.

- They will be specially trained to represent a specific company. Representing several different clients at once will become less common than at present.

- Call center agents will know a lot more about their client company than they do now. They will have authority delegated to them, and the ability to transfer calls within the organization.

- Customer service, marketing, sales, and technical support will all merge into a single group of very professional, knowledgeable people who will think, feel, and act as if they were the company. They will be the voice, ears, and soul of database marketing.

CTI is part of what makes the telephone rep's job not only more productive but also less stressful and more enjoyable. Another aspect of a good quality of worklife in a telephone center is a pleasant and efficient working environment.

DESIGNING A PRODUCTIVE WORK ENVIRONMENT

The telephone work station and the overall work environment are important parts of successful telephone marketing. Reps can become stressed and fatigued, both mentally and physically, as a result of the constant nature of telephone contact with customers and prospects. The result can be poor service and can lead to rapid turnover. This may be considered acceptable in a project-oriented consumer marketing setting, but it spells disaster for

---

[21]Robert C. Varney, "New Dimensions in Predictive Dialing," *Telemarketing* (January 1993): 53–57.

[22]Arthur Middleton Hughes, "Database Marketing . . . And the Teleprofessional in the 1990s," *TeleProfessional* (January 1992): 98.

a business-to-business center engaging in professional selling and relationship management. One way to mitigate these problems is to provide a suitable work environment. Designing an ergonomically correct work environment—essentially, creating an interface between workers and their equipment and surroundings that makes them more productive and at the same time protects them from harm—requires careful consideration of a number of important factors.

The design of the call center will have to accommodate certain necessary facilities besides the reps themselves. There must be adequate space for telecommunications and computer equipment and perhaps for fulfillment operations. Offices for managers and supervisors will also be required. The supervisor's office should be visible to as much of the floor as possible. A lounge is a virtual necessity. Reps need a comfortable, accessible place to take a break when things get too intense. A conference room for meetings and training sessions is important.

Each rep should have a designated work area, either an office or a cubicle. Privacy is desirable, but not isolation. There should be adequate desk and storage space and a comfortable adjustable chair. Lighting and ventilation should be optimal, not merely "adequate." Special attention must be paid to the height and placement of the monitor and keyboard for each rep to minimize the occurrence of the repetitive-motion injury known as carpal tunnel syndrome and other stress-related physical problems. Quietness, along with good headsets, is essential; sound must not carry from one rep's area to another. This requires partitions made of sound-absorbing material, carpeted floors, and sound-absorbing materials on walls and ceilings.

A call center requires a substantial amount of space and a sizable front-end investment in equipment and systems. Careful design will result in a productive work environment that returns the investment many times over.

Testing Systems and Procedures

Because a call center is a complex operation, assume that Murphy's law applies. Things will go wrong; there will be bugs in systems; procedures, from scripts and guides to reporting formats, will not produce the desired results on the first try. Plan for intensive testing and allow sufficient time for tests to be completed and revisions made (and retested) before attempting a full-scale operation. Supervisors and managers must be actively involved in all aspects of testing.

The structure of a test and the time it will take depend on what is being tested. A completely scripted program in an established telephone center can be thoroughly tested in a few hours to a few days. For this type of program, one or more lead telephone reps will usually test the new routine and work with supervisors and managers on needed revisions. When new programs (especially those that involve professional selling) or new equipment or systems are being tested, much more time is required. It may take three to six months for a test of this magnitude to be completed. Supervisors and managers should take an active role in the testing of new operations; often they actually perform the initial tests themselves.

One more word of warning: if multiple operations are planned—for example, incoming calls in response to media advertising as well as for customer service, plus outgoing calls for account servicing and prospecting—test each application separately. If you are testing multiple operations, it may require 12 months or more for the tests to be completed.

One activity that will take time is developing measurements of productivity, profitability, and customer satisfaction that accurately reflect the activities and accomplishments of the center.

DEVELOPING MEASUREMENT SYSTEMS

As in all other direct marketing applications, the most appropriate measures for any program depend on its objectives. Some of the typical measures include

- number of dialings per hour
- number of completed calls per hour
- cost per call
- ratio of completed to attempted calls
- number of orders or leads per hour
- average order size
- time per call

Many of these—any many more statistics—can be automatically compiled by the telephone switch or ACD. These include number of dials per hour, number of completed calls per hour, number of abandoned calls, number of lost calls, time per call per rep, and so forth. From the abundance of statistics that is available, carefully choose the ones that are meaningful to program success. Also, be sure you are measuring what you want to measure. What does a longer average call time mean, whether it is for an individual rep compared to others in the center or for one marketing program compared to a similar past activity? Longer call time for an individual rep could signal a person that needs additional training or it could identify someone who provides superior service or who achieves significant cross-selling or up-selling. Longer average call time for a program could simply suggest that the two programs are not really comparable or it could suggest a problem with the product or with the offer. On the one hand, call time is an important measure of productivity. On the other hand, focusing on it to the exclusion of other important measures may fail to uncover important issues and lead to poor rep morale and resulting poor service.

REPORTING AND CONTROLLING THE OPERATION

Good reporting procedures are critical to the measurability that is so much a part of direct marketing. The basic reporting form is the customer call report that is filled out for each customer contact. There are literally hundreds of other reports, including summary call activity reports by rep, by shift, and by location; account activity reports; and profitability analyses by product, by account, and by call duration. The list seems endless and the amount of information available can create a problem unless it is carefully managed.

There should be few paper reports produced and distributed automatically. Instead, the system could include a good query system, one that allows supervisors and managers themselves to request the specific data they wish in the format they wish—on the computer screen, hard copy, numbers, graphics, and so forth. Most of the data will be summary data compiled at the end of a shift or a day. Some information must be available in real time—rep availability, for example. The necessary reporting and control processes must be designed into the system.

Developing and operating a state-of-the-art call center is clearly a major undertaking. As we have already pointed out, the technology that makes call centers possible also makes them a global reality.

GLOBAL TELEMARKETING

The formation of both in-house call centers and commercial telephone service bureaus is growing rapidly throughout the world, in concert with the growth of other direct-response media. International 1-800 numbers are promoting this growth. It is occurring from Australia, to Japan, to Canada, where the inexpensive Canadian dollar makes rates especially attractive to U.S. marketers. Nowhere, however, does the growth appear to be as explosive as in Europe, where the progress of the European Union has led to the imminent deregulation of telecommunications and the anticipation of lower telephone rates. Increasing use of toll-free numbers in Europe has also fueled the growth rate. The experience of two Dutch firms suggests both the opportunities and some of the problems:

- The SNT Project Support firm, headquartered in Zoetermeer, The Netherlands, is the result of a merger between two Dutch call centers, one specializing in consumer financial services and DRTV and another specializing in the marketing programs of high-technology companies. It has other centers in New York and San Mateo, California, one soon to open in Singapore, and plans for others in the Netherlands and overseas. Some of the services they offer to their clients are
  - 200 multilingual work stations that can handle responses in a multitude of languages
  - direct billing of customers in the correct currency of 44 different countries without need for costly conversion on the part of the clients
  - the opportunity for clients to use the same toll-free numbers on all packaging materials, "whether the products are on shelves in Germany, France, or Spain"

The firm expects to attract many foreign clients who want to outsource telemarketing and database marketing activities.[23]

"Truly global" describes the intent of the Hulsink Direct Marketing company, headquartered in Almelo, The Netherlands, to set up a call center in the United Kingdom to service U.S. clients who are marketing products and services throughout Europe. Its existing call centers are located in Germany, France, and Denmark as well as The Netherlands. A new telemarketing facility to be located in the United Kingdom would be linked by computer to Hulsink's fulfillment operation in Almelo. The goal is to set up seamless operations in Europe's major direct-response markets.

> German consumers, for example, need only call a local number to order a product they saw on TV or heard about on the radio.
>
> A native German speaker takes the order and enters all the pertinent information about the customer in his work station. The order is then transferred electronically to Hulsink's Dutch warehouse where the product is packed and shipped within seven days.
>
> Once in Germany, the Deutsche Post AG takes over and delivers the order to the German buyer. "The consumer has the feel that he is dealing completely with a German company," Hulsink said. "That is the structure we want to expand with in the future."[24]

Telecom Ireland is actively promoting the establishment of Pan-European call centers in this country which has experienced significant unemployment for many years. The opportunity and the achievement so far is documented in promotional literature.

---

[23]"Dutch Call Centers to Merge, Offer Greater Clout," *DM News International,* 16 September 1996, 4.

[24]Matthew Rose, "Dutch Firm to Launch UK Call Center," *DM News International,* 8 September 1997, 10.

Technology and Systems Options	Key Site-Selection Criteria	How Many Call Centers Do You Need?
• Call handling options— inbound or outbound	• Track record	• A single, centralized center
• ACD	• Telecommunication costs and support services	• Two or more regional centers
• CTI	• Availability of skilled, multilingual labor	• One center for each country
• NR	• Labor costs and turnover rates	
• Host computer, databases	• Reliable telecommunications	**Trends to Consider in Europe**
• Integrated European and U.S. call centers	• Tax breaks	• Well-established call centers
What Level of Set-up Assistance Is Available?	• Government grants	• Pan-European numbering
• From inward investment agencies	• Regulatory environment	• Growth in direct marketing and teleculture
• From telecommunications providers	• Distribution infrastructure	• Falling costs
• From independent consultants	• Banking system	• European legislation
• From recruitment firms	• Quality of life	

FIGURE 14.3 Factors to Consider in Planning a European Call Center

Source: Reprinted with permission of Ireland Telecomm.

In 1994, 67 million Americans purchased a product over the telephone. By contrast, the European telemarketing industry is just beginning to develop, but during the past 5 years the use of toll free numbers (equivalent to 1-800 numbers in the U.S.) for customer service, order processing, sales and technical support has experienced exponential growth. For example, Telecom Ireland's international toll-free traffic achieved a record growth of 600% in 1995 over and above the previous year.[25]

Figure 14.3 summarizes the factors to consider when planning a call center in Europe. It can be generalized to any international direct marketing situation. Notice that many of the technological issues are the ones discussed earlier in the chapter. Many other considerations of language, regulation, infrastructure, culture, and economic development incentives, however, apply in the international setting.

It is easy to believe that this is the future of telemarketing—seamless operations that support marketing programs and provide customer service around the globe.

---

[25]Margaret Molloy, "Establishing a European Call Center," www. telemkt.com/ireland/, 30 July 1997, 1.

Summary

The telephone is a valuable marketing medium, and its use is growing rapidly in consumer and business markets around the world. Its very prevalence, however, makes it vulnerable to abuses that damage the entire fabric of direct marketing. Whether the objective is to market test a program using an outside service bureau, to use international call centers to facilitate global expansion, or to establish an in-house call center to handle either inbound or outbound calls or a combination of both, telephone marketing needs to be carefully planned and executed. Successful telemarketing requires integration with other media and extensive integration of the supporting technological infrastructure. It also requires the backing of top management and other functional areas of the organization to reach its full potential to increase productivity and lower costs at the same time it provides a significantly higher level of service to customers.

Discussion Questions and Exercises

1. In your own words, define *telemarketing*. What is it able to do especially well? Not so well?
2. What are the basic types of interaction that are possible between a telephone representative and a prospective customer? In what situations is the use of each type appropriate?
3. The telephone is rarely used as a stand-alone medium in direct marketing programs. Why do you think this is true?
4. What circumstances suggest the use of a telephone service bureau?
5. What are the steps that must be taken in establishing an in-house telephone call center?
6. Have you used a toll-free number recently or been solicited as part of an outbound calling program? Be prepared to discuss your experiences in class.

Suggested Readings

Domanski, Jim. "Plain, Simple and Effective Telephone Marketing." *TeleProfessional* (February 1992): 31–33.

Roman, Ernan. *Integrated Direct Marketing,* 2nd ed. Lincolnwood, IL: NTC Business Books, 1995.

CHAPTER

15 Direct Response in Print Media

At a Glance

Direct marketing in the print media may not be the most glamorous side of the industry, but is the lifeblood of many smaller firms and an important part of the media strategy of mid-sized and giant companies, consumer and business alike. In addition, as media reach becomes more global, important print titles are engaged in major international expansion that benefits direct marketers.

Consider the ads from *Sports Illustrated* (*SI*) in Figure 15.1 (p. 358) as an example of the impact and flexibility magazines can offer direct-response marketers. We discuss newspapers as a direct-response medium later in this chapter.

In the same issue that reported the results of the 1997 World Series, *SI* made the two offers shown in Figure 15.1. The postage-paid card is a subscription offer to the magazine itself that actually appeared three times in the issue: twice as a bind-in and once as a blow-in. It offers two incentives for a paid one-year subscription—a World Series video and a Marlins sports watch. This illustrates good offer and incentive strategy by making the incentive relevant to the offer. On the page facing one of the cards is a full-page ad offering

FIGURE 15.1 Direct-Response Advertising for Sports Products

Source: Used with permission of *Sports Illustrated*.

Marlin's specialty items—from a signed team bat to caps and sweatshirts. The incentive for these products is an "Exclusive Florida Marlins Collector's Edition" of *Sports Illustrated*. Near the 1-800 number, *SI* also promotes a Web site—www.ultimatelockerroom.com.

Although the fact that this is advertising for the magazine and its own sports-related products undoubtedly enhanced *SI*'s ability to insert this advertising so quickly, who is to say that a well-prepared advertiser—with the media buy made and ads prepared for both eventualities—could not have done the same?

Magazines as a Direct-Response Medium

Magazines are an advertising medium used by both general advertisers and direct marketers. In deciding to use this medium and then deciding in which magazines to advertise, the direct marketer confronts many of the same issues faced by general advertisers plus a few unique to direct marketing.

We consider four major issues as they confront the direct marketer:

1. determining whether magazines are an appropriate medium
2. deciding which magazines to test
3. specifying additional requirements such as regional editions and split runs
4. designing and executing the advertisement

THE CONTEMPORARY MAGAZINE ENVIRONMENT

In recent years magazines have become very much a specialty medium. There are few mass-circulation magazines left—*TV Guide* and *Reader's Digest* are the two primary ones in the United States. Other staples of the 1940s and 1950s, such as *Look* and the *Saturday Evening Post* (fondly remembered for its Norman Rockwell covers, among other things), have disappeared, unable to compete with television for mass-media advertising. *Life* magazine disappeared from the shelves for almost six years and reemerged with a much smaller rate base and a highly pictorial format that was feature oriented rather than news oriented. General newsweeklies such as *Time* and *Newsweek* have also shifted toward a more in-depth feature and investigative format as the dissemination of news has become instantaneous via cable television and the Internet. Other survivors include *McCall's* and *Ladies' Home Journal,* womens' magazines that refocused their editorial material on concerns of contemporary women, including their status as working wives and mothers.

The large-circulation magazines now face intense competition from a host of specialty magazines that appeal to well-defined target markets from apartment dwellers to organic gardeners. Competition continues to intensify, with dozens of new specialty titles being added each year. *Bob Vila's American Home* competes with *This Old House* and both compete with the well-established *Architectural Digest.*[1] Niche titles such as *American Patchwork* and *Quilting* search for their place in the market.[2] Another niche title, *Cigar,* has taken advantage of the popularity of high-end cigars and includes cigar retailers such as liquor stores in its distribution strategy. A new entrant called *Notorious* aims to attract females as well as males in competition with *Cosmopolitan* and *Playboy.*[3] The music category continues to spawn new titles—*The Source, Vibe,* and *XXL.*[4]

At the same time, major publishers are expanding well-known titles internationally. France's Hachette Filipacchi Presse established *Elle China* in 1988, offered first as a quarterly, then as a bimonthly, and by 1997 as a monthly. By that time, Hachette had a total of 30 titles in Asia, ranging from *Car and Driver* to *Top Model.*[5] U.S. publisher Condé Nast has

---

[1]Keith J. Kelly, "Bob Vila Tries to Build Niche in Magazine World," *Advertising Age,* 26 August 1996, 4.

[2]William Spain, "In General, Where Are the Readers?" *Advertising Age,* 15 October 1996, s6.

[3]Carol Krol, "'Notorious' Stakes out Own Niche in Sexuality Category," *Advertising Age,* 27 October 1997, 8.

[4]Kathryn Drury, "Entrepreneurs Find New Source of Inspiration," *Advertising Age,* 27 October 1997, s18.

[5]Scarlet Cheng, "Hachette's Barometer Is 'Elle' When Entering Any New Market," *Advertising Age International* (October 1997): 27.

successfully introduced *Vogue* into Korea, Taiwan, and Japan. After initial success in Korea, it added *Glamour* to its offering. Previously that title had been marketed only in the United States and Italy.[6]

Other changes have occurred in magazine publishing in recent years. The physical appearance of many magazines has been greatly enhanced with modern typefaces, more sophisticated photography, streamlined graphics, and more use of color—all on heavier paper that provides a better look and more impressive feel. Editorial policy has changed too. Recognizing that time pressure makes lengthy articles unappealing to many people, many magazines have been featuring shorter articles. Others, such as *The New Yorker,* have made small alterations in layout or type without changing their primary focus on the written word. Still others feature an occasional lengthy, in-depth article interspersed among many shorter ones. Special-feature issues, such as *Sports Illustrated*'s annual swimsuit issue, are also used by many magazines. All these changes have been accompanied by increasingly aggressive marketing of both subscriptions and single copies.

One relatively new title, *Martha Stewart Living,* illustrates subscription marketing and the development of a customer base that is receptive to direct-response offers:

> Martha Stewart is one of the phenomenally successful "brands" of the 1990s. Beginning her media career as a frequent guest on talk shows including Letterman and Today, she launched the *Martha Stewart Living* magazine under the auspices of Time Inc. in 1990. It has since become independent.
>
> In January 1991 the first subscription mailing was sent to about two-dozen magazine lists. They tested lists that targeted middle-income women (such as *Ladies' Home Journal*) and upscale women (such as *Elle Decor*). The upscale lists drew better, and the magazine had established its niche.
>
> Soon they began to package editorial content into books on topics like gardening or seasonal specialties such as Christmas entertaining. In 1994 she launched a weekend television program which included a plug for the magazine at the end of each segment. In 1997 the media empire further expanded with a daily television program and a Web site. Each medium cross-promotes the others.
>
> Much of the subscriber acquisition for the magazine has been by direct mail with a mailing of 3 to 4 million packages each December. According to Lauren Stanich, director of marketing for Martha Stewart Enterprises, they continually test creative, but "the only thing that works for us is a complicated package with a four-color outer envelope, colorful order form and long letter. We're not like *Sports Illustrated,* where everybody knows what it is."
>
> Ms. Stewart also has a Martha by Mail catalog which has been cross-promoted in the magazine with an eight-page catalog insert. Buyers are added to the catalog list.
>
> Ms. Stanich adds that as the brand has grown, "the amount of available names that work for us has dramatically increased" with successful use of mail order lists like Williams-Sonoma (kitchen equipment and food) and Jackson & Perkins (gardening). They plan to begin coding subscribers who order merchandise as mail-order buyers and database records will indicate whether they were originally acquired through mail or television.
>
> By early 1997 the magazine's subscriber base was over 2 million, making database building successful enough to allow them to develop demographic and lifestyle models to drive future acquisition mailings.[7]

---

[6] Scarlet Cheng, "If Conde Nast Can't Enter at Top, It Won't Enter at All," *Advertising Age International* (October 1997): 27.

[7] "Eight in the Top Corner," www.mediacentral.com, 27 August 1997; Keith J. Kelly, "Publishers Fixing Problems with Single-Copy Sales," *Advertising Age,* 24 February 1997, 15.

A magazine that acquires a substantial portion of its customer base from mail-order lists should be a prime vehicle for direct marketers of relevant products and services.

MAGAZINES AS A MAIL-ORDER AND LEAD-GENERATION MEDIUM

Magazines allow the direct marketer to reach relatively large audiences at a cost per contact (but perhaps not a cost per order or per lead) that is generally lower than direct mail. Like direct mail, they allow for detailed presentation of sales appeals and high-quality color photographs and artwork. Magazines are presumed to require considerable attention from the reader, which may lead to more careful consideration of the advertising in them. Nash suggests that there are several considerations when determining whether magazines are an appropriate medium for a particular offer:[8]

- *Economics.* If the margin is very low, or if it is a two-step offer whose objective is to get information to many prospects, magazines may be appropriate because of their low cost per contact.

- *Credibility.* If the firm or product are unknown, the offer may need the "halo effect" of the magazine's own credibility to appear believable to prospects. Magazines that are known to be selective in accepting advertising and to stand behind the claims of their advertisers have high credibility with readers. Those that lack credibility (for example, the sensationalist tabloids sold at supermarket checkout counters) are poor vehicles for mail-order advertising of reputable products.

- *Lack of Satisfactory Lists.* If there are no good lists for a particular type of offer, it will be necessary to build lists by initial promotion in media that reach large audiences. This may be true for a genuinely innovative product. It is frequently true for business products that may be purchased by many different people within the same organization. Today consumer magazines carry database-building direct-response ads for pharmaceuticals ranging from cardiac medications to birth control aids. In addition, direct-mail marketers and catalog marketers frequently add magazines to their media mix when they see their ability to rent high-performance lists declining. It is also possible that space advertising will attract customers who do not tend to respond to direct-mail offers. Because of cultural issues, restrictions, and the overall scarcity of rental lists, European direct marketers have found it necessary to use mass media, including magazines and newspapers, to build product-specific databases.

Which Magazines?

Like the general marketer, the direct marketer looks at three basic criteria when deciding in which magazine to place advertisements: circulation, special services, and editorial policy. The direct marketer then adds a fourth criterion: receptivity to direct-response offers.

CIRCULATION

Magazine circulation has three components:

1. subscriptions
2. single-copy sales
3. pass-along readership

---

[8]Edward L. Nash, *Direct Marketing: Strategy, Planning, Execution* (New York: McGraw-Hill, 1982), 115–116.

Some magazines (for example, *National Geographic*) are sold primarily by subscription, whereas others obtain most of their sales at newsstands and store checkout counters. Some magazines have high pass-along readership (have you been in a doctor's office lately that did not have *People* magazine in the waiting room?), whereas others do not. Magazine subscriptions can be either paid or unpaid, the latter—called *controlled circulation*—is primarily an issue in business markets.

There is no single answer to which type of magazine is best for a particular application. It depends on the product itself and the objectives and requirements of the specific direct marketing program. An offer that needs the credibility conferred by the magazine itself will benefit from a magazine with a strong image and a loyal subscriber base. An offer that has as one objective building a new mailing list or adding genuinely new respondents to an existing list will benefit from a magazine with either high single-copy sales or pass-along readership or both. Lead-generation programs, consumer or business, will also benefit from the wider exposure provided by single-copy sales and pass-along readership.

The size and composition of the magazine's circulation are also important. The most comprehensive sources of detailed data on magazine circulation are the consumer and business publications of Standard Rate and Data Service (SRDS). In these publications, magazines are listed according to category (general editorial, women's, men's, card decks, and so forth). Besides circulation data, each listing contains detailed information on advertising rates, sales office locations, and special services offered by the magazine. In addition, you can find detail on the statistics they offer and see sample magazine and newspaper rate cards and circulation data on the SRDS Web site (www.srds.com).

SPECIAL SERVICES

Magazines offer many special services, most of which involve additional charges, that may be important to the direct marketer.

Position

Basic rates for magazine space are for ROP (run-of-paper) advertising in which the publication controls the placement of the ad. Advertisers can negotiate some aspects of placement; for example, placement on right-hand pages only (left-hand pages have been found much less desirable for direct-response advertising).

For the most desirable pages in the magazine, there will be an additional charge, if those positions are even available. The best positions are highly prized and are usually offered first to repeat advertisers. Position may not be very important as far as readership is concerned, but direct marketers feel it is extremely important in terms of response. Table 15.1 presents a list of the most important positions in a magazine and an evaluation of their relative worth.

If a response coupon is used, it should be on the right-hand side (of a right-hand page) so it will be highly visible and easy to remove—not lost in the "gutter" at the center of the magazine. Likewise, if the ad is less than a full page, negotiate placement on the outside of the page rather than on the inside.

Many magazines have shopping pages near the end of the publication. These are similar to the classified pages in a newspaper and offer exposure to readers who are particularly interested in mail-order shopping opportunities. The ads are usually rather small, making them feasible for the very small or beginning mail-order marketer.

	TABLE 15.1 Position Preferred Sequence	
Position Pre-ferred Sequence	*Position*	*Index*
1	First right-hand page and back cover	100
		Approximate Response Reduction from First Choices Above, %
2	Second right-hand page	−5
3	Third right-hand page and inside third cover	−10
4	Fourth right-hand page and page opposite third cover	−15
5	Midbook (preceding editorial matter)	−30
6	Back of book (following main editorial section)	−50

Source: Walter S. McKenzie, "Magazine Advertising," in Edward L. Nash, ed., *The Direct Marketing Handbook* (New York: McGraw-Hill, 1984), 312. Reproduced with permission of the McGraw-Hill Companies.

Split Runs

Split runs allow the advertiser to insert different versions of the ad in the same issue of the magazine. The ads are actually inserted in every other issue of the magazine as it comes off the press, so the advertiser receives a random sample of the magazine's audience. The ability to test in the same issue of a magazine decreases both the cost and the time necessary to evaluate a new product, offer, or creative execution. When engaging in split-run testing, keep two things in mind. First, vary only one element—for example, the offer, the manner in which the product is positioned, or the price. Second, responses to the different versions of the ad must be carefully tracked. A code number printed on the response device or different toll-free telephone numbers are two common ways of tracking. Helpful hints for developing code numbers, commonly referred to as "keys," are shown in Figure 15.2 (p. 363). The number of splits that can be tested in a single edition of a magazine is primarily a function of the circulation and, consequently, the sample size available for each version.

Inserts

Inserts provide high visibility for direct-response offers by "breaking" the magazine, that is, by causing the magazine to fall open at the insert. Inserts can be done in many ways. Some popular formats are postcards or business-reply envelopes that are either bound in or blown in, full-page inserts with detachable response coupons, and multipage inserts that are either the same size as the publication or smaller. Remember, though, an insert adds to both the cost of the ad and its lead time. Therefore the economics of inserts must be considered carefully.

Magazines limit the number of inserts that will be placed in a single edition and where inserts can be placed. Position is just as important for inserts as it is for other direct-response ads. The closer to the front of the magazine inserts are placed, the better. The one exception is the inside back cover, which has been found to be equal in pulling power to the third insert placement.

The functions the key in an ad must perform are:

Provide unique identification of the ad to which the individual is responding. It is helpful to know the publication that generated the response. It is preferable to know the exact issue.

Be easy to locate and identify by the fulfillment staff or the telephone respondent.

Be easy for the publication to advance with each issue. When an ad is run consistently day after day or month after month, new copy is not submitted for each insertion. The responsibility of changing the key for each insertion will be the publication's.

Make it easy to tabulate returns. This necessitates either a numerical or an alphabetical code in each key.

The key may include any or all of the following information:

- The number of the post office box.

- A code that identifies the publication. A large number of magazines suggests something like "M14"—the 14th magazine in the "M's" in list of magazines. Use the SRDS index or develop your own list. There are fewer newspaper possibilities: a simpler code like "WSJE" (*The Wall Street Journal* eastern edition) will usually suffice.

- A number for the specific issue of the publication. "M145" would identify the fifth insertion in the 14th magazine in the "M" list. Again, this can be more straightforward for newspapers: "110587" —simply month, day, year.

- A code that identifies the product. This is especially helpful when the number of ads is very great or there are multiple ad insertions in a single issue of a publication.

Two other keying issues are:

- Different telephone numbers may be used for different publications.

- The key in direct-mail pieces identifies the list from which the name was taken. It may also be helpful to include other information such as the date of the mailing in the key. The key is printed on the response envelope or card.

FIGURE 15.2 How to Key Advertisements

Source: Adapted from Julian L. Simon, *How to Start and Operate a Mail-Order Business,* 4th ed. (New York: McGraw-Hill, 1987), 147–150.

Regional and Demographic Editions

Most major magazines offer several regional editions. Using regional editions results in a higher cost per contact but a lower total cost, which may be especially important to the small direct marketer. It allows the larger firm to gather information about the responsiveness of particular geographical markets and provides a cost-effective media buy for products with known regional appeal.

Advertising in regional editions may also be used to support a television campaign or mail-order drop within that particular area. In addition, splits are often available within regional editions, allowing for testing of new products or copy, for example, within that geographic region. The drawback to using regional editions is that the position options within the magazine are usually limited, so the advertisement often ends up in a less favorable position. Demographic editions offer the opportunity to reach only subscribers who possess a

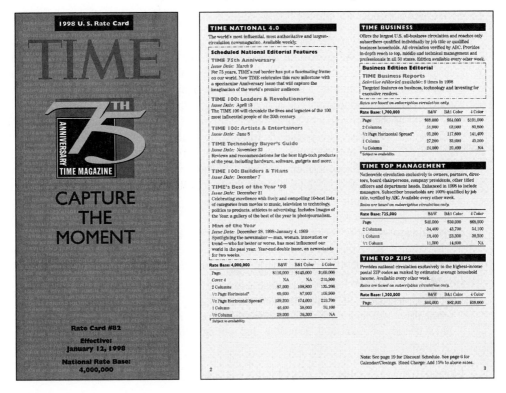

FIGURE 15.3 Part of *Time* Magazine Rate Card

Source: Reprinted with permission of Time, Inc.

particular demographic characteristic, such as households with an income over $100,000 or working women. The cost of advertising in these editions is proportionally higher than in regular editions, but testing may confirm that the more targeted audience is worth the added per prospect cost. Part of the rate card of *Time* magazine is shown in Figure 15.3. It shows several of the many special editions offered by this magazine. The targeted editions are made possible by the existence of identifiable market segments within its four million household rate base.

Discounts

Direct marketers should also be aware that magazines offer several types of discounts, most of which are available to all advertisers and some of which are especially designed for direct marketers. If any of these apply to a particular media buy, they should be used:

- special mail-order rates
- dollar-volume discount
- frequency discount
- discount based on the total number of pages purchased
- discount based on purchase of space in several magazines owned by the same publishing house
- remnant space (space unsold just prior to the magazine's closing date)
- per inquiry rates

EDITORIAL POLICY

Editorial policy refers to the general tone of the feature articles in the magazine as well as to the actual editorials. When you pick up a copy of *The New Yorker,* you expect detailed articles on social affairs, politics, and the arts written for a well-educated and socially aware audience. When you pick up a copy of *Wired,* you expect to find articles for computer-savvy readers as well as feature material and advertising with a distinct edge.

Both of these magazines are popular with direct-response marketers. *The New Yorker* contains numerous direct-response ads for upscale clothing and home furnishings, travel and entertainment, and gourmet foods and gifts galore. *Wired,* as you would expect, contains direct-response ads for computers, software, peripherals of all types, and a wide variety of supporting products and services. Clearly, both are effective for direct-response advertisers who need to reach quite different target audiences.

The overall viewpoint of a magazine may be politically liberal or conservative or downright iconoclastic, but remember that the advertiser's concern with editorial policy does not necessarily refer directly to political ideology. It refers to the tone of the content and to the context it provides for both general and direct-response advertising. The publisher of *Harper's* summarized it well:[9]

> A reader who trusts the editorial content, if not in all of its particulars at least in its intent, presumably will look upon the ads in a similarly open-minded way. Maybe not without a trace of envy or a pause of suspicion—but willing to read the message and listen to the argument.

RECEPTIVITY TO DIRECT-RESPONSE OFFERS

For the direct marketer the single most important criterion in choosing a magazine for promotional purposes is the receptivity of the publication's readership to direct-response offers. Bob Stone points out some of the characteristics of the "best" magazines for direct marketers to test:[10]

> A magazine that performs consistently well for a variety of direct response advertisers is like a store in a low-rent, high traffic location. It's far more profitable than a store selling the same merchandise on the wrong side of town.
>
> Such a magazine just seems to have an atmosphere that is more conducive to the mail response customer. The mail order shopping reader traffic is high in relation to the publication's cost per thousand. Magazines in this category (and this is by no means a complete list) are *National Enquirer, Parade,* and the mighty *TV Guide.* Women's publications also doing well for mail-order advertisers are *Family Circle, Better Homes & Gardens, Good Housekeeping, Cosmopolitan, Woman's Day, Seventeen,* and *Redbook.* Men's publications include *Home Mechanix, Moose, Playboy,* and *Penthouse.*

Stone also notes that the list of mail-order responsive magazines changes significantly over time, and there can even be variations from year to year.

---

[9]Lewis H. Lapham, "Why Integrity Tastes Better than a Belgian Chocolate," *Advertising Age,* 27 October 1997, s2.

[10]Bob Stone, *Successful Direct Marketing Methods,* 6th ed. (Lincolnwood, IL: NTC Business Books, 1996), 59.

Changing demographics (primarily working women) and changing lifestyles certainly account for some of these shifts. The increasing willingness of a large segment of the population to purchase by mail the more expensive items appropriate for inclusion in upscale magazines is also a factor. The important question is not: What magazines are good for mail-order and lead-generation advertising? Rather, it is: What magazines are good for mail-order and lead-generation advertising for my product category? Some magazines may work well for certain product categories but poorly for others. *Yankee* magazine has long been regarded as one of the most effective vehicles for mail-order advertising. It has a relatively upscale and devoted readership that stretches throughout the United States. Mail-order ads for foods, household items, clothing, crafts, and other products with a decidedly New England ambiance generate high response rates. However, the value of the average order generated by advertising in *Yankee* is lower than that obtained through advertising in *The New Yorker.* Products that can succeed in *Yankee*'s digest-sized format might not succeed in *The New Yorker.* The reverse is not necessarily true, though. Although some products that are at home in the sophisticated environment of *The New Yorker* would be seriously out of place in the more informal setting of *Yankee,* a few appear to do equally well in both—L.L. Bean and The Company Store (down products), for example. This seems to be because of the general mail-order receptivity of the subscriber bases of the two publications.

The direct marketer must look not only for magazines that contain substantial amounts of direct-response advertising, but also for those that continually feature direct-response advertising for similar products. One way to ascertain this is to buy a lot of magazines and track their advertising for several months. Certainly the direct marketer should make a practice of studying the advertising of competitors and leaders in the field, but a quicker and more efficient way of finding out which magazines carry ads for products similar to your own is to consult the magazine advertising schedules complied by the Publishers Information Bureau for member publications.

WHICH MAGAZINES . . . ONE MORE TIME

So, after taking into consideration all these factors, which magazines (and a direct marketer of any size will use several) should you chose? The rule is the same as it is for any other direct marketing situation: Make the most informed choice possible and test your choice. Once you learn which type of magazine tends to work best for your product, it will become easier to select other magazines that are similar on the key characteristics. Just avoid making any long-term advertising commitments until you are sure that a particular magazine will generate a profitable level of sales or the quality and quantity of sales leads you desire.

Designing and Executing Direct-Response Space Ads in Magazines

There are many similarities between developing copy and artwork for direct-mail pieces and for space advertisements in magazines. The ad must attract attention, arouse interest, stimulate desire, and inspire action. At the same time, an ad does not operate in the one-to-one environment of direct mail, so it cannot have the exact characteristics of a direct-mail piece.

THE ELEMENTS OF A DIRECT-RESPONSE SPACE AD

A direct-response space ad has four basic elements: the headline, copy, graphics, and coupon. Joel Blattstein makes strong recommendations about each of these four elements as well as other aspects of designing and executing print ads.[11]

Headline

In general, short headlines of nine words or less work better. However, length is not the most important issue. Rather it is how well the headline motivates the reader by promising a desired benefit. A motivating headline leads to careful reading of the copy and then to taking the desired action.

Copy

Again, the issue in copy is not length; it is content. "If the body copy is well written and carries the reader along, it can't be too long. If it's clumsy and boring, it can't be too short!" If the copy is lengthy, however, consider using boldface captions at intervals throughout or breaking the copy up into separate blocks. And remember to make crystal clear what action you wish the reader to take and to make it easy to take that action.

Graphics

Print is a more visual medium than direct mail; the graphics are important. Blattstein distinguishes between "classy" and "klutzy" graphics. This is not a matter of high-quality versus low-quality graphics, it is a question of the target market to which you wish to appeal.

According to Blattstein, "classy" advertising has a clean, perhaps even sophisticated, layout. The typeface used and the photographs or artwork contribute to the image of high quality and prestige. "Klutzy" ads, on the other hand, feature "an informal layout, heavy use of spot illustration, aggressive use of headlines and captions, and a lavish sprinkling of exclamation points and arrows [to] convey to the prospect the sense that he's looking at a real bargain opportunity."

Coupon

The principle for a coupon is the same as for an order form in a catalog or a direct-mail piece: Make it easy to fill out and return. Leave plenty of room for the name and address. Four lines are preferable. Saying "please print" is not superfluous; many orders or requests for information go unfilled because the name and address are illegible. Include the mailing address on the coupon because the reader may tear it out and separate it from the ad. The placement and emphasis given to the toll-free telephone number, if one is used, can affect the number of readers who respond by telephone as opposed to by mail.

We have already mentioned the importance of having the ad on the right-hand page and the coupon on the right-hand side of the page. If the magazine will not promise right-hand placement, you can either prepare a second version of the ad with the coupon on the left side or move the coupon to the bottom center of the page. The coupon should not be at the top of the page. It should be a simple rectangle; would you go to the trouble of cutting out a coupon shaped like a Christmas tree and figuring out how to mail it? Finally, the coupon should have a white background so it can be written upon easily.

If you are using a bind-in card instead of a coupon, all of these design rules still hold true. In addition, the card size and height-to-width ratio must conform to postal regulations

---

[11]The ideas and quotations in this section on elements are from Joel J. Blattstein, "Creating Successful Direct Response Print Ads," DMA Release No. 310.4, January 1984.

and the card stock must be heavy enough to qualify for mailing. The rule here is the same as for direct mail: When in doubt, consult your local postmaster. The design of the card should complement the ad itself. Prepaid postage will increase the response rate. Whether it increases it enough to justify the cost is a good variable to test.

SIZE AND COLOR

The general principle concerning size is: to use the amount of space necessary to present your offer effectively and profitably. The cost of space varies greatly from one publication to another, but you should neither take larger ads than are necessary in the less expensive publications nor compress an ad into too small a space to be effective in the more expensive publications. An interesting guideline is attributed to Robert Baker: "if the item is of genuine interest to 25 percent or more of a particular medium's readership, you can effectively use as much as a full page. But if your item is of limited interest, probably you should confine yourself to small units."[12] For example, stamp and coin collectors ferret out very small space ads that contain an appealing offer. Test extensively to find out which sizes work best for your offer.

Just as space costs money, so does color. It increases the expense of inserting each ad, as well as the original cost of producing the ad. There are some products that virtually require color—fashion items and foods, for example. Others, such as staple household items or office supplies, may be presented effectively in black and white. All other things being equal, the use of four-color will increase the response rate. But will the greater response be sufficient to recover the added expense? Only testing will tell you for sure.

TIMING AND FREQUENCY

In general, Stone says that the timing choices for direct-response space advertising can be described as follows:

- best months: January, February
- next best: October, November

The nature of the product or offer has an effect. He also points out that the purchase of Christmas gift items begins as early as September and that September is also good for schools and book continuity offers.[13]

The same warning that applies to direct mail applies here: These are useful generalizations, but the seasonal characteristics of your products may cause a dramatically different response pattern. Test!

Stone presents some guidelines for gauging the appropriate advertising frequency:

If the cost per response is in an acceptable range or up to 20 percent better than expected, wait six months and follow with a second insertion. If that insertion produces results within an acceptable range, you probably are a twice-a-year advertiser. If the first insertion pulls well over 20 percent better than the planned order margin, turn around and repeat within a

---

[12]Quoted in Julian L. Simon, *How to Start and Operate a Mail-Order Business,* 4th ed. (New York: McGraw-Hill, 1987), 217.

[13]Stone, *Successful Direct Marketing Methods,* 68.

three- or four-month period. If the response to the test insertion in January or February was marginal, it usually makes sense to wait a full year before returning for another try in that publication.

Stone's approach assumes that the readership of a magazine is finite and can quickly become saturated by a particular mail-order offer. However, if your objective is to generate leads or to build your database, you can probably run the ad more frequently. The level of response is the best indicator.

RESPONSE PATTERNS

The response pattern to your ad will vary according to the type of magazine. If its sales are primarily by subscription, response will peak quickly and fall off rapidly. If there is considerable pass-along readership, responses may come in over a considerable period of time. If the publication is time-sensitive, such as *TV Guide,* you can also expect a quick peak and short tail.

Stone indicates that for a weekly publication you can expect 50 percent of the responses by the end of the first two weeks. For a monthly, the average response has the following pattern:[14]

after the first week	3–7%
after the second week	20–25%
after the third week	40–45%
after one month	50–55%
after two months	75–80%
after three months	85–92%
after four months	92–95%

Study the response pattern for your product in each magazine. The patterns for different types of publications will be different, but you will soon learn what the patterns are and will therefore be able to predict total response with considerable accuracy long before the final response arrives.

SHOPPING AND CLASSIFIED PAGES

Hundreds of magazines offer either shopping pages that take ads as small as one column inch or classified sections that have the same format as newspaper classifieds. With a very few exceptions, such as *The Wall Street Journal,* mail-order advertising is rarely successful in the classified sections of newspapers. Ads in shopping pages and magazine classifieds, on the other hand, can be very successful, especially for the entrepreneur on a tight budget. The general principles for developing ads for both types of pages are the same, although shopping pages usually have illustrations whereas the classifieds do not.

William Cohen summarizes the advantages of classified advertising (most of which apply as well to shopping pages) as follows:[15]

- *Low cost.* Cost can be as low as a few dollars per word.
- *High profit potential.* According to one source, "these ads generate dollar for dollar more inquiries or sales than any other method."

---

[14]Stone, *Successful Direct Marketing Methods,* 67.

[15]William A. Cohen, *Building a Mail Order Business* (New York: John Wiley & Sons, 1985), 161–165.

- *Excellent for new businesses.* The low cost means less risk.
- *No need for layout or artwork* for a classified ad. Simply type the ad exactly as you wish it to read and submit it. Ads in shopping pages usually incorporate illustrations and are laid out like display ads.
- *Good place to test.* If successful, roll out to other magazines or progress to display advertising.
- *Builds mailing list.* Because readers of classifieds are often looking for that specific type of product or service, the quality of the responses is surprisingly high.
- *Useful supplement to display advertising.* If the response rate from the publication will not support an ROP display ad, it may well support a classified or shopping page ad. Some regular users of display ads choose to place their ads in shopping pages when available, apparently because of the quality of attention they receive from readers of those pages.
- *Lower dropoff.* The decline in response rate that ordinarily occurs with repeated use of a magazine is slower. This seems to be because not all the readers of the magazine examine these pages in every issue.

This type of advertising has disadvantages also:

- *Limited applicability.* High-cost products or others that require extensive information cannot be sold in this manner. However, even very small ads may be sufficient to generate a request for more information.
- *Limited possibilities for growth.* There are not likely to be many magazines that will be successful for any one product or service.

Cohen also points out that the classified ad must contain sufficient information and a request for action. His suggestion is to write out the ad as if you were writing copy for a display ad and then cut out every word that is not absolutely necessary.

Whatever the type of advertising the direct marketer chooses to place, magazines offer a variety of ways in which to reach audiences that range from large and heterogeneous to small and highly targeted. Consequently, they are part of the media plan of most direct marketers and the chief medium of many. However, today magazines face a threat of uncertain magnitude from new media, especially the Internet.

MAGAZINES AND THE INTERNET

Magazines have faced threats, first from broadcast television and then from cable; now they face a threat of unknown magnitude from the Internet. Don Schultz of the Medill School of Journalism at Northwestern University described the situation this way in the 1997 study, "The Role of Magazines in the New Media Age":

> Historically, we have been able to look out and if not always accurately, at least generally, predict the media future. We saw, for example, mass magazines give way to more specialized and local publications. Black and white television predictably moved to color. Network domination declined predictably as a result of cable. Direct mail challenged mass media for advertiser dollars and the like. In short, most of the changes we could see coming, and in some cases, even do something about influencing their impact. That was because change was commonly slow and often predictable. Today, that is not the case. One innovation leads quickly to another. Speed is of the essence. Companies, technologies, concepts and even media forms are born and die in months, not years or decades. It is this change in speed which, in my opinion, makes concrete analysis of the media scene so difficult. It is the transition which makes the challenge so great. It is the lack of solid, historical evidence, experi-

ence or background which challenges publishers, advertisers and even educators. In the words of Star Trek, "we are going where no man has gone before." And, that is scary.[16]

Speaking to magazine publishers, one Internet expert described some of the challenges in late 1996 in the following terms:[17]

- Less than 0.3 percent of total advertising expenditures are for on-line.

- Standards for major issues such as legal requirements, ad size, and payment conditions are not clear.

- Magazine publishers are finding little profitability on the Web thus far. (In fact, a top executive of one large media company is reported to have described the costs of its site as "giving new meaning to the concept of a black hole.")

- It is out of control and could damage media brands. "Publishers cannot control the size of a user's browsers; color palettes across different operating systems are far from uniform; people can grab any images you create and take them out of context; authentication passwords are circulated around the office in a matter of seconds; many web technologies are unstable and unreliable; and computers crash on a regular basis."

It is clear, however, that magazines, like other branded products, cannot afford to ignore the Web. The key questions center on how they should use it and what their financial expectations should be. The 1997 "Role of Magazines" report has a number of tentative conclusions and recommendations:

- **Content will continue to be the primary draw on-line for magazines as it is for other products and services**.   Because magazines are content rich, they have an advantage; yet they cannot give content away free of charge on the Web and still expect to have people pay for it. Many of the trade publications on the direct marketing and general business fields deal with this issue by putting up only summaries and features of general interest (see the various trade publications on www.mediacentral.com and the promotion of the current edition of the *Harvard Business Review* on www.hbs.com for good examples). Print media can deal with this issue in the opposite fashion, by making additional content—such as the research and notes of their reporters— available to the public for selected articles. Providing content on a regular basis that is not available elsewhere will help publishers develop and maintain loyal audiences for their Web sites.

- **No one yet has a clear idea of how magazines are going to make a profit on the Web.**   At present advertising alone does not hold much promise for supporting expensive sites. Two other possibilities are on-line and off-line transactions. Providing content to users on-line seems to have interesting possibilities. Both PointCast (general news) and Jupiter Communications (digital research) have sites where you can register free of charge and experience this type of service if you have not already done so (www.pointcast.com and www.jupiter.com respectively). PointCast relies on advertising revenue to support its service, whereas Jupiter sells the detailed reports of its research. Most information providers charge for these services. *Newsweek* and *Time* provide the ability to customize by country, a service of obvious value to international marketers and students alike. Some magazines not only provide customization by topic but also provide additional services such as early-morning news summaries to the desktop. Numerous others offer merchandise off-line. For example, *Rolling Stone* magazine (www.rollingstone.com) has a "store" in its Web site. The merchandising section (www1.viaweb.com/rsstore/) offers products

---

[16]Cowles Business Media and the Medill School of Journalism, "The Role of Magazines in the New Media Age," 1996 report, www.mediacentral.com, 7 August 1997.

[17]Adapted with quotation from Tom Wang, "Magazine Publishing's New Media Chameleon: Immature and Irresistible," www.organic.com, 17 October 1997.

including related magazines, books, T-shirts and hats, calendars, and CD collections, all with themes that reflect the nature and content of *Rolling Stone.*

One publishing executive contends, "The Web offers the ability to help advertisers develop direct, more profitable relationships with customers. The kinds of measurements that need to be in place for this will track lifetime customer value, not eyeballs. They'll go beyond demographics to offer advertisers real opportunities to develop those customer relationships in new and creative ways."[18]

- **Advertisers need meaningful measures of results.**   So far, most of the measurement of Web activity has been by the number of "hits" a site receives during a given period of time. Other possible measures include the number of inquiries received via the Web site or the number of transactions generated or even the number of times the site is bookmarked. We talk more about the current difficulties of measuring Web results in chapter 16.

- **Separation of advertising from editorial content is an issue.**   There has always been concern about how advertising might influence the editorial content of magazines. One way of controlling this problem has been to clearly separate advertising and editorial content. It is especially easy for the two to become blurred on the Web, and publishers need to be vigilant. Remember the quote earlier in this chapter about the credibility of the magazine medium and the importance of that credibility to advertisers. There is no reason to believe that the same does not hold true of Web sites.

- **What role does consumer privacy play?**   Publishers, like marketers of all other types, must pay attention to the way in which they collect and disseminate information about their customers.

It is clear that there are currently more questions than answers about how magazines can successfully coexist with the Internet. It also seems equally clear that electronic communication is a part of the future that no magazine can afford to ignore. The future of the print media is linked to that of the Internet and the nature of the relationship will become more obvious as time passes.

Let us now turn to the other major print medium, newspapers. They share with magazines the potential for reaching large audiences, but differ on many other characteristics.

Direct Response in Newspapers

Newspapers, too, are an important medium for many direct marketers. Once the dominant mass medium, newspapers have found competition, especially from television, to be intense in recent years. However, newspapers still reach a majority of all adults in the United States every day. According to a study conducted for the Newspaper Association of America, almost 59 percent of people over age 18 read a daily newspaper in 1996, and more than 68 percent read a Sunday paper. Readership increases with education, household income, occupational status, and home value. However, it is undeniable that overall readership levels have decreased during the past 25 years.[19]

Numerous factors have contributed to the decline of newspapers as the primary medium for conveying both national and local news. Network and, more recently, cable television have assumed first place as providers of news for a majority of consumers. Radio is able to

---

[18]David Shnaider, Ziff-David Publishing Co., in "The Role of Magazines in a New Media Age," 1997 report, www.mediacentral.com, 27 October 1997.

[19]"Most U.S. Adults Read Newspapers," www.naa.org, 11 November 1997.

respond more quickly to fast-moving events. Magazines, increasing in number and ever more targeted on editorial material, also provide competition. Rising paper costs and distribution problems place continuing pressure on newspaper prices. Changing lifestyles, especially time pressure and the increase in single-person households (which are less likely to subscribe to a newspaper), have also contributed to static circulation figures. Finally, the success of *USA Today* as the first "national newspaper," with its short articles and colorful graphics, has challenged many basic tenets of the newspaper industry.

A national study of consumer media use conducted for the Newspaper Association of America and the American Society of Newspaper Editors in early 1997 portrays newspapers as strong in local content, some image areas, and in advertising that provides utility in daily living. The study indicates that consumers want newspapers to do more in areas that include helping communities find solutions to problems, helping consumers understand issues, focusing on and investigating important issues, and providing depth of content. The report concludes that newspapers must be intensely local, useful, and relevant while reporting on solutions and capturing the interest and engaging the emotions of readers.[20]

Newspapers have also looked at ways in which they can better serve advertisers. As a result, they now offer direct marketers a variety of ways in which to successfully reach their customers.

There are four basic types of placement within the newspaper, ROP advertising, free-standing inserts (FSIs), Sunday supplements, and classified advertising. Papers in major markets tend to offer regional editions at least once a week. Others offer special services to important accounts, services that may involve other advertising media. Each of these advertising approaches has its own particular strengths and each tends to appeal to a different type of direct marketer. We consider each in detail in this chapter. First, however, let's look at the general characteristics of the newspaper medium.

Newspapers as a Direct-Response Medium

Newspapers offer a number of special advantages to any advertiser, including the direct marketer:

- *Frequency.* Most newspapers, with the exception of small suburban and rural papers, publish six or seven times per week, and a few large urban papers offer both morning and evening editions.

- *Immediacy.* For black-and-white advertising, the close (the time by which the ad must be submitted for inclusion in a particular edition) is often only hours prior to publication for camera-ready copy.

- *Reach.* Newspapers offer high penetration of households in their primary geographical area. A 50 percent penetration of households in the locality is not uncommon, and some newspapers have a penetration of 70 percent or more.

- *Local shopping reference.* No other medium has been able to supplant the newspaper as the primary reference to local shopping opportunities. Readers expect to learn of merchandise availability, sales, and special events in the pages of their newspapers. Special sections, such as the midweek food sections, provide a focused environment for the advertiser of related product categories.

- *Fast response.* Because most newspapers are a daily medium, the direct marketer knows quickly whether a particular offer is producing a satisfactory response.

---

[20]Newspaper Association of America, "Consumer Media Usage," www.naa.org, 11 November 1997.

At the same time, newspapers have drawbacks as an advertising medium. The primary one is the poor color reproduction in the main portion of the paper. Mass-circulation newspapers also fail to reach some particular subgroups effectively. Non–English-speaking people and single-person households are two good examples. In larger cities, however, there are many newspapers that cater to speakers of other languages and offer special opportunities to marketers who target that segment.

In addition, the cost of newspaper advertising has risen sharply in recent years. Add to that their high level of household penetration, and newspaper advertising can easily become too expensive for advertisers who need to reach a specialized or neighborhood market. Because newspapers are essentially a local medium, the type of advertising that does well in them is more limited than it is in some other media. Finally, newspapers have a life span of only about 24 hours; they are not kept around the house to give people multiple opportunities to see an offer and respond to it.

Many of the services added by newspapers in recent years have been aimed at dealing with some of these disadvantages.

ROP Advertising in Newspapers

Because newspapers reach a large, heterogeneous market, they do not provide the precise targeting that most direct marketers require. Still, they are a useful medium for some types of direct-response offers.

Direct marketers who serve national or regional markets use ROP advertising in newspapers for two primary purposes: (1) offers that are of interest to or are related to a local market and (2) tie-ins with local retailers. Direct-response offers in newspapers are frequently for services that are being offered in a local area—for example, a seminar on buying real estate with little or no down payment or a stop-smoking clinic. Direct-response display (as opposed to classified) advertising is also used by local retailers. This advertising often has dual objectives: to generate sales and, often more important, to build traffic in the local retail establishment. The retail ad may include an incentive for coming into the store or a telephone number for additional information or retail locations.

Freestanding Inserts

Freestanding inserts (FSIs), also called preprints and freefalls, have been in widespread use for many years. These ads are prepared and printed in a central location and shipped to the newspapers for insertion, primarily in Sunday issues. Circulation of FSIs has fallen somewhat in recent years as newspaper circulation has slipped, but almost 45 billion are estimated have been distributed in 1996.[21]

Large retailers such as Sears and JC Penney and mail-order firms with extensive product lines such as Columbia Record Club and Time-Life Books were among the first to make consistent use of inserts. Inserts in envelope form also achieved popularity with publishers and photofinishing concerns. Billions of coupons for food and household products are distributed in this medium each year. Small, flat items can be sampled through FSIs. They are also effective for some one-shot direct response offers, notably collectibles.

---

[21]"Newspaper Preprint Insert Volume," www.naa.org, 11 November 1997.

Marketers like FSIs because costs are lower as a result of the centralized production. Centralized production also allows better control over the creative design and execution of the ads. Perhaps most important of all, FSIs are printed on heavier, glossier paper stock than the newspaper itself and can therefore provide high-quality color reproduction.

ADVANTAGES OF FSIs

According to *The New York Times,* the advantages of FSIs to the advertiser are

- Because they are distributed in the Sunday paper, readers have time to consider their propositions at leisure.
- FSIs offer a great deal of flexibility. Virtually any kind of print promotional format (e.g., reply cards or envelopes, single sheets, tabloids, catalogs, brochures) can be adapted to FSIs.
- Geographic and demographic editions offer flexibility in the site and type of market reached.
- FSIs reach the loyal readership of a particular newspaper and confer the credibility of that publication on the advertisement.
- Large and sophisticated advertisers, including retailers, travel and financial services firms, non-profit organizations, and manufacturers of consumer packaged goods have consistently used FSIs successfully.

FSIs remain popular with consumers who find both information content and special offers, including those carrying price reductions, in the FSI section of newspapers.

Newspaper Supplements

Newspaper supplements are virtually brief magazines that, like FSIs, are produced at a central printing facility and distributed to local newspapers for insertion in Sunday editions. They combine the frequency, reach, and rapid response of newspapers with the high-quality graphics reproduction of magazines. Because their content is feature articles as opposed to news, they are retained longer than newspapers, giving more opportunity for exposure to the advertisements they contain. However, they lack the immediacy of the newspaper itself because closing dates can be as much as 90 days prior to publication. There are four major Sunday supplements, and they have little circulation overlap because they are designed for newspapers in different markets.

- The largest is *Parade* magazine, which is featured in Sunday newspapers in the suburbs of large cities and in smaller cities. It contains articles on subjects of national interest, regular features and columns, and theme sections on subjects such as food and health. Its editorial content is not localized, but it offers regional and demographic buys and split runs. *Parade* offers other services of interest to direct marketers, including a reader service card.
- The next largest newspaper supplement is the *Sunday Magazine Network,* distributed in newspapers in larger metropolitan areas. Its editorial content is local and its advertising is a combination of local and national ads sold through the network.
- *Family Weekly* is distributed through newspapers serving smaller towns and rural America. It is found in a large number of papers, but because of their small sizes its overall circulation is relatively low.
- The newest of the supplements is *USA Weekend,* which is published by *USA Today* and distributed by other newspapers throughout the United States (the newspaper *USA Today* has no

Sunday edition). It features articles on topics of general interest, including personal finances, entertainment, sports, lifestyles, and celebrity interviews. There are regular columns and sections on health, automobiles, literature, and travel. *USAWeekend* offers regional buys.

Remnant space—space unsold as the closing date nears—is also available in some of these supplements. It is offered at a considerable discount, but the direct marketer may have to wait several weeks for it to become available, especially if a selective buy is desired. If there is no urgency, however, the economics of remnant space are very attractive, especially for an untried product.

Sunday supplements work very well for a wide variety of direct marketers both in testing situations and for products with mass appeal over a long period of time, such as collectibles, or for products that need to reach a wide audience in order to build a database of qualified buyers. This means, however, that new advertisers may have difficulty obtaining the placement or even the particular edition desired. Because of the differences in reader demographics of the circulations of the four major supplements, they will probably not all work equally well for all product categories and should be tested just as carefully as any other media vehicle.

Total Market Coverage

Traditional newspaper advertising, whether ROP or in some type of insert, does not completely satisfy the needs of local retailers and national manufacturers for two reasons:

1. No newspaper reaches all the households in any given geographical area; 30 to 40 percent are not likely to be reached by a specific newspaper. In markets where there is more than one daily newspaper, of course, the marketer can advertise in more than one newspaper, but this is likely to be duplicative and prohibitively expensive.

2. For retailers who serve only part of the newspaper's geographical area or for manufacturers who market to specific market segments, newspapers represent a great deal of waste circulation. For example, a seasonal promotion for snow blowers should be received by suburbanites, not urban dwellers with no driveway and very little sidewalk.

The "classic" approach to solving the problem of total coverage is to publish a weekly edition that is carrier-delivered to the entire market or mailed to all nonsubscribers. There are many variations on this basic theme. These special editions can be targeted selectively. They can be used as delivery vehicles for other types of advertising such as samples, catalogs, or coupon packs. This type of service to advertisers has been growing rapidly in recent years, with most daily newspapers offering some type of service to reach nonsubscribers.

DATABASE MARKETING SERVICES

Another glimpse of the type of service that newspapers of the future will offer to advertisers is found in the experience of the *Salina* (Kansas) *Journal.*[22] A program was begun in 1996 as a way to both acquire new subscribers and advertisers. According to the newspaper's advertising director, "we needed more specific information by households before we could comfortably feel we were going to be able to do it right. . . . We bought some life-style data that included, for instance, household income, type of home ownership, and the presence of

---

[22]Adapted with quotations from Scott Hample, "Front Page News," *Marketing Tools* (April 1997): 8–11.

children in the household." They also used computer mapping technology to produce a visual representation of the information in the database. They found the maps to be especially well received by clients who prefer them to statistical reports.

Their first application was to their own subscription marketing. They mapped subscription rates by block group and color-coded them to show where penetration was strong and where it was lower. Low-penetration areas with demographics that matched those of high-penetration areas were prime prospects for circulation campaigns. With this program a success, they were ready to offer their database capabilities to advertisers:

> "A salesperson from the advertising department approached the furniture store owner about the availability of the database and mapping services the newspaper offers, including the renting of our subscriber and nonsubscriber database," says [direct marketing head] Atkinson. "We mapped out his clients, primarily looking at five demographics—their age, their income, their education level, whether or not they are homeowners, and the type of furniture they purchased in the past." The newspaper's subscriber and nonsubscriber databases were overlaid with the furniture store's database of people who bought a specific brand of furniture. . . . The client mailed 10,000 catalogs in four cities, using a mailing list consisting of current customers who have purchased the specified type of furniture in the past, and prospective customers with matching demographics generated from the Proximity [mapping software] database.

The results of this campaign were not given, but the newspaper is enthusiastic about the potential of database marketing. "Basically, we are trying to help our customers know who their customers are," according to the newspaper's advertising director.

With the high penetration they offer in many markets, newspapers seem to be well positioned to offer database marketing services to their advertisers. This is another circumstance in which understanding lifetime value will be useful in planning cost-effective direct-response programs.

THE LIFETIME VALUE OF A NEWSPAPER CUSTOMER

Table 15.2 presents a model for determining lifetime value (LTV; also known as Customer Lifetime Value) for a newspaper.[23] This model assumes that the publication has defined zones based on subscriber demographics that permit it to charge different rates to advertisers looking for particular demographic targets. The process for calculating LTV is as follows (numbers in parentheses refer to columns in Table 15.2):

- Determine the number of households in each zone (1) and the number of subscribers in each (2) to obtain the penetration rate (3).

- Calculate the total revenue per customer (8) by adding ROP (nonzoned advertising that runs in all editions) advertising revenue (4), revenue from zoned editions (5), and circulation revenue (6), and subtracting from this sum the costs attributed to customer attrition or churn (7).

- Determine the average customer lifetime for each zone (9).

- Use the acquisition cost for the most recent acquisition program in each zone because the marginal customer acquisitions tend to be the most expensive (10).

- Calculate the total revenue (11) for each zone [(1) × (8)].

---

[23] Adapted from Timothy J. Keane and Paul Wang, "Applications for the Lifetime Value Model in Modern Newspaper Publishing," *Journal of Direct Marketing* (spring 1995): 59–66.

TABLE 15.2 Lifetime Value Model for Newspapers

Zones	[1] No. of Subscriber Households	[2] Total No. of Households	[3] Penetration ([1]/[2])	[4] Nonzoned Advertising Sales per Customer	[5] Zoned Advertising Sales per Customer	[6] Average Circulation Revenue per Year	[7] Average Annual Churn Costs	[8] Total Sales per Customer ([4] + [5] + [6] + [7])
North	10,000	15,000	67%	$135	$200	$135	$(24)	$446
South	15,000	20,000	75	135	35	155	(13)	312
East	9,000	30,000	30	135	140	115	(34)	356
West	25,000	50,000	50	135	140	105	(45)	335
Rural	6,000	28,000	21	135	100	135	(44)	326
Total	65,000	143,000	45	135	123	129	(32)	355

[9] Average Customer Lifetime (Years)	[10] Most Current Acquisition Cost	[11] Total Sales ([1]*[8])	[12] NPV (Year 1) ([8] − [A] − [B] − [10])	[13] NPV (5 Years) Based on Average Life and 6.5% Inflation Rate	[14] Total NPV (5 Years) Based on Average Life ([1]*[13])	[15] Percentage of Total NPV (5 Years) ([14]/SUM[14])	[16] Percentage of Total Subscribers ([1]/SUM1])
6	$35	$4,460,000	$116.00	$969.49	$9,694,852	32%	15%
3	55	4,680,000	(38.00)	267.29	4,009,372	13	23
4	35	3,204,000	26.00	512.44	4,611,961	15	14
6	75	8,375,000	(35.00)	401.81	10,045,234	33	38
4	25	1,956,000	6.00	385.43	2,312,601	8	9
5	45	22,675,000			30,674,019	100	100

Source: Timothy J. Keane and Paul Wang, "Applications for the Lifetime Value Model in Modern Newspaper Publishing," *Journal of Direct Marketing* (spring 1995): 60–61. Copyright © 1995 by John Wiley & Sons. Reprinted by permission of John Wiley & Sons.

Note: [A] = Direct product cost per customer Year 1: $250. [B] = General and operating cost per customer Year 1: $45.

- Calculate the net present value (NPV) per customer for each zone:
  - Year 1 (12) includes the acquisition cost.
  - Follow the cash flow (income minus total costs of servicing each customer in each zone) for the average customer lifetime (13).
  - The net present value of those yearly cash flows is the total net present value for each zone (14).
- Determine the percentage of NPV produced by each zone (15).
- Determine the percentage of subscribers in each zone (16).

The newspaper has learned, for example, that the north zone produces 32 percent of its net present value with only 15 percent of its subscribers, whereas the west zone produces 33 percent of NPV but requires 38 percent of the subscribers to do so. The newspaper will now be able make better decisions about how much to spend on acquiring certain types of subscribers, and it will be able to price advertising in its zoned editions so that advertisers receive a better return on their promotional dollar.

As we can see, newspapers are taking a number of approaches to retain their readership and their value as an advertising medium in the face of the rapidly changing media environment. Another strategy is to join the electronic age.

ON-LINE NEWSPAPER PUBLISHING

Like magazines, newspapers are having to contend with the explosion of the Internet. Many newspapers, both large and small, have established on-line editions. Like magazines, they are looking for innovative ways to integrate on-line with print publishing and to add value to the material that goes on-line. The following are just a few examples:[24]

- The *Chicago Tribune* (www.chicago.tribune.com) runs a Beat Siskel (of the Siskel and Ebert movie review team) contest at Oscar time each year, which is flourishing since being on the Web. It runs in both the print and on-line versions of the paper, as does much of the paper's content, but they now receive more "pick the Oscar winners" contest entries by e-mail than they do by regular mail.

- New Jersey Online partners with the *Newark Star-Ledger* on a project called Interact (www.nj.com/interact/). A photo and a background piece on a current-interest topic are entered on the site each week. Users can respond and view the responses of other visitors to the site. The following week the editor chooses Web postings to print in the paper. At that time the topic for the following week is introduced and readers are urged to go on-line to learn more and to express their views.

- The *San Jose Mercury News* (www.sjmercury.com), which often breaks stories about the high-technology industry, has reporters on major stories file to the on-line version even before the print edition appears. Readers are encouraged to read the paper or to visit the site again for the final version.

- On a lighter note, the *Syracuse Post-Standard* (www.syracuse.com) publishes a business-related cartoon each Monday, which it then posts on-line. Viewers can customize the cartoon with their names and then turn it into a fax cover sheet, send it as an electronic postcard, or use it as a monthly calendar.

---

[24]Adapted from Melinda Gipson, "Integration Strategies," www.naa.org, 11 November 1997.

- Taking advance of the Texas mania for high school football, the *Austin Chronicle* has an on-line project that provides detailed high school game stats and pictures topped with a huge inflatable football and throws out "hundreds" of T-shirts with the logos of both the print and on-line versions of the newspaper.

Also like magazines, newspapers have yet to identify a clear model for making a profit on the Web. All accept advertising, but, remarkably, a number do not make it easy for a visitor to the site to find out how to purchase advertising. All seem to use their Web site as a subscription-generating activity, and there are some scattered reports of results that are deemed satisfactory. Some are generating revenue from subscriptions to the on-line version. *The Wall Street Journal Interactive* (www.interactive.wsj.com) is subscription based, and the *San Jose Mercury News* (www.sjmercury.com) provides its archival services only to subscribers. At the other end of the spectrum, *The Washington Post* (www.washingtonpost.com) and *USA Today* (www.usatoday.com) provide content free of charge. Both *The Times* (London) (www.the-times.co.uk) and *The New York Times* (www.nytimes.com) require that visitors register to access the site but do not charge for the privilege. Based on what we have learned, they may anticipate selling database services at some future time.

Summary

Magazines and newspapers are important vehicles for many direct-response marketers. They may well assume greater prominence as their presence on the Internet becomes established. What has now emerged as four separate but related media vehicles will each offer specific target markets and promotional advantages. In addition, each has drawbacks that make them more useful to most direct marketers as part of an overall media plan than as stand-alones. These media also offer special opportunities for the small direct marketer and the innovative or untried product. Each of them will continue to evolve as part of the rapidly changing media environment.

Discussion Questions and Exercises

1. What are the major characteristics of magazines as a direct-response medium? Of newspapers?
2. What criteria should a direct marketer use in selecting magazines to test?
3. Explain the different ways in which direct marketers can advertise in newspapers.
4. Bring some direct-response ads from magazines and newspapers to class and be prepared to discuss their content and execution.
5. Visit the Web sites of a number of magazines and newspapers with which you are familiar in their print format. Be prepared to discuss the similarities and differences between the print and on-line versions.

Suggested Reading

The current year's report on "The Role of Magazines in the New Media Age," www.mediacentral.com.

CHAPTER 16 Direct Response in Broadcast Media

It is midmorning on Saturday. You are surfing the television channels, looking for entertainment to take your mind off the paper you have to write this weekend. After clicking your way through all the channels, you still have not found anything you want to watch. Thinking about why that is, you realize that sandwiched between all the cartoons are programs that look like entertainment and that sell everything from exercise equipment to cosmetics to food preparation devices.

What is going on? Do people really watch these infomercials? Do they buy the products being advertised? When did this explosion of direct marketing on television take place?

Before we answer these questions directly, let's take a look at the nature of the direct-response television industry—how it began and its current status.[1]

The Development of Direct-Response Television

The tone of many early direct-response television (DRTV) commercials can be attributed to Daniel Rubin, who sold Florida Fashions via television beginning in 1946. Rubin imitated the style of the pitchmen who worked the boardwalk in Atlantic City. He taped their sales pitches and brought them to New York to use in filming simple direct-response spots. Why did these crude commercials with their rapid-fire narration, minimal sets, harsh lighting, and simple camera angles set the standards for early direct-response television? The reason is simple—they sold products. Their success attracted many imitators, but it also quickly attracted reputable advertising specialists, some of whom are still working in the field today.

Record companies, the first major direct-response television advertisers, developed the classic 120-second direct-response commercial. During the 1950s and 1960s, they were joined by companies selling products for the home—kitchen gadgets and equipment, books, tools, and inexpensive home decorating items. Another development during this period was the appearance of celebrities as spokespersons, some of whom worked for modest fees plus a percentage of sales.

In the early years of television, the supply of advertising time was considerably greater than the demand. Crude production techniques combined with cheap airtime yielded a very inexpensive advertising medium. A commercial could be produced and aired on one or two test stations for as little as $2,000. Results were available quickly; orders began to arrive in the mail about 48 hours after the commercial aired.

Another factor that stimulated the early growth of direct-response television was per-inquiry (PI) advertising. As the term implies, the PI advertiser's payment to the station is based on a negotiated fixed payment per response. Because stations typically use these spots to fill unsold airtime, marketers have no control over the date and time at which they are run. This makes planning for order fulfillment difficult. In addition, responses must be carefully "sourced" by the station for payment purposes. Although PI deals provided inexpensive advertising opportunities during the 1950s and 1960s, they became less common as network advertising time became more desirable and therefore much more expensive.

The next major change came about as the cable television industry grew in size and scope. Cable TV originated to serve isolated areas that could not be reached by regular television signals. Cable grew slowly for many years, but by the 1980s it became a serious challenger to network television as an advertising medium. Television shopping channels began with the formation of the Home Shopping Network in 1992. The 30-minute infomercial became a recognizable force about the same time; its positioning is discussed in chapter 2.

---

[1]The material on the development of direct-response television is based on John Witek, *Response Television: Combat Advertising of the 1980s* (Chicago: Crain Books, 1981), 1–18; Sandy Davis, "Television Direct Response," in Edward L. Nash, ed., *The Direct Marketing Handbook* (New York: McGraw-Hill, 1984), 317–322; Jerrold Ballinger, "The Changing Role of DR Broadcast," *DM News*, 1 July 1986, 36–39; "Advertising Age's History of TV Advertising," www.adage.com, 16 August 1997; David Kyffin, "The Assessment of a Direct Response Television Campaign," *Journal of Database Marketing* 1, no. 4 (1994): 334–342.

There are now four identifiable types of DRTV advertising on the airwaves. *Direct-response spots* are most often produced in 60- or 30-second (:60 and :30) time frames. Spots of 120 and 90 seconds (1:20 and :90) were once popular, but the cost of television time makes their use less frequent today. The *infomercial* is most often 30 minutes in length, but can vary. *Home shopping networks* are aired 24 hours a day in major markets. Infomercials and home shopping channels offer a wide variety of products for sale. Direct-response spots often have sales as their objective, but they may also be used with an objective of generating inquiries and building databases, or they may be used to support direct-response promotions in other media. Finally, we often see what one author calls *added-value commercials*—brand advertising that takes the opportunity to promote a 1-800 telephone number or a Web site where viewers may obtain additional information.

ENABLING CONDITIONS FOR DIRECT-RESPONSE TELEVISION

Once the power of direct-response television became widely understood, it became commonplace during all times of the day. Major advertisers, however, brought a quality orientation that was almost totally lacking in early direct-response TV. Day and prime-time airing demanded different products and marketing approaches as well as production values that were consistent with the surrounding entertainment programming. The increasing quality and credibility of direct-response TV commercials for consumers also brought business-to- business advertisers into the arena, using prime time and weekend television for lead-generation spots and further increasing the credibility of this type of promotion.

Perhaps the single greatest growth stimulant for DRTV has been the availability of a national 1-800-number service. Without a toll-free telephone number to encourage impulse purchasing, it is doubtful that the industry would have enjoyed its substantial growth of recent years. However, some advertisers have learned to their sorrow that impulse buying can result in high return rates, especially if order fulfillment is slow. A related factor is the prevalence of credit cards among consumers. The ability to charge a purchase facilitates television buying, just as it does in other media.

At the same time that major national advertisers were doing their part to upgrade the quality of DRTV, the Federal Communications Commission and the Federal Trade Commission were engaging in regulatory and consumer protection activities that lessened the abuses of earlier days, and this has also added to the credibility of the medium. Although there are still some products of questionable value and advertisers of questionable repute featured in this medium, both the broadcast and the direct marketing industries have made substantial efforts to prevent genuine abuses.

As a result, the consumer's image of direct-response TV appears to have improved in recent years, although there is little empirical evidence on the subject. One study found limited support for a relationship between consumer reactions to several DRTV spots and a set of demographics, attitudes toward the advertiser and the commercial, and past shopping behaviors.[2] As seen in Table 16.1, many consumers do report watching DRTV, and a substantial number have purchased. Notice also, that these consumers report later purchasing at retail stores as a result of DRTV commercials.

---

[2]Glen Nowak, "TV Viewer Characteristics and Results Beyond Response," *Journal of Direct Marketing* (spring 1992): 18–31.

TABLE 16.1 Consumer Attitudes Regarding Direct-Response Television

Group	Ever Viewed Direct-Response TV					Where Bought Product (% of Last Purchases)[a]		
	Any Type	Infomercial	DR Spot	Home Shopping Show	Bought Any Product[b]	1-800 Number	Later at Retail	From Catalog
Gender								
Male	74%	45%	59%	44%	29%	61%	30%	6%
Female	79	50	61	55	31	66	28	5
Age								
16–24	85	57	66	63	16	46	54	0
25–34	84	54	64	50	34	60	29	9
35–44	84	58	69	54	32	61	34	5
45–59	76	50	64	49	37	74	21	5
>60	55	21	40	34	25	69	15	8
Household Income								
< $20,000	73	44	54	51	28	70	22	5
$20,000–$39,999	79	48	63	50	35	59	32	6
$40,000–$59,999	80	54	64	49	30	60	35	5
>$60,000	83	57	71	55	31	70	24	4
Total	77	48	60	50	30	64	29	6

Source: Data from NIMA International, 1995. From *Direct Marketing Association's Statistical Fact Book, 1996* (New York: Direct Marketing Association, 1996), 165. Reprinted with permission of the Direct Marketing Association, 1998.

Note: This telephone study was conducted for NIMA International by Leisure Trends and the Gallup Organization in January and February 1995 among a representative sample of 1,013 adults aged 16 and older.

[a]"Thinking only of the last time you bought a product that was offered [through direct-response television], did you buy it calling the 800 number, buy it later in a store or buy it later from a catalog?" (Total may not add up to 100% because of "don't know" or "refused" answers.)

[b]"Have you ever purchased a product that was offered [through direct-response television]?"

When to Use Direct-Response Television

Planning and producing DRTV spots requires all the detailed knowledge of the medium that a general advertiser must have plus a thorough understanding of the special requirements of direct response. In addition, producing infomercials or shopping channel segments requires skills generally expected of entertainment programmers. These are substantial skill sets, and to provide an in-depth review of the complexities of television advertising, not to mention programming, would take more space than we can devote to it here. Textbooks on advertising and marketing communications cover the advertising aspect in detail. Remember as you read the remainder of this chapter that it covers only those aspects of planning and executing television commercials that are essential to direct response.

DRTV FORMATS

The 120-second commercial is the preferred format for continuity offers because there is so much to communicate that a full two minutes of time is needed. It is difficult to make a 60-second continuity spot successful. In the same way, a minimum of 60 seconds is generally required to communicate the information for a one-shot offer. Because a lead-generation commercial does not have to present a complete offer—just sufficient information to entice the viewer to request more—it can usually be confined to 30 seconds. Although these are generalizations rather than absolute rules, it would be a false economy to squeeze a direct-response spot into a shorter time to save money and end up with a commercial that does not pull. Remember, it is also necessary to allow a substantial block of time to show the toll-free number and mailing address on the screen, although the audio repetition of this information can be shorter. The most important thing to remember is that DRTV spots can and should be tested, just like promotions in other media.

The formats in Figure 16.1 have withstood the test of time, and to ignore them could be dangerous. That is not to say that a knowledgeable direct marketer with a creative idea cannot structure a direct-response spot differently—as long as it is done on the basis of creativity, not ignorance!

Media Planning for Direct Response

Network and cable television compete directly for advertising revenue. There was a time when the competition seemed to tilt in favor of network, but as more homes have subscribed to cable, it has become a powerful competitor. With the ability to support many channels, each of which caters to a somewhat different demographic and interest group, cable is able to reach niche audiences in a way that mass-appeal broadcast networks are not. In the not-too-distant future, cable may provide households access to as many as 500 different channels. This will offer an even greater opportunity to reach specialized audiences.

The conventional wisdom says that cable audiences are more upscale than those of the mass-appeal broadcast networks. According to *American Demographics,* "For the past decade, cable television has been stealing the most desirable consumers away from broadcast network[s]."[3] The DMA adds, "Cable viewers are younger, better educated, more affluent, hold higher level employment, and live in larger households."[4]

Whether broadcast or cable networks offer the best target audience for a specific offer, the key media planning and buying concepts are the same. They are gross rating points (GRPs), dayparts, and availability. Let's look at each in turn.

---

[3]Rebecca Pinto, "New Markets for Cable TV," *American Demographics* (June 1995).

[4]Cabletelevision Advertising Bureau, Inc., quoted in *Direct Marketing Association's Statistical Fact Book, 1996* (New York: Direct Marketing Association, 1996), 169.

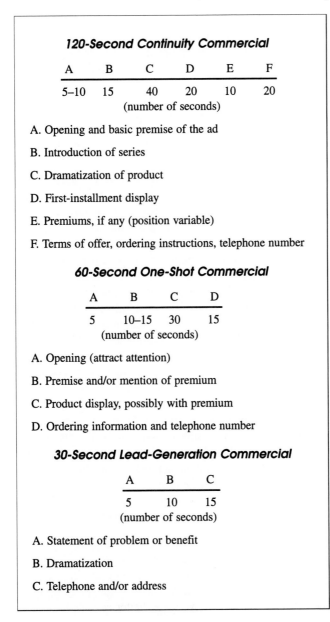

120-Second Continuity Commercial

A	B	C	D	E	F
5–10	15	40	20	10	20

(number of seconds)

A. Opening and basic premise of the ad

B. Introduction of series

C. Dramatization of product

D. First-installment display

E. Premiums, if any (position variable)

F. Terms of offer, ordering instructions, telephone number

60-Second One-Shot Commercial

A	B	C	D
5	10–15	30	15

(number of seconds)

A. Opening (attract attention)

B. Premise and/or mention of premium

C. Product display, possibly with premium

D. Ordering information and telephone number

30-Second Lead-Generation Commercial

A	B	C
5	10	15

(number of seconds)

A. Statement of problem or benefit

B. Dramatization

C. Telephone and/or address

FIGURE 16.1 Basic Formulas for Direct-Response Commercials

Source: Adapted from John Witek, *Response Television: Combat Advertising of the 1980s* (Chicago: Crain Books, 1981), 24–32.

GRPs are the basic measure of television efficiency—the cumulative number of households receiving the spot during a given period of time. This measure is computed by a simple formula:

Reach (the percentage of households tuned in) × Frequency (the number of times the spot is aired) = Gross rating points

The objective of the direct-response media buy is to obtain as many GRPs in the most desirable dayparts as possible for the amount of money budgeted. This buying criterion is essentially the same as for general advertising. Remember, however, that the direct marketer will then be able to measure success of the commercial by product sales or qualified leads generated.

Broadcasters have divided the day into sections that are relatively homogeneous in terms of the type of programming offered. Finer divisions are possible, but the basic dayparts are morning, day, prime, and night. The significance of dayparts is that both the size and the composition of the viewing audience differ by daypart and, consequently, so do the rates charged for time in each.

Availability of time is a major concern to the direct-response TV advertiser because there are relatively few :120s or :60s spots available. This is not only because of sheer length but also because the networks and stations do not put directly competing products in the same commercial block, or "pod." Independent stations often have more long segments to offer than either the broadcast or cable networks.

Media cost is affected by issues other than length. Local advertising is proportionally more expensive than network. Buying specified time slots is more expensive than purchasing within a broader time frame. Less expensive alternatives are "preemptibles" (the advertiser chooses a specific time but the station can replace it with a full-rate advertisement if one becomes available) and run-of-the-station (ROS) spots (the station itself chooses the time). Per-inquiry deals, if available, lessen the risk that exists even when airtime is purchased at very favorable rates.

You may have recognized that this list of key media planning concepts omits one considered very important by the general advertiser—program ratings. Whereas general advertisers are eager to place their commercials on highly rated programs, direct marketers generally avoid them because they are not usually good vehicles for direct-response advertisements. It is possible that viewers of popular programs are too absorbed in the entertainment to pay much attention to the commercials. It is also possible that viewers tend to resent the intrusion of a commercial more when they are watching a program they like and that they do not want to chance missing any of the program while placing an order. The same reasoning in reverse explains why independent stations have been such successful vehicles for direct-response spots: it is not as much of a sacrifice to miss part of a rerun to place an order for an attractive product.

The concepts of GRPs, dayparts, and availability are all important to the direct-response TV advertiser, but the most important concept of all is profitability, which is usually measured in terms of cost per order or per lead. Because profitability can be measured on a station-by-station basis, direct-response television time is purchased with a clause allowing for cancellation at any time with 48 to 72 hours notice. Direct marketers must not hesitate to cancel unprofitable advertising, but they should give the spot a chance to perform.

Edward L. Nash points out that response builds over time with a television campaign, but because it builds erratically, it is difficult to forecast results. A successful campaign will reach a peak after 2 to 3 weeks, plateau for several weeks, and then start to decay. The direct marketer must show some patience in the beginning, but track results carefully so the spot can be removed once results decline below the minimum acceptable profitability level.[5]

---

[5]Edward L. Nash, *Direct Marketing: Strategy, Planning, Execution* (New York: McGraw-Hill, 1982), 163.

Creating Direct-Response Spots

The aim of direct-response television creative is to take advantage of the visual imagery unique to TV while conveying a convincing sales message. Products that lend themselves to demonstration are particularly appropriate for this visual medium. A unique product with benefits not easily obtainable elsewhere is also desirable because of television's high cost.

Having been assured that the product is well suited for television, the direct marketer should concentrate on creating an attractive offer. All the relevant elements of the offer (as discussed in chapter 3) must be described in sufficient detail to be clearly understood by the viewer. In addition, some products, such as financial services and medications, require disclosure of certain information, which must be shown on the screen in type that can be read by the viewer. Portraying the details of the offer will require a substantial portion of the allotted time. As with all other direct-response media, if customers misunderstand any of the terms of the offer, returns are likely to be high and back-end results are apt to be disappointing. Variations in the offer, such as changes in price or incentive, can have a substantial effect on the pulling power of the spot and should be carefully tested.

Having constructed the offer, there are a number of issues that must be dealt with to create a successful direct-response commercial, according to John Witek:[6]

- A detailed script is the first step. The script includes not only copy, but all the stage directions, so completeness and clarity is essential if the product is to be displayed to fullest advantage.

- A storyboard is the next step. It displays some of the key scenes in the commercial in some detail so that everyone involved in the production cangrasp the tone and mood desired and visualize some of the instructions given in the script.

- A skilled and experienced production team is essential to translate the creative concepts and directions onto the medium of film.

- Choose the on-air talent carefully because the actors or celebrities will have substantial impact on the portrayal of the product and the kind of image established for it.

- Use motion (for photographic images such as magazine covers) or action (for any product that can be demonstrated) when filming the commercial. "Motion helps hold an audience's attention. Direct response visuals have interest in proportion to the degree of action they incorporate."[7] The visuals must, of course, be synchronized with the audio, and they must also be integrated with the copy that appears on the screen.

- When deciding between film and videotape, remember that film produces a higher-quality visual image, but video gives a sense of immediacy.

Witek concludes by reminding us that today's audience has been raised on a steady stream of commercials that have great visual impact. The impact has further increased in recent years with the widespread use of computer graphics in advertising. To hold its own in this environment, direct-response advertising must use creative and production techniques that generate their own impact and believability. He goes on to say:

---

[6]Adapted from John Witek, "Direct Response Graphics—The Look of Direct Response TV Commercials," DMA Report 505.01A, July 1989, 1–3.

[7]Ibid., 2.

Direct response spots tell you to go to the telephone. But they often show little to prove that the trip will be worth it. And a big part of the audience won't know that it's worth it until the flash and style taken for granted in general advertising becomes typical of direct response graphics and until the ability to build an image blends with the skills it takes to get an order.[8]

Testing Direct-Response Spots

Testing DRTV spots bears many similarities to test-marketing a product. Choosing representative markets and determining the length of the test must be done correctly if test results are to be valid. One DRTV executive recommends the following:[9]

- three broadcast markets, two stations in each market
- one or two cable networks
- a three- to four-week test
- at least 15 spots per week per station

Response rates are higher during the first and third quarters of the calendar year. It is therefore desirable to test during the second and fourth quarters in order to be ready to roll out during the more productive quarters.

A test must be monitored very carefully to measure its degree of success and to find ways, such as a better media buy, in which it might be improved. The time of the call and the station on which the spot ran are both essential pieces of data. It simplifies the tracking problem to assign each station a different 1-800 telephone number. David Kyffin presents a detailed methodology used in testing direct-response television spots in Great Britain.[10]

In preparing, first, to test a DRTV spot and, later, to roll it out, remember that part of the planning is to have both the telemarketing and the fulfillment operation ready to play their roles in the program.

SUCCESSFUL USE OF DIRECT-RESPONSE TELEVISION

Christian Children's Fund (CCF) is a not-for-profit organization that has used DRTV successfully for more than a decade. CCF, founded in 1938, originally used the mail, as do most other nonprofits, for its fund-raising efforts. In its case, fund-raising equates to convincing people to contact CCF for additional information about sponsoring a child in need. It runs spots on both cable and broadcast networks as well as local and syndicated stations, based on affordability. CCF receives 16,000 to 20,000 inquiries per month and finds that as many as 30 percent of the inquirers do convert into sponsors. CCF spends about 90 percent of its fund-raising on television.

CCF uses little outbound telemarketing except to place a call to prospects who have not converted into sponsors 15 days after receiving the information. They use card packs and package inserts for prospecting. They have tested prospecting on the on-line services, which do bring in some leads, but those leads have a low conversion rate. CCF uses its database when an emergency strikes in a geographical area in which it is active. They contact people

---

[8]Ibid.

[9]Diana Vogel, "DR Television Makes Marks with Marketers," *DM News,* 21 October 1991, 21–22.

[10]Kyffin, "Assessment of a Direct Response Television Campaign," 334–342.

who are sponsoring children in that particular area with an appeal for special assistance and find that the sponsors are receptive.[11]

A much newer entrant into the realm of DRTV is Xerox Corp., which aired its first infomercial in 1997. The product was a new line of digital copiers, a product that the company felt would be difficult to explain adequately in conventional spots. The offer in both the 30- and 60-second versions of the direct-response spot is for a video demonstrating in detail the company's Document Centre line of digital copiers. One reason for using television is to reach multiple decision makers for a copier product that may be integrated into computer networks. According to a communications manager for Xerox:

> The way the office is today, it's kind of hard to say who makes the purchase decision. . . . Is it someone who's involved with network services? Is it a CIO [chief information officer] or a manager of a data center? Or is it an administrative head or purchasing manager who traditionally has been part of the copier decision-making process? The purpose of DRTV is to let people know there's a new day in technology. DRTV is very complementary to everything we're doing.[12]

This concept was developed as an integrated campaign leading with publicity, followed by print, and later by direct mail. Its direct-response objectives were to generate leads for the Xerox sales force and to build a database of responders. Xerox planned to spend $10 million on the campaign.[13]

Infomercials

What the industry often refers to as "long-form" promotions grew from its beginning in the late 1970s to more than $1 billion in sales in the United States and more than $8 billion worldwide in 1997.[14] The way was opened when the television industry in the United States was deregulated in 1984, removing the restriction of 12 minutes of advertising time per half hour. Public attention was drawn to the format in 1992 when presidential candidate Ross Perot used it as an important element of his media strategy. Traditional DRTV products such as Jay Kordich's "Juiceman" flourished in the new format. According to *Advertising Age,* "Yuppies ordered $500 exercise machines by phone and more than half the orders for Tony Robbins' $149.95 'Personal Power' self-improvement course came from people with incomes of more than $50,000 a year."[15] Well-known national advertisers from Lexus to Club Med have used the format with success. How is it possible to produce 30-minute programs, purchase air time, and still sell enough products to make money? There are several answers to this question, including the nature of the prospective consumer market, the types of products that work in this format, and the economics of infomercials.

---

[11]"Eight in the Top Corner," *Direct,* www.mediacentral.com, 1 October 1996.

[12]Rob Williams, "Xerox Launches First DRTV Campaign," *DRTV News,* 1 July 1997, 6.

[13]Ibid.

[14]Direct Marketing Association, *Handbook* (New York: Direct Marketing Association, 1996), 174; www.nima.org, 27 August 1997.

[15]Kathy Haley, "The Infomercial Begins a New Era as a Marketing Tool for Top Brands," *Advertising Age,* 25 January 1993, M3.

	Light Viewers (n = 66)	Heavy Viewers (n = 68)
TABLE 16.2 Motives for Viewing Infomercials		
Learning about new products	30.88%	51.89%
Interest in specific product	20.58	32.91
Enjoy celebrities	8.82	11.39
Entertainment value	17.64	17.72
Bored (switching channels)	58.82	58.22

Note: Classification as light or heavy is based on an index that combined viewership scores with familiarity scores on 24 infomercials.

Source: Adapted from Michael T. Elliot and Paul Surgi Speck, "Antecedents and Consequences of Infomerical Viewership," *Journal of Direct Marketing* (spring 1995): 39–51.

INFOMERCIAL VIEWERSHIP AND PURCHASING BEHAVIOR

Surveys in 1994[16] and 1995[17] suggested that about 70 percent of respondents had watched at least one infomercial in the preceding six months. Elliott and Speck reported that 31 percent of respondents said they never watched infomercials, whereas 21 percent watched them once or twice a month, and 7 percent watched them several times per month. The infomercial viewers in this study were more likely than nonviewers to be younger, unmarried, financially optimistic, and willing to try new products. An industry study in 1996 found viewers to have an average age of 41 and an average household income of $50,250. This study also found viewers to be employed full time, have children under age 16 living at home, and to live in the suburbs.[18] Note that these studies do not agree on whether infomercial viewers are more likely than nonviewers to be married. Nonetheless, the overall profile of informercial viewers appears to be relatively upscale.

The Elliott and Speck study asked about viewing experience with respect to 24 different infomercials. It found that "all of the infomercials in our sample were viewed completely by at least some respondents, and many were completely or partially viewed by a substantial part of the sample. Some had completion rates three times as high as others but [perhaps surprisingly] none had completion rates lower than 17%."[19] In other words, many viewers watched all or a substantial portion of the infomercial. This study also asked about viewer motivations (Table 16.2).

---

[16]Hudson Street Partners, in Haley, "The Infomercial Begins a New Era."

[17]Michael T. Elliott and Paul Surgi Speck, "Antecedents and Consequences of Infomercial Viewership," *Journal of Direct Marketing* (spring 1995): 39–51.

[18]Cathy Asato, "NIMA Chief Views Future of DRTV," *DM News,* 4 November 1996, 10.

[19]Elliott and Speck, "Antecedents and Consequences," 43.

PRODUCT AND INFOMERCIAL FIT

There are two different situations with respect to the question of whether a product lends itself to the infomercial format. The companies that derive their livelihood from the DRTV industry are constantly on the lookout for products that will work well in the long format. National advertisers ask themselves whether it makes sense to add infomercials to the media strategy for a particular product.

The importance of choosing a product that is unique and that lends itself well to demonstration is true in the long-form just as it is in short-form direct response commercials. In addition, one agency executive recommends that the product should have broad appeal (to match the broad appeal of the medium), offer a solution to a problem, have an excellent price to value relationship (to encourage impulse purchasing), and have a minimum five-to-one mark-up.[20]

The entertainment component of infomercials (which Table 16.2 suggests is not very high) does not override the need for a compelling offer. Another executive points out that few products priced at less than $29.95 or more than $300 are successful. In the higher price ranges most offers state price in terms of three to five equal monthly payments. Shipping and handling costs average $8.95 except for high-priced exercise equipment or housewares.[21]

Within these general guidelines, are there some product categories that do well in infomercials and others that do not? Certainly some product categories, such as fitness equipment, personal care products, and self-improvement programs, have many successful models. However, many other products and services—from automobiles, to household cleaning equipment and devices, to telephone services and equipment—have been used in at least limited markets with success.

One way of answering this question is to look at the types of products that are selling well at any given time. The information in Table 16.3 (p. 394) is compiled on a monthly basis, so be careful about implying too much from one set of results or even from a several month time period. The media buys that drive the results may have seasonal patterns, or you could simply be seeing a short-term phenomenon. It is certainly true that over a few months in 1996 and 1997 offers as varied as Dionne Warwick's "Psychic Friends Network" and Richard Simmon's "Sweatin' to the Oldies" led the infomercials parade.

The data in Table 16.3 are interesting also because they show that this particular list of hosts includes few celebrities. There are some differences of opinion on the value of celebrity hosts to infomercial success. Celebrities do have attention-getting value, but some viewers appear to doubt their credibility. This may be especially true if the celebrity seems to have little affinity with the product in question. However, when the celebrity has a clear standing with regard to the product category (Bob Vila of *This Old House* promoting tools) or is the originator of the product (Victoria Principal and her line of cosmetics), their presence seems to work in the product's favor. If celebrities have, or can demonstrate in the infomercial, no obvious relation to the product, they might actually be counterproductive.

In addition to these product considerations, national advertisers of branded products have to ask themselves whether infomercials make sense in terms of their overall promo-

---

[20]Peter Spiegel, "The Eight Most Frequently Asked Questions about Infomercials," www.smartbiz.com, 27 August 1997.

[21]"Guide to DRTV Advertising," www.tracomm.com, 27 August 1997.

TABLE 16.3 Infomercial Product Ranking for July 1997

	Product Name	Show Host	Cost	Category	Marketing Company	Product Description
1	Autobike Classic	Robb Weller	$359.96 plus $49.99 S&H	Health and fitness	CSA Inc.	Bicycle
2	Total Gym	Chuck Norris and Christie Brinkley	$599.40 plus $50 S&H	Health and fitness	American Telecast	Exercise equipment
3	Smart Wrench	Beau Rials and Bob Circosta	$39.90 plus $6.95 S&H	Household	The Media Group/ American Direct Marketing	Tool
4	Sweet Simplicity Body Smoothing System	Wendi Rogers	$29.95 plus $6.95 S&H	Beauty	HSN Direct	Hair removal system
5	Bun Trainer	Tracy Effinger and Lisa Lamendola	$79.80 plus $19.95 S&H	Health and fitness	Marson Media LLC	Exercise equipment
6	Great North American Slim Down	Larry North	$79.80 plus $9.95 S&H	Health and fitness	Quantum Television	Diet system
7	Sobakawa Pillow	Jennilee Harrison	$29.95 plus $8.95 S&H	Household	Kent & Spiegel Direct	Specialty pillow
8	WebTV Internet Terminal by Philips Magnavox	Unidentified male	$249.99 plus $19.95 S&H	Computers and electronics	Philips Magnavox	Internet–TV interface
9	Quick 'N Brite	Larry Gourlie	$29.95 plus $8.95 S&H	Household	Quick 'N Brite	Concentrated cleaner
10	Brown & Crisp	Darla Hahn	$29.95 plus $6.95 S&H	Kitchen	The Media Group/American Direct Marketing	Microwave cooking bags

Source: DRTV News, 11 August 1997.

Note: Ranking includes only hard good product infomercials. Business opportunity, brand awareness, and lead generation infomercials have been excluded. This ranking is based on gross media rates. Information provided by Infomercial Monitoring Service, Inc., 810 Parkway Boulevard, Broomall, PA 19008. To contact IMS, 610-328-6902, fax 610-328-6791, or http://www.imstv.com.

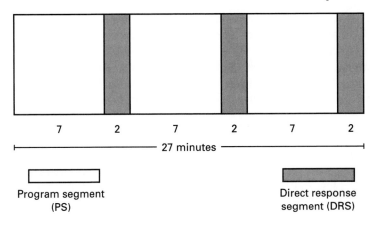

FIGURE 16.2 Anatomy of an Infomercial Program

Source: Michael T. Elliott and Pamela Lockard, "An Analysis of Information Content in Infomerical Programs," *Journal of Direct Marketing* (spring 1996). Copyright © 1996 by John Wiley & Sons. Reprinted by permission of John Wiley & Sons.

tional strategy. Infomercials may provide additional attention-getting power for a brand, and they are one answer to management's demand for more accountability in advertising. National advertisers may use infomercials to sell products as well as to produce leads and to build databases, but they may also have more complex objectives, which include image building and differentiating the brand from its competition.

PLANNING AND PRODUCING INFOMERCIALS

Like the short form, infomercials have a basic format, which is shown in Figure 16.2. This standard format is three equal-length programming segments, each of which is followed by a direct-response segment that presents the offer, ordering information (including the 1-800 telephone number, which may also be displayed for segments of time during the program sections), and encourages the viewer to take immediate action. Because it does not appear that most viewers watch the complete infomercial, it is important to make the "sales pitch" at intervals throughout the program. Our students have also pointed out that the three-segment approach tends to place the direct-response segments at the same time commercials are appearing on regular programming; a situation that inhibits channel surfing.

There are several types of infomercial programming. *Demonstrations,* often used for fitness equipment and food preparation devices, focus on showing how the product is used and benefits of usage. *Testimonials* feature an expert or celebrity who brings his or her own credibility to the sales message. Self-help or self-improvement programs use this format, which often includes interviews with obscure individuals who describe how their lives have been changed by the product. *Documercials* use a journalistic format to present the product in a way that may create audience confusion about whether the program is paid advertising or nonpaid programming. *Talk shows* use this popular format in ways very similar to traditional programming. Celebrity interviewers are often used and audience participation is important. One variant of the format has the host interviewing a group of product users or prospects; another has a host interviewing the product's developer. Finally, there is the *dramatization,* which may look very much like traditional programming, including attempts to use the situation comedy format.[22]

The format chosen guides the scripting of the program. Producing the infomercial will involve all the considerations of other DRTV formats. It will require longer to produce than a spot, perhaps several months. This brings us to the question of costs.

THE ECONOMICS OF INFOMERCIALS

The cost of producing an infomercial can range from as little as $75,000 to as much as $1 million, with most falling in the $160,000 to $250,000 region.[23] Table 16.4 shows how those costs break down for a low-end infomercial, and confirms that the $250,000 estimate is a common one. This is just for the production of a 30-minute infomercial; it does not include media costs. There are many variables that can impact production costs, such as the use of food stylists, audiences, customization, dubbing, and celebrities. Re-edits are common and costly.

According to the president of Kent and Spiegel Direct:

> Media [costs are] generally broken into two categories; the test and the roll-out. Media tests run anywhere from $25,000 to $100,000. We usually get our feet wet with about $10,000 and start doubling it every week. You pretty much know what you have after you spend $50,000. A decent test should include a mix [of] broadcast and national cable.
>
> The roll-out is another story. Our bare minimum for a successful infomercial is $50,000 per week—generally we spend between $100,000 and $500,000 per week for a successful infomercial.[24]

These costs appear quite substantial—and they are. However, when they are compared to the cost of traditional brand image commercials for network television, they begin to look quite reasonable. Production costs for 30-second brand-image spots are easily as much as $250,000 to $1 million. Media costs for top-rated entertainment programs and sporting events can approach $1 million per minute.[25]

The direct marketer knows the gross margin for the product going into the testing phase. At this point it would be useful to decide on an allowable cost per order (CPO) in order to help decide whether to continue testing and rolling out. The allowable CPO varies. "A low price offer may have a CPO of $2, $3, or $4, but a product with a $100 price tag may have a $10 to $14 allowable CPO. But even those thresholds may not apply to a specific product."[26]

According to Spiegel, only one out of four infomercials is successful. He identifies a successful infomercial as one with sales of $10 million, with $50 million being a real winner.[27]

---

[22]Michael T. Elliott and Pamela Lockard, "An Analysis of Information Content in Infomercial Programs," *Journal of Direct Marketing* (spring 1996): 44–55.

[23]Spiegel, "The Eight Most Frequently Asked Questions," 2.

[24]Ibid., 3.

[25]Joe Mandese, "Seinfeld Is NBC's $1M/Minute-Man," *Advertising Age,* 18 September 1995, 1.

[26]Laurie Freeman, "Formula Mixes Numbers, Intuition, Tests," *DRTV News,* 24 February 1997, 3.

[27]Spiegel, "The Eight Most Frequently Asked Questions," 4.

TABLE 16.4 Infomercial Production Cost Worksheet (for 30-minute Spot, Not Including Air Time)	
Script	$15,000
Talent (Host/Hostess)	15,000
Commercial Agency (20%)	3,000
Testimonial Development	5,000
Shoot (2 cameras, 2 days—Rehearsal & Shoot Day. Plus 1 camera, 2 days—testimonials and commercial)	30,000
Videotapes (Beta SP, 20 @ $45. ea.)	900
Teleprompter (2 days)	2,000
Production Assistant (5 days)	2,000
Director (5 days)	5,000
Make-up Artist (4 days)	1,600
Catering (5 days)	1,500
Location/Studio/Set Design	15,000
Props	2,000
Wardrobe	2,000
Voiceover	1,000
Audio Studio	900
Audio Materials	50
Music Score	1,000
Time-coded Dubs	575
Off-Line Edit	3,000
On-line Edit (30 hrs. @ $325 per)	9,750
1-inch Tape Stock	175
Protection Master	150
VHS Dubs (4 @ $25 ea.)	100
Animation (logo & body of show)	5,000
Administrative Costs	4,000
Production Fee	25,000
Total Cost	150,700

Source: Data from Concepts Video Productions, 1996. From *Direct Marketing Association's Statistical Fact Book, 1997* (New York: Direct Marketing Association, 1997), 174. Reproduced with permission of the Direct Marketing Association, 1998.

EXAMPLES OF SUCCESS

An interesting but atypical application of the infomercial format by a national advertiser occurred when Quaker State motor oil realized that it had a problem with both sales and perception of the brand in the southern part of the United States. They hit on an infomercial as a way to "build brand image and to develop a more positive perception of Quaker State motor oil in that part of the country." The show was entitled the "Winning Formula" and featured stars from the Hendrick Motor Sports racing team. The story line included the team preparing for a race and discussing their trust in the product. The offer included a sweepstakes for a new car, a trip with a racing crew, and merchandise if the viewer called a toll-free number.

The company used focus groups to assess changes in perception of the product, which they found to be greatly improved as a result of the infomercial. They also reported that in one chain, retail sales increased by 7.2 percent during the eight weeks that the infomercial ran. The director of marketing for Quaker State says, "The show was a risk for us, in a sense, because it's not cheap, especially in this format. . . . We shot not in the typical videotape. We did a combination of high-quality film and high-quality production values that enhanced the total program." It was not clear, however, whether Quaker State planned to continue airing the infomercial.[28]

Another unusual application of the infomercial format was developed by the Arthritis Foundation. The offer is for subscriptions for their publication, *Arthritis Today,* membership in the foundation, and resources including a guide called "101 Tips for Better Living" and a videotape of exercises for arthritis suffers—all priced at $39.95. What makes the infomercial unusual is that it is sponsored by Tylenol, MIC Communications, and HealthSouth, a national chain of outpatient service providers. Both Tylenol and MIC aired existing commercials in identified sponsorship segments. The story line involves real people who have conquered or learned to live with the pain of arthritis. The infomercial moved from test markets into a regional roll-out, although no specific measures of success were given.[29]

THE FUTURE OF INFOMERCIALS

The long-form format has seen rapid growth in the United States and in other countries including Japan, Western Europe, and Australia. What the future holds is not clear. It has proven its drawing power, but it is vulnerable to cost increases, especially for airtime.

Will the format continue to grow and to expand internationally, drawing even more national advertisers? Will most infomercials in the future be sales oriented or will more be used as image and database builders? Or is the infomercial a short-term phenomenon, soon to be replaced by other types of promotional activity? Does the future include delivery of infomercials on demand over the Internet? No one knows the answers for sure at present.

One certainty, however, is that infomercials face competition from another type of electronic retailing—the home shopping channel.

Home Shopping Channels

Home shopping channels are another phenomenon fostered by the multiplicity of broadcast opportunities available on cable television. Originating in the United States, the two major channels are expanding their efforts into Europe, primarily the United Kingdom, Germany, and Austria, and also into Japan.

THE ORIGIN OF HOME SHOPPING CHANNELS

This aspect of direct marketing began with the founding of the Home Shopping Network (HSN) in 1985 and QVC (which stands for Quality, Value, and Convenience) in 1986. Both networks had their origins in established spheres of direct marketing. The founders of HSN had operated a radio shopping station in Clearwater, Florida, and the creator of QVC had ear-

---

[28]Rob Williams, "Williams Sells Quaker State on 'Guerrilla' Tactics," *DRTV News,* 9 June 1997, 4.

[29]Kim Cleland, "Arthritis Foundation Turns to Infomercial," *Advertising Age,* 14 June 1997, 14.

lier established The Franklin Mint, a well-known direct mail marketer of collectibles.[30] In the past decade a number of other electronic home shopping services have come and gone, while HSN and QVC and their subsidiaries have emerged as the key players in the industry. Other viable smaller networks also exist, and they all operate in essentially the same manner and tend to sell a similar array of merchandise.

THE HOME SHOPPING PRODUCT MIX

Consumer Reports provides an apt description of the merchandise mix: "Today, the fare of most TV-shopping channels is the same as it has been for years: collectibles, clothing, small electronics, housewares, and jewelry, jewelry, jewelry."[31] Fully half the total volume of the channels is represented by jewelry. There are several reasons for this. Jewelry qualifies as an impluse purchase, especially important in this medium where comparison shopping is not really an option. Jewelry is attractive and shows well on the screen, especially if well lit and exhibited against dark, rich backgrounds. Often it is displayed on live models to show how it dramatizes an ensemble. Jewelry also has attractive margins.

The same *Consumer Reports* article points out that the merchandise itself has changed from the early days when most of the items were closeouts and the quality was unpredictable. There is a greater variety of merchandise, chosen to appeal to a broader target audience. High-end department stores such as Saks Fifth Avenue have sold products through this medium and designers have created exclusive lines for the networks.[32] In 1996, the fashion director of QVC said that clothing accounted for 25 percent of the network's sales.[33] Competitor HSN, having experimented with recognized clothing brands, commented, "We've been trying to get back to our customer, the customer that we know. We're selling lots of denim, lots of embellishment." The vice president for ready-to-wear and fashion accessories added that the collections created exclusively for them by U.S. designers were selling well.[34] HSN, which has two channels with a broad merchandise mix, also has a 24-hour jewelry channel, America's Jewelry Store. QVC's Q2 channel targets a younger, more upscale audience with a mix of merchandise.

Table 16.5 (p. 400) presents a thumbnail sketch of the two largest networks, including some data on their product lines and audience composition. It also shows combined sales for the two largest networks at more than $2.5 billion in 1995.

THE FORMAT OF HOME SHOPPING CHANNELS

The programming on the home shopping networks is predominately live, although there are occasional taped segments. Programming is divided into 30- and 60-minute segments, just like entertainment programming. There are a few longer regularly scheduled segments, such as the QVC "Sampler Hour." The networks also run special programming. Referring to his larger competitors, Mark Payne, chief financial officer of third-ranked ValueVision, com-

---

[30]Tim Allis, "Cable's Home Shopping Network Holds This Truth to Be Self-Evident: No American Should Pay Retail," *People,* 11 August 1986, 107; www.qvc.com, 27 August 1997.

[31]"Shopping by Television," *Consumer Reports,* January 1995, 8.

[32]Ibid.

[33]Sharon Edelson, "HSN, QVC: Another Fine-Tuning," *Women's Wear Daily,* 16 October 1996, 12.

[34]Ibid.

	QVC Network	Home Shopping Network
	TABLE 16.5 HSN/QVC Snapshot	
Annual sales	$1,600,000,000 (FY 2/1/95–1/31/96)	$1,019,000,000 (FY 1/1/95–12/31/95)
Number of homes reached	55 million U.S. 5 million international	69 million U.S.
Number of active customers	12 million	5 million
Percent of repeat customers	60	69
Number of calls per day	192,000	158,000
Average number of packages shipped a day	130,000	58,000
Merchandise mix	Jewelry 35% Home and lifestyle 45% Apparel accessories 20% Other 10%	Jewelry 41% Hardgoods 34% Softgoods 14% Cosmetics 10%

Source: Data from NIMA Fact Book, 1996. From *Direct Marketing Association's Statistical Fact Book, 1997* (New York: Direct Marketing Association, 1997), 176. Reproduced with permission of the Direct Marketing Association, 1998.

ments, "When you're in 50 million homes you can put on lots of things with adequate success. . . . QVC did an hour of throw pillows."[35] Both of the major networks have experienced success with day-long specials featuring broad categories such as "Yukon Gold."

The regular segments are hosted by one or a pair of on-air personalities. Celebrity hosts are often featured: Vanna White selling shoes or Bobby Unser promoting an engine treatment. Joan Rivers sells a line of jewelry and collectibles she has designed based on her own collection of fine jewelry and Faberge eggs. In general, however, the hosts are television professionals who have become quite skilled at exploiting the capabilities of the medium. The on-air personalities have become well known to, and extremely popular with, their loyal viewing audiences.

Some shows are primarily a presentation of one product after another with air time allotted in proportion to expected or demonstrated sales. To vary the format, the developer of the featured product or the author of the book often joins the host to discuss his or her product. Sometimes the format resembles a talk show, but generally it is a straightforward sales pitch, enlivened by demonstrations and lively chatter. Audience call-in has also become a major feature of many program segments, with customers providing testimonials about their enjoyment of the medium and satisfaction with the products. The networks maintain that testimonials are unsolicited and spontaneous or that callers are selected randomly to speak with the hostess. One caller recently bragged to HSN that she had bought 23 rings from the network![36] Some shows are filmed in front of a live audience. QVC built a special facility to accommodate more live-audience shows. It also contains a stage set called QVC Home, an actual house set up to allow filming to move from room to room according to the nature of the product being featured at a given time.[37]

---

[35]"TV or Not TV," *Inc.,* June 1994, 64.

[36]"Shopping by Television."

[37]Rob Williams, "QVC Revs Up with $100M Complex," *DRTV News,* 11 August 1997, 1.

Response to the featured product begins very quickly after it goes on the air. Behind the scenes, producers are able to monitor the rate of sales and inventory in real time. If the product is a hit and inventory is almost depleted, the host will be instructed to move on to the next product before the allotted time elapses. If the product is doing well and inventory is available, the time may be extended. If it is a real bomb, the producer can pull it off and move on to something with more potential.

Recently, the networks have begun to use a bank of monitors to feed this information to the on-air personalities. The monitors show graphs of real-time data for important parameters such as call volume, number of calls on hold, inventory, and so forth. A skilled presenter can use these data to modify the on-air sales pitch. For instance, if call volume falls while one product feature is being discussed, the host can switch to another feature. The data can also be used to trigger sales support graphics or even prerecorded videotapes, again depending on the reaction to the depiction of specific product characteristics. Incentives can also be introduced, based on real-time audience reaction. One journalist has observed, concerning the use of the databanks, that

> this information allows the producer of the segment to alter the amount of time allotted to a specific product based upon the data presented. Intuitively, higher sales rates should justify an increase in on-air time. However, this is not always the best case scenario. Inventory availability and, occasionally, inbound operator availability may also effect the choice of timing and sales pitch. I have observed offers that were so successful that all available operators were taking calls and hundreds of customers were on hold, the producer of the segment immediately switched to a more expensive product with a complex series of features to slow down incoming call volume until the operators could catch up.[38]

Although the technology involved in this latest refinement is not terribly sophisticated, it provides an opportunity to remove some causes of customer dissatisfaction and to maximize the sales effectiveness of the medium. At the same time, it takes real skill on the part of the production team and the on-air talent to make smooth, seamless transitions.

This vignette raises another interesting question: Who are the people calling in and waiting on the lines to order merchandise from the television shopping programs?

THE AUDIENCE FOR HOME SHOPPING CHANNELS

The original home shopping channel audience was perceived as being somewhat downscale. After all, the initial merchandise was primarily factory overruns and discontinued items. Both QVC and HSN have worked to upgrade their audience to a younger, more affluent one as well as to attract males.

OTHER HOME SHOPPING CHANNEL DEVELOPMENTS

Both QVC and HSN continue to extend their reach in a number of ways, including the Internet and international expansion.

Internet Shopping

Both of the major channels have established on-line retailing operations. The QVC site offers more than 20,000 products similar to those offered on TV, including jewelry, home office supplies, and furniture. Kitchen items make up the best-selling category on the Web. QVC states that, in late 1996, it was averaging more than 100,000 hits per day and had an

---

[38]David J. Katz, "On-Air Databanks," *DM News Home Shopping Supplement,* 19 May 1997, 14.

average order size in excess of $100, which is higher than from television. The Internet Shopping Network (ISN) is a wholly owned subsidiary of HSN that focuses on computers, software, and computer supplies. HSN reports 30,000 to 40,000 hits per day and revenue of about $1 million per month. In both cases, Internet sales are only a small fraction of television sales.[39] Little is known about the demographics of Web shoppers on either site, but it seems likely that they are quite different from their television customers.

International Expansion

Both major shopping channels have expanded into other countries. HSN operates in Germany in an alliance with GmbH & Co. The channel is called "HOT." It broadcasts 24 hours a day, 12 of which are live. It reached 8.3 million households in Germany and Austria in 1997. In Japan, HSN has partial ownership of the Tokyo-based Shop Channel. This channel also broadcasts 24 hours a day, but only 18 hours of live programming per week. In early 1997 this channel was reaching 845,000 Japanese households.[40] QVC has a joint venture with BskyB, which reaches four million households in the United Kingdom with 17 hours of live programming seven days a week.[41]

Direct-Response Radio

The use of radio as a direct-response or support medium bears many similarities to the use of television. Radio's special ability to reach targeted groups of people as they pursue many aspects of their daily lives has made it a useful direct-response medium from its inception.

EARLY DIRECT-RESPONSE RADIO

One author describes an early direct-response radio operation as follows:

> Back in the wonder years of radio, in the late 1930s, the 1940s, and early 1950s, one of the most popular direct-response ads running over WCKY in Cincinnati peddled a lamp shade impregnated with insecticide. When the lamp was turned on, the announcer promised, the heat would activate the insecticide and kill all the bugs in the room. . . .
>
> WCKY was one of several 50,000 kilowatt, clear-channel stations which, since many stations were required to go off the air at sundown, were able to "skyway" their signals at night over as many as 30 states. L. B. Wilson of WCKY was one of the most colorful station managers. At one time, he was said to have 16 to 18 people in the mailroom just filling orders for products that included baby chicks and a very popular plastic statue of Jesus. Stories of closets full of "crystal-like" table cigarette lighters or leftover "collapsible" hula hoops were common station gossip through the years.[42]

Radio and the sophistication of its audience have changed a great deal since those early days. One practical difference is that stations no longer perform the fulfillment function.

---

[39]"Cable TV Shopping Networks Face Online Retailing Realities," *Electronic Marketplace Report,* 1 October 1996.

[40]HSN 10K Filing, www.sec.gov, 14 April 1997.

[41]QVC Corporate Facts, www.qvc.com, 27 August 1997.

[42]Terry Considine Williams, "Will Direct Response Radio Return to the Golden Ad Days?" *Direct Marketing* (October 1986): 50–52.

Marketers who do not have fulfillment capabilities hire independent fulfillment specialists to handle responses from their radio advertisements. An even more important change is that radio has lost its status as the only mass medium capable of attracting a large national audience with broad-appeal programming. The days of long-running situation comedies, dramas, and variety shows on the radio are gone forever. Those formats are now almost exclusively the province of television. With the widespread adoption of television in the 1950s, radio evolved into a low-reach, high-frequency medium that offers its own unique advantages to the direct marketer.

RADIO TODAY

At present there are as many as 10,000 radio stations selling commercial airtime in the United States.[43] According to the DMA, radio attracted $5.1 billion in direct-response advertising revenue in 1997, split about evenly between consumer and business markets. Of this, $3.5 billion was spent on lead generation in this medium, $1 billion was allocated to direct sales spots, and the remainder to retail traffic generation. The 3.5-to-1 ratio for lead generation to direct sales advertising dollars is considerably higher than the roughly 2-to-1 ratio for all direct-response media combined. Direct-response sales attributed to radio in 1996, when total direct marketing advertising revenue was $4.7 billion, were $31.8 billion. Direct-response advertising accounted for more than one-third of radio advertising revenues in that year.[44] In spite of the perceptions of many people that radio is not a good direct-response medium because listeners are often engaged in other activities while they are tuned in to the radio, clearly the medium is an important one for direct marketers.

The reasons that radio is effective in producing sales and leads as well as attracting traffic to retail locations include

- *Cost efficiency*. Radio is a local medium and major markets are extremely competitive, keeping rates in check. In addition, it is quite inexpensive to prepare and produce radio advertising, compared to other media.
- *Excellent targeting*. Part of the competitiveness of radio markets is the proliferation of stations appealing to well-defined target markets by age, listening preference, ethnic background, and language. The ability to selectively target adds to the cost efficiency of radio.
- *Availability*. Radio can be accessed at times and places where other media are not readily available.
- *Flexibility*. It is often possible to place and withdraw radio spots on short notice, and the script can be changed almost immediately to reflect current developments.
- *Involvement*. Radio is a local medium that attracts and involves its audience.

THE RADIO AUDIENCE

The Radio Advertising Bureau (RAB) data for 1996 indicate that 77 percent of all consumers listened to radio every day, and fully 95 percent listened each week. Persons over age 12 listened more than three hours a day during the week and five and three-quarters hours each

---

[43]Gary Kretchmer, "The Right Ingredients for Successful Radio," www.smartbiz.com, 27 August 1997.

[44]DMA Report, "Economic Impact: U.S. Direct Marketing Today, 1996," www.dma.org, 14 September 1997.

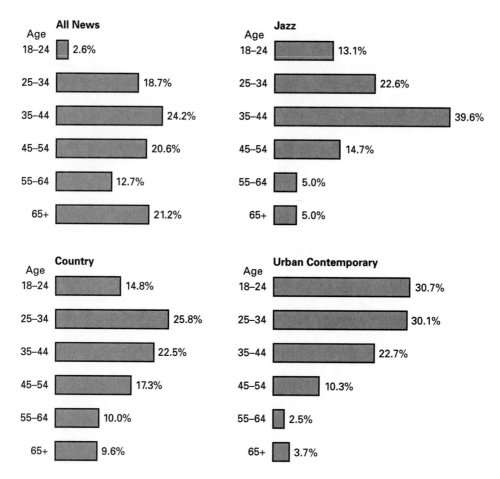

FIGURE 16.3 Listenership by Age of Selected Radio Formats

Source: *Radio Marketing Guide & Fact Book for Advertisers, 1996.* Reprinted with permission of the Radio Advertising Bureau.

weekend day. The RAB data also show more than 80 percent of all adults listen to the car radio each day.[45]

Perhaps even more important to an understanding of radio listenership is the recognition that there are as many as 20 identifiable radio formats in the United States today.[46] Each format appeals to an identifiable target audience with a unique profile that can be used by the direct marketer to target the sales message. Figure 16.3 shows four profiles from a large number to show how audience composition differs between format. Keep in mind two things as you examine this data. One is that it is national data and local profiles for the same format may differ slightly. The second is that for some stations, especially those for which drive time listenership is very high, profiles may differ by daypart (time of day).

---

[45]www.rab.com, 12 September 1997.

[46]Kretchmer, "Right Ingredients for Successful Radio," 3.

When to Use Direct-Response Radio

Although radio is an electronic medium like television, the requirements for successful direct-response radio are quite different from those for DRTV.[47] For one thing, the successful use of radio does not require a product with broad mass appeal. Products that serve niche markets can be ideal candidates if customer characteristics have a good match with the profile of a particular format. Second, response to radio spots does not usually begin immediately, as it does with DRTV. It may require two or three exposures for any given individual to be convinced to respond and to be in a place to conveniently do so. That means that a great deal of frequency is needed to reach a specified audience.

The requirements for successful direct-response radio include

- *A suitable product,* preferably one that can be explained without visual demonstration. A product category with which the listener is familiar may still work without demonstration, however.
- *A simple offer.* This is why the statistics show so much lead generation on radio. If a product or the overall offer really requires more than 60 seconds of explanation to give listeners a clear and compelling reason to buy, a lead generation spot, featuring a 1-800 number, will be more successful. This presents a particular problem for product categories such as financial services and medicines, where disclosure requirements are important. These categories do not lend themselves well to radio sales, although a two-step process may be used.
- *Good creative* that exploits the strengths of radio. A good script, with a strong lead-in, strong offer, copy that stresses benefits, and a clear call to action, is required (see Figure 16.4 for an analysis of a script). In addition, Kretchmer says,

when you play to the intimate, one-on-one qualities of radio and the loyalty people have to their favorite radio stations, then your creative will go the extra mile for you. And it doesn't take expensive, highly-produced commercials to go the distance. Just make sure your approach is informational and personal, with copy crafted for the spoken word and repetition of the most important points. Without visuals, radio can often paint a much more dramatic and convincing picture than other media.

- *Pacing* is another important issue. If you try to cram too much information into too brief a time, the delivery will become very fast and hard to comprehend. "Normal, conversationally paced commercials with pauses will be understood and comprehended better than a spot that becomes a race with time."

Finally, Kretchmer warns that humor does not usually work in direct-response radio spots. Presumably, the humor distracts from the sales message.

RECENT DEVELOPMENTS IN DIRECT-RESPONSE RADIO

On-Line Experiments

Estimates of how many U.S. radio stations have Web sites vary greatly, but it is clear that most stations in major markets are experimenting with this new medium. Finding out how the Internet can support audience acquisition and the experience of listeners has not been easy, though. Beyond the obvious—programming schedules, rate cards, and job post-

---

[47]This section is based on Kretchmer, "Right Ingredients for Successful Radio."

Can you recognize your body's danger signals? Which of those aches, pains, or changes in your body should your doctor know about at once? With Better Homes and Gardens' FAMILY MEDICAL GUIDE in your home, you'll always have practical, easy-to-understand health and first-aid information on hand—when you need it. When you're confused . . . when you're frightened . . . when there's a medical emergency. Written by 29 of America's most prominent physicians, the FAMILY MEDICAL GUIDE gives you frank advice on hundreds of health problems—on female disorders, irregular heartbeat, loss of vigor, arthritis, strokes, cancer, allergies, and much, much more. It's profusely illustrated and contains more than 2,000 clear, simple explanations of often-confusing medical terms. Yes, you owe it to yourself and your family to examine Better Homes and Gardens' FAMILY MEDICAL GUIDE and right now you can do just that—absolutely free.

The opening attracts attention and excites interest in the minds of the target market.

An important benefit is promised early in the script.

The participation of experts add credibility.

Considerable detail is given about the attributes and benefits of the product.

In fact, to encourage you to take advantage of this no-obligation opportunity you'll receive from Better Homes and Gardens not one but two FREE gifts . . . an amazing see-through Atlas of the Human Body and Better Homes and Gardens' EAT AND STAY SLIM cookbook.

A free trial is offered as one way to reduce perceived risk.

Two free gifts are offered as incentives.

All you need do is call toll-free, 800-228-2200 and ask to have a copy of the FAMILY MEDICAL GUIDE sent to you. Then, if you agree the FAMILY MEDICAL GUIDE is a book that will prove its great value in your home time and time again, you may pay the full and complete price of $16.95 plus $1.45 postage and handling in four easy monthly payments. Four easy payments of only $4.60 each—which covers all costs. Or return it within 14 days and not owe a single penny. But no matter what you decide, the two gifts from Better Homes and Gardens are yours—free . . . just for examining the MEDICAL GUIDE! So act now. Operators are standing by! Call 800-228-2200, today. Better Homes and Gardens pays for the call, 800-228-2200 . . . call today!

The toll-free number is mentioned well before the end of the script to alert listeners to the fact that this is a direct-response ad.

Since the objective of this ad is to close a sale, the terms of the offer must be completely spelled out.

The call to action gives specific instructions on how to take action. The toll-free number is repeated two more times.

The ending is another call to action.

FIGURE 16.4 Analysis of a Direct-Response Radio Script

ings, for example—a wide variety of content can be observed on station Web sites. It ranges from background on on-air personalities and featured performers to concert schedules to event promotion. As a general rule, however, the content of sites does not seem to be very good. Worse, it is not at all clear that many stations are benefiting from the investment in a Web site. One solution may be to use industry-sponsored sites such as Electric Village and Rock Daily.

Exploiting the Widespread Use of Cell Phones

One of the difficulties that has always been associated with direct-response radio is that listeners in automobiles or other locations outside their homes or offices could not readily respond. Cellular telephones, either hand-held or in automobiles, obviously offer a solution to this problem. Industry data indicate that 85 percent of all cellular phone calls are made from automobiles and that 65 percent of them are personal, not business, calls. However, because cellular rates are relatively high, response to radio spots from cell phones does not appear to have grown rapidly. A solution is to provide cellular 1-800 numbers, which require advertisers to pay all charges. Although this service is in its infancy, according to a supplier called Radio 2000,

> The service is effective for decisions that pertain to using a car, such as a new car lease or purchase, automotive services, or food deliveries. For example, . . . it's late and a person is driving home from work and hears an ad for pizza delivery. He dials *800 and has the pizza arrive at his house shortly after he does.

No further number is required because the calls all go to a center where a "concierge" answers and either collects the necessary information or reroutes the call directly to the advertiser.[48] No data are available yet on this type of service, but it represents an innovative solution to a vexing direct marketing problem.

Summary

Television and radio are not new media to the direct-response marketer, but both have gained considerably in use and credibility in recent years. Both continue to be successful in selling a wide variety of products, and television, especially, has evolved important new formats—the infomercial and the home shopping channel. The direct marketer's approach to using broadcast media is more structured than that of the general marketer. The direct marketer finds the same opportunity to test, refine, and measure the effectiveness of broadcast commercials that exists in the other direct marketing media. These electronic media also provide interesting opportunities to integrate promotional activities with newer media, including the Internet.

Discussion Questions and Exercises

1. What are the similarities and differences between general and direct-response advertising on television? On radio?

---

[48]Cathy Asato, "Partnership Targets Cell-Phone Users to Boost Radio Direct Response Ads," *DM News,* 8 September 1997, 4.

2. What are the major considerations when buying direct-response television time? Direct-response radio time?

3. The formularized approach described in this chapter for direct-response television spots and infomercials unnecessarily hinders creativity in their development. Comment.

4. What are the similarities and differences in the audiences for DRTV spots, infomercials, and home shopping channels?

5. Watch an infomercial all the way through and a program segment on a homeshopping channel. Be prepared to discuss your observations.

Suggested Readings

Arlen, Gary. "DRTV: Beyond the Fringe!" *Marketing Tools* (October 1997): 37–42.

Brady, Frank R., and J. Angel Vasquez. *Direct Response Television*. Lincolnwood, IL: NTC Business Books, 1995.

Cannella, Frank. *Infomercial Insights*. Burlington, WI: Cannella Response Television, 1995.

Eicoff, Al. *Direct Marketing through Broadcast Media*. Lincolnwood, IL: NTC Business Books, 1995.

Hawthorne, Timothy R. *The Complete Guide to Infomercial Marketing*. Lincolnwood, IL: NTC Business Books, 1997.

CHAPTER 17

Interactive Media

Looking into the future is, to put it mildly, an imprecise science. Still, let's consider one view of what the living room of the average consumer might look like in a few years:

Walk into the living room of 2007, and at first glance it may not look that different from Archie Bunker's two-chairs-and-a-box setup.

But in 2007, the box with a screen isn't just a TV, it's a teledevice. It's an Internet-connected PC, a videophone, an answering machine, and a stereo. It's also the interface to your household network server, which sets the thermostat for maximum energy efficiency, turns on a room's lights whenever someone enters, monitors the security alarm, and alerts you at work when your kids come home from school.

The Internet is the main connection between your home and the outside world, replacing even the telephone. "It's my prediction that Americans will live a Web lifestyle within a decade," said Microsoft chairman Bill Gates, way back in 1997. Consumers will "simply have incorporated the Web into everything they do."

There are Web browsers throughout your house, including one on the display attached to your refrigerator. You open the fridge and notice you're out of milk, so you browse the grocery store site right there for the items you need, and then send off your request for a delivery.

Every family member has a <u>smart card</u> containing their preferences for the household network. Once you've checked your email while driving your <u>network vehicle</u> home from work, you grab your personal card and pop it into the teledevice. A video server then compiles your nightly news broadcast based on your interests: all international news, anything about advances in cancer treatment, any sports stories involving your favorite team, but no weather or features about animals. Knowing you want to sit down and relax, your smart card has already set the thermostat to your preferred temperature, adjusted your favorite chair to the most comfortable position, and turned on the nearest reading lamp.

If you don't have your smart card handy, you simply talk to the teledevice, which recognizes your voice and follows your commands. The living room of 2007 is all about letting you communicate in a personal way with the electronic devices you probably already have, a TV and a Web-connected PC.[1]

Whether this vision does or does not come true, it is all technologically feasible. Direct marketers—along with many other businesses, organizations, and individuals—are exploring the fringes of this brave new world.[2] They are beginning to make discoveries about what works and what doesn't—and how to measure it.

Although what works on the Internet does have something to do with technology, it seems to have more to do, however, with who is using it and for what purposes.

The Demographics of the Internet

Many groups are interested in how many people are on the Internet and how fast that number will grow. There seem to be as many different numbers as there are forecasters. Internet market research company eMarketer (formerly e-land) looked at several published sources and made a conservative middle-of-the-road forecast of 19 million users worldwide by the end of 1996 and 142 million by the year 2000. Growth is occurring rapidly throughout the world, but e-land believes that the United States will still yield half the users, about 71 million, in 2000. Figure 17.1 shows the proportion of Internet users by geographic region. eMarketer finds that Internet infrastructure is least well developed in Asia, and that Finland is the "most wired" country, with a server for every 25 people. The United States comes in second with a server for every 50 people.[3] The increasing diversity of the Web is also illustrated by the fact that in 1997 AltaVista, the major purveyor of Web content for the commercial search engines, reported that 50 percent of its page returns requested a language other than English.[4]

One detailed study of Internet use comes from FIND/SVP. They studied 1,000 users and an equal number of nonusers in the United States and projected 31.1 million adults using the Web in mid-1997. More than 9 million have tried it, but are not currently users, presumably because they found it difficult or unproductive. An additional 55 million more were poised to become users, again presumably because they owned or plan to own a personal

---

[1]"The Living Room of 2007," www.cnet.com, 11 December 1997.

[2]There are media other than the Internet that have interactive characteristics, especially the CD-ROM. In this chapter we concentrate on the Internet, but bear in mind that the basic principles discussed can be applied to any interactive medium.

[3]www.e-land.com, 1 January 1998.

[4]Dana L. Tower et al., "The Internet in 1998," www.forrester.com, November 1997.

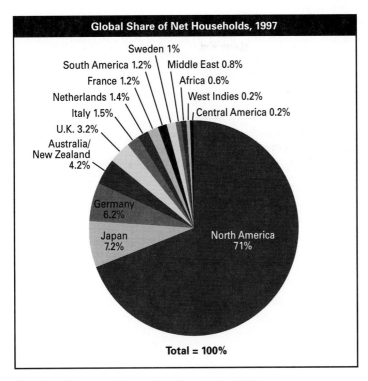

FIGURE 17.1 Global Share of Net Households, 1997

Source: Used with permission of eMarketer.

computer. On the other hand, 41 percent of respondents who do not use the Internet perceive no use for it. Specific findings included

- Almost half the respondents reported using the Web daily. Sixty percent of business users indicated that they used the Web daily.
- 27 percent reported they had made a purchase on-line during the past 12 months.
- 30 percent said they were likely to begin on-line banking in the next 12 months.
- An increasing proportion of users in 1997, as compared to 1995, say their Internet use is decreasing the time spent with other media.[5]

Marketers are interested in the profile of Internet users, and there is considerable agreement on the general outline of that profile and the directions in which it is moving:

- Users are relatively young, with a majority being younger than age 44 or even 34, depending on the study.
  - College students and teenagers comprise the largest age segment of Internet users, estimated to be as great as one-third of all users.
    - They also spend the most time on-line—4.9 hours per week.
    - The majority of users spend less than 3 hours each week on-line.

[5]"The 1997 American Internet User Survey," www.findsvp.com, 19 November 1997; "Highlights from FIND/SVP's 1997 American Internet User Survey," *Marketing Tools* (July 1997): 11.

- More males than females are users, but female usage is growing faster.
- Users are well-educated, with more than 70 percent having at least some college education.
- Half or more have household incomes in excess of $50,000.
- They are equally likely to be married or single.
- More than 60 percent are employed in white-collar occupations.
- The most frequent Internet activities are
  - getting information (76 percent)
  - sending and receiving e-mail (58 percent)
  - reading news about current events (43 percent)
  - getting product information (36 percent)
- In another study only 10 percent reported having bought something. Most frequently purchased items were
  - software
  - clothing
  - books
  - computer hardware
  - CDs
  - flowers
  - hotel reservations
- Another survey found that 25 percent of Internet users have purchased something on-line, although only 1 percent say they do so frequently.
  - On-line buyers were older, with 42 percent of respondents age 65 and older having purchased and 39 percent of those ages 50 to 64.
  - Younger respondents tended to make more use of the Internet for entertainment, including games and discussion forums. Of the women surveyed, 21 percent said they played games often compared to 9 percent of the men.[6]

Which Marketers Are Successful on the Web

Since the mid-1990s there has been a rush, particularly on the part of firms in the United States, to be on the Web, often without a strong sense of what they intended to accomplish there. The good reason for doing this appeared to be to experiment and to learn, so the company would be ready when use of the Web increased to the point that profitable operations were possible. A less good reason has often been stated as something such as "our competitors are there so we must be also."

That sort of reasoning will rapidly become a thing of the past as managers demand accountability of their Internet marketing expenditures, just as they demand it of other marketing communications activities. Forrester Research says there are three basic Web advertising approaches—build a *destination site* that users will visit again and again; create a *micro*

---

[6]"Internet Statistics," http://research.chilton.net, 2 October 1997; "Net User Demographics," www.e-land.com, 1 January 1998; "As College Marketing Hits the Web, Jupiter Predicts Billion-Dollar Turf War," www.jupiter.com, 19 September 1997; "A Census in Cyberspace," *Business Week,* 5 May 1997, 84.

site, a small set of brand pages hosted by a content provider or network; or simply use *banner ads* (to be discussed later in this chapter). According to Forrester, advertisers need to ask

1. *Can it be sold on-line?* Products that can be sold on-line and shipped economically or delivered digitally—such as music, tickets, books, software, and mutual funds—can use a destination site to support everything from brand awareness and consideration through post-sales support. But if the Net doesn't enable your company to offer a product faster, cheaper, or better, rule out a destination site.

2. *Is it a considered purchase?* Sellers of complex products like computers, cars, and industrial coatings can use a Web site to squeeze costs, allowing prospects to check specifications, configure their purchase, and get product support on-line. . . . But if your customers are more likely to ask their neighbors than you about your product, you don't need a Web site.[7]

Products that fit into each of four quadrants based on these two considerations are shown in Figure 17.2.

Experts tend to agree that most consumer packaged goods and relatively undifferentiated retailers such as gas stations and convenience stores have little use for a Web site and would, in fact, be better off putting their money into traditional mass media advertising. In

FIGURE 17.2 Who Should Build What

Source: Reproduced with permission of Forrester Research, Inc.

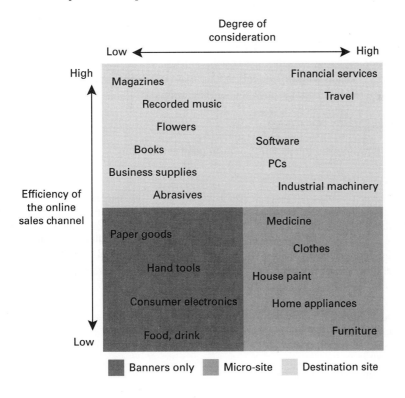

[7]Bill Doyle, Mary A. Modahl, and Ben Abbott, "What Advertising Works," www.forrester.com, 1 March 1997.

chapter 11 we pointed out that the bulk of Internet commerce is expected to take place in business markets. Marketers of consumer goods and services may find a profitable new channel or profitable new markets on the Web. On the other hand, they may find a bottomless sinkhole for their promotional dollars. It all depends on how well suited their activities are for the Web and how well they execute their site.

How Marketers Are Using the Web

It is clear that it is no longer enough to simply have a presence on the Web. Organizations must have a clear strategy that is based on customer needs and behaviors and integrated into the overall communications and marketing strategies of the firm. The Web strategy must also be based on a clear understanding of what the medium can do especially well. The Web's special capabilities all center around the inherently interactive nature of the medium. Direct marketers can make good use of this capability to build and enhance databases. They may also, in time, find that it has become a major forum for transactions.

In a generic sense, there appear to be three primary marketing activities that are well suited to the Web:

- making information available to prospective customers
- providing customer support and service
- enabling transactions

Before we examine marketing activities in each of these areas in detail, we need a framework for thinking about how the Web should be used. We have models such as the hierarchy of effects and various learning models that apply to traditional mass media advertising; what is needed is a model that takes into account the unique characteristics of the Web.

THE WEB MARKETING PROCESS

In introducing their model, the authors, consultants at McKinsey & Company, refer to research that shows

> that many consumer marketers approach interactive media in the same way they might approach traditional media like television, magazines, or even direct marketing channels. Yet there are fundamental differences between the two. For example, traditional media involves one-way communication from the marketer to the customer, while interactive media allows marketers to establish a dialogue. Further, marketing through traditional media takes place in a mass-market environment, while interactive media allows marketers to reach [and interact with] individual consumers.[8]

Their model (Figure 17.3) is built around five elements that are essential for successful digital marketing. It asserts that marketers must

- *attract* users
- *engage* their interest and participation

---

[8]Alexa Kierzkowski, Shayne McQuade, Robert Waitman, and Michael Zeisser, "Marketing to the Digital Consumer," *McKinsey Quarterly* 3 (1996): 12.

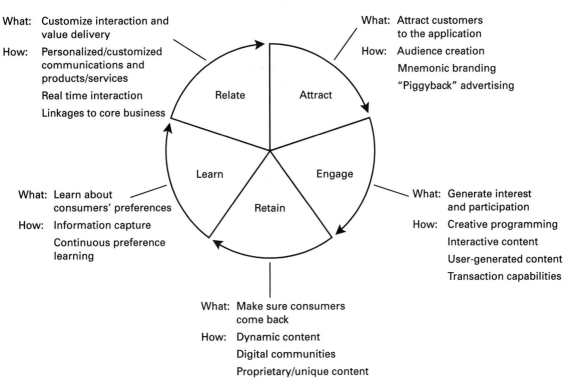

What: Customize interaction and value delivery

How: Personalized/customized communications and products/services

Real time interaction

Linkages to core business

What: Attract customers to the application

How: Audience creation

Mnemonic branding

"Piggyback" advertising

Relate Attract

Learn Engage

Retain

What: Learn about consumers' preferences

How: Information capture

Continuous preference learning

What: Generate interest and participation

How: Creative programming

Interactive content

User-generated content

Transaction capabilities

What: Make sure consumers come back

How: Dynamic content

Digital communities

Proprietary/unique content

FIGURE 17.3 Digital Marketing Framework and Levers

Source: Alexa Kierzkowski, Shayne McQuade, Robert Waitman, and Michael Zeisser, "Marketing to the Digital Consumer," *McKinsey Quarterly* 3 (1996): 12. Used with permission of McKinsey & Co.

- *retain* users, ensuring that they return to an application
- *learn* about user preferences
- *relate* to them with customized, personalized approaches that add value to the interaction

The implication is that, like successful marketing in any other medium, marketing on the Web is a process in which the marketer moves a prospect through a series of stages with the objective of creating a long-term loyal customer. The first step is to attract visitors to the site.

Attract Users to the Site

Unlike mass media, which is able to expose an existing set of viewers, readers, listeners to an ad, Web sites must draw visitors to them. To put it another way, consumers must take the initiative to visit a specific site. Among the hundreds of thousands of sites that exist, how does a marketer attract consumers? There are a number of ways:

- Some marketers come onto the Web with an already *well-known brand name*—Nike or Pepsi, for example. Surfers should be more prone to visit the site of a "favorite friend" than one of an unknown. If, however, the brand name is already associated with direct response—say, L.L. Bean or 1-800-Flowers—they may be perceived as having a particular affinity with the new interactive medium.

- Marketers are well advised to *advertise their URL* (universal record locator) in all their other communications—everything from business cards to sales support material, and certainly all media advertising. Consider this incremental and virtually free advertising. Do not, however, consider it sufficient.

- Marketers who rely heavily on their Web sites may use *advertising campaigns* in broadcast and print media to create user awareness of the site. Yahoo!, as the first widely available search engine, used advertising with some apparent success. Other search engines also continue to advertise extensively, especially in computer-related publications. It is not clear whether this later "brand" advertising is as effective as Yahoo!'s initial advertising, which was informing about a new concept instead of merely trying to create preference for one of several search engines, all of which are equally accessible.

Creating awareness is only a first step; how does the marketer persuade the viewer, reader, or listener to leave that medium, fire up his or her browser, and visit the site?

- Direct marketers know that it requires *an offer of some kind* to compel prospects to take action. The offer may simply be superb content. Archives of highly useful material, attractive games, an opportunity to interact with like-minded people—these are some of the options. (Consider for a moment: Will the same features attract business users as consumers? Probably not.)

However, in this age of intense competition for visitor "eyeballs," a known brand name or the promise of exceptional content alone may not be enough. *Incentives* may be necessary. There are contests and sweepstakes all over the Internet. This is an obvious invitation for Web surfers to visit the site and register. One incentive program offers frequent flier miles to visitors who purchase, register for an on-line service, or complete an electronic survey. Part of the objective here is to attract consumers with upscale demographics. Other programs offer various kinds of points or "cybercurrency," which can be converted into gift certificates or redeemed for merchandise. One well-known promotional program, CyberGold, offers small amounts of cash as an incentive.[9] The issue here is one long familiar to direct marketers—are people responding because they are interested in the product or just to get the incentive? Not much is known in a general sense about the demographics of people who respond to incentives on the Internet, but individual marketers need to exercise the usual caution to be sure they are attracting their target market. Web marketers should be able to do this with relative ease compared to promotional programs in the mass media. Web activities produce an instant database of highly useful facts about visitor behavior, which we examine at several points in this chapter.

If you stop to think about it, though, these promotional approaches—a strong brand, a corporate tag line, advertising campaigns, or marketing programs that include incentives—are very traditional. Marketers have been doing these things pretty much since we coined the term *marketing*! None of them makes use of the unique ability of the Internet to promote interaction.

- At one level, which is probably better termed *connectivity* instead of *interaction,* there is the ability to link directly to other sites. In content, this is done with "hot links," which transfer the user directly to another site with related content. In advertising, it is "banners," which invite the viewer to click and move to promotional content on another site. We discuss banner advertising in detail later in this chapter.

---

[9]"Attracting Consumers with Trinkets," *Internet World* (January 1998): 22.

- At another level, there is the ability of the user to interact with the site—to answer questions about needs and preferences or to play a game. We provide examples of this type of interaction in the next section when we talk about engaging the visitor.

- Still another type of interaction is the ability the Internet has to facilitate communication between users through chat rooms and discussion groups. Marketing researchers are taking advantage of this capability by learning how to conduct focus groups on the Web.

- At a very high level there is a kind of interactivity that the user may not even recognize. That occurs when, based on information about the individual user, content or advertising is "pushed" directly to that single person.

The highly interactive nature of the Web also means that word of mouth travels like wildfire in the cybercommunity:

Amazon.com was founded in 1994 by Wall Street investment strategist Jeffrey Bezos. He realized that "to sell anything on a medium as emotionally cold as the Internet, he would have to offer a product that was so superior that customers would brave the obstacles of the technology to get it.

The key, Bezos decided, was to sell products in so many formats that no single place could offer them all. He drew up a list of 20 possibilities, including magazines and PC hardware and software. But he settled on his early love: books. Even the biggest physical bookstore can't purvey more than a fraction of the 50,000 books printed every year. But a virtual bookstore could, in theory, offer every book in print. Bezos decided to call his bookstore Amazon—a mighty river of text." By 1997 it offered over 2.5 million titles.[10]

While Bezos describes the three main attractions of the site as "selection, selection, selection," it also typically offers books at a 10 to 40% discount on the retail selling price.

Convinced that booksellers with known brand names like Barnes & Noble and Borders would set up Web sites and find it relatively easy to attract people, Bezos ploughed a substantial portion of revenues into advertising from the beginning. Amazon.com ads appeared in everything from *Slate* (Microsoft's online magazine) to the *New York Times Book Review.* However, the success of amazon.com in attracting buyers to the site must be attributed in part to the peculiar powers of the Web. "'In our business plan, we projected a 10-times impact from word of mouth,' according to Bezos, meaning one satisfied customer's experience would influence ten other people. Instead, he estimates that the site gets a 100-times impact."[11]

By 1997 Amazon.com was attracting 80,000 visitors a day[12] and the site generated sales of $16 million in the first quarter of 1997 alone. Jeff Bezos's early Web vision had created a lead that would be difficult for competitors to overcome.[13]

So, the marketer has numerous options to consider when deciding how to attract users to the Web site. Most marketers will probably use a combination of tactics. What is important, however, it that they break free of conventional mass media approaches and use tactics best suited to the unique nature of the Internet.

Having coaxed visitors to the site, the marketer must then engage them in the content of the site, involving them in pursuits that are interesting and satisfying.

---

[10]Charles C. Mann, "Volume Business," *Inc. Tech,* no. 2 (1997): 56.

[11]Evan I. Schwartz, *Webonomics* (New York: Broadway Books, 1997), 100.

[12]Mann, "Volume Business."

[13]Adapted from Mann, "Volume Business," 54–61; Schwartz, *Webonomics,* 98–101; Mark Cuban, "Having a Big Name Is Not Everything," cma.zdnet.com, 2 January 1998.

Engage Visitors in the Content of the Site

Although there are numerous sports-related sites on the Web, ESPN SportsZone (www.espn.sportszone.com) is invariably highly rated.[14] Its array of content is mind-boggling—from the National Hockey League to women's college basketball to soccer to auto racing to health and fitness and special events such as the Olympics. The site provides a great deal more than stats on every sport imaginable. It contains current news on sports-related topics. It has information about television coverage of sporting events. It has chat rooms, many of which are hosted by well-known personalities, and it has polls ("Who do you think will be the next coach of the Dallas Cowboys?" Of the 39,169 responses, 44.8 percent voted for George Seifert) as well as games (anyone for Fantasy Basketball?) and, of course, a ZoneStore. The sports enthusiast is invited to make SportsZone his or her start-up page. The visitor is also invited to subscribe to *ESPN—The Magazine* with the incentive being a free issue. All this—and much, much more—is available free.

The premium service offered by this is called ScoreTracker. In addition to customizing the information on the site, it allows the subscriber to access cybercasts of NBA basketball, which remain available for 48 hours after the game was played. The subscriber can either watch the entire game or fast forward to a specific portion.

According to on-site promotion, SportsZone is:

> the ultimate custom scoreboard from the people who brought you NFL Drive Charts, NBA Game Flows, big league Hit Charts, *and more.*
>
> ScoreTracker is a powerful Java applet that gives you complete control over your own personal professional sports scoreboard. . . .
>
> **You get instant, real-time updates**
> Every pitch, every hoop, every handoff, you'll be there. ScoreTracker updates automatically. . . . Every 15 seconds if you're that kind of fan. . . .
>
> **You customize it**
> Bend ScoreTracker to meet your own demanding specifications. While other guys comb through extra stats, you get exactly what you want, when you want it. . . .
>
> **You get the whole story**
> ScoreTracker is not only your own, personalized, up-to-the second sports scoreboard. It's also your gateway to incredible SportsZone coverage of your favorite teams and their biggest games. Clock on a ScoreTracker score to get previews, schedules, continually updated game logs. If it's on SportsZone, ScoreTracker takes you there. . . .
>
> ScoreTracker runs in its own window, and updates every 15 seconds by default.[15] It continues to update as long as you have it running. If you leave it open overnight, it will display yesterday's scores and upload the new day's schedule and game updates. Leave it running all the time and you'll always have the latest scores for every game.[16]

To the casual visitor, somewhat bewildered by the vast quantity of content available on this site, it is not surprising that the real sports fanatic is willing to pay $4.95 per month for a premium service to help him make sense out of this abundance.

---

[14]"A Year of Stars," www.adnet.com, 2 January 1998.

[15]Among the many options, such as selecting a favorite team, sport, or college conference, the service allows the subscriber to update at 30-second, 1-minute, or 2-minute intervals.

[16]www.scores-espn.sportszone.com, 10 January 1998.

The Sony Web site (www.sony.com) also receives commendation from critics and repeat visits from users. The site describes itself as "Your Connection to Entertainment and Information about Electronics Products" and, among others, has sections on its electronics products, music, and movies. It has, however, become best known for its access to games. Sony PlayStation can be accessed from the corporate site as well as directly (www.playstation.com). It has recent releases of popular games that game aficionados find highly intriguing.

The Warner Brothers site (www.warnerbros.com) and the MTV site (www.mtv.com) were the top two music sites in 1997, according to Yahoo![17] Warner Brothers has an incredibly rich site, filled with information about its current television, movie, video, and music offerings. As might be expected of a company that has a chain of retail outlets, it also has an extensive on-line store. In the store, you can select by merchandise category (e.g., toys, or watches and jewelry) or by department (e.g., kids and baby), or by cartoon character (e.g., Bugs Bunny).

The MTV site is full of information about music and the people who make it. Somewhat unusual among large corporate sites, it has a local section containing music news in the viewer's area. This is an interactive site and its LiveLine section had an interesting cross-promotion in early 1998. A banner area carried the MTV logo and the message, "The Live Link Needs You. Come and do your part! Brought to you by Intel." When the visitor clicked on the link, it opened with a screen saying, "Welcome to the Live Link. Brought to you by Intel." Beside the message was one of the Intel "Bunny People" carrying a Pentium II banner as featured in Intel print and TV advertising. Consider for a moment the targeting that caused a manufacturer of computer operating system chips to buy sponsorship on a music site that appeals to adolescents and young adults.

These four sites are quite different in content but quite similar in two important ways. First, they have ever-changing content, which originates from their primary lines of business. Second, they all have a great deal for the visitor to do—chat with a member of a music group, play a game, get information about movie or video releases, or follow a favorite sports team. These activities, centered around entertainment of various types, provide compelling reasons for people to return to these sites on a frequent basis.

A feature that may lie on the boundary between engaging visitors and bringing them back to the site time after time is the ability to complete transactions on the site. Users may find it frustrating to look at attractive merchandise but not to be able to buy it. After all, when you are shopping in a store, do you want to be told that you can look but not touch, or that you certainly cannot purchase the product and take it home with you?

Chapter 11 mentioned that Cisco Systems allows purchasers of its networking products to arrange for FedEx shipping without ever leaving the Cisco Web site. This seems like a good idea, both as a convenience to customers, and to keep those customers from leaving "the store." After all, sometimes when you leave, you don't get around to going back.

A good example of using the unique capabilities of the Web that allow customers to do something in virtual reality more easily than they can in the physical world is Eddie Bauer's on-line furniture catalog. It encourages users to download a piece of 3-D software that permits them to design a room by putting furniture into it and moving the furniture around. When the customer is satisfied, he or she clicks on the product and links to the furniture mer-

---

[17]"Year on the Net 1997," *Yahoo! Internet Life,* www.yahoo.com, 2 January 1998.

chant's site, where the customer is presumably able to complete the transaction.[18] This is a wonderful example of adding value to the attempt to sell a product, in this case, furniture. However, quite a few items of technology (e.g., a sophisticated piece of software) and of marketing action (e.g., does the furniture retailer's Web site fulfill its part of the promise?) have to work—and have to work together—to make the customer's experience a satisfying one.

Retain Users by Ensuring That They Return to the Site

Continue with the store analogy for a moment. If you return to a store, and it is still featuring the same old, tired merchandise that it had the last time you visited, will you return again? Probably not. Retailers have long known that they must have fresh, exciting merchandise each time a shopper he returns to the store. Web marketers must learn the same lesson.

Warner Brothers, Sony, and MTV all have a continuing source of interesting, unique content from their movie and music business. What we learned in the previous section is that consumers will not simply visit a Web site just for promotions for new movies and CDs. They want the material packaged in intriguing and involving ways that enable them to interact with the content. Continuing to come up with new ways to package content from other sources will be one of the ongoing challenges of successful Web sites.

One way to keep the content fresh is to use visitors as a resource:

> Amazon.com has only a small staff of reviewers who generate editorial material for its pages. Instead of professional reviews, it provides an opportunity for readers and authors to comment on books. Not only does this generate free commentary, it is another way in which visitors can interact with the site.
>
> Booksellers have long featured the recommendations of the prestigious *New York Times Book Reviews* as part of their merchandising, and Amazon.com does this also. In addition, they feature Oprah Winfrey's personal picks, and it is said that a recommendation from Oprah can give sales a huge lift.[19]

Chat rooms and discussion groups are, of course, another way of furnishing visitor-generated content and providing a reason to return to a site over and over again.

Another technique that may encompass both the attraction and retention phases is to go, in effect, where the visitors are. This would be akin to locating a retail store in a high-traffic location, perhaps in a mall. On the Web, one equivalent of a physical mall is America Online (AOL). As the largest provider of on-line services, AOL had 10 million subscribers in late 1997, which qualifies it as a high-traffic location.[20] In 1997 both 1-800-Flowers and Amazon.com signed marketing agreements with AOL:[21]

> Under the terms of the agreement, amazon.com will be the exclusive bookseller on AOL.com and its NetFind search engine (Barnes & Noble already had an exclusive in the mall section of AOL). Revenue to AOL will be based on a flat fee plus commissions over a base level of sales.
>
> As part of the exclusive agreement Amazon received a permanent front screen button on the AOL home page that links the viewer to amazon.com. The agreement also provided

---

[18]Ken Magill, "Eddie Bauer Uses 3-D Graphics to Entice Online Consumers," *DM News,* 24 November 1997.

[19]Adapted from Mann, "Volume Business."

[20]Barton Crochett, "America Online Sets New Round of 'Carpet-Bombing' Software," *Wall Street Journal Interactive Edition* (September 24, 1998).

[21]"From Computers to Soap, Web Is the Place to Be," www.adage.com, 28 December 1997.

for links to relevant Amazon content from NetFind search pages. This is similar to cross-marketing arrangements that Amazon has with many other sites where there is a button encouraging visitors to go to amazon.com for additional references on the topic being investigated.

1-800-Flowers, a company founded on direct response, expected to tap into new market segments via AOL. Their traditional segment had been professional males in their 30s and 40s, but they were reaching out to college students, military personnel, and Americans living abroad. These groups are made up almost entirely of people who are away from home and therefore need to make purchases in nontraditional ways. They are good candidates for on-line shopping, especially because college students and military personnel tend to have good access to computer facilities.[22]

Learn about Consumer Preferences

The Internet is the quintessential direct-response medium because every move a visitor makes leaves an "electronic footprint." This obviously creates tremendous privacy implications, to which we return later in this chapter. For the moment, we concentrate on the equally tremendous database implications.

There are two basic ways to get information about individuals in cyberspace: either ask them directly or collect information electronically. Of course, marketers can do both, and many do. You see evidence of this from the moment you log onto the Web.

Versions of the Netscape browser, for example, offer personalized content on the home page. From the consumer's viewpoint, the "catch" is that you must register and provide demographics as well as information about your interests to receive e-mail newsletters that have been customized for you. From the marketer's viewpoint, information of real value is being collected. For that the customer is offered a reward—information of real value. Put that way, does it not seem like a reasonable transaction?

That is one of the keys to persuading consumers to provide the information—give them something of value in return. A bank furnishes a good example of how this can work:

> Summit Bank in Princeton, New Jersey, has a Web site that requests detailed data about its visitors and repays them with targeted product information.
>
> After registering for their own file by submitting their name, e-mail address, a password and ID, customers are asked to complete a checklist specifying categories they're interested in. They're then asked to provide personal information; age, childrens' ages, income, housing and expected expenditures within the next year.
>
> After the information is submitted, the site automatically fills the file with content tailored to the customer and continues to keep customers posted on new products, including the latest mortgages or CDs that fall within their interests.
>
> Customers can use up to 12 tools to make personal calculations that estimate new worth, predict mortgage payments and determine what type of investor they are. They can save those calculations for future use. . . .
>
> "The industry is moving toward a push-down marketing philosophy," said Summit Internet manager John Harding, referring to the new Internet practice of delivering content directly to the customer rather than waiting for the customer to access the site. "We are marketing to a segment of one rather than mass marketing."[23]

Amazon.com, on the other hand, does a great deal of its information collection electronically, "remembering," in effect, what the customer has done previously. Once the cus-

---

[22]"AOL to Draw More than $94 Million from New Commerce Agreements," cma.zdnet.com, 15 July 1997; "America Online Gets $44 Million in Flower/Book Deals," cma.zdnet.com, 9 July 1997.

[23]Denise Duclaux, "Bank Uses Web Site to Build Database," *DM News,* 14 April 1997, 6.

tomer has identified himself by making a purchase, the site greets him by name whenever he visits. A bit obvious, yes, but a small signal that the customer is valued in an anonymous world. The site also makes suggestions about other books the customer might enjoy that are based on previous purchases and the choices of other customers who have picked that book. If the customer is predictable in his selections, the recommendations quickly become eerily accurate. The site is also quite polite. It checks to make sure you are the person it identifies with the particular computer, and it frequently asks if you want something, rather than presenting you with information you do not want. It also asks if you wish to have new book announcements e-mailed to you, not wanting to be a purveyor of junk e-mail.

Summit Bank asks for information by means of a registration form (see Figure 17.4 for a set of guidelines for setting up registration procedures) and almost certainly by collecting additional data as people use the site. Amazon.com collects data electronically with no information requested except what is essential to make a purchase. The term that is most often applied to the activity of gathering data electronically is the *cookie*.

Cookies are pieces of software that are deposited in the computer of the Web surfer, remaining there to transmit information about where the surfer goes and what he or she does while there. Many Web users are taken aback to discover that this is going on. Their first inclination is often to try to prevent it. Some Web browsers have alternative levels of protection against cookies that can be selected by the user, although it seems fair to say that the user has to look diligently to find this particular set of preferences. There is also software, along the lines of virus protection programs, that can sweep the hard disk for existing cookies and prevent new ones from being deposited. Only the user can decide what to trade off. Cookies enable Web sites to push targeted content and advertising to the user, which should furnish a more productive and satisfying Internet experience. They are also useful in measuring Web activity, a precursor of setting advertising rates. If advertisers know the Web to be an effective medium, more advertising will be placed there, which should, in turn, keep usage fees down. Cookies are, however, an example of collecting data without the user's conscious knowledge or consent, and probably represent a practice the industry will, in time, have to confront openly.

FIGURE 17.4 Rules for Web Site Registration Programs

Source: Adapted from Dana Blankenhorn, "How to Profit from Registration," *NetMarketing* (April 1997): M-3.

- Do not ask for data unless you are going to use it.
- Get names, addresses and telephone numbers so you can match them to the existing database.
- Every question cuts the response rate.
- Ask just a few questions at a time. Build a relationship, not a registration file.
- Tell visitors how the data will be used—more important, how it will benefit them.
- Respect their privacy. Do not transmit data without telling customers up front.
- Integrate registration data with internal and commercial databases.
- Respond to customer queries in the medium they used; assume this is their media preference.
- Use the data to offer value-added information to customers.

However marketers do it, though, the ability to "learn" about its users is the key factor that allows a Web site to relate to them in a manner that promotes profitable long-term customer relationships.

Relate to Customers with Personalization and Customization

In the preceding pages you have read about one of the mantras of successful Internet marketing—collect data and give users value in return. Value-added information is a common solution, and we have given numerous examples to show how compelling this can be. There are also instances of customization in the physical world that offer fascinating insights into how the Web might, in time, be used to achieve true one-to-one customer relationships:

> The average female tries on 13 pairs of jeans before making a purchase. Why? Simple, they do not fit. Ironically, even after this considerable amount of effort spent, a substantial proportion of women leave the store without purchasing what they came to buy. Even more profound, approximately 30% of women do not buy pants at all because they cannot find any that fit properly. . . .
>
> Proper sizing for women's jeans is . . . complex—a function of waist size, hip size, rise, inseam, and most important, the wide variance in the difference between waist and hip sizes. The number of combinations is so vast than an outlet carrying all possible combinations of sizes, styles, and colors would be the retail-clothing equivalent of Home Depot . . . Custom Clothing Technology Corp. . . . is destined to lead major changes in the apparel industry with a collaborative design-and-selection system that addresses all of these issues.
>
> The Personal Pair system . . . is being rolled out in conjunction with the Old Levi's Store chain. . . . The customer's measurements are taken by a salesperson in an in-store boutique and then fed into a computer. Within minutes, the customer can select from 14,280 fit variations for Levi's jeans, instead of the 52 choices available off the rack in traditional Levi's stores. Within two weeks, the customer receives a custom-cut pair of jeans for $15 more than off-the-rack alternatives.[24]

A bar code on the jeans could provide all the data necessary for reorders. This type of customization is dependent on reengineered operations as well as reengineered marketing, as illustrated by the following example:

> The National Bicycle Industrial Co., a subsidiary of Matsushita in Japan, provides individually customized bicycles through cut-to-fit and component-sharing modularity combined. Its factory, as *Fortune* relates, "is ready to produce any of 11,231,862 variations on 18 models of racing, road, and mountain bikes in 199 color patterns and about as many sizes as there are people." The process starts with a shopkeeper who determines a customer's model, color, and design preferences, which define the sharable components to use; then precisely measures him or her on a special frame for the cut-to-fit components. All the specifications are faxed to the factory, where a computer creates custom blueprints for both craftsmen and robots. The latter measure and cut each piece of the frame to fit the individual's measurements, weld the pieces together, and apply the base coat of paint. The skilled workers perform most of the assembly work and all of the final touches, including silk-screening the customer's name on the frame.[25]

---

[24]Christopher W. Hart, "Made to Order," *Marketing Management* (summer 1996): 16–17.

[25]B. Joseph Pine II, *Mass Customization* (Boston, MA: Harvard Business School Press, 1993), 203–204.

As more companies around the world move key parts of their business to the Web, this integration of marketing and manufacturing may be seen in many other categories. Companies that have based their entire business on the "direct model" are far ahead of most others in meeting the needs of individual consumers in ways that seamlessly blend marketing and manufacturing. A prime example is Gateway 2000. This company had its origins in 1984 when Ted Waitt, a salesclerk in a retail computer store in Iowa, recognized the inefficiencies of the retail channel, "I became fascinated with the idea that if you knew what you were talking about, you could sell somebody a $3,000 product over the phone in a 20-minute conversation."[26]

The company Waitt built, Gateway 2000, is headquartered in North Sioux City, South Dakota, and uses a holstein cow as its mascot. The cow theme permeates Gateway's promotional activities. However, the down-home folksiness of Waitt's manner masks a no-nonsense approach that propelled Gateway to number four in the home PC market in 1996.[27] The business model was described as late as 1997 in this way:

Here's how it works: Except for a few showrooms, Gateway customers see its computers strictly through advertising—a lot of advertising, about $90 million worth a year. The customer calls in and, over the phone, custom-designs a computer with the specific features he wants. In about five days, his system is built and shipped in the company's trademark white boxes with the black cow spots.

In an industry where speed is a critical advantage, Gateway moves like lightning. Computers are not built until the orders are in. There's no inventory to speak of. Gateway often changes product configurations every three days. It can change prices every day. There's no middleman, so Gateway can deliver a lot of bang for the buck—what Waitt calls "the value equation."[28]

Each of Gateway's 5 million customers becomes a member of "Club Gateway." Membership entitles them to the quarterly publication *GW2k: Gateway Magazine,* mailers announcing the latest offerings and a product catalog covering everything from game packs to printers. Prospective customers who call Gateway's hotline receive the catalog and an informational video.[29]

This business model seems to be ideally suited to the Internet. One evaluation described Gateway's Web site as follows:

For any first-time visitors to this site who are unfamiliar with PC marketer Gateway 2000, one immediate question they'll likely have is: "What's with the cows?" Cow cartoons—a cow wearing headphones, talking on a phone, and wearing a beanie, e.g.—marks every significant area on the home page. . . .

Amid the cows, the home page is jam-packed with options. Viewers can connect to listings of Gateway 2000 computer models, technical help areas, and Gateway information sections ranging from the story of the company and executive bios to press releases and awards. There are also hot links to Gateway's international sites, articles about the company, and plenty more. And for those looking to be entertained, there's "The Cow Zone"—a series of whimsical cow-related areas. This is a content-rich Website with a zillion options. . . .

---

[26]Brian Dumaine, "America's Smart Young Entrepreneurs," *Fortune,* 21 March 1994, 34.

[27]"Can Gateway Round Up the Suits?" *Business Week,* 26 May 1977, 134.

[28]Michael Warshaw, "Guts and Glory: From Farm Boy to Billionaire," *Success,* March 1997, 28.

[29]Denise Duclaux, "Gateway Casually Builds Booming Business in Direct Sales," *DM News,* 17 February 1997.

As for *serving prospective PC buyers,* Gateway is tops at allowing the visitor to create his or her own system configurations. When you open many of its offerings . . . a sophisticated onscreen form lets you build a system from a multitude of options and then gives you an estimated price for the full package.[30]

At Gateway the customer-oriented approach to product customization carries over to a comprehensive approach to customer service. All desktop models have a three-year warranty and there is free technical support for all software applications that are bundled with the system. Service and support systems can be customized for an additional charge.[31]

This entire cycle—from attracting viewers through relating to them with customized content—makes use of the interactive nature of the Internet to create one-to-one customer relationships. Keep this in mind as we look at the basic marketing activities on the Web—advertising, customer service, and sales.

Advertising on the Web

Both direct marketers and traditional marketers are still in the process of learning how to make Web advertising effective and how to integrate it with other marketing and communications activities. Procter & Gamble, the perennial largest mass media advertiser, has tried a variety of approaches. One television ad showed a father looking on the Tide detergent Web site for advice on stain removal. Check-out station couponing technology produced messages encouraging purchasers of baby products to visit the site of Pampers diapers. In partnership with other companies P&G has helped to finance, and has advertised on, a site designed to reach working parents and another targeting women who are concerned with health and fitness.[32]

In the midst of all this experimentation, standard types of advertising on the Web have emerged. These ads are almost exclusively designed to be placed on one high-traffic or related-content Web site in an attempt to attract visitors to the advertiser's site. Let's consider each briefly in turn:[33]

- *Banner ads* are ads, usually rectangular in shape and varying in size depending on where they are placed on the page, that contain a very limited message. Often the message is little more than the corporate logo and a phrase inviting the viewer to click on the banner and visit the corporate site. The message may simply be static, it may have motion, or it may have "streaming" text that moves across the banner as the viewer watches. The owner of the Web site specifies what types of spaces are available (small spaces on the side of a page; one large space stretching across the top of the home page, and so forth), and, of course, sets the rates for each space.

- *Button ads* are generally smaller than banner ads and more likely to be square. They often contain only the corporate name, or perhaps the logo and the name. Clicking on either a button or a banner ad takes the viewer directly to the corporate site.

- *Sponsorships or cobranded ads* are found on targeted Web sites. They represent attempts to identify corporations and their products with certain types of content. The Intel Pentium II ad on the MTV site is a good example of this kind of sponsorship.

[30]"The Cybercritic," *Catalog Age,* 4 April 1996; www.mediacentral.com, 5 January 1998.

[31]"Gateway 2000," *Computer Shopper,* 1 January 1996, www.cma.zdnet.com.

[32]"From Computers to Soap, Web Is the Place to Be," www.adage.com, 18 December 1997.

[33]Based on "Web Ads Start to Click," *Business Week,* 6 October 1997.

- *Keyword ads* are featured on commercial search engines such as Yahoo! or search engines embedded in a network site such as Manufacturing Marketplace or IDG.Net, described in chapter 11. The ads are linked to search keywords so that, for example, when the surfer enters "beer," an ad for a popular brand of beer appears.

- *Interstitials* are separate windows that often have both audio and video. They are keyed to a move to a specific site and may appear while the viewer is waiting for the site to appear on the screen. The visitor must close the ad in order to view the site.

MEASURING THE EFFECTIVENESS OF WEB ADVERTISING

From the beginning, we have emphasized that direct marketing is trackable, and therefore measurable, and that measurability is one of its chief advantages compared to traditional mass media. The Web is, as we have already pointed out, completely trackable. However, because the vast majority of activity on the Web does not now result in a transaction, the measurement issues are more like mass media than direct marketing. That may change as commerce continues to develop on the Web, but for the time being the need is to develop measures of exposure that are somewhat parallel to the reach and frequency measures of traditional media. The electronic and interactive nature of the Internet, coupled with the fact that most of the content is accessed by viewer initiative, have created an interesting measurement challenge.

The measurement model that has gained acceptance is based on the concept of a *clickstream*. A clickstream is "the database created by the date-stamped and time-stamped, coded/interpreted, button-pushing events enacted by users of interactive media." Five elements can form the unit of measure in a clickstream:[34]

- *Hits* are the equivalent of an advertising impression; that is, given that a person is viewing a particular page at a particular time, how many files did he have an opportunity to see? If you think about a vibrant home page, or the main screen of a search engine, or even a page with several banner advertisements, there are several "hits" whether the viewer attends to the banners, buttons, and so on, much less whether she clicks on one and moves to the material linked to it. Each link on the page counts as a hit, no matter how short the visit to the page and regardless of whether the viewer accesses the link. You might reasonably assume that hits are easy to measure but relatively meaningless to the advertiser.

- *Pages* are a measure of the number of pages downloaded from a specific site at a particular time. One link may access many pages. The viewer may or may not scroll through all of the pages, and therefore may or may not have an opportunity to be exposed to the material. Again, this is a measure that is relatively easy to collect but that has little relationship to the potential effectiveness of the advertising.

- *Visits* count the total number of times a user accessed a particular site during a given period of time. This corresponds to the concept of "frequency" in mass media advertising.

- *Users* measure of the number of different people who visit a particular site during a given period of time. It corresponds to the concept of "reach" in mass media advertising.

- *Identified Users or Visits* is the demographic profile of either visits or users of a site during a given period of time. Again, this corresponds to the demographic profiles of readers, listeners, or viewers that mass media provide to their advertisers.

---

[34]Based on Coalition for Advertising Supported Information and Entertainment, "CASIE Guiding Principles of Interactive Media Audience Measurement," www.commercepark.com, 2 April 1997.

When possible, Web sites are moving toward advertising charges based on sales leads acquired or sales made as a result of the initial Web ad. This is obviously attractive to direct marketers who are accustomed to basing their results measures on customer and prospect behavior, not on mere exposure.

There are two important points to make about this brief overview of Internet audience measurement. First, these simple definitions greatly oversimplify the problem of obtaining accurate measures of advertising efficiency and effectiveness on the Internet. The reasons that even these straightforward-sounding measures are not always accurate are primarily technical, having to do with the way Internet service providers handle and store data in an effort to give their customers speedy access to the material they desire. The second point is that Internet audience measurement is in its very primitive stages, and better, more accurate measures of effectiveness may become available. Measurement on the Web is a moving target as well as an issue of great importance to marketers as they place increasing proportions of their advertising dollars there.

Buying Advertising on the Web

The general principle for buying advertising on the Internet is the same as for buying mass media advertising. Put simply, it is to get the most exposure to the target market for the dollars spent. The most common measure of efficiency in mass media is gross rating points, calculated as follows:

$$GRP = \text{Reach} \times \text{Frequency}$$

The principle is the same, but as suggested in the preceding section, the newness of Internet advertising and the difficulties of measuring it have created challenges for the marketer who is trying to get the greatest benefit from advertising dollars spent. Traditional advertising agencies or media buying services can do the analysis and make Internet placement purchases for their clients. However, you would probably not be surprised to learn that specialized agencies have grown up to deal with the intricacies of Internet advertising and the tremendous number of promotional vehicles available there.

One type of agency closely parallels the traditional advertising agency, or at least the creative department of it. These are specialized agencies that build and manage Web sites for clients. As Web advertising has taken off, a large number of entrepreneurial firms have been established, and traditional agencies have established interactive departments. You can also expect that the successful entrepreneurial concerns will, in time, be acquired by large agencies in their continuing quest to service the entire spectrum of marketing communications needs for their clients.

The second type of agency parallels the media buying firm or the media department of a traditional agency. These agencies are described as "networks" because of the intermediary function they play. The basic functions performed are holding a stock of "space" inventory, performing analysis of site traffic and demographics, placing client advertising, monitoring advertising performance, and making adjustments to optimize advertising performance.

According to Forrester Research, five different types of networks have emerged:[35]

- *Ad-reach networks* can make placements on hundreds, or even thousands, of sites. The job of the network is to understand the nature of each site as an advertising vehicle and make appropriate media buys for clients. The ads can be generic banner ads, ads targeted to a particular segment

---

[35]Mary A. Modahl and Ruth MacQuiddy, "Internet Advertising," www.forrester.com, 1 September 1996.

of site visitors, or ads that deliver personalized content to targeted visitors. The better-known agencies in this category are DoubleClick, WebConnect, SOFTBANK, and FlyCast, among many others.

- *Local networks* are made up of a few hundred sites such as Digital Cities and CityScape that provide local content. Because the content is key to a particular geographical area, these sites are especially attractive to local retailers and service providers. They also attract national brands looking for reach.

- *Personal broadcast networks* are the providers of personalized content delivered directly to the user's desktop. There will be a limited number of these "push" channels, some of which are Individual, PointCast, and WSJ Interactive. Because these content channels are predicated on customized content, they can provide targeted demographics that are very attractive to advertisers.

- *Content networks* link together a number of content-rich sites. Chapter 11 discussed IDG.net, and other sites, such as ZDnet, TechWeb, CNET, and MediaCentral, have been referenced throughout the text. Most of these sites require first-time visitors to register, even though the content is free. By now you are well aware that the primary purpose of registration is to provide advertising demographics. Many of the sites have premium services that require a subscription fee, providing another level of knowledge about persons who choose to subscribe to a particular area of content.

- *Navigation hubs* are seen as the next generation of current search engines, such as Yahoo!, Excite, and Lycos. Forrester predicts that the numerous search engines available in the late 1990s will consolidate into two or three central locations that support Internet traffic and search activities. They see these hubs as the "mass media" of a maturing Internet.

Two examples from ad-reach agencies give a sense of the types of services that are emerging to serve Internet advertisers:

SOFTBANK Interactive Marketing (www.simweb.com) offers clients an opportunity to reach consumers through an array of well-known sites such as Hotmail, Netscape, and Playboy. Their on-site promotional material states that they sold over 1 billion Web ad impressions in their first year of operation. They analyze the client's needs and develop a media plan that incorporates promotional activities that go beyond simple banner advertising.

For clients who need to reach well-defined target markets, SOFTBANK offers portfolios of sites that specialize in reaching those markets. "The SOFTBANK Network[SM] provides advertisers with state-of-the-art ad serving, *targeting, campaign testing,* inventory management, *performance optimization, reporting,* near real-time post-buy analysis, and auditing and billing systems." Content areas include Arts/Entertainment, Games, and Travel as well as the generic Run of Network.

They state that their College Portfolio "covers a wide range of content aimed at both the college and college-bound student and their families. With 14 million students in the United States spending over $60 billion every year, these active Web-oriented consumers are an attractive market for any business, ranging from credit cards to merchandise." This network generates 7.6 million impressions per month and includes sites that have content ranging from career planning to scholarship information to college planning and lifestyles. Examples include College Insider, Electric Library, and Hotmail.

In addition to banner advertising, the firm develops programs such as on-line contests and sweepstakes that establish targeted databases and provide sales leads for large-ticket products like automobiles.[36]

---

[36]Adapted with quotations from www.simweb.com, 12 January 1998.

DoubleClick[37] is a pioneer of in the area of ad-reach networks. The DoubleClick Network is described as "a collection of the most highly trafficked and premium branded sites on the Web (AltaVista, Dilbert, US News, Macromedia and over 60 more)."

DoubleClick has developed a number of proprietary technologies, including its DART technology, which it describes as being a full-service advertising management solution that is available globally as a result of servers located around the world. The DART software matches the profile of the target market that the advertiser desires to reach to the profile of the individual Web user and delivers targeted advertising content in less than 20 milliseconds. The system gives clients log-on access to advertising performance measures that are compiled in almost real time. This service is available to both advertisers and Web sites on a 24-hour-a-day basis.

DoubleClick also has a separate network for direct marketers who wish to drive additional traffic to their sites and who want to pay on a per response basis. This network is made up of sites willing to run ads on a cost-per-lead, cost-per-download, or a cost-per-transaction basis, giving direct marketers a response-based advertising option in which they pay only for visitor action, not on the basis of exposure.

It is important to recognize that, although the underlying principles derived from mass media advertising apply to Web advertising, the execution is radically different, as we have just seen. First, there is the great number of individual Web sites, which is growing on a daily basis. Some of these are credible vehicles for advertising; many are not. The advertiser needs Web specialists to keep track of sites and assess their potential value as advertising vehicles. Second, there are the issues of measuring effectiveness that we have already discusssed.

Third, Web advertising operates in a real-time atmosphere—and at warp speed! The ads themselves do not have a long life; DoubleClick estimates that an ad is "worn out" after two exposures.[38] In addition, the performance of ads can often be improved by moving them around in a site or moving them from site to site. Finally, client expectations have greatly accelerated. Clients expect to be able to log-in to the monitoring software used by the agencies, examine performance in real time, and request instantaneous changes to advertising content or the media buy. They also expect to submit content electronically so that it is instantly available for placement. This is not the way in which—nor is it the speed at which— traditional advertising agencies are accustomed to working. Hence the growth of the specialized agencies to support advertising programs and media buys on the Internet.

Advertising on the Web, just as it is in traditional mass media, is the most visible aspect of marketing to many Web surfers. However, providing service and support is an area that offers great potential to many marketers.

Using the Web to Provide Customer Service and Support

When asked whether many companies would begin to find their Web sites profitable in 1998, strategist Esther Dyson answered, "Some will; more will *save* money or provide better service using the Web."[39] This is probably, at least in part, a reference to the anticipated predominance of business marketing activities on the Web. However, there are many ways in

---

[37]DoubleClick promotional material, www.doubleclick.net, 12 January 1998.

[38]Modahl and MacQuiddy, "Internet Advertising."

[39]"In 1998 . . . ," www.cnet.com, 11 January 1998.

which consumer marketers can provide a greater level of satisfaction to their customers via the Internet.

We have already discussed some of the great customer service and support successes on the Web. Both Federal Express and Dell were able to move activities previously handled over the telephone to the Web. They saved money for the company at the same time they increased the level of service for their customers through instant access and availability 24-hours a day, seven days a week. This is truly a win-win—for both the marketer and the customer!

Many consumer marketers have been unsure how quickly they could migrate important service and support activities to the Internet, because they did not know how many of their customers were on-line. Businesses that were established to serve the on-line market were more fortunate; they knew their customers were "wired."

The @Home Network was founded by a group of established cable companies to supply high-speed information service over the existing cable television infrastructure.[40] It describes its service as "hundreds of times faster than possible with traditional telephone modems." @Home is not a supplier of cable modems; it uses network technology to provide this extremely fast service. @Home further states that it "provides a high level of network management and customer support, which is complemented by multimedia content that is tailored to the network's high bandwidth capabilities."

@Home has made its entire user guide available on its home page. In addition, it offers the following categories of help that can be accessed on the site:

- Internet basics
- overview of the @Home Service
- using member services (change password, etc.)
- Netmail customer support
- system preferences
- frequently asked questions (FAQ)
- troubleshooting tips
- error messages
- contacting customer support

The firm also provides high-bandwidth data transmission to business customers through a division called @Work. Technical support representatives (TSRs) are available to business customers on a 24-hour-a-day, 7-day-a-week, 365-day-a-year basis. Business customers will be referred to operations or engineering personnel if their assistance is required. These levels of support are published on the @Home home page and accessed directly through the home page.

Business customers are receiving Internet-based service and support in an individualized manner through the creation of *extranets*. An extranet is a private site, or portion of a site, that can be accessed only by users who have a valid password. Some areas of the Web that cannot be entered by casual visitors are, of course, subscription-based services. Many others, however, are available only to users who are, for example, members of an organiza-

---

[40]Information on @Home is adapted with quotations from www.home.net/support, 11 January 1998.

tion or customers of a particular firm. Business marketers, once again, seem to be leading the way in providing this kind of service. A company can create a special page for each major account so that, "When Ford logs on to the Compaq account, Ford gets a special site that says, 'Compaq Welcomes Ford Motor Co.' . . . It puts only the product support info for the products that Ford currently owns; for example, if there is a new upgrade to the Proliant 4500, they will get the notification of that upgrade. All of the other upgrades will be hidden from them, because they don't care about those."[41]

Firms can also look at on-line operations as a way to provide excellent service to customers whose business is not large enough to warrant substantial amounts of personal attention. CoreStates Bank, headquartered in Philadelphia, has set up an extranet for small business customers that makes use of Intuit's QuickBooks software:[42]

> Customers can use the software to check balances, transfer funds between bank accounts, and pay vendors online. In addition, the software offers easy and comprehensive accounting capabilities in lay form, so that users do not need to understand accounting jargon or debit-credit accounting. Users can create custom invoices, enter sales, record customer contracts, track time, perform job costing, manage inventory, handle payroll, and prepare for tax season.

Bank officials believe that a system of this type strengthens relationships between the bank and its customers. There seems little doubt of that. Customers are using the bank's Web site to perform many of their routine business duties—a powerful reminder of the relationship. The bank is saving money on paperless transactions, especially vendor payments. It is offering routine business assistance that it could not otherwise make available. Perhaps most important of all, it is an example of what high-tech consultant Regis McKenna describes when he talks about the emergence of the never-satisfied customer who expects suppliers to "eliminate time and space constraints on service, to give customers the means to satisfy and serve themselves and obtain access to products and services anytime, anywhere."[43]

Some companies will develop sophisticated, customized Web sites to provide customer service and support. Others, like CoreStates, will build a site around a tested, successful software package. These companies are likely to benefit from faster—and probably also cheaper—Web site development. They may well choose to partner with a supplier who puts marketing effort behind a brand name such as Quicken, thereby making site promotion cheaper and more effective.

Remember two important points about providing service and support on the Web. The first objective should be to provide better, faster, more complete service to all qualified customers. The second objective should be to save money as compared to labor-intensive customer service operations. The good news is that a successful Web site can accomplish both objectives. The less good news is that it is not free. The Web site itself carries a development cost, which is usually recognized in advance. The cost of ongoing maintenance—especially in the light of heightened customer expectations—is often not recognized in advance. L.L. Bean is said to maintain a team of several customer service representatives whose sole responsibility, 24 hours a day, is to respond to customer e-mail. Another marketer is report-

---

[41]Gene Koprowski, "Only Connect," *Marketing Tools* (January/February 1998): 30.

[42]Ibid., 32.

[43]Ibid.

ed to have completely shut down the feedback portion of a Web site. The volume of e-mail was more than the assigned personnel could handle and the inattention was causing a substantial amount of customer ill will.

Remember that the Internet customer is upscale and sophisticated with a very high set of expectations, whether the issue is on-line service or on-line sales.

Using the Internet to Sell Goods and Services

We have already said that the Internet is the quintessential direct-response medium. It allows the marketer to interact with customers and prospects on a one-to-one basis. Some of these interactions will be fulfilled in other sales channels, but transactions are gradually moving onto the Web. Security is still an issue in the minds of many people, but the data quoted at the beginning of this chapter indicate that some people are buying. The number of on-line shoppers is growing, and it seems likely that it will continue to do so.

Virtual shopping is not going to replace shopping in the physical world, however. Some people shopping for some types of products still want to touch, feel, see, smell, and try out the product before they buy it. Other people enjoy the social and sensory aspects of shopping and do not want to give that up. Still, there are some product categories that seem ideally suited to on-line shopping.

Travel services are one such category. The information that allows customers to make reservations for planes, trains, hotels, and rental cars has been available electronically to suppliers of travel services and travel agents for many years. The next step was to give corporate customers, and later consumers, access to the same information systems that professionals use. Customers were then able to get the same information without an intermediary, and many have begun to do so. This is one area in which intermediaries seem to be genuinely threatened.

On the other hand, consider the case of PC sales. Dell and Gateway 2000 have proven that the "direct model" is successful in both business and consumer markets, yet the established computer manufacturers have been slow to emulate their success. The first generation of personal computer manufacturers, from IBM to Compaq to Apple, worked long and hard to develop strong channels of distributors, dealers, and retailers. They sold to their large accounts, both intermediaries and end users, by means of large, expensive sales forces. It has been difficult for them to move to direct sales in the face of resistance from their channels and sales forces.

Finally, consider the case of automobile manufacturers, most of whom have large, glitzy Web sites. They offer a great deal in the way of audio, video, and even virtual reality technology that lets a prospective buyer take a "virtual test drive." Still, in the face of all this technology, most customers will go to an automobile dealer to make the actual purchase. Some automobile dealers are already noticing that Web surfers are a different type of customer when they arrive—well prepared with information, very likely to have a "best price" offer located with the assistance of one of the automobile sites, and totally uninterested in negotiating. These customers know what they want, the price they are willing to pay, and may even have located the dealership that will fulfill their requirements before they ever enter the automobile showroom. In one sense, all the Internet is doing is to generate sales leads; in a more profound sense, it may change the nature of the shopping experience for many customers and the nature of automobile retailing for many dealers.

With different scenarios for doing business on the Web, let's look at a prediction for the size of electronic commerce. Jupiter Communications predicts that total Internet revenue will exceed $9 billion by 2002, but that only $1.3 billion will be in direct marketing revenues. The other $7.7 billion will be in media placements.[44]

We have already suggested that some products are more suited than others to interactive marketing applications (see Figure 17.2). We have also reiterated frequently throughout this and other chapters that interactive marketing is different from traditional mass media marketing and even from direct marketing as we have known it. *PC Magazine* examined the 30 best e-commerce sites and came to some generic conclusions about the technological characteristics of the best on-line commerce sites. According to that magazine, the best transactional sites

> meet most if not all of the following criteria: They have fast-loading pages, elegant and easy-to-use layouts, extensive selections or hard-to-find merchandise, and robust search engines. Some include features that add a sense of community, such as forums and chats; others focus on personalization features, including customized accounts and e-mail reminders.
>
> The most successful sites have a clear understanding of their mission. For stores that manage huge inventories, for example, a streamlined interface coupled with robust search capabilities is paramount. The best smaller specialty stores understand the importance of creating a unique atmosphere, often enhanced by useful information or historical background. Many of the best sites—Amazon.com, CompUSA, and Virtual Vineyards among them— manage to do both. . . . The best sites also target both kinds of shopper; the one who comes ready to buy and the one who takes time to browse around.[45]

There have been several attempts to develop "shopping malls" on the Internet, but most have not been successful. The customer realizes very little advantage from going to a virtual mall over simply moving from site to site, totally unlike the physical world. On-line services such as America Online offer a variety of shopping options to their customers as part of the service package. As we have already pointed out, many of these are accomplished through links to cyberretailers such as Amazon.com and 1-800-Flowers.

Here again, however, a direct marketer who has a distinctive retailing concept and can execute it well may find a home on the Web. One such direct marketer is Cendant Corp. This company was formed as the result of a merger between CUC, an operator of membership clubs including Traveler's Advantage and Shopper's Advantage, and HFS, which owned a number of well-known franchise brands including Avis Rental Cars and Century 21 real estate. That gave Cendant several million members as well as established brand names on which to base Internet operations. Their site is called netMarket (www.netmarket.com) and offers merchandise, travel, and automobile shopping services as some of the major areas within the site. They promote their merchandise offerings as being 10 to 50 percent off list prices and offer a $1.00 three-month introductory membership on the Web page; regular membership is $49.95 per year. They offer bargain areas—a flea market and a silent auction, with a live auction soon to come. Members earn netMarket cash of up to 5 percent on their purchases and they promote many other member specials.

The jury is still out as to whether virtual malls are a viable concept, but *Business Week* says, "CUC's real leg up may be its proven computer system for taking huge volumes

---

[44]www.jupiter.com, 1 January 1998.

[45]Toni F. Kistner, "Let's Go Shopping," *PC Magazine,* 18 November 1997, www.cma.zdnet.com.

of orders and delivering in a timely manner. 'Most of what will make Internet commerce successful is the blocking and tackling,' says analyst Christopher A. Feiss of Alex Brown & Sons Inc."[46]

What Really Makes a Site Work?

We are now beginning to develop an understanding of what makes a site effective. By *effective* we mean a site that accomplishes stated business objectives, not one that is merely technologically or creatively awesome. But remember that "effective" may also mean creating awareness or disseminating information, providing customer service or support, as well as selling products or services.

One measure of effectiveness is how well the site interacts with visitors. Forrester Research has a sample set of questions that marketers can use to rate how well their site interacts with visitors, a key ingredient of effectiveness (Figure 17.5). They recommend rating each feature on a scale of 1 = uncompelling to 5 = very compelling.

As it is in all marketing activities, being really effective on the Internet is a result of understanding the customer's needs and behaviors first, foremost, and always. One of the most thoughtful analyses of what consumers are looking for in cyberspace comes from Evan Schwartz, a former editor of *Wired* magazine. He has formulated nine principles of the emerging discipline of "webonomics." These nine principles summarize many of the issues discussed in this chapter:[47]

1. The *quantity* of people who visit a Web site is less important than the *quality* of their experience.

2. Marketers should be on the Web for *results,* not for exposure.

3. Consumers must be compensated for disclosing data about themselves.

4. Consumers will shop on-line only for information-rich products.

5. Self-service gives customers the highest comfort level.

6. Web-based transaction systems enable marketers to create their own payment systems, using principles of either credit or debit cards.

7. Trusted brand names are even more important on the Internet, where visitors must be attracted to a site through a veritable forest of other sites competing for their attention.

8. The Web creates a global "marketspace" in which small firms can compete on a relatively even footing with much larger competitors.

9. Agility rules! Activities of all kinds take place on the Web in real time, and marketers must be swift and flexible to participate successfully in this new medium.

In just a few years, the Internet has emerged from obscurity to become an important fourth channel for distributing goods, services, and ideas. Although most marketers still have a distance to travel in terms of taking fullest advantage of the opportunities offered by the Internet, there is no turning back. The Internet is a fact of life in both business and consumer markets. One of its accomplishments has been to force marketers to confront issues related to customer privacy, although not all those issues have yet been entirely resolved.

---

[46]Based on "Point, Click—and Spend," *Business Week,* 15 September 1997, 74–75; "CUC to Consolidate Web Efforts through Aggregate Site," www.mediacentral.com, 9 December 1996; On-site promotional material, www.netmarket.com, 16 January 1998.

[47]Adapted from Evan I. Schwartz, *Webonomics* (New York: Broadway Books, 1997).

Engaging

Does the site greet return visitors by name?

Are customers enamored with the design of the site?

Unique

Does the site allow visitors to customize their view?

Can customers set up filters that sort and retrieve real-time information?

Responsive

Is the information delivery convenient and are notifications prompt?

Can customers immediately reach and interact with a human being?

Complete

Are prospects given all the information they need to make a choice?

Can customers complete the entire sales cycle on the site?

Valuable

Do prospects have powerful tools for overcoming the complexity of large sites?

Is the site faster to respond and more polite than comparable sites?

Reliable

Is all information on the site accurate at all times?

Does the site protect customers against fraud, including misappropriation of customer information?

FIGURE 17.5 Rating a Site's Intelligent Interactivity IQ

Source: Adapted from John M. Robb, John C. McCarthy, and H. Daniel Sheridan III, "Intelligent Interactivity," *Interactive Technology Strategies* 1, no. 12 (1 February 1997), www.forrester.com.

Privacy and the Internet

The potential benefits of the Internet to both customers and business will not be realized unless customers have a level of trust that creates a willingness to provide information and conduct transactions. This is true in the United States, where privacy has been less highly regulated, as well as in Europe, where privacy has been more closely regulated. There is disagreement about specific details and statistics, but there is little disagreement on major aspects of the problem. First, consumers are concerned about privacy as it relates to their activities in cyberspace, but they are not completely informed about what the issues are. Second, while some businesses are setting an excellent example, others simply "haven't gotten it" yet.

One comprehensive study used an on-line focus group and e-mail surveys of a panel of 300 to 500 respondents each month for five months.[48] The focus group elicited the following themes:

- concern for the protection of identities and being able to remain anonymous in order to assure personal safety and security
- the general perception that companies' requests for information are self-serving
- apprehension that offering personal information will result in receiving "junk" e-mail
- some willingness to provide limited information on interests, opinions, product and service needs, and demographics in return for a tangible reward

The researchers concluded that overcoming these concerns will require assurances of confidentiality, the establishment of personal relationships between businesses and their customers, and building a brand image in other media instead of relying on Internet-based brands, which are not trusted by consumers.

The survey indicated that customers were aware of the role of information in providing more targeted and customized services, but were concerned about privacy issues. Some of the specific findings were

- Respondents felt that submitting personal information online is
  - the best way for companies to learn about customers (76 percent)
  - only to sell you products and services (66 percent)
  - an invasion of privacy (52 percent)
- They were nevertheless willing to share information in return for customized content.
- Only 10 percent deemed site registration an invasion of privacy.
  - Ninety percent were willing to provide information on hobbies and interests at registration.
  - Only 4 percent were willing to provide credit card information.
- Users did not receive what they expected as a result of registration (see Figure 17.4).

A study in April 1997 by Louis Harris & Associates with the assistance of privacy expert Alan Westin gives us additional perspectives:[49]

- Fifty-two percent of computer users who do not now use the Internet would be more likely to do so if the privacy of their personal information and communications were protected.
- Of the 58 percent of the users who have been asked to provide information on a site, 79 percent declined and 8 percent supplied false information.
- Eighty-seven percent of users say it is very important or somewhat important that Web sites obtain users' permission before placing cookies.

The Boston Consulting Group (BCG) carried out a study for the not-for-profit privacy advocacy group TRUSTe in March 1997 that gave even more direct evidence that privacy

---

[48]"An Investigation into the Businesses's Need for Information vs. The Consumer's Need for Privacy," March 1997, www.cyberdialogue.com.

[49]"Louis Harris/Westin Survey," www.etrust.org, 16 January 1998.

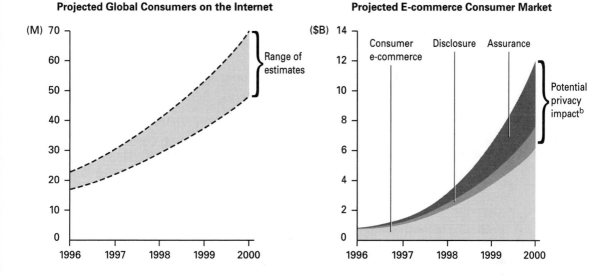

Note: Data from Forrester, Computer Reseller News, Computerworld, IDC, BCG estimates and analysis.
[a]Assumes 40 percent of e-commerce merchants adopt eTRUST by 2000 (on a transaction basis).
[b]Estimates based on eTRUST consumer survey results, adjusted to reflect overlapping security concerns and rate of adoption.

FIGURE 17.6 Privacy Assurance Could Have Up to a $6 Billion Impact on E-Commerce by 2000 (*If* Privacy Programs Are Adopted by Commerce Sites[a])

Source: The Boston Consulting Group, Inc. © 1997.

concerns are retarding the growth of Internet use. Their data give a strong indication that both familiarity with the company and privacy policy disclosure and privacy assurances are crucial in convincing consumers to reveal information (Figure 17.6). This study also addressed an important issue not covered in other studies. BCG found that many consumers do not distinguish between the *privacy* of their personal information and the *security* of information transmitted over the Web. Security is primarily a technical issue, which can be accomplished by the correct technology and vigilance against hackers, and the protection of personal information about individuals is a matter of corporate and governmental policy about the sharing and sale of information about individuals. Public confusion about these issues only complicates the problem.

BCG concludes that:

CONSUMERS ARE CONCERNED ABOUT CONTROLLING THE PRIVACY OF THEIR PERSONAL INFORMATION ON THE INTERNET:

- Privacy concerns generate multiple negative effects on e-commerce:
  - low rates of consumer participation
  - falsification of personal information given on-line
  - potential for governmental intervention

- Consumers would welcome Internet privacy assurance, indicating that they would modify their behavior accordingly.

ON-LINE BUSINESSES MOSTLY SEE BROAD, SOCIAL VALUE IN ADDRESSING THESE CONCERNS:

- They perceive less direct value to their business than indicated by consumers.
  - Many may mistake privacy concerns for security issues.
  - Some believe that their brands will carry them through.

ON-LINE BUSINESSES WILL NEED TO TAKE ACTION TO BUILD CONSUMER TRUST IN ELECTRONIC COMMERCE AND FURTHER THE DEVELOPMENT OF THE ELECTRONIC MARKETPLACE:

- beyond technical solutions
- beyond security and authentication
- addressing consumer concerns about the privacy of their information
  - disclosure of information practices
  - assurance of good business practices generally

AN INDEPENDENT PRIVACY ASSURANCE ENTITY COULD GENERATE SIGNIFICANT BENEFITS FOR E-COMMERCE AS WELL AS FOR CONSUMERS AND ON-LINE BUSINESSES:

- increased consumer trust and confidence in on-line businesses
- higher accuracy of consumer information provided on-line
- Increased consumer on-line activity—valued at up to $6 billion by 2000[50]

Note that BCG's estimate is an *incremental* $6 billion in on-line transactions, a substantial increase over the forecast given earlier in this chapter. A potential sales increase of that magnitude has attracted the interest of various Internet entities who have supported the establishment of TRUSTe (www.etrust.org). This nonprofit group describes its mission as being "to establish a trusting environment for you to make purchases and share and gather information on the Internet." It has developed a set of policy principles and allows businesses that subscribe to these policies to display the TRUSTe seal on their Web site. It remains to be seen how successful this effort will be.

One final study, by the Electronic Privacy Information Center (EPIC), reveals that business has a long way to go in this regard. EPIC reviewed 100 of the most popular Web sites and found that

- 49 of the 100 sites evaluated collect personal information through on-line registration, mailing lists, surveys, user profiles, or order fulfillment requests; EPIC could not determine whether the Web sites link collected information with other databases.
- Only 17 of the sites had actual privacy policies, and most were difficult to locate.
- Every site provided user anonymity when accessing the home page; most sites let users browse without disclosing personally identifiable information.

---

[50]"TRUSTe Internet Privacy Study," www.etrust.org, 16 January 1998.

- 24 of the 100 sites enabled cookies (however, not all pages or links were checked for each site); cookies were used mostly for registration and password storing, and sometimes to create logs of user interests and preferences.
- None of the 100 Web sites informed users of the cookies.[51]

In the United States, the Direct Marketing Association has taken a leading role in encouraging businesses to maintain high standards in terms of protecting the personal data of their customers. The DMA's own privacy statement, as found on their Web site, is shown in Figure 17.7 (p. 440). It provides an excellent model for businesses who still need to develop and display a policy of their own.

Summary

After a number of years of uncertainty about the impact of interactive marketing on business of all kinds, it has become clear that the impact is going to be great. It also seems evident that the impact is not going to be felt equally by all types of business, governmental, and non-profit organizations. However, any concern that needs to interact with its various constituencies—and that may include virtually all organizations—could benefit to some degree from having a Web site. Many consumer packaged goods companies, however, may derive benefits far less than the costs of maintaining a credible Web site. Any business that cannot make a commitment to designing and maintaining a Web site that reflects positively on its image is better off without one. At the same time, transactions in business markets are moving onto the Web very quickly, and business marketers who do not avail themselves of opportunities, or do not meet the requirements of customers who insist on on-line commerce, may soon see a negative impact on their results.

The conclusion that an increasing number of transactions will be either conducted on or facilitated by the Internet seems inescapable. From that we can draw the equally inescapable conclusion that more marketers are going to find themselves actively engaged in direct marketing over the coming years.

Discussion Questions and Exercises

1. Be prepared to describe, in your own words, what we mean by interactive media and how they are different from traditional mass media and direct-response media.
2. Why should marketers develop programs for interactive media that are different from marketing programs in traditional media?
3. What is the hierarchical process through which marketers must lead prospective customers on the Internet?
4. What does it take to be successful in the interactive media? Do direct marketers have special capabilities that will be helpful in the interactive marketspace?
5. Talk to someone who has recently made a purchase on the Internet. Find out about the nature of the purchase and their postsale experience.

---

[51]"EPIC Survey," www.etrust.org, 16 January 1998.

DMA Web Site Privacy Policy

This is the web site of The Direct Marketing Association (The DMA).

Our postal address is:

1120 Avenue of the Americas
New York, NY 10036-6700

We can be reached via e-mail at dma@the-dma.org or you can reach us by telephone at 212.768.7277.

For years The DMA has developed guidelines and programs to help marketers meet consumer privacy expectations. By providing consumers with notice of information practices and the ability to remove their names from lists, marketers have demonstrated their commitment to protecting consumer privacy. As interactive media evolve, The DMA and its membership renew their commitment to offer notice and opt-out in this new medium.

Note: The DMA does not compile, buy, sell, rent or trade consumer mailing lists. All marketing efforts we undertake are targeted toward a business audience only.

For each visitor to our Web page, our Web server does not recognize information regarding the domain or e-mail address.

We collect the e-mail addresses of those who communicate with us via e-mail, and any information volunteered by the customer, such as survey information and/or site registrations. The information we collect is used to improve the content of our Web page and to contact customers for marketing purposes.

If you do not want to receive e-mail from The DMA in the future, please let us know by sending us an e-mail, calling or writing us at the above address.

Marketers that supply The DMA with their postal address on-line may receive periodic mailings from us with information on new DMA products and services or upcoming DMA events. They may also receive mailings from other reputable companies.

If you do not wish to receive such mailings, please let us know by sending an e-mail, calling or writing us at the above address. Please provide us with your exact name and address and we will be sure your name is removed from our marketing list and/or the list we share with other organizations. Persons who supply The DMA with their telephone numbers on-line may receive telephone contact from us with information regarding orders they have placed on-line, new products and services or upcoming events. They may also receive periodic telemarketing calls from other carefully screened business-to-business marketers.

If you do not wish to receive such telephone calls, please let us know by sending e-mail to us at the above address or calling us at the above telephone number or writing to us at the above address. Please provide your correct phone number and we will be sure your name is removed from our marketing list and/or the list we share with other organizations.

Companies that wish to create a privacy policy page and post it to their Web site can use The DMA's Privacy Policy Creation Tool.

FIGURE 17.7 DMA Web Site Privacy Policy

Source: Reprinted with the permission of the Direct Marketing Association, 1998.

Selected Internet Research Sites

CyberAtlas	www.cyberatlas.com
Cyber Dialogue/Yankelovich Partners	www.cyberdialogue.com
eMarketer	www.emarketer.com
Find/SVP	www.findsvp.com
Forrester Research	www.forrester.com
Internet Advertising Bureau	www.iab.net
Jupiter Communications	www.jup.com
Nua, Ltd.	www.nua.net/surveys/
The Yankee Group	www.yankeegroup.com

Suggested Readings

Baldock, Robert. "The Virtual Bank: Four Marketing Scenarios for the Future." *Journal of Financial Services Marketing* 1, no. 3 (1997): 260–268.

Cartellieri, Caroline, Andrew J. Parsons, Varsha Rao, and Michael P. Zeisser. "The Real Impact of Internet Advertising," *McKinsey Quarterly* 3 (1997): 44–62.

Katz, Jon. "The Digital Citizen," www.hotwired.com, 1 Janaury 1998.

Kelly, Kevin. "New Rules for the New Economy," www.wired.com, September 1997.

McKenna, Regis. *Real Time: Preparing for the Age of the Never Satisfied Customer.* Boston, MA: Harvard Business School Press, 1997.

Staff of the Federal Trade Commission. "The Online Marketplace: Challenges and Opportunities," www.ftc.gov/reports/privacy, 15 January 1998.

Index

A

Aaker, David A., 26, 56
Abbott, Ben, 413
Abramson, D., 159
Advertising, Internet, 425–29
Agrawal, R., 139
AIDA, 280–81
Allis, Tim, 399
Alpert, Shell, 33
American Domain Name Registry, 6
American Express, 67, 161–62
American Institute of Certified Public Accountants, 190
Ames, Pamela, 98
Analysis of variance (ANOVA), 220–30
Anderson, Virgil, 233
Arlen, Gary, 408
Armour, G., 148
Armstrong, Gary, 192
Arthur Andersen Consulting, 150
Asato, Cathy, 392, 407
Asia, direct marketing in, 326, 360, 410–11
AT&T Universal Card Services, 152
Australia, direct marketing in, 254, 326, 411
Automatic Interaction Detection (AID), 101, 105–6, 115
Automatic shipment plans, 40

B

Bailey, Marci, 85
Baker, Kim, 295
Baker, Sunny, 295
Baldock, Robert, 441
Ballinger, Jerrold, 383
Ballou, Ronald, 148
Batra, Rajeev, 26, 56
Bauer, Connie, 2, 116
Baughan, Cynthia, 85
Beard, John D., 278
Bencin, Richard L., 337
Berenson, Mark, 233
Berger, Paul, 90–91, 99–100, 107–113, 150, 233, 247
Berman, Barry, 30
Berry, Leonard, 151, 159
Bertrand, Kate, 245
Best Mailing Lists, 68, 71, 85

Beta error, 212
Bissel, Brent John, 320
Bjorncrantz, C. E., 297
Blankenhorn, Dana, 263
Blattberg, Robert, 105–6, 112, 191–92, 201
Blattstein, Joel J., 368
Bly, Robert W., 333
Bodenberg, Thomas M., 42
Borland, John, 254
Boston University, 107
Bowersox, Donald, 148
Brady, Frank R., 408
Bricker, Roger W., 61
Brightman, H., 233
Bringe, Paul, 278
Brochure, 281–82
Brookstone Company, 70
Brown, Eryn, 264
Brown, Herbert E., 61, 348
Buchanan, R., 114
Budgeting, 31–33, 397
Buffa, Edward, 148
Burnett, Ed, 289
Business Lists, 64, 65, 85
Bylinsky, Gene, 261

C

Cahners Business Information, 258–60
Caldwell, Bruce, 255
Call center, establishing and managing, 343–53
Canada, direct marketing in, 296, 354
Cannella, Frank, 408
Cartellieri, Caroline, 441
Carter, J. F., 106
Carter, Kent, 302
Catalog Age, 191–92
Catalog development and marketing process, 304
Catalog success factors, 303, 324
Cheng, Scarlet, 359, 360
China, direct marketing in, 59
Chi-Square Automatic Interaction Detection (CHAID), 101–3, 112, 115
Churchill, Gilbert, 159
Clancy, Kevin, 153–54, 159
Claritas, Inc., 75, 101